W9-ABG-329

Use and Abuse
of
America's Natural Resources

Use and Abuse
of
America's Natural Resources

Advisory Editor

STUART BRUCHEY
Allan Nevins Professor of American
Economic History, Columbia University

Associate Editor

ELEANOR BRUCHEY

Franklin D. Roosevelt
& Conservation
1911-1945

Compiled and Edited by EDGAR B. NIXON

-{ VOLUME TWO }-

ARNO PRESS
A NEW YORK TIMES COMPANY
New York • 1972

Reprint Edition 1972 by Arno Press Inc.

Reprinted from a copy in The Wesleyan University
Library

Use and Abuse of America's Natural Resources
ISBN for complete set: 0-405-04500-X
See last pages of this volume for titles.

Manufactured in the United States of America

Library of Congress Cataloging in Publication Data

Roosevelt, Franklin Delano, Pres. United States,
1882-1945.
    Franklin D. Roosevelt & conservation, 1911-1945.

    (Use and abuse of America's natural resources)
    Reprint of the 1957 ed.
    CONTENTS.:--v. 1. 1911-1937.--v.2. 1937-1945.
    1. Conservation of natural resources--United States.
I. Nixon, Edgar Burkhardt, 1902-   ed. II. Title.
III. Series.
[S930.R66 1972]   333.7'2'0973   72-2861
ISBN 0-405-04525-5

Franklin D. Roosevelt
and Conservation, 1911-1945

—»»«←—

VOLUME TWO • 1937-1945

Franklin D. Roosevelt

& Conservation

1911-1945

Compiled and Edited by EDGAR B. NIXON

-⟦ VOLUME TWO ⟧-

GENERAL SERVICES ADMINISTRATION

NATIONAL ARCHIVES AND RECORDS SERVICE

FRANKLIN D. ROOSEVELT LIBRARY

HYDE PARK, NEW YORK : 1957

UNITED STATES

GOVERNMENT PRINTING OFFICE

WASHINGTON : 1957

Contents.

Part III

The Second Term: 1937-1941

The Second Term: 1937-1941

576 Morris L. Cooke, Chairman, Great Plains Committee,
     to Stephen T. Early, Assistant Secretary to the
     President

Washington, *January 22, 1937*

My dear Mr. Early: Following up our conversation of a few days ago I hand you herewith a Summary of the Report of the Great Plains Committee. I understood you intended to give this to the newspapers twenty-four hours or so in advance of the report going to Congress.

An adequate supply of the reports will be available on Monday in case it should be decided to send the report to the Hill on Tuesday next.

Yours very sincerely,

Morris L. Cooke

[*Notation*: A] Cooke to put out release

[13:OF 2285:TS]

577 [*Enclosure*]

Confidential

Summary of the Final Report of the Great Plains Committee on the
Future of the Great Plains

The problem of the Great Plains is not merely one of relief of a courageous and energetic people stricken by drought and economic depression; it is the problem of arresting the decline of an agricultural economy not adapted to the climatic conditions and of readjusting that economy in the light of experience and scientific information now available, the President's Great Plains Committee reported today.

The settlers of the Plains brought with them agricultural practices developed in the more humid regions from which they came. By coincidence, the period of settlement was generally one of above average rainfall and these practices, therefore, at first appeared suitable. Experience has shown that the rainfall hovers around and often falls below the critical point at which it is possible to grow crops by the agricultural methods common to humid regions. A new economy based on conservation and effective use of all the water available is called for. Intelligent adjustment to the ways of Nature must take the place of attempts to "conquer" her.

The success of a long-time plan for essential readjustments in the Great Plains economy depends in the final analysis upon coordinated cooperation between Federal, State and local agencies. Federal agencies may advise, assist and coordinate; State agencies may administer permissive or mandatory legislation; local agencies and individuals will have to assume the final responsibility in effecting the necessary changes.

Pointing out that there is no simple solution to the problem, the Great Plains Committee has presented a three-part program of Federal, State and local action:

I. Lines of Federal action should include (1) a ten-year program of additional investigations and surveys; (2) the continued acquisition of land in range areas and the control and use of publicly owned range land in accordance with the objectives of general rehabilitation as well as of existing priorities; (3) measures to increase the size of farms too small for efficient operation; (4) the development of the water resources of the region, including small irrigation systems; (5) resettlement both within and without the region, when and if detailed readjustment plans indicate the necessity; (6) compensation to local governments where Federal land acquisition results in a shrinkage of the local tax basis; (7) the control and possible eradication of insect pests; and finally, (8) the exploration of the possibilities of developing other resources such as the vast lignite deposits to provide alternative occupation for some people.

II. Lines of State action should include (1) immediate surveys of present legislation affecting land and water use and conservation to determine the need for revision and extension; (2) the application to rural territory of the principle of zoning; (3) the encouragement of cooperative grazing associations as one method of alleviating the results of too-small holdings and checkerboard ownership patterns; (4) legislation permitting the formation of county soil conservation districts; (5) making tax-delinquent range lands available for coordinated use with other public lands instead of re-selling to private individuals; (6) the encouragement of local communities to make broader use of legislation permitting consolidation of local governments; (7) revision of the taxing system to take account of the current or average income from the land; (8) measures to promote ownership and permanent occupancy of the land and to make more equitable the position of those who continue as

[4]

tenants; and finally, (9) assistance to farmers in meeting the basic water problems of the region, including aid in developing local water supplies for stock through tax reductions, simplified procedures for adjudicating water rights and encouragement of small or medium sized irrigation projects.

III. Lines of local action—which can be guided by Federal and State action, but cannot be coerced—should include (1) the enlargement of undersized operating units and the establishment of cooperative grazing ranges; (2) major shifts in the cropping plans to reduce the single "cash crop" and restore the more stable "balanced farm"; (3) flexible cropping plans to permit the adaptation of each season's crop to the amount of moisture in the soil at planting time; (4) the creation of feed and seed reserves against dry years; (5) the conservation of soil moisture by such means as contour plowing and listing, contour strips, terracing, leaving of stubble and crop residue in the ground, and planting of sweet clover and winter rye on sandy soils; (6) supplemental irrigation where practicable; (7) fuller utilization of springs and wells where stock are to be pastured; and finally, (8) the planting of trees and shrubs as windbreaks on borders of fields and around houses.

Noting that over fifty Federal agencies in addition to State, county and municipal governments and various types of districts which have been or will be formed under State legislation touch the problems of the Great Plains at one point or another, the Great Plains Committee concludes its recommendations with the suggestion that a Federal agency be established to promote readjustments and coordinate the activities in this field. Such an agency should not displace existing agencies or assume any administrative control over the operations those bodies normally carry on. Its field should be that of a continuing study of the Great Plains problem and of endeavoring by consultation, education, persuasion and guidance to integrate the efforts of all forces. It should report annually with recommendations as to Federal legislation bearing on the Great Plains and should be prepared to recommend, after appropriate consultation, to State and local political subdivisions such legislation as may be deemed desirable. The precise manner in which the proposed agency should be woven into the administrative fabric of the Federal government is left for later determination. In conclusion, the Report states:

Public opinion throughout the Great Plains appears to be ripe for this step . . . during recent years the economic drift in the Great Plains has been steadily downward. If the deplorable consequences, recently heightened as a result of the depression and drought, are to be arrested, it will only be because the entire Nation takes the situation in hand promptly, emphatically, and competently. There is no controversy as to ultimate objectives and there should be none as to immediate means.

In a sense the Great Plains afford a test of American ways of dealing with matters of urgent common concern. They have not responded favorably to a purely individualistic system of pioneering. The Committee is confident that they will respond to an altered system which will invoke the power of voluntary cooperation without sacrificing any of the virtues of local initiative and self-reliance.

The Great Plains Committee was appointed by the President in September, 1936, after the Great Plains Drought Area Committee of last summer had reported. The Committee was instructed to bring in a comprehensive Report which should serve as the basis for legislation by the new Congress. The Committee includes: Harlan H. Barrows, Professor of Geography, University of Chicago, Member, Water Resources Committee, National Resources Committee; H. H. Bennett, Chief, Soil Conservation Service, Department of Agriculture; L. C. Gray, Assistant Administrator, Resettlement Administration; F. C. Harrington, Assistant Administrator, Works Progress Administration; Richard C. Moore, Colonel, Corps of Engineers, U. S. A., Division Engineer, Missouri River Division; John C. Page, Acting Commissioner, Bureau of Reclamation, Department of the Interior; Harlow S. Person, Consulting Economist, Rural Electrification Administration; Morris L. Cooke, Administrator, Rural Electrification Administration (Chairman).[1]

[13:OF 2285:T]

[1] The first two paragraphs of this summary were used as the basis of the first two paragraphs of Roosevelt's message to Congress of Feb. 10, 1937, transmitting the report, *post*, 588.

578   HENRY A. WALLACE, SECRETARY OF AGRICULTURE, TO
       ROOSEVELT

[WASHINGTON] *January 22, 1937*

DEAR MR. PRESIDENT: I told Mr. Richey, Chief of the Bureau of Plant Industry, of your feeling about the failure of the farmers of the Great Plains to utilize the results of the investigational work of the Bureau. Of course, it is true that the Bureau is more of a research agency than an action agency but nevertheless it has engaged in a number of cooperative shelterbelt plantings as shown by the enclosed maps.[1]

Respectfully,

[HENRY A. WALLACE]

[13:OF 1–C:CT]

[1] Not present.

579   Roosevelt to Henry A. Wallace, Secretary of Agriculture

[Washington] *January 23, 1937*

Memorandum for the Secretary of Agriculture: I do not desire to be critical of the experimental work of the Bureau of Plant Industry because I am sure that they have learned much during the past twenty years in regard to tree or shrub coverage on arid or semiarid land. This experimental work should go on, testing an even larger number of potential tree or shrub plants from every part of the world and including, for example, more species from South America and Africa and Central Asia than we have tested before.

The enclosed report [1] proves, however, that I was right in thinking that the acreage in private and public ownership, which has so far benefitted from the experimental work, is negligible. I have personally seen numbers of individual farms included in the total of four thousand farmers now "cooperating" with these shelter-belt experimental test plantings. On these farms, in many cases, only a few acres running down to only a few hundred square feet are planted and many of the plantings are ornamental rather than soil conserving. The total net result in acreage is negligible from the point of view of soil conservation and water retention.

I wish the Department would study and give me a report on this whole subject from a large acreage point of view. In the State of New York alone, for example, over forty million trees a year are produced by the State and planted either on State owned land or on privately owned land.[2] This means a total of forty thousand acres a year planted to trees. If the State of New York can do this for a very small annual cost, it is time that the Federal Government did it, especially on the vast public domain, the title of which is still in the Federal Government.[3]

F. D. R.

[13:of i–c:t:copy]

[1] Not identified.
[2] Actually, 52,000,000 trees in 1935 and 48,000,000 in 1936, according to the *Annual Reports* of the New York State Conservation Department for these years.
[3] Answered *post*, 600.

580   Roosevelt to the New York Rod and Gun Editors Association

[Washington] *January 25, 1937*

To the Members of the New York Rod and Gun Editors Association: It is a pleasure to present to the New York Rod and Gun

Editors Association and its assembled guests, who have dedicated themselves to the cause of conservation, my official greetings and personal wishes for success in their undertaking. I appreciate your confidence in selecting me to receive your first annual conservation award and I am glad to accept your invitation to send this message of greeting.[1]

Long ago, I pledged myself to a policy of conservation which would guard against the ravaging of our forests, the waste of our good earth and water supplies, the squandering of irreplaceable oil and mineral deposits, the preservation of our wild life and the protection of our streams. We must all dedicate ourselves for our own self-protection to the cause of true conservation.

Much progress has been made during the past four years but the full significance of conservation as related to our national welfare is not yet clear to all of our people. I believe, however, that more and more of our citizens are coming to appreciate that the natural resources of America, while vast, are neither limitless nor inexhaustible. I also am encouraged to believe that today there is a better understanding of the problems that are faced by the government in this respect than at any previous time in our history.

I gratefully acknowledge and accept your aid in this enterprise.

[FRANKLIN D. ROOSEVELT]

[13:PPF 4301:CT]

[1] This award (a model of an eighteenth-century Hudson River packet) was given to Roosevelt for having made "the greatest individual contribution to conservation in the United States during 1936" through his sponsorship of the Civilian Conservation Corps and of other conservation measures (Fred Fletcher, chairman, banquet committee, New York Rod and Gun Editors Association, to Roosevelt, Dec. 18, 1936, PPF 4301). The statement here printed was drafted by the Interior Department, but references in the draft to the desirability of a conservation department and a permanent national resources board (amounting to about a third of the text) were removed by the White House (Michael W. Straus to Hassett, Jan. 15, 1937, enclosing the draft, PPF 4301). Ickes read the statement at the dinner of the association. The ship model is now in the Franklin D. Roosevelt Library.

581   PRESS CONFERENCE, Executive Offices of the White House, January 26, 1937, 4:05 P. M.

[Excerpt] Q: Is this flood going to give a stronger interest to more permanent flood control work in that area? [1]

The President: I would rather put it on a broader basis. We had an editorial this morning that pointed out that whenever we have a flood we have three or four different groups who rush to the Government to get money for this, that or the other thing.[2] There are the people who are downstream, who want more and better levees, and then the next group that wants dams in the rivers, and another group that wants to go up into the headwaters and plant trees, and another group that says it is entirely a question of soil erosion. So you get all these different groups that say their own particular pet theory will stop the flood.

I have come to the conclusion that we have to pursue all of these things simultaneously. They all tie in in a general picture and, for the first time, we have in the last three or four years been developing a synchronized program to tie in the entire field of flood prevention and soil erosion. That is one reason why I hope, in the Reorganization Bill, we can have a Central Planning Authority, which will be responsible for, let us say in the case of all of the waters of the Mississippi, responsible for a plan which will cover all of the watersheds that go into the Mississippi.[3] And then all the work that is being carried on will have some relationship to the work that is being carried on at some other point.

[13 : PRESIDENT'S PRESS CONFERENCES : T]

[1] The Ohio Valley.
[2] The leading editorial of the New York *Times* of Jan. 26, 1937, was on this subject and was probably the one meant.
[3] The "Reorganization Bill" had yet to be introduced. On Jan. 12, 1937, Roosevelt sent to the Congress the report of the President's Committee on Administrative Management, appointed by him in 1936 to consider means to improve the administration of the executive branch of the Government. (The message accompanying the report and a summary of it are printed in Rosenman, ed., *Public Papers*, V, 668–681.) Among other things, the report recommended the establishment of a permanent national resources planning board to plan the development and use of the country's resources, and the creation of a department of conservation to administer the public lands and parks and the conservation laws. To prepare the necessary legislation, the Congress appointed the Joint Committee on Government Organization, with Senator Robinson of Arkansas as chairman. On June 23 Robinson introduced S. 2700, embodying certain of the recommendations of the committee. This was not acted upon nor was a bill of the same title, S. 2970, introduced by Byrnes (S. C.), on Aug. 16, 1937. The reorganization bill finally enacted was H. R. 4425, introduced by Cochran (Mo.) on Feb. 23, 1939 (*Cong. Rec.*, 75th Cong., 1st sess., 81:6, 6207; 81:8, 8939, 9327; 76th Cong., 1st sess., 84:2, 1850). This was approved April 3, 1939, as the Reorganization Act of 1939 (53 *Stat.* 561).

582   SENATOR ELBERT D. THOMAS OF UTAH TO ROOSEVELT

[WASHINGTON] *January 29, 1937*

MY DEAR MR. PRESIDENT: A situation has arisen in the Western mining states regarding prospecting and location under the United States mining laws within the boundaries of game preserves which I believe is in need of correction.

Since the creation of game preserves by Executive order, the General Land Office of the Department of the Interior has taken the position that the creation of a national game preserve is a withdrawal of the lands for an exclusive purpose, and prevents other disposition of the land under the public land law. The General Land Office has consistently held that national game preserves are not open for prospecting and location under the United States mining laws.

It is my belief that prospecting and location under the United States mining laws should be permitted within the boundaries of national game preserves. I do not believe that such mining activities will interfere with the purposes of the creation of the game preserves, and application of the present ruling of the General Land Office constitutes a formidable drawback to mining development in the Western states.

Inasmuch as the national game preserves were created by Executive order, I believe a reservation of mining rights in such preserves may be effected in like manner.

Therefore, I request that consideration be given to this matter to the end that an Executive order may be issued if it is practicable to do so.[1]

Respectfully submitted,

ELBERT D. THOMAS

[13:OF 378:TS]

[1] Answered *post,* 603.

583   ROOSEVELT TO HENDRIK WILLEM VAN LOON, South Norwalk, Connecticut

[WASHINGTON] *February 2, 1937*

DEAR HENDRIK: The "Missis" showed me that gem of a broadcast of yours on January nineteenth. You are a wise adviser and your advice is much needed by the American people.

There is only one little thought to which I, as a Dutchess County, New York and Meriwether County, Georgia, farmer, take exception. When you suggest that this Nation could feed two billion people, my conservationist self rises up.[1] I am no great naturalist like T. R. but I do know that with every known modern device we would be very fortunate in this country if we could grow enough food to feed three hundred million people. The reason is this: all of what you so delightfully term the "promontory of Asia"—Europe—happens to have an amazing climate. For century after century your Netherlandish ancestors and mine, whether they lived near the mouth of the Rhine or further up the river or still further east, could count on an almost complete lack of erosion for the very simple reason that the European rains drop constantly but gently from heaven and the wash of topsoil from the cultivated land which replaced the forest has been, on the whole, negligible.

In almost every part of the United States, on the other hand, an equal amount of rain comes from the heavens in vast torrents and has taken away in three hundred years on this East Coast, about half of the original topsoil. I forget my figures, but I think I am approximately correct in saying that it takes one hundred years to restore one inch of topsoil through reforestation. Perhaps that is over optimistic.

Let me tell you the tale of a part of my farm at Hyde Park for which I have a fairly clear record. It was settled about 1740; the trees were cut; the stumps removed, the fields planted. The Old Dutch and New England owners used rotation of crops—corn and wheat and rye and grass. They had cows and manure from the barnyard was spread on the land. As late as 1840 that farm grew prize corn. But the toll had been taken and from then down to 1910, when I took hold of it, went from bad to worse. While it did not lie on steep land, the topsoil grew thinner and thinner each year through snow-melting floods and later torrents. In 1910 it grew only about one half the crops that it could have grown in its earlier days. I can lime it, cross-plough it, manure it and treat it with every art known to science but it has just plain run out—and now I am putting it into trees in the hope that my great-grandchildren will be able to try raising corn again—just one century from now.

That is the story of raising food supplies in America. At least one hundred million acres of land now under the plough ought not to be cultivated again for a whole hundred years.

I shall feel deeply insulted if you come to Washington again without letting me know, especially as I want to make a dirt farmer out of you.

As ever yours,

[FRANKLIN D. ROOSEVELT]

FDR/TMB

[13:PPF 2259:CT]

[1] A copy of van Loon's broadcast (made over WEAF in New York) was sent by him to Mrs. Roosevelt in a letter of Jan. 26, 1937 (PPF 2259). The broadcast dealt with the perils inherent in the overcrowding of Europe; the part referred to by Roosevelt reads: "Meanwhile, at the other side of the ocean there is our country, rich in everything that Europe lacks. It has 125,000,000 inhabitants. If it had the density of population of western Europe, it would have two billion people, the total population of the earth, and it could feed them."

584   ROOSEVELT TO THE CONGRESS

THE WHITE HOUSE, *February 3, 1937*

TO THE CONGRESS OF THE UNITED STATES: During the depression we have substantially increased the facilities and developed the resources of our country for the common welfare through public works and work relief programs. We have been compelled to undertake actual work somewhat hurriedly in the emergency. Now it is time to develop a long-range plan and policy for construction—to provide the best use of our resources and to prepare in advance against any other emergency.

[11]

In a previous message, I have suggested a permanent planning agency under the Chief Executive in order that, among other things, all public works proposals may filter from the many individual departments and bureaus to a central planning place and thence to the President.[1]

I have also suggested to the Congress that following this course of planning the President will annually submit to the Congress a list of projects which have been studied and approved and, at the same time, inform the Congress, through the Budget, of the total amount of Federal funds which, in his judgment, should be appropriated for public works during the following fiscal year.

The list of public works submitted by the President in the Budget Message would, of course, be wholly advisory, for it is within the discretion of the Congress to eliminate projects from this list, to alter the scope of projects or to add other projects.

The report of the National Resources Committee on public works planning [2] which I submit today should, of course, be read in conjunction with the recommendations for highways, bridges, dams, flood control, and so forth, already under construction, estimates for which have been submitted in the Budget, and also should be read in conjunction with other special reports, such as the report of the Great Plains Committee which I expect to submit to the Congress in a few days.[3]

The National Resources Committee submits a six year program, based on selection and priority of public works. The period of six years is arbitrarily chosen and can, of course, be made to fit into annual future appropriations made by the Congress.

The report also contains recommendations on the timing of public works and division of costs in their relation to the necessary organization of future continued planning. I have already referred to this in my message relating to the reorganization of the Executive Branch of the Government.

As an example of the kind of reservoir of projects constituting the six-year program, a Drainage Basin Study is included in the report. This summary list of projects involving the uses of water is not to be regarded as fixed or final, as the report itself notes, but rather indicates a great forward step in the development of the planning process, considering not one project alone but the relationships between a great group of projects dealing with water use and control.

Through the formulation and annual revision of a program of all types of construction, revision and adoption of the program by Congress and appropriations under regular budgetary procedure timed in part in relation to economic needs we can provide for the orderly development of our resources and the provision of needed facilities for our people.[4]

FRANKLIN D. ROOSEVELT

[W. H. PRESS RELEASES : M]

[1] The message of Jan. 12, 1937 (Rosenman, ed., *Public Papers*, V, 668–674).

[2] Printed, with this message, as *Message from the President of the United States Transmitting a Proposed Plan of a Six-Year Program Submitted by the National Resources Committee Based on Selection and Priority of Public Works Projects* (Washington, 1937).

[3] *Post*, 588.

[4] In the Senate the message was referred to the Committee on Education and Labor; in the House, to the Committee of the Whole House (*Cong. Rec.*, 75th Cong., 1st sess., 81:1, 743, 817–818).

585   ROOSEVELT TO ROBERT H. WOOD, TEXAS HOUSE OF REPRESENTATIVES, Austin

[WASHINGTON] *February 5, 1937*

MY DEAR MR. WOOD: This is in reply to your letter of January twenty-fifth, inquiring about State administration of the soil conservation work now administered by the Department of Agriculture.[1]

Your letter does not make entirely clear whether you are referring to the program of the Agricultural Adjustment Administration or that of the Soil Conservation Service, both of which are administered by the Department of Agriculture.

Under the Soil Conservation and Domestic Allotment Act, as it now stands, the AAA conservation program would go on a State-aid basis not later than January 1, 1938. This feature was included in the law enacted by Congress last winter and was then thought to be a promising experiment. However, the nearer the date for transferring the program to a State-aid basis has approached, the greater and more complex the difficulties in this kind of operation appear to be. It is the opinion of many people in the various States, and it is my own opinion, that we cannot depend on parallel and simultaneous action by forty-eight States to assure a just return for agriculture. Therefore, it seems wise to postpone the date when the State-aid provisions in the present law become effective.

If you have in mind the program of the Soil Conservation Service involving erosion control and water conservation on watersheds, I would refer you to the Department of Agriculture, and the Standard State Soil Conservation Districts Law which has been recommended by the Department of Agriculture to facilitate the operation of that program.[2]

Very sincerely yours,

[FRANKLIN D. ROOSEVELT]

[13:OF 1–R:CT]

[1] Wood said that he wanted the information so that he could present it to a committee of the Texas Legislature (OF 1–R).

[2] Drafted by the Agriculture Department.

[WASHINGTON] *February 8, 1937*

MY DEAR GOVERNOR: In thinking over matters connected with the probable establishment of the Civilian Conservation Corps on a permanent basis it seems to me desirable to call attention to several phases of this work.

When I sent a special message to Congress in March 1933, proposing the creation of this new organization there were very few who visualized just what the new organization was intended to accomplish. Few states were prepared to accept their proper part of responsibility in the tasks that the new organization was intended to accomplish.

In this emergency we did not hesitate to authorize the use of federal funds to assist the states in receiving their proper share in this work. Letters, however, were sent to all state governors in May of 1933 and again in 1934 and in 1935, calling attention to this situation and urging that states which had not properly provided for their part in this work should immediately do so by enacting legislation where necessary and in appropriating necessary funds.

In the first place it is vitally important that each state should make adequate arrangement to maintain the physical improvements that have been accomplished by CCC camps on state property. This is with especial reference to state parks and state forests.

I would be glad to learn what measures your State has taken to insure the proper maintenance and orderly development of this work in your State.

Secondly but of equal importance it is necessary to maintain a competent staff to supervise and direct this maintenance and development work.

Because of the reasons referred to at the beginning of this letter many states did not have a technical staff set up to cooperate with the Federal Government in this work. In order that the high type of supervision considered necessary for the success of the work could be maintained federal funds were made available for the employment of technical and other personnel where state funds were not available.

It seems to me that the time has come for each state to make proper provision for taking over this part of the work. In preparation for the probable establishment of the CCC as a permanent federal agency consideration is now being given to what has been accomplished. Many camps are completing their approved work projects and it will be necessary in the coming months to find new work projects to which companies can be assigned. It will naturally follow that those states which show a proper concern for their part in this cooperative work with the Federal Government will be entitled to receive first consideration.

[14]

In order that we may have a clear picture I will appreciate your informing the Director, Robert Fechner, Post Office Department Building, Washington, D. C., of what your State has done or will agree to do in this important matter.   If additional information is desired I am sure Mr. Fechner will be glad to supply it.[1]

Very sincerely yours,

[FRANKLIN D. ROOSEVELT]

[13:OF 268:CT]

[1] This letter, which was drafted by Fechner, was sent to all the governors.   In his letter sending the draft (Jan. 18, 1937, OF 268), Fechner said that because the Emergency Conservation Work had been set up so suddenly, few states had had the funds or the authority to assume their share of the responsibility for the CCC work. In consequence the Government had been providing funds for the entire CCC activity in practically all the states.

587   PRESS CONFERENCE, Executive Offices of the White House, February 9, 1937, 4 P. M.

[*Excerpt*] Q: Mr. President, has anyone introduced an Arkansas Valley Authority Bill?

The President: Oh, I think there have been bills last session and this for two or three dozen authorities.   I will tell you what we are talking about at the present time in regard to natural resources and public works.   After looking at a dozen different schemes and examining into these individual bills for authorities like a Potomac River Authority, an Ohio River Authority, et cetera, we have come around to this point of view: I told this to the Senators this morning,[1] that in the interest of orderly planning it seems best to set up perhaps eight regions—not necessarily eight, it might be seven, nine, or ten, but eight regions, in a general way, seemed to cover the country without any one region having too large an area and at the same time avoiding too many small watersheds and thereby keeping the overhead down.

Each of these regional authorities or administrations or whatever Congress wanted to call them, would have the task every year of submitting a list of projects for flood or drought or soil erosion or navigable channels or reforestation within their region, listing them in the order of preference.

After all the regional reports were in—oh, say July or August—we would add up the figures of their recommendation and, based on the condition of the Treasury—in other words, a careful check-up by the Budget as part of the Budget Message—determine how much the President could recommend to the Congress for the Nation as a whole in his budget.   Thereupon, under the reorganization plan the third agency under the President, the National Planning Agency, would get hold of these eight regional agencies and say to them, "The President can only approve so many dollars to go into his budget; therefore, will you all cut (of course it would be every year a cut) your recommendations down to fit into the total budget figure that is possible, and give us a list for each region of the things that would fit into the budget sum; then put down at the same time a B list of projects that you approve, that you have recommended, that are all ready to shoot on the following fiscal year."

The President thereupon submits both lists to Congress, the first list being within the budget, and the second list being what might be called alternative projects, leaving it to Congress to determine whether they want to go along with the original recommendation or lift anything out and put something else in—wholly a matter of congressional discretion.

That makes for early planning and ties in all of these problems that are before us because of acts of God and man during the past few years—drought, dust storms, floods; the control of floods by levees, reservoirs, and soil erosion control. They all tie into one general planning picture every single year—that is the important part. I shall probably have a few more conferences with members of the House and Senate in regard to it with the hope we will get some kind of legislation. It is a procedure that costs comparatively little money.

Q: What will be the cost, Mr. President?

The President: The cost will be very low.

Q: What will be the expenditure?

The President: Approximately what is being spent now on national planning—probably actually making a saving over what we are doing now on national planning because we have a dozen different agencies.

Q: How much will be spent on projects?

The President: That depends on what can go into the budget. It will come in under that $500,000,000 limitation that I talk about so often. That, of course, includes public buildings, highways, harbor work, and things of that kind.

Q: These would be regional divisions not corporate authorities?

The President: They would be regional divisions. In working it out, possibly in some cases the regional divisions would also have administrative duties—as, for instance, in the case of the T. V. A.—but in most instances they would be planning authorities.[2]

Q: When you talked to us about two years ago, when you used the phrase "reshaping the face of nature," you mentioned $500,000,000, but we did not understand that would include harbors.

The President: Yes, all public works.

[16]

Q: Would this new plan change the omnibus flood control bill enacted by Congress?

The President: It ties in with it. As you know, that bill authorized all kinds of things—about $300,000,000 worth. The taking up of those things depends each year upon the amount appropriated by Congress, and this fits right into that. It is possible that in the course of two or three years there may be coming from the planning division a recommendation that some of those projects rather hastily thrown together be eliminated and others put in their place.

Q: Do you plan strict adherence to the principle established in that omnibus bill with reference to local contributions?

The President: That's a headache. I will give you a very good illustration. Yesterday I approved a letter that the Secretary of War is going to send out. We had those terrible floods up on the Connecticut River—very serious, but didn't do as much damage as on the Ohio River; but they were front-page on the newspapers for two weeks, at least, and in New England longer than that. Congress appropriated $10,000,000 for immediate construction of reservoirs and things of that kind, conditioned on the four states involved—Vermont, New Hampshire, Massachusetts, and Connecticut—buying the land. The land cost was estimated at three and one-half million dollars, and the problem came, because most of the land was in Vermont and New Hampshire, as to how much Massachusetts and Connecticut would contribute. Vermont and New Hampshire didn't want to buy all the land for benefits that would accrue as far south as Hartford; so the state contract [3] method was tried.

The first week in August we were trying to work out a prorata of the cost of that land. We are now nearing the middle of February and they haven't bought any land; so the $10,000,000 which we are ready to spend is held up. We are ready to go ahead. That is the question brought up last week. It is discretionary on my part. We will start the work as soon as we get the land. That method doesn't seem to be working. That is as far as we have gone, except the Secretary of War is asking the governors of these four states whether they can get together, and they are sending up our engineers to assist the states.

Q: What is the cure, Mr. President, for this headache you spoke of?

The President: I don't know. It obviously seems clear that the states and the localities ought to bear some of the burden; but when you come down to the prorating of it, it is an awfully difficult problem. I hesitate very definitely involving the Federal Government in bearing the whole expense, because I think we should have some local contribution.

Q: Some of these senators today said that power and reclamation would be tied in together.

The President: It all ties in together. One dam may be a dam solely for reclamation; another dam may be for reclamation and navigation: another dam may be for navigation and power. It depends on the individual project.[4]

Q: Mr. President, would these regional administrations deal only with Federal projects, or would they also plan what the states and localities might do with Federal aid?

The President: The message on drought has this sentence that goes up tomorrow: "All the different programs must be cooperative and will require complementary lines of action by the Federal Government, state governments, and all the states of the region." Don't use that in quotes, because the message has not gone to Congress yet.

[13:PRESIDENT'S PRESS CONFERENCES:T]

[1] Roosevelt apparently here referred to a White House conference with "Sen. Pope and western Senators", according to the appointments list for this day (PPF 1-O).

[2] Some indication of Roosevelt's thinking with respect to the administrative organization of the proposed agencies is found in his letter to the Tennessee Valley Authority Board of Directors, Feb. 25, 1937 (OF 42): "As I have known for several weeks that Mr. Blandford has been working on a tentative report on administrative organization of the TVA, I have asked him to show me what he now has. I do this because whatever final report he makes to the Authority itself will have a direct bearing on the form of set-up proposed for other regional Authorities in other parts of the country. . . ." (John B. Blandford, Jr., was general manager of the Authority.)

[3] "Compact" is obviously meant.

[4] Roosevelt, on Jan. 27, 1937, had discussed the plan for a nation-wide system of regional authorities with Senator Norris. He had also discussed it with Ickes and other members of the special power policy committee (as distinct from the National Power Policy Committee), appointed on Jan. 18, 1937, to make recommendations on power policy legislation for the Bonneville project and all new power developments. Ickes, chairman of the special committee, said that the President's idea was to have the authorities do whatever sound conservation policies demanded, "all of them . . . to head up through the new Department of Conservation" (*Ickes' Diary*, II, 60–61; Roosevelt to Ickes, Jan. 16, 1937, OF 2575). Ickes submitted a draft bill on Feb. 9, 1937. In his covering letter to Roosevelt of that date (OF 2575), he said that the bill did not attempt to define a power policy for all Government projects, as it was the understanding of the committee that the formulation of such a policy could await the drafting of the bill the President had mentioned for the creation of eight conservation authorities.

The draft bill had to do only with the temporary administration of the Bonneville project. (Introduced Feb. 19, 1937, as H.R. 4948 it was not reported from committee.) Morris L. Cooke, a member of the power committee until his resignation as Rural Electrification Administrator on Feb. 6, 1937, was disturbed over the fact that power policy should be considered without reference to the problem of conservation in general. He prepared a long and carefully documented memorandum on the general thesis that, "In the use of vast resources of water power . . . considerations of policy run far beyond mere proprietorship and must embrace the public functions for which governments exist." In his covering letter to Roosevelt of Feb. 20, 1937 (OF 2575), he said that he was strongly convinced that some such general discussion should precede the drafting of any far-reaching power program. "Conservation and power are indissolubly linked. Should we proceed without this fact fully in mind we are likely to make an error of the first order."

THE WHITE HOUSE, *February 10, 1937*

TO THE CONGRESS OF THE UNITED STATES: I transmit herewith for the information of the Congress, the report of the Great Plains Committee under the title, "The Future of the Great Plains." [1]

The report indicates clearly that the problem of the Great Plains is not merely one of relief of a courageous and energetic people who have been stricken by several years of drought during a period of economic depression. It is much more fundamental than that. Depression and drought have only accentuated a situation which has been long developing. The problem is one of arresting the decline of an agricultural economy not adapted to the climatic conditions because of lack of information and understanding at the time of settlement, and of readjusting that economy in the light of later experience and of scientific information now available.

The settlers of the Plains brought with them agricultural practices developed in the more humid regions from which they came. By historic circumstance the period of settlement was generally one of rainfall above the average, and, although water was known to be scarce, these practices then appeared to be suitable. The long-run experience, however, has disclosed that the rainfall of the area hovers around, and, for considerable periods, falls below the critical point at which it is possible to grow crops by the agricultural methods common to humid regions. A new economy must be developed which is based on the conservation and effective utilization of all the water available, especially that which falls as rain and snow; an economy which represents generally a more rational adjustment of the organization of agriculture and cropping plans and methods to natural conditions.

The whole subject of drought on the Great Plains dovetails into the studies made by the National Resources Committee in the larger aspect of public works planning. Previous and current studies of land and water problems have been undertaken on a nation-wide basis. In this report they have been re-worked and applied by the Great Plains Committee in cooperation with other Federal agencies and with State and regional planning agencies as a component part of our desire to develop a program of constructive action for the drought area.

Whatever program is adopted must be cooperative and will require complementary lines of action by the Federal Government, State Governments and all the citizens of the Region individually. Each has material interests at stake and can no longer afford to defer constructive action; each has moral responsibility for unwitting contributions to the causes of the present situation; and especially each has responsibility for undertaking lines of action essential to effectiveness of action by the others.

The problem is one that can be solved, but the solution will take time. Therefore a policy should be determined, a long-run program formulated, and execution begun without undue delay.[2]

FRANKLIN D. ROOSEVELT

[W.H. PRESS RELEASES:M]

[1] *Future of the Great Plains. Report of the Great Plains Committee* (Washington, 1936). The *Report* was also printed, with this message of transmittal, as House Document 144, 75th Cong., 1st sess. (Washington, 1937).

[2] Morris L. Cooke submitted three drafts of this message: the text as here printed, minus paragraph 4; a draft omitting paragraph 3; and one omitting paragraph 5 (Cooke to Roosevelt, Jan. 22, 1937, OF 2285). Paragraph 4 was added by Ickes to the original Cooke draft to explain the relationship of the Great Plains Committee to the National Resources Committee (Ickes to Roosevelt, Jan. 25, 1937, OF 2285). Ickes' paragraph was revised in the White House, probably by Roosevelt. Senator Pope of Idaho, in a letter to McIntyre of Feb. 9, 1937 (OF 2285), referred to a White House conference of that date attended by him and other western senators: "At the conference this morning it was understood that we would submit to the President for his consideration a suggestion to be included in his message to Congress at the time of the transmittal of the report of the Great Plains Committee." He enclosed a one-page draft statement emphasizing the importance to the nation of reclamation; his covering letter, however, bears McIntyre's notation: "Recd too late."

In the Senate the message was referred to the Committee on Agriculture and Forestry; in the House, to the Committee on Agriculture (*Cong. Rec.*, 75th Cong., 1st sess., 81:1, 1070, 1113).

589   ROOSEVELT TO REPRESENTATIVE HENRY C. LUCKEY OF NEBRASKA

[WASHINGTON, *February 11, 1937*]

MY DEAR MR. LUCKEY: Receipt is acknowledged of your letter of February 4, 1937, requesting a revision of the Budget estimates for the fiscal year 1938 for the Department of Agriculture so as to provide the sum of $100,000 for the establishment of a Forest Experiment Station in the Great Plains region.[1]

I am informed that the question of providing funds for the establishment of this experiment station was considered when the 1938 Budget was in course of preparation and it was the opinion of the Department of Agriculture that, because of other more pressing needs of the Department, the establishment of such a station could be deferred until the 1939 Budget.

In these circumstances I do not feel that the Budget for 1938 should be revised to include provision for this station. If the Department of Agriculture again presents the item for inclusion in the Budget for 1939 I can assure you that it will receive careful consideration.

Very truly yours,

[FRANKLIN D. ROOSEVELT]

[*Notation*:A] 2/11/37
[*Notation*:AS] DWB [2]

[13:OF 1–C:CT]

[1] Luckey said in part (OF 1–C): "Recent developments have shown the need for a separate station to serve the Great Plains and Prairie region. During the last fifty years some 700,000 acres of trees have been planted by farmers in this area, although they have not had information available on tree types which would survive in their particular localities." A forest experimental station had been authorized by an amendment, approved June 15, 1936, to the Forest Research Act of 1928. A similar request from Governor Robert L. Cochran of Nebraska, April 23, 1937 (OF 1–C), was answered in the same language.

[2] Acting Budget Director Daniel W. Bell, in whose agency this letter was drafted.

590   HENRY A. WALLACE, SECRETARY OF AGRICULTURE, TO ROOSEVELT

WASHINGTON, *February 16, 1937*

DEAR MR. PRESIDENT: A soil and water conservation program is a community enterprise and to be effective should be developed on a watershed basis. The landowners should have a legally authorized procedure by which they may get together to agree upon common action to meet a common problem, and to accept their responsibilities for the execution of a corrective program. Then too, as a matter of policy, the Federal Government should deal with a responsible public agency rather than with a large number of private individuals.

The Act which established the Soil Conservation Service, Public No. 46 of 1935, empowers the Secretary of Agriculture to require the States to enact legislation authorizing local cooperation in soil conservation, as a condition of his spending Federal money in any State for erosion-control work. Because the work is now in a demonstration stage, this requirement has not been fulfilled, although a number of States are now asking the Department for advice.

Most States do not have legally constituted agencies authorized to cooperate with the Federal Government for this purpose. To meet this situation a proposed Standard State Soil Conservation Districts Law has been prepared by the Land Policy Committee of the Department of Agriculture, and has been cleared with the National Emergency Council. This proposed Act provides the authority to create local conservation districts with power to establish and administer local programs for waterflow retardation and soil erosion prevention. The Act is broad enough to provide the basis for local cooperation in watersheds to alleviate floods.

It seems highly desirable that standard State legislation be enacted. Its adoption will aid in developing uniformity of legislation. It is also constitutionally imperative, because only the States can deal with this phase of erosion control. It will further establish a proper basis for Federal, State, and local cooperation in a National soil and water conservation program.

Many State legislatures are now in session. Most of them are considering legislation which would enable them to cooperate with the Federal Government in flood and erosion control programs. It occurs to me that it may be appropriate for you to send a letter to the Governors requesting their consideration of the proposed legislation. A draft of a proposed letter to the Governors is attached, together with a digest and complete text of the Standard State Soil Conservation Districts Law.[1]

Respectfully,

H. A. WALLACE

[13:OF 1:TS]

[1] The digest (typed) is entitled, "Basic Provisions of the Standard State Soil Conservation Districts Law." The text is *A Standard State Soil Conservation Districts Law* (Washington, 1936). Letters modeled on the draft enclosed were sent to the governors on Feb. 23, 1937; see *post*, 597.

591   HENRY A. WALLACE, SECRETARY OF AGRICULTURE, TO ROOSEVELT

WASHINGTON, *February 16, 1937*

DEAR MR. PRESIDENT: The Department of Agriculture has responsibilities for work on watersheds for waterflow retardation and soil erosion prevention under the Omnibus Flood Control Act of 1936; similarly, the War Department is responsible for work on the waterways.

In the discharge of these responsibilities satisfactory assurance of cooperation from the States must be obtained. State and local cooperation adequate to meet the needs of the War Department is provided in the Flood Control Act. There is no provision for any State or local cooperation with the Department of Agriculture, although much of the control work must be done on farms and other private lands.

The Flood Control Act should be amended at an appropriate time. Legislation specifically authorizing the Department of Agriculture to require such cooperation should be included. Likewise any new flood control legislation should similarly provide for State and local cooperation. The necessity for these provisions and the suggested language for incorporation in legislation are given in the attached statement.[1]

Sincerely yours,

H. A. WALLACE

[13:OF 732:TS]

[1] "The Position of the United States Department of Agriculture on State and Local Cooperation in Flood Control." This included a draft amendment to the 1936 Flood Control Law to bring about the cooperation sought. The draft was incorporated (as section 4) in the act approved Aug. 28, 1937 (50 *Stat.* 876).

[22]

Summerville, S. C., *Feb. 17, 1937*

Personal.　Attention of Miss LeHand

Dear Mr. President: Our interview was cut so short, that I feel I should try to make clear in as few words as possible the matter I particularly had on my mind.[1]

The National Parks Association, formed when only the older National Parks and Monuments were in the care of the National Park Service, is naturally chiefly concerned about the future of these reservations. Recent enlargement of the field of the Service has added various duties which are not concerned with preservation.　While we recognize the value of these new activities, we are frankly fearful that they will claim such a large part of the Bureau's attention in the future as to bring about a change in its major function from preservation to mere playground development.　The result might be that the unique institution we now call the National Primeval Parks, possessing values which most other areas either never have had or have lost—values which cannot be restored once they have been impaired or destroyed—would be completely submerged in a purely recreational promotion.

You will remember that the duty originally laid upon the Park Service was to "regulate the use of the Federal areas known as National Parks * * * by such means and measures as conform to the fundamental purpose of the said Parks, which purpose is to conserve the scenery and the natural and historic objects and the wild life therein, and to provide for the enjoyment of the same *in such manner and by such means as will leave them un-impaired for the enjoyment of future generations.*"[2]　We believe that the objectives here so well stated should remain the chief objective of the National Park Service.

In the reorganization of the government, which you undoubtedly will be empowered to make, it is my confident belief that you will have in mind the welfare of our matchless heritage of the Creator's masterpieces.

Sincerely yours,

Wm. P. Wharton

[*Notation*:A] ackd 2/20/39[3]

[13:OF 6–P:TS]

---

[1] Wharton had talked with Roosevelt on February 12 (PPF 1–O).

[2] From the National Park Service Act of Aug. 25, 1916 (39 *Stat.* 535).　The italicized words were underscored by Wharton.

[3] By LeHand (OF 6–P).

593   Roosevelt to Richard G. Tyler, Chairman, Department of Civil Engineering, University of Washington, Seattle

[Washington] *February 18, 1937*

My dear Professor Tyler: I am grateful for your letters of December 12 and February 6, and for your continuing interest in the problem of engineering education presented in my letter of October 7 to presidents of educational institutions.[1]

Responses to my letter indicate that there is a substantial group of educators who agree that, notwithstanding notable recent progress, engineering education generally does not yet give graduates an adequate understanding of the social problems which result from the impact of engineering technology on our culture.

Your suggestion—that further discussion of the problem would be promoted by consideration of specific courses which should be added to curricula—is constructive. Believing strongly in democratic processes, I believe that action along this line should be begun and carried on within the profession. I hope that you and colleagues of the same mind can succeed in having such concrete proposals presented and discussed at appropriate professional meetings.

Very sincerely yours,

[Franklin D. Roosevelt]

[13:OF 2450:CT]

[1] See *ante,* 563.

594   Roosevelt to Harold L. Ickes, Secretary of the Interior

Washington, *February 19, 1937*

Memorandum for the Secretary of the Interior: What is the latest news about the Sugar Pine Grove next to the Yosemite?[1]

F. D. R.

[13:OF 6–P:CT]

[1] See *post,* 621.

595   Roosevelt to C. Blackburn Miller, President, Salt Water Anglers of America, New York City

[Washington] *February 23, 1937*

My dear Mr. Miller: Thank you very much for your letter of January eighteenth.[1] My intense interest in the conservation and development of our natural resources of every character is, I believe, quite generally known.

The Budget for the coming fiscal year has been completed and is now before Congress. I have accordingly instructed the Acting Director of the Bureau of the Budget to give careful consideration to an estimate of appropriation for a sound program of salt water fisheries research work, if submitted by the Department of Commerce for the fiscal year ending June 30, 1939, which gives reasonable promise of results commensurate with its need and cost.

I congratulate you upon your achievements in promoting harmony among the commercial and sports fisheries and the real progress you and your associated agencies are making in the interest of effective conservation.

Very sincerely yours,

[FRANKLIN D. ROOSEVELT]

[13:OF 3–E:CT]

[1] Miller's letter was sent to the Bureau of Fisheries for draft of reply and was not returned to the White House. It proposed that funds be made available to the Bureau of Fisheries so that a thorough study could be made of ocean fish and measures taken by the Government to ensure their abundant supply (McIntyre to Bell, Feb. 1, 1937, OF 3–E). Commissioner Frank T. Bell of the Bureau of Fisheries prepared a draft reply which would have had the President say that he was asking the Department of Commerce to reassess the financial needs of its research program (Bell to McIntyre, Feb. 5, 1937, OF 3–R). This draft was prepared for Roosevelt's signature and was signed by him but was then sent to Acting Budget Director Bell for review (McIntyre to Daniel W. Bell, Feb. 12, 1937, OF 3–R). The Acting Budget Director was of the opinion that "the reply contemplated might, and probably would, be construed as endorsement of a research program considerably broader than . . . necessary," and called attention to the President's veto, in the previous session of Congress, of a bill for construction of a vessel for fishery research work in the Pacific, and of his withholding of approval of a fishery research bill (Daniel W. Bell to McIntyre, Feb. 18, 1937, OF 3–R). The Acting Budget Director submitted another draft, the letter to Miller here printed.

596   PRESS CONFERENCE, Executive Offices of the White House, February 23, 1937, 4:05 P. M.

[*Excerpt*] The President: I was just showing the Dean [1] my bill which has just come in for 26,000 trees which are going to be planted next month.

Q: Spruce trees, aren't they?

The President: In other words, I am practising what I preach.

Q: Are these the Christmas trees?

The President: Yes. 23,000 Norway spruce, 2,000 balsam firs and 1,000 Douglas firs. That is experimental. That is an awful lot of trees.

Q: Those are the ordinary Santa Claus trees?

The President: Yes. They are on another ten acres of waste land. That is stopping erosion.

Q: You did not tell us the amount of the bill.

The President: $130.00.

Q: Did you say, sir, whether they are to be planted in Georgia or in New York?

The President: At Hyde Park.

Q: $130.00 for all of them?

The President: Yes, $5.00 a thousand.

Q: Are they seedlings?

The President: They call them three-year old transplants. In other words, they have been transplanted once already from the original bed.

Q: Do you get them from the State Conservation Department?

The President: Yes.

Q: You had the others down at Valkill?

The President: In back of the cottage, yes. Outside of that I don't think there is any news at all.

[13: PRESIDENT'S PRESS CONFERENCES: T]

[1] John Russell Young, one of the newspapermen present.

597   ROOSEVELT TO GOVERNOR JAMES V. ALLRED, Austin, Texas

[WASHINGTON] *February 23, 1937*

MY DEAR GOVERNOR: The dust storms and floods of the last few years have underscored the importance of programs to control soil erosion. I need not emphasize to you the seriousness of the problem and the desirability of our taking effective action, as a Nation and in the several States, to conserve the soil as our basic asset. The Nation that destroys its soil destroys itself.

In the Act of Congress approved April 27, 1935 (Public No. 46 of the 74th Congress), the Federal Government, through the Soil Conservation Service of the Department of Agriculture, initiated a broad program for the control of soil erosion. Demonstration work has ben undertaken but much remains to be done. The conduct of isolated demonstration projects cannot control erosion adequately. Such work can only point the way.

The problem is further complicated by the fact that the failure to control erosion on some lands, particularly if such eroding lands are situated strategically at the heads of valleys or watersheds, can cause a washing and blowing of soil onto other lands, and make the control of erosion anywhere in the valley or watershed all the more difficult. We are confronted with the fact that, for the problem to be adequately dealt with, the erodible land in every watershed must be brought under some form of control.

To supplement the Federal programs, and safeguard their results, State legislation is needed. At the request of representatives from a number of States, and in cooperation with them, the Department of Agriculture has prepared a standard form of suitable State legislation for this purpose, generally referred to as the Standard State Soil Conservation Districts Law. The Act provides for the organization of "soil conservation districts" as governmental subdivisions of the State to carry on projects for erosion control, and to enact into law land-use regulations concerning soil erosion after such regulations have been approved in a referendum. Such legislation is imperative to enable farmers to take the necessary cooperative action.

I am sending to you several copies of the Standard State Soil Conservation Districts Law, with a memorandum summarizing its basic provisions. I hope that you will see fit to make the adoption of legislation along the lines of the Standard Act part of the agricultural program for your State.[1]

Very sincerely yours,

[FRANKLIN D. ROOSEVELT]

[13:OF 732:CT]

[1] This letter originated in the draft statement sent to Roosevelt by Wallace on Feb. 16, 1937 (*ante*, 591). With this draft is a memorandum, Roosevelt to Early, February 19: "Will you work out with Wallace a letter to all the Governors based on this type letter but shortened from three pages to two, and I will sign them?" Early submitted the draft on which the letter here printed was based with a note (February 19) saying that the new draft had Wallace's approval. The material omitted consisted of a statement of the work of the Soil Conservation Service, a paragraph on the results of improper land-use practices, and a warning that unless suitable state machinery were provided, "the full benefits of Federal expenditures and cooperation" could not be realized. Identical letters were sent to all the governors on Feb. 23, 1937.

598   HENRY A. WALLACE, SECRETARY OF AGRICULTURE, TO ROOSEVELT

WASHINGTON, *March 4, 1937*

DEAR MR. PRESIDENT: Because of your very deep and sincere interest in the cause of conservation, I am bringing to your attention the dilemma in which the Biological Survey finds itself in its land purchase program.

The Survey has obligated as much of the six million dollars for land as it is possible to do until present condemnation cases have been concluded. After that any balance will be very small.

During the past three years they have built up a competent and well-trained personnel for the appraisal and purchase of lands best suited for wildlife refuge purposes, capable to handle with economy and good judgment a purchase program of from three to five million dol-

[27]

lars a year. They are now facing the necessity of dissolving it in the near future if no more land purchase money is allowed. You have on your desk a brief of the program submitted recently by the Biological Survey for continuing this program. Would it be possible for you to indicate, in the near future, whether money would be forthcoming to continue this program so that plans may be made accordingly?

The Biological Survey program submitted to you expresses the minimum needs to effectively carry out the conservation of waterfowl undertaken three years ago. In the future it will have to be supplemented by smaller subsidiary refuges and perhaps by the acquisition of lands adjacent to existing refuges as economic changes make feasible the purchase of such areas at present too expensive to acquire. However, the early fulfillment of the program submitted to you is necessary if the perpetuation of the migratory waterfowl is to be realized and it will also save some of the rare species, notably the Carolina paroquet and the ivory-billed woodpecker which head the list of those that need assistance.

In case no money is available for allocation now or in the immediate future, may we have permission to attempt to secure funds from Congress? However, we do not feel very optimistic about this possibility and would much prefer that the money come through you, although the increasing number of friends of wildlife in Congress might make a special appropriation possible if it would not conflict with your conservation program.[1]

Sincerely,

H. A. WALLACE

[13:OF 1–F:TS]

[1] Answered *post,* 615.

599   MILBURN L. WILSON, ACTING SECRETARY OF AGRICULTURE, TO ROOSEVELT

WASHINGTON, *March 6, 1937*

DEAR MR. PRESIDENT: I am advised that S. 206 has passed both the Senate and the House of Representatives and is now before you for approval. This bill provides for a preliminary examination and survey by the War Department of the Snake River and its tributaries in Idaho, Washington, and Oregon, with a view to control of floods in accordance with the provisions of the Omnibus Flood Control Act, approved June 22, 1936. Several weeks ago, the Department of Agriculture prepared an amendment to S. 206 for the consideration of the Chairman of the House Committee on Flood Control but, unfortunately, the report did not receive the required Administration clearance before final action was taken by Congress.

S. 206 is deficient in that no authorization is given the Department of Agriculture to make the necessary preliminary examination and survey of the watershed of the Snake River.

Congress declared in the Flood Control Act of 1936, to which S. 206 is related, that hereafter investigations and improvements of waterways for flood control shall be under the jurisdiction of the War Department, and investigations of watersheds and measures for run-off and water-flow retardation and soil-erosion prevention on watersheds shall be under the jurisdiction of the Department of Agriculture. Pursuant to this declaration, Section 6 of the Act authorized the Secretaries of War and of Agriculture to make such preliminary examinations and surveys on the waterways and watersheds respectively of 222 designated localities. Thus Congress, for the first time, recognized the necessity of tackling the flood control problem simultaneously on the land and in the streams. This was a remarkable step forward and it would be unfortunate if we now began sacrificing or handicapping this policy.

I therefore hope that, in approving S. 206, you will call the attention of the Senate Committee on Commerce and the House Committee on Flood Control, to the deficiency in that legislation and recommend to the Congress: (1) That it enact legislation which will authorize the Department of Agriculture to examine and survey all watersheds of rivers which the War Department, under previous legislation and including S. 206, has been authorized to survey; (2) that this principle be adhered to in any future legislation which relates to the Flood Control Act of 1936. I am attaching a suggested bill which would suffice for the first purpose and suggested language for inclusion in future flood-control legislation.[1]

Sincerely yours,

M. L. WILSON

[13:OF 1:TS]

[1] These two drafts, of one page each, are present. S. 206 was approved March 4, 1937 (50 *Stat.* 26), without comment by Roosevelt.

600 HENRY A. WALLACE, SECRETARY OF AGRICULTURE, TO ROOSEVELT

[WASHINGTON] *March 13, 1937*

DEAR MR. PRESIDENT: .With reference to your memorandum of January 23, 1937, concerning the possibilities of tree planting in the Great Plains region, the Forest Service, Soil Conservation Service, and the Bureau of Plant Industry, of this Department, submit the following:

In Zone 1, to the westward (map attached), lack of rainfall and moisture, and particularly wind in relation to evaporation, restrict the opportunities for tree planting to (a) limited areas having particularly favorable conditions and (b) individual farmsteads where special care can be given and where small windbreaks will make the prairies a better place to live, though not affecting mass wind movement or soil erosion. Only some 500,000 acres in Zone 1 are considered favorable for tree planting, mostly in small units.

In Zone 2, to the eastward, additional rainfall and moisture, with lessened wind and evaporation, provide more favorable conditions for tree planting, some 5,500,000 acres in this Zone being considered favorable for such purpose. It is within Zone 2 that the National shelterbelt was projected. Conditions for tree growth are sufficiently favorable in many parts of this area to promise success for relatively large-scale tree plantings. The locations must be selected, however, and tree planting alone can not be counted on for erosion control.

Although there are over 20,000,000 acres of publicly-owned lands within the Great Plains, these occur in Zone 1, and only a very small part is suitable for tree planting. Most of it is in grass, and grass must be relied upon primarily to control erosion. Within Zone 2, where large-scale tree planting is considered practicable by the Forest Service, there is no public domain.

Experimental and demonstrational plantings, under many conditions, in both Zones 1 and 2 should be continued and expanded to provide a background of fact for planning the continued program of small-scale and large-scale planting, and also to promote by example the private plantings of windbreaks around the farmsteads which will be conducive to better social conditions for our Great Plains families.

The recommendations by the Great Plains Committee offer definite support for tree planting as an integrated part of the larger erosion-control program. The Presidential Order authorizing a large-scale shelterbelt planting provided for the first time a plan for comprehensive action. Over 32,000 acres have been planted in two years with emergency funds in spite of limitations by the constant questioning of legal and fiscal authority. The Norris-Doxey Farm Forestry Bill (S. 1504 and H. R. 4728), if enacted, would furnish such additional legislative authority as is needed. With provision of the necessary funds, the Department is prepared to undertake the planting on a scale leading very rapidly to at least 125,000 acres a year on farm lands in Zone 2.

It is estimated that annual appropriations of $3,250,000 for planting in Zone 2, and $100,000 for an adequate program of research and demonstration in Zones 1 and 2, would be needed.

The planting can be done. It is essential, however, that the organic legislation now in process be passed and that there be continuity of financing.[1]

Respectfully yours,

[HENRY A. WALLACE]

[13:OF 1–C:CT]

¹ An attached memorandum, Roosevelt to the Acting Director of the Budget, written at Warm Springs, March 17, 1937, reads, "Will you speak to me about this on my return?"

601   HAROLD L. ICKES, CHAIRMAN, NATIONAL RESOURCES COMMITTEE, TO ROOSEVELT

WASHINGTON, *Mar. 16, 1937*

MY DEAR MR. PRESIDENT: For your information I am forwarding herewith a copy of a second report on Water Pollution, prepared by a special committee of the National Resources Committee.

The members of the National Resources Committee have not yet had an opportunity to examine this document, and it is transmitted in advance of their consideration only because hearings are proposed on bills concerning this matter during the next week.[1]

Sincerely yours,

HAROLD L. ICKES

[13:OF 1092:TS]

[1] *Second Report on Water Pollution by the Special Advisory Committee on Water Pollution* (Washington, 1937). The report was endorsed by the National Resources Committee and officially submitted to Roosevelt by Ickes in a letter of March 22, 1937 (OF 1092). It recommended that Federal financial assistance in pollution abatement be continued, that pollution control work be integrated with other water conservation activities, and that no new Federal regulatory legislation be enacted. A bill before Congress at this time (H. R. 2711, introduced by Representative Vinson of Kentucky on Jan. 12, 1937) proposed the establishment of a Division of Water Pollution Control in the United States Public Health Service, and the authorization of annual grants or loans amounting to as much as $700,000 for the construction of pollution-abatement facilities by public and non-public agencies and corporations. In the debate in the House, Faddis (Pa.) criticized the bill on the ground that it lacked teeth and would be ineffectual in stopping pollution of streams by industries. Vinson defended it as being a gradual approach to the problem.

In connection with Ickes' reference (in the letter here printed) to pending legislation, it may be noted that in the debate it was brought out that the Budget Bureau had reported to the Treasury Department that enactment of the bill would not be in accord with the President's program. Vinson replied that he was not aware of this and that so far as he knew, the President was not against the measure. He also said that the National Resources Committee was behind his bill "with all their power and strength." It is clear from the debate, however, that Administration support was not in evidence. The bill was passed by both House and Senate but in different forms and at the end of the session it was before a conference committee (*Cong. Rec.*, 75th Cong., 1st sess., 81: 1, 196; 81: 4, 3679–3700; 81: 8, 8947–8951, 8954–8957, 9182–9183). Passed in the following session, the bill was vetoed by Roosevelt; see his veto message, *post*, 799.

WARM SPRINGS, GEORGIA, *March 17, 1937*

MEMORANDUM FOR THE SECRETARY OF AGRICULTURE: I think this
will interest you. The nub of the whole question is this: if a farmer
in up-State New York or Georgia or Nebraska or Oregon, through bad
use of his land, allows his land to erode, does he have the inalienable
right as owner to do this, or has the community, i. e., some form of
governmental agency, the right to stop him?

F. D. R.

[*Notation*:T] Letter from Mrs. Caroline O'Day, MC, 3/12/37 to Miss
LeHand, enclosing letter to Mrs. O'Day from Dorothy Straus, 475
Fifth Ave., NYC, 3/2/37, in re Standard Soil Erosion Act and its
possible effects in New York.[1]

[13:OF 732:CT]

---

[1] These letters were presumably retained by Wallace. The act referred to was
the Standard State Soil Conservation Districts Law.

603   ROOSEVELT TO SENATOR ELBERT D. THOMAS OF UTAH

WASHINGTON, *March 29, 1937*

MY DEAR SENATOR THOMAS: I have received your letter of January 29, requesting that an Executive order be issued permitting prospecting for minerals and the locating of mining claims under the United
States mining laws on lands withdrawn and included in national game
preserves.

National game preserves have been established by Executive order
either by virtue of the authority vested in the President or pursuant to
specific acts of Congress, and jurisdiction thereover is conferred by law
upon the Secretary of Agriculture. The Congress did not provide that
the United States mining laws shall be applicable to lands included in
such game preserves but, on the contrary, application of the mining
laws thereto is seemingly precluded by the provisions of Section 10 of the
Migratory Bird Conservation Act of February 18, 1929 (45 *Stat.* 1222).
Consequently, I believe that your objective may be effected only through
an act of Congress.[1]

Sincerely yours,

[FRANKLIN D. ROOSEVELT]

[13:OF 378: CT]

---

[1] Drafted by the Interior Department.

[Washington] *Apr. 3, 1937*

My dear Mr. Secretary: It is my understanding that following a resolution of the Flood Control Committee of the House of Representatives, the United States Engineer Corps was delegated to review the flood control programs of the Ohio River and the Lower Mississippi River.

It is my further understanding that General Markham is prepared in the immediate future to submit a report on that subject.

In view of the great importance of this enterprise and its probable relationships to other water resources problems in the same areas, I am requesting that the report of General Markham be submitted to me for review before it is finally submitted to Congress and that it be withheld from any public use or release until it has been submitted to me.

It is my intention to submit this preliminary document to the National Resources Committee for review and for careful clearance and discussions with other Federal agencies having major water interests in both of these basins.

It is my wish that this procedure be followed with respect to any future similar reports which you may be called upon to submit to the Congress or to any Committee or member thereof.

Sincerely yours,

[Franklin D. Roosevelt]

[*Notation*:AS] DWB[1]

[13:OF 25–N:CT]

[1] Acting Budget Director Daniel W. Bell, in whose agency this letter was drafted. Answered *post,* 610.

605　Roosevelt to Harold L. Ickes, Secretary of the Interior, and Arno B. Cammerer, Director, National Park Service

[Washington] *April 5, 1937*

Memorandum . . . In regard to the Great Smoky Park, I understand that North Carolina has made all of its necessary land purchases and that we are held up by Tennessee's failure to complete its acreage. Would it be possible, under the law, to open the North Carolina side of the Park? Perhaps this would encourage Tennessee to complete their purchases as agreed on.[1]

F. D. R.

FDR/DJ

[13:OF 6–P:CT]

[1] A report on this query was made by Cammerer to Ickes, April 17, 1937 (OF 6–P); see *post,* 652.

THE WHITE HOUSE, *April 5, 1937*

TO THE CONGRESS OF THE UNITED STATES: On March 21, 1933, I addressed a message to the Congress in which I stated:

I propose to create a civilian conservation corps to be used in simple work, not interfering with normal employment, and confining itself to forestry, the prevention of soil erosion, flood control and similar projects. I call your attention to the fact that this type of work is of definite, practical value, not only through the prevention of great present financial loss, but also as a means of creating future national wealth.

The prompt consideration given to this message by Congress resulted in the enactment, on March 31, 1933, of Public No. 5, to provide for the relief of unemployment through the performance of useful public work; and on April 5, 1933, by Executive Order, I set up the office of Emergency Conservation Work to carry the above Act into effect.

It is not necessary to go into detail regarding the accomplishments of the Corps. You are acquainted with the physical improvements that have taken place in our forests and parks as a result of the activities of the Corps and with the wealth that is being added to our natural resources for the benefit of future generations. More important than the material gain, however, is the improvement we find in the moral and physical well-being of our citizens who have been enrolled in the Corps and of their families who have been assisted by monthly allotments of pay.

The functions of the Corps expire under authority of present law on June 30, 1937.

In my Budget Message to Congress on January 5 of this year I indicated that the Corps should be continued and recommended that legislation be enacted during the present session to establish the Corps as a permanent agency of the Government. Such continuance or establishment is desirable notwithstanding the great strides that have been made toward national recovery, as there is still need for providing useful and healthful employment for a large number of our youthful citizens.

I am convinced that there is ample useful work in the protection, restoration and development of our national resources, upon which the services of the Corps may be employed advantageously for an extended future period. It should be noted that this program will not in any respect reduce normal employment opportunities for our adult workers; in fact, the purchase of simple materials, of food and clothing and of other supplies required for the operations of the Corps tends to increase employment in industry.

I recommend, therefore, that provision be made for a permanent Corps of 300,000 youths (and war veterans), together with 10,000 Indians and 5,000 enrollees in our territories and insular possessions. It would appear, after a careful study of available information, that, with improved business conditions, these numbers represent the maximum expected enrollment. To go beyond this number at this time would open new and difficult classifications of enrollment, and the additional cost would seriously affect the financial position of the Treasury.

I trust that the Congress will deem it wise to enact legislation making permanent the Civilian Conservation Corps.[1]

FRANKLIN D. ROOSEVELT

[W. H. PRESS RELEASES: M]

[1] A draft of a bill along the lines suggested by Roosevelt in his letter to Fechner of Oct. 26, 1936 (*ante*, 567), was prepared by the Emergency Conservation Work. In submitting the draft, Acting Director McEntee said that much of the language was based on previously issued executive orders relating to the administration of the Civilian Conservation Corps (McEntee to Roosevelt, Feb. 10, 1937, OF 268). This bill (presumably) was the one introduced in the Senate on April 7 as S. 2102, and in the House on April 21 as H. R. 6551. (Four other bills to establish a permanent CCC were introduced in the House between Jan. 5 and April 6, 1937, but none was reported from committee.) The Senate passed over its bill in favor of the House bill. The debate in both houses was protracted and the bill as approved June 28, 1937 (50 *Stat.* 319), was the result of numerous amendments and several House and Senate conferences. The act did not provide for a permanent agency although the President's wishes in this regard were emphasized by the bill's sponsors. Instead, the life of the Corps was fixed at three years beginning July 1, 1937. It was to be employed in (among other things) the protection and restoration of the lands and waters "and the products thereof" of the United States; it could work on lands of counties and municipalities, and on private lands under the arrangement sanctioned by the original act.

Much of the debate on the bill centered on the value of the proposed agency as a means of rehabilitating and educating unemployed young men. Some criticism was made, however, of the value of the work done in soil erosion and forestry, and Representative Rich of Pennsylvania said that in his state much of the work was "made work" (*Cong. Rec.*, 75th Cong., 1st sess., 81:4, 3705, 4349–4353, 4353–4401; 81:5, 4762–4769, 4825–4831, 4831–4845, 5371–5373; 81:6, 6095–6102, 6203–6205, 6299–6306).

607 PRESS CONFERENCE, Executive Offices of the White House, April 6, 1937, 4:10 P. M.

[*Excerpt*] Q: Mr. President, are your plans for flood control nearing completion now? There are several schemes up on the Hill to create authorities of various sorts, and they seem to have boiled down in the last —

The President: That's it. I am trying to boil them down and see if we can't get them in somewhat orderly shape, which they are not in now.

As you know, there has been a habit—I suppose it has been in existence forty or fifty years, as far as I know—on any flood control project or any river or harbor improvement, on any suggestion that has been made either by a committee or by a member of a committee that they would like such and such a river deepened or such and such a harbor dredged out, they have had a habit of sending directly for a report and recommendation from some Government agency involved. It may be the Reclamation Service, or it may be the Army Engineers or it may be any one of half a dozen different agencies. Then the particular agency so asked has been in the habit, in the past, of sending back their recommendations to the Committee of the Congress, in many cases without even referring it to the head of their own Department. Well, of course, the net result is that you get favorable recommendations from different Government bureaus for perfectly obvious reasons. They would like to do the additional work. That is only human. It is a perfectly natural thing. But there has never been any organization to tie the whole thing in together as part of a national program.

I took up the other day with the Secretary of War and the Chief of Army Engineers many requests that have come down this year in regard to recommendations for different flood control projects. I also took it up with the Secretary of the Interior and got the recommendations from the Reclamation Service.[1] From now on such recommendations will be made, in complete form, by the bureau involved—that is all right—but they will come via the Secretary of the department to me. Then, pending the Reorganization Bill—until that goes through and goes into effect, as I hope it will, until that time—I will then take the bureau recommendation, which may have on it some comment from the head of the department, and send it to some appropriate reviewing authority, such, for example, as the National Resources Committee, for their comment. It won't take long, only a matter of a few days. It will then come back to my desk and then I may or may not add my comment and send the whole works up to the committee of the Congress so that they will have a complete picture, starting with the original recommendation of the bureau plus the comments on it all the way through to the responsible planning agency, and in that way I hope we will get a little more order out of it.

Q: When you say these will come to you through the secretary, do you mean the Secretary of War?

The President: Any one of the secretaries. It may be the Secretary of Agriculture, the Secretary of War, the Secretary of the Interior.

Q: Would this mean taking the Army Engineers out of the picture to some extent?

The President: No. Their recommendation will go as they make it to the Hill, absolutely. There was a fool editorial about a week ago about how the Army Engineers were going to be taken out of doing any public works. Of course that is crazy—perfectly silly.

[13:PRESIDENT'S PRESS CONFERENCES:T]

608   HENRY A. WALLACE, SECRETARY OF AGRICULTURE, TO
        ROOSEVELT

[WASHINGTON] *April 6, 1937*

DEAR MR. PRESIDENT: Congressman Whittington, Chairman of the Flood Control Committee of the House of Representatives, has invited the Department of Agriculture to offer suggestions for advancing the flood control program under the Flood Control Act approved June 22, 1936. I understand that hearings will probably be held by that Committee during the week of April 5, and that at these hearings consideration will be given to proposed amendments to the Act approved June 22, 1936, and to bills providing for additional examinations, surveys, and flood control operations, to take advantage of the experience of the past year.

I have prepared a letter for transmission to Congressman Whittington raising three considerations which the Department wishes to present for the attention of the Committee at these hearings. The proposed letter is attached hereto. May I ask you to advise me whether it is satisfactory to you that that letter be submitted? [1]

May I call your attention especially to the third point, discussion of which begins on page four of the accompanying proposed letter? In your recent letters to the Governors of the forty-eight States you recommended the adoption by State legislatures of legislation along the lines of the Standard State Soil Conservation Districts Law, to provide for State and local cooperation in erosion control. That same statute is appropriate to enable States and localities to provide similar cooperation in the watershed phases of the flood control programs of the Federal Government. Section 3 of the Flood Control Act of June 22, 1936, now requires State and local cooperation with the War Department in its operations for flood control, but that Act does not now require such cooperation in the work that the Department of Agriculture will be doing on the watersheds in aid of flood control. It is the purpose of the third point mentioned in the attached proposed letter, to suggest an amendment to Section 3 of the Act of June 22, 1936, to provide for such State and local cooperation with the Department of Agriculture in work on the watersheds for flood control purposes.

I am informed that at this writing ten States have adopted legislation along the lines of the Standard Act which you recommended to the Governors, and that there is good prospect that about ten more States will take this action during the present sessions of the legislatures. Amendment of the Flood Control Act of June 22, 1936 in the manner

I have suggested, will authorize the Secretary of Agriculture to require the adoption of such legislation in aid of flood control work on the watersheds, as a condition to the performance of such work in the State by the Federal Government, and will measurably facilitate the adoption of such legislation in the remaining States. The States will then be in position to cooperate both in erosion control and in the watershed phases of flood control.

Sincerely yours,

[HENRY A. WALLACE]

[*Notation*: A] HAW OK FDR 4-7-37

[13:OF 25-N:CT]

¹ Wallace's letter made three proposals. The first was that the Congressional policy declared by the 1936 Flood Control Act, that the Agriculture Department should have charge of Federal investigations of watersheds and of measures for waterflow retardation and soil erosion prevention, be made effective in all pending flood control bills. The second was that such authorization be given to the Agriculture Department in cases where legislation had already been enacted. The third was that the 1936 Flood Control Act be amended to provide for state and local cooperation in watershed surveys to be conducted by the Agriculture Department.

609   ROOSEVELT TO HENRY A. WALLACE, SECRETARY OF AGRICULTURE, AND OTHERS

WASHINGTON, *April 8, 1937*

MEMORANDUM FOR THE SECRETARY OF AGRICULTURE, THE RESETTLEMENT ADMINISTRATOR, THE ACTING DIRECTOR OF THE BUDGET, THE SOLICITOR OF THE INTERIOR DEPARTMENT: Will you please meet and discuss what is apparently the only remaining question in regard to this proposed bill (assuming that the bill method is preferable to the estimate of appropriation method): this question is whether Federal funds should be appropriated for the purchase of lands in the Columbia Basin?

One of the principal reasons for the development of this Basin has been the settling of families from other parts of the country who have migrated for economic reasons from submarginal farms, or who will be removed from submarginal farms because of the purchase of these lands by the Government, thus eliminating the lands from crop production.

We have always discussed the possibility of the Government buying new irrigable lands and settling submarginal farmers on them. It is, in fact, closely akin to the conflict in the House Agricultural Committee now pending.¹

F. D. R.

[13:OF 360:CT]

¹ The bill referred to was S. 2172, to prevent speculation in the Columbia Basin lands to be made irrigable by the Grand Coulee dam, approved May 27, 1937 (50 *Stat.* 208). This placed restrictions on the size of farms and provided for the recapture by the Government of excessive profits in the sale of land but did not provide for the purchase of lands by the Government.

610   HARRY H. WOODRING, SECRETARY OF WAR, TO ROOSEVELT

WASHINGTON, *April 8, 1937*

DEAR MR. PRESIDENT: I submit herewith, in compliance with the instructions contained in your letter of April 3, 1937, the report of the Chief of Engineers containing a comprehensive flood control plan for the Ohio and Lower Mississippi Valleys called for by Resolution of the Committee on Flood Control of the House of Representatives.

Under former procedure this report would be submitted direct to the Chairman of the Committee on Flood Control. The Department has been of the view that the scope of the project makes it of such significance in the national program as to warrant deviation from the established procedure. Accordingly, the report was prepared prior to the receipt of your letter of April 3, with a view to its transmission to Congress with an appropriate message from you. A draft of such a message is also submitted herewith.¹

Respectfully yours,

HARRY H. WOODRING

[13:OF 25–N:TS]

¹ This draft was not used; see below.

611   ROOSEVELT TO THE NATIONAL RESOURCES COMMITTEE

WASHINGTON, *April 8, 1937*

MEMORANDUM FOR THE NATIONAL RESOURCES COMMITTEE: I enclose letter from the Secretary of War accompanying report of Chief of Engineers relating to flood control plan for Ohio and Lower Mississippi Valleys.¹

As this report must be transmitted to the Committee on Flood Control of the House of Representatives, I should like to have the comment of the National Resources Committee on it.

At the same time it occurs to me that you will desire to consult with members of the former Great Plains Drought Committee and the former Water Resources Committee, both of whom made reports relating at least in part to the general subject of flood control.²

I hope I may have your report within a week, as I desire to advise the Committee of the House of Representatives as soon as possible.[3]

F. D. R.

[13:OF 25–N:T]

[1] Above.
[2] The report of the Great Plains Committee, *The Future of the Great Plains* (Washington, 1936), makes little mention of flood control. By "former Water Resources Committee" Roosevelt apparently meant its predecessor, the Water Planning Committee of the National Resources Board. This committee issued a report entitled, *Floods in the United States, Magnitude and Frequency* (Washington, 1936).
[3] April 28, 1937, *post*, 618.

612   MARVIN H. MCINTYRE, ASSISTANT SECRETARY TO THE PRESIDENT, TO SENATOR HATTIE W. CARAWAY OF ARKANSAS

[WASHINGTON] *April 14, 1937*

MY DEAR MRS. CARAWAY: The President asks me to thank you for your letter of April tenth, calling attention to the letter you received.[1]

May I say, quite frankly, the President feels as you do that the Corps of Engineers is competent, capable and qualified to handle flood control matters. However, the whole policy of flood control, as handled by the Army engineers, involves also the problems of agriculture and forestry.

You are familiar, of course, with the studies and consideration given, over the past few years, to the whole question. The problem is being treated in its entirety, and the questions of soil conservation, forestry, etc., are as much a part of flood control as is the building of dams and reservoirs. For this reason, the President feels that the National Resources Board should have the opportunity to study and make recommendations on all flood control projects.

Sincerely yours,

[MARVIN H. MCINTYRE]

MHM/K/MWD
[13:OF 25–N:CT]

[1] Senator Caraway (OF 25–N) said that her correspondent opposed referral of the Army Engineers' flood control plan to the National Resources Committee for review and insisted that the plan should be turned over to the Army Engineers for immediate action. Senate Joint Resolution 57, introduced by Senator Caraway on Jan. 30, 1937, provided for the direct submission to Congress by the Chief of Engineers of a comprehensive national flood control plan (*Cong. Rec.*, 75th Cong., 1st sess., 81: 1, 605).

CHARLES E. MERRIAM, ACTING CHAIRMAN, ADVISORY COMMITTEE TO THE NATIONAL RESOURCES COMMITTEE, TO ROOSEVELT

WASHINGTON, *April 19, 1937*

MY DEAR MR. PRESIDENT: In accordance with your memorandum of April 8, requesting the comments of the National Resources Committee on the Report of the Chief of Engineers relating to a flood control plan for the Ohio and Lower Mississippi Valleys, the Advisory Committee requested our Water Resources Committee to consult with members of the former Mississippi Valley Committee and the Great Plains Drought Committee. As a result of their deliberations the Water Committee submits the attached recommendations and comments, which are concurred in by the Advisory Committee.

In addition to the points raised by the Water Committee, the Advisory Committee wishes to call your attention to the relation of the activities proposed in the Report of the Chief of Engineers to problems of fiscal policy and public works planning. The data submitted by the Chief of Engineers does not give sufficient information to judge the effect of these construction projects on the market for materials of construction and on the nature and location of the labor required for building dams and dikes.

The Advisory Committee recommends:

(1) That the Report of the Chief of Engineers be returned to the War Department for further consideration, review and development in collaboration with other interested agencies, as outlined in paragraph 7 of the Water Committee Report; and

(2) That, in order to secure effective participation in this proposed collaborative reconsideration of the plan, modest additional resources be made available to the several agencies, other than the War Department, for employment of special consultants and for appropriate contacts with State and local groups. The aggregate sum need not exceed $175,000 and might be made available either through the National Resources Committee or direct to the agencies concerned.

In the absence of Chairman Ickes and Vice Chairman Delano, and in view of your request for a report within a week, it has not been practicable to secure the views of the members of the National Resources Committee. It has therefore fallen to me to submit these statements by the Advisory Committee and the Water Resources Committee.

Sincerely yours,

CHARLES E. MERRIAM

[13:OF 25–N:CTS]

WASHINGTON, *April 17, 1937*

Memorandum by the Water Resources Committee on the Report by the Chief of Engineers on a "Comprehensive Flood Control Plan for Ohio and Lower Mississippi Rivers," Under Date of April 6, 1937

The Water Resources Committee has reviewed the Report of the Chief of Engineers on a "Comprehensive Flood Control Plan for Ohio and Lower Mississippi Rivers," dated April 6, 1937, and, after consultation with members of the former Mississippi Valley Committee, Water Planning Committee, and Great Plains Committee, presents the following findings and recommendations:

I. Summary of Report of the Chief of Engineers

1. The Report of the Chief of Engineers is in response to a resolution of the Committee on Flood Control of the House of Representatives, dated February 10, 1937. The Report is dated April 6, 1937.

2. The Report submits revised plans for protective works against floods in the Ohio Valley and plans to insure further protection in the Mississippi Valley in the light of the January–February 1937 flood.

3. The Report proposes, in addition to projects already authorized, additional reservoirs, levees, flood walls, and other works, and the purchase of lands and rights-of-way, at an estimated cost of more than $800,000,000, of which approximately one-third would be borne by local interests under existing policy.

II. Previous Plans

4. On the Lower Mississippi River the present levee system had its beginning in the New Orleans area as early as 1717. The United States had expended less than $1,000,000 up to 1879. By 1927 $340,000,000 had been spent by the Federal Government and local groups on the Mississippi River below Cairo, of which sum only $80,000,000 were Federal funds. The Flood Control Act of May 15, 1928, authorized additional Federal appropriations for this River of $325,000,000. The Act of June 15, 1936 (known as the Overton Act), amended the Act of 1928, modifying the physical plan, and authorized an appropriation of $272,000,000 in addition to unexpended balances under the 1928 Act. In addition to the work authorized by the Overton Act of June 15, 1936, flood control works on tributaries of the Mississippi are authorized in the Flood Control Act of June 22, 1936, to the extent of $92,000,000 (exclusive of Ohio River reservoirs).

On the Ohio River approximately $130,000,000 has been expended or authorized for flood control reservoirs, such as in the Miami Conservancy District, the Muskingum Watershed Conservancy District and for a reservoir system authorized under the·Flood Control Act of June 22, 1936 ($33,000,000 was for the Miami Conservancy District plan).

To these authorized or completed expenditures of $1,200,000,000 the Report of April 6, 1937, contemplates adding further expenditures of approximately $805,000,000 covering both Federal and local contributions.

III. Some Underlying Considerations

5. The Committee recognizes the fact that the scope of the Report of the Chief of Engineers is circumscribed by the resolution adopted by the Committee on Flood Control of the House of Representatives on February 10, 1937, but it feels impelled, nevertheless, to consider flood control as only one phase of the interlocking problems related to the control and use of water.

6. From this point of view, the plan proposed in the Report appears to be neither truly comprehensive nor effectively integrated.

7. The Report is silent on various problems of water and land that are inherent in or related to flood control and that are represented by such other Federal agencies as the Tennessee Valley Authority, the Federal Power Commission, the United States Public Health Service, the Bureau of Biological Survey and the Soil Conservation Service. It views these uses of water and land as only incidental to flood protection. It leaves their proper integration in later years too much to the future discretion of the War Department.

8. The Report appears to suggest important modifications in the principles of local participation in the costs of flood protection as established in the Flood Control Act approved June 22, 1936, and it undoubtedly will stimulate renewed efforts in various quarters to shift to the Federal Government entire financial responsibility for the amelioration of flood conditions.

9. The Report fails to present convincing economic and social justification for the huge expenditure it proposes (more than $800,000,000 in addition to existing unexpended authorizations of more than $400,-000,000). It states merely that "the real justification for this large expenditure is to be found in the saving of human life and suffering and in the prevention of the disturbances of the affairs of the nation brought about by a flood disaster." The Committee emphasizes the obvious fact that the expenditure in other ways of more than a billion dollars could bring far greater returns in reduction of deaths. Certainly, more definite bases for the justification of the proposed program are desirable.

10. The Report does not consider the flood regulation effects of the work now under way or proposed in the Tennessee Valley, in spite of the fact that the system of flood-control reservoirs now under construction or planned by the Tennessee Valley Authority on the Tennessee River system is expected to reduce crest flood flows at Paducah and Cairo by 200,000 second feet.

[43]

11. In the absence of basic supporting data regarding costs of construction, estimated damages, benefits and the like, it is impossible to separate tributary benefits from main river benefits. A clear exposition is desirable of exactly what benefits are to be attained at different places under various conditions of flood flow.

12. The Report makes no recommendations concerning such methods of reducing flood hazards as improved flood forecasting, the zoning of flood plains, the relocation and duplication of important key public utilities and the establishment of programs to prevent unwise encroachment upon river channels and their flood plains. Adequate forecasts of flood stages and effective plans for the evacuation of lowland dwellers in times of emergency could largely prevent, at comparatively trivial cost, the destruction of human life by floods.

IV. Recommendations

13. Since reasonably rapid progress in the control and alleviation of floods in the Mississippi Basin may be accomplished by measures indicated below, the Committee recommends that Congress withhold authorization of the plan involving works costing over $800,000,000 as recommended by the Chief of Engineers pending the completion of investigations herein proposed.

14. The Committee recommends that the 14 reservoir projects for the Ohio Basin, previously recommended by this Committee and already authorized by Congress, be listed for immediate construction, when the studies by the Corps of Engineers in collaboration with other Federal agencies have been completed. These reservoirs already have been authorized by the Congress and appropriations for them would involve approximately $85,000,000 in projects for construction during the next two years.

15. The Committee recommends that the construction of levees, flood walls and other works for the protection of cities and towns on the main Ohio River be undertaken whenever practicable plans are available and wherever appropriate local participation is assured, as required by the Flood Control Act approved June 22, 1936. Such a program should be woven into any new work relief policy, and it might aggregate $190,000,000 according to the Report of the Chief of Engineers.

16. The Committee recommends that any further participation by the Federal Government in cooperative flood control be made contingent upon proper action by state and local governments, satisfactory to the Secretary of War, restricting new and uneconomic encroachments upon flood plains. Only by such restrictions will it be practicable to prevent further encroachment, some of which would be encouraged by the construction of reservoirs.

17. The Committee has previously recommended purchase in fee simple of floodways along the Lower Mississippi and it now recommends

that authority be granted the Secretary of War to make such purchases in cases where the cost of flowage rights approximates the full cost of the land.

18. With respect to the other features of the plan proposed in the Report, aggregating over $600,000,000, the Committee finds that further analysis and appraisal of the entire plan by the interested agencies, and by the employment of special consultants are necessary. If and when these are undertaken additional funds will be necessary.

19. The Committee also suggests that such analysis should be made in consultation with state and local authorities from time to time on the various aspects of the comprehensive program herein discussed, inasmuch as many phases of the flood control problem obviously affect diversified interests.

20. The Committee recommends that the Department of Agriculture be authorized, in extension of a procedure sanctioned by the Flood Control Act of June 22, 1936, to extend its surveys of watershed areas to all parts of the Mississippi Basin with a view to determining desirable measures for retarding runoff, controlling soil erosion, and reducing the shoaling of river channels with erosional debris. The Committee is informed that the Secretary of Agriculture has already requested such authority.

Respectfully submitted,

[ABEL WOLMAN, Chairman]

[13:OF 25–N:CT]

615   ROOSEVELT TO HENRY A. WALLACE, SECRETARY OF AGRICULTURE

[WASHINGTON, *April 20, 1937*]

MY DEAR MR. SECRETARY: Reference is made to your letter of March 4, 1937, in which you advocate the acquisition of additional lands for wildlife refuges and request permission to attempt to secure funds for this purpose from Congress, in case no money is available for allocation now or in the immediate future.

I am sure you are well aware of my interest in the conservation of wildlife but, in the light of our financial condition as I see it now and as I am able to see it for this and the next fiscal year, I do not feel justified at this time in giving my approval to the land-purchase program which you have submitted. You will readily appreciate this after consideration of my message to the Congress on the subject of our fiscal affairs.

As to the allocation of emergency relief funds for the purchase of additional lands for wildlife refuges, I find that there are no balances from prior appropriations available for such purposes and due to the necessity of holding to the minimum the amount which I must ask Congress to appropriate for work relief of the unemployed during the fiscal year 1938, no provision can be made for the purchase of land from such funds.[1]

Sincerely yours,

[FRANKLIN D. ROOSEVELT]

[*Notation*:A] 4/20/37
[*Notation*:AS] DWB

[13:OF 1–F:CT]

[1] Drafted by the Budget Bureau. Acting Budget Director Bell, in a letter to Roosevelt enclosing the draft, April 20, 1937 (OF 1–F), said that the Biological Survey was not the only Government agency that wished to add to its land holdings. "There is the Forest Service, for instance, backed by strong groups interested in forestry, insisting upon material additions to the national forests. To approve the request for one activity would open the door for numerous requests which it would be difficult to resist."

616   ROOSEVELT TO HAROLD L. ICKES, SECRETARY OF THE INTERIOR

[WASHINGTON] *April 21, 1937*

MEMORANDUM FOR THE SECRETARY OF THE INTERIOR: Representative Caroline O'Day of New York is asking about the possibility of making Admiralty Island a wild life sanctuary until such time as it may be turned into a National Park. Will you and the Secretary of Agriculture talk this over and let me have a recommendation?[1]

F. D. R.

FDR/TMB
[13:OF 378:CT]

[1] Mrs. O'Day, writing April 17, 1937 (OF 378), had urged that something be done about Admiralty Island before the opening of the bear hunting season. See *post,* 645.

617   ROOSEVELT TO DANIEL W. BELL, ACTING DIRECTOR, BUREAU OF THE BUDGET

WASHINGTON, *April 28, 1937*

MEMORANDUM FOR D. W. B.: I have already told several leaders in House and Senate that in any new flood control work the state, county or municipality should pay for all lands, easements and rights of way for flood control works and that the U. S. Government would pay only for the flood control works and nothing for the land.

Please pass that along to the necessary Chairman, etc.[1]

F. D. R.

(Dictated but not signed)
FDR/DJ

[13:OF 132–C:CT]

[1] This was in reply to a memorandum on the subject from Bell, April 27, 1937 (OF 132–C).

618   ROOSEVELT TO REPRESENTATIVE WILLIAM M. WHITTINGTON
       OF MISSISSIPPI, CHAIRMAN, HOUSE COMMITTEE ON FLOOD
       CONTROL

EN ROUTE TO NEW ORLEANS, *April 28, 1937*

MY DEAR JUDGE WHITTINGTON: I enclose the report of the Chief of Engineers made in pursuance of Resolution of the Committee on Flood Control dated February 10, 1937.

Under the Resolution, this report covers a review of the reports submitted in House Documents Nos. 259 and 306, which relate to plans for a comprehensive reservoir system in the Ohio and Mississippi River basins. It also covers a review of Flood Control Committee Document No. 1, 74th Congress, relating to a revision and perfection of flood control for the alluvial valley of the Mississippi.

The present report relates especially to further flood control measures in the light of the Ohio River flood of January, 1937.

It will be noted, of course, that the present report, like the three previous reports, takes up only the subject of flood control works such as levees and reservoirs, all of these works being intended to keep out or to hold back waters after they have reached the main stem of the Mississippi or one of the principal tributaries thereof.

Forty-five new reservoirs in addition to those already authorized are recommended. The cost of the additional reservoirs would be $245,958,000.

The total cost of the works proposed for the protection of the Ohio River Basin would run, in round numbers, $440,000,000; in the Missouri River Basin to $132,000,000; in the Middle Mississippi Basin to $153,000,000, and on the Arkansas and White Rivers to $81,000,000.

Mention is made of securing fee simple title to floodways on the Mississippi River. It occurs to me that, in view of the history of previous legislation and its results, this is advisable in order that no questions may arise if it is found necessary to flood these lands. At the same time, it may be well to consider the possibility of renting these lands, once fee simple title is acquired, to neighboring farmers, with the definite understanding that tillage of these lands is solely at the risk of the individuals renting them.

Finally, the Chief of Engineers recommends, for additional flood control and fee simple purchases in the Mississippi Valley proper, an additional sum of $52,000,000.

To sum up the report, it proposes additional projects over and above those already authorized at an estimated cost of more than eight hundred million dollars, of which approximately one-third would be borne by local interests under existing authority.

Recognizing the fact that the report of the Chief of Engineers is limited by the Committee Resolution to large works such as levees and reservoirs, I have consulted with other agencies of the Government concerned with the control and use of water.

The report of the Chief of Engineers considers, of course, only one phase of the very large interlocking problem. For this reason it may be considered neither truly comprehensive nor effectively integrated. No opportunity has been possible, in this short space of time, to consider the report in relation to other Federal agencies, such as the Soil Conservation Service, the Forestry Service, the Tennessee Valley Authority, the United States Public Health Service, the Federal Power Commission and others.

For example, the report apparently does not consider the flood regulation work now under construction or planned by the Tennessee Valley Authority, which system is expected to reduce crest flood flows at Paducah and Cairo by 200,000 second feet.

No serious delay can come if the present Session of the Congress appropriates funds to undertake and continue some of the projects already authorized by previous Congresses for the Mississippi and Ohio Rivers. The amount of these appropriations should, of course, be viewed in the light of the budgetary necessities of the Government.

In the light of all the circumstances attaching to this report, I am requesting that a further and complete study be made by all of the Government agencies involved, sitting together as a group to make recommendations for a complete picture. This report should be available to the Congress by next January.

One other subject remains—the participation of state and local authorities in the cost of any of these projects. It is my belief that, for many reasons, the Federal Government should not be charged with the cost of the land necessary for levees, dams and reservoirs. This policy was adopted by the Congress last year in connection with the projects in the Connecticut River Valley. In that case, while no work has yet been started, it is my understanding that the states of Vermont, New Hampshire, Massachusetts and Connecticut are substantially in agreement in regard to the purchase of the necessary land. It should be made clear, however, that if any electric power results from the erection of dams and reservoirs, the Federal Government alone should have complete authority over the sale of this power.

I am returning about May 12th, at which time I shall be glad to discuss this whole subject with you and the members of your Committee in case you should care to do so.[1]

Very sincerely yours,

[FRANKLIN D. ROOSEVELT]

[13:OF 25–N:CT]

[1] Whittington replied in a long letter of May 5, 1937 (OF 25-N), defending the Chief of Engineers' plan:

"The proposed plan appears to be comprehensive for flood control. It would not conflict with the design and initiation of other improvements for water and soil conservation. The authorized beneficial activities of the several departments of the Government with respect to water and land conservation up to the present time have scarcely come in contact. When they do approach I feel that the War Department will fully cooperate with other governmental departments."

619   ROOSEVELT TO HARRY H. WOODRING, SECRETARY OF WAR

EN ROUTE TO NEW ORLEANS, *April 28, 1937*

DEAR HARRY: I have transmitted Gen. Markham's Flood Control Report to Chairman Whittington with a letter, of which I enclose a copy.[1]

Will you be good enough to have a meeting with Sec. Ickes and Sec. Wallace in order that the three Departments (including the Water Resources Committee, National Resources Committee) may work out a plan for the comprehensive report which I propose be made to the Congress next January.

It seems to me that in the future, instead of authorizing any new list of projects for some incredible sum, such as the eight hundred million dollars recommended herein, we should get Congress to approve, but not authorize, a five year or ten year plan, authorizing only those works which we are all agreed on should be commenced within the next two years and appropriating only for those works to be commenced within the next year.

Please explain this to General Markham. The present system is an impossible one and because of budgetary considerations would necessitate my disapproval of any huge authorization.

When I get back we can all talk this over.

Very sincerely yours,

[FRANKLIN D. ROOSEVELT]

[13:OF 25–N:CT]

[1] Above.

EN ROUTE TO NEW ORLEANS, *April 28, 1937*

MEMORANDUM FOR SECRETARY ICKES: Please read the enclosed copies of letters to the Secretary of War and Chairman Whittington of the Flood Control Committee of the House and get together with Henry Wallace so that by the time I get back we shall be ready to proceed with a comprehensive, long-distance plan.

I enclose my own file of correspondence with Wolman and the Merriam memoranda. Please bring it to me on my return.[1]

F. D. R.

[13:OF 25–N:CT]

[1] The first two enclosures mentioned are printed above. The Wolman correspondence consists of a copy of a letter from Roger B. McWhorter, chief engineer of the Federal Power Commission, to Abel Wolman, chairman of the Water Resources Committee of the National Resources Committee, April 19, 1937, commenting on a draft report of the WRC on the Army Engineers' flood control plan. The Merriam letter, April 19, 1937, is printed *ante*, 613. With the second paragraph omitted, the letter here printed was also sent to Wallace.

621   HAROLD L. ICKES, SECRETARY OF THE INTERIOR, TO JAMES ROOSEVELT, ADMINISTRATIVE ASSISTANT TO THE PRESIDENT

WASHINGTON, *April 29, 1937*

MY DEAR MR. ROOSEVELT: I have received your memorandum of April 27 and the enclosed correspondence from Congressman Englebright, concerning H. R. 5394 and Senate 1791 which propose to add a certain area of sugar pine forest to Yosemite National Park.[1]

In reply I am submitting the following information to refute the statements contained in Congressman Englebright's letter. This same information will be presented before the Public Lands Committee of both the House and Senate today by representatives of the Department.

The statement that a serious unemployment situation would almost immediately develop and that other dire consequences would result from the proposed purchase is grossly exaggerated. In the first place, the area of timber to be purchased is only 6,700 acres which is a relatively small area. It is difficult to understand how the purchase of so small an area of forest as this can seriously affect so many industries. The timber involved is enough to supply the sawmills of the lumber company for a period of only four to six years. The proposed purchase does not include all of the timber owned by the lumber company. It will have left enough timber to continue its operations for a period of from five to ten years.

The labor employed by the lumber company is very largely of a migratory type. This is due partly to the seasonal character of certain portions of their work. A census of the employees of this company taken within the last few days shows the total number of employees to be 422. Of this number 98 are aliens, the majority being Mexican and Italian. There are considerably more than 400 men employed during the summer season and considerably fewer than that during the winter. The employees own no property in the sawmill town. The lumber company owns all the cottages and cabins occupied by the laboring people. The employees have only a transitory interest in their homes and are little concerned about the proper maintenance of them. They move readily from place to place in search of employment or more congenial surroundings.

As pointed out by Congressman Englebright, there are many other stands of sugar pine forests in California. There are also many other logging operations in progress in sugar pine forests of less outstanding character. Even in Tuolumne County, the same County in which the proposed purchase is to be made, there are other logging operations which can furnish employment for the same laborers if they leave their employment at Merced Falls.

The claim that the proposed purchase will render it impossible for the Yosemite Valley Railway to continue operation is based on the assumption that the purchase will cause the Yosemite Sugar Pine Lumber Company to cease operation almost immediately. As pointed out above, this is not likely to happen for a period of some years. An examination of the financial statements of the Railway Company shows that it has succeeded in earning its operating expenses except in the worst years of the depression. Its income statement shows that it can continue to do this without the revenue from the lumbering operations. Officials of the Railroad Company claim there is a reasonable prospect for the development of mineral industries within a period of 15 or 20 years. They anticipate revenues from such industries to replace revenues now derived from the lumber traffic.

As it will be possible for this railroad to continue in operation, the claims that other important industries representing capital investments of approximately ten million dollars will be wiped out are entirely without foundation.

It is predicted by Congressman Englebright that the proposed purchase probably will cost in excess of three million dollars. It is our belief that if a reasonable price cannot be arranged through negotiation with the owners of the timber, condemnation proceedings will result in a price which should not exceed two million dollars.

On the other hand, as an alternative, it has been suggested by the California State Chamber of Commerce that the area be purchased by the Federal Government and the timber be harvested under a plan whereby roadside strips would be left and the remainder of the timber would be cut by selective logging. The plan has one serious defect: whether the forest is logged selectively or by any other method, it is the very finest trees—the ones it is desired to save—that would be cut down. Moreover, forests of such huge trees do not thrive in narrow strips because the trees are subject to wind-throw and, when disturbed, are more susceptible to the ravages of insects and disease. Such a plan would be conservation in name only.

It has been stated that the proposed purchase will have little, if any, effect in attracting additional tourists to Yosemite Park. While this may be correct, the matter should be considered in another light. It is quite within reason to expect that the cutting of the timber may have a very unfavorable effect upon travel to Yosemite Park over the Big Oak Flat Road. Many people drive to Yosemite Park over that road because of the charming drive through the sugar pine forest. If the forest is logged, thereby creating the usual scene of devastation along this road, visitors will be very severe in their criticism of the Government because of its failure to protect the beauty which has caused this drive to be so noteworthy. Economic losses to the towns along this road because of fewer Yosemite visitors travelling that way may have more far-reaching effects than the immediate loss of tax revenue in the county.

The bills providing for the saving of this forest are sponsored in Congress by Senator McAdoo and Congressman McGroarty, both of California, and they are very strongly in favor of the measures. They have found that there is very widespread sentiment in California favoring this bill. The only opposition from a California Congressman which has come to our attention is that of Congressman Englebright, in whose district the timber lies. We believe most of his opposition is due to the protests of county officials who anticipate tax losses. An amendment agreeable to this Department has been suggested to the House Public Lands Committee providing reimbursement of the counties for tax losses.

I am enclosing several photographs showing some of the large trees we are trying to save and others showing what is happening as the result of the logging operations of the Yosemite Sugar Pine Lumber Company on its lands adjoining the area we propose to purchase.[2]

Sincerely yours,

HAROLD L. ICKES

[13:OF 6–P:TS]

[1] James Roosevelt asked if Ickes thought that he (Ickes) should write to the chairman of the House Public Lands Committee about the bill. Englebright's letter to James Roosevelt, April 26, 1937 (OF 6–P), protested the enactment of the bill: the nature of his objections is indicated by the letter here printed.

[2] A copy of this letter was sent to Representative Englebright by James Roosevelt with a note (May 3, 1937, OF 6–P), saying that in view of Ickes' report there was

nothing more he could do. The bills in question, H. R. 5394 and S. 1791, "for the acquisition of certain lands for, and addition thereof, to the Yosemite National Park," were identical; both were introduced on March 8, 1937. Extensive hearings were held on the House bill by the Public Lands Committee (*Acquisition of Lands for, and Addition thereto, Yosemite National Park in California*, Hearings, 75th Cong., 1st sess., on H. R. 5394, Apr. 20–23, 1937, Washington, 1937). Englebright had succeeded in persuading the House committee to include a provision in the bill to reimburse Tuolumne County for the tax loss it would suffer by the taking of its lands. This, however, was rejected by the House after extended debate. He charged that the bill was supported principally by the Emergency Conservation Committee of New York City of which Rosalie Edge was chairman, Davis Quinn was secretary, and Irving Brant treasurer, and that this committee had no other membership.

The arguments brought against the bill by Englebright are adequately indicated by the Ickes letter here printed. Representative McGroarty (Calif.), sponsor of the bill, pointed out that the destruction of the forest would, in a few years, also result in unemployment and the destruction of capital values, but with nothing left in its place. The only debate in the Senate was over a minor matter of language which was settled in conference (*Cong. Rec.*, 75th Cong., 1st sess., 81:5, 5473–5490; 81:6, 6293, 6375, 6429, 6662, 6733, 6739). The act was approved July 9, 1937 (50 *Stat.* 485).

622   Harold L. Ickes, Secretary of the Interior, to Roosevelt

Washington, *Apr. 29, 1937*

Memorandum for the President: Reference is made to Senator Hayden's letter of March 12 to you, which was referred to this Department by Mr. Marvin H. McIntyre, regarding the possibility of making funds available for the purchase of certain lands within Saguaro National Monument, Arizona.[1]

The Saguaro National Monument was established by proclamation of March 1, 1933. It contains an area of 72,884 acres of which 63,284 acres are publicly owned, leaving 9,600 acres of alienated lands. There are 5,920 acres of State-owned lands and 3,680 acres of privately-owned lands comprising the 9,600 acres of alienated lands. Unfortunately, the major portion of the finest Saguaro cactus stand in the United States is located in the area not now controlled by the Federal Government.

Dr. H. L. Shantz, until recently president of the University of Arizona, has described the area as follows:

Nowhere in the world is there so fine a stand of the giant saguaro (Carnegia gigantia) as in the area included in the University Cactus Forest. Here the plants rise so close together that at times it is difficult to see through them for any great distance. Unique as is the area because of the close stand of saguaro, it is none the less remarkable for the fine stand of cholla, vignaga, ocotilla, palo verde, and hackberry, as well as hundreds of other interesting plants. Those who know every portion of the great Southwest maintain that the area surpasses them all.

To allow this area to pass to private ownership and allow these great plants to be destroyed or shipped and sold, would not only be a calamity to Arizona, but to the Nation and to science as well. Unfortuniately, the area had already been homesteaded, but the vegetation still remains in its virgin state.

It is recommended that the Federal Government undertake the purchase of the privately-owned lands, provided the State will agree to exchange its land for lieu lands of the public domain. It is also recommended that the Federal Government negotiate with the individual owners of the properties involved rather than with Mr. J. E. Harrison who claims to have options on all of the land. It is believed the 3,680 acres of privately-owned lands can be acquired for approximately $85,000.

If you approve, a supplemental item of $85,000 for inclusion in the pending Interior Department Appropriation Bill, conditioned upon the State of Arizona exchanging its lands for lieu lands of the public domain, will be submitted to the Bureau of the Budget for approval.

HAROLD L. ICKES

[13:OF 928:TS]

[1] Senator Hayden's letter was apparently not returned to the White House.

623 THE ORGANIZING COMMITTEE OF THE UP-STREAM ENGINEERING CONFERENCE TO ROOSEVELT

WASHINGTON, D. C., *April 30, 1937*

DEAR MR. PRESIDENT: We have the honor to submit in the form of a volume entitled "Headwaters Control and Use," the report of the Up-Stream Engineering Conference held in Washington, D. C. September 22nd and 23rd, 1936,[1] in accordance with instructions in your letter of June 16, 1936 appointing us as a committee to organize and conduct such a conference.

As stated in your letter, "Up-Stream engineering will have a major part in efforts to save the land and control floods, and for that reason it offers a broad field of opportunity for the engineering profession. There are indications that a substantial body of technical information on the control of little waters is now available in the scattered records of American experience. The urgent problem is to bring these data together in a coordinate body of engineering knowledge."

This report, we believe, is noteworthy in that it assembles under one cover for the first time a fairly complete treatment of the subject in the light of present knowledge: the basic scientific concepts and data; the specific objectives and techniques of application of these concepts in the control of waters in the various forms they take before becoming large streams; and general considerations of the social values to be realized through a comprehensive program of control and use of headwaters.

General interest in the subject was manifest in cordial cooperation from many sources and in the attendance. Attached is a list of cooperating agencies and individuals, both within and without the Government. The registered attendance—not including many members of Government organizations who "dropped in" for short periods to hear particular papers and discussions—was over six hundred. There were present eminent geophysicists, hydrologists, hydraulic engineers, civil engineers, agricultural engineers, geographers, biologists, economists, and political scientists, as well as other students and people of affairs who have become concerned with the problem of erosion and flood control, and with conservation in all its aspects.

Supplementary to the conference reported in this volume, the Committee organized a third days' program entitled "Young Men's Conference: On Behalf of a Continent." The purpose of this supplementary conference was to interest potential future leaders from all parts of the United States in the problems of soil and water conservation. This supplementary conference, which attracted a substantial audience, presented a program arranged by representatives of Four-H Clubs of America, the National Grange, the Future Farmers of America, the Junior Chamber of Commerce, and the National Youth Administration.

It is hoped that a new impulse has been given to the search for additional scientific data concerning the behavior of waters between the rain-drop and the river stages, and to the development of new techniques for application of fundamental principles to beneficial control and use of little waters.

Sincerely,

HUGH H. BENNETT, Chief, Soil Conservation Service
F. A. SILCOX, Chief, Forest Service
MORRIS L. COOKE [2]

[13:OF 2450:M]

[1] This was published by the Soil Conservation Service and the Forest Service with the cooperation of the Rural Electrification Administration as *Headwaters Control and Use; a Summary of Fundamental Principles and Their Application in the Conservation and Utilization of Waters and Soils* (Washington, 1937).
[2] Cooke had resigned as Rural Electrification Administrator on Feb. 6, 1937.

624   ROOSEVELT TO SENATOR CARL HAYDEN OF ARIZONA

ON BOARD U. S. S. "POTOMAC," *May 8, 1937* [1]

MY DEAR SENATOR HAYDEN: I have your letter of March 12, 1937, regarding the possibility of making funds available for the purchase of certain lands within the Saguaro National Monument, Arizona.

The general policy with respect to the acquisition of private lands for national parks and monuments has been to require their donation or purchase from donated funds. While it is true that there have been a few departures from this policy, I think that as a general policy it is a wise one, and that I would not be justified in submitting an estimate to Congress for an appropriation from the general fund of the Treasury to purchase the privately-owned land within the monument.[2]

Sincerely yours,

[FRANKLIN D. ROOSEVELT]

[13:OF 928:CT]

[1] Roosevelt was on vacation from April 28 to May 13, 1937. He left Washington on April 28 and boarded the *Potomac* at New Orleans on April 29. After a fishing cruise in the Gulf he returned to Washington by way of Galveston.

[2] Drafted by the Budget Bureau, to whom Ickes' letter to Roosevelt, April 29, 1937 (*ante*, 622), was referred. Acting Budget Director Bell's report to Roosevelt on the policy involved, May 6, 1937, is with the letter here printed.

625   ROOSEVELT TO HENRY C. TURNER, New York City

GALVESTON, TEXAS, *May 8, 1937*

MY DEAR MR. TURNER: This is in reply to your letter of April twenty-first,[1] concerning your check for $9.70 received from the Government in payment for plowing under 9.7 acres of a cover crop in a citrus grove in Florida, which you own.

I am informed by the Department of Agriculture that the check was issued after application for grant under the Agricultural Conservation Program had been made in the regular way by the Lake Wales Citrus Growers Association, acting as your agent. The application followed the filling out of a work sheet covering operations on your farm. Before the check was issued proof of compliance was given by your agent to the local committee.

Apparently the association acting as your agent was not informed of your desire not to receive any Government assistance in carrying out good conservation practice on your farm. Had it been so informed, the waste of effort by the local committee and the Government, in connection with the application made in your name, could have been avoided.

The majority of payments made to farmers under the program are larger than the one you received. While a payment of $9.70 may seem trivial to you, nevertheless there are many small farmers to whom even a payment of that size makes the difference between being able to finance a conservation practice and being forced to continue exploiting their soil.

If all landowners, unaided, could and would carry out proper soil conservation practice on their land, there would be no need for a soil conservation program sponsored by the Government. However, experience has shown that the pressure of competition forces most farmers,

[56]

in the absence of government assistance, to mine and exploit their soil, so as to increase their immediate cash return, even though it might be in their own long-time interest to avoid such exploitation. The government grants are intended to help the farmer avoid the cash sacrifice he would otherwise have to make in order to carry out good conservation practice.

The problem of stopping soil waste is especially acute on absentee-owned land which is occupied by tenants. The tenant naturally has little interest in conserving the soil for the benefit of some future occupant of the farm. The same is true of owners who are holding the land primarily for resale at a speculative profit.

Since the soil is the ultimate source of a large part of the Nation's wealth, the Nation cannot afford to permit the soil over large areas to be irretrievably ruined through the unrestrained operation of the competitive system. The Government's Agricultural Conservation Program represents the first serious and comprehensive effort by this Nation to save the good soil that is left. Expenditures by the Government which assure the conservation of the soil are in the interest of national economy in the truest sense of that word.[2]

Very sincerely yours,

[FRANKLIN D. ROOSEVELT]

[13:OF I–R:CT]

[1] Turner said that he had done nothing to earn the payment made to him because the planting and plowing under of the cover crop had been done as a regular procedure.

[2] Drafted by the Agriculture Department.

626   HENRY A. WALLACE, SECRETARY OF AGRICULTURE, TO ROOSEVELT

WASHINGTON, *May 11, 1937*

DEAR MR. PRESIDENT: When I learned from your son James that he was leaving Washington on May 11 and could take a message from me direct to you, I hastened to avail myself of the opportunity because I wanted to give you the background of my wire of May 8.[1]

You are fully informed, I believe, of how much I sympathize with you in your endeavors to bring about an effective integrated program of national and regional planning. Furthermore, I believe such planning should have to do with flood control, conservation and power projects. In your public life for many years you have driven straight toward the objective of an integrated program in these fields and I want to do what I can to help you attain your objective.

Now in this letter I would like to write you as frankly as though I were speaking with you face to face. The draft of the bill as prepared by the

National Power Policy Committee and also such bills as the Barkley-Bulkley Bill and the Norris Bill, while dealing with the broad program which is of such great interest to both of us, cannot possibly in my opinion attain the objective which means so much to you.[2]

Two months ago I received from the National Power Policy Committee a proposed draft of a bill and on March 17 I sent to Secretary Ickes a strong objection to the procedure and machinery outlined in the bill. Last Saturday when I learned that most of the provisions of the tentative draft prepared by the National Power Policy Committee had been incorporated in the Norris Bill, I thought the matter sufficiently urgent to send you the wire. While I have talked very little with Secretary Woodring about the matter, I am confident that he will join me in proposing an alternative method of achieving national power development, flood control, conservation and related objectives. I believe this alternative will appeal to you as workable, sound and attractive. I think you will like it.

In response to your letter to Secretary Woodring and me,[3] our two Departments are now at work on a comprehensive plan for the Ohio and the Mississippi drainage basins. Unfortunately, however, we have not been able to obtain the cooperation of Secretary Ickes and the National Resources Committee in carrying out your instructions. When we endeavored to obtain this cooperation, a situation developed which illustrates the need for making the National Resources Committee directly responsible to you, but not to you through a Cabinet Member. Secretary Ickes and Mr. Eliot refused to cooperate in doing the work which you asked us to do unless the job could be turned over to them.

It seems to me that the situation with respect to the National Resources Committee as well as with respect to the whole Government, would be very greatly strengthened if you could move the Committee from the Interior Building, put it in an independent location and then have the Chairman report direct to you and not through a Member of the Cabinet. This would make overall planning a Presidential staff function as it should be. Most of the other Departments, I think, share my view in this respect. Also I am inclined to think that many of the Members of the National Resources Committee would concur in this view if they were in position to speak their minds freely.

The greater part of this letter was written before I received your wire late Monday afternoon, but in view of Secretary Woodring's experience with Secretary Ickes last week, I do not feel it wise to ask him to call the three of us into conference at this time. Between now and the time you get back Secretary Woodring and myself will confer with Director Bell and will also work on the approach referred to later in this letter. We hope to have the opportunity of talking to you about the whole problem on your return.

What we are all interested in, of course, is a constructive method of obtaining with the least friction possible the objectives for which you have so steadily fought.

I wish now, therefore, to discuss an idea which seems the nucleus of what I believe to be a thoroughly constructive proposal for legislation in the field of national and regional planning, flood control, soil conservation, power, and the development of human resources. The first essential is that overall planning should not be permitted to get mixed up with administration. If a regional or national agency both plans and executes, it is in a position no different from that of the several Departments. And if planning is under a single Member of the Cabinet, there will not be very much sound cooperation. Like now, planning will be antagonistic to administration.

Further, if the regional authorities, encompassing the entire area of the United States, were empowered to administer the projects they plan, then there would eventually be a complete regional duplication of identical national programs.

For example, all the bills to establish regional authorities include soil conservation as one of the basic functions. Soil conservation is mainly the adoption by farmers of improved farm techniques. These practices must be in accord not only with the farm's physical requirements, but also with the farmer's economic requirements. As you know, farm income is the largest single factor in the difference between soil exploitation and soil conservation. If soil conservation were managed by seven or eight regional authorities, as contemplated in most of the bills on this subject, it is almost inconceivable that all eight plans would fit harmoniously into a national farm program that would yield an adequate farm income and that would, at the same time, induce soil conservation practices.

It seems to me unnecessary to violate sound principles of organization to accomplish the purposes that motivate those who prepare such bills as the Barkley-Bulkley, Norris, and other proposals.

In the light of the discussions now under way with the War Department, I may wish to modify the following recommendation in small details but, essentially, I think it is administratively and politically possible to have the Congress authorize a program of power development, true overall planning, flood control, and conservation, somewhat along these lines:

(1) Establish regional planning agencies, with a substantial part of the membership drawn from the Departments concerned and with a few other members appointed by the President from the region. This will keep the regional agencies from working in an administrative vacuum and will at the same time bring in a viewpoint wider than that of the immediate agencies involved.

[59]

(a) The plans developed by these agencies should include the development of navigation, drought alleviation, flood prevention, and power development and distribution, and, in addition, the whole field of conservation of natural and human resources.

(b) The regional planning agencies should report to the National Planning agency which should, as I indicated before, be a part of the Presidential staff; a substantial part of its membership, too, should be drawn from the Departments concerned.

(2) Such plans as are approved by the President and for which appropriations are granted, should definitely become part of the action programs of the established administrative agencies, but under no circumstances should the national or regional planning agencies themselves have authority to administer the programs.

(a) Among the overall plans would be, of course, plans for power development. These would become mandatory upon the administrative agencies concerned.

(3) Special provision should be made for the administration of the generation, transmission, and distribution of electric power, developed as an incident of projects for navigation, flood control, and reclamation.

(a) When engineering structures in streams are completed, the electric energy produced should be turned over, at the power house, to an administrator. There might be one or more administrators for each region to suit specific power requirements.

(b) Rates to be charged for such power should be subject to the approval of the Federal Power Commission. Furthermore while the Federal Power Commission is now mainly a regulatory body, I am inclined to believe that the administrators should be administratively responsible to the Federal Power Commission to insure a coordinated national power policy.

The Departments of War and Agriculture are already agreed upon the essentials of a comprehensive plan for the Ohio and Mississippi and are now moving to obtain the cooperation of the Public Health Service, T. V. A., and others for the preparation of that report. The outline of this plan will be ready for you when you return next Friday. Beginning tomorrow morning, the two Departments will go to work on a specific proposal for a comprehensive national program. I think Harry Woodring and I will be sufficiently in accord by the time you return that we can present a common recommendation to you.

I am sending this to you in the meantime because I think the issue at stake is sufficiently great that you will wish, before supporting any particular plan, to consider all possible alternative methods of achieving the desired objective. If you should agree with the general outline presented here, we could within a very few weeks perfect a bill that would provide suitable coordination of planning on a regional and national basis, would provide for the necessary separation of overall planning from actual administration, would avoid needless and dangerous duplication of the activities of the Federal departments, and would make possible effective administration of public power projects, as incidents of projects for navigation, reclamation, and flood control.

Respectfully,

H. A. WALLACE

[13:OF 1:TS]

[1] Wallace asked Roosevelt to defer endorsement of any flood control or conservation legislation until they could discuss it. Roosevelt agreed to do this in a radio message from the *Potomac* of May 10, 1937 (OF 132).

[2] The Barkley-Bulkley bill (S. 1440), "To provide for the control of the floodwaters of the rivers of the United States, for the improvement of navigability of such rivers, for the reforestation and conservation of natural resources, and for other purposes," was introduced Feb. 10, 1937. It was not reported (*Cong. Rec.*, 75th Cong., 1st sess., 81:1, 1081). On the Norris bill, see *post*, 636 n.

[3] The former is printed *ante*, 619; the latter has not been found.

627   ROOSEVELT TO THE CONGRESS

THE WHITE HOUSE, *May 12, 1937*

TO THE CONGRESS OF THE UNITED STATES: I transmit herewith for the information of the Congress a letter from the Organizing Committee of the Up-Stream Engineering Conference held September 22 and 23, 1936, with the accompanying record, under the title "Headwaters Control and Use," of the proceedings of the Conference.[1]

This volume of proceedings is a sequel to the report "Little Waters," which was transmitted to the Congress with my message of January 30, 1936. Whereas "Little Waters" was an initial elementary analysis of the relations between precipitation, run-off and soils, and of accompanying problems, the proceedings of the Up-Stream Engineering Conference constitute a more exhaustive treatment of the subject, and bring together under one cover the basic hydrologic data and principles, experience in applying these principles to land-water problems, and appraisals of the significance of this experience.

"Headwaters Control and Use" should be of service to the Congress in connection with its consideration of measures looking towards conservation of waters, prevention of erosion, and control of floods. It is becoming increasingly apparent that big waters are not the only part of our water resources presenting problems and requiring constructive treatment. Little waters also are of critical importance. In fact, with respect to some problems, drainage basins must be treated as a whole, both headwaters and main channels of any river system being brought into an integrated program of regulation.[2]

FRANKLIN D. ROOSEVELT

[W. H. PRESS RELEASES: M]

[1] *Headwaters Control and Use; A Summary of Fundamental Principles and Their Application in the Conservation and Utilization of Waters and Soils Throughout Headwater Areas. Papers Presented at the Upstream Engineering Conference ...* (Washington, 1937).
[2] Two typescripts of this message are present (OF 2450): one is dated May 1, 1937; the other bears the dates May 6, May 8, and May 12, 1937, the first two being crossed out. Except for the dates, they are identical with the text here printed. With the May 1 copy is a memorandum, McIntyre to Early, May 2, 1937, sent from Galveston, Texas, and reading, "I am keeping a copy of this. Since news is so damn scarce here do you think it would be all right to hold this and give it out down here when I get a release from you that it has gone to the Congress? This may not be practical since I'd have to tell the boys the report itself is available in Washington." Early replied by telegram of May 4, 1937 (OF 2450), that he had no objection.
In the Senate the message was referred to the Committee on Commerce; in the House, to the Committee on Flood Control (*Cong. Rec.*, 75th Cong., 1st sess., 81:4, 4413-4414, 4445).

628   ROOSEVELT TO HENRY A. WALLACE, SECRETARY OF AGRICULTURE

WASHINGTON, *May 15, 1937*

MEMORANDUM FOR THE SECRETARY OF AGRICULTURE: Please let me have a memorandum as to just how this bill will work and where. Also, what is the Department's definition of the size of a farm forest or forest and shrub plantation? Also, will the plantings be limited to drought areas? Also, how will the act work out in those states like the state of New York which already have large reforestation programs and sell state-raised seedlings, but do not give them away? [1]

F. D. R.

[*Notation*:T] Re: H. R. 4728, An Act to authorize cooperation in the development of farm forestry in the States and Territories, and for other purposes.

[13:BUDGET BUREAU ENROLLED BILLS:CT]

[1] Answered *post*, 630.

629   ROOSEVELT TO MARVIN H. McINTYRE, ASSISTANT SECRETARY TO THE PRESIDENT

WASHINGTON, 5/17/37

MEMO FOR MAC: I want a conference with Wallace, Ickes, Woodring and the National Resources Board if they are ready to report to me on the Flood Control plan.

F. D. R.

[13:OF 25-N:T]

WASHINGTON, *May 18, 1937*

DEAR MR. PRESIDENT: Reference is made to your memorandum of
May 15.

The cooperative farm forestry bill, H. R. 4728, was designed to give
a legislative basis for the Shelterbelt Project, the handling of which has
been very much handicapped by the lack of such a basis. The continuation of this project depends on aproval of this bill. The bill was made
broad enough, however, to cover the entire farm forestry field.

Approximately one-half of the fund authorized by the bill will be
used in the critical drought areas of the Middle West for shelterbelt
plantings. These forest and shrub plantings are in strip form and for
single farm units will not ordinarily exceed one-half mile in length.

The greater part of the remainder of the fund authorized by the bill
will be used for farm woodlots, which aggregate about 185 million acres
and are located almost entirely east of the plains. The work will consist
of advice to farmers to make their forests productive and of assistance
in planting. The Department's conception of farm woodlots would
confine them to bona fide farm enterprises. Areas exceeding 50 acres
in individual units are rare, except in the South. Plantations on individual holdings will not ordinarily exceed 10 acres. The total area
requiring reforestation is estimated at 35 million acres.

A relatively small part of the fund authorized by the bill will be used
for investigative work dealing with the Shelterbelt and farm woodlots.

In this entire undertaking the maximum practical cooperation will be
required from the landowners. In planting, the drought area will probably require the extreme of Federal contribution but even here it is
planned to require farmers to furnish the land, to do the necessary ground
preparation, essential fencing, and a large part of the cultivation. New
York probably represents the other extreme where the Federal Government should cooperate with the State in furnishing seedlings at cost.
For other States, an equitable arrangement will be worked out which
will take into account the difficulties in planting, existing State policies,
etc. The difficulties of establishing plantations will be the controlling
factor which will determine the degree of Federal cooperation.[1]

Sincerely,

H. A. WALLACE

[*Notation*:A] Approved 5/18/37

[13:BUDGET BUREAU ENROLLED BILLS:TS]

[1] The Norris-Doxey bill (Cooperative Farm Forestry Act) was approved May 18,
1937 (50 *Stat.* 188). By amendment, the act as passed differed from the Norris-
Jones bill of the previous session (see draft enclosed in Wallace to Roosevelt, June 1,
1936, *ante,* 515) in the following particulars: (1) the Secretary of Agriculture was

directed to give effect to the act by cooperation with the land-grant colleges and state forestry agencies rather than through the Forest Service; (2) competition of Government nurseries with commercial nurseries was specifically forbidden, and (3) the original requirement that half the cost of the trees be borne by the recipients was removed. An appropriation of $2,500,000 was authorized.

Introduced in the Senate by Norris (Nebr.) on Feb. 15, 1937, as S. 1504, and in the House by Doxey (Miss.), on the same day, as H. R. 4728, the bill was passed by the Senate on April 20. There was little opposition in the Senate but the debate was prolonged in the House. There it was passed May 5 by a vote of 171 to 152 (*Cong. Rec.*, 75th Cong., 1st sess., 81:2, 1194, 1227; 81:4, 3617–3625, 3630–3631; 4128–4131, 4189–4209.) Reports on the bill by the Senate and House Agriculture Committees are printed *ibid.*, 81:4, 3622–3623, 4130–4131. Succeeding appropriations for the Cooperative Farm Forestry Act barred the use of such funds for the establishment of new nurseries.

631   ROOSEVELT TO GOVERNOR ELMER A. BENSON, St. Paul, Minnesota

[WASHINGTON] *May 19, 1937*

MY DEAR GOVERNOR BENSON: Your letter of April ninth, urging that I make available $1,000,000 for immediate acquisition of the lands included in the Kabetogema Purchase Unit, has been read with a sympathetic appreciation of the Forest problems of Northern Minnesota.[1] You know of my interest in furthering a sound and constructive program of forest conservation for the Nation as a whole. The restoration and protection of the forest area along the northern boundary of Minnesota, particularly because of its international aspects, is unquestionably a worthy project.

Unfortunately, the conditions which dictate affirmative federal action in the Kabetogema Area exist in equal or greater degree within many other of our forest regions, where not only the preservation and restoration of physical resources, prevention of soil erosion, and the reduction of floods, but also the welfare of people stranded on submarginal lands and in communities whose basic economic resources have become exhausted, depends upon federal action to acquire, protect, and develop the land and to aid the people in shifting from poor land to better land, or otherwise finding needed sources of livelihood and economic security.

I am very anxious that the Federal government shall continue to bear an adequate share of such work. But as you know, the heavy requirements for the more immediate task of human conservation in the form of unemployment relief, combined with other inescapable costs of government, have made such demands upon federal revenues that it has been impossible to do many things that obviously are very desirable.

An item for forest-land acquisition is included in the 1938 budget, which will meet some of the above needs. I am confident Secretary

Wallace, in expanding such appropriation, will see that an equitable portion of it is used to meet the situation described in your letter.[2]

Very sincerely yours,

[FRANKLIN D. ROOSEVELT]

[13:OF 1–C:CT]

[1] Governor Benson said that these lands were a fire hazard because neither the state nor the Federal Government was providing fire prevention facilities (OF 1–C).

[2] Drafted by the Agriculture Department. Wallace, in his letter to Roosevelt enclosing the draft, May 18, 1937 (OF 1–C), said that his agency recognized the merit of Benson's proposal but that there were numerous other National Forest Purchase Units where the need for fire prevention measures was equally acute, and "in the matter of social relief, flood prevention, soil erosion control, and aid to industrial stabilization," even more acute.

632   NELSON C. BROWN, NEW YORK COLLEGE OF FORESTRY, TO ROOSEVELT

SYRACUSE, NEW YORK, *May 22, 1937*

DEAR PRESIDENT ROOSEVELT: The 26,000 trees were planted on your place during the last week of May, just ahead of some bright warm sunshine and good spring rains. Last Friday I made a careful inspection of the planting work and the results. I believe excellent survival will attend this planting as great care was exercised in putting the trees in the ground, especially in the second lot near the woods where, due to the stony nature of the ground cover, unusual care was necessary.

In the first lot, in order to finish out the planting not completed in 1936, 2000 balsam fir, 1000 Douglas fir, and 1100 Norway spruce were planted, making a total of 4100 plants. In the second lot, 21,750 Norway spruce were planted 3½' x 3½' apart. In the home garden or nursery, about 50 each of Douglas fir, balsam fir, and Norway spruce were placed as a reserve for fillers in case of any losses. It is estimated there are 9½ acres in the second lot next to the woods and of these about three-fourths were planted this spring. With the recent heavy rains I am very much encouraged and believe that results of planting should be very successful. Even the trees stricken by the drought last year have shown excellent survival due to the emergency watering which we did during July. . . .[1]

Sincerely,

NELSON

[13:PSF:HYDE PARK:TS]

[1] See *post,* 646.

ROOSEVELT TO HENRY A. WALLACE, SECRETARY OF AGRICUL-
TURE, AND HARRY H. WOODRING, SECRETARY OF WAR

[WASHINGTON] *May 26, 1937*

Personal

MEMORANDUM . . . I have read over your letter of May twenty-
fourth and the accompanying material,[1] and suggest that in order not to
complicate legislative procedure of getting the thing started that you
let the bills that Senator Norris and Congressman Rayburn are going to
introduce, go ahead and be referred to the committees.   Then take up
your suggestions with the committees and have them considered as
amendments to these bills in committee rather than in separate bills.

I think this will help all concerned.

F. D. R.

[13:OF 1:CT]

[1] Not present.

634   JEAN SHERWOOD HARPER TO ROOSEVELT

SWARTHMORE, PA., *May 26, 1937*

DEAR MR. ROOSEVELT: When you made possible last year the Government's acquisition of Okefinokee Swamp as a wild-life refuge, Francis
felt that his struggle of nearly a quarter of a century for the preservation
of the swamp ought to be at an end.   But evidently it is not.

The Biological Survey is showing either a woeful ignorance or a
profound disregard of certain fundamental principles in the proper administration of a natural wilderness, still largely in a primeval state.
Every real naturalist knows that the paramount policy in such an area
should be non-interference with nature.

It is true that the Chief of the Survey, in a recent letter to Dr. John C.
Phillips (brother of the Ambassador), professed that the Survey's aim
was to preserve the "pristine quality" of the Okefinokee.   Furthermore,
in a letter of February 16, 1937, the Survey's technical adviser, W. L.
McAtee, wrote to Francis that "no planting of anything not native to
the region is planned."

Apparently both letters were mere "scraps of paper."

For we have just learned that 114 Asiatic chestnut trees have already
been planted in the refuge, apparently on Floyd's Island, one of the
choicest areas in the swamp.   A copy of Francis's letter of protest to one
of the Survey officials is enclosed.[1]   The only excuse offered in reply is
that "the Department is experimenting with the growing of these trees
to replace the native chestnuts wiped out by the blight."   Apparently the

Survey is in total ignorance of the fact that no native chestnuts ever have occurred in the entire Okefinokee region! In any event, the wilful introduction of exotics into a natural wilderness is nothing short of a biological crime.

In its anxiety to cater to the politically powerful duck-hunters, and in disregard of the opinions of competent biologists, the Survey is also planning the introduction of certain non-native aquatic plants as duck food. There is already sufficient native duck food.

Is there no way to stop this sort of bungling by the Biological Survey in its administration of a unique and priceless wilderness?

It is most unfortunate that the CCC, with its record of devastation in other wilderness areas, has had to be turned loose on the Okefinokee, too. (This is another matter which the Chief of the Survey professed not to be planning last year.)

The National Research Council's Committee on Wild Life and Nature Reserves (H. E. Anthony, chairman) is quite in sympathy with Francis's views on the Okefinokee, but feels that its style is rather cramped when it comes to criticizing a federal agency. But isn't that what the National Research Council is for? Couldn't you ask for its opinion?

Always sincerely.

JEAN SHERWOOD HARPER

[13:PPF 1091:TS]

[1] To James Silver, May 20, 1937.

635 ROOSEVELT TO HENRY A. WALLACE, SECRETARY OF AGRICULTURE

[WASHINGTON] *June 2, 1937*

MEMORANDUM FOR THE SECRETARY OF AGRICULTURE: A friend of mine on his way back from Florida came through the Okefinokee Swamp and told me that the Biological Survey is introducing plant and animal life not native to the region. Of course, the original object of the Biological Survey in acquiring the swamp, was to keep the fauna and flora in an absolutely original state. He tells me that Japanese chestnuts have been planted to replace the native chestnuts but that it is well-known that no native chestnuts ever grew in the swamp. Further, he tells me that aquatic plants not native to the swamp have been introduced as duck food. Further, he says that some kind of Japanese squirrel have been turned loose, apparently to go with the Japanese chestnuts.

Please let me have a definite report on these rumors. If they are true, the chestnuts should be removed, the squirrels should. be shot and the duck food eliminated.   Why, oh why, can't we let original nature remain original nature![1]

F. D. R.

FDR/TMB
[13:PPF 1091:CT]

[1] Answered *post*, 642.

636   ROOSEVELT TO THE CONGRESS

THE WHITE HOUSE, *June 3, 1937*

TO THE CONGRESS OF THE UNITED STATES:[1] Nature has given recurrent and poignant warnings through dust storms, floods and droughts that we must act while there is yet time if we would preserve for ourselves and our posterity the natural sources of a virile national life.

Experience has taught us that the prudent husbandry of our national estate requires far-sighted management.   Floods, droughts and dust storms are in a very real sense manifestations of nature's refusal to tolerate continued abuse of her bounties.   Prudent management demands not merely works which will guard against these calamities, but carefully formulated plans to prevent their occurrence.   Such plans require coordination of many related activities.

For instance, our recent experiences of floods have made clear that the problem must be approached as one involving more than great works on main streams at the places where major disasters threaten to occur.   There must also be measures of prevention and control among tributaries and throughout the entire headwaters areas.   A comprehensive plan of flood control must embrace not only downstream levees and floodways, and retarding dams and reservoirs on major tributaries, but also smaller dams and reservoirs on the lesser tributaries, and measures of applied conservation throughout an entire drainage area, such as restoration of forests and grasses on inferior lands, and encouragement of farm practices which diminish runoff and prevent erosion on arable lands.

Taking care of our natural estate together with the stopping of existing waste and building it back to a higher productivity is a national problem.   At last we have undertaken a national policy.

But it is not wise to direct everything from Washington.   National planning should start at the bottom or, in other words, the problems of townships, counties and states, should be coordinated through large geographical regions and come to the Capitol of the nation for final coordination.   Thus the Congress would receive a complete picture in which no local detail had been overlooked.

It is also well to remember that improvements of our national heritage frequently confer special benefits upon regions immediately affected, and a large measure of cooperation from state and local agencies in the undertaking and financing of important projects may fairly be asked for.

Any division of the United States into regions for the husbandry of its resources must possess some degree of flexibility. The area most suitable as a region for the carrying out of an integrated program designed to prevent floods is the basin including the watersheds of a pivotal river. But other problems dependent upon other combinations of natural economic and social factors, may require a somewhat different area to permit the most effective functional program. For instance, the problem of the Great Plains area is a problem of deficient rainfall, relatively high winds, loose, friable soils, and unsuitable agricultural practices. The natural area for solution of the Great Plains drought problem is different from that for the solution of dynamic water problems presented by the rivers which traverse that area. The rational area for administration of a Great Plains rehabilitation program crosses the drainage areas of a number of parallel major tributaries of the Mississippi River. It should therefore be kept in mind that in establishing a region for one type of comprehensive program, parts or all of the same area may be included in a different region for another type of comprehensive program with the result of a federal system, as it were, of programs and administrative areas for solution of basically different yet interrelated problems.

Neither the exact scope nor the most appropriate administrative mechanism for regional husbandry can at the start be projected upon any single blue print. But it is important that we set up without delay some regional machinery to acquaint us with our problem.

I think, however, that for the time being we might give consideration to the creation of seven regional authorities or agencies; [2] one on the Atlantic Seaboard; a second for the Great Lakes and Ohio Valley; a third for the drainage basin of the Tennessee and Cumberland Rivers; a fourth embracing the drainage basins of the Missouri River and the Red River of the North; a fifth embracing the drainage basins of the Arkansas, Red, and Rio Grande Rivers; a sixth for the basins of the Colorado River and rivers flowing into the Pacific south of the California-Oregon line; and a seventh for the Columbia River Basin. [3] And in addition I should leave undisturbed the Mississippi River Commission which is well equipped to handle the problems immediately attending the channel of that great river.

Apart from the Tennessee Valley Authority, the Columbia Valley Authority, and the Mississippi River Commission, the work of these regional bodies, [4] at least in their early years, would consist chiefly in developing integrated plans to conserve and safeguard the prudent use of

[69]

waters, water-power, soils, forests and other resources of the areas entrusted to their charge.

Such regional bodies [4] would also provide a useful mechanism through which consultation among the various governmental agencies working in the field could be effected for the development of integrated programs of related activities. Projected programs would be reported by the regional bodies [4] annually to the Congress through the President after he has had the projects checked and revised in light of national budgetary considerations and of national planning policies. When the National Planning Board is established, I should expect to use that agency to coordinate the development of regional planning to ensure conformity to national policy, but not to give to the proposed National Planning Board any executive authortiy over the construction of public works or over management of completed works. [5]

Projects authorized to be undertaken by the Congress could then be carried out in whole or in part by those departments of the Government best equipped for the purpose, or if desirable in any particular case by one of the regional bodies. [4] There should be a close coordination of the work done by the various agencies of government to prevent friction, overlapping and unnecessary administrative expense and to ensure the integrated development of related activites. There should be the closest cooperation also with the developing state and local agencies in this field, particularly the state, regional and local planning boards and the commissions on interstate cooperation which work through interstate compacts ratified by the Congress and through interstate administrative arrangements. And provisions should be made for the effective administration of hydro-electric projects which have been or may be undertaken as a part of a multiple purpose watershed development. The water-power resources of the nation must be protected from private monopoly and used for the benefit of the people. [6]

This proposal is in the interest of economy and the prevention of overlapping or one-sided developments. It leaves the Congress wholly free to determine what shall be undertaken and provides the Congress with a complete picture not only of the needs of each one of the regions but of the relationship of each of the regions to the whole of the Nation.

If, for example, the Congress could have had before it at this session a complete picture of immediate and long-term needs I think its task in providing for flood prevention and drought emergencies would have been an easier one. [7]

For nearly a year I have studied this great subject intensively and have discussed it with many of the members of the Senate and the House of Representatives. My recommendations in this message fall into the same category as my former recommendation relating to the reorganization of the Executive Branch of the Government. I hope, therefore, that both of these important matters may have your attention at this session.[8]

FRANKLIN D. ROOSEVELT

[W. H. PRESS RELEASES: M]

[1] This text is that of the mimeographed White House press release of the message. It derives from four drafts: (1) a draft entitled "Notes for Message on Regional Authorities," authorship not indicated, with a number of pencilled deletions and additions by Roosevelt; (2) a "clean copy" of the first draft, typed in final form and signed by Roosevelt; (3) the second draft plus revisions noted as having been made by the President's Committee on Administrative Management (the Brownlow Committee), plus certain other revisions noted as "having been inserted to avoid the inference that the Message indorses one bill rather than another and to avoid comment on the omission of any special reference to power"; and (4) draft 3, plus four insertions that were apparently composed by Roosevelt. With the fourth draft is a memorandum, Roosevelt to Early, James Roosevelt and Forster, May 31, 1937: "To show to Tommy Corcoran. Have him check with Norris and the Congressman who is to introduce it and have final draft for me Wednesday morning when I get in." (This was written in Hyde Park.) Since some of the textual changes in the several drafts have more than ordinary interest as showing Roosevelt's decision (arrived at, apparently, between the preparation of drafts 1 and 2) not to press for regional authorities exclusively, they have been noted.

[2] "Or agencies" was added by draft 3.

[3] Crossed out by Roosevelt in draft 1, "and an eighth authority for the territories and possessions of the United States."

[4] Draft 3 substituted "regional bodies" for "authorities."

[5] The Brownlow Committee contributed the first part of this sentence; the qualifying clause is from draft 4.

[6] The preceding three sentences were added by draft 3 (the first by the Brownlow Committee).

[7] This and the preceding paragraph were added by Roosevelt to draft 1.

[8] Bills were at once introduced to give effect to the recommendations of the President: S. 2555, by Senator Norris (Nebr.), on June 3, 1937, to provide for the creation of seven "corporate Conservation Authorities"; H. R. 7392, by Representative Rankin (Miss.), June 4, 1937, companion bill to Norris'; H. R. 7365, by Representative Mansfield (Texas), on June 3, 1937, providing for seven regional planning agencies and for the creation of regional power authorities which would be operating agencies; and H. R. 7863, "to provide for the creation of conservation authorities," also by Rankin, on July 14 (*Cong. Rec.,* 75th Cong., 1st sess., 81:5, 5281, 5335, 5341; 81:7, 5157).

Hearings were held on the bills: *Creation of Conservation Authorities,* Hearings before a Subcommittee of the Committee on Agriculture and Forestry, U. S. Senate, 75th Cong., 1st sess., on S. 2555, June 21 to July 7, 1937 (Washington, 1937); *Regional Conservation and Development of National Resources,* House of Representatives, Hearings, 75th Cong., 1st sess., on H. R. 7365 and H. R. 7863, July and August, 1937 (Washington, 1937).

Roosevelt's reference to the Norris bill at his press conference of the day following the transmittal of his message to Congress (see below) did not indicate any great enthusiasm for it, nor did he attempt, in the months following, to secure public support for either the Norris or the Mansfield bill. He did, it is true, make a general reference to the desirability of regional planning and the creation of regional planning boards in his Bonneville Dam speech of Sept. 28, 1937 (Rosenman, ed., *Public Papers,* VI, 390–391). Concerning Administration policy and the regional authority bills, see William E. Leuchtenburg, "Roosevelt, Norris and the 'Seven Little TVA's' " in *The Journal of Politics,* 14 (August, 1952), 418–441, and his *Flood Control Politics* (Cambridge: Harvard University, 1953), pp. 72–73, 77–89, 102, 103.

[71]

PRESS CONFERENCE, Executive Offices of the White House, June 4, 1937, 11 A. M.

[*Excerpt*] Q: To go back to the National Planning Bill: [1] What is its relation to the St. Lawrence Waterway and Quoddy?

The President: That is a pretty broad question. It depends entirely how they set up these planning commissions. I don't know whether the St. Lawrence Waterway would come under the Ohio and Great Lakes or whether it would come under the Eastern Seaboard. In other words, it is one jump ahead of the game. I don't know. But it would have nothing to do with the treaty with Canada, of course, because these are only planning commissions and that would be only a planning commission. You see, of all these agencies that are proposed, there would only be three—really only two—that would have any administrative functions at all. One would be the TVA in that area and the other would be the Columbia Basin when the Bonneville Dam Bill goes through. Another is the existing agency of the Mississippi Valley Commission. [2]

Q: Are you referring to the House Bill as distinct from the Norris Bill when you say that?

The President: To tell the honest truth, I have not read either so I cannot answer the question.

Q: Would the bill cover Quoddy?

The President: Only the planning.

[13: PRESIDENT'S PRESS CONFERENCES: T]

[1] See preceding note.
[2] Mississippi River Commission.

638   HARCOURT A. MORGAN, VICE CHAIRMAN, BOARD OF DIREC-
       TORS, TENNESSEE VALLEY AUTHORITY, TO ROOSEVELT

WASHINGTON, *June 11, 1937*

MEMORANDUM TO THE PRESIDENT . . . PHOSPHATE DEPOSITS: The Tennessee Valley Authority's efforts, stimulated by your emphasis upon the slipping away of our land capital, have produced results of great national significance. For more than three years the Authority has undertaken at Muscle Shoals experiments in the production of phosphate products and their use. Equipment has been designed and methods have been developed by which new products and new processes have been made available. As a result of these experiments, the importance of phosphate products has been thoroughly established and their proper use greatly stimulated. At the same time, the experiments have emphasized the limited resources available and the folly of our present day commercial use of this essential element. Adequately to protect the land, a program of conservation must be considered for the two major phosphate areas in the United States, Florida and the West.

Florida Deposits

The deposits of Florida, though less than ten per cent of the total reserves in this country, are today supplying almost all of the phosphate being applied to our soil, and a third of their output is exported to foreign countries. They are now held in private corporate ownership, with profit as the motive in their exploitation. The accessibility of commercial water transportation accelerates their use, and the TVA experiments, when generally utilized, will add another factor encouraging their speedy exhaustion. For the protection of the land in this country, consideration should be given to purchase by the Government of the entire Florida phosphate area, or at least the million tons produced therefrom which are now being exported annually, in order that the products may be available for the soil conservation and adjustment program of the U. S. Department of Agriculture.

The Deposits of the West

The western deposits are located in the States of Idaho, Utah, Wyoming, and Montana, largely on public lands. So far, they have been developed by leasing to private interests. As the TVA experiments are now directed particularly to the liberation of these resources, it is important that consideration be given to a program which would permit the leasing of these deposits by the Department of the Interior to the Department of Agriculture for use in a national program of land restoration.

It will be a tragedy if steps cannot be taken to conserve all the benefits of the TVA experiments for a program looking toward the rehabilitation and maintenance of the exhausted soils of this country. Unless our national phosphate resources are protected by public policy, the success of the work at Muscle Shoals may prove an advantage only to those who have for so long exploited the land and those who live upon it in order that industry should profit.

At your earliest opportunity, I should like to discuss with you a specific proposal for meeting these problems.[1]

[HARCOURT A. MORGAN]

[13:OF 42:T]

[1] Answered *post,* 640.

639   ROOSEVELT TO MAUDE STOUTENBURGH ELIOT, New York City

[WASHINGTON] *June 12, 1937*

MY DEAR MRS. ELIOT: I am so glad to have your letter and to know that you and Ellie [1] have seen each other. I understand that "The Pines" have not yet been taken over by the churches. When that takes place I think that there should be created some kind of park authority on the same principle as the State Park Authorities so that the property and its use are permanently labeled with a public interest. Such an Authority would have the right to ask for the help of a CCC camp.

I heartily agree with you that it would be a fine thing if the reforestation work could be undertaken and that in a few years we would have a real park in its natural setting for the use of future generations.

When I go home next month I will talk with the church people about it.

Very sincerely yours,

[FRANKLIN D. ROOSEVELT]

[13:PPF 751:CT]

[1] Ellen C. Roosevelt, a cousin of Roosevelt. The letter, June 8, 1937 (PPF 751), concerned Mrs. Eliot's plans for the future use of the former seat of the Stoutenburgh family, "The Pines," a wooded area east of the village of Hyde Park. This was given by Mrs. Eliot to the Protestant churches of Hyde Park for development as a park.

640   ROOSEVELT TO HARCOURT A. MORGAN, VICE CHAIRMAN, BOARD OF DIRECTORS, TENNESSEE VALLEY AUTHORITY

WASHINGTON, *June 16, 1937*

MEMORANDUM FOR DR. HARCOURT MORGAN: I want to talk with you about these phosphate deposits. Can you bring me a map showing location of the Florida deposits? [1]

F. D. R.

[13:OF 42:CT]

[1] See *ante,* 638.

641   ROOSEVELT TO REPRESENTATIVE JAMES F. O'CONNOR OF MONTANA

[WASHINGTON] *June 19, 1937*

MY DEAR MR. O'CONNOR: I am impressed by the account of drought conditions in Montana which you indicated in your letter of May twenty-fourth,[1] and the desire of the people for construction of more small earthen dams and drilling of wells. I realize the necessity of conserving the scanty water supply of the Great Plains and the importance of small dams to impound water for livestock and for stabilizing production of farm gardens and supplemental stock feed.

The Works Progress Administration is now carrying on an extensive water conservation program in Montana and in other States subject to drought. This program includes the construction of a considerable number of small dams, and, where conditions are favorable, the installation of wells.

The Works Progress Administration of Montana is prepared to handle additional water conservation projects of this type for which certified relief labor is available. Public agencies of the State desiring to sponsor such projects should be advised to make application to the State Administrator, Mr. Joseph E. Parker, at Helena, or to the Director of the Works Progress Administration district in which they are located, who will be pleased to advise and assist them in the preparation of their applications.

The program of the Department of Agriculture in Montana also includes both actual construction of small dams and aid to farmers in constructing them. Hundreds of small earthen dams have been constructed by the Resettlement Administration to furnish stock water on publicly owned range land in Montana. This program has furnished beneficial work for thousands of needy people of the State. The 1937 range practices program of the Agricultural Adjustment Administration for Montana includes payments to farmers for construction on private land of earthen pits and reservoirs, and for digging or drilling wells.

In some parts of Montana as well as elsewhere in the Great Plains, limited supplies of ground water exist. The Resettlement Administration is carrying on a program of locating these areas and the determination of available supplies and the properly coordinated utilization with other natural resources of the area. This work has been confined largely to the Southern High Plains but it is intended to extend it to the Northern Great Plains, including eastern Montana, during the next fiscal year. Such investigations prepare the way for comprehensive ground water development programs.

I think you would be interested in reading the report of the Great Plains Committee, which was recently transmitted to Congress and which outlines a long range program for proper utilization and conservation of the land and water resources of this area, and I have asked that a copy be sent to you.

The enclosures received with your letter are returned herewith.

Very sincerely yours,

[FRANKLIN D. ROOSEVELT]

[13:OF 987:CT]

¹ O'Connor's letter (OF 987) enclosed a number of letters he had received from his constituents concerning the drought in Montana. He urged the construction of

small earth dams and artesian wells as the most effective way to meet the emergency. The importance attached to O'Connor's letter by the White House is indicated by the care taken in drafting the reply. The Department of Agriculture and the Works Progress Administration were asked to prepare a reply, and this draft (sent to Roosevelt by Wallace, June 17, 1937, OF 987) was then sent to the Budget Bureau for review (Bell to Roosevelt, July 22, 1937, OF 987). No changes were made in the draft and it was sent as the letter here printed.

642   HENRY A. WALLACE, SECRETARY OF AGRICULTURE, TO ROOSEVELT

WASHINGTON, D. C., *June 22, 1937*

DEAR MR. PRESIDENT: Reference is made to your memorandum of June 2 in which you indicate that the Biological Survey apparently is not conforming to the original policy adopted for the maintenance and development of the Okefenokee Wildlife Refuge in Georgia.

From the time negotiations started for the acquisition of this area it has been and still is the intention of the Biological Survey to maintain the area primarily as an inviolate wilderness, with a minimum of disturbance of the natural balance of the plant and animal life.

The balance of nature for some of our bird and animal life has been upset on many millions of acres of land formerly occupied by the chestnut and chinquapins by the introduction from abroad of the chestnut blight and the Phytophthora root disease. These two exotic diseases have resulted in the loss of an outstanding source of food supply for wild turkeys, deer, and other game. The Department is introducing and breeding strains of chestnut and chinquapins which are resistant to these diseases. Some of these that seem especially valuable as a source of game food are being planted in the Eastern States in an attempt to restore nature to its original condition so far as the food supply of some of our important native birds and animals is concerned. A part of this breeding work is being conducted at our Plant Introduction Garden near Savannah, Georgia, and we are using in this work some of the remaining plants of these species of chinquapins that are native to the coastal region of Georgia. The small experimental planting of chestnuts and chinquapins that was made on the Okefenokee Refuge included some hybrids between chinquapins and the resistant Asiatic chestnuts. It is not known definitely whether chinquapins formerly extended naturally into the drier parts of the Refuge but they do occur in that general region. Instructions have been issued to remove this experimental planting.

No introduced aquatic plants have been planted on the area by the Biological Survey, although we have definite information that such aquatic plantings were made by the Hebard Lumber Company officials prior to our acquisition.

[76]

There is no truth in the rumor that Japanese squirrels have been introduced on the Okefenokee Refuge.

I desire to thank you for calling my attention to this matter, and I assure you that it is the intention of the Chief of the Biological Survey, as well as the undersigned, to maintain the Okefenokee Wildlife Refuge as an inviolate wilderness area. Only such few trails, quarters, and boundary markings as are necessary to provide for proper protection of the area will be approved.

Respectfully yours,

H. A. WALLACE

[13:PPF 1091:TS]

643　SENATOR ALVA B. ADAMS OF COLORADO TO MARVIN H. McINTYRE, ASSISTANT SECRETARY TO THE PRESIDENT

[WASHINGTON] *June 23, 1937*

MY DEAR MAC: As I told you on the phone, I am extremely anxious to have the Budget Commissioner submit an estimate of not less than $1,000,000 to start the construction of the Colorado-Big Thompson Reclamation Project.

Colorado has had no reclamation project nor any major project during the present administration. Every state in the west has one or more major projects. The lack of such a project is highly prejudicial to the standing of the administration. This matter was taken up with the President on two occasions during the preceding session of Congress. We were then advised, and properly advised, that none of the projects which we presented had met the requirements of the Reclamation Law and the Reclamation Service. Now, however, the present project has met each and every one of these requirements.

The surveys and plans of the project are complete. The project is recommended as highly desirable by the Reclamation Service. The project is feasible from an engineering standpoint. The repayment to the Reclamation Fund of the cost of the project is assured.

The project will not bring into cultivation new lands but will furnish a supplemental supply for some 600,000 acres of the finest land in the United States, which is now under cultivation but for which there is an occasional shortage of water in the late summer to complete the crop. Not less than 175,000 people will be benefited by the project. In addition, the City of Denver and all of northern Colorado will derive great indirect benefits.

The cost of the project can be easily borne by those benefited by it. Water of the kind which the project will furnish is now being paid for upon both public and private projects at from six to ten dollars per acre per year, while the cost of this water during the forty-year period for repayment of reclamation costs will not exceed two dollars per acre. The last session of the Colorado Legislature authorized the formation of water users' associations or districts for the purpose of contracting with the Reclamation Service in order to insure the repayment of the costs of the construction to the Reclamation Fund so that those who will make use of the water to be supplied by the proposed reclamation project are now in a position to make and perform whatever contracts may be necessary to comply with the Reclamation Law or the desires of the Reclamation Service. In addition a tax of one-half mill per annum will be levied upon the property in the district for the purpose of aiding in meeting the costs of the project. The assessed valuation of the territory within the district is in the neighborhood of $150,000,000.

In the past there has been considerable controversy over the proposed construction of this project between residents of the eastern and western sections of Colorado. The western group, led by Congressman Taylor, vigorously opposed the project. During the past few weeks a series of conferences have been held and a complete agreement has been reached between the representatives of the two areas of the state and both regions now urge the construction of the project. Congressman Taylor has withdrawn his objection.

Congress, at the time of the passage of the act creating the Rocky Mountain National Park, was advised of the ultimate desirability of a project such as the one now proposed and in order that there might be no hindrance to such construction by the creation of the park, incorporated the following provision in the Act: "The United States Reclamation Service may enter upon and utilize for flowage or other purposes any area within said Park which may be necessary for the development and maintenance of a Government reclamation project" (Chap. 19, Sec. 1, Vol. 38 *Statutes* 798: enacted January 26, 1915).

Some objections to the construction of the project have been made by those interested in national parks. These objections are based upon complete misunderstanding and in some cases, misrepresentations of the character of the project and the effect if its completion. Some of the objections have their origin in the fact that the project will develop a large amount of hydroelectric power which will be of great benefit to the communities to be served by the project, but which will inevitably lower the cost of hydroelectric energy in that section of our State now served by private corporations.

The water which is to be carried from the western slope to the eastern slope is taken through a tunnel, neither portal of which is within the Rocky Mountain National Park, though the tunnel itself passes under the Continental Divide which is within a portion of the Park. Construction of the project will improve and not impair the scenic beauties of the Park.

[78]

Grand Lake, at the western portal of the tunnel and from or through which the waters are derived will be enlarged and improved, and its shoreline leveled and stabilized at a point greatly to the improvement of the lake from every standpoint.

On the western slope provision is being made by replacement reservoirs to equalize the flow of water for irrigation purposes so that the irrigable lands in that section will no longer be in danger from a shortage of water during any portion of the irrigation season.

The Senate incorporated an authorization for the construction of this project in the Interior Department Appropriation Bill during the last session but due to the controversy which then existed the authorization was defeated in the House.

From a careful study of the project, both on the ground and from the engineering reports, I can assure you that the project is desirable and beneficial from every aspect and so far as I know, there is no single feature of it which will be detrimental socially, economically, financially, or from the standpoint of scenic beauty and attraction.

The time is very pressing as I am desirous of having an appropriation for the commencement of the project included in the Interior Department Appropriation Bill which is under consideration by the Senate Appropriations Committee. This bill will probably be presented to the Senate for consideration on Monday, June 28; consequently if a budget estimate is to furnish a basis for the appropriation it should be made immediately.

I will be appreciative and deeply indebted if the President would request the Director of the Budget to submit the necessary estimate. I am informed that the Interior Department made a request for an estimate some time back.

With best regards, Sincerely,

ALVA B. ADAMS

P. S. I am attaching herewith a copy of Senate Document No. 80 which is a synopsis of the report of the Reclamation Service on the project,[1] and also a copy of the report of the Irrigation and Reclamation Committee of the Senate recommending the passage of the bill authorizing the construction of the project and summarizing the provisions of the report.[2] The facts concerning this project as stated will be corroborated by Mr. Page, Commissioner of Reclamation, and I suggest that he be called upon if there be any question about them. A. B. A.

[Notation: AS] West Slope legislators have withdrawn objections Alva says. MHM [3]

[13: OF 402: TS]

¹ *Synopsis of Report on Colorado-Big Thompson Project, Plan of Development and Cost Estimate Prepared by the Bureau of Reclamation* . . . 75th Cong., 1st sess., S. Doc. 80 (Washington, 1937).
² *Senate Report 775 to Accompany S. 2681,* 75th Cong., 1st sess. (Washington, 1937).
³ Writing again to McIntyre on July 14, 1937 (OF 402), Adams said that if provision for the project should be taken out of the House Interior Department appropriation bill, it would be difficult to explain to the people of Colorado, especially when it was understood "that word has gone out from the White House to some of the leaders in the House that it is desired that this project be eliminated from the appropriation bill."

644   ROOSEVELT TO MARVIN H. McINTYRE, ASSISTANT SECRETARY TO THE PRESIDENT

WASHINGTON, *June 25, 1937*

MEMO FOR MAC: Will you talk with Bell about this ¹ and tell him I do not think we should submit an estimate this year and for him to tell Adams that the matter should go over until next year?

F. D. R.

[13:OF 402:T]

¹ Above.

645   CHARLES WEST, ACTING SECRETARY OF THE INTERIOR, TO ROOSEVELT

WASHINGTON, *June 25, 1937*

MEMORANDUM FOR THE PRESIDENT: In conformance with your memorandum of April 21 concerning the possibility of making Admiralty Island a wildlife sanctuary until such time as it may be turned into a national park, I have asked the Secretary of Agriculture to appoint a representative who, with a representative of the Department of the Interior, will study the problem in Alaska.

I have suggested this method of procedure because I am advised by the National Park Service that Admiralty Island is believed to be of doubtful national park quality; that the Forest Service and the Alaska Game Commission have effected a wildlife management plan of apparent merit for Admiralty Island; and, that a desirable extension of Glacier Bay National Monument would provide comparable wildlife sanctuary in a region of great scenic beauty and scientific interest.

The proposed joint study should be completed by the middle of the summer.¹

CHARLES WEST

[13:OF 378:TS]

¹ The Agriculture Department was reluctant to enter upon a joint survey until the newly created Alaskan Territorial Board (whose object was the development of Alaskan resources) was fully organized. Interior then decided to go ahead with its

own survey, and Agriculture promised the aid of Forest Service officers at Juneau (West to Roosevelt, Oct. 9, 1937, quoting Acting Secretary of Agriculture Wilson to West, July 24, 1937; Roosevelt to Bell, Nov. 22, 1937, OF 378). No further reference to the President's query of April 21, 1937, appears in the Roosevelt papers.

646   ROOSEVELT TO NELSON C. BROWN, New York State College of Forestry, Syracuse University, Syracuse, New York

[WASHINGTON] *June 29, 1937*

DEAR NELSON: Many thanks for yours of June twenty-sixth.[1] I shall be delighted to try the experiment of the Asiatic chestnuts next Spring.

When you next make a check on the woods I wish you could have someone from the College go through the woods, especially the woods around the oldest white pine grove back of the farm to see if there are many young chestnuts growing. I have seen a number of them— possibly forty or fifty—ranging from five feet to twenty feet in height.

Back on the top of the hill at the extreme east end of the place I think there are some others.

If you want something definite to do in Europe, get information about community owned forests in France, Germany, Austria, etc., showing the actual annual profit which the communities make from the sale of fagots, cord wood, lumber and hunting licenses.

If you could get up a little book in popular vein with photographs and a catchy title and cover, it would sell like hot-cakes. The important thing is to confine the story to small communities which have not got much capital to invest.

I hope you will have a wonderful time and I will see you both when you get back.

Always sincerely,

FRANKLIN D. ROOSEVELT

[13:PPF 38:CT]

[1] Brown said that he was going to plant some Asiatic chestnuts on the Roosevelt grounds in the spring in an effort to develop a blight-free variety, and that he was going to Europe to look into some recent forestry and conservation developments there (PPF 38).

647   CHARLES WEST, ACTING SECRETARY OF THE INTERIOR, TO MARVIN H. McINTYRE, ASSISTANT SECRETARY TO THE PRESIDENT

WASHINGTON, *June 30, 1937*

MY DEAR MR. McINTYRE: Further reference is made to a letter of January 29 to you from Representative Frank W. Boykin, relating to the proposed diversion of water from Yellowstone Lake in Yellowstone National Park to the Snake River for use in Idaho. The above-mentioned letter was transmitted to Secretary Ickes with your memorandum of February 9, which was acknowledged by my letter of February 20 to you.[1] It has required considerable time to assemble and analyze the data related to this important problem.

This particular proposal originated, as Mr. Boykin indicates, with the people of the upper Snake River valley in Idaho through the Commissioner of Reclamation of Idaho, and has been discussed with this Department for some time.

The principal question in the case is whether or not the policy of the Congress and of this Department, of protecting from any change in their natural condition park areas which exemplify natural history values of national and international significance, is of more benefit to the public as a whole than it would be if modified to allow the alteration of natural conditions in those areas because of purely local industrial urgency. Local agitation in favor of proposals to divert waters of Yellowstone National Park for irrigation and power development has occurred frequently during past years, but no projects have materialized because they have not, upon careful study, proven to be of greater benefit to the public than the park values they would destroy.

Mr. Boykin is apparently misinformed regarding the previous status of the lands included within Yellowstone National Park. None of those lands were at any time under the jurisdiction of the State of Wyoming. As the property of the United States, they were part of the public domain when they were reserved for national park purposes by the Act of March 1, 1872 (17 *Stat.* 32). By the Act of July 10, 1890 (26 *Stat.* 222), admitting the State of Wyoming into the Union, Congress specifically reserved the ownership of all lands included within the park, and provided that the park should remain under the exclusive jurisdiction of the United States. The Wyoming Constitutional Convention had already adopted an ordinance forever disclaiming all right and title to the unappropriated public lands lying within the park boundaries.

It has long been recognized that the waters upon the public domain are subject to disposal in accordance with the laws of the several States. There was no special guarantee for the benefit of Wyoming, other than the provisions of general statutes relating to waters on the public domain. However, it is equally well recognized that the States, in exercising their authority to dispose of water, may not grant any right or privilege to use lands of the United States. From time to time, acts of Congress have provided the exclusive means by which rights-of-way over the public lands and reservations may be obtained for the purpose of constructing diversion works, dams, reservoirs, and conduits. There is no authority for the granting of such rights-of-way within the national parks.

There is some impression that the water flowing from Yellowstone Lake contributes materially to the periodic floods on the Mississippi and Missouri Rivers. Such is not the case. On the contrary, the lake acts as a natural impounding and restraining reservoir during the season when those floods occur. The reports of the United States Geological Survey, based upon observations made from 1923 to 1934, inclusive, show that the maximum discharge from Yellowstone Lake occurs usually about two weeks after the date of maximum flow of the Yellowstone River at Miles City, Montana. During the twelve-year period, the earliest date of maximum discharge was May 31, and the latest date was July 18. The mean date of maximum discharge for the 12 years was June 26, long after the disappearance of any danger of floods on the lower streams.

The maximum flow from Yellowstone Lake amounts to only a small part of the flow of the Yellowstone River at Miles City, Montana. During the six years from 1929 to 1934, inclusive, the percentages were as follows: 1929, 6%; 1930, 9%; 1931, 6%; 1932, 8%; 1933, 8%; 1934, 9%.

It will readily be seen that the outflow from Yellowstone Lake cannot be considered an important contributing factor in any floods in the Mississippi and Missouri valleys, and that any flood control measures undertaken at Fishing Bridge or elsewhere on the lake or along the river within the park boundaries would be almost wholly ineffective.

With reference to the idea of augmenting the flow of the Snake River for irrigation and power purposes by water from Yellowstone Lake, the policy governing national parks, as mentioned above, again comes to mind. It is assumed that no one today questions the premise that the natural features which the national parks and monuments were established to preserve are of incalculable recreational and economic value. Years of public service experience in the national park system adequately prove this. Raising the level of Yellowstone Lake and tunneling through to an outlet on the headwaters of the Snake River would have the effect of relegating the lake to a position of comparative recreational and economic unimportance to the park.

Not only would the natural character of the lake be destroyed, but other undesirable changes would certainly result from the permanent stabilization of the lake at its present high-water mark. The destruction of the Molly Islands, where the white pelicans and numerous other waterfowl nest under protection, would be complete. The remarkably fine sandy shores of Yellowstone Lake would be permanently submerged, and the effect of wave action above the present high-water mark would be incalculable. It would be necessary to raise a large part of the road along the shore and to protect it by riprapping. Some of the hot springs would be permanently submerged. The present high recreational value of Fishing Bridge and the adjacent camp would be destroyed, and the natural character of the lake at its outlet would be fundamentally changed if a dam or weir were to be installed to control the level. The Yellowstone River and the falls within the park would, upon their being converted to an artificially controlled display, lose their appeal to the many thousands of visitors who now visit them annually during the peak flow in June and July. The same unfortunate results would follow any arrangement whereby the lake level would be subject to artificial fluctuations, and, in addition, the shores of the lake would tend to become unsightly mud flats, such as those observed at Jackson Lake, a few miles to the south of Yellowstone Lake, resulting from the establishment of an irrigation reservoir.

If an irrigation and power project such as Mr. Boykin suggests were ever approved, local people in the upper Snake River Valley would profit at the expense of hundreds of thousands of actual and potential park visitors. A precedent would be established for utilization of resources in national parks throughout the country in connection with purely local irrigation, power development, and other schemes, and the economic values of the high public service to which the parks have been dedicated would shortly be gone. In view of the interest the Congress and this Department have consistently maintained in protecting the national park system, I cannot at this time view Mr. Boykin's recommendations favorably.

Mr. Boykin's letter of January 29 is returned herewith.

Sincerely yours,

CHARLES WEST

[13:OF 590:TS]

[1] Representative Boykin (Ala.), on behalf of "a friend of many years standing," urged consideration of a proposal to dam Yellowstone Lake for irrigation purposes. He denied that the appearance of Yellowstone Park would be harmed and said that the "attitude of the National Park Service should be revised because of present and future necessity" (OF 590). McIntyre in his memorandum to Ickes (OF 590) said that the President had suggested that he take up the Boykin matter with him. Apparently no reply was made to Boykin.

648 WILLIAM P. WHARTON, PRESIDENT, NATIONAL PARKS ASSOCIATION, TO ROOSEVELT

WASHINGTON, D. C., *July 1, 1937*

(*Personal, Attention of Miss LeHand*)

DEAR MR. PRESIDENT: Senate bill 2681, authorizing the Colorado-Big Thompson Transmountain Water Diversion Project, which passed the Senate hurriedly without opportunity for public hearings, is, in the estimation of this Association and others concerned with protecting the integrity of the National Parks, a serious menace to the entire National Park System. By permitting economic use of natural resources within the Rocky Mountin National Park, it would set a precedent which might easily lead to breaking down the barriers which have been set up against similar projects in the other Parks. If the National Park System is to be maintained as a unique American institution, it is clear that economic development within every Park must be prevented. Since National Forests offer every opportunity for economic development under wise restrictions, surely we can afford to maintain a few relatively small areas of supreme natural beauty wholly in their original condition for the enjoyment and inspiration of our people.

Since the real issue tends to become obscured by the claim of the Reclamation Service that this project would have no effect on the primeval conditions and natural beauty on the surface, it may be well to add here that the National Parks Association is satisfied that the necessary work cannot be carried on without actual impairment of these values in the vicinity of the location of the proposed tunnel.

We shall do everything we can to defeat this authorization, as well as any appropriation which may be made pursuant to it, or in anticipation of it, in the Interior Department Appropriation bill. I hope that we may have your help in our effort to stop this project in the House, or, if that fails, a ringing veto in defense of complete preservation for the National Primeval Parks.

With kind regards, Sincerely yours,

WM. P. WHARTON

[APS] There appears to be an entirely practicable route to carry the needed water around the south end of the Natl Park, and wholly outside of it. This route should be surveyed.

[*Notation*:A:LEHAND] Mac to ack & hold it in case the Bill comes down—[1]

[13:OF 402:TS]

[1] Acknowledged by McIntyre, July 6, 1937 (OF 402).

649 ARNO B. CAMMERER, DIRECTOR, NATIONAL PARK SERVICE, TO ROOSEVELT

WASHINGTON, *July 6, 1937*

MEMORANDUM FOR THE PRESIDENT: Reference is made to your memorandum of June 17, requesting a memorandum on former Governor Baxter of Maine.[1]

In *Who's Who in America*, Mr. Baxter is credited with being a "champion of State's rights." In the *Portland Press Herald*, May 3,

1937, he refers to the Baxter State Park, which he purchased and donated to the State, as follows: "In planning for this over all those years my sole interest was in the State of Maine, not in the National Government."

These evidences, as well as the correspondence that we have received from Mr. Baxter protesting the Mount Katahdin National Park project, indicate that he is so staunch an advocate of State's rights that he would consider even a national park as an undesirable invasion. We are unable to understand his point of view since the proposed national park, if ultimately established, would increase the park area at Mount Katahdin from the present 7,000 acres of Baxter State Park to about 300,000 acres, which would provide a much more effective recreational area, wildlife sanctuary and scenic wilderness, the very resources that he is seeking to preserve for the State of Maine. . . .

We are informed by Mr. Myron H. Avery, President, Appalachian Trail Conference, that the public facilities at Baxter State Park are inadequate and poorly planned. The State legislature this year refused to appropriate the requested $2,000 for the care of the park. Last year, at the request of Governor Brann, this Service conducted a preliminary investigation of the Mount Katahdin region and recommended that approximately fourteen townships, including the Baxter State Park, would be suitable for national park status, if the lands could be donated in fee simple. Congressman Brewster has introduced the Katahdin Park bill (H. R. 5864) at the request of people in Maine and not at the request of this Department. It is contemplated that final report upon the bill will be withheld until we have made further and detailed study of the project, which study will be undertaken this summer.

The correspondence that was attached to your memorandum of June 17 is returned.[2]

ARNO B. CAMMERER

[13:OF 6–P:TS]

[1] (OF 6–P.)   Percival Baxter was governor of Maine from 1921 to 1925.
[2] Baxter to Mr. and Mrs. David Gray, April 26, 1937, enclosing copies of Baxter's letters to E. A. Pritchard of the National Park Service, Aug. 15, 1936, and to Senator Hale of Maine, April 8, 1937 (OF 6–P). Baxter asked the Grays to intercede with Roosevelt to prevent the establishment of a national park in the Katahdin area. (Mrs. Gray was an aunt of Mrs. Roosevelt.)   In his letter to Hale, he asked that H. R. 5864, to create a Mount Katahdin national park, be "killed," and said that he had plans of his own for the improvement of Baxter State Park.   H. R. 5864 had been introduced on March 23, 1937, by Representative Brewster (Me.); H. R. 6599, apparently a modification of the former bill, was introduced by him on April 22. No action was taken on either measure (Cong. Rec., 75th Cong., 1st sess., 81: 3, 2664; 81: 4, 3772).
The case for a national park to include Katahdin was given in a statement by Myron H. Avery, chairman of the Appalachian Trail Conference (ibid., 81: 10, 1411–1412).   Avery said that the Baxter State Park took in only the mountain top and that proper protection of the scenic values of the mountain could be given only by the addition of extensive areas surrounding it.   He also said that the state was in

no position to care for the area. Several years before, Governor Louis J. Brann of Maine had attempted to interest the Administration in a national park in the Katahdin-Moosehead Lake region (Fechner to Roosevelt, Aug. 24, 1933, OF 6-P). At that time the Park Service recommended that the President move slowly in approving such projects, since large cut-over areas did not make a national park. See below.

650   ROOSEVELT TO MR. AND MRS. DAVID GRAY, Portland, Maine

[WASHINGTON] *July 8, 1937*

MY DEAR MAUDE & DAVID: I did not get the letter to you from Governor Baxter until about two weeks ago and sent it at once to the Interior Department for a memorandum. Here it is. Will you be good enough to send it to the Governor and tell him, incidentally, that I know of the splendid work which he has done for conservation and wild life.[1]

I hope all goes well.

Affectionately,

[FRANKLIN D. ROOSEVELT]

[13:OF 6-P:CT]

[1] The "memorandum" is the preceding letter. The Mount Katahdin park proposal came up again in 1938 and 1939; see *post, 925.*

651   JOSEPHINE ROCHE, ACTING SECRETARY OF THE TREASURY, TO SENATOR ROYAL S. COPELAND OF NEW YORK, CHAIRMAN, SENATE COMMITTEE ON COMMERCE

[WASHINGTON] *July 12, 1937*

MY DEAR MR. CHAIRMAN: Reference is made to H. R. 7051, a bill "Authorizing the construction, repair, and preservation of certain public works on rivers and harbors, and for other purposes." This bill, as passed by the House of Representatives, contains in section 5 provisions which are the same as those of H. R. 2300, a bill "To provide for a survey of the Ohio River and its tributaries with a view to preventing their pollution." Under date of April 19, 1937, this Department, in a letter to the Chairman of the Committee on Rivers and Harbors, House of Representatives, reported adversely on H. R. 2300, as follows:

The Treasury Department has given careful consideration to H. R. 2300, a bill "to provide for a survey of the Ohio River and its tributaries with a view to preventing their pollution."

This bill would authorize and direct the Secretary of War to cause to be made a survey of the Ohio River and its tributaries, to ascertain the sources and extent of pollution, with a view to determining the most feasible method of correcting and eliminating pollution, and to make such recommendations for remedial legislation as is deemed advisable.

[87]

The Secretary of War would be authorized, in carrying out this proposed study, to secure the cooperation and assistance of the Public Health Service.

The Public Health Service has been engaged in scientific studies of stream pollution problems for nearly twenty-five years. Methods of field and laboratory procedure have been developed that are in general use today. In addition the Public Health Service is, and has been for many years, cooperating in a limited way with the State health departments in connection with stream pollution studies. The work of the Public Health Service in this field has been limited only by the appropriations made available.

During the period 1913 to 1917 a careful study was made of the sources and extent of pollution entering the tributaries and the main stream of the Ohio River, and extensive laboratory studies were made of the Ohio River throughout its length. During the period elapsing since this study many changes have taken place with increasing population and industrial development. The canalization of the Ohio River has changed completely the pollution conditions in the main stream during low water periods. Some effects of this canalization on pollution conditions have been studied more recently in the stretch of river between Cincinnati and Louisville.

Were the War Department to undertake a study of this drainage basin it would be necessary for that department to develop the required technical force and duplicate much of the work that has already been done by the Public Health Service, as well as to establish contacts with the State agencies, such as already have been established by the Public Health Service over a period of many years.

It would appear more logical that the Public Health Service, the federal agency authorized by the Congress to make such studies under the Act of August 14, 1912 (37 *Stat.* 309, U. S. C. Title 42, sec. 7) should make the survey if it is required.

In view of the fact that the Public Health Service is the agency authorized by the Congress to carry on stream pollution studies and is the only federal agency properly qualified to make such studies, and since stream pollution control is essentially a public health problem, the Treasury Department does not recommend the enactment of H. R. 2300.

For the reasons stated in the report on H. R. 2300 this Department recommends that Section 5 pertaining to the pollution survey of the Ohio River be stricken from H. R. 7051.[1]

Very truly yours,

(Signed) JOSEPHINE ROCHE

[13:BUDGET BUREAU ENROLLED BILLS:T]

[1] This letter was sent to McIntyre by Acting Budget Director Bell under cover of a letter dated Aug. 21, 1937, in which Bell reported on the bill referred to. Bell noted that the Secretary of War and the Acting Secretary of the Interior recommended that the bill be approved, and enclosed their letters to this effect, dated respectively Aug. 17 and 21, 1937. Bell said he was "wholly in accord with the Treasury position" that stream pollution was essentially a public health problem, and that the Public Health Service was the agency authorized by Congress to carry on stream pollution studies, but he felt that the matter could be "satisfactorily worked out between the two departments," and therefore recommended that the bill be approved. Roosevelt approved the bill Aug. 26, 1937, but took note of the objection made by the Treasury Department in a press release issued on the same date, *post,* 682.

[WASHINGTON] *July 26, 1937*

MY DEAR GOVERNOR BROWNING: During your recent visit you called my attention to the fact that the acquisition of all lands in North Carolina within the boundary lines of the Great Smoky Mountains National Park project had been completed with funds made available by Executive Order 6542 of December 28, 1933, but that some 26,000 acres in Tennessee, estimated to cost approximately $745,000, needed for the completion of the park, had not been acquired due to lack of funds. You asked me why the Government should not complete the program in Tennessee as it did in North Carolina.

The sum of $1,550,000.00 was made available by the above-mentioned Executive Order after North Carolina had advised that $1,145,-540.08 was necessary to acquire two remaining timber parcels in the park area, and Tennessee advised that $858,828.64 was necessary to acquire all lands on the Tennessee side. This made a total of $2,004,-368.72. There remained $506,557.86 of Rockefeller donated funds which were also made available subject to certain conditions that were met. This made a total of $2,056,557.86 available to complete the land acquisition program.

The reliability of the estimates and the adequacy of the funds were first questioned when court awards on the two remaining North Carolina parcels were over $300,000 higher than the estimates. Checking of the Tennessee estimates also found them far too low. The court awards in North Carolina, however, had to be paid at once to stop accrual of interest charges. Of course, these high awards resulted in a greater shortage of funds for land acquisition in Tennessee. The National Park Service estimates that the amount yet needed to complete the park is approximately $745,000. Under the law and the agreements with the chief private donor to the park fund it is contemplated that all of the park lands in North Carolina and Tennessee must be acquired before development of the park may be undertaken.

The provision in previous laws permitting the acquisition of lands with Federal funds for CCC and other purposes, which would be applicable to this project, were not continued by the Congress in the new emergency legislation, and, consequently, there is now no existing authority under which funds may be allocated to complete the land acquisition in Tennessee for the Great Smoky Mountains National Park project.[1]

Very sincerely yours,

[FRANKLIN D. ROOSEVELT]

[13:OF 6–P:CT]

[1] Drafted by the National Park Service.

653 Roosevelt to Daniel C. Beard, Chairman, National Court of Honor, Boy Scouts of America, Suffern, New York

[Washington] *July 28, 1937*

Dear "Uncle" Dan: You are a grand Scout in every sense of the term and I am thrilled to know the story of the characters in "The Yankee in the Court of King Arthur." [1] I am especially thrilled to recognize the faces of Annie Russell and Sarah Bernhardt—even I remember them in their youthful or at least their prime days—and as for Lord Tennyson, who could mistake it?

I wish I could join you in the joy of your camp. I am still searching out bits of original wilderness. Two weeks ago we bought the last of the sugar pine groves in California near the Yosemite.

By the way, up at Hyde Park we have thirty or forty acres of real primeval forest between our house and the river. Some day I shall show it to you.

Always your friend,

[Franklin D. Roosevelt]

[13:PPF 1104:CT]

[1] Referring to Beard's letter of July 23, 1937 (PPF 1104), dealing mostly with his manner of illustrating Mark Twain's *A Connecticut Yankee in King Arthur's Court.* Beard said that he rejoiced to see that the President had "the wisdom and foresight to see the necessity of protecting bits of wilderness in this great land of ours . . ."

654 Roosevelt to Robert Fechner, Director, Civilian Conservation Corps

Washington, *July 28, 1937*

Memorandum for Hon. Robert Fechner: I have signed the Executive Order and I want only to make one suggestion in regard to its administration.[1]

While it is legal to undertake projects on land belonging in private ownership, I think it is a great mistake to do any more of this than we can possibly help. There are some cases where the cutting of firebreaks, for example, the privately owned forest lands, will safeguard publicly owned lands against fire, but it is difficult to say to one private owner "We will work on your land" and to his neighbor say "We will not work on your land."

Furthermore, in view of the fact that there is so much work to be done in the national parks, the national forests, the national monuments and the game refuges, I hope we can confine the CCC work almost

entirely to these areas and to similar areas owned by states and municipalities.

F. D. R.

[13:of 268:ct]

[1] Executive Order 7677–A, signed July 26, 1937, authorized the Civilian Conservation Corps to do work on certain county, municipal and private lands.

655   FREDERIC A. DELANO, VICE CHAIRMAN, NATIONAL RESOURCES
       COMMITTEE, TO JAMES ROOSEVELT, SECRETARY TO THE
       PRESIDENT

WASHINGTON, D. C., July 31, 1937

MY DEAR JIMMIE: I have been down here in Washington attending
meetings, and yesterday afternoon learned of a Joint Resolution that had
been passed by both houses but in different form, the House form being
very objectionable. As a Joint Resolution cannot be vetoed by the
President,[1] it is especially difficult to deal with, and I therefore send you
a copy of this resolution and a copy of the *Congressional Record* with
the passage marked on page 10127.

The resolution as passed by the House would give the War Department authority to prepare a comprehensive plan for utilization of all
water resources in the United States. Reports on run-off retardation will
be prepared by the Department of Agriculture, and studies of reclamation
projects would be made in conjunction with the Department of the
Interior. The Senate Resolution would authorize the preparation of a
comprehensive flood control plan by the War Department. Authority
for the preparation of such a plan by the Departments of War and Agriculture already has been granted, in large measure, under the flood control act of 1936. It appears that the House resolution, if agreed to by
the Senate, would result in a national water plan which would have
been prepared without reference to important Federal interests such as
represented in the power activities of the Federal Power Commission and
the pollution abatement activities of the Public Health Service. It also
might ignore the State water planning activities which were initiated
throughout the country last year when, at the request of the President,
the National Resources Committee undertook the preparation of a comprehensive water program in cooperation with all Federal and State
agencies. A revision of the first report on "Drainage Basin Problems
and Programs" is now in progress.

In view of these facts it seems to me that it would be desirable to
attain agreement to the resolution as passed by the Senate with allowance
for participation by the Department of Agriculture in preparing reports
on run-off retardation. The resolution as passed by the House would

[91]

be an obstacle to the comprehensive water resources planning by all Federal and State agencies which was initiated last year.

I hesitate to bother the President at this time, and would not even call his attention to the matter if it did not seem to me very important.[2]

Very sincerely yours,

FREDERIC A. DELANO

[13:OF 132:TS]

[1] Delano was in error; see *post*, 663.

[2] Senate Joint Resolution 57, "to authorize the submission to Congress of a comprehensive plan for the prevention and control of floods of all the major rivers of the United States," was introduced Jan. 30, 1937, by Senator Caraway (Ark.) The companion measure, House Joint Resolution 175, introduced by McClellan (Ark.), was amended by the House to give the War Department very broad planning powers in the fields of conservation and hydroelectric power. The amendment was incorporated in the Senate resolution and this was passed on Aug. 2, 1937 (*Cong. Rec.*, 75th Cong., 1st sess., 81:1, 601, 604; 81:5, 5654; 81:7, 7822–7841, 7963–7964, 8163). On August 4 Roosevelt asked for a report on the measure from the Budget Bureau, and on August 11 Acting Budget Director Bell submitted statements requested by him from the agency heads most affected by the act (Bell to McIntyre, Aug. 11, 1937, Budget Bureau Enrolled Bills). Acting Secretary of Agriculture Wilson, in his letter to Bell of Aug. 6, 1937, said that the resolution would aid his agency in carrying out its responsibilities for flood control surveys as authorized by the act of June 22, 1936. He was aware, however, that the proposed law might not be in accord with the President's general program. Ickes, writing August 9 as head of the National Resources Committee, and August 10 as Secretary of Interior, urged disapproval for reasons essentially those stated in the memorandum sent by him to Roosevelt on Aug. 4, 1937 (*post*, 660). Secretary of War Woodring, writing Aug. 10, 1937, said that the War Department had not objected to the resolution in its original form. As amended, however, the War Department would be required to evaluate flood control projects for hydroelectric development and other conservation purposes, and would "call for plans for all works necessary for an effective soil and water conservation [*sic*] for all rivers and their watersheds." He considered such an extension of responsibilities more appropriately assumed by the Federal Power Commission and the Agriculture and Interior Departments and he therefore recommended disapproval.

Acting Federal Power Commissioner Draper, in his letter of Aug. 6, 1937, recommended neither approval nor disapproval but pointed out that the resolution would transfer to the War Department functions hitherto exercised by the Power Commission. Draper said that it was apparent that the "underlying purpose" of the measure was "to confer upon the War Department the broad planning functions which, under other legislation now pending . . . would be conferred upon newly created regional conservation or power authorities." This view was openly expressed in the House debate; for example, Chairman Whittington of the House Committee on Flood Control said, "We hear much about planning and planning agencies. Much of the planning and many of the agencies would be duplications . . . The establishment of additional agencies for flood control would result in delay." (*Cong. Rec.*, 81:7, 7831). (Cf. Maass, *Muddy Waters*, pp. 87–93.) On the basis of the reports, Bell recommended that the resolution be disapproved.

656   ROOSEVELT TO HAROLD L. ICKES, SECRETARY OF THE INTERIOR

[WASHINGTON] *August 2, 1937*

MY DEAR MR. SECRETARY: I am approving, with some reluctance, the enrolled bill S. 2086, "To authorize the construction of a Federal reclamation project to furnish a water supply for the lands of the Arch Hurley Conservancy District in New Mexico." [1]

The necessity for, or desirability of, this legislation is not apparent in view of the statement in the letter of Acting Secretary West which accompanied the enrolled bill, that: "The plans so far made entail a total cost of $8,278,000, or $184 per acre, which under present Reclamation laws would render the project infeasible. However, by a revision of plans or by some other means, the repayment of the investment may become possible."

It seems to me that a determination of the feasibility of the project and of the probability of its repayment of construction costs, through the use of funds that are available to the Bureau of Reclamation for such investigations of proposed Reclamation projects, should have been a prerequisite to the consideration of legislation authorizing the construction of the project.

I am persuaded, however, to approve this bill only because of the provision which it contains forbidding the initiation of construction work on the project unless and until you are able to make a finding, under Subsection B of Section 4 of the Act of December 5, 1924, that the project is economically feasible and will in all probability return its construction cost.

In view of the fact that the Reclamation Fund will be exhausted by the end of the present fiscal year and that its income for the next few years will be no more than enough to provide for the projects now under construction, I shall not be disposed to hereafter submit an estimate of appropriation for beginning the construction of the project covered by the enrolled bill until I am thoroughly satisfied that this project is feasible and will repay the cost of its construction.

Sincerely yours,

[FRANKLIN D. ROOSEVELT]

FJB/ABP [2]
[Notation: AS] DWB
[13: OF 402: CT]

[1] Act approved Aug. 2, 1937 (50 *Stat.* 557).
[2] Drafted in the Budget Bureau, presumably by Frederick J. Bailey, chief of the Division of Research and Investigation.

657   VERNON G. DAVIS, SPEAKER OF THE ARIZONA HOUSE OF REPRESENTATIVES, TO ROOSEVELT

PHOENIX, ARIZONA, *August 3, 1937*

[*Telegram*] HONORABLE SIR: The following Memorial was unanimously passed by the Legislature of the State of Arizona:

A House Memorial Protesting Against the Proposed Withdrawal of Land in Southwest Arizona as Game Refuge

The Secretary of the Interior, and The Chief of the Bureau of Biological Survey of the United States of America:

Your Memorialist respectfully represents: The total area of land within the State of Arizona is 72,838,400 acres. Of this area Indian reservations occupy 19,566,339 acres. National forests 11,203,438 acres. National Parks and monuments 671,610 acres. Military reservations 73,008 acres. The Public Domain consists of something less than thirteen million acres. Two-thirds of the State's area is controlled by Federal bureaus; less than one-fourth is subject to taxation. It is understood that the Bureau of Biological Survey has requested the Department of the Interior to have withdrawn from entry two large bodies of land in the southwestern portion of the State, totalling approximately 3,400,000 acres for the use and propagation of mountain sheep and goats and as game refuges. A large portion of the area which it is proposed to have placed in these two game refuges is grazing land and being used by local stockmen, while other portions thereof will soon be irrigated by water from the Colorado River under the Gila project. These proposed withdrawals if made will work undue hardships on the users of said lands especially those persons engaged in the livestock business, which is one of the biggest industries of the State and will also greatly retard the development of the State, and in large measure prevent these lands from being developed and improved and placed upon the tax rolls. It is overwhelmingly the public sentiment of the people of Arizona that these proposed game refuges be not established.

Wherefore, your Memorialist, the House of Representatives of the State of Arizona, urgently requests that the proposed withdrawal of public lands in southwestern Arizona for the purposes above stated be not made.[1]

VERNON G. DAVIS

[13:OF 633:T]

[1] Answered *post,* 672.

658   ROOSEVELT TO ALBERT Z. GRAY, Locust Valley, New York

WASHINGTON, *August 4, 1937*

DEAR MR. GRAY: I am glad you took the time to write me as you did in your letter of July 8, relative to Senate Bill 2681, introduced by Senator Adams, to authorize the construction of the Colorado-Big Thompson project.[1] A companion bill has also been introduced in the House but has not yet passed. The Interior Department Appropriation Bill carries an item for commencing the construction of this project.

You may care to read a synopsis of the Bureau of Reclamation's report, which has been printed as Senate Document No. 80, a copy of which I enclose.[2]

Please be assured that I share your appreciation of the national park policy and will not by any Presidential act even remotely jeopardize this national policy declared in 1916.[3]

Very sincerely yours,

[FRANKLIN D. ROOSEVELT]

[13:OF 402:CT]

[1] Gray opposed the project because he said he understood it would drain the lakes and springs within Rocky Mountain National Park (OF 402).

[2] *Colorado-Big Thompson Project, Synopsis of Report on Colorado-Big Thompson Project Plan of Development and Cost Estimate . . .* S. Doc. 80, 75th Cong., 1st sess. (Washington, 1937).

[3] S. 2681 was approved by the Senate without debate on June 24, 1937 (*Cong. Rec.*, 75th Cong., 1st sess., 81: 6, 5953, 6016, 6294–6295). The House Irrigation and Reclamation Committee held hearings on the Senate bill and made a report but the House took no further action. Senate backers of the Big Thompson project then added an amendment to the pending Interior Department appropriation bill which appropriated $900,000 to proceed with construction. The House conference committee refused to agree to this amendment and the measure came before the House for debate.

Opponents of the project said the park scenery would be harmed; debris from the tunnel borings would be an eyesore; lake levels would be affected; power lines, canals and other installations would line the approach roads. Representative Dirksen (Ill.) said the contemplated invasion of the park would establish a precedent: next would come demands to open the park for mining and grazing and for the building of railroads and air fields; in the years to come posterity would lament the lack of vision that had permitted the spoliation. He pointed out that the hearings had shown that alternate routes for the tunnel outside the park were available. Representative Zimmerman (Mo.) voiced the general reaction of the western members when he said that the only opposition to the bill came from "certain organizations throughout the country that wanted to act as godfathers for the people of Colorado, and other Western States in looking after our natural parks" (*ibid.*, 81:7, 7408–7429). The amendment was approved by the House July 22 by a vote of 174 to 154 with 103 not voting, and became law with the signing of the Interior Department appropriation bill on Aug. 9, 1937 (*50 Stat. 595*).

659   HAROLD L. ICKES, SECRETARY OF THE INTERIOR, TO ROOSEVELT

WASHINGTON, *August 4, 1937*

MY DEAR MR. PRESIDENT: I thought you might be interested in this memorandum with reference to House Joint Resolution No. 175, which has been prepared by the Water Resources Committee of the National Resources Committee, by direction of Dr. Merriam.

Sincerely yours,

HAROLD L. ICKES

[*Notation*:A] S. J. Res. 57 passed in lieu

[13:BUDGET BUREAU ENROLLED BILLS:TS]

Memorandum re House Joint Resolution 175 and Senate Joint Resolution 57: This joint resolution, if approved by the President, would authorize a national water-planning program which would be carried out independent of much planning work already in progress by Federal agencies other than the War Department, and by state and local agencies now actively concerned with water-resources plans. The effect of the resolution would be to centralize in the War Department a water-planning function which now is and should continue to be distributed among many Federal agencies. It would result in a single, static plan presented to Congress without provision for continuing revision on a regional basis in the light of changing national policy. For these reasons it would establish a system directly contrary to the program of integrated regional planning outlined by the President in his message of June 3, 1937.

A national water plan was requested by the President during the early part of 1938 and was submitted by the National Resources Committee in December, 1936. It was intended to set forth the major problems of water resources use, broad programs for the development of water resources, and specific construction and investigation projects consistent with the broad program. It resulted from the cooperative studies of all Federal, state, and local agencies concerned. It was directed at an integration of the multiple aspects of water use and control, and recognized that flood-control in a given drainage area should not be considered independently of hydroelectric power, navigation, irrigation, pollution abatement, municipal water supply, recreation, and wildlife conservation. In this respect, the plan carries forward for the first time on a national scale, the plans for smaller areas or for restricted problems prepared by the Corps of Engineers, the President's Committee on Water Flow, the Mississippi Valley Committee, the Great Plains Committee and other groups.

The resolution, as passed by the Senate originally, was intended to provide Congress with a comprehensive statement on flood-control projects in major drainage areas. Such a statement is needed as an aid in the consideration of individual projects. However, as the recent experience with the Ohio-Lower Mississippi comprehensive flood-control plan has shown so forcefully, strictly flood-control plans are of little value unless integrated with larger programs for use and control of water for other purposes. The House amendments extended the authority to include "provisions for . . . utilization of water resources through the building of power dams or a combination of power, reclamation, conservation, and flood-control dams, and all work necessary for an effective soil and water conservation." Therefore the amendments were in the right direction, but along lines which are unsatisfactory for the following reasons:

1. The planning of wise use and control of water resources and related land resources is distributed by law among numerous agencies not included in the resolution. The Federal Power Commission, the U. S. Public Health Service, the International Boundary Commission, the Tennessee Valley Authority are among the more important ones. Moreover, several bureaus within the Department of Agriculture are concerned with water utilization from standpoints other than run-off retardation and erosion control. Although all of these agencies are actively engaged in water-planning work, they would not have a formal part in preparing plans under the joint resolution. The current controversy between the War Department and the Federal Power Commission over hydroelectric and flood-control development on the Connecticut and Merrimack Rivers illustrates the difficulties which might be expected to result from the procedure outlined in the resolution. It should be noted that the resolution does not indicate clearly whether or not the War Department and Department of Agriculture reports would be integrated.

2. In preparing the report on "Drainage Basin Problems and Programs" (the national water plan) at the direction of the President last year, all interested state agencies as well as Federal agencies were brought into the work. For example, state sanitary engineers and conservation commissioners submitted proposals through the state planning boards. Water-planning activities were initiated in most states as a result of that first national survey. Continued cooperation with those state and local groups in the planning of developments which affect those groups primarily is to be desired. Such cooperation is not authorized or directed in the joint resolution.

3. In his message of June 3, 1937, the President outlined a program for planning of national resources on a regional basis. The essential features were a group of regional planning bodies which were to be integrated through a national planning board and the Bureau of the Budget. If the joint resolution were to be approved in its present form, the authority for such planning would in effect be delegated to the Secretary of War. He would report directly to Congress. The planning would not be organized on a regional basis. It would not "start at the bottom" with the state and local groups as suggested by the President. The results would not necessarily be coordinated with the work of more than a few other agencies. There would be no provision for revision and checking the program in the light of national budgetary considerations and of national planning policies. Once authorized, this new planning venture would be used as an argument against the regional organization proposed by the President.

The joint resolution would substitute a new water-planning structure for that which was developed during 1935. In so doing, it would ignore certain interested Federal agencies, it would eliminate the present joint State-Federal planning relationships, and it would establish an organization contrary in structure to that proposed by the President in his message on regional planning.

In view of these considerations, it would seem that if the President wishes to develop the program outlined in that message, the joint resolution should not be approved.

G. F. WHITE [1]

[13:BUDGET BUREAU ENROLLED BILLS:TS]

[1] Gilbert F. White, a geographer specializing in conservation problems, from 1946 to 1955 president of Haverford College.

661   ROOSEVELT TO DANIEL W. BELL, ACTING DIRECTOR, BUREAU
       OF THE BUDGET

WASHINGTON, August 5, 1937

MEMORANDUM FOR THE ACTING DIRECTOR OF THE BUDGET: Please prepare veto message after consultation with Interior, Agriculture, War Department and National Resources Committee.

F. D. R.

[*Notation*:T] Let. from Secy. Ickes 8/4/37, with memo. re H. J. Res. 175 and S. J. Res. 57.

[13:OF 132:CT]

662   REPRESENTATIVE JOHN L. McCLELLAN OF ARKANSAS TO
       ROOSEVELT

WASHINGTON, D. C., August 11, 1937

MY DEAR MR. PRESIDENT: At the suggestion of Honorable Daniel W. Bell, Acting Director, Bureau of the Budget, I am writing this as a memorandum in support of SJR 57, which now awaits Executive approval.

I have just returned from my home in Arkansas, and am much surprised to learn that any opposition had been expressed to this bill. It passed both the House and Senate without a dissenting vote.

From the best information I have been able to obtain since my return, it seems some are apprehensive that undue authority is given to the Army Engineers in connection with hydro-electric development, and that objection is directed to this provision: "and (the report) shall set forth the values of such projects for hydroelectric development and other conservation purposes."

The original bill did not contain this and other provisions that were incorporated by the House Committee amendments, but these amendments to the bill regarding hydro-electric power were incorporated at the instance of members on the Committee and other members of the House who expressed an opinion that no dams should be constructed for flood control purposes with disregard to their availability and the possibility of their utilization for power development. To satisfy those who are favorable to the development of our power resources, the power provision was incorporated in this resolution by the House Flood Control Committee.

It must be borne in mind that this resolution authorizes and directs nothing that will be binding on the Congress. When the report or reports called for by the resolution have been prepared and submitted, they will be in effect, if the letter and spirit of the bill are followed, a recommendation for a comprehensive flood control plan, national in scope, and covering all of the major streams of the Nation, and in addition there will be pointed out incidental values and benefits that may accrue by reason of the construction of such projects. If the Congress cares to, it may from time to time by further legislation authorize and appropriate money for the construction of any project that may have been so recommended. It could enact legislation authorizing the construction of all or any part. It is my thought that a comprehensive report of this character will be very valuable in the study of this problem as we undertake to find an adequate solution in future legislation.

It can do no harm, but rather, will be an aid to the Administration's program of creating a number of authorities for the different drainage basins. Such authorities in formulating their plans and the National Resources Board in formulating its plans may well avail themselves of such information and recommendations as the War Department may submit in this report, or reports, pursuant to the direction and authority contained in this resolution.

It is positively not the intention of this act to place any new authority over power legislation with the Army Engineers other than it shall be their duty in their reports to point out, where a dam is recommended for flood control purposes, whether in their opinion it has any value or possibilities as a power project in addition to the purposes it will serve in connection with the control of floods.

I especially wish to respectfully call your attention to our conference regarding this resolution on the 15th of June. At that time the Flood Control Committee of the House had reported favorably HJR 175 with amendments, but which as originally introduced was identical with SJR 57. On June 10 I had written you, calling your attention to HJR

175 and SJR 57, and among other things, I stated: "Before proceeding further in an effort to obtain passage, I should like to have you consider the merits of the proposal, and if you feel it does not seriously conflict with the program you have recommended, I would be pleased to have you give it your approval, or, at least, advise there is no objection to its enactment," and requested an opportunity to discuss the measure with you at your convenience. On June 15, when you extended me the courtesy of a conference, after discussion, you assured me that you had no objection to the measure and that you preferred the House bill with the Committee amendments rather than SJR 57, which had passed the Senate and which was identical with HJR 175 in its original form. Therefore, bearing in mind your preference and after you advised you had no objections, I proceeded to obtain favorable action in the House on HJR 175, and then called up SJR 57 and amended it by inserting the House bill after the enacting clause. The Senate thereafter promptly concurred in the House amendments.

After you had advised me that you had no objection to this legislation, I asked if I might have the liberty to so state, and you replied in the affirmative. The press in my state has carried a number of articles regarding this measure, and one to the effect that after my conference with you, I stated that you had assured me you had no objection to its enactment. Since its passage I have received many congratulatory messages from my constituents and others in the State of Arkansas.

I sincerely hope you will not veto this bill. It is good legislation, sound and wise from every viewpoint. I trust you will let it become a law.

Sincerely yours,

JOHN L. McCLELLAN

[13:OF 132:TS]

663   ROOSEVELT TO FREDERIC A. DELANO, VICE CHAIRMAN,
       NATIONAL RESOURCES COMMITTEE

[WASHINGTON] *August 12, 1937*

DEAR UNCLE FRED: Jimmy has shown me your letter.[1] It is a joint Resolution; it is on my desk, and I am going to veto it!

You will hear from me in a day or so in regard to a committee to be formed to bring in a comprehensive plan by January.

Affectionately,

[FRANKLIN D. ROOSEVELT]

[13:OF 132:CT]

[1] *Ante,* 655.

664   Daniel W. Bell, Acting Director, Bureau of the Budget,
        to Marvin H. McIntyre, Secretary to the President[1]

[Washington] *8/12* [*1937*]

Mr. McIntyre: Here is draft of memo. the President wanted in connection with S. 57. Will you put in day and hour.

DWB

[*Notation*:as] How soon do you want to have this conference?

MHM

[13:of 132:as]

[1] McIntyre's title was changed from Assistant Secretary to the President to Secretary to the President on July 1, 1937.

665   [*Enclosure*] Draft Memorandum, Roosevelt to the Secre-
        tary of War and Others

Washington

To—The Secretary of War, The Secretary of the Interior, The Secretary of Agriculture, The Secretary of the Treasury, The Acting Director of the Budget: Will you be good enough to come to my office at   on   , for the purpose of discussing with me a plan that I have in mind for the creation of a committee, upon which you would serve, to make a comprehensive study of, and develop a program for, the conservation and utilization of the water resources of all our watersheds from the tops of the watersheds to the ocean.

It would be my purpose to have this committee bring to me a complete program of water conservation and utilization for the next several years, in time for the inclusion in the 1939 Budget to be submitted to the Congress early in January, of the items for the first year of such a program. These items would form a part of the total estimate of appropriation of not to exceed $500,000,000 for all kinds of public works that would be included in the 1939 Budget.

It is suggested that you have representatives of the following agencies under your supervision accompany you to this conference: Corps of Engineers, United States Army; Reclamation Service; Public Land Agencies; Forest Service; Soil Conservation Service; National Resources Committee, and Procurement Division of the Treasury Department.[1]

[13:of 132:ct]

[1] An attached memorandum, Roosevelt to Bell, Aug. 22, 1937, reads, "Will you speak to me about this?" No further reference to the proposed conference has been found.

THE WHITE HOUSE, *August 13, 1937*

To THE SENATE: I return herewith without my approval, Senate Joint Resolution No. 57, entitled "Joint Resolution to authorize the submission to Congress of a comprehensive national plan for the prevention and control of floods of all the major rivers of the United States, development of hydroelectric power resources, water and soil conservation, and for other purposes."

In my message of June 3, 1937, I proposed for the consideration of Congress, a thoroughly democratic process of national planning of the conservation and utilization of the water, and related land, resources of our country. I expressed the belief that such a process of national planning should start at the bottom through the initiation of planning work in the State and local units, and that it should contemplate the formulation of programs on a regional basis, the integration of fiscal and conservation policies on a national basis, and the submission of a comprehensive development program to the Congress by the President.

The reverse of such a process of national planning is prescribed in Senate Joint Resolution No. 57. By this resolution the War Department would become the national planning agency, not alone for flood control, but for all the other multiple uses of water. Although the Department of Agriculture would prepare reports on runoff retardation and soil erosion prevention, and the Department of the Interior be consulted on reclamation projects, the War Department would report for these coordinate agencies directly to Congress instead of to the Chief Executive. The local and regional basis of planning would be ignored, and there would be no review of the whole program, prior to its presentation to Congress, from the standpoints of national budgetary considerations and national conservation policies.

The corps of Army Engineers has had wide experience in the building of flood control projects and has executed the projects entrusted to it with great skill and ability. Its experience and background is not alone sufficient, however, for the planning of a comprehensive program for the development of the vast water and related resources of the Nation.

The planning of the use and control of water and related resources is distributed by law among numerous governmental agencies, such as the Departments of Agriculture and Interior, the Federal Power Commission, the United States Public Health Service, the International Boundary Commission, and the Tennessee Valley Authority. The Joint Resolution encroaches upon the functions of these agencies, and ignores and duplicates the coordinated planning work already in progress under the general guidance of the National Resources Committee.

I find it impossible to subscribe, therefore, to the proposal that has been embodied in this Joint Resolution.

This does not mean, however, that the objective of this Joint Resolution cannot be attained without the need of any legislation whatsoever. I propose to present to the Congress in January a comprehensive national plan for flood control and prevention and the development of water and soil conservation, such plan to be prepared by all of the many Government agencies concerned.

I trust that this will meet all of the desires of the Congress.[1]

FRANKLIN D. ROOSEVELT

[W. H. PRESS RELEASES:M]

[1] (Drafted by the Budget Bureau.) Read in the Senate Aug. 13, 1937, this message was referred to the Committee on Commerce (*Cong. Rec.,* 75th Cong., 1st sess., 81: 8, 8823).

667 ROOSEVELT TO MARVIN H. McINTYRE, SECRETARY TO THE PRESIDENT

WASHINGTON, *August 17, 1937*

MEMORANDUM FOR MAC: Will you prepare a nice letter to Congressman McClellan explaining why I vetoed his Bill?[1]

F. D. R.

[13:OF 132:T]

[1] See *post,* 674.

668 STEPHEN T. EARLY, SECRETARY TO THE PRESIDENT, TO ROOSEVELT

WASHINGTON, *August 17, 1937*

MEMORANDUM FOR THE PRESIDENT: According to Secretary Wallace, you promised the Wild Life Committee to issue, *this week,* a Proclamation designating a week in which the importance to the nation of wild life preservation is to be given emphasis.

Please edit the attached, and I will circulate it for the approval of the various Departments. I can't do this without your approval first.

S.E.

[*Notation*:A] STE I don't think I promised it for this week—Please check

[*Notation*:AS] Both Secretary Wallace and Senator Pittman say the President is correct in this—no promise was made that the Proclamation would be issued this week. My information came from Henry P. Davis, Secretary, Am. Wildlife Institute. W. D. H.[1]

[13:OF 378:TS]

[1] William D. Hassett, at this time special assistant to Early. The proclamation was issued Feb. 15, 1938, *post*, 745.

669 S. B. LOCKE, CONSERVATION DIRECTOR, IZAAK WALTON LEAGUE OF AMERICA, TO MARVIN H. McINTYRE, SECRETARY TO THE PRESIDENT

CHICAGO, ILLINOIS, *August 18, 1937, 10:22 p. m.*

[*Telegram*]   M. H. McINTYRE: Acceptance in the House of water pollution Act HR—2711 [1] as amended by Senate by agreement between Senators Lonergan and Barkley will give the Administration opportunity to claim real progress in field of pollution control as a contribution to public health and economic welfare of the country. Am informed Representative Vinson favors amended bill but Mansfield who gave original bill strong support somewhat doubtful about amendments. If the President could indicate his approval of amended bill to Congressmen Vinson and Mansfield it would be of great service and a real contribution to public welfare. Your personal assistance greatly appreciated.

S. B. LOCKE

[13:OF 114–A:T]

[1] The Vinson Water Pollution Bill.

670 DANIEL W. BELL, ACTING DIRECTOR, BUREAU OF THE BUDGET, TO ROOSEVELT

WASHINGTON, *Aug. 19, 1937*

MEMORANDUM FOR THE PRESIDENT: I believe that the only matters which have been eliminated in the Third Deficiency Bill as it passed the House that you would be interested in talking to Senator Adams about are the following:

Department of Agriculture: Farm Forestation and Woodland Management, Salaries and Expenses—We submitted an estimate of $1,000,000 which has been eliminated. This, you will recall, is the shelter belt project. The House Committee took the view that there is available from emergency funds for the fiscal year 1938 the sum of $700,000, which should be sufficient to last until the end of the fiscal year and that it would then be a proper item for inclusion in the 1939 Budget. Congressman Ferguson attempted to get the bill amended on the floor of the House for half of the estimate submitted but was unsuccessful. I understand that Agriculture is asking the Senate Appropriations Committee to restore this. . . .[1]

D. W. BELL

[13:OF 79:TS]

[1] Representative Woodrum (Va.) opposed Ferguson's amendment on the ground that no emergency or deficiency was involved and that the matter should go to the regular subcommittee on agricultural appropriations (*Cong. Rec.*, 75th Cong., 1st sess., 81: 8, 9170–9171). The Shelterbelt (from 1937 on the Forest Service called it the "Prairie States Forestry Project") was carried on by the Forest Service with emergency funds from the Works Progress Administration.

671   ROOSEVELT TO HAROLD L. ICKES, CHAIRMAN, NATIONAL
       RESOURCES COMMITTEE

WASHINGTON, *August 20, 1937*

MY DEAR MR. ICKES: In order to implement my message to Congress withholding approval of Senate Joint Resolution No. 57,[1] I am hereby requesting the National Resources Committee to proceed with its review and revision of the report on Drainage Basin Problems and Programs. It is my hope that the Committee will be prepared to present to me in January 1938 a comprehensive national plan for flood control and prevention and the development of water and soil conservation.

In undertaking this revision it is understood that the Committee will cooperate with and have the benefit of the activities of all the government agencies concerned. In addition, the reviews of state and local agencies interested in these problems should be carefully canvassed in connection with the preparation of the revised program.

Sincerely yours,

[FRANKLIN D. ROOSEVELT]

[*Notation*: STAMPED] (Sgd) Ickes Draft reply sent to the White House for signature Aug 20 1937 [2]

[13:OF 132:CT]

[1] *Ante*, 666.
[2] Drafted by the National Resources Committee.

672   ROOSEVELT TO VERNON G. DAVIS, SPEAKER OF THE ARIZONA
       HOUSE OF REPRESENTATIVES, Phoenix

[WASHINGTON] *August 21, 1937*

MY DEAR MR. SPEAKER: I have received your telegram of August third, regarding the protest of the Legislature of the State of Arizona against the withdrawal of certain areas in the southwestern part of that State for use by the Department of Agriculture as game refuges.

The Secretary of the Interior informs me that in lieu of game refuges the present proposal of the Department of Agriculture is to place the area in that part of the State which is to be included in a grazing district also under game range administration in order that the grazing of the domestic livestock and game therein may be regulated and adjusted.

He also informs me that this proposal has his approval insofar as it does not conflict with the plans of his Department for the development of the Colorado River and Gila Valley reclamation projects and that no action is proposed until consideration has been given all the facts and the objections of interested persons.

It appears that in areas in other States in which the same problem is involved, the form of dual administration contemplated is satisfactory to the stockmen and affords adequate protection to the game.[1]

Very sincerely yours,

[FRANKLIN D. ROOSEVELT]

[13:OF 633:CT]

[1] (Drafted by the Interior Department.) The Arizona-Colorado River Commission, Phoenix, Arizona, also protested the proposed withdrawal of lands in a telegram to Roosevelt of Aug. 3, 1937, and received the same reply, dated Sept. 3, 1937 (OF 633).

673 ROOSEVELT TO HARRY L. HOPKINS, WORKS PROGRESS ADMINISTRATOR

WASHINGTON, *August 21, 1937*

MEMORANDUM FOR HON. HARRY L. HOPKINS: Will you please tell all of your Regional Directors that as a matter of administration policy no further WPA projects will be approved for improving or repairing or adding to sewers which dump into any creek or river?

On the other side of it, we will encourage projects for the building of sewage disposal plants.

The same order has gone out to the PWA Administrator.

This is of the utmost importance.

F. D. R.

[13:OF 444–C:CT]

674 ROOSEVELT TO REPRESENTATIVE JOHN L. MCCLELLAN OF ARKANSAS

[WASHINGTON] *August 21, 1937*

MY DEAR CONGRESSMAN: This is the first opportunity I have had for a personal reply to your letter to me of August eleventh with respect to S. J. R. 57.

In my veto message I outlined fully my reasons for disapproving the Bill. I just want you to know that I read your letter very carefully and gave much consideration to this measure.

Confidentially, however, the objectives of this measure will be carried out anyhow and will be an important part of the complete report of the whole subject of flood control. The survey, of course, will be made by the Corps of Engineers and simultaneously, conservation, reforestation and the other factors entering into the problem will also be available.

Some time when we both have a little more leisure, I will be very glad to talk over this subject with you.[1]

Very sincerely yours,

[Franklin D. Roosevelt]

MHM/TMB

[13:OF 132:CT]

[1](Drafted by McIntyre.) McClellan wrote again on Dec. 6, 1937 (OF 132), asking for an appointment to discuss future flood control legislation. He saw the President on Jan. 14, 1938 (PPF 1-O).

675   Robert Fechner, Director, Civilian Conservation Corps, to Roosevelt

Washington, D.C., *August 21, 1937*

Dear Mr. President: On July 28, 1937 you sent a memorandum to this office in connection with Executive Order No. 7677–A, July 26, 1937, which you had just signed. In this memorandum you made the following statement:

While it is legal to undertake projects on land belonging in private ownership, I think it is a great mistake to do any more of this than we can possibly help. There are some cases where the cutting of firebreaks, for example, the privately owned forest lands, will safeguard publicly owned lands against fire, but it is difficult to say to one private owner "We will work on your land" and to his neighbor say "We will not work on your land."

I have discussed the contents of this paragraph with the several technical agencies of the Federal Government cooperating in Civilian Conservation Corps work and each of them assures me that they will be guided by the policy that you suggest.

There are some phases of this situation, however, which I feel I should bring to your attention. Under the work program for the Tenth Period beginning October 1, 1937 we will have 113 CCC camps operating primarily on privately owned forest lands. These camps are engaged in the construction of firebreaks, truck trails, telephone lines, lookouts and administrative facilities designed to protect the privately owned forests from ravages of fire, insects, and disease. The basic authoriza-

[107]

tion for this activity is contained in the Act of June 7, 1924 which provides that the Federal Government may reimburse states for monies expended by the states or by private landowners under state supervision in a statewide system of forest protection.[1] In no case, however, can the Federal Government exceed fifty percent of the total expenditure made by the states and private landowners. All states which have extensive acreage of forest lands now have forest protection systems supported wholly or in part through state appropriations.

As a general statement, all the states from the District of Columbia north, and west to the Great Plains region support and finance protective systems wholly through the appropriations of state money raised through ad valorem taxes. In the far West, and in most of the Southern states the state appropriations are supplemented by funds contributed through associations of forest landowners. In all of these states, the state organization either handles directly the protective work, or supervises the protection work done by forest protection associations. In no case has any state or federal appropriation, to my knowledge, been used for the single purpose of protecting lands of any individual or corporation.

There must always be a state-wide or at least a community-wide protection system to which landowners in the West and South contribute through payment of monies to the treasurer of an association. All work done on land belonging to any private owner is, therefore, for the purpose of carrying out state or community-wide protection plans. For example, a road, telephone lines, or lookout structures on any owner's land may or may not be of more value to that landowner than it is to his neighbors.

The majority of the states have recognized the protection of forests as a public responsibility—financing and going about the job in much the same way as municipalities finance and go about the job of fire protection in cities. It is impossible for individual landowners to protect their forests against the ravages of fire, insects, and disease excepting through state-wide or community-wide cooperative systems. I am informed that no less than 75% of the forest lands that are important to the Nation in watershed protection, timber production and public recreation are privately-owned.

A small part of our work has to do with the rehabilitation and to a limited extent the reconstruction of drainage systems. During the Tenth Period of work beginning October 1 we will have 41 CCC camps engaged in this type of work. All of these camps are located in some of the most valuable agricultural lands in this Nation. Partly on account of the depression in agricultural prices, and partly because of a lack of adequate maintenance programs, a very large part of these drainage ditches have become largely or wholly inoperative. Landowners claim that these drainage systems are quasi-public organizations in many of the states that have given them a legal status conferring the authority to levy assessments or taxes and to force their collection to provide for maintenance.

As stated above, however, it has been impossible to maintain most of these drainage systems during recent years. There is also a lack of understanding about the best or the most economical methods of carrying on maintenance work necessary on these ditches. Under the supervision of the Bureau of Agricultural Engineering, we are attempting to devise methods and machinery that will reduce the cost of maintenance work on drainage ditch systems to a figure that can be met by the landowner. On this type of work, as is the case in forest protection, no one owner could maintain his drainage system separately. It has to be a combined effort. The work benefits each landowner individually, although not necessarily in proportion to the amount of work done on his particular land.

The other large activity in which CCC camps engage on private property is in connection with soil erosion. In the Tenth Period of work beginning October 1, 1937, 374 CCC camps will engage in soil control work under the supervision of the Soil Conservation Service. Every one of these camps will operate on privately owned lands for demonstrating methods of erosion control. A definite effort is being made to establish a system whereby all CCC camps engaged in work of this character will be working in cooperation with local erosion control associations. Here, too, there is a lack of understanding on the part of landowners and tenant farmers as to how soil erosion can be prevented. The Soil Conservation Service is using every effort to get the private landowner to make as large a contribution as possible toward the cost of CCC work on his land. All of the valuable agricultural land of the country is in private ownership and wastage of soils is probably the biggest loss that is occurring in the natural resources of the country. There is no way to demonstrate proper methods of farming to save soils excepting that it be done on privately-owned lands.

There appears to be no doubt that private landowners appreciate the work that the Federal Government is doing to assist in the proper use and protection of privately owned land. I hope our program will meet with your approval.[2]

Sincerely yours,

ROBT. FECHNER

[13:OF 268:TS]

[1] The Clarke-McNary Act.
[2] Answered *post*, 681.

WASHINGTON, *August 21, 1937*

MEMORANDUM TO THE PRESIDENT: I am taking the liberty of sending you a prepared veto message on S. 2863, which has passed both Houses before the report of the Department could be presented to the committee. The Acting Director of the Budget advises that the proposed legislation would not be in accord with your program at the present time. Further than this, it affects the activities of the Department of the Interior so materially that I feel it would be unwise to allow the bill to become a law. So far as I know, there were no hearings either by committees of the Senate or the House. It may be possible that through a joint resolution the bill may be recalled and referred back to committee. I understand an effort to this end is being made this afternoon.

HAROLD L. ICKES

[13:BUDGET BUREAU ENROLLED BILLS:TS]

677   [*Enclosure*] DRAFT BY ICKES OF A PROPOSED VETO MESSAGE

TO THE SENATE: I return herewith, without my approval, S. 2863, a bill to promote conservation in the arid and semiarid areas of the United States by aiding in the development of facilities for water storage and utilization.

The bill provides for conservation of water resources in the arid and semiarid areas of the United States, resulting from inadequate facilities for water storage. It directs the Secretary of Agriculture to formulate and keep current a program of construction and maintenance projects, to construct and to sell or lease these projects with or without a money consideration, and to carry out certain other operations in connection with the construction program.

I am heartily in accord with the principle of conservation set forth in the bill, but the work directed to be done therein is already being accomplished by suitable agencies. The National Resources Committee, of which the Secretary of the Interior is the chairman, has completed a study of the water resources of the entire United States and formulated plans for an integrated program of construction in all the drainage basins. This program is currently revised as conditions indicate.

The construction of facilities and the conducting of investigations concerned with water resources in the arid and semiarid region of the United States are already being undertaken, among others, by the Bureau of Reclamation, National Park Service, and Office of Indian Affairs. The Bureau of Reclamation in particular, has been the leader in the conservation of water resources and has an excellent organization for continuing this work.

The bill covers a wide field of activity in the conservation and utilization of the water resources of the nation, and as stated in the last two paragraphs of my Message to Congress of August 13, vetoing Senate Joint Resolution No. 57, in which I indicate that I propose to present to Congress in January a comprehensive national plan for flood control and prevention and for the development of water and soil conservation, it is my view that water and soil conservation plans should await the formulation of such comprehensive policy.

The bill is disapproved on account of its conflict with the present program for the development of water conservation under the jurisdiction of the Interior Department, and on account also of the expected formulation in January of a comprehensive national flood control policy, with which S. 2863 might possibly be in conflict.

Sincerely yours,

[13:BUDGET BUREAU ENROLLED BILLS:T]

678   ROOSEVELT TO DANIEL W. BELL, ACTING DIRECTOR, BUREAU OF THE BUDGET, HARRY L. HOPKINS, WORKS PROGRESS ADMINISTRATOR, AND HENRY MORGENTHAU, JR., SECRETARY OF THE TREASURY

[WASHINGTON] *August 22, 1937*

MEMORANDUM . . . Sometime ago we discussed initiating a project to survey all Government buildings, etc., throughout the United States in relation to water pollution in respect to water supply and sewage. I understand a survey of this kind was made for New York City and Detroit.

What is the result?

Should this kind of study be extended?

I want to write Congressman John D. Dingell about it.[1]

F. D. R.

ILP

[13:OF 114-A:CT]

[1] No letter on the topic mentioned has been found although Roosevelt had been corresponding with Dingell, who was from Detroit, on a Public Works Administration sewage disposal project for Wayne County, Michigan (OF 1788).

679   Roosevelt to Marvin H. McIntyre, Secretary to the President

Washington, *August 23, 1937*

Memo for Mac: Tell him that we have already initiated a Federal policy against stream pollution by refusing to approve PWA projects for sewers that dump into rivers or bays, with the exception of the Mississippi River, which is a problem all by itself.[1]

F. D. R.

[13:OF 114–A:T]

[1] Roosevelt referred to Locke's telegram of Aug. 18, 1937, *ante,* 669. McIntyre wrote to Locke as directed Aug. 25, 1937 (OF 114–A).

680   Roosevelt to Representative A. Willis Robertson of Virginia, Chairman, House Select Committee on Conservation of Wildlife Resources

[Washington] *August 23, 1937*

My dear Mr. Robertson: I have received your letter of August fifth, in reference to the bag limit for sora.[1]

A decrease in the bag and possession limit on sora was justified due to the fact that these birds are strictly migratory and become abundant only in a few restricted areas during their migration. It was determined that the previous bag limit of 25 is more than the species can bear with any hope of perpetuating the sport of sora shooting throughout the range of the bird in the United States. As you realize it has been necessary from time to time to reduce the bag limit on waterfowl, the reasons for which are as familiar to you as to any one else in the country. I am sure you will find that the Department of Agriculture is not alone in its appraisal of the situation with reference to the sora. I have reason to know that such sportsmen, well known to you, as former Senator F. C. Walcott, Dr. George Bird Grinnell and Mr. Thomas H. Beck share the Department's apprehension for the future sport of sora shooting.

The Federal bag limits are as liberal on all species of migratory game birds as their present status will admit and I feel, in view of the widespread sentiment throughout the country that shooting of all migratory game birds should be prohibited, at least for a year or so, that the real sportsmen should be willing to accept with good grace reasonable limitations on their hunting.[2]

Very sincerely yours,

[Franklin D. Roosevelt]

[13:OF 378:CT]

¹ Robertson protested the reduction of the bag limit on sora, a bird he described as "delicious to eat" but "not much larger than an English Sparrow" (OF 378).
² Drafted by the Agriculture Department.

681   ROOSEVELT TO ROBERT FECHNER, DIRECTOR, CIVILIAN
       CONSERVATION CORPS

WASHINGTON, *August 24, 1937*

MEMORANDUM FOR HON. ROBERT FECHNER: I have your letter of
August twenty-first in regard to work on private land.   Your program
meets with my approval.

F. D. R.

[13:OF 268:CT]

682   STATEMENT BY ROOSEVELT ON SIGNING THE 1937 RIVERS AND
       HARBORS BILL

THE WHITE HOUSE, WASHINGTON, *August 26, 1937*

FOR THE INFORMATION OF THE PRESS, AUGUST 27, 1937: In signing
H. R. 7051, the so-called Rivers and Harbors Bill, I note that in Section
5 thereof provision is made for a pollution survey of the Ohio River by
the War Department.¹
Obviously a survey of this nature falls properly under the jurisdiction
of the Public Health Service.   I am, however, asking the Secretary of
War and the Secretary of the Treasury to join in the appointment of a
committee of three to conduct this survey—an army engineer, a representative of the Public Health Service and a non-government expert on
pollution problems.

FRANKLIN D. ROOSEVELT

[13:OF 25:T: COPY]

¹ Act approved Aug. 26, 1937 (50 *Stat.* 844).

683   ROOSEVELT TO HAROLD L. ICKES, SECRETARY OF THE
       INTERIOR

WASHINGTON, *August 26, 1937*

MEMORANDUM FOR THE SECRETARY OF THE INTERIOR: In the administration of H. R. 2512, An Act for the construction of small reservoirs under the Federal reclamation laws,¹ please submit a plan to me
under which, in the construction of these reservoirs, all possible labor
will be taken from the work relief or the Resettlement home relief lists
of needy persons.

Also, I think it is important that efforts be made to select projects in drought areas or areas where there is much need for soil erosion prevention. Please submit list and places of projects.[2]

F. D. R.

FDR/DJ

[*Notation*:A] Mr. Hess[3] has the department's report on H. R. 2512.

[13:OF 402:CT]

[1] Approved Aug. 26, 1937 (50 *Stat.* 841).
[2] Answered *post,* 703.
[3] Clarence T. Hess, head of the Office of Chief of Records in the White House.

684   DANIEL W. BELL, ACTING DIRECTOR, BUREAU OF THE BUDGET, TO MARVIN H. McINTYRE, SECRETARY TO THE PRESIDENT

WASHINGTON, *Aug. 27, 1937*

MY DEAR MR. McINTYRE: By your memorandum of August 23, 1937 you referred to me, by direction of the President, for advice as to whether there is any objection to its approval, the following bill:

S. 2863, An Act To promote conservation in the arid and semiarid areas of the United States by aiding in the development of facilities for water storage and utilization, and for other purposes.

I have referred this bill to the Secretaries of Agriculture and Interior and am transmitting herewith the letter of the Secretary of Agriculture and the letter of the Acting Secretary of the Interior, each dated August 26, 1937.[1]

The Secretary of Agriculture states that he believes that the provisions of the bill are well adapted to accomplish the purposes of the program recommended by the Great Plains Committee and recommends that the bill be approved.

The Acting Secretary of the Interior states that he does not think that the bill should be approved for the reasons set forth in a memorandum of the Secretary of the Interior to the President, dated August 21, 1937, enclosing a suggested draft of veto message. This memorandum and its enclosure, which were referred to this office, are returned herewith.

There is also returned herewith copy of a letter dated August 21, 1937, addressed to me by the Acting Secretary of Agriculture with respect to this bill and his letter of the same date transmitting such copy to the President.[2] A rather complete statement of the aims and purposes of the bill are set forth in this letter of the Acting Secretary of Agriculture.

While I have not studied the matter thoroughly, it appears to me that what is sought to be accomplished by the present bill is, as stated by the Secretary of Agriculture, in accord with the recommendations contained in the report of the President's Great Plains Committee, which report the President transmitted to Congress with his message of February 10, 1937. I do not believe that the enactment of the bill will cause any embarrassment with respect to the President's regional planning or reorganization programs.

The bill authorizes an appropriation of "such sums as Congress may from time to time determine to be necessary." The Secretary of Agriculture states that he is at present inclined to the opinion that an appropriation of from $1,000,000 to $5,000,000 per year, until the purposes of the act have been accomplished, should be adequate. It would be my purpose, if the bill be approved by the President, to hold the amount to be provided in the annual Budgets to the lowest possible figure consistent with a reasonable administration of the act.

I recommend that the bill, which is returned herewith, be approved.

Very truly yours,

D. W. BELL

[*Notation*:A] Approved 8/28/37
[13:BUDGET BUREAU:ENROLLED BILLS:TS]

[1] Both are present.
[2] The second letter only is present.

685   [*Enclosure*] HENRY A. WALLACE, SECRETARY OF AGRICULTURE, TO DANIEL W. BELL

WASHINGTON, *Aug. 26, 1937*

DEAR MR. BELL: I have Mr. Bailey's letter of August 25 asking for my comments on the enrolled bill, S. 2863, entitled "An Act to promote conservation in the arid and semiarid areas of the United States by aiding in the development of facilities for water storage and utilization, and for other purposes."

S. 2863 was the companion bill to H. R. 7697. Under date of July 9, 1937, I submitted to the Chairman of the Committee on Agriculture of the House of Representatives a favorable report on H. R. 7697. That report was cleared with the Bureau of the Budget. See your letter to me of July 3, 1937. Subsequently, on August 11, 1937, I submitted to the Chairman of the Senate Committee on Agriculture and Forestry a favorable report on S. 2863, and in that report referred to the clearance of the companion bill with the Bureau of the Budget.

S. 2863 and H. R. 7697 were not amended in Congress subsequent to the submission of my reports referred to above.

The present enrolled bill authorizes the Secretary of Agriculture to assist in providing within the arid and semiarid areas of the United

States facilities for water storage or utilization, including ponds, reservoirs, wells, check-dams, pumping installations, and similar facilities. These are to be located where they will promote the proper utilization of lands, and the bill expressly provides that "no such facilities shall be located where they will encourage the cultivation of lands which are submarginal and which should be devoted to other uses in the public interest." The Secretary is authorized to sell or lease such facilities upon such terms and conditions as will advance the purposes of the Act, and to require State and local cooperation in the program as a condition of extending benefits under the Act to other than Federal lands. These operations are to be financed by such appropriations "as Congress may from time to time determine to be necessary."

As I stated in my favorable reports to the Committees of Congress, legislation along the lines of the present enrolled bill was one of the major recommendations of the Great Plains Committee in its report entitled "The Future of the Great Plains" which the President submitted to the Congress. I believe that the provisions of the present enrolled bill are well adapted to accomplishing the purposes of this program, and I recommend approval of the bill.

A few days ago, on August 21, 1937, I wrote you, in response to your letter of August 18, concerning the present enrolled bill. In that letter I stated to you that it is my belief that the present enrolled bill is consistent with the program of the President as set forth in his message to the Congress on June 3, 1937, recommending the creation of regional authorities. As I stated in that letter, the present enrolled bill is necessary to the effective development of the Department's land utilization program. I have sent to the President, under date of August 21, a copy of my letter to you of the same date.

May I add a final word about the probable cost. The enrolled bill merely authorizes the appropriation of "such sums as Congress may from time to time determine to be necessary." I am at present inclined to the opinion that an appropriation of from $1,000,000 to $5,000,000 per year, until the purposes of the Act have been accomplished, should be adequate.[1]

Sincerely yours,

H. A. WALLACE

[13 : BUDGET BUREAU ENROLLED BILLS : TS]

[1] S. 2863 was introduced July 28, 1937, by Senator Pope (Idaho). There was no debate on the bill in the Senate, and in the House the only adverse comment was made by Representative Taber (N. Y.) who said that it was bad enough having one reclamation service, let alone two (*Cong. Rec.*, 75th Cong., 1st sess., 81:7, 7719; 81:8, 8670, 8921, 9540–9541). The act was approved Aug. 28, 1937 (50 *Stat.* 869). See below.

HYDE PARK, NEW YORK, *August 29, 1937*

MEMORANDUM FOR THE ACTING DIRECTOR OF THE BUDGET: I have
signed S. 2863, an Act to promote Conservation in Arid Areas by the
development of facilities for water storage. I understand there is no
money appropriated. Please call it to my attention when we make up
the Budget this autumn.

At the same time, I should like to have from the Department of
Agriculture a plan for the carrying out of the purposes of the Bill; this
plan to list the projects with the location and cost of each.

Reclamation projects should not be undertaken.

As I understand it, most of the projects will be for what are described
as, "farm ponds." If I am right in this assumption, why should we not
set a top limit on the construction of each.

The Department of Agriculture should get in touch with PWA and
other agencies which have been doing the same work in the past.[1]

F. D. R.

FDR/TMB
[13:OF 177:CT]

---

[1] Copies of this memorandum were sent to Wallace and to Ickes. A detailed
statement of the policies that the Agriculture Department proposed to follow in
carrying out the act was sent by Wallace to Roosevelt on Sept. 29, 1937 (OF 177).

687   DANIEL W. BELL, ACTING DIRECTOR, BUREAU OF THE BUDGET,
TO MARVIN H. MCINTYRE, SECRETARY TO THE PRESIDENT

WASHINGTON, *Aug. 30, 1937*

MY DEAR MR. MCINTYRE: By your memorandum of August 23,
1937 you referred to me, by direction of the President, for advice as to
whether there is any objection to its approval, the following bill:
"S. 2670, An Act To provide that the United States shall aid the States
in wildlife restoration projects, and for other purposes." [1]

I have referred this bill to the Secretary of Agriculture and to the
Secretary of the Treasury and am transmitting herewith the letter of the
Secretary of Agriculture dated August 26, 1937 and the letter of the
Acting Secretary of the Treasury dated August 28, 1937.[2]

The Secretary of Agriculture recommends that the bill receive the
approval of the President.

The Acting Secretary of the Treasury advises that, while the Treasury
is opposed to the method of appropriating tax receipts provided in the

bill, since this method does not afford Congress an opportunity to review contemplated expenditures and annually appropriate such sums as may be justified in the light of subsequent conditions, and does not permit the President to maintain an effective budgetary control over expenditures, nevertheless he does not consider this objection a sufficient justification for recommending that the President withhold approval of the bill.

It is provided in section 3 of the bill that "An amount equal to the revenue accrued during the fiscal year ending June 30, 1939, and each fiscal year thereafter, from the tax imposed by section 610, title IV, of the Revenue Act of 1932 (47 *Stat.* 169), as heretofore or hereafter extended and amended, on firearms, shells, and cartridges, is hereby authorized to be set apart in the Treasury as a special fund to be known as 'The Federal aid to wildlife restoration fund' and is hereby authorized to be appropriated and made available until expended for the purposes of this act."

The foregoing provision of the bill is so objectionable that I recommend the President withhold his approval of the bill solely on that ground, without giving consideration at this time to whatever merit the bill may possess in connection with the conservation and preservation of wildlife.

It will be recalled that during the first session of the 74th Congress the Agricultural Adjustment Act was amended so as to appropriate a sum equal to 30% of customs receipts to the Secretary of Agriculture to encourage exportation and domestic consumption of agricultural commodities. In his Message transmitting the Budget for the fiscal year 1937 the President recommended the repeal of that amendment in language reading as follows:

By appropriating directly instead of authorizing an appropriation the amendment denies to the President the opportunity to consider the need and include appropriate estimates in the Budget, and it denies to the Congress the opportunity to review such estimates in their relation to the whole program of the Government. The amendment violates the principles of the Permanent Appropriation Repeal Act of 1934, and of the Budget and Accounting Act of June 10, 1921. It is in conflict with sound administration in that it provides in advance for large annual expenditures without any attempt to coordinate income and expense.

Except as to the amount involved, the Agricultural Adjustment Act case and the one now before us are identical in principle and the above quoted comments of the President apply equally to both.

While no accurate estimate can be made of the amount of the revenue which will accrue in future years from the tax on firearms, shells, and cartridges, the Treasury Department advises that the revenue from such tax in the fiscal year 1937 amounts to $3,234,357.22.

I recommend that the bill, which is returned herewith, be not approved. A draft of a proposed memorandum of disapproval is transmitted herewith.[3]

Very truly yours,

D. W. BELL

[13 : BUDGET BUREAU ENROLLED BILLS : TS]

[1] The Federal Aid to Wildlife Restoration Bill, or Pittman-Robertson Wildlife Bill, was introduced in the Senate by Pittman (Nev.) on June 17, 1937, and in the House (as H. R. 7681) by Robertson (Va.), on June 28, 1937 (*Cong. Rec.*, 75th Cong., 1st sess., 81:5, 5856–5857; 81:6, 6490).

[2] The second letter is not printed because it is adequately summarized here.

[3] The draft veto message states the objections expressed by Bell in this letter. Roosevelt approved the act without comment on Sept. 2, 1937 (50 *Stat.* 917). It became effective July 1, 1938, with an appropriation of $1,000,000, to be administered by a newly organized division of the Bureau of Biological Survey, a Division of Federal Aid in Wildlife Restoration. See *Report of the Chief of the Bureau of Biological Survey, 1939*, pp. 35–36.

688 [*Enclosure*] HENRY A. WALLACE, SECRETARY OF AGRICULTURE, TO DANIEL W. BELL

WASHINGTON, D. C., *August 26, 1937*

DEAR MR. BELL: We have your request of August 25 for our comments on S–2670, "An Act To provide that the United States shall aid the States in wildlife-restoration projects, and for other purposes," which has been enacted by Congress and submitted to the President.

It is observed that the general scheme of the act follows quite closely that of the Act of July 11, 1916 (39 *Stat.* 355) commonly known as the Federal Aid Road Act which was designed to aid the States in the construction of highways and roads. Federal aid to the States under this act is proposed for wildlife-restoration projects which are defined in section 2 as the selection, restoration, rehabilitation, and improvement of areas of land or water adaptable as feeding, resting, or breeding places for wildlife, including acquisition by purchase, condemnation, lease, or gift of such areas or estates or interests therein as are suitable, or capable of being made suitable therefor, and the construction thereon or therein of such works as may be necessary to make them available for such purposes, and including also such research into problems of wildlife management as may be necessary to efficient administration affecting wildlife resources, and such preliminary or incidental costs or expenses as may be incurred in and about such projects.

The act forbids expenditure in a State of any money apportioned to that State until its legislature shall have assented to the provisions of the act and until it shall have passed laws for the conservation of wildlife which meet the minimum requirements of the Secretary of

Agriculture, one of which shall be a prohibition against the diversion of license fees paid by hunters to any other purpose than the administration of the State's fish and game department.

Section 3 provides that there .is authorized to be set apart in the Treasury as a special fund to be known as "The Federal aid to wildlife-restoration fund" an amount equal to the revenue accruing during the fiscal year ending June 30, 1939, and each fiscal year thereafter, from the tax on firearms, shells, and cartridges imposed by Section 610, title IV of the Revenue Act of 1932 (47 *Stat.* 169), as heretofore or hereafter extended and amended, which fund is authorized to be appropriated and made available until expended for the purposes stated in the act.

Section 4 authorizes the Secretary of Agriculture to deduct not to exceed 8 per centum of the revenue covered into the Federal aid to wildlife-restoration fund in each fiscal year for expenses in administering and executing the act and the Migratory Bird Conservation Act, the remainder to be apportioned among the several States, one half in the ratio which the area of each State bears to the total area of all the States and the other half in the ratio which the number of paid hunting license holders of each State in the preceding fiscal year bears to the total number of paid hunting license holders of all States, with the proviso that not more than $150,000 shall be apportioned to any one State and that if the apportionment to any State is less than $15,000 annually the Secretary of Agriculture may allocate not more than $15,000 to that State when the State certifies that it has set aside not less than $5,000 from its fish and game funds or has appropriated that amount, for the purposes of the Act.

Wildlife-restoration projects in any State accepting the benefits of the act must be agreed upon by the Secretary of Agriculture and the State fish and game department and must conform to the standards fixed by the Secretary of Agriculture and to that end the State fish and game department is required to submit to the Secretary full and detailed statements of the proposed projects, which, if approved by the Secretary, may receive not to exceed 75 per centum of the total estimated cost thereof from the apportionment made to the State.

The act imposes upon the States accepting its benefits the entire duty of maintaining wildlife-restoration projects established under the act and provides that if they are not properly maintained the Secretary of Agriculture shall withhold further apportionments to the State until the project is put in proper condition of maintenance.

The foregoing is the substance and essence of the act. The scheme of Federal aid to the States in constructing highways and roads has worked well and it is believed will work equally well and advantageously in the matter of wildlife projects as defined in the act. . . .[1]

This act, if it becomes law, will undoubtedly stimulate the States to action in the establishment of sanctuaries, reservations, or refuges vitally necessary in a well-rounded-out nation-wide plan for the restoration and conservation of our useful wildlife. The act is sponsored and earnestly advocated by practically all of the conservation organizations, official and unofficial, in the United States. It is recommended that it receive the approval of the President.

You ask that we include estimate of the probable cost. As will have appeared from the foregoing summary of the essential features of this Act, the monies authorized to be appropriated thereunder are amounts equal to the revenue accruing during the fiscal year ending June 30, 1939, and each fiscal year thereafter, from the tax imposed by section 610, title IV, of the Revenue Act of 1932 (47 *Stat.* 169), not exceeding 8 per centum whereof being authorized to be deducted by the Secretary of Agriculture for expenses in the administration and execution of the Act and the Migratory Bird Conservation Act. We are informed by the Treasury Department that the revenue from this tax in the fiscal year 1937 was $3,234,357.22.

Sincerely,

H. A. WALLACE

[13:BUDGET BUREAU ENROLLED BILLS:TS]

[1] In the part omitted, Wallace described past efforts of the Government to protect wildlife, including the Lacey Act of 1900, the act establishing the Upper Mississippi Wildlife and Fish Refuge of 1924, and the Migratory Bird Conservation Act of 1929. Wallace pointed out that the act under discussion proposed to aid the states in setting up wildlife refuges that could not, because of their small size and scattered location, be administered by the Federal Government.

689 THE ACTING SURGEON GENERAL, PUBLIC HEALTH SERVICE, AND HARRY L. HOPKINS, WORKS PROGRESS ADMINISTRATOR, TO ROOSEVELT

[WASHINGTON] *September 2, 1937*

MEMORANDUM FOR THE PRESIDENT: Reference is made to your memorandum to Mr. Hopkins dated August 21st, regarding the Administration's policy in reference to sewer projects. We are fully sympathetic to the objectives in your memorandum and are submitting for your approval the following outline of procedures which will promote the construction of sewage treatment plants.

In practically every State the sanitary laws prohibit the construction or extension of any sanitary sewer or sewage treatment plant until a permit has been secured from the State health authorities. In many instances permits for sewer construction are given only when the municipality includes in the plans provision for sewage treatment at a later date.

Prior to the construction of sewage treatment plants it frequently is necessary for intercepting sewers to be constructed, for antiquated sewer systems to be brought up to date by providing for separating storm water from the sanitary flow, for an increase in size of sewers and other construction which does not tend to increase the pollution of the stream through the discharge of additional amounts of sewage. In view of the fact that the installation of sewage collection and treatment in a municipality usually involves construction extending over a period of time, it is desirable for Works Progress Administration projects to include such construction as is an integral part of comprehensive plans which include sewage treatment.

It is recommended, therefore, that the following procedure be adopted in connection with the construction of Works Progress Administration projects involving sanitary sewer systems: That no further Works Progress Administration projects be approved for the construction of new sanitary sewer systems or for the extension of existing systems in such a way as to increase the amount of untreated sewage discharged into creeks or rivers from such systems unless the sewage from such systems is treated in disposal plants, or unless general plans or programs which include provisions for sewage treatment plants are submitted with the applications for the projects; that Works Progress Administration proposals which involve reconstruction or repair or extension of sanitary sewer systems will be approved even though such sewer systems discharge into water courses, provided the amount of untreated sewage being discharged will in no way be increased by the work to be performed on the project. In no event will such sanitary sewer construction be approved by the Works Progress Administration unless the projects have had the prior approval of the proper State health authorities.

We shall, of course, do everything possible to encourage projects for the building of sewage disposal plants.

[13:OF 444–C:T:COPY]

690   ROOSEVELT TO FREDERIC C. WALCOTT, PRESIDENT, AMERICAN
       WILD LIFE INSTITUTE, Hartford, Connecticut.

HYDE PARK, N. Y., *September 8, 1937*

DEAR FRED: Many thanks for your telegram.[1] Naturally I was all for the objectives of the Wild Life Bill. There were strenuous objections to it from the Treasury and Budget, however, because it set up what amounts to a continuing appropriation and this is contrary to the laws of the Medes and Persians among the experts! However, the pros outweighed the cons.

I do hope to see you one of these days soon.

As ever yours,

[FRANKLIN D. ROOSEVELT]

[13:OF 378:CT]

[1] Sept. 3, 1937 (OF 378), thanking Roosevelt for signing the Pittman-Robertson Wildlife Bill. Walcott (senator from Connecticut from 1929 to 1935) said that he was personally as well as officially grateful to Roosevelt for "this outstanding boost" he had given the cause of conservation.

691   ROOSEVELT TO ARTHUR E. MORGAN, CHAIRMAN, BOARD OF DIRECTORS, TENNESSEE VALLEY AUTHORITY, Wilson Dam, Alabama

HYDE PARK, NEW YORK, *September 9, 1937*

[*Telegram*] The entire nation has a vital interest in the dedication today of this important link in one of our great hydro-highways. Wheeler Dam, the second Tennessee Valley Authority navigation and flood control structure to be completed and placed in service since the inception of this project in 1933, meets the popular desire expressed through Congressional mandate for planned conservation and utilization of the natural resources of a complete watershed. Through unified control, the Tennessee River is stepped up for navigation and, in the reverse order, stepped down for flood control. At the same time incidental generation of power by these "steps" provides a means of reimbursing the Government in large measure for monies expended for the development and control of our interior waterways. As all sound conservation projects should do Wheeler Dam makes an incidental contribution to the public welfare by adding another important unit to the nation's parks and providing sanctuary for the conservation of wild life.

It is particularly appropriate that this dam, undertaken in the South and destined to play a large part in the life of the nation as a whole should bear the name of fighting Joe Wheeler, an earnest advocate of conservation who in and out of Congress was an ardent champion of the development of the Tennessee River. The inauguration of this work marks another step in the great task of organizing the household of the nation to meet growing social and economic needs.

FRANKLIN D. ROOSEVELT

[*Notation*:A] Approved by President and given to TVA in advance [1]

[13:OF 42:CT]

[1] Apparently drafted by Hassett (Early to Hassett, Aug. 20, 1937, OF 42).

Hyde Park, N. Y., *September 10, 1937*

My dear Miss Gillmore: Thank you for your letter [1] and the report of the Hudson River Conservation Society.

I am in heartiest sympathy with all of the fine efforts being made to protect the scenery of the Hudson. I only wish it were possible for me to be of more direct help.

Very sincerely yours,

[Franklin D. Roosevelt]

[13:PPF 4853:CT]

[1] Sept. 7, 1937 (PPF 4853), asking for Roosevelt's help in stopping the destruction by quarrying of Mount Taurus (on the Hudson below Beacon). On another occasion Roosevelt replied to a similar plea that he do something to stop the quarrying by saying that he could take no part in New York State legislation (Roosevelt to Mayer, March 9, 1935, PPF 2321).

693   Aubrey Williams, Acting Works Progress Administrator, to James Roosevelt, Secretary to the President

Washington, D. C., *September 10, 1937*

Dear Mr. Roosevelt: Attached is a copy of a memorandum to Mr. Hopkins from the President dated August 21st, and copy of a memorandum dated September 2nd for the President, from the Works Progress Administrator and the Acting Surgeon General.[1] This memorandum deals with the conditions under which sewer projects could be approved for the Works Progress Administration.

The original of the memorandum for the President, which has Harry's approval and has been signed by the Acting Surgeon General, is in Harry's possession. He intended to take it up with the President on the trip but for some reason did not do so. He suggested that I send you this copy and ask you to present the matter to the President and if possible, secure his approval.

We are, of course, in hearty agreement with his purposes in making the order, but after consulting with the Public Health Service, we feel that his purposes can be carried out and at the same time permit certain work which has heretofore comprised a large part of our program, especially since in the northern states sewer work is practically the only type of out-door construction which can be done during much of the time in the winter months.

We are now holding up about fifty sewer projects involving about 3,500 men, so if it is possible to get this cleared right away it will be greatly appreciated.[2]

Sincerely yours,

AUBREY WILLIAMS

[13:OF 444–C:TS]

[1] Printed *ante*, 673, 689.
[2] Answered *post*, 695.

694   SPEECH BY ROOSEVELT TO THE ROOSEVELT HOME CLUB, Val-Kill Farm, Hyde Park, September 11, 1937, 3:15 P. M.

[*Excerpt*] MINE HOST, PRESIDENT ARTHUR AND JOHNNY:[1] . . . In an old Poughkeepsie newspaper of 1841—I think it is just about a hundred years ago—the man who owned this farm that we are standing on at this time produced the largest yield of corn of any farmer in Dutchess County, a very much larger yield than almost anybody in Dutchess County could possibly raise today. Well, Moses knows and I know what this farm was like when we came here. It was brought to a condition that was caused by lack of planning. Well, you could not blame them seventy-five and a hundred years ago for putting nothing back into the land because the land was virgin land and, after all, the main thing was to get all the cash you possibly could out of the land. Dutchess County was the granary of New York City and the more corn you could ship down there the richer you were. But of course we know today that if our ancestors and the original owners of this land of ours had known enough about agriculture, as much as we do, and had put things back into the soil, we would be a whole lot better off in these modern times. And so it goes; we have had a lot of narrow escapes because we haven't thought much beyond the end of our own noses.

I was driving through the middle part of the county the last time I was here in early August and I was struck by the number of lovely streams we have in the county, not only the larger creeks, like the Wappingers, but also the Krum Elbow and a lot of the smaller creeks, and it occurred to me what a wonderful escape we had. I don't suppose there are more than a dozen people who remember the escape we had. John Mack will because he, to a certain extent, and I were responsible for the escape. Back only about fifteen years ago there was a bill introduced in the legislature by the New York City representatives to give the city of New York the right to come up into Dutchess County and create a great water system, the watershed with reservoirs on the headwaters of Wappingers Creek, the main branch and the branch that runs up towards Clinton Hollow, and the same thing with the headwaters of the Roeliff Jansen

Kill, which runs along the boundary, a large part of the boundary, between Columbia and Dutchess Counties. The bill, as I remember it, passed one House and yet there was hardly anybody in the County of Dutchess that woke up to the fact that our resources were being taken away from us.

I was south at the time. I telegraphed to John and John went up to Albany and we succeeded in preventing the passage of the bill. In other words, we were just thinking to the ends of our own noses and no further. As I remember it, the newspapers of the county took the view that the purchase of these lands for the reservoirs would bring a lot of money into the county, forgetting entirely that while it might bring some cash into the county, and while it might put a lot of people to work for two years or three years or four years, it would take, after that was over, most of the water supply out of the county, and also the water level and make a vast acreage, thousands and thousands of acres, unhabitable. There would be no purchasing power left, there would be reservoirs that nobody could use—you could not swim or boat on them. There would be no agriculture, nothing at all and nobody employed except a few people to watch the dams. And all for a few dollars today, not thinking about the future.

Well, that was an escape that the county had and there were very, very few people in the county that woke up to the danger at that time. I think most of us are very happy today that we saved the water of this county because, as we see things now, we know the real demand there is on the part of the people from the outside, New York City and other places, to come up here and establish homes, the real chance there is to plan for permanent lakes in the county, for a better water supply, to bring people out to join us and increase, incidentally, not only our population but the wealth of the county.[2]

[SPEECH FILE: T]

[1] Respectively, Moses Smith, tenant of the Roosevelt Val-Kill farm; Arthur Smith, his son, newly elected president of the Franklin D. Roosevelt Home Club; and Judge John E. Mack, of Poughkeepsie. The Home Club was formed in 1929 to further Roosevelt's political fortunes. It is now a social organization devoted to honoring his memory.

[2] This speech was extemporaneous; the part not here printed also dealt, informally, with the virtue of county planning. The text is that of the stenographic transcript.

695   Roosevelt to Aubrey Williams, Acting Works Progress Administrator

Hyde Park, N. Y., *September 13, 1937*

Memorandum for Hon. Aubrey Williams: I realize that sewer projects are useful but I think we should adhere strictly to my memorandum of August twenty-first, directing that no future WPA projects shall be approved for improving, repairing or adding to sewers which dump into any creek or river.

The only modification, or, to be more accurate, interpretation, of this order would be in a case where the sewer project has nothing to do with the ultimate disposal of sewage. In other words, if it is merely relaying sewer pipe in a town at a location where the new pipe would continue to be used, if a sewage disposal plant were put in, such a project would be all right.

But, at the same time, if such a project is proposed, there should be a definite demand on the municipality calling for a plan for sewage disposal and engineering assurance that the immediate project would dovetail in with a new method of disposal.

In order to be absolutely on the safe side in these cases, I wish you would submit to me any projects which seem to come within the above interpretation.

F. D. R.

[13:OF 444–C:CT]

696   FREDERIC A. DELANO, VICE CHAIRMAN, NATIONAL RESOURCES
          COMMITTEE, TO ROOSEVELT

WASHINGTON, *September 16, 1937*

MY DEAR MR. PRESIDENT: In accordance with your letter of August 20 to Chairman Ickes, copy enclosed, our Advisory Committee has approved preliminary steps for the preparation of the revised Drainage Basin Report as outlined by our Water Committee in the attached draft statement.[1]

Mr. Wolman, Chairman of the Water Committee, proposes to utilize our field offices for contact with State Planning agencies and other local interests. A series of Basin Committees is being set up, operating out of these offices and with the former Water Consultants serving as Special Advisers. The cooperation of Federal agencies, both in the field and in Washington, has already been assured.

Because of the special problems of the Ohio and Lower Mississippi Valleys, the Water Committee desires also the opinion of a special group or committee to advise as to flood control and other water projects. Mr. Wolman proposes to ask Dr. H. H. Barrows, of the University of Chicago, to serve as chairman of this special advisory group, consisting of Dr. A. E. Morgan, of the Tennessee Valley Authority; Gen. E. M. Markham, Chief of Engineers; Gen. Harley B. Ferguson, of the Mississippi River Commission; Col. H. M. Waite, formerly Deputy Administrator, Public Works Administration; Charles E. Paul, formerly of the Mississippi Valley Committee, and M. S. Eisenhower, of the

Department of Agriculture. Their progress report will be embodied with the other recommendations of the Water Resources Committee in the document you have requested before January 1.

The expense of this project has been estimated around $125,000, including printing. Our Advisory Committee has already authorized immediate inauguration of the work, using the reserve funds which we have allowed in our budget for just such a special project. These funds, however, fall considerably short of covering the cost. If we can assume that assistance will be provided from other Federal bureaus without charge against the Committee's funds, we believe that we can complete this undertaking at an additional cost not exceeding $50,000 over our present reserve funds. We are therefore appealing to you for a further allocation of that amount, since all our other funds have already been obligated to other projects.[2]

Respectfully submitted,

FREDERIC A. DELANO

[13:OF 1092:TS]

[1] The enclosure is an eight-page, single-spaced typescript entitled, "Proposed work of Basin Committees and Water Consultants in revision of 'Drainage Basin Problems and Programs.'" It is dated "Draft September 15, 1937" but the date "September 20, 1937" also appears in the heading. This document describes the plan and objectives of the revision, for which the Water Resources Committee of the National Resources Committee was given immediate responsibility. The specific objective was the preparation of a report in two parts: "The first will be a summary of recommended programs and policies for the country as a whole. The second will comprise a detailed report on each of the 95 drainage basins as defined in the last drainage basin report, each basin report to be published separately."

[2] This letter and its enclosures were first sent to Ickes for his approval (Delano to Ickes, Sept. 16, 1937, OF 1092).

697 ROOSEVELT TO FREDERIC A. DELANO, VICE CHAIRMAN, NATIONAL RESOURCES COMMITTEE, AND MORRIS L. COOKE, CHAIRMAN, GREAT PLAINS COMMITTEE

[WASHINGTON] *September 17, 1937*

MEMORANDUM . . . I do not want to get into a crossing of wires in regard to immediate studies of the water and soil and budget appropriation problems.

Let me put it this way (see my letter to Chairman Whittington of the House Committee): [1] I want to send in my Budget Message a complete recommendation for the appropriation of between $450,000,000 and $500,000,000 covering all forms of public works. These include obligations and expenditures for highways, public buildings, rivers and harbors, flood control, reclamation, acquisition of land for parks and forests, etc.

Because the Reorganization Bill has not gone through, all of the planning work and the estimates of many departments and bureaus must be coordinated (a) from the National Resources planning standpoint and (b) from a financial standpoint. Next year, if the Reorganization Bill goes through, all of this will be done by the planning and budget sections directly under the President.

In the meantime, while I am away, will you work out and go ahead with machinery to carry us through for the next few months? It is my thought that Mr. Cooke's committee will consider itself primarily an agency of the President and the Budget, and that the National Resources Committee will assist in preparing and coordinating the projects in the order of their importance—all of the interested departments being represented on that committee.

Finally, it seems simplest to work out two lists—(a) list totaling between $450,000,000 and $500,000,000 and (b) list for a similar amount. The Congress can then, if it wishes, transfer a project from the (b) list to the (a) list, eliminating a project from the (a) list which approximates the same cost.

Meanwhile, in regard to this problem of the Water Committee of which Mr. Wolman is Chairman, please take it up with the Budget Bureau.

F. D. R.

[13:OF 1092:CT]

[1] *Ante,* 618.

698 ROOSEVELT TO HENRY A. WALLACE, SECRETARY OF AGRICULTURE

WASHINGTON, *September 17, 1937*

MEMORANDUM FOR THE SECRETARY OF AGRICULTURE: In regard to yours of September fourteenth [1] about the Ohio-Mississippi flood-control report, this must, of course, be coordinated with the more extensive report on all drainage basins.

Furthermore, flood control in general must be coordinated to other public works in budget making. Perhaps you will have a talk with the following during my absence: Secretary Woodring, General Schley (the new Chief of Engineers), the Secretary of the Interior, Mr. Delano, Mr. Wolman and Mr. Morris L. Cooke.

F. D. R.

[13:OF 25–N:CT]

[1] Not found.

WASHINGTON, *September 17, 1937*

MEMORANDUM FOR THE SECRETARY OF THE INTERIOR: Owen Johnson, as you know, made a gallant run against Treadway in the Massachusetts Berkshire district last autumn. He is continuing the fight and will, I think, run next year. I told him in general of the plan for an eventual parkway from the Canada line to Georgia. He feels that this would be a great asset to the Berkshire region.

Could you prepare for him a description of what we have talked about and of the procedure under which this parkway could be gradually extended from North to South?

By the way, I hear that Vermont people are now beginning to be sorry they did not give us better cooperation.

F. D. R.

[*Notation*:T] Let. from Owen Johnson, Stockbridge, Mass., 9/15/37 req. information re proposed North-South Mountain Highway.[1]

[13:PPF 611:CT]

---

[1] Not present. See *post*, 704.

700   IRVING BRANT, EDITOR OF EDITORIAL PAGE, ST. LOUIS *Star-Times*, TO ROOSEVELT

[ST. LOUIS] *September 22, 1937*

DEAR MR. PRESIDENT: I hope you may find time to read a brief note on the Olympic Park situation before you make the drive to Lake Quinault.

You may possibly remember that last year, when you told me you wanted to visit the area, I made the remark that if you had the same experience Secretary Wallace did, local Forest Service officials would see to it that you saw nobody who wanted a real park. I hope your party will include Preston Macy, custodian of the Olympic National Monument,[1] though I do not know his views.

The Olympic situation is badly complicated now because Congressman Wallgren, who sponsored a good bill a year ago and had it approved by committee, abandoned it this year and offered a new bill cutting down the boundaries so as to eliminate the great Douglas firs, Sitka spruces and giant cedars that most needed preservation. He claimed that he followed the wishes of the Interior Department, but the attitude of Secretary Ickes does not support that claim.

The cut-down Wallgren bill was reported for passage this year under remarkable circumstances. Neither the Interior Department nor the

Department of Agriculture made a report on it, though it involved a transfer of land from one department to the other.

Secretary Ickes omitted a report, I believe, because he hoped for a better bill next year.

Secretary Wallace omitted a report, judging from what I was told in advance, because he feared the Forest Service was taking a wrong attitude.[2]

The Washington State Planning Council, including and apparently dominated by a big lumber representative, is fighting to keep these national forest lands out of the park. The plain purpose is to turn government timber over to the Grays Harbor mills, to postpone their shutdown.

The Forest Service arguments against preservation of these last virgin forests are utterly specious. President Wilson was persuaded to cut the national monument to half its size on the claim that this was necessary to permit manganese mining. The only manganese mines in the region are outside this area, and the only ore in the proposed park is a small amount to bementite, a manganiferous ore from which it is impossible to extract the manganese by any chemical method now known.

The Forest Service claims that by a new technique in lumbering, involving application of the permanent yield principle to the wood pulp industry, it would be possible to sustain 6,630 persons on the crop-yields of lumber in the area of the reduced Wallgren bill. I took their figures and showed, by them, that it would be possible to sustain over 200,000 persons on the cut-over lands of the Olympic peninsula, so why cut down the last virgin forest of the Northwest to get more cut-over land to reforest.

They also claim that there are 3,000,000,000 board feet of merchantable timber in the reduced Wallgren area, but the largest of it appears to be No. 6 Douglas fir, in no way comparing with the gigantic trees of the lower valleys. In general, the lower the slope, the larger the trees. The farther the park is pushed up the mountains, the smaller the trees. It can't be a real park unless it takes in the areas the Forest Service is trying to keep out, and unless these areas are brought in, there will be no protection for the winter range of the Roosevelt elk herd.

If you are able to go even a short distance up the Quinault River toward Enchanted Valley, you will see forests of the kind it is desired to preserve, though these happen to be in private ownership.[3]

Yours respectfully,

IRVING BRANT

[*Notation*:A] Anna B

[13:OF 1–C:TS]

[1] Mount Olympus National Monument.
[2] On the contrary, Wallace submitted a 3000-word statement on the bill dated

Aug. 13, 1937, to Rep. Rene L. DeRouen, chairman of the House Committee on Public Lands (OF 1–C). He concluded his statement by saying that the Agriculture Department wished to avoid "any arbitrarily negative attitude" toward the bill:

"Belief that the lands involved appropriately might continue under the administration of the Department is supported by many considerations . . . If, however, the Congress is convinced that a national park should be established in the Olympic Range, more suitable boundaries than those now described in H. R. 4724 should be adopted, so as to establish the best attainable balance between the inspirational and recreational needs on the one hand and the economic needs of the dependent population on the other."

The copy of this statement in the Roosevelt Library is a ribbon typescript, bound in a folder of photographs and text descriptive of the Olympic National Forest, entitled, "Forest Facts/Olympic National Forest/Washington," prepared by the North Pacific Region of the Forest Service, 1937. H. R. 4724 was introduced Feb. 15, 1937, and reported Aug. 16, 1937, but no action was taken (*Cong. Rec.*, 75th Cong., 1st sess., 81:2, 1226; 81:8, 9061).

[2] Roosevelt left Hyde Park for his trip to the West on September 23 and returned October 6. On September 30–October 1 he went by automobile from Port Angeles to Tacoma, staying overnight at Lake Crescent. The letter here printed was sent by Brant to Anna Roosevelt Boettiger in Seattle. In a covering letter of September 22 to Mrs. Boettiger (OF 1–C), Brant said: "I have talked with the President a number of times about the Olympic situation, and at his suggestion have tried to secure an understanding between the two departments involved. Secretaries Ickes and Wallace do not seem to be far apart in their desires, but the Portland office of the Forest Service seems to be causing a tremendous amount of trouble."

701 SPEECH BY ROOSEVELT, Bonneville Dam, Oregon, September 28, 1937

[*Excerpt*] [1] Governor Martin, my friends of the Northwest: Today I have a feeling of real satisfaction in witnessing the completion of another great national project, and of pleasure in the fact that in its inception, four years ago, I had some part. My interest in the whole of the valley of the great Columbia River goes back seventeen years to 1920 when I first studied its mighty possibilities. And again, in 1932, I visited Oregon and Washington and Idaho and on that visit I took occasion in Portland to express certain views which have since, through the action of the Congress, become a recorded part of American national policy.

Almost exactly three years ago, I inspected the early construction stages of this dam at Bonneville.

The more we study the water resources of the Nation, the more we accept the fact that their use is a matter of national concern, and that in our plans for their use our line of thinking must include great regions as well as narrower localities.

If, for example, we Americans had known as much and acted as effectively twenty or thirty or forty years ago as we do today in the development of the use of land in that great semiarid strip in the center of the country that runs from the Canadian border all the way down to Texas, we could have prevented in great part the abandonment of thousands and thousands of farms in portions of ten states and thus prevented the migration of thousands of destitute families from those areas into the States of Washington and Oregon and California. We would have done this by avoiding the plowing up of great areas that should have been kept in grazing range and by stricter regulations to prevent over-grazing. And at the same time we would have checked soil erosion, stopped the denudation of our forests and controlled disastrous fires.

Some of my friends who talk glibly about the right of any individual to do anything he wants with any of his property take the point of view that it is not the concern of Federal or state or local government to interfere with what they miscall "the liberty of the individual." With them I do not agree and never have agreed, because unlike them, I am thinking of the future of the United States. Yes, my conception of liberty does not permit an individual citizen or a group of citizens to commit acts of depredation against nature in such a way as to harm their neighbors, and especially to harm the future generations of Americans.

If many years ago we had had the necessary knowledge and especially the necessary willingness on the part of the Federal Government to act on it, we would have saved a sum, a sum of money which, in the last few years, has cost the taxpayers of the Nation at least two billion dollars.[2]

[RL RECORDINGS: 114]

[1] The text of this excerpt, which comprises the first third of the speech, is that of the radio broadcast transcription. Also present (Speech File) are: a draft, dated Sept. 27, 1937, containing a number of revisions in Roosevelt's hand; the reading copy; and the official mimeographed press release of the reading copy. The language and form of the draft suggest that it was composed by Roosevelt; paragraph 5 of the excerpt (which appears in the reading copy but not in the draft) was undoubtedly composed by him. The entire speech is printed in Rosenman (ed.), *Public Papers*, VI, 387–392; this follows the reading copy.

[2] The remainder of this speech deals with the social and economic implications of the potentially wide distribution of cheap power from Bonneville and other dams in the West, and the advantages of a regional approach to the planning of the country's development.

702   SPEECH BY ROOSEVELT AT TIMBERLINE LODGE, Mount Hood National Forest, Oregon, September 28, 1937

GOVERNOR MARTIN, LADIES AND GENTLEMEN: Here I am on the slopes of Mount Hood where I have always wanted to come.

I am here to dedicate Timberline Lodge and I do so in the words of the bronze tablet which is directly in front of me on the coping of this very wonderful building:

"Timberline Lodge, Mount Hood National Forest, dedicated September 28, 1937, by the President of the United States as a monument to the skill and faithful performance of workers on the rolls of the Works Progress Administration."

In the past few days I have inspected many great governmental activities—parks and soil protection sponsored by W. P. A.; buildings erected with the assistance of the Public Works Administration; our oldest and best-known National Park, the Yellowstone, under the jurisdiction of the National Park Service; great irrigation areas fathered by the Reclamation Service; and a few hours ago a huge navigation and power dam built by the Army engineers.

And now I find myself in one of our many national forests, here on the slopes of Mount Hood.

The people of the United States are singularly fortunate in having such great areas of the outdoors in the permanent possession of the people themselves—permanently available for many different forms of use.

In the total of the acreage of the national forests, all of those many acres in many, many states of the Union already play an important part in our economy and as the years go by their usefulness is bound to expand.

A good many of us probably think of the National Forests as having the primary function of saving our timber resources, but they do far more than that; much of the timber in them is cut and sold under scientific methods, and replaced on the system of rotation by new stands of many types of useful trees. The National Forests, in addition, provide forage for livestock and game, they husband our water at the source; they mitigate our floods and prevent the erosion of our soil. Last but not least, our National Forests will provide constantly increasing opportunity for recreational use. This Timberline Lodge marks a venture that was made possible by the W. P. A. Emergency Relief work, in order that we may test the workability of recreational facilities installed by the Government itself and operated under its control.

Here, to Mount Hood, will come thousands and thousands of visitors in the coming years. Looking east toward eastern Oregon with its great livestock raising areas, these visitors are going to visualize the relationship between the cattle ranches and the summer ranges in the forests. Looking westward and northward toward Portland and the Columbia River, with their great lumber and other wood using industries, visitors will understand the part that National Forest timber will play in the support of this important element of northwestern prosperity.

Those who follow us to Timberline Lodge on their holidays and vacations will represent the enjoyment of new opportunities for play in every season of the year. And I mention specially every season in the year, because we as a nation, I think are coming to realize that the summer isn't the only time for play. And I look forward to the day when many, many people from this region of the Nation are going to come here in the winter for skiing and tobogganing and various other forms of winter sports. Among them, all of these visitors, winter and summer, spring and autumn, there will be many from the uttermost parts of our Nation, from the Atlantic seaboard, from the Gulf of Mexico, from the Middle West, travelers from every one of the other forty-seven states; travelers, in addition, from the Territories of Hawaii and Alaska—territories also from that part of America [sic]—Puerto Rico and the Virgin Islands.

I am very keen about travel, not only personally—you know that, but also travel for as many Americans as can possibly afford it because those Americans will be fulfilling a very desirable objective of our citizenship, getting to know their own country better, and the more they see of it, the more they will realize the privileges which God and nature have given to the American people.

And so I take very great pleasure in dedicating this new adjunct, not only of national prosperity, but also as a place for generations of Americans to come in the days to come.[1]

[RL RECORDINGS: 116]

[1] This text is that of the radio broadcast transcription; it varies inconsequentially from the stenographic transcript. Also present (Speech File) are the reading copy and the mimeographed press release of the reading copy, the latter containing Kannee's shorthand notes of Roosevelt's departures from the prepared text. In addition to numerous changes of words and phrases, Roosevelt added all of paragraphs 1, 2, 3, the greater part of 10, and all of 11 and 12. Cf. Rosenman (ed.), *op. cit.*, VI, 392–394, which follows the stenographic copy for the most part.

703   THEODORE A. WALTERS, ACTING SECRETARY OF THE INTERIOR, TO ROOSEVELT

WASHINGTON, *Sept. 28, 1937*

MY DEAR MR. PRESIDENT: I have your memorandum of August 26 concerning the administration of H. R. 2512, an Act for the construction of small reservoirs under the Federal Reclamation laws, in which you request the submission of a plan whereby all possible labor for the construction of the dams will be recruited from work relief rolls. You also call attention to the desirability of selecting projects in the drought areas and in regions where there is great need for soil erosion prevention.

H. R. 2512 authorized an appropriation of $500,000 to carry out the provisions of the act, but the appropriation was not made. It is planned to request an appropriation as soon as Congress convenes, but this will not permit construction to be undertaken at an early date. However, if it is deemed desirable to commence the building of these dams with the least possible delay, work could be started with funds from Emergency Relief appropriations.

Regardless of the source of funds, it will first be necessary to expend about $50,000 to review the list of several hundred projects that have been submitted to the Bureau of Reclamation, to make an investigation of the feasibility of some of these, and to prepare plans and designs for the dams selected to be built. Relief labor cannot be used to any appreciable extent for these surveys as the personnel primarily will be engineers and engineering aides.

In the construction of those projects which investigations show to be feasible, repayment of all construction charges under the reclamation law probably should not be required if the dams are built strictly in accordance with the limitations of the Emergency Relief Appropriation Act of 1937.

This Department will carry out your suggestion that the dams to be built at this time should be located principally in the drought areas or where fertile lands are being rapidly destroyed by soil erosion.

Sincerely yours,

T. A. WALTERS

[13:OF 402:TS]

704   HAROLD L. ICKES, SECRETARY OF THE INTERIOR, TO OWEN
       JOHNSON, Stockbridge, Massachusetts

WASHINGTON, *Sept. 29, 1937*

MY DEAR MR. JOHNSON: The President has told me of your interest in the plan for a parkway which will run eventually from the Canadian line through the eastern states to Georgia, and he has asked that you be furnished a description of the route and of the procedure to be followed in its gradual extension.

This Department's conception of a national parkway is ". . . an elongated, Federally-owned area devoted to recreation which features a pleasure vehicle road through its entire length, bordered by adequate buffer strips, on which occupancy, commercial development, and access are restricted." The roadway itself under this definition becomes an incidental feature of the elongated recreational area and the traveller passing through it is protected from the dangers, annoyances and ugliness of the usual highway. The acquisition of the much wider right-of-way likewise serves as a means of preserving and protecting scenic beauty and of presenting the scenery, with the variations due to change of topography and latitude, in a continuity of form both interesting and instructive. The primary purpose is to make accessible the best scenery in the region which the parkway traverses, and consequently the choice of the most direct route is not considered of the greatest importance. . . .

The proposal in which you are particularly interested has been termed the "Appalachian Parkway," and would provide a recreational scenic route through New England, the Middle Atlantic States, and south to Atlanta, Georgia, from which existing highways will give access to Boston, New York, Philadelphia, Baltimore and Washington. The nucleus of the scheme is the Blue Ridge Parkway now under construction in the states of Virginia and North Carolina between the Shenandoah National Park and the Great Smoky Mountains National Park. From the northern end of the Shenandoah National Park the National Park Service has made a reconnaissance study and survey of a line which follows roughly the eastern slopes of the Blue Ridge Mountains through Virginia, Maryland and Pennsylvania; thence through northern New Jersey and through a portion of New York connecting with a Bear Mountain Park road and crossing the Bear Mountain bridge; thence to Fahnestock Park, Putnam County, New York; thence following the existing Eastern State Parkway a few miles; and then east to the Berkshire region. Just east of the Taconic Tri-State Park, a fork is proposed, one branch of which would proceed directly to Worcester, Massachusetts, and would utilize the existing State Highway to Boston. The other branch would continue north through the Berkshire Hills to the Green Mountains, following that range to Canada. A logical extension of the Blue Ridge Parkway in a southerly direction would be to continue from near Asheville, North Carolina, direct to Stone Mountain, Georgia, which is but a few miles from Atlanta over existing highways.

The mountain top and flank location reduces land acquisition cost and provides a recreational area with considerable wilderness character easily accessible from metropolitan areas. Thus is projected a parkway of great scenic beauty, tapping regions of scenic wealth and traversing the eastern states along a natural route through the entire Appalachian range at a generally high, cool, healthful altitude.

There is attached a map showing the proposed location of the line all of which has been reviewed in the field and has been found to be entirely feasible from a planning and construction standpoint.[1]

Sincerely yours,

[HAROLD L. ICKES]

[13:PPF 611:CT]

[1] Ickes' letter is a fair statement of Roosevelt's concept of scenic parkways. Many conservationists deplored his enthusiasm for mountain ridge roads because of their invasion of wilderness areas and because of the violence done the natural scene by the construction of the roads themselves. Roosevelt saw them as a means of permitting mass access to scenic areas. How much his own disability contributed to his interest in such highways is conjectural. One of Roosevelt's few public references to his inability to walk occurs in his speech dedicating the Whiteface Mountain Memorial Highway of Sept. 14, 1935. Here he noted that the road made ascent of the mountain possible for the aged and said also: "I wish very much that it were possible for me to walk up the few remaining feet to the actual top of the mountain" (Rosenman, ed., *Public Papers*, IV, 361).

[*Excerpt*] Governor Langer, my friends of North Dakota and of the nearby state of Minnesota as well: . . . In seeking the betterment of our farm population, no matter what part of the country they live in, no matter whether they raise cotton or corn or wheat or sugar beets or potatoes or rice, the experience we have today teaches us that if we would avoid the poverty of the past, we must strive today—not tomorrow—toward two objectives.

The first is called "better land use"—using the land in such a way that we do not destroy it or harm it for future generations, using it in such a way that it will bring to us the best year-in and year-out return as a reward for our labors. This we are doing at least in part today by various methods, by helping to educate the users of land, by putting back into grass or trees land which should not be under the plow, by bringing water to dry soil which has immense possibilities for profitable use, and by helping farm families to resettle on good land. The money we are spending on these objectives is already coming back in increased national income and will be repaid, in the long run, many, many times over.

The other objective is the control, with the approval of what I believe is the overwhelming sentiment of the farmers themselves, of what is known as crop surplus.

Any one crop, wheat or cotton or corn, is like any widely used manufactured commodity, like bricks or automobiles or shoes. If, for instance, every shoe factory in the United States were to run on a three-shift basis, turning out shoes and nothing but shoes day and night for two or three years, we would have such an enormous surplus of shoes in the United States that that surplus would have to be sold to the public, in order to get rid of it, at far less than the actual cost of manufacturing the shoes, and the same thing goes for wheat. Yes, the principle is the same whether it is shoes or wheat or cotton or corn or hogs.[1]

[SPEECH FILE:T]

---

[1] The text of this excerpt, which comprises somewhat less than one-fourth of the speech, is that of the stenographic transcript. Roosevelt made numerous departures from the reading copy (Speech File) in making the speech; cf. Rosenman (ed.), *Public Papers*, VI, 399–403, which follows the reading copy. This speech was one of a series made by Roosevelt in a trip to the West Coast and back, beginning with brief remarks at Clinton, Iowa, September 23, and concluding at Cleveland on October 5. He called the trip an "inspection trip": "I have taken one every year for the last four years and I have felt that it was right for me once more to go through the country and see how things are getting on . . ." (Clinton, Iowa, Sept. 23, 1937, Speech File).

[*Excerpt*] Q: Are we safe in assuming that wages and hours would come in for consideration by that Special Session, if there is one?

The President: If I were writing the story I would mention the principal things such as the crop thing, wages and hours, reorganization, regional planning and, by the way, on regional planning, of course it is easy to say "the little TVA's" but of course they are not.

Q: They are not?

The President: No, they are not TVA's. They are not at all TVA's. In other words, the TVA, under the Act, is given complete charge over a whole region, a whole watershed and, if a dam is to be built, the TVA builds it. When an electric transmission line is to be run, the TVA runs it. When there is soil erosion work to be done, the TVA does it, and the TVA is doing quite a lot of that replanting. When it is a question of building certain communities, you will notice that the TVA is doing it. In other words, it is a complete administrative agency for that region.

Now, the bill which Senator Norris has is an entirely different thing. It does not create any Board or Commission with administrative authority. It is merely a planning agency and, as the bill is drawn, it is nothing more than a planning agency.

Of course on the administrative end, things depend a good deal on how the reorganization bill goes through. Of course the idea of the reorganization plan originally was that there would be a Public Works Department. Now that has been eliminated but we can arrive at the same objective by an entirely different method by coordinating all of the public works agencies of the Government through the President's office so that after a plan for a region is made, the Congress and the President would then determine who would carry out the plan. Now, it would not be in one agency, necessarily. There might be a dam on the Columbia River, a new one, three or four or five years from now which had been recommended and which Congress appropriated for. Now, in all probability, that dam would be built by the Army Engineers or the Reclamation Service and not by the Columbia Valley Authority because that is only a planning agency. Do you see the distinction?

Q: The agency would determine how much of the program is to be carried out at any one time?

The President: No, the agency would only make recommendations to the planning agency of the President—the national planning agency under the White House.

[13: PRESIDENT'S PRESS CONFERENCES: T]

707   Roosevelt to J. Frederick Ham, Millbrook, New York

[Hyde Park] *October 20, 1937*

Dear Mr. Ham: I am delighted to have your note,[1] especially because of my long friendship for your splendid father.

We saw your pines the other day and your trees are nearly as old as the ones I first put in a great many years ago. Some day when you are driving up this way I hope you will take a look at the experimental plantings I have made at Tompkins Corner where Violet Avenue and the old Creek Road meet.

Very sincerely yours,

[Franklin D. Roosevelt]

[13:PPF 4935:CT]

[1] Oct. 18, 1937 (PPF 4935). Ham, a dairy farmer and at this time a field officer of the New York State Agricultural Conservation Program, referred to Roosevelt's visit on October 16 to a planting of pines near Washington Hollow, New York, set out by Ham's father.

708   Henry A. Wallace, Secretary of Agriculture, to Roosevelt

Washington, *October 25, 1937*

Dear Mr. President: As you know, one of the most significant recent industrial developments in the South is that represented by an investment—which has already reached some 100 million dollars or more—in new pulp and paper plants now being built there.

This new development depends on southern forests which for decades have furnished raw material for naval stores and many other forest industries vital to the South's present and future social and economic welfare, and competitive demands on those forests are now such that I have felt impelled to sound a distinct note of warning.

I am sure you have this situation in mind, in connection with your conference at Warm Springs with southern Governors. But pulp and paper developments have been so rapid in the South, and consequences may well be so far reaching and so unfortunate, that it occurs to me you may wish to review the situation, very briefly, before you leave for Warm Springs. I have asked Mr. Silcox, Chief of the Forest Service, to prepare a brief summary, and a map showing the new pulp and paper mills in relation to existing forest industries and forest resources. We will be glad to lay them before you whenever you wish us to do so.

Sincerely,

H. A. Wallace

709   PRESS CONFERENCE, Hyde Park, October 26, 1937, 4:30 P. M.

[*Excerpt*]   The President: I will give you a story.   I received the other day twelve flower pots from the Sequoia National Forest, and a lot of cones of various West Coast evergreen trees, and tomorrow I am having a ceremony and planting them.   They are about eight inches high.   I am going to plant them out by the tennis court to see whether they will grow.   They are sugar pine, western cedar, sequoia, lodge pole pine, and some other kind of pine.   And we are having a planting ceremony tomorrow and we are also taking the cones apart and trying them in the greenhouse.   You remember in Yellowstone, those hillsides where there were those perfectly straight trees?   They are lodge pole pines. They may not grow in this climate, for they came from a level where they have snow and ice, and we hope they will grow here.

Q: Are you planting redwood?

The President: Yes, I am expecting some seeds from the Olympic peninsula and I thought I would take them to the pond in the back woods and plant the redwoods around it and call it Lake Crescent.

I don't think anything is going to happen this week except Morgenthau and Bell.[1]   I think for the rest of the week, except for Friday evening, I am going to be almost free.   It will be very dull, getting lots of sleep and driving around planting lots of trees.

[13:PRESIDENT'S PRESS CONFERENCES:T]

[1] Secretary of the Treasury Morgenthau and Acting Director of the Budget Bell had an appointment with Roosevelt on October 29, and Bell had a second appointment on November 1 (PPF 1–O).

710   IRVING BRANT, EDITOR OF EDITORIAL PAGE, ST. LOUIS *Star-Times*, TO ROOSEVELT

[ST. LOUIS] *November 19, 1937*

DEAR MR. PRESIDENT: I have received enthusiastic reports about the sentiment for the Mt. Olympus National Park which you stirred up in the state of Washington.   It also appears that what you said about selective cutting is being interpreted in ways that must have been far from your meaning, and this is creating a dangerous situation.

The Port Townsend Chamber of Commerce national park committee has sent you a letter (published in the Port Angeles *Evening News*
of October 29) which in half a dozen details is too artistic a work of
deceit to have come from any source except the Forest Service.[1]

The main trouble appears to be that selective cutting as you understand it—the Black Forest variety—and selective cutting as practiced
on the Olympic peninsula—are two entirely different propositions.

A few years ago I went to the Forest Service office in Portland and
urged the adoption of selective cutting of the kind you have in mind.
They told me that in forests of the Olympic type this was an impossibility. Owing to the enormous size and dense growth of trees, the fell-
ing and dragging out of one tree destroys or damages scores of others.
The slash is so tremendous that it cannot be piled, but must be burned
as it lies on the ground. Opening the forest by partial cutting exposes
the remaining trees to windthrow. Finally, Douglas fir will not repro-
duce in shade. All of these factors, they said, force them to cut down
everything if they cut anything. This is true even where tractors are
used in place of high leads—tractors merely increase the salvage.

So, the Forest Service officials told me, they had developed a special
kind of selective cutting in the Olympic region. It consists of cutting
everything on selected areas. It is the only kind of selective cutting
that can be practiced in these huge, dense forests, but it absolutely destroys the forests as scenic assets.

When you talked with the Forest Service officials about selective cutting, did they tell you the same thing about it that they told me? Or
did they indorse selective cutting, saying nothing about what they mean
by it in the Olympic National Forest, and thus encourage you to make
a statement which they are now using to put over a plan of commercial
use that would destroy the forests you want to save?

Since the forests within the proposed park are not needed for the
economic life of the Olympic peninsula, where sawmills are doomed
anyway and pulpwood is growing four times as fast as it is being cut, I
hope you will capitalize on the principal effect of your trip around the
peninsula, which was to put emphasis on a large park, and that you
will check the misuse of your other statements. This can be done, I
think, by a few words to Congressman Wallgren. The people of the
state of Washington, aside from the lumber interests, want the finest
park obtainable.

I believe that the National Park Service ought to be kept clear of
commercial activities, except for the public visiting the parks. If the
Park Service cuts timber and sells it commercially, it will open the way
to the same gradual infiltration of a commercial point of view that has
been taking place in the Forest Service during the past twenty years.
If this is permitted in one park, it will be an entering wedge for com-

mercial encroachments elsewhere, and it is only by rigid adherence to non-commercial uses that the park system has been saved from a breakdown of standards. A breakdown would come more quickly if the Forest Service should be given jurisdiction within the parks. I know that these are results you do not want.

Last Wednesday I attended a meeting in Chicago devoted to aiding your program of government reorganization. Some of the others who were there are hoping to talk with you about it, but I cannot be with them. I believe that the most far-reaching results will flow ultimately out of changing the name of the Interior Department to Department of Conservation, by establishing standards which the department must live up to under all Presidents, but this will not come about unless you get the power to regroup bureaus without hampering restrictions by Congress. I hope you will stick to this feature of your proposals, no matter what compromises may prove necessary in the entire undertaking.

Yours sincerely,

IRVING BRANT

[13:OF 6–P:TS]

[1] Not found in the Roosevelt papers.

711   ROOSEVELT TO NELSON C. BROWN, New York State College of Forestry, Syracuse University, Syracuse, New York

[WASHINGTON] *November 22, 1937*

DEAR NELSON: Many thanks for yours of the sixteenth.[1] I think much the best thing for us to do is to get five hundred beeches from the F. W. Kelsey Nursery Company at $45.00 per thousand or a total of $22.50.

That means that Mr. Plog could set them out in the two places indicated, putting in each location two hundred and fifty trees spaced nine or ten feet apart, thus covering about half an acre in each locality.

I am glad you found the trees doing so well and I am delighted with your plans for the winter woods work and spring planting.

As ever yours,

[FRANKLIN D. ROOSEVELT]

[13:PSF:HYDE PARK:CT]

[1] Brown had written concerning future tree planting on the Roosevelt estate and had enclosed a "Summary of Plans for Winter Woods Work and Spring Planting in 1938, Roosevelt Place, Hyde Park" (PSF:Hyde Park). He discussed the difficulties of getting beeches wanted by Roosevelt, and concluded: "Altogether the trees made a most excellent showing during the past favorable year and I am very happy to report that most of them are doing very well, excepting in the tamarack swamp where the growth of weeds and sprouts was so vigorous last year that the planted trees had a pretty tough time of it."

Washington [*November 27, 1937*] [1]

Dear Mr. President: Both directly and indirectly I have been informed that the leading farm and conservation organizations are greatly concerned about one phase of your proposal to reorganize the government. These organizations approve about 99 per cent of your reorganization proposal. They have appreciated enormously your unprecedented interest in agriculture and conservation. Nevertheless, their opposition to one phase of your reorganization plan furnishes an opening which may seriously split your forces and even endanger other phases of your program. They are against the proposal to change the name of the Department of the Interior to the Department of Conservation.[2]

The following organizations are among those against the proposal: American Farm Bureau Federation, National Grange, National Cooperative Council, National Farmers' Union, Farmers' National Grain Corporation, American Agricultural Editors Association, Association of Land Grant Colleges, Izaak Walton League (and other wildlife organizations), American Forestry Association (and other forestry and conservation organizations.)

(And may I add that I know of no agricultural, or forestry, or conservation organization of any strength or standing that is in favor of the Conservation Department proposal.) To be honest, I must admit that I am in sympathy with the point of view of these organizations toward the Conservation Department proposal. I do not see how agriculture and conservation can be divorced, nor why they should be. Nevertheless, I have refrained from stating my views publicly. I have asked all officials of the Department of Agriculture to adopt the same course. This course, however, is rendered increasingly difficult by two facts:

1. The Department of the Interior has carried on a concerted campaign of propaganda which clearly urges the transfer of many land use functions of the Department of Agriculture to another government department. This campaign has grown bolder under the guise of upholding your endorsement of the Brownlow Committee report which calls for the establishment of a Department of Conservation. The campaign has culminated in a radio speech by the Secretary of the Interior, who has again attacked all opponents of the idea as agents of special interests and enemies of conservation. Whatever Secretary Ickes' intentions, the result of his campaign has been to stir the farm and conservation organizations to deep resentment and united action.

2. The farm and conservation organizations have construed my silence to mean consent. They are asking where I stand. The letter from H. H. Chapman, President of the Society of American Foresters,

which I handed you several days ago illustrates the situation. I attach hereto another copy of this letter and my proposed reply.[3] In ordinary circumstances they might subscribe to my feeling that differences of opinion between administration officials should be settled inside the administration, but they protest that Secretary Ickes has gone too far for that attitude to govern the present situation.

Let me say at once that I have given and will give the warmest possible support to your effort to reorganize the government. The need is pressing. I agree that we must have more efficiency and greater harmony in government. I feel keenly that you are harassed, day in and day out, by jurisdictional disputes which ought never to arise.

The long-standing conflicts between the Departments of Agriculture and the Interior usually have involved the land use functions of government. Somehow we shall have to solve the problem of properly locating these major land use functions within the government if we are to end the conflict.

I wish therefore to propose for most serious consideration a plan which in my judgment would finally bring harmony into the relations of at least the Departments of Agriculture and the Interior.

The premises of the plan are these:

Our government is engaged in a vast land use program looking toward the wise husbandry of our land resources, both public and private. In such a program some land must be in trees, some in grass, some in farm crops. Whether the land be in public or private ownership the problems are the same, the solutions demand scientific and economic information, and the programs must be manned by persons trained in the agricultural and related sciences.

Erosion must be controlled on grass land, forest land and crop land. No matter who owns the land, the scientific techniques are the same. Grazing must be controlled on both grass land and forest land, public and private. Fertility must be conserved on all. Human needs must be considered. Most of the people who live on and use the land are farmers. The Federal government cannot do the job alone. It must have the cooperation of state governments and millions of farmers and stockmen. That cooperation in solving our land use problems cannot be obtained if the federal part of the effort lacks unity and harmony.

I can see but one solution: the transfer to the Department of Agriculture of the Grazing Administration, the agricultural phases of the Reclamation Service, the General Land Office, and the National Parks. That would at once bring harmony and unity in land use programs. On the other hand, harmony in land use cannot be achieved by transferring three or four bureaus from the Department of Agriculture to a Department of Conservation. Such transfer would only increase the disunity, frictions and duplication of effort now extant. The Department of Conservation would have to have its own plant experts, its own animal experts, its own soil experts, its own agricultural economists, its own research organizations. If it used the resources of the Bureau of Plant Industry, of Animal Industry, of Soils, etc., the present frictions still would exist but in an intensified form. As it now stands, the Department of the Interior, in order to administer grazing, national parks and railroad lands, has added plant experts, livestock experts, foresters, agronomists, etc., all of whom perform functions better done in the Department of Agriculture.

To accomplish these transfers to the Department of Agriculture two small modifications in the bill now before Congress would be required:

1. Deletion of the section which provides for renaming the Department of the Interior the Department of Conservation.

2. A change in the definition of agriculture as expressed in the bill.

I am not urging an increase in the size of the Department of Agriculture. I am perfectly willing to surrender such parts of it as do not contribute to what I conceive to be the functions of a department of agriculture—to administer those branches of government which have to do with land use, the welfare of people on the land, and with growing things and living things that depend for life upon the soil and what grows from it. The budgets of certain bureaus in this department which could reasonably be transferred greatly exceed those of the bureaus which I suggest be transferred from Interior to Agriculture.

I believe that the majority of farm and conservation groups would heartily support reorganization if their concern respecting agriculture and conservation were eliminated. But if the bill remains as it is, my own silence and the silence of officials of my department will not restrain the active opposition of these groups. They feel that agriculture will be split wide open, that conservation will be endangered, that a wise land use program will be impossible. They do not see how private and public lands can provide a basis for divided jurisdiction when the two are so inextricably interwoven physically, economically, and socially. They fear that such a basis for division would in effect result in two departments of agriculture—one for public lands, to be known as "Conservation," the other for private lands, to be known as "Agriculture,"—with eastern farmers looking to one and western farmers looking to the other, with interminable conflicts and overlapping of functions. They are certain that changing the name of the Department of the Interior to the Department of Conservation will make it certain that in future administrations Secretaries of that Department will have a legal sanction for continuing efforts to gain control of many of the myriad functions which the Department of Agriculture properly should exercise.

You, Mr. President, are at present recognized as the real conservation leader in this Nation. I do not wish to see any change in public sentiment in this regard, particularly on the part of the farm and conservation organizations which long have fought for conservation principles and which on many counts are among your most earnest supporters.

The opposition so rapidly developing against this one phase of your reorganization plan may result in deep-seated resentments. The conservation organizations wield considerable power and their opposition may easily be a rallying point in Congress against you and the possible defeat of the whole reorganization plan. That opposition can be turned to support by the two modifications of the pending bill suggested on the preceding page.

May I have your permission to approach congressional leaders on the two changes above proposed?

In this way I believe you can attain the most harmony and efficiency in government and the widest support from farm and conservation groups in carrying out your reorganization and other programs.

Respectfully yours,

H. A. WALLACE

[*Notation*:A] F 11/27/37

[13:OF 285–C:TS]

[1] In the absence of a date, the filing date has been used.
[2] The President's Committee on Administrative Management (see *ante,* 581 n.) had proposed that a department of conservation be created to administer the public lands and to enforce the conservation laws. Wallace opposed this because it meant the transfer of the Forest Service to the new department and for the other reasons stated in this letter. The Reorganization Act of 1939 did not, however, make the creation of a conservation department mandatory and it was not included in any of the reorganization plans adopted under the act.
[3] Chapman's letter to White of Oct. 26, 1937, attacked Ickes' proposal for a conservation department and raised the question whether the Department of Agriculture had "ever really grasped the significance and importance of the broad program of soil conservation" that was implicit in its responsibility for the public lands. Wallace, in his proposed reply (present as an undated carbon copy), said that conservation was "not the function of one agency but a fundamental underlying social principle of governmental action," and that there would be opportunity in the Congressional debate on the plan for consideration of all points of view.

713   JAMES D. LeCRON, ASSISTANT TO THE SECRETARY OF AGRICULTURE, TO ROOSEVELT

[WASHINGTON, *November 29, 1937*] [1]

DEAR MR. PRESIDENT: Reference is made to Miss LeHand's note of November 23 and the attached copy of a letter to Senator Fletcher of October 1, 1935. [2]

The matter of forest credits has been of active interest to this Department for several years. Our first formal action was the inclusion of a forest credit item in the forest program of the Department reported to the Senate March 30, 1933 (Senate Document 12, 73rd Congress).[3]

National Recovery Administration legislation and the inclusion of Article X in the Lumber Code resulted in two conferences on forest conservation, held in October, 1933 and January, 1934, by representatives of the lumber and timber products industries and of public agencies. A proposal for forest credit legislation was part of the programs recommended by the Forest Service and by the industrial agencies at these conferences and included in the continuing legislative effort which, with your general approval, followed the conferences.

It having been early concluded that a self-supporting credit institution (probably a division of the Farm Credit Administration) rather than one drawing continuously on tax funds would be the most appropriate agency, the Farm Credit Administration and the Forest Service of this Department entered into a careful study of the appropriate and most economical methods of providing credits for sustained yield forestry. The general conclusions were given to Senator Fletcher by the FCA early in 1935 and made the basis of a tentative draft of legislation submitted to you with his letter of May 25, 1935. Senator Fletcher's letter with draft of the bill was submitted, on June 4, 1935, to this Department by Acting Director Bell of the Budget Bureau with a request for a report. Our report favoring the legislation subject to certain minor changes was submitted to Mr. Bell on June 26. On July 29, 1935, S. 3417 was introduced by Senator Fletcher embodying the general provisions of the draft previously submitted to you. On August 25, 1935, Representative Caldwell introduced an identical bill, H. R. 9197, in the House of Representatives.[4]

On September 28, Acting Director Bell returned the above-mentioned report to this Department with the statement that it was your desire that this matter be discussed with the Treasury with a view to determining a satisfactory method of handling the financial aspects of this problem. Such discussion was held on October 10, 1935 between Governor Myers of the Farm Credit Administration, Mr. Silcox of the Forest Service of this Department, and Mr. Coolidge of the Treasury, together with other officials of these agencies. A financial program apparently satisfactory to the Treasury was formulated. On December 13 Secretary Morgenthau wrote Governor Myers that after due consideration there seemed no objections to extending the credit facilities of the FCA for the purposes of S. 3417 providing no new bond issues were authorized.

Following further intensive study by the interested agencies revisions needed in the Fletcher bill were agreed upon between the FCA and this Department and embodied in reports by Governor Myers of the FCA to Senator Fletcher as chairman of the Senate Committee on Banking and Currency, and to Chairman Jones of the Agricultural Committee in March, 1936. Reports concurring in the recommendations of the FCA were also prepared by this Department. These reports were, however, never released by the Budget Bureau to the Senate and House committees.

This Department believes that a new bill embodying the general principles of the Fletcher bill but containing the revisions recommended by the FCA and this Department early in 1936 and such other changes as may now seem necessary should be prepared. Cooperative arrangements between the FCA and this Department are in effect whereby such a draft can be prepared on short notice.

The proposals of this Department from the very beginning have been that the forest credit agency should be set up for the sole purpose of financing both large and small forest properties definitely managed under sustained yield practices in order to support stabilized employment and contribute continuously to community welfare.

Very sincerely yours,

[JAMES D. LeCRON]

[13:PPF 64:CT]

[1] The supplied date is that of LeCron's covering note to Miss LeHand.
[2] Miss LeHand's note (Nov. 23, 1937, PPF 64), asked for information about the Fletcher bill in connection with the preparation by Rosenman of the *Public Papers and Addresses*. The letter to Fletcher is printed *ante*, 428.
[3] *A National Plan for American Forestry* (Washington, 1933).
[4] The two bills were introduced on Aug. 14 and 21, 1935, respectively (*Cong. Rec.*, 74th Cong., 1st sess., 79:12, 13032; 79:13, 14042).

714   FRANCIS C. HARRINGTON, ASSISTANT WORKS PROGRESS ADMINISTRATOR, TO JAMES ROOSEVELT, SECRETARY TO THE PRESIDENT

WASHINGTON, D. C., *December 6, 1937*

DEAR MR. ROOSEVELT: In memoranda of August 21 and September 13, 1937, to the Works Progress Administrator, copies of which are attached, the President gave certain instructions regarding projects for the construction of sanitary sewers. In substance these instructions were to the effect that such projects should not be constructed where untreated sewage would be discharged into creeks and rivers.

In the application of the instructions a number of questions have arisen which I hope to have an opportunity to discuss with you in some detail. In general, however, it may be said that a literal application of the instructions will result in the disapproval of certain projects which, if carried out, would bring a definite improvement in health conditions.

The governmental agency which is best fitted to pass upon the technical questions in this regard is the Public Health Service and, to a somewhat lesser degree, the Water Resources Committee of the National Resources Committee. I have, therefore, discussed this matter with Dr. Thomas Parran, Jr., Surgeon General of the Public Health Service, and Mr. Abel Wolman, Chairman of the Water Resources Committee of the National Resources Committee.

As a result of this discussion, I am attaching a suggested memorandum for the President's signature which, in effect, would permit the submission of projects for sewer construction in those cases where the Public Health Service believes that a definite improvement in public health conditions would result, and would permit carrying to a useful state of completion the unfinished projects on which the Works Progress Administration is now working.

The suggested memorandum has the concurrence of Dr. Parran and Mr. Wolman.[1]

Very truly yours,

F. C. HARRINGTON

[*Notation*:A:FDR] *No* Except as Tie in on Permanent Sewage Sewage [*sic*] disposal.[2]

[13:OF 444–C:TS]

[1] The proposed memorandum would have modified the President's directives so as to permit the construction of sewer projects which tended "to eliminate conditions which are a menace to public health without adding appreciably to the volume of untreated sewage which now enters creeks and rivers."
[2] Answered *post,* 716.

715   MORRIS L. COOKE TO ROOSEVELT

PHILADELPHIA, *December 8, 1937*

MY DEAR MR. PRESIDENT: The revised Drainage Basin Report, which will presently be before you, is a very great improvement on its predecessor.[1] But it will not be, I believe, in your sense a comprehensive plan for flood control. Apparently it will again be mainly an inventory of separate, unrelated projects—a reservoir here, a dam there—and will not, on the basis of intelligent, farsighted planning, present a balanced picture of what really needs to be done downstream, upstream, and *on the land.*

Criticism of the previous report has been so severe, of course, that some discussion on erosion control and run-off retardation will no doubt be included. But the engineers who worked on the redraft have not changed in their complete reliance on dams and levees downstream.

Everything else seems to them unimportant largely because you cannot now forecast quantitatively, to the decimal point, the effect that a co-ordinated system of upstream engineering and land management will have on major flood crests. Upstream data does not yet figure in the engineers' handbooks.

My information is that the report will not propose for a single area, a coordinated upstream development.

You fully realize that if we are to survive we must eventually learn to harness the streams from the headwaters to the sea, keeping as much water as we can in the natural reservoir of the soil. We shall build dams in the smaller streams firstly, to replenish our water reserves and then to provide for flood and low water control, irrigation, recreation, and power. Further I will not expect important progress until we have passed the stage of "jobbing" work upstream. We must standardize these developments and so make mass construction possible.

I hope in your covering message, you will find it possible to speak both hopefully and forcibly of the upstream problem with or without the immediate cooperation of my profession.[2]

Yours very sincerely,

MORRIS LLEWELLYN COOKE

[13:OF 1092:TS]

[1] Water Resources Committee, *Drainage Basin Problems and Programs: 1937 Revision* (Washington, 1938). The original report was issued December, 1936.
[2] Answered *post*, 719.

716 JAMES ROOSEVELT, SECRETARY TO THE PRESIDENT, TO FRANCIS C. HARRINGTON, ASSISTANT WORKS PROGRESS ADMINISTRATOR

[WASHINGTON] *December 10, 1937*

DEAR COLONEL HARRINGTON: In discussing your letter of December sixth, the President has asked me to transmit the message to you that he will not approve any projects for construction of sanitary sewers unless the work to be done is of a permanent character and lending itself to ultimate development of sewage disposal plants and will not become obsolete or have to be torn up at a later date.

With my best wishes to you, Very sincerely,

[JAMES ROOSEVELT]

JR–KG

[13:OF 444–C:CT]

WASHINGTON, D.C., *December 10, 1937*

DEAR MR. PRESIDENT: On July 28, 1937, you sent me a memorandum part of which reads as follows:

While it is legal to undertake projects on land belonging in private ownership, I think it is a great mistake to do any more of this than we can possibly help. There are some cases where the cutting of firebreaks, for example, the privately owned forest lands, will safeguard publicly owned lands against fire, but it is difficult to say to one private owner "We will work on your land" and to his neighbor say "We will not work on your land."

Immediately on receipt of this memorandum I took up with the technical agencies cooperating in CCC work the question of the amount of work that our CCC camps were doing on private land. When I had received a report from the Department of the Interior and the Department of Agriculture I wrote you under date of August 21st, 1937, setting forth in considerable detail just what our camps were doing on private land. On August 24, 1937 you sent me a memorandum approving the program as I had outlined it. On November 17, 1937 Senator Pat McCarran of Nevada personally called at my office in company with several gentlemen from his state and presented a petition from the Walker River Irrigation District, Yerington, Nevada, in which we were asked to place one or more CCC camps on the Irrigation District area to build new irrigation ditches and repair already existing irrigation ditches.

This was purely a privately owned irrigation district. Any work that we did on the area would be for the sole benefit of the private landowners or landusers in the district. I doubted if work of this character would come within the scope of what you felt would be desirable and justifiable for the CCC to engage in. Therefore on the same date November 17, 1937, I addressed a letter to you briefly outlining what the Senator and his constituents wanted to do. On November 21, 1937, you sent me a memorandum reading as follows:

The answer is "no." Do not extend these irrigation projects on private lands except in very rare cases in dry areas where the farmers are practically on relief." [1]

This confirmed my understanding of the type of work which you did not feel was proper for us to engage in. An identical condition exists in privately owned drainage ditch associations. These associations are organized for the identical purpose of reclamation districts except that they are designed to accomplish the opposite purpose. Reclamation ditches put water on the land, drainage ditches take water off of the land. The drainage ditch associations are wholly privately owned and any work we did on them would be solely for the benefit of private landowners.

On receipt of your memorandum of November 21, I addressed a joint letter to the representatives of the Secretary of the Interior and the Secretary of Agriculture on my Advisory Council directing that in the further reduction of operating CCC camps to discontinue all Civilian Conservation Corps work on privately owned reclamation districts and drainage ditch districts.

On December 9th during a conference that you had with several members of Congress including Honorable T. Alan Goldsborough of Maryland, Mr. Goldsborough brought up the subject of discontinuing CCC work on privately owned drainage ditches. The Congressman understood from you that you were not opposed to CCC work on this type of project.

We have at the present time approximately 42 CCC camps engaged wholly on drainage ditch projects and a total of approximately 34 camps engaged wholly on Bureau of Reclamation projects. In order that I may clearly understand your desires in the matter I will appreciate it if you will let me know whether or not we should continue these two types of work.

Sincerely yours,

ROBT. FECHNER

[13:OF 268:TS]

[1] The memorandum is quoted in full (OF 268). See below.

718   ROOSEVELT TO ROBERT FECHNER, DIRECTOR, CIVILIAN CONSERVATION CORPS

[WASHINGTON] *December 13, 1937*

MEMORANDUM FOR MR. FECHNER: Will you get me the information in regard to Congressman Goldsborough's privately owned drainage ditches. Is it a cooperative association? How are they financed? What kind of land are they using, etc?

F. D. R.

[13:OF 268:CT]

719   ROOSEVELT TO MORRIS L. COOKE, Philadelphia

[WASHINGTON] *December 14, 1937*

DEAR MORRIS: I am glad to have your slant on the coming Drainage Basin Report.[1] When it is completed I wish you would let me have a two or three page memorandum on where it fails to cover the whole subject.[2]

Always sincerely,

[FRANKLIN D. ROOSEVELT]

[13:OF 1092:CT]

[1] *Ante,* 715.
[2] Answered below.

720   MORRIS L. COOKE TO ROOSEVELT

PHILADELPHIA [*December 20, 1937*]

MY DEAR MR. PRESIDENT: The Drainage Basin Report deals with reclamation, drainage and other subjects not directly related to flood control. Possibly you will want to comment on some of these other phases. The enclosure, sent in answer to your letter dated December 14, is a suggestion as to what might possibly be said in comment on the flood—and erosion—control aspects of the report. After all, this is, or should be, the dominant theme in our watershed thinking and planning. I have assumed that you would want to stress soil and water conservation.

My contacts with this subject to date recall a comment of a former colleague in a different field: "We make progress steady by jerks." Thanking you for this opportunity to serve a good cause, I am,

Yours very sincerely,

MORRIS LLEWELLYN COOKE

[13:PPF 1820:TS]

721   [*Enclosure*]

On April 28, 1937, I indicated that I would present to the Congress in January 1938 a plan for flood control in the Ohio-Mississippi Basin. Again, on August 9, 1937, I said that I would also present to the Congress a comprehensive national plan for flood control and prevention and the development of water and soil conservation. These plans are included as a part of the revised report on Drainage Basin Problems and Programs.

The text of this report describes the importance of land management and engineering works in tributaries as well as in the main streams, as measures for water control and use. However, the projects recommended for immediate consideration deal for the most part with the engineering phases of water regulation in the downstream channels. These projects constitute a 6-year program, which will be revised each year to make it more comprehensive and to keep it current.

Experience and exhaustive data on downstream engineering have been acquired over a period of many years. More recently experience and data relating to conservation farming practices which control run-off and reduce erosion are being added to our information bearing on downstream control—even though such information has not yet reached the engineering handbooks.

Improper land-use practices increase both the speed and volume of run-off, with injurious consequences to agriculture, the range, volume and purity of the water supply, river ways and channels, dams, reservoirs, and the control of floods. Proper land-use practices and upstream engineering such as contour cultivation, terracing of sloping fields, check-damming of gullies, appropriate crop rotations, reforestation, and dams and other works in smaller streams, will hold much of the water where it falls, and retard the flow of the rest, so as to derive its benefits and avoid its contributing to hazards.

If we can learn to view as a unit each river, its watershed sources, and the rainfall that flows off the adjacent lands, then by supplementing engineering structures downstream with measures for wise land use on the watershed, we can provide for the integrated development of the river and its watershed and secure the benefits of improved navigation, flood control, a stable agriculture, abundant electric power, and greater security for the people.

The objectives of the Ohio-Mississippi project, for example, may be reached more rapidly and completely if the great structures downstream are supplemented by widespread land management practices on the watersheds and engineering works in the tributaries of these great streams. The man along the river dreads the floods. But these terrifying masses of water do not simply fall into the river. The water falls on millions of acres upstream, downstream, all along the great basin. The man on the land upstream can contribute to the program of engineering downstream by slowing and timing the journey of the raindrop and keeping the soil out of stream channels and reservoirs. Vegetation, and engineering measures on the farm and in the small tributaries of the larger streams protect the soil, conserve water for crops and power development, and reduce the intensity of the waterflow.

The report properly recommends funds for additional study of this whole problem, especially for the Mississippi basin. The knowledge thus developed can be utilized to great advantage in further development of the program.

The report on Drainage Basins and Programs recognizes that it is essential to develop engineering projects downstream to avoid immediate hazards from floods, and to facilitate navigation and power development. Year by year this plan should be broadened to take into consideration the smaller tributaries of the large streams, the watersheds, and the

[155]

people on the land. I believe this development must be continued until the scope of the single coordinated program extends from the headwaters to the sea.

[13:PPF 1820:T]

722   ROOSEVELT TO J. J. McENTEE, ACTING DIRECTOR, CIVILIAN CONSERVATION CORPS

WASHINGTON, *December 20, 1937*

MEMORANDUM FOR J. J. McENTEE, CIVILIAN CONSERVATION CORPS: In view of your memorandum of December seventeenth,[1] it seems clear that the main Maryland drainage ditches are operated by a public non-profit making authority and therefore C. C. C. work on them does not fall into the category of work on private land. We should be careful, therefore, not to do any work on the lateral ditches which are built and maintained by private landowners.

F. D. R.

[13:OF 268:CT]

[1] Describing CCC work on privately owned drainage ditches in Maryland (OF 268).

723   ROOSEVELT TO HENRY A. WALLACE, SECRETARY OF AGRICULTURE

[WASHINGTON] *December 20, 1937*

MEMORANDUM FOR THE SECRETARY OF AGRICULTURE: I am seeing the Southern Governors at lunch on January seventh. Can you let me have some more information about the alarming possibility of over-cutting in the Southern States, as a result of the large number of new pulp mills?[1]

F. D. R.

[13:OF 149:CT:COPY]

[1] Answered *post*, 729.

724   HAROLD L. ICKES, SECRETARY OF THE INTERIOR, TO ROOSEVELT

WASHINGTON, *December 20, 1937*

MY DEAR MR. PRESIDENT: The following reports on the Colorado-Big Thompson project in the State of Colorado is made to you under the provisions of Section 4 of the Act of June 25, 1910 (36 Stat. 835) . . .[1]

[156]

The Colorado-Big Thompson project contemplates the construction of a system of reservoirs, canals, and a pumping plant on the western slope, a long tunnel through the Continental Divide, and a system of reservoirs, canals, and power plants on the eastern slope. By this means, the waters of the Colorado River and certain tributaries will be conserved on the western slope, diverted by tunnel to the eastern slope, re-stored there in a system of reservoirs, and later released to the Poudre, Big Thompson, and South Platte rivers, and to St. Vrain Creek for subsequent distribution through existing canals and ditches to 615,000 acres of land which now have an inadequate water supply.

Water Supply

The Colorado River and tributaries feeding the system have an average annual divertible water supply of 320,000 acre feet, derived principally from the spring melting of snows, which will be caught in a reservoir constructed on the Colorado River and will be used almost entirely as a supplemental water supply for the lands on the eastern slope. A replacement reservoir of 152,000 acre feet is to be built on the Blue River, a tributary of the Colorado River, to furnish an ample water supply for vested and future rights for irrigation and power that exist on the Colorado River below the mouth of the Blue River. By this means, the entire supply of 320,000 acre feet, mentioned above, will be made available for eastern slope use.

Reservoirs also will be built on the eastern slope. The storage in these reservoirs and the water diverted from the western slope will provide an adequate supplemental water supply so that the 615,000 acres of land in the project will have a sufficient irrigation supply except in very infrequent seasons. The furnishing of this supplemental supply will permit the raising of crops of a higher per acre value than those grown at present and will, as well, allow the production of more abundant crops . . .[2]

Objections to the Project

Attention has been given to the objections to this project by various persons and organizations interested in national parks. On November 12, 1937, I held a hearing which was well attended by the proponents and opponents of the project who were given an opportunity for open discussion. Regardless of the point of view of those who would preserve national parks unimpaired, the Organic Act which established Rocky Mountain National Park, approved January 26, 1915, reserved the right to utilize the park for irrigation purposes as follows: "The United States Reclamation Service may enter upon and utilize for flowage or other purposes any area within said park which may be necessary for the development and maintenance of a Government reclamation project."

Congress again expressed its will when it authorized the construction of the project and appropriated $900,000 in the Department of the Interior Appropriation Bill approved August 9, 1937.

Certain agreements which will benefit the park have been entered into informally and will be made binding before the commencement of the construction. These agreements involve the furnishing of a firm supply of water from the project to the park; free electricity for Government purposes; abstention from construction work within the park boundaries; and the right of the Park Service to pass upon plans and specifications where lands authorized to be added to the park are involved.

The objections of the persons on the western slope of the Rocky Mountains from whose watershed the water will be diverted to the eastern slope were withdrawn when the plans provided for a compensatory reservoir on the western slope where feasible.

At the conclusion of the morning hearings on November 12, after the principal arguments had been presented for and against the project, I made a statement summing up the situation which is faced by the Secretary of the Interior and the President. I am enclosing a copy of this statement for your information.

Findings Regarding Feasibility of Project

In view of all of the circumstances, the changes in the plans, and the care which will be exercised to avoid injury to the park, I find that the project is feasible from an engineering and economic standpoint and so declare.

In order to prevent the abandonment of developed lands, and also to improve economic conditions involving a population of 175,000 people in northeastern Colorado, I recommend that construction of the Colorado-Big Thompson project be approved and that construction be started at an early date.

Sincerely yours,

[HAROLD L. ICKES]

Approved: [*Stamped*] FRANKLIN D. ROOSEVELT 12/21/37

[13:OF 402:CT]

---

[1] An act to authorize advances to the reclamation fund. Omitted here is a quotation from the act.

[2] Omitted are several pages on the engineering features and construction costs of the project.

725 [*Enclosure*]

Statement by Secretary Ickes

Secretary Ickes: I would like to make a short statement. I would like all of you to put yourselves in the position of the Secretary of the Interior. I do not say that I am speaking for the conservationists of America, but I believe that I am a conservationist. I have tried to carry out the principles of conservation since I took this office.

Many misrepresentations have been made about this project. It is not easy to make a decision, but I will ask you to put yourselves in my position. It seems to be forgotten by a good many of those who have spoken that Congress has spoken through statute, not once but more than once. We talk about the sanctity of treaties in the Rocky Mountain National Park. Senator Adams will testify with what disfavor he was received when he came into my office to propose this tunnel. Like Mr. Delano, I am not convinced that there should be the taking of water from one watershed to another. I am opposed to it, but it goes further than the National Park Service.

Now, no one will go further than I in preserving wilderness areas. We have too many roads in the National Parks, too many approach roads. I wish we had more wilderness areas; but this park came in with a condition, the condition being the creation of an irrigation project in the future. Now that is not open to dispute. Such a situation does not exist with respect to any other National Park. Under this Administration there have been proposed certain areas for parks with mineral rights reserved, but I have no interest in having some one digging up a National Park, no more than you do. This same situation exists at Big Bend. I have insisted as a condition precedent that mineral rights must be extinguished before it be brought in. But this condition was made and was accepted by the United States Government, and the condition is either good today or it is not good today.

Now, it might be said that the declaration of policies in two subsequent acts would be binding as against the original reservation. I am also able to see that that is arguable. But the reply would be that the appropriation of $900,000 for the specific purpose of starting to build this tunnel would be the most recent declaration of policy with respect to the Rocky Mountain National Park.

I do not see this eye to eye with Senator Adams. I think there is danger of creating a bad precedent. I agree also with Mr. Delano, and not with some of the others, that if we start a tunnel and have to have an air shaft, the argument of necessity will be made. I can hear the argument ring that we have been spending too much money already. I do not want to throw money away—there is danger in this thing.

The question has been raised as to whether this might drain the lake. I raised the question long ago, and had a careful investigation made by the Geological Survey.

I am not in agreement with the insinuations which have been made against the Bureau of Reclamation in the past, but I know under this Administration it is and has been an agency of conservation, and Mr. Page was not recommended for Commissioner until it was assured that he was a conservationist, nor until I satisfied myself on that point; and the President would not have made the appointment if he had not been sure of it. I have no reason to believe that Mr. Page is a proponent of this, he is only an instrumentality for this, and I agree with Mr. Delano, and not with Senator Adams, that this may not pay out.

The Congress can make and Congress can unmake laws. It can pass a law that a project must be self-liquidating, and Congress can change that law; the next session or two or five years from now, Congress can change it. I have said to western Congressmen who come to me on western Reclamation project matters, especially when they come in on the abatement of payments, that they were doing the greatest disservice and damage to Reclamation that could possibly be done. Just to the degree that it becomes necessary to ask the Government for a project on the assurance that it will be self-liquidating, and come in later years and say, "We cannot pay out, we want you to reduce our principal payments," just to that degree the people whose lives are dependent on reclamation are the people who are injuring reclamation. But they are doing it.

The Congress has passed a law authorizing the Secretary to set up a commission of three for studying the whole question as to whether there should be an abatement of payments—well, sooner or later, Congress will not be appropriating any more money for so-called self-liquidating reclamation projects that are not self-liquidating in fact.

I cannot follow my own will in this matter. I have to follow the law and I tell you very frankly that between the Bureau of Reclamation and the Park Service, I am for the Parks, but I am sworn to obey the law. Congress definitely appropriated $900,000 to start that Reclamation project. Now suppose I, for some trivial reason, would have to find that it was infeasible—I am afraid it would have to be trivial—would I be performing my duty? Are you not asking me to usurp powers that clearly belong to Congress? Congress says, "We will let the Park in on this condition," and then says, "You must go ahead and build a Reclamation project as provided by law, reservation for which was made by Congress."

Now, if I do this, I will probably go to the guillotine, but if I do go to the guillotine, how many of you would go with me? I am willing to go if any good would be served, but would I stop this project? What are we going to do about it? I have to follow the law. I wish the baby had not been laid on my doorstep, but it is there.

Now what I can do, and none of you are helping me in this, is to bring pressure to bear on Congress to get concessions, to get Congress to enlarge this area and take in a section of the National Forest. I know there is no reason why it should not go in. The National Forest Association comes in here and asks me to do something that it knows I cannot do. We can get contributions if we insist on them and I will go to the point where I would be an annoyance to Senator Adams and the rest of the Colorado delegation in insisting that we get it in, but—taking this attitude won't get any of us anywhere. I can resign as Secretary of the Interior with a grand gesture. I could do this, but my successor would be confronted with the same problem and would have to do it. Now that is what I am up against. Pray for me.[1]

[13:OF 402:CT]

[1] Cf. *Ickes' Diary,* II, 248–249. (The date of this statement is derived from the *Diary* entry.)

726   ROOSEVELT TO MORRIS L. COOKE, Philadelphia

[WASHINGTON] *December 29, 1937*

DEAR MORRIS: I am inclined to think that a Conservation Congress would be a good thing for the autumn of 1938—and I would suggest that it be held prior and not subsequent to election—in other words, about October tenth or fifteenth.

In regard to who should call it, I am not quite clear—certainly not a private organization.

If any decision can be held up for a week or two, I shall be glad to talk with you about it when you next come down. Any time after January eighth is all right.[1]

My best wishes to you for the New Year.

Always sincerely,

[FRANKLIN D. ROOSEVELT]

[13:OF 177:CT]

[1] This was in reply to Cooke's letter of Dec. 27, 1937 (OF 177), to the effect that the American Academy of Political Science was contemplating the holding of a conservation conference late in 1938, the program to be devoted to outlining the measures necessary to stop "current depletions." Cooke referred to the proposal of the Mississippi Valley Committee in 1934 that a large-scale conservation congress be held in Washington, a proposal that was not pressed because some Government agencies did not favor it. He said that if the Administration had in mind the calling of a conference, he would persuade the Academy to delay an immediate announcement of its own plans.

727 ROOSEVELT TO JOHN H. BAKER, EXECUTIVE DIRECTOR,
NATIONAL ASSOCIATION OF AUDUBON SOCIETIES, New York City

[WASHINGTON] *December 31, 1937*

MY DEAR MR. BAKER: I have received your letter of December 8,
explaining the urgency of the great white heron situation in Florida Bay.[1]

Apparently, under the terms of the Antiquities Act the urgency cannot
be met by proclamation and, since we have no assurance that the proposed amendment to that Act can be consummated in time to serve this
particular purpose, I believe special legislation is required.

I am prepared, therefore, to approve an Act of Congress extending
the Fort Jefferson National Monument for the specific purpose of fa-
cilitating adequate, permanent protection of the great white herons and
other wildlife of that environment.

Work of the National Association of Audubon Societies in the wildlife
protection field is one of the worthy conservation enterprises in which I
am personally interested.

Very sincerely yours,

[FRANKLIN D. ROOSEVELT]

[13:OF 378:CT]

[1] Baker urged that either a national monument or a wildlife refuge be promptly
established (OF 378). His letter was sent to both Ickes and Wallace for preparation of reply. Wallace replied Dec. 27, 1937 (OF 378), that he had asked the Interior Department's approval of an executive order to create the Great White Heron
Refuge on Jan. 13, 1937, but that Interior had asked that this order be held in
abeyance until it could "study the matter more thoroughly with reference to the
inclusion of the area in the nearby Fort Jefferson National Monument." Wallace
said that the establishment of the refuge would give protection to the great white
heron, roseate spoonbill, American flamingo, and other birds, "some of which are
on the verge of extinction." Ickes replied Dec. 29, 1937 (OF 378), that the area
could not be included within the Fort Jefferson National Monument under the
Antiquities Act, and that he had therefore prepared legislation for immediate introduction for the extension of the Fort Jefferson National Monument. A national
monument would provide the best form of sanctuary because it would afford complete protection for all forms of life and for the environment as well. He enclosed
a draft of reply, the letter here printed.

The Act for the Preservation of American Antiquities, enacted in 1906, empowered
the President to set aside by proclamation public lands that contained "historic
landmarks, historic or prehistoric structures, and other objects of historic or scientific interest" (34 *Stat.* 225).

728 JOHN C. PAGE, COMMISSIONER, BUREAU OF RECLAMATION, TO
JAMES ROOSEVELT, SECRETARY TO THE PRESIDENT

WASHINGTON, *Dec. 31, 1937*

MEMORANDUM FOR COL. JAMES ROOSEVELT: This memorandum and
the attached data are written in an attempt to describe the CCC program now under way and proposed by the Bureau of Reclamation and

to reassure you and others that the operations conform to the principles governing CCC operations established by the President.

The CCC operations for the Bureau fall generally into two classes. First, the rehabilitation of the older irrigation systems and, second, assistance in the construction of new projects or new features supplementing facilities on old projects.

The original Reclamation law required the return of the Federal investment in irrigation projects in ten years, later extended to twenty years and now to forty years. Construction under the early law was done as cheaply as possible, expecting that when the investment was retired local funds could rebuild and replace the short-lived structures without hardship. Wooden headgates, culverts, bridges, etc. were installed instead of concrete and steel as is now the practice. With the repayment period extended to forty years the Federal investment is seriously jeopardized by the deterioration of the cheaper type of construction. A major CCC activity has been this replacement which is so essential to the Government because repayment by the water users does not transfer ownership or control of Reclamation projects from the Government. The end of the repayment period does not mark the end of an irrigation project. The irrigation systems are truly permanent assets of the state and of the nation and must be maintained in operating condition forever.

Federal reclamation was inaugurated only when the simpler, cheaper projects which were attractive to private investments had been largely developed. During the life of the Bureau the projects have become increasingly complex and expensive. Structure designs now contemplate a minimum maintenance cost over long periods and the construction is of as permanent a type as can be justified. Feasible projects by old standards are more difficult to find and CCC help in reservoir clearing, small dam and canal construction often makes the difference between a cost which can be repaid in forty years, the present criterion of feasibility, and one which cannot, thus forcing the abandonment of very worthy projects and preventing the proper conservation of the water resources. This type of work is a major CCC activity of the Bureau and one which was specifically approved by the President in the particular case of the Deschutes project in Oregon.

Many lesser but still very important activities include the control of rodents and noxious weeds on irrigation property, the improvement of recreational opportunities on project reservoirs so sorely needed in the desert areas, the emergency assistance to communities stricken by flood and drought, and others of similar benefit.

Because of the diversified work programs in pleasant healthful surroundings, the maximum benefits accrue to the boys themselves. The Bureau camps are universally commended for behavior and accomplishment.

To summarize, the Bureau camps with very rare exceptions work on property permanently owned and developed by the Government on tasks to protect and enhance the security of the Federal investment. In times of emergency some work has been done which has reduced the expense of water users organizations, but these instances are rare and are incidental to the major activities.

The consequences of a curtailment of the Bureau CCC program are so serious and I so earnestly feel that the program truly conforms to the intent of the CCC act that I hope no curtailment will be necessary. I am confident that there would be no danger if the program were fully understood and appreciated.

May I ask your concurrence in my recommendation that the activities of the CCC camps be continued in accordance with the attached memorandum, which summarizes in some detail the program we wish to follow? [1]

JOHN C. PAGE

[13:OF 268:TS]

[1] Policy regarding CCC work on reclamation projects was settled by a memorandum, Fechner to James Roosevelt, Jan. 31, 1938, approved by the President Feb. 5, 1938 (OF 268). This memorandum restricted CCC reclamation work to Federally owned lands except where through "adversity" local interests could not finance the program. An effort by Fechner to secure equal treatment for reclamation and drainage projects was, however, unsuccessful (James Roosevelt to Fechner, Feb. 19, 1938, OF 268). Congressmen from states where the CCC had been operating drainage projects (in May, 1938, there were thirty-nine such camps in twenty-two states), protested the proposed closing of the camps, and on April 15, 1938, Senator Ellender (La.) introduced a bill (S. 3851) to amend the CCC act to permit work in organized drainage and irrigation districts. This bill died in committee. The policy finally established was that the CCC could do drainage work only in connection with lands "in organized drainage or ditch districts or associations" (McIntyre to Rep. Lewis Boyer of Illinois, June 2, 1938, OF 268).

729   HENRY A. WALLACE, SECRETARY OF AGRICULTURE, TO ROOSEVELT

WASHINGTON, *January 5, 1938*

DEAR MR. PRESIDENT: I enclose the additional material about recent pulp and paper developments in the South, and the timber situation there, for which you asked on December 20. You may also want to consider the following highlights.

1. Except for Russia (which according to recent investigations will use all her own pulp for the next few decades), southeastern and northwestern United States, western Canada, and Alaska, there are no major reserve stands of softwood timber for pulp left in the world.

2. Pulp and paper developments in the South assume particular significance in view of this world-wide situation.

3. Added significance is given by the fact that world consumption of cellulose products from wood is estimated to have increased by some 3,400,000 tons in 1936 over 1935; that production of yellow pine for lumber (95% in the South) increased from about 3 billion ft. B. M. in 1932 to more than 7 billion ft. in 1936; that this increase may well be intensified by the need to meet the present housing shortage.

4. Pulp and paper developments in the South offer opportunities to establish firm foundations for a new and enduring prosperity there. But timber resources—both capital stock and growing stock—must be safeguarded for that and all other wood-using industries.

5. General approach to the forest situation in the South has been similar to past approaches in other regions—that forests are unlimited. This is not true.

6. There are indications of pulp and paper developments in the Piedmont territory (a rayon mill in North Carolina, a newsprint mill at Rome, Georgia, another at Lufkin, Texas) but most pulp and paper operations in the South are concentrating on the coastal plains. It is unsound to apply to this restricted area figures for forest growth and drain for the South as a whole.

7. Besides capital investments in wood utilizing industries, the situation involves employment of a large proportion of the southern population. It also affects associated agriculture.

8. The situation is serious. Protection of public interests is required. In this, we must face (a) extension of public ownership to certain key areas; (b) extension of public cooperation with private owners (protection from fire and diseases) including farmers; (c) public regulation, both to protect vital public interests and to assure protection to the private owner who wants to crop his forest on a sustained yield basis but now has no protection from unfair competition by those who continue forest exploitation.

You realize, I know, that the situation is involved, and that many figures from many sources can and may be used. I have, therefore, asked Mr. Silcox to stand by on January 7, in case you wish him to attend your conference.[1]

Sincerely,

H. A. WALLACE

[13:OF 1—C:TS]

[1] According to press reports, the principal purpose of the January 7 meeting was to persuade the southern governors to support the Administration program for minimum wages and hours. Referring to the meeting at his January 14 press conference, Roosevelt said, "There seemed to be a very favorable reaction to all the things we are working towards, including wages and hours and the saving of the forests" (President's Press Conferences).

WASHINGTON, *January 10, 1938*

[*Telegram*] Those concerned with planning for the conservation of
our resources in the Southeast have an opportunity to further sound
forestry practices in connection with the growing pulp industry. I wish
your conference success in the furtherance of broad scale planning and
conservation work.[1]

FRANKLIN D. ROOSEVELT

[13:OF 1092:CT]

[1] (Drafted by Frederic A. Delano, vice chairman of the National Resources Committee.)   The telegram refers to a conference of State Planning Boards and governors in Atlanta on Jan. 11–12, 1938, arranged by the National Resources Committee.   At a conference with the NRC Advisory Committee on Jan. 8, 1938, Roosevelt "expressed his interest and concern over the forestry practices developing in
the Southeast through the establishment of pulp mills" (Delano to James Roosevelt,
Jan. 10, 1938, OF 1092).

731   JEAN SHERWOOD HARPER TO MRS. ROOSEVELT

SWARTHMORE, PA., *January 10, 1938*

DEAR MRS. ROOSEVELT: Another emergency has just arisen in Okefinokee Swamp. We don't want to bother the President at a time like
the present, but something simply must be done at once, to stop the
Biological Survey in its insane destructiveness.

The Government acquired the Okefinokee for a wild-life refuge, and
the Chief of the Biological Survey has protested time and again that they
aim to preserve the "pristine quality" of the swamp.

Last year, however, they planted a lot of Asiatic chestnut trees in
various parts of the swamp. When we protested to the President, the
chestnut trees had to be grubbed out again, while the Survey renewed
its pledge about keeping the swamp primeval.

That pledge was evidently quite worthless. For we have just received
word of another and far greater project of insane vandalism—to cut
down all the big pine trees on Chesser's Island. This is one of the very
few islands in the swamp where the timber has remained largely untouched, and we and other naturalists have made very special efforts
to keep it so. We ourselves own 15 acres of those lovely piney woods on
Chesser's Island, and go there to enjoy them at every possible opportunity. We simply can't bear the idea of having the pines cut down all
around our tract. The scheme is so utterly senseless that it taxes the
imagination to understand the type of mind that could plan it.

Furthermore, we hear that the Government plans to build a paved highway right across Chesser's Island to its western edge. This alone would ruin the island for ourselves and our friends the Chessers. There is no conceivable use for such a road that would justify the expenditure of Government funds on it. It is not only quite needless, but its construction would be thoroughly detrimental to the wilderness value of the area. It looks like just another case of giving the CCC something to do, no matter how much destruction it involves. It is just as important to stop this road-building as to stop the timber-cutting.

The Biological Survey, as at present organized, is a thoroughly unfit guardian of our wilderness areas and wild life. And no CCC camp should be tolerated in a place like the Okefinokee.

May I implore you to do whatever you can to preserve natural conditions in the Okefinokee from this new and senseless attack? [1]

Sincerely yours,

JEAN SHERWOOD HARPER

[13:PPF 1091:TS]

[1] See *post,* 734.

732 MORRIS L. COOKE TO MARVIN H. MCINTYRE, SECRETARY TO THE PRESIDENT

[WASHINGTON] *January 13, 1938*

MEMORANDUM FOR MR. MCINTYRE: The American Academy of Political and Social Science have, after a year's consideration, tentatively decided that they are ready to go ahead with a two or three day conservation congress to be held in Florida next fall with the proceedings to be published early in 1939. The thought is to build a program around the whole cost of conservation. They will assume that the tragic need for it has been demonstrated and through the program they intend to build up what is necessary in order to win out—legally, financially, educationally, economically and socially.

The President has indicated his desire to have such a congress take place but he thinks it should be held under public auspices and has suggested the date as October 10–15, 1938.[1]

The suggestion for a conservation conference in the past has been negatived by the feeling on the part of some of the Departments that they might not get a break. As a preliminary committee, the President has suggested M. S. Eisenhower of Agriculture [2] and Beardsley Ruml,[3] who is to represent Interior and the National Resources Committee. There was a suggestion that these two talk with me and get the background and then decide what is feasible. Without having given it much thought, the President suggested a divided chairmanship of a pure scientist and somebody else not too closely identified with the scientific field.

[MORRIS L. COOKE]

[13:OF 177:CT]

[1] See *ante,* 726.
[2] Head of the information office of the Agriculture Department.
[3] At this time treasurer of R. H. Macy and Co.

733   PRESS CONFERENCE, Executive Offices of the White House, January 18, 1938, 4:30 P.M.

[*Excerpt*] The President: I don't think there is any news at this end.

Q: In your judgment have the difficulties of getting local cooperation on flood control reservoirs become so manifest as to justify a one hundred percent Federal financing?

The President: That is too general a question. I think you will have to come down to specific cases.

Q: Would you mind restating your flood control policy?

The President: That is too general a question. It would take several hours. I would have to make a speech on it. What are you driving at? What do you want to know?

Q: A bill was introduced this week modifying the 1936 Act so as to authorize full Federal financing of reservoirs.

The President: They are discussing that on the Hill at the present time. Congressman McCormack introduced the bill.[1] You see, it is much clearer and quicker to come to the point. Judge Whittington is considering it and it will be brought before his committee, the theory being this: That in the future Government policy will be to draw a line between those flood control works which hold back the water, such as a reservoir and dam, and contribute thereby to something that will produce future income, such as water power or reclamation or irrigation, those being income producing, and in those cases to change the Government policy so that the Government would own the land overflowed and the site of the reservoir, thereby having control of the water which would be gradually let out, either for power or irrigation, the Government thereby getting a return, there being no question about the right, title and interest of the Government to that water.

The other category would be the category of levees which do not return any dividends to the Government and which are merely to keep water from overflowing the land while it is in the process of going past a given point. In that case the community, being benefited without any possible return in the way of income, would continue under the present policy to pay a portion of the cost of the land that would be temporarily overflowed, spill basins and the land the levee goes on, things of that kind.

Now, that is all under discussion in Judge Whittington's committee, and I cannot give you the answer. They are discussing it. It seems a plausible and reasonable thing to do.

Q: What about a state that has to take care of the water from a number of other states above, such as Louisiana?

The President: Well, all the other states above have to take care of it too.

[13:PRESIDENT'S PRESS CONFERENCES:T]

[1] H. R. 8997, introduced Jan. 17, 1938, was referred to the House Committee on Flood Control, which took no action (*Cong. Rec.*, 75th Cong., 3d sess., 83:1, 677).

734   ROOSEVELT TO HENRY A. WALLACE, SECRETARY OF AGRICULTURE

[WASHINGTON] *January 19, 1938*

MEMORANDUM FOR THE SECRETARY OF AGRICULTURE: I am told that the Biological Survey is "at it again" in Okefinokee Swamp—and that this time they are about to cut down the big pine trees on Chesser's Island.

I hope the report is not true for, as you know, you and I have agreed that the Swamp is to be kept definitely in its untouched pristine condition.

Will you let me have a report. I do not want any trees cut down *anywhere* in the Swamp.

F. D. R.

MAL/TMB

[13:PPF 1091:CT]

735   HENRY A. WALLACE, SECRETARY OF AGRICULTURE, TO ROOSEVELT

WASHINGTON, *January 22, 1938*

DEAR MR. PRESIDENT: This Department acknowledges the receipt of your memorandum, dated January 19, 1938, which was written to ascertain the facts in a report that the Biological Survey is cutting down the big pine trees on Chesser's Island, Okefenokee Wildlife Refuge, Georgia.

With the exception of certain timber leases in effect at the time the Okefenokee Swamp was purchased by the United States and with which we cannot interfere, the Department has not authorized the cutting of

[169]

pines or other trees on any part of the entire refuge save a limited number of carefully selected dead or dying trees which prior to our acquisition had been killed by turpentining in the old-fashioned way. These trees were not taken from the swamp itself but from the higher lands of the refuge in the vicinity of Camp Cornelia where we propose to build our administrative headquarters of lumber sawed from these trees.

Development within the swamp itself is restricted to cleaning out some channels to facilitate water transportation to permit the necessary travel of officers charged with the responsibility of protecting the refuge's wildlife resources.

On January 12, 1938, letters from interested conservationists reporting the alleged cutting of pine trees on Chesser's Island and in the swamp, were received by the Biological Survey. A telegram immediately was dispatched to our Agent of the Okefenokee Refuge advising him to cease cutting any timber whatever, even away from the swamp, until we could get the facts in the case.

Dr. Ira N. Gabrielson, Chief, Bureau of Biological Survey, is making a personal inspection of the Okefenokee Refuge prior to February 1, 1938. If you so desire, he will be pleased to submit a report of his inspection findings to you and further, the Department will be glad to submit the proposed plans of the Okefenokee Wildlife Refuge to you for your personal approval.[1]

Respectfully,

H. A. WALLACE

[13:PPF 1091:TS]

[1] Answered *post,* 737.

736   ROOSEVELT TO REPRESENTATIVE J. MARK WILCOX OF FLORIDA

WASHINGTON, *January 22, 1938*

MY DEAR MR. WILCOX: I have received your letter of January 6 regarding the proposal of the Department of the Interior to extend the boundaries of Fort Jefferson National Monument to include two additional areas in the vicinity of Key West, Florida, for the purpose of affording greater protection for the great white heron.[1]

Secretary Ickes and I are concerned over the need of additional protection for the great white heron, an important but almost extinct species that occurs only in southern Florida. It was determined that the boundaries of Fort Jefferson National Monument could not be extended to accomplish this purpose under the terms of the Antiquities Act. For this reason, legislation is necessary to accomplish the desired extension of the monument.

The proposal to extend the boundaries of Fort Jefferson National Monument has my full approval. It is my hope that legislation may be enacted during the present session of the Congress to accomplish this purpose.

Very sincerely yours,

[FRANKLIN D. ROOSEVELT]

[13:OF 928:CT]

¹ Wilcox's letter was sent to the Interior Department for preparation of the reply here printed.

737   ROOSEVELT TO HENRY A. WALLACE, SECRETARY OF AGRICULTURE

WASHINGTON, *January 25, 1938*

MEMORANDUM FOR THE SECRETARY OF AGRICULTURE: Thank you for your letter of January twenty-second in regard to the preservation of Okefenokee Swamp. I shall be delighted to see the proposed plans for the Wildlife Refuge.

F. D. R.

[13:PPF 1091:CT]

738   ROOSEVELT TO HENRY A. WALLACE, SECRETARY OF AGRICULTURE

WASHINGTON, *January 27, 1938*

MEMORANDUM FOR THE SECRETARY OF AGRICULTURE: It seems to me that every consideration of an adequate conservation policy should include the land and water areas within the Aberdeen Proving Grounds, Edgewood Arsenal and Fort Hoyle as a migratory waterfowl sanctuary.¹

The fact that the canvasback duck and indeed other ducks have so diminished in numbers that we have had to prohibit all hunting of them and the fact that the Government is engaged in bringing back the numbers of migratory waterfowl to a point well above the danger of extinction lead me to believe that as a general policy of the government, all government owned or controlled areas should be closed to hunting where such closing would benefit the general policy.

Will you, therefore, please take up with the War Department the question of closing the above areas in Maryland.

F. D. R.

[13:OF 378:CT]

¹ This refers to Wallace's letter of Jan. 18, 1938 (OF 378). Roosevelt had referred to Wallace a joint resolution of the Maryland legislature, approved by the

[171]

governor on June 26, 1937, requesting the President to set aside as a waterfowl refuge the areas at the head of Chesapeake Bay included within the Aberdeen Proving Grounds, Edgewood Arsenal and Fort Hoyle. (The resolution is filed with Wallace's letter.) Wallace said that Susquehanna Flats, in the area, were probably the most important concentration place for migratory waterfowl, especially canvasback duck, on the eastern seaboard. He proposed that the Agriculture Department try to work out with the War Department a mutually acceptable conservation policy for military reservations.

739   ROOSEVELT TO HENRY A. WALLACE, SECRETARY OF AGRICULTURE

WASHINGTON, *January 27, 1938*

MEMORANDUM FOR THE SECRETARY OF AGRICULTURE: Would you prepare for me a comparatively short Message to the Congress, calling their attention to the general forestry situation in the country, with a separate section relating specifically to the danger in the Southern States?

It is my thought that this Message would act as a preliminary to a study by a joint committee of the Congress, looking to legislation next year.

I recognize the fact that outside of the method of purchasing land by the Federal Government (which takes too long and costs too much) the principal method of getting immediate action is by State legislation. Therefore, if the information is broken down by States, I could send a copy of my Message and a copy of the memorandum accompanying it to each Governor, with a request for study and the expression of hope that action would be taken by the State. I think such a Message could probably go up in the course of the next two or three weeks.[1]

F.D.R.

[13:OF 1–C:CT]

[1] Wallace replied Feb. 5, 1938 (OF 1–C), that material on the forestry situation, with a draft for a short message, would be sent within a week or ten days. See *post*, 758.

740   ROOSEVELT TO ANTHONY J. DIMOND, DELEGATE FROM ALASKA

WASHINGTON, *January 28, 1938*

MY DEAR MR. DIMOND: I am glad you found the report on *Alaska, Its Resources and Development*, a useful document.[1] Whatever disappointment you have felt concerning Part I of the report may perhaps be counterbalanced when you have had an opportunity to examine the second part. In the very limited time between passage of Concurrent Resolution No. 24 and the date of transmittal required in that resolution, the committee has secured quite a surprising amount of planning information and projects.

I share your interest in the proposed Pacific-Yukon Highway, but since the major part of the construction lies in Canada, it would hardly be appropriate for an official report of the United States Government to insist upon the immediate construction of a thousand miles of road in a neighboring country. Representations have already been made to the Canadian Government concerning the proposed highway.

Unfortunately your suggestions on this matter came too late for incorporation either in the report or in my message to the Congress.[2]

Very sincerely yours,

[FRANKLIN D. ROOSEVELT]

[13:OF 400:ALASKA:CT]

[1] Issued by the National Resources Committee as part 7 of *Regional Planning* (Washington, 1938).
[2] (Drafted by the National Resources Committee.) This letter is a reply to Dimond's letter of Jan. 18, 1938 (OF 400), in which he criticized the Alaska report because of its failure to emphasize the importance of the proposed U. S.-Alaska highway, and because of its emphasis on conservation: "The conservation policy carried to its extreme and entirely unreasonable limit would leave any land a wilderness, and would deny any use whatsoever, and would forbid all development."

741   ARNO B. CAMMERER, DIRECTOR, NATIONAL PARK SERVICE, TO HAROLD L. ICKES, SECRETARY OF THE INTERIOR

WASHINGTON, *February 3, 1938*

MEMORANDUM FOR THE SECRETARY: Your memorandum of January 26 inquiring whether anything has ever been done to bring in the Quetico National Forest as a national park has been received.

It is assumed you refer to the Superior National Forest in northern Minnesota adjacent to the Quetico Provincial Park of Canada. We have been interested in the preservation of this area for the past 12 years. In 1927 you wrote Mr. Mather from Chicago telling him of Mr. Ernest C. Oberholtzer's interest in the region and his efforts to protect it from encroachment by the water power interests. He has been an unfailing worker for the preservation of both the Superior area in the United States and the Quetico Park of Canada, and too much credit cannot be given to him. In 1930 Collaborator Harlan P. Kelsey inspected Isle Royale and the Superior National Forest, and in September 1937 we made an investigation of the Superior area, a report on which is now being prepared. While the area appears to warrant national park status, because it is probably the greatest water wilderness remaining in the United States, there are certain complications which make it inadvisable to advocate a national park at this time.

Public No. 539, 71st Congress, approved July 10, 1930, as you know, made it obligatory upon the Forest Service to conserve for recreational use the natural beauty of the lake shores of all of the lakes and streams within the areas which are now, or which eventually will be, in general use for boat or canoe travel, and prohibited logging within 200 to 400 feet of the lake shores.[1] It also required that no further alterations of the natural water level of any lake or stream within, or bordering upon, the designated area shall be authorized, except by specific act of the Congress.

In accordance with this legislation, Executive Order 6783 of June 30, 1934, set up the Quetico-Superior Committee, consisting of E. C. Oberholtzer, S. T. Tyng, C. S. Kelly, one person designated by the Secretary of Agriculture, and one person designated by the Secretary of the Interior. Because of our interest in the eventual national park status for the area, and also to advise on recreational matters, we have twice attempted to have a representative of this Service appointed to the Quetico-Superior Committee but each time a representative of the Office of Indian Affairs has been appointed.

The most pressing problem now is the preservation of the remaining stands of virgin timber. Much of the finest timber is located on the shores and islands of some of the largest and most beautiful lakes adjacent to the international boundary, and is in danger of being cut within the next few years. The primitive area in the Superior National Forest is comprised of 959,000 acres, of which the Government owns 598,000 acres, the State of Minnesota 118,000 acres, and private interests 243,000. The problem is so complicated by numerous interests that the injection of the national park question now would almost certainly wreck what has been accomplished. Mr. Oberholtzer has so advised us recently, and has also informed us that cutting is now in process in the Quetico Provincial Park of Canada and that he is trying to have this cutting stopped. The Superior National Forest and the Quetico Provincial Park of Canada are integral parts of a natural unit.

Accordingly, it is respectfully urged that you recommend to the President that the Quetico-Superior Committee, which expires on June 30, 1938, in accordance with the Executive Order of June 30, 1934, be extended for an additional four years and that this Department should not advocate a national park at present, but should lend all possible assistance toward the preservation of this great wilderness area.

ARNO B. CAMMERER

[13:OF 1119:TS]

[1] The Shipstead-Nolan Act "to promote the better protection and highest public use of lands of the United States and adjacent lands and waters in northern Minnesota for the production of forest products" (46 *Stat.* 1020).

PHILADELPHIA, *February 3, 1938*

MY DEAR MR. PRESIDENT: In reference to your suggestion that a Conservation Congress be held early in October, 1938, and under public auspices: [1]

Possibly a preliminary organizing committee about as follows would be a good substitute for the two-headed leadership mentioned in our talk:

1. William F. Durand, Stanford University, Chairman
2. Isaiah Bowman, President, Johns Hopkins University (Representing Pure and Applied Science)
3. Hugh Baker, President, Mass. Agricultural College or Clarence A. Dykstra, President, University of Wisconsin (Representing Education in Agriculture)
4. General Robert E. Wood (Representing business)
5. Someone having no official position in the Administration but with knowledge of the Government conservation activities—past and present—and without interdepartmental bias.

We used Dr. Durand both for the World Power Congress and the Upstream Engineering Conference with entire satisfaction to everybody. The suggested group is well distributed geographically. My preference would be for Dykstra except that I have no reason to believe he is as much interested in conservation as Hugh Baker.

After your small interdepartmental committee has cleared the way by assuring reasonable co-operation on the part of Federal agencies you could ask the five mentioned above to the White House and at this conference ask them to proceed with the organization of the Congress. You may not think it necessary even to have such a preliminary conference. If you would prefer to write a letter and so avoid this, and you request it, I shall be glad to suggest a tentative draft. This committee would in due course be superseded by a large General Committee under whose auspices the Congress would be held. If I can help further, please let me know.

Yours very sincerely,

MORRIS L. COOKE

[13:PPF 940:TS]

[1] *Ante,* 726.

743   ROOSEVELT TO MORRIS L. COOKE, Philadelphia

[WASHINGTON] *February 12, 1938*

DEAR MORRIS: I have talked about the proposal for a Conservation Congress this Autumn but, frankly, I find much opposition and little sympathy for the idea.

The principal factor is the Reorganization Bill. When and if that passes there should be a period of at least a year before any general airing of views is held. For example, if one were held this coming October it would create a beautiful platform for Pinchot and other wild men, just prior to election.

I know you will understand.

As ever yours,

[FRANKLIN D. ROOSEVELT]

[13:PPF 940:CT]

744 ROOSEVELT TO HENRY A. WALLACE, SECRETARY OF AGRICULTURE

WASHINGTON, *February 12, 1938*

MEMORANDUM FOR THE SECRETARY OF AGRICULTURE: Would you be good enough to let me have a brief report on the Superior National Forest and its timber situation? [1]

F. D. R.

[13:OF 1119:CT]

[1] Acting Secretary of Agriculture Wilson replied Feb. 26, 1938 (OF 1119), with a 4000-word report. He emphasized the need of the Midwest for the timber and ore resources of the region and noted that the Quetico-Superior Committee had assisted in developing, and had approved, a forest management policy for the Superior National Forest. This policy barred all roads, commercial enterprises, summer homes and other special uses, and provided for definition of legal controls over cutting and water levels, and for "definite standards for trails, portages, administrative and protective structures, etc."

745 PROCLAMATION OF NATIONAL WILD LIFE WEEK

[WASHINGTON, *February 15, 1938*]

Whereas one of the most important phases of the conservation of our natural resources is the protection and preservation of our wild life; and

Whereas this is a work in which virtually our entire citizenship can participate wholeheartedly and enthusiastically, whether resident in the large metropolitan centers, with limited access to the great out-doors, or permitted to enjoy at first hand the wonders of nature; and

Whereas the carrying into effect of any program for the conservation of our hereditary wild life—in the past seriously diminished and depleted by destructive exploitation and lack of proper understanding and sympathy—must enlist the support of all of our citizens if the mistakes of the past are to be avoided in the future in dealing with this important resource of incalculable social, economic, esthetic, and recreational value:

Now, Therefore, I, Franklin D. Roosevelt, President of the United

States of America, do hereby proclaim and designate the week beginning March 20, 1938, as National Wild Life Week and do earnestly appeal to all of our citizens first to recognize the importance of the problem of conservation of these assets in wild life, and then to work with one accord for their proper protection and preservation. To this end I call upon all citizens in every community to give thought during this period to the needs of the denizens of field, forest, and water and intelligent consideration of the best means for translating good intentions into practical action in behalf of these invaluable but inarticulate friends. Only through the full cooperation of all can wild life be restored for the present generation and perpetuated for posterity.

In Witness Whereof, I have hereunto set my hand and caused the seal of the United States to be affixed.

Done at the City of Washington this 14th day of February, in the year of our Lord nineteen hundred and thirty-eight, and of the Independence of the United States of America the one hundred and sixty-second.[1]

FRANKLIN D. ROOSEVELT

SEAL   By the President:
CORDELL HULL, Secretary of State

[W. H. PRESS RELEASES: M]

[1] Apparently drafted by either Hassett or Early from information supplied in a letter of Carl D. Shoemaker, secretary of the Senate Special Committee on Conservation of Wildlife Resources, to Hassett, Jan. 13, 1938 (OF 378). Attorney General Cummings, in reviewing a draft of the proclamation, changed the original title of "National Wild Life Restoration Week" to "National Wild Life Week" because, he said, "the proclamation deals with the broad subject of conservation of wild life rather than mere restoration" (Cummings to Roosevelt, Feb. 10, 1938, OF 378).

746   ROOSEVELT TO REPRESENTATIVE JOHN LUECKE OF MICHIGAN

[WASHINGTON] *February 15, 1938*

MY DEAR MR. LUECKE: Your memorandum of February first concerning the Great Lakes cut-over area[1] raises many interesting questions which I am referring to the National Resources Committee. As you say, the problems involved have been subjected to study by several Federal agencies and much effort has been put in by State agencies seeking appropriate solutions. Several state institutions in Michigan, Wisconsin, and Minnesota have been or could be interested. We should find a way to bring them all together.

This is a good example of the need for regional planning which I outlined in my message to the Congress last June. The National Resources Committee has made some progress in similar cases, in the valley of the Red River of the North, and with the States of Colorado, New

Mexico, and Texas on the Upper Rio Grande. At my suggestion the Committee has recently secured the cooperation of a group of southern States on a study of the Pine and Pulp Resources of that area with a view to furthering sound conservation practices.

I am sure that you will find all the agencies of the Government interested in developing cooperation among the Lake States on an economic survey of the cut-over areas.[2]

Very sincerely yours,

[FRANKLIN D. ROOSEVELT]

[13:OF 834:CT]

[1] A five-page typescript, "Economic Survey Great Lakes Cut-Over Area of Northern Michigan," enclosed in Luecke to Roosevelt, Feb. 1, 1938 (OF 834), describing the exhaustion of the forest and mineral resources of Upper Michigan and the need for reforestation and development of water power. Luecke urged the creation of a "Northern Michigan Authority" to study the development of the remaining resources.

[2] Drafted by the National Resources Committee.

747   DANIEL W. BELL, ACTING DIRECTOR, BUREAU OF THE BUDGET, TO ROOSEVELT

WASHINGTON, *Feb. 16, 1938*

MEMORANDUM FOR THE PRESIDENT: The Administrative Assistant to the Secretary of the Interior has referred to this office the attached draft of legislation to provide for the establishment of the Green Mountain National Park in the State of Vermont and the proposed letter of transmittal from the Secretary of the Interior to the Speaker of the House of Representatives.[1] This letter contains a brief statement of the provisions of the proposed legislation, and a considerable amount of information in support of the establishment of the park.

A hearing on this legislation has been held in this office but it was not developed that this area is superior in scenic beauty or natural wonders to many areas in New England, and, thus, the question naturally arises if we agree to the establishment of this park, will we not shortly be requested to concur in the establishment of national parks in several if not all of the New England States.

The proposed legislation provides that the land required for the park shall be acquired by donation or from donated funds, but it must also be borne in mind that a considerable sum for administrative expenses will become an annual charge on the Treasury. Furthermore, the proposal contemplates a parkway 50 miles long and the cost of constructing a road of this length is estimated at $3,000,000.

Since this matter has been pending in this office, I have received the attached copy of a letter from Mr. Delano regarding it, and I am advised that on March 9, 1937 Secretary McIntyre wrote a letter to Dr. Guy

W. Bailey, President of the University of Vermont, which concluded with the following paragraph:

I understand that if Governor Aiken will write to Secretary Ickes, advising that the State of Vermont will agree to acquire the necessary lands for donation to the United States, the President will authorize submission to the Congress of a draft of legislation to accept the lands for the proposed Green Mountain National Park.

In view of the present state of the Government's finances, I hesitate to recommend approval of this legislation, but I would be less opposed to the enactment of it if the authorization for the parkway were eliminated. This could be done by striking out the words "including an adjoining right-of-way for parkway development purposes" in lines 5 and 6 of the draft of legislation, and thus the Government would be relieved of responsibility for the construction of the parkway, including the road, and for its maintenance. This proposed parkway, except for touching the proposed park at several widely separated points, is not a necessarily integral part of the proposed park, and is separated from it for most of its length by wide areas of cultivated private land that would not under any circumstances be contemplated for inclusion within the boundaries of the park.

Since Mr. Delano's and Mr. McIntyre's letters indicate that this proposal has already received your attention, I shall await your instructions.

D. W. BELL

[13:OF 6–P:TS]

[1] These enclosures were returned to Bell with Roosevelt's reply of Feb. 24, 1938, *post*, 749.

748 HARCOURT A. MORGAN, VICE CHAIRMAN, BOARD OF DIRECTORS, TENNESSEE VALLEY AUTHORITY, TO ROOSEVELT

KNOXVILLE, TENNESSEE, *February 18, 1938*

DEAR MR. PRESIDENT: The Tennessee Valley Authority has been informed of the probability of a considerable reduction in the number of Civilian Conservation Corps camps. This is of particular importance to the Authority because of the integral place which the corps has earned in the broad program for soil and water control in this area.

You have taken leadership in calling attention to the importance of control of water upon the land and its place in the ultimate control of flood waters in the rivers and in the conservation of a basic natural resource, the land. We feel that, in view of the proposed curtailment, we should bring to your attention our conviction that these camps are vitally important in the Authority's long range program. The CCC camps furnish virtually the only means of supplementing the land owner's efforts in dealing with those badly eroded lands which are a public menace and a public responsibility, and the control of which is beyond the means and ability of the average farmer.

There are now 19 CCC camps engaged in erosion control work in the Valley-wide program, either in reforestation or in "up-stream engineering" such as the building of check dams, the construction of diversion ditches and terrace outlets, and the creation of small retention reservoirs on headwaters. This work is a vital link between the major engineering projects on the Tennessee River and its tributaries and the land owner whose conservation activities are limited for both economic and technical reasons.

In many areas in the Tennessee Valley the erosion problem is acute, threatening not only the destruction of the land but the silting of reservoirs. This work may thus be regarded as insurance in some measure for the investment which the government is making in its engineering projects on the river. We feel that these camps are demonstrating effectively the place and importance of the CCC in an integrated river control program.

Surveys throughout the Valley have shown that there is a need for from thirty to sixty months work in areas in which camps are now established. In some areas work which was started has had to be dropped because of discontinuance of camps.

At one time, the Authority had a total of 38 camps engaged in this soil erosion work in the Valley area. This has now been reduced to nineteen camps. We feel that the need is urgent for at least twenty-five CCC camps.

Further reduction of our erosion control camps at this time would make it impossible to continue much of the Authority's cooperative program of upstream engineering.[1]

Respectfully yours,

HARCOURT A. MORGAN

[13:OF 42:TS]

[1] Answered *post,* 756.

---

749   ROOSEVELT TO DANIEL W. BELL, ACTING DIRECTOR, BUREAU OF THE BUDGET

WASHINGTON, *February 24, 1938*

MEMORANDUM FOR THE DIRECTOR, BUREAU OF THE BUDGET: As I understand it this legislation will cost the Government no money for several years.[1]

It is desirable legislation because:

(a) There is no national park in New England except Mount Desert, which should be called a monument rather than a park, because it is used by very few people each year and benefits principally the rich summer residents. It is logical to select the Green Mountains for a national park because today they are rather inaccessible but contain wonderful scenery and forests. This does not mean another national park in the White Mountains—the only other suitable locality—because the White Mountains are already highly developed for tourists, and the price of land is high.

(b) The matter of the parkway fits in definitely with the proposed national parkway starting at the Canada line and running down through the Green Mountains and the Berkshires, across the Hudson at Bear Mountain Park and thence following the Blue Ridge through northern New Jersey, Pennsylvania and Maryland to the Skyline Drive, just south of Washington; thence along the Skyline Parkway to a point east of the Great Smoky Park, thence south to the end of the Appalachian system at Stone Mountain, Georgia.

(c) The proposed parkway in Vermont lies most of the way outside the park, but this is necessary in order to get the view of the mountains and of Lake Champlain, and to run the parkway through the park itself would be physically difficult and costly.

For all these reasons I am inclined to favor the whole proposal.

F. D. R.

[*Notation*:T] Memo from Mr. Bell, Budget, 2/16/38 for the President (copy retained in files), copy of letter from F. A. Delano, 12/21/37 to Victor M. Cutter, National Resources Committee, Boston, copy of letter from Acting Secretary of the Interior to Speaker of the House of Representatives (no date), and a copy of a Bill to provide for the establishment of the Green Mountain National Park in the State of Vermont, and for other purposes. Also accompanying memo are two maps showing proposed national park or national monument area in Vermont, and proposed national park in Vermont.

[13:OF 6–P:CT]

¹ See *ante,* 747.

750   IRVING BRANT, EDITOR OF EDITORIAL PAGE, ST. LOUIS *Star-Times,* TO ROOSEVELT

[ST. LOUIS] February 25, 1938

DEAR MR. PRESIDENT: Here is some information I thought you might like to have before your talk with Congressman Wallgren;¹ also three small maps:²

No. 1. Boundaries of Mt. Olympus National Park as agreed to at meeting of Park Service, Forest Service, Wallgren, Smith, two weeks ago.

No. 2. Boundaries Wallgren suggested yesterday, after getting protests from Port Angeles. (You will get these two maps on larger scale at meeting.)

No. 3. A suggestion I offered to meet Port Angeles objections, if it seems necessary to make concessions.

At the meeting held to draw boundaries, at your direction, there was no conflict between the Park and Forest Services. Silcox supported a good park. Wallgren retreated before Congressman Smith right from the start, though why he should choose Smith to retreat from is beyond me. Wallgren said he wanted a park satisfactory to Smith, who is against any park. Cammerer, Silcox and I kept Wallgren from cutting the park way down, to meet Smith's views, and the upshot was that only one important region was cut out, on the lower Queets river.

This was taken out as an [sic] incident to the exclusion of some heavily timbered ridges between the Queets river and Lake Quinault, desired by Gray's Harbor for the pulp industry. I think it is advisable to leave these ridges out, to reduce Smith's opposition, but the Queets area (I am advised by Irving Clark of Seattle) contains some fine scenic stands of timber that ought to be in the park, and it is also needed to protect the winter feeding grounds of the Olympic elk. Cammerer does not seem to see the value of this tract. He judges it by the shape of the map, but he would take a strong stand for it if he thought you wanted it in. Wallgren also would agree to it if you asked for it. Cammerer has emphasized your desire to protect the courses of the rivers, so you could naturally urge it on that grounds. This area on the Queets is in the national forest, and can be lumbered by destructive methods only. It is marked B on Map No. 3.

In the last few days a new complication has arisen. Chris Morgenroth of Port Angeles, Washington, a good friend of the park, a well-informed and thoroughly honest man, has come to Washington with a Port Angeles protest against the two corridors to the sea. He says that owing to past misrepresentations by the Forest Service, news of inclusion of these corridors in the park created a panic among the owners of land in them. They have been told that creation of a park would take away their property rights, cause loss of school taxes, etc. Morgenroth says that this could be offset by a clear statement about protection of private and county rights on private land within a park. More important than this, the Port Angeles pulp mills fear that establishment of these corridors will lead to government purchase of bottom lands on which they own spruce needed to whiten and toughen the writing paper they produce. And they also fear the isolation of timber in an "island" between the two corridors.

I think there is some merit to the pulp mill position. It could be met in two ways. First, by a statement that the right to lumber on private lands in the park is fully protected by law, and that it is recognized that the method of lumbering for pulpwood is not destructive. This would reduce the new opposition, but still would leave the fear that future spruce supplies would be cut off by government purchase of the lands within the corridors.

The second method is outlined in Map No. 3. It is to leave the lower Bogachiel river out of the park, but to retain the Hoh corridor. This would eliminate the timber "island," greatly reduce private holdings in the park, give Port Angeles mills a permanent supply of spruce, and still maintain a continuous park from mountain top to ocean.

You will notice that Maps 2 and 3 both contain much more ocean frontage than No. 1. This was added, in the first place, to offset the effect of eliminating the corridors; but also, Morgenroth said that the ocean front to the north, with Lake Ozette, was far more attractive than that to the south, and that the land could be bought for $10 an acre.

Wallgren was ready to eliminate the ocean front altogether. In fact, he would eliminate anything. But he says he is determined to get the bill passed. What he needs is a good stiff push from you.

There is also need for a public statement to clear up fears and rumors in Washington state (where general sentiment for the park is stronger than ever). It should include a statement about protection of private rights, tax revenues, etc., and a statement that both the Forest Service and Park Service are for the park. Also, it would be very valuable if you would say publicly what you did to me, that you were against all cutting by private contractors in the national forests. (Silcox is against that too.) Such a statement—the last two in fact—would take the heart out of the opposition.

Sincerely,

IRVING BRANT

[13:OF 6-P:TS]

[1] The meeting was suggested by Roosevelt (Wallgren to Roosevelt, Feb. 1, 1938, OF 6-P). On February 8 he conferred with Senators Bone and Schwellenbach and Representatives Wallgren and Smith of the Washington delegation (PPF 1-O).
[2] The maps are from a pamphlet published by the Emergency Conservation Committee, 734 Lexington Ave., New York, headed by Rosalie Edge.

751   ERNEST C. OBERHOLTZER, EXECUTIVE SECRETARY, QUETICO-SUPERIOR COMMITTEE, TO ROOSEVELT

[MINNEAPOLIS] *Feb. 25, 1938*

MY DEAR MR. PRESIDENT: The Quetico-Superior Committee was created by Executive Order of June 30, 1934, to study and make recommendations for the preservation of an international wilderness sanctuary in the border lakeland of Minnesota and Ontario.

To that end the Committee submits its accompanying Report [1] and recommends:

1. Federal acquisition of the remainder of the area lying within the United States.

2. Negotiation of a treaty with the Dominion of Canada, agreeing:

(1) To keep all lakes and streams, with their islands, rapids, waterfalls, beaches, wooded shores, and other natural features undisturbed in a state of nature;

(2) To administer the forests under modern forestry practices for a sustained yield;

(3) To manage all game, fish, and fur-bearing animals for maximum natural production; and

(4) To set up an advisory board or committee made up of biological, forestry and park officials from both countries to help coordinate practices under the principles agreed upon in the treaty.

The Committee believes that the early execution of these recommendations is desirable in order to forestall the vesting of adverse private interests and ensure permanent conservation of the area as a natural recreational resource.

Respectfully yours,

ERNEST C. OBERHOLTZER

[13:OF 1119:CTS]

[1] *Report to the President of the United States on the Quetico-Superior Area by the Quetico-Superior Committee* (1938). This is an illustrated pamphlet, this copy bearing the autograph signatures of the committee members. The place of publication is not given.

752   ROOSEVELT TO NORTH DAKOTA STATE PLANNING BOARD, Bismarck

WASHINGTON, *March 2, 1938*

GENTLEMEN: Your letter of February 11, 1938,[1] directs attention to water conservation problems which are acute in many sections of the Great Plains. Obviously, it is essential that the expenditures for relief in areas of drought should be utilized insofar as practicable for the permanent rehabilitation of those areas.

The Great Plains Committee last year pointed out the need for preservation of the soil and water resources of the Great Plains, and the general lines of action required to bring about their most effective use. A more specific program of action now is necessary. Many Federal as well as state agencies are concerned, and readjustments of administrative procedures and national policies may be involved.

I am requesting the National Resources Committee, therefore, to make a special review of the land and water conservation problems in the Northern Great Plains, to give attention to your suggestions for improvement of conditions there, and to advise me on those specific changes in Federal procedure and policy affecting land and water conservation which might be carried out promptly in order to promote the rehabilitation of the area. The Committee will act as a coordinating agency for Federal agencies, and it will consult with the interested state agencies.[2]

Sincerely yours,

[FRANKLIN D. ROOSEVELT]

[13:OF 1092:CT]

[1] Not present; presumably referred to the National Resources Committee, the drafter of this letter.

[2] The National Resources Committee created the Northern Great Plains Committee, made up of representatives of the Federal departments and the states concerned, with Harlan H. Barrows of the University of Chicago as chairman. For the accomplishments of the committee, see the National Resources Committee's *Progress Report, 1939* (Washington, 1939).

753   BENJAMIN V. COHEN, GENERAL COUNSEL, NATIONAL POWER POLICY COMMITTEE, TO MARGUERITE A. LEHAND, PRIVATE SECRETARY TO THE PRESIDENT

WASHINGTON, *March 2, 1938*

DEAR MISS LEHAND: The attached bill [1] is about to be reported out by the House Rivers and Harbors Committee, as a substitute for the original Regional Conservation bill introduced by Judge Mansfield. The substitute is a pretty weak, mealy-mouthed sort of bill which does little more than set up a National Resources Board with more limited powers than those provided by the Byrnes Reorganization bill.[2]

My guess is that the present National Resources Board and the Brownlow Committee would much prefer the set-up in the Byrnes Reorganization bill to that provided in the Mansfield substitute. On the other hand, it might be desirable to let the Mansfield bill be reported out so that if Senator Norris gets his bill through the Senate something could be worked out in conference. But Senator Norris does not seem optimistic as to the chances of getting his bill through the Senate this session. Senator Smith's [3] absence makes it difficult, if not impossible, for him to secure a meeting of the Senate Committee on Agriculture to report out his bill. Senator Norris seems to think it would be just as well if the Mansfield bill were kept in the House Committee for the present.

I spoke to Sam Rayburn who said he would suggest to Judge Mansfield that he hold the bill in committee for a few days, and Judge Mansfield has agreed to hold the bill until Friday.

I should be grateful if you would advise me of the President's wishes.[4]
Yours sincerely,

BEN V. COHEN

[13:OF 834:TS]

[1] H. R. 10027, "to provide for the regional conservation and development of the national resources." In its statement of policy, the bill covered the development of navigation, flood control, pollution abatement, and the conservation of the water, soil, mineral and forest resources of the nation. A national resources board was provided for, with eight members appointed by the President, one by the Secretary of Agriculture, one by the Secretary of the Interior, and one by the Secretary of War. Seven conservation planning regions were set up, each with a regional conservation planning committee; the chairman of each regional committee was a member of the national resources board. The proposed board was purely a planning and advisory agency and possessed no authority to require coordination of governmental conservation planning activities. Introduced by Representative Mansfield (Texas) on March 25, 1938, the bill was reported from the House Committee on Rivers and Harbors on March 29 and referred to the Committee of the Whole House (*Cong. Rec.*, 75th Cong., 3d sess., 83:4, 4180, 4339). No further action was taken. A copy of the bill is with the letter here printed.

[2] S. 2970, introduced Aug. 16, 1937, was not acted upon during the session. Brought up again March 31, 1938, it was indefinitely postponed (*Cong. Rec.*, 75th Cong., 1st sess., 81:8, 8939, 9327; 3d sess., 83:4, 4437).

[3] Senator Ellison D. Smith (S. C.) was chairman of the Senate Committee on Agriculture and Forestry.

[4] An attached referral sheet, LeHand to Benjamin V. Cohen of the National Power Policy Committee, March 8, 1938, reads: "President's memorandum to Miss LeHand asking that she tell Ben Cohen that he thinks it is probably better strategy to have Judge Mansfield get his bill reported out in a few days. It gives us something to work on."

754   ROOSEVELT TO HENRY MORGENTHAU, JR., SECRETARY OF THE
       TREASURY

WASHINGTON, *March 8, 1938*

MEMORANDUM FOR THE SECRETARY OF THE TREASURY: Will you speak to me about this?

F. D. R.

[13:OF 1092:CT]

755   [*Enclosure*] FREDERIC A. DELANO, CHAIRMAN, ADVISORY
       COMMITTEE TO THE NATIONAL RESOURCES COMMITTEE, TO
       ROOSEVELT

WASHINGTON, *March 8, 1938*

Confidential

MEMORANDUM FOR THE PRESIDENT: Mr. Abel Wolman, who was with Doctor Parran of the Public Health Service at a recent conference with you in regard to pollution,[1] has reported the very interesting suggestion you have made in regard to a Public Works revolving fund which might be used as a loan fund advanced to the States and other local governmental units under contracts for repayment to the Federal Government over a term of fifty years. This, it appears to me, is an exceedingly interesting suggestion and in no way inconsistent with views which the Resources Committee has expressed in dealing with flood control, reclamation and other important Federal projects including, of course, water power development, pollution abatement and road construction. As I write, there are no members of the Advisory Committee available to discuss this project, but in order promptly to report on the message relayed to me by Mr. Wolman, I assure you that I see nothing in this plan which would violate the principles which we have worked upon and advocated. I will take the matter up with my colleagues immediately with a view to preparing a confidential memorandum for you on this subject, if you desire it.

I am also informed that Mr. Wolman spoke to you of the memorandum his Committee had prepared in regard to the New England Compacts and the proposed McCormack amendments to the Flood-control Act of 1936.[2] As Mr. Wolman told you, a report covering some six closely knitted pages has been submitted on this subject, but it has not been studied by the Advisory Committee nor transmitted to the general Committee. While we regard the opinions of the Water Committee on the question of the New England Compacts and the McCormack Amendment as entirely sound, I would like to have them pretty carefully considered by the Advisory Committee, and perhaps the full Committee, before transmitting them to you. Of course, if you desire the Wolman memorandum, even though not cleared by our Committee, I will send it over at once. Undoubtedly the suggestions that you have made in regard to loans to State and local governments in carrying out public works projects could be applied perfectly well to the New England problem.

Respectfully submitted,

FREDERIC A. DELANO

Approved: HAROLD L. ICKES, Chairman, Mar. 8, 1938.

[13:PPF 1820:TS]

[1] On March 7, 1938 (PPF 1–O).
[2] Representative McCormack (Mass.) introduced H. R. 8997 on Jan. 17, 1938. This would have amended the 1936 Flood Control Act by requiring that the Federal Government bear the whole cost of dams and reservoirs. It was not reported from committee (*Cong. Rec.*, 75th Cong., 3d sess., 83: 1, 677).

[187]

ROOSEVELT TO HARCOURT A. MORGAN, VICE CHAIRMAN, BOARD OF DIRECTORS, TENNESSEE VALLEY AUTHORITY, Knoxville

[WASHINGTON] *March 9, 1938*

MY DEAR VICE CHAIRMAN MORGAN: Following receipt of your letter of February eighteenth, I called on the Director of the Civilian Conservation Corps to submit information regarding the work of the Civilian Conservation Corps on the area controlled by the Tennessee Valley Authority.

I am informed that Civilian Conservation Corps camps have been assigned to TVA territory since the fall of 1933. At that time twenty-five camps were assigned directly to the Tennessee Valley Authority area. I am informed that in addition to these twenty-five camps, there were an undetermined number of other camps working under the supervision of the United States Forest Service and the National Park Service whose work was of value in the general development and protection of the area.

During 1934 and 1935 when the original Civilian Conservation Corps was expanded, the number of camps engaged on TVA area was increased in proportion to the general increase in the size of the Corps. When it became necessary to curtail the size and activities of the Corps, I am informed that a proportional reduction was made in the number of these camps. At the present time the size of the Corps is somewhat smaller than it was in the winter of 1933, at which time twenty-five camps were assigned to the Authority area.

In view of your statement that nineteen camps are still in operation on the area, it does not seem to me that the interests of the Authority have been neglected. Unfortunately, a further reduction in the number of operating camps will have to be made this spring, in which case I am informed by the Director of the Corps the present number of camps operating on the Authority area will have to be still further reduced. It is regretted that this necessity arises, but it cannot be avoided.

I am informed that there are still a number of camps operating under the United States Forest Service and the National Park Service whose work is of considerable value to the Tennessee Valley Authority area, although it is not credited directly to the Authority.

I am assured by the Director that he will continue to give fair consideration to the needs of 'the Tennessee Valley Authority in assigning CCC camps.[1]

Very sincerely yours,

[FRANKLIN D. ROOSEVELT]

[13:OF 42:CT]

[1] Drafted by the Civilian Conservation Corps.

THE WHITE HOUSE, *March 10, 1938*

TO THE CONGRESS OF THE UNITED STATES:[1] In accordance with my message of August 13, 1937 (in returning without my approval Senate Joint Resolution 57), I am presenting herewith for your consideration a comprehensive national plan for the conservation and development of our water resources.

This report on Drainage Basin Problems and Programs has been prepared by the National Resources Committee in consultation with other Federal Agencies.[2]   It suggests policies, investigations, and construction necessary to carry forward a broad national program for water conservation and utilization.[3]

It is based upon the findings of 45 joint State-Federal basin committees, composed of more than 500 local, State, and Federal officials. These drainage basin committees have met in the field and have drafted plans for their local areas.   Arrangements have been made to publish the detailed reports on individual drainage basins at a later date.

The proposals in the report provide a guide for authorizations of surveys and construction of irrigation, flood-control, navigation, rural water supply, wildlife conservation, beach erosion control, hydroelectric power, and other water projects.   Because it was necessary to confine the program to projects that are primarily for water control and use, many related land-use projects are not included.   Land policy has significant water implications but it pertains to a large sphere of activities requiring separate though related treatment.

The preferred water projects have met the test of conformity to a general regional program, and, although they are set forth in terms of a six-year program, they are susceptible to completion during either a shorter or longer period, as fiscal policy may dictate.   The total cost of the recommended work at both Federal and non-Federal levels is about equal to the average annual expenditures for these purposes during recent years.   The six-year program suggested in the report should be read in the light of budgetary requirements and must, of course, be adjusted each year to correspond with budget recommendations and with action by the Congress.

Our knowledge of the Nation's water resources and our ideas on their best use and control change rapidly in the light of new investigations and of dynamic economic conditions.   Water plans should be flexible. The history of flood-control plans for the alluvial valley of the Mississippi River affords many examples of plans, once considered comprehensive, which soon were replaced by others.   Water plans should be revised annually.

Changing public interest, first in navigation, then in irrigation, and then in flood-control, water power or pollution, has produced a collection of unrelated water policies.   The recommendations in this report define in broad strokes an *integrated* water policy for the country as a whole. Such a Federal water policy is needed.

Notwithstanding the small amount of time available for the revision of earlier Federal programs, the planning mechanism which was developed for this report seems to have given gratifying results.   Starting with local and State groups, organized through the regional offices of the National Resources Committee, plans and programs have been prepared in the field and reviewed in Washington.   The process has not interfered with the normal and established duties of the agencies charged by the Congress with construction and surveys of water conservation projects.   Rather it has promoted cooperation both among such agencies in Washington and with State and local interests as well.

I recommend careful study of these documents by the Congress because they present a frame of reference for legislative programs affecting water conservation, and because they illustrate an approach to the systematic husbandry of our natural resources on a democratic, regional basis.[4]

[FRANKLIN D. ROOSEVELT]

[W. H. PRESS RELEASES : M]

[1] The text here printed is that of the White House press release.   Other texts (Speech File) are: (1) a draft by Ickes, sent by him to Roosevelt with a letter of Feb. 14, 1938, enclosing the drainage basin report; (2) a redraft of the first two paragraphs of the Ickes draft by Chairman McNinch of the Federal Communications Commission, enclosed in his letter to Roosevelt of Feb. 16, 1938; (3) a draft by Ickes incorporating McNinch's revisions, enclosed in Ickes' letter to James Roosevelt of Feb. 21, 1938.   The text of the last draft is that of the message as sent to the Congress (and as here printed).

[2] *Drainage Basin Problems and Programs: 1937 Revision* (Washington, 1937).

[3] In Ickes' first draft this sentence reads: "This report on Drainage Basin Problems and Programs has been prepared by all of the many Federal agencies concerned, and represents their joint views on the policies, investigations, and construction necessary . . ." McNinch suggested this revision because he objected to the assertion that all the agencies consulted were in accord with all parts of the report.   He also added the phrase, "for your consideration," in the first sentence.

[4] The message was read in the Senate March 10, 1938, and referred to the Commerce Committee.   Read in the House on the same day, it was referred to the Committee on Rivers and Harbors (*Cong. Rec.*, 75th Cong., 3d sess., 83: 3, 3149–3150, 3180–3181).

758   ROOSEVELT TO THE CONGRESS

THE WHITE HOUSE, *March 14, 1938*

TO THE CONGRESS OF THE UNITED STATES: I feel impelled at this time to call to the attention of the Congress some aspects of our forest problem, and the need for a policy and plan of action with respect to it.

Forests are intimately tied into our whole social and economic life. They grow on more than one-third the land area of the continental

United States. Wages from forest industries support five to six million people each year. Forests give us building materials and thousands of other things in everyday use. Forest lands furnish food and shelter for much of our remaining game, and healthful recreation for millions of our people. Forests help prevent erosion and floods. They conserve water and regulate its use for navigation, for power, for domestic use, and for irrigation. Woodlands occupy more acreage than any other crop on American farms, and help support two and one-half million farm families.

Our forest problem is essentially one of land use. It is a part of the broad problem of modern agriculture that is common to every part of the country. Forest lands total some six hundred and fifteen million acres.

One hundred and twenty odd million acres of these forest lands are rough and inaccessible—but they are valuable for the protection of our great watersheds. The greater proportion of these protection forests is in public ownership. Four hundred and ninety-five million acres of our forest lands can be classed as commercial. Both as to accessibility and quality the best four-fifths, or some three hundred and ninety-six million acres of these commercial forests, is in private ownership.

This privately owned forest land at present furnishes 96% of all our forest products. It represents 90% of the productive capacity of our forest soils. There is a continuing drain upon commercial forests in saw-timber sizes far beyond the annual growth. Forest operations in them have not been, and are not now, conducive to maximum regrowth. An alarming proportion of our cut-over forest lands is tax-delinquent. Through neglect, much of it is rapidly forming a new but almost worthless no-man's land.

Most of the commercial forest lands are in private ownership. Most of them are now only partially productive, and most of them are still subject to abuse. This abuse threatens the general welfare.

I have thus presented to you the facts. They are simple facts; but they are of a character to cause alarm to the people of the United States and to you, their chosen Representatives.

The forest problem is therefore a matter of vital national concern, and some way must be found to make forest lands and forest resources contribute their full share to the social and economic structures of this country, and to the security and stability of *all* our people.

When in 1933 I asked the Congress to provide for the Civilian Conservation Corps I was convinced that forest lands offered one source for worth-while work, non-competitive with industry, for large numbers of our unemployed. Events of the past five years have indicated that my earlier conviction was well founded. In rebuilding and managing those lands, and in the many uses of them and their resources, there exists a major opportunity for new employment and for increasing the national wealth.

Creation of the National Forest system, which now extends to thirty-eight States, has been a definite step toward constructive solution of our forest problem. From national forest lands comes domestic water for more than six million people. Forage, occurring largely in combination with timber, contributes stability to one-fourth the western range live-stock industry. Through correlated and coordinated public management of timber and all other resources, these public properties already help support almost a million people and furnish healthful recreation to more than thirty million each year. By means of exchanges and purchases, the Congress has for many years encouraged additions to this system. These measures should very definitely be continued as funds and facilities are available.

The Congress has also provided that the national government shall cooperate with the various States in matters of fire protection on privately owned forest lands and farm woodlands. The States are in turn cooperating with private owners. Among other measures the Congress has also authorized an extensive program of forest research, which has been initiated and projected; Federal cooperation in building up a system of State forests; cooperative activities with farmers to integrate forest management with the general farm economy; the planting of trees in the Prairie-Plains States—an activity which has heretofore been carried on as an emergency unemployment relief measure with outstanding success and material benefit; and—under the Omnibus Flood Control Bill—measures to retard run-off and erosion on forested and other watersheds.

Progress has been made—and such measures as these should be continued. They are not adequate, however, to meet the present situation. We are still exploiting our forest lands. Forest communities are still being crippled; still being left desolate and forlorn. Watersheds are still being denuded. Fertile valleys and industrial cities below such watersheds still suffer from erosion and floods. We are still liquidating our forest capital; still cutting our accessible forests faster than they are being replaced.

Our forest budget still needs balancing. This is true in relation to future as well as present national needs. We need and will continue to need large quantities of wood for housing, for our railroads and our telephone and telegraph lines, for newsprint and other papers, for fiber containers, for furniture and the like. Wood is rich in chemicals. It is the major source of cellulose products such as rayon, movie films, cellophanes, sugars of certain kinds, surgical absorbents, drugs, lacquers, phonograph records. Turpentines, rosins, acetone, acetic acid, and alcohols are derived from wood. Our forest budget should, therefore, be balanced in relation to present and future needs for such things as these. It should also be balanced in relation to the many public services that forests render, and to the need for stabilizing dependent industries and communities locally, regionally, and nationally.

I am informed, for example, that more than one hundred million dollars has recently gone into development of additional forest industries in the southeastern section of our country. This means still more drain from southern forests. Without forestry measures that will insure timber cropping there, existing and planned forest enterprises must inevitably suffer. The Pacific Northwest contains the greatest reserves of virgin merchantable timber in the continental United States. During recent years many private forest lands have been given better fire protection there, and there are more young trees on the ground. But the cutting drain in our virgin Douglas fir forests is about four times current growth, and unless existing practices are changed the old fir will be gone long before new growth is big enough for manufacture into lumber.

I recommend, therefore, study by a joint committee of the Congress of the forest land problem of the United States. As a nation we now have the accumulated experience of three centuries of use and abuse as guides in determining broad principles. The public has certain responsibilities and obligations with respect to private forest lands, but so also have private owners with respect to the broad public interests in those same lands. Particular consideration might therefore be given in these studies, which I hope will form the basis for essential legislation during the next session of Congress, to the situation with respect to private forest lands, and to consideration of such matters as:

1. The adequacy and effectiveness of present activities in protecting public and private forest lands from fire, insects, and diseases, and of cooperative efforts between the Federal government and the States.

2. Other measures, Federal and State, which may be necessary and advisable to insure that timber cropping on privately owned forest lands may be conducted as continuous operations, with the productivity of the lands built up against future requirements.

3. The need for extension of Federal, State, and community ownership of forest lands, and of planned public management of them.

4. The need for such public regulatory controls as will adequately protect private as well as the broad public interests in all forest lands.

5. Methods and possibilities of employment in forestry work on private and public forest lands, and possibilities of liquidating such public expenditures as are or may be involved.

Facilities of those technical agencies that, in the executive branches of the government, deal with the many phases of our forest problem will of course be available to such committee as the Congress may appoint. These technical agencies will be glad to assist the Committee in assembling and interpreting facts, indicating what has been done, what still needs to be done, and in such other ways as the Committee may desire.

I make this suggestion for immediate study of our forest problem by the Congress in the belief that definite action should be taken by the Congress in 1939. States, communities and private capital can do much to help—but the fact remains that, with some outstanding exceptions, most of the states, communities and private companies have, on the whole, accomplished little to retard or check the continuing process of using up our forest resources without replacement. This being so, it seems obviously necessary to fall back on the last defensive line—Federal leadership and Federal action. Millions of Americans are today conscious of the threat. Public opinion asks that steps be taken to remove it.

If the preliminary action is taken at this session of the Congress, I propose to address letters to the Governors of those States in which the amount of state and privately owned forest land is substantial, enclosing to them a copy of this Message to the Congress and asking their full cooperation with the Congress and with the Executive Branch of the National Government.[1]

[FRANKLIN D. ROOSEVELT]

[W. H. PRESS RELEASES:M]

[1] This message was drafted by the Agriculture Department in accordance with Roosevelt's request of Jan. 27, 1938 (*ante,* 739). Acting Secretary of Agriculture Wilson sent a draft to Roosevelt on Feb. 25, 1938 (OF 149). The President made some half-dozen minor changes in this draft and added the seventh and last two paragraphs of the text as here printed. In the Senate the message was referred to the Committee on Agriculture and Forestry; in the House, to the Committee of the Whole House (*Cong. Rec.,* 75th Cong., 3d sess., 83:3, 3317–3318; 3320–3322). For the subsequent action taken, see note in Rosenman (ed.), *Public Papers,* VII, 149, and Wallace to Roosevelt, April 6, 1938, *post,* 772.

759   HENRY A. WALLACE, SECRETARY OF AGRICULTURE, TO ROOSEVELT

WASHINGTON, *March 15, 1938*

DEAR MR. PRESIDENT: I am enclosing for your consideration a proposal of the Forest Service with far-reaching implications. This proposal involves two major public problems: the immediate use of private forest lands at a minimum expense, for purposes of unemployment relief; and the increased production of forest crops, particularly from cutover lands held in private ownership. The plan of action proposed is similar in many respects to that so successfully used in the British Isles. There is enclosed a brief summary covering the British System.

The plan to enter into cooperative agreements with landowners providing the use of their lands for forest production, with the recapture of a large portion of the Federal expenditures through sale of the products grown, places the proposal on a basis that should assure uniform public support. The plan appears to offer many advantages in that it integrates unemployment relief and the prevention of unemployment with a partially liquidating enterprise. In addition, it would result in the production of a raw material that would offer an opportunity for employment that, in the long run, should absorb large numbers of workers.

I am glad to concur in the proposal and to recommend it for your consideration.

There is attached a brief report covering the plan, an outline of procedure that might be followed, and a short bill, the enactment of which would facilitate action.[1]

Respectfully,

H. A. WALLACE

[13:PPF 1820:TS]

[1] The draft bill, dated March 1, 1938, is present. Also present is a summary (four pages, typed) of a report of the Reconstruction Ministry of Great Britain on forest conditions in the United Kingdom.

760   [*Enclosure 1*]

March 10, 1938

Summary

(1) The Federal Government will manage private forest land under contractual agreement with the owner.

(2) The Federal Government will pay all costs of forestry operations over the period of the contract.

(3) The Federal Government is reimbursed by retention of from 50 to 90 per cent of the receipts from sale of products.

(4) The owner pays all taxes and management of the land is returned to him upon completion of the contract.

(5) People on relief and subnormal income farmers would be used for the improvement of the land through forestry operations.

(6) The plan combines the desirable objective of rehabilitation of people with rehabilitation of private forest land. It proposes an expanded program during times of distress and contraction to a minimum during normal times.

(7) The cost of the plan will vary with the number of men employed. As a minimum, $15,000,000 per year will be required for 80,000 men on a 3-month basis; $95,000,000 for employment of 500,000 men on the same basis; $500,000 will be required for initiation, including planning, organization of the work and contract negotiations.

[13:PPF 1820:T]

March 10, 1938

Analysis of Sample Area

In the southern pine area west of the Mississippi River, embracing over 45,000,000 acres in Arkansas, Louisiana, Oklahoma and Texas, shown on the map following, there is an annual requirement, above growth, of about three million cords of pulpwood.

Within this area are over 268,000 farms. Cotton is their principal cash crop. Overproduction and foreign competition, with the resultant depressed price, have made it impossible for many farmers to meet their absolute needs without outside assistance and have left these farmers in dire circumstances.

During the past year W. P. A. expenditures in these four States were $196,000,000; during the past three years, A. A. A. expended $32,000,-000 in the forest area within the four States.

There is an under-production of wood in the area. Ten pulp and paper mills, utilizing pine, and over 1,300 pine sawmills, and other demands, now require approximately 10,000,000 cords of wood including over $2\frac{1}{3}$ billion board feet of logs each year. There are nearly 29,000,-000 acres of forest land not in public ownership, over 7,000,000 acres of which are on farms. Timber farming offers the only apparent solution.

[13:PPF 1820:T]

March 10, 1938

A National Cooperative Reforestation Plan for the Promotion of Forest Land Management and the Prevention and Relief of Unemployment

As yet, no adequate national policy or program has been developed for forest lands not under Federal control. The following report and recommendations propose such a policy and program.

Under long-time lease or cooperative agreement the government would utilize forest land as a cushion to offer employment in times of distress to persons requiring assistance and to farmers needing supplemental cash income, in carrying out forest land management activities. These would include tree planting, thinning and other woods work designed to increase the income from forest land by establishing a forest crop on denuded forest and submarginal agricultural land and by increasing the productivity of existing second growth forest stands.

Funds appropriated for relief purposes would be used to finance the program. Fifty per cent or more of the expenditures would be recovered from receipts for products sold from the land.

Present Situation

1. The total area of forest land not under public control is 474,000,000 acres. Of this acreage, 429,000,000 acres has been cut over and generally burned or erroneously placed under cultivation. It is with the latter classes of land that this report is primarily concerned although there is some opportunity for forestation and improvement of State and community forest areas.

2. It is inevitable that the United States will face a shortage of timber of suitable quality in the future unless the situation is met by an adequate program at this time. In fact, because of long distance to major consuming centers and particularly to large agricultural centers, the price of lumber is now materially restricting building construction and indirectly lowering standards of living. New uses of wood are developing at a tremendous rate and the establishment of plants for the fabrication of wood, particularly in the South and in the Northwest, renders necessary a comprehensive approach to the problem of a permanent supply if those industries are not to be transitory.

3. In the United States, forestry on forest lands has not been generally accepted by private enterprise as a profitable undertaking and of grave concern is the fact that in the regions where tree growth is natural, the supplemental income that should be available on every farm has not been available because forestry has not been understood and has not been integrated with the farm enterprise.

It appears sound judgment, purely from an economic standpoint, to devote considerable acreages of low-grade agricultural land to a forest crop, to reforest areas of denuded forest land, and to increase the productivity of existing second growth stands by cultural operations.

Such a program, to be carried out as proposed herein, would accomplish this and would:

(a) Provide employment for persons on the relief rolls;

(b) Provide supplemental cash income through employment to needy farmers;

(c) Make strides toward a balance between growth and utilization of wood;

(d) Make productive use of otherwise idle land and eliminate it as a hazard from an erosion and flood control standpoint;

(e) Develop a condition of stabilized employment in growing and harvesting a continuous crop of wood.

4. The bearing of the plan recommended upon flood and erosion control and the use of submarginal agricultural land is of great importance. When effectuated, the plan will offer the opportunity to reforest watersheds with ultimate liquidation of better than 50% of the cost.

[197]

5. The production of raw material from forest lands and farm woodlands of the United States offers a major opportunity to liquidate unemployment now and in the future. It should form a part of any permanent Public Works Program.

Recommended Action

The proposed policy and plan, it is believed, will give part-time employment to not less than 500,000 workers in the regeneration and management of forest lands. Costs will be liquidated in part from returns. The ultimate result will be the liquidation of unemployment, the elimination of potential relief clients and the creation of new sources of employment in private enterprises.

The following recommendations are made:

(a) That timberlands carrying commercial timber, other than farm woodlands, be brought under regulatory control.

(b) That the forest and sub-marginal agricultural land of the United States be used as a cushion to offer employment in times of distress, the forestry program to be expanded during such times and reduced to a minimum during times of prosperity.

(c) That authority be granted the Department of Agriculture to enter into cooperative agreements with owners of forest land, over long periods, such cooperative agreements to provide for forestry enterprises that will result in maximum wood production and thereby maximum returns.

(d) That the provisions of this program include cooperation with public agencies in the forestation and management of State and community forest areas.

(e) That no cooperative agreement or lease be entered into without provision that at least 50% of the total expenditures in the management of the land shall be returned to the Government.

(f) That the undertaking be developed insofar as practicable in cooperation with the State forestry agencies.

(g) That for immediate purposes, funds now appropriated directly or indirectly, for the relief of unemployment and for farm stabilization and improvement, be diverted in amounts necessary to effectuate these recommendations under the general plan proposed.

(1) The Forest Service, working through State Forestry agencies, is prepared to initiate and carry on the recommended program which, if placed in effect, will represent the greatest step forward in forest conservation since creation of the National Forest system.

(2) The recommended policy and plan can be initiated in three months and the objective should be a minimum of 50,000,000 acres covered by agreements.

(3) Fifteen million dollars per year, as a minimum, would be required to establish and carry on a basic skeleton program, giving part-time

(three months per year) employment to 80,000 men, which could be expanded to employ at least 500,000 men part-time, on the same basis, for about $95,000,000 per year as acreages came under agreement and it became necessary to extend relief to available people. An immediate allocation of $500,000 would be required for localized plans, organization of the work and initial negotiation for contracts.

[13:PPF 1820:T]

763   ROOSEVELT TO GOVERNOR FRANK MURPHY, Lansing, Michigan

[WASHINGTON] *March 15, 1938*

MY DEAR GOVERNOR: I believe you know of my long-time interest in the forest land problem of the nation, particularly as it applies to stabilized employment, farm income, and all the other benefits inherent in forests. I am firm in the belief that there is a vital public interest involved in the proper protection and management of the forests, and I am convinced that under such management these areas can add materially to the national wealth and well-being. Without proper management, the reverse is true.

Michigan, together with its sister Lake States, has long since passed the peak of lumber and forest products production. In some ways the problem of vast areas of non-productive land, which actually become a burden to the general public, has been attacked aggressively in the Lake States region. For example, the system of fire protection on forest lands in Michigan is one of which the State can well be proud. Your method of placing tax-delinquent land under State ownership and management is, I understand, one of the best yet evolved. In spite of this, there is still a large percentage of the area of the State which is today adding little, if anything, to the wealth and well-being of its people.

Information given me indicates that of a total land area of 36,787,000 acres, more than 19,000,000 acres, or 51.5% is classified as forest land, of which 61% is still in industrial ownership, 23.5% is owned by farmers, with the balance in public ownership. The relative importance of the forests in Michigan in the industrial and employment picture has been reduced materially, and at the present time only 5% of the total industrial establishments, representing 1.5% of the total wages paid, are dependent on the forests for their raw material. In spite of this, the forest products industries in the State are still the life-blood of many of its communities, and so far as I can determine but little progress has been made in the application of good forest practices on the remaining timber stands.

In order to fully protect the public interest involved, I have no doubt you agree that the State might well exercise its sovereignty to an extent that will insure all the benefits possible from the proper management of a great natural resource.

I am writing the Governors of the other Lake States suggesting the desirability of some common plan of action which might well include public regulation of private operations on forest land.[1]

Since the forest land problem of the Lake States is of regional character and since this regional situation has obvious national implications, I am enclosing for your information a copy of the Message I have recently addressed to the Congress. In this Message I have recommended a study by a Joint Congressional Committee looking towards the development of essential legislation during the next session of Congress.

I ask your cooperation in fulfillment of the objectives set forth in the Message.[2]

Very sincerely yours,

[FRANKLIN D. ROOSEVELT]

[13:OF 149:CT]

[1] Letters similar to this one (all dated March 15, 1938), but differing according to the special forest problem of each state, were sent to the governors of all states having appreciable forest areas except where the forests were largely in Federal ownership. All the letters were drafted by the Agriculture Department; copies are present with the one here printed. Replies were referred to the Agriculture Department.

[2] Answered *post,* 787.

764   ROOSEVELT TO CORDELL HULL, SECRETARY OF STATE

WASHINGTON, *March 17, 1938*

MEMORANDUM FOR THE SECRETARY OF STATE: I have approved this report [1] and the letter from the Secretary of the Interior. Will you, therefore, be good enough to cooperate with the Secretary of the Interior and other officials in presenting the matter through official channels to the Government of the Dominion of Canada?

F. D. R.

[13:OF 1119:CT]

[1] *Report to the President of the United States on the Quetico-Superior Area by the Quetico-Superior Committee* (1938).

765   [*Enclosure*] HAROLD L. ICKES, SECRETARY OF THE INTERIOR, TO ROOSEVELT

WASHINGTON, *Mar. 16, 1938*

MY DEAR MR. PRESIDENT: By Executive Order of June 30, 1934, upon the joint recommendation of the Secretaries of the Interior and of Agriculture, you established the Quetico-Superior Committee, which has prepared its first report for submission to you. I have long been in sympathy with the major objective sought by the Committee, which is to set aside as an international wilderness sanctuary the Pigeon River and Rainy Lake watersheds, including countless streams and lakes, in northern Minnesota and adjacent Ontario. I am fully convinced that such a wilderness area, within easy reach of 35,000,000 citizens of the United States, is socially and economically desirable. It is proposed that the area be dedicated as "a peace memorial to the service men of both countries who served as comrades in the Great War." The Committee's program has the endorsement of veterans' organizations both in the United States and Canada. I believe that the establishment of this sanctuary would call world-wide attention to the continuing peaceable relations between these two good neighbor nations of North America.

To make its program effective, the Committee makes two basic recommendations, with both of which I am in accord. First, it will be necessary to place under Federal control all of the lands within the proposed sanctuary. This end can be achieved under existing law; except for the Grand Portage Indian Reservation, at the eastern tip of the area, all of the lands will then be within the Superior National Forest. The National Forest Reservation Commission and the State of Minnesota, through its Conservation Commission, have already approved this part of the plan.

The Committee's second recommendation is that the international character of this sanctuary be established and maintained by treaty with the Dominion of Canada. The Committee's Executive Secretary, Ernest C. Oberholtzer, has held numerous informal meetings with representative Canadian citizens and officials, who believe that the Dominion Government would welcome your initiative in the matter. At my suggestion, Mr. Oberholtzer also consulted Honorable R. Walton Moore, Counselor of the Department of State, who indicated that upon instruction from you the Secretary of State would be pleased to present the matter through official channels to the Dominion Government. I believe that the Committee's report clearly indicates the desirability and the feasibility of its program, and I urge that proper inquiries be now addressed to the Dominion Government.

Although the Quetico-Superior Committee has submitted its recommendations, I am certain that its proposal can not be carried out before June 30, 1938, the date on which its existence would end in accordance with your Executive Order. I intend, therefore, in the near future, to submit for your approval a draft of a new order to extend the existence of the Committee to June 30, 1942.

Sincerely yours,

[Harold L. Ickes]

[13:OF 1119:CT]

766   HENRY MORGENTHAU, JR., SECRETARY OF THE TREASURY,
       AND DANIEL W. BELL, ACTING DIRECTOR, BUREAU OF THE
       BUDGET, TO ROOSEVELT

WASHINGTON [*March 17, 1938*]

MEMORANDUM FOR THE PRESIDENT: At a conference had with you by the Acting Director of the Bureau of the Budget on Monday, March 7th, last, with respect to your policy on flood control, you suggested that serious thought be given to the proposition of having Congress enact a billion-dollar flood control program; the work to be done by the Army Engineers; the funds to be raised by the Treasury through the sale of Government bonds in the regular manner; such funds to be loaned to those States desiring the prosecution of flood control projects, repayable over a period of fifty years, without interest, such repayments to be used in retiring the bonds sold by the Government.

By your memorandum of March 8, 1938, you referred to the Secretary of the Treasury a memorandum of the same date addressed to you jointly by the Secretary of the Interior and Honorable Frederic A. Delano, upon the subject of a public works revolving fund.

With respect to the subject first above mentioned the following facts and observations are submitted: Disregarding the flood control of the main stem of the Mississippi River, which is really in a class by itself, there are now on the books flood control projects, authorized by the Omnibus Flood Control Act, as amended, estimated to cost the Federal Government, for construction, a total of $344,000,000 and to cost local interests, for lands, easements, rights-of-way, and damages, a total of $107,000,000, or a grand total of $451,000,000.   In addition, Congress has authorized and directed the making of examinations and surveys of some 335 additional streams and localities with a view to the adoption of projects for the control of floods.   How many of such projects will actually be adopted and what their total cost will be cannot, of course, be even approximated at this time.   Other such examinations and surveys will undoubtedly be provided for in the future.   We think it safe to predict, therefore, that the ultimate cost of a nation-wide plan for flood control will certainly amount to a billion dollars, and probably more.   While we have not had time to go into the matter thoroughly from every angle, your suggested plan for financing national flood control would seem to us to have a great deal of merit and one worthy of detailed collaborative study by the Treasury Department, the Bureau of the Budget, the National Resources Committee, and interested Departments, particularly, War and Agriculture.   The following phases of the matter are of particular interest:

(1) We are now committed to an annual expenditure of about $50,-000,000, with the great probability that this sum must be materially increased if the demands of local interests are acceded to and if the

existing policy of local cooperation is discarded. Hence, the payment of annual interest on one billion dollars of Government bonds would probably be cheaper than our annual outlay for flood control. Assuming that the Treasury would have to pay an average interest rate of 3 per cent over a period of fifty years on a $1,000,000,000 bond issue, we would pay out in interest over that period, if the bonds are retired at the rate of $20,000,000 a year, the sum of $765,000,000. It is seen, therefore, that the total cost of flood control would be $1,765,000,000, of which the States would pay $1,000,000,000, or about 57 per cent, and the Federal Government $765,000,000, or about 43 per cent. On the present basis of $451,000,000 of projects now authorized, of which the Federal Government pays $344,000,000 and the States $107,000,000, the ratio is Federal Government about 76 per cent, and the States about 24 per cent. This is based upon a continuation of local cooperation; otherwise the Government cost would, of course, be 100 per cent.

(2) The country at the present time is apparently flood control conscious and with every recurring flood demands upon the Government for relief will become more insistent and far-reaching. The adoption of a scheme of financing, such as you suggest, would at once indicate whether the pressure comes from those who will eventually pay the bills or from politicians. It would also, without doubt, we believe, result in the prosecution only of projects of real merit, in which the cost of construction bears a proper relation to the benefits to be derived. Pork-barrel tactics would thus be eliminated.

It is proper to point out that there would necessarily be some delay in getting under way a program such as the one under consideration and that in the interim the Government would have to continue the program now in effect. Assuming that Congress would enact the required legislation early in the calendar year 1939 (serious doubt being entertained that action would be taken during the present session, with the 1938 elections coming on), it would then be necessary for the legislatures of the various States to enact enabling legislation and for compacts to be entered into between States with respect to projects interstate in character and such compacts would probably have to be sanctioned by the Congress.

There are two angles to this matter which are of particular concern to us, to wit: (a) the handling of the funds loaned to the States, and (b) their repayment to the Treasury. As to (a), while loans should be allocated to States, the funds should remain in the Federal Treasury and be drawn upon to meet the costs of prosecuting the projects for flood control, an account being kept for each State and periodic statements furnished to it. Otherwise there might be a danger that the funds would in some instances, be diverted. And with respect to (b), there should be some assurance to the Federal Government that the loans made

[203]

to the States would be repaid and that such repayments would be made in the annual installments conutemplated by the plan. Just how this may be accomplished would have to be worked out and provided for in the legislation to be enacted by the Congress.

Adverting now to the suggestion that a revolving fund be created for the handling of public works, we wish to register our opposition to such a plan. Revolving funds violate the principles of proper budgeting and are highly objectionable in many ways and for many reasons. Such a plan would necessarily include projects for flood control and would, of course, displace the plan for financing this class of public works which we have discussed in the forepart of this memorandum. If it be your desire to make loans to States and local governments for public works authorized not only by Federal law but by State and municipal law, it is our definite recommendation that the authority of the Reconstruction Finance Corporation be broadened so as to enable it to make such loans in the manner set forth in the accompanying draft of an Act prepared by Jesse Jones of that Corporation. This would be more businesslike and we believe the loans would be better administered. Moreover, we believe that Congress would be less likely to make grants to the States out of funds of the Reconstruction Finance Corporation than it would out of a revolving fund.

H. MORGENTHAU JR.
D. W. BELL

[13: PPF 1820: TS]

767   ROOSEVELT TO MONSON MORRIS, PRESIDENT, AIKEN COUNTY RURAL ELECTRIFICATION ASSOCIATION, Aiken, South Carolina

WARM SPRINGS, GEORGIA, *March 25, 1938*

DEAR MONSON: I was delighted to receive your letter of March eighteenth [1] and particularly to know of your activities along forestry lines. This, as you know, is a subject that has had my deep concern for many years, and I have watched with a great deal of interest and some foreboding the large industrial expansion, based on wood as a raw material, which has taken place in your section of the country.

I am tremendously interested in the Bill which you say was enacted by your Legislature. While I do not have a copy, it apparently approaches the forest-land problem of South Carolina on a cooperative basis whereby an association, semi-public in character, is to take over the management of the tax-delinquent lands within the county. Presumably, after this land has been rehabilitated by the Association, the resulting net revenue will accrue to the benefit of the county as a whole. Working cooperatively with the State and Federal forestry agencies, this seems to me to be commendable.

You will be interested in knowing that I am now giving consideration to a somewhat similar plan on a National basis. This contemplates productive work on forest land as a cushion for unemployment, and on a semi-liquidating basis in cooperation with private owners and State agencies.

On March fourteenth, I sent a special message to the Congress on the forestry problem of the Nation and requested that a Joint Committee be appointed to make a study so that definite action could be taken by the next session of Congress. I stated that ". . . States, communities, and private capital can do much to help . . ." and the action taken by your Legislature, together with the idea proposed in the resolution passed by your County Forestry Committee, seems to me to be a fine example of the type of help that can be rendered locally. I believe that, after it has been appointed, this Joint Committee should study the plan about which you have written me, and I hope you will, at the proper time, suggest such action.

It gives me pleasure to note that we are both thinking along the same lines.[2]

Best wishes to you.

Very sincerely yours,

[FRANKLIN D. ROOSEVELT]

[13:PPF 2637:CT]

[1] Morris enclosed a copy of the resolution submitted by the Aiken County Forestry Association to the Aiken County delegation in the South Carolina General Assembly asking that the state authorize a reforestation plan. His letter (PPF 2637) stated that "all the county land bought-in for nonpayment of taxes is to be turned over to our Association, and we are going to plant pines on all the worthless lands thereon and hope within fifteen years our county will need no county taxes, as the sale of the products from this land will pay them all."

[2] Drafted by the Forest Service. Silcox, in his letter to Rowe, March 24, 1938, covering the draft, said that he thought the plan offered a real opportunity to turn nonproductive into productive land "with least violation to the local set-up." He thought, however, that the estimate of fifteen years for recovery of the investment was too optimistic.

768   ROOSEVELT TO REPRESENTATIVE EDWARD T. TAYLOR OF COLORADO

WASHINGTON, *March 25, 1938*

MY DEAR MR. TAYLOR: Since the Congress has authorized the Colorado-Big Thompson Transmountain Water Diversion Project, which involves lands and waters previously authorized for addition to Rocky Mountain National Park, I consider it important and desirable that boundary adjustments and other compensatory measures included in your bill (H. R. 8969) be enacted into law as early as possible.

The areas proposed for addition to the park are of outstanding scenic value. I am convinced that the proper safeguarding of such resources, which would be provided by the enactment of your bill, will result in great public benefit to the State of Colorado and to the Nation.[1]

Very sincerely yours,

[FRANKLIN D. ROOSEVELT]

[*Notation*:A] Copy sent to Interior 3/26/38 hm

[13:OF 6–P:CT]

[1] Drafted by the Interior Department. Ickes, in his letter of March 23, 1938, sending the draft, said that enactment of the bill was particularly desirable because of the authorization of the Colorado-Big Thompson Transmountain Water Diversion Project. He said that local groups who opposed enlargement of the park had protested to Taylor and that the latter had said he would not press for the enactment of the bill during the current session of Congress. H. R. 8969, introduced Jan. 14, 1938, was referred to the House Committee on Public Lands but was not reported (*Cong. Rec.*, 75th Cong., 3d sess., 83:1, 566).

769   ARNO B. CAMMERER, DIRECTOR, NATIONAL PARK SERVICE, TO ROOSEVELT

WASHINGTON, *March 28, 1938*

MEMORANDUM FOR THE PRESIDENT: In your memorandum of March 21 to Mr. Silcox and myself, you said: "I understand you are in substantial agreement in regard to the Mount Olympus National Park project. If this is true, will you join in giving the bill a push in both Houses? Let me know at Warm Springs how things are coming on." [1]

The Budget this morning received clearance for the project from the Secretary of Agriculture, and promptly gave it Budget clearance. Silcox and I are in complete agreement, and Secretary Ickes has reviewed the boundaries developed under your instructions. From now on every effort will be centered on putting it through Congress. Certainly I shall do my very level best to help push it along.

Copies of Agriculture's and the Budget's clearance letters are attached for your information.[2]

ARNO B. CAMMERER

[13:OF 6–P:TS]

[1] The entire memorandum is here quoted.

[2] The Olympic National Park Bill (H. R. 10024) was introduced by Representative Wallgren (Wash.) on March 25, 1938. The hearings before the House Committee on Public Lands are printed: *To Establish the Olympic National Park in the State of Washington*, Hearings, 75th Cong., 3d sess., on H. R. 10024, April 19, 1938 (Washington, 1938). For the history of the bill see *post*, 801.

OLYMPIA, *March 31, 1938*

MY DEAR MR. PRESIDENT: The people of this state and I share your keen appreciation of the great forest wilderness on the Olympic Peninsula, and your desire to preserve an adequate part of this unsurpassed wonderland in its primitive state. However, I believe that the boundaries proposed in House Resolution 10024 by Congressman Wallgren, embracing nearly one million acres and nineteen billion feet of standing timber are too large, and such extensive reservation would unnecessarily curtail the state's economic advancement. The desired scenic and recreational advantages can be preserved within a smaller area.

The boundaries, as proposed, will seriously interfere with sustained yield management of approximately 200,000 acres of school and granted lands immediately adjoining, with the tax structure of the state, and with the economic use of mineral, fish and waterpower resources.

I fully concur with you in your statement (contained in your letter of March 15 and message to Congress of March 14) that "Some way must be found to make forest lands and forest resources contribute their full share to the social and economic structures of this country." This, however, cannot be accomplished nor can employment opportunities be maintained or enlarged by withdrawing from utilization such vast areas and resources.

I heartily favor a park of adequate proportions that includes and preserves the important scenic and recreational features, including large stands of mature forests, but not one so extensive as to prevent controlled development and reasonable use of natural resources so vital to the welfare and progress of this state.

The accompanying map contains my recommendations for an Olympic National Park of aproximately 450,000 acres, which I believe adequate. The proposal for a park along the ocean beach is omitted from this recommendation since this area is impractical for park purposes.

This proposal is based upon careful investigation and study by the State Department of Conservation and Development and the State Planning Council. I therefore respectfully urge your further consideration and the opportunity to present a complete statement of my position to you and the Congress.[1]

Sincerely yours,

CLARENCE D. MARTIN

[13:OF 6–P:TS]

[1] Answered *post,* 778.

771 ROOSEVELT TO ROBERT FECHNER, DIRECTOR, CIVILIAN CONSERVATION CORPS

[WASHINGTON] *April 5, 1938*

MY DEAR BOB: I regret very much that it is impossible for me to be present at your celebration of the fifth anniversary of the Civilian Conservation Corps. However, I want to tell you once more how keenly I have followed the successes of the CCC from its initiation in the Spring of 1933 to the present time.

It should be a source of gratification to the country that in the Corps we have an organization that conserves and develops our natural resources and at the same time gives unemployed young men practical training and health advantages which return them to their home communities better equipped for private employment. While your reports show a huge job has already been done in advancing a sound conservation program, the studies of the National Resources Board indicate that a tremendous lot of needed conservation work remains to be accomplished. It is my earnest hope that the Corps may continue its fine work for many years to come.[1]

Very sincerely yours,

[FRANKLIN D. ROOSEVELT]

[13:PPF 2265:CT]

[1] Drafted by Hassett.

772 HENRY A. WALLACE, SECRETARY OF AGRICULTURE, TO ROOSEVELT

WASHINGTON, *4/6/38*

Secretary Wallace:[1]

"DEAR MR. PRESIDENT: With regard to the Forestry Message which you sent up a couple of weeks ago (March 14th), Sen. McAdoo is now requesting the Forest Service to prepare for him a resolution which he would introduce.[2]

"I would like to know if it is all right for the Forest Service to play ball with Sen. McAdoo on this matter."

K

[*Notation*:AS] Yes but would like to see the resolution. JR[3]
[*Notation*:A] telephoned to Sec'y Wallace's office.

[13:OF 149:T]

[1] This is in the form of a White House memorandum. Presumably Wallace read his note to Kannee over the telephone.
[2] This was passed June 14, 1938, as Senate Concurrent Resolution 31 (52 *Stat.* 1452). The resolution set up a joint committee of the House and Senate to investigate the condition, ownership and management of forest land in the United States

with respect to the adequacy of protective measures against fire, disease and insects; continuous timber production of private lands; need for expanded public ownership; and the need for public regulation. Hearings were held in various parts of the United States, beginning in September, 1938, in Idaho, and concluding in February, 1940, in Washington, D. C. Transcripts of the hearings are printed: *Forest Lands of the United States*, Hearings before the Joint Committee on Forestry, 75th Cong., 3d sess., on S. Con. Res. 31, Parts 1–8 (Washington, 1939, 1940).

³ James Roosevelt, Secretary to the President.

773   KENNETH A. REID, GENERAL MANAGER, IZAAK WALTON LEAGUE OF AMERICA, TO ROOSEVELT

CHICAGO, *April 14, 1938*

DEAR MR. PRESIDENT: As you may know, the Izaak Walton League of America has since its conception in 1922 steadfastly stood for the correction of the nation wide abuses of our streams by pollution from both municipal and industrial sources.

Our fight has been productive of beneficial results in a number of states, but we are convinced that the only eventual solution is Federal control on a watershed basis. The very nature of water flowing by gravity with an utter disregard for man-made political boundaries makes the logic of this position self evident.

We started the movement for control of pollution on a national basis with the "Dern-Lonergan" Conference in 1934 in Washington, D. C. We supported the Pure Streams Bill introduced by Senator Lonergan [1] and are now supporting the compromise bill HR 2711 which resulted from a conference between Senator Lonergan and Senator Barkley.[2] While we do not feel that this Bill is as desirable as Senator Lonergan's Bill, we were agreeable to support it in order to avoid a stalemate and hope that something may be done to get it out of conference for action this session.

Certainly water has been the orphan stepchild of the entire conservation picture, and our polluted streams have been a national disgrace for many years.

We can think of nothing that could be of more broad public benefit than the sensible correction of these abuses and when we consider the tremendous losses that the nation suffers every year by reason of rampant pollution of streams and coastal waters, we have every reason to believe that correction of this evil would in the long run not cost the nation a thin dime. It would mean a different distribution of costs to be sure, but the pollution penalty load that we are paying today would likely offset the needed investment for treatment.

In connection with your new plans for pump-priming, will you not give Pollution of Streams the consideration that it justly deserves? The passage of HR 2711 as amended by the Senate would be a first and logical step. Allocation of funds to put men back to work for municipal sewage plants and industrial waste treatment plants would be a second logical step. May we suggest that it would both simplify the allocation of these funds and accomplish much needed and lasting public benefits if you could make a ruling to the effect that "unless and until a municipality that has a sewage system either has an adequate sewage treatment plant or bonafide plans for installing one" it will not be eligible for Federal funds for any other purpose?

May we respectfully suggest that you give this matter your careful attention in the public interest? [3]

Sincerely yours,

KENNETH A. REID

[13:OF 114–A:TS]

[1] The Lonergan Water Pollution Bill, introduced in 1936 as S. 3958 and in 1937 as S. 13.
[2] The Vinson Water Pollution Bill of 1937.
[3] Answered *post,* 780.

774   HENRY A. WALLACE, SECRETARY OF AGRICULTURE, TO ROOSEVELT

WASHINGTON, *April 15, 1938*

DEAR MR. PRESIDENT: In answer to your memorandum of March 18 [1] in which you ask certain questions relative to a hypothetical case which might come up under the proposed National Cooperative Reforestation Plan, I wish to submit the following:

Your hypothetical case was: "I am a poor man owning a farm of 200 acres in the Ozarks. I farm 50 acres—100 acres are in brush or eroded pasture. The balance of 50 acres is in 20 year old second growth mixed hardwoods."

Your questions and the answers are:

1. Q. What contract do I make with the Government? A. Attached is a sample form of contract of the sort we propose.

2. Q. How long does the contract run? A. The contract runs until receipts from sale of products produced on the forest land repay the Government 50 per cent of the expenditures made by the Government for its improvement. In you specific case it would be approximately 30 years.

3. Q. What do I get in cash? A. Fifty per cent of the receipts from sale of products produced on your forest land until such time as the Government has been reimbursed in an amount equal to 50 per cent of its expenditures for its improvement and after that the full income from the land. During the period of the contract, priority of opportunity for employment is contemplated in connection with work on your own and

other similar neighborhood projects, which should result in a cash income of perhaps $100.00 to $200.00 in the near future.

4. Q. What does the Government spend? A. The Government would spend approximately $1,500 over a period of 15 years.

5. Q. What is the ultimate return to the Government and to me? A. The ultimate return to the Government, derived from sale of products produced on your forest land, would be $750. In addition, in this case a sounder tax base for continuous revenue would be developed. The return to you over the period of 30 years would be approximately $950.00. At that time the land would be in such condition that it should be capable of producing approximately $1.35 per acre annually.

In your hypothetical case no expenditure for, or income from, harvesting operations is included. There are shown only the values in the form of stumpage to be derived from increased productivity of the land as a result of its improvement. In some instances it is contemplated that the Government may carry on the harvesting operation, which would result in a change in the financial set-up, involving increased expenditures, more employment and greater income.

There is enclosed an Operation and Expenditure Plan showing the basis for your contract.

In addition to the hypothetical Ozark Farmer case you set up, I am enclosing a contract and an Operation and Expenditure Plan covering a hypothetical case involving 10,000 acres of southern Arkansas pine land such as might be owned by a lumber company. Operations to increase its productivity would afford work for unemployed persons in nearby towns.[2]

Respectfully,

H. A. WALLACE

[13:PPF 1820:TS]

[1] Roosevelt's memorandum (OF 1-C) asked: "Please let me have answer to the following hypothetical case which might come up under the proposed National Cooperative Reforestation Plan." The rest of the memorandum consists of the five questions here quoted by Wallace.
[2] See post, 777.

775 DANIEL W. BELL, ACTING DIRECTOR, BUREAU OF THE BUDGET, TO ROOSEVELT

WASHINGTON, Apr. 22, 1938

MEMORANDUM FOR THE PRESIDENT: On the 19th instant you handed me, for comment, a copy of a study (minus its appendices), dated January, 1938, prepared in the Office of the Chief of Engineers, entitled "Information on Flood Control in the Mississippi River Basin," together with certain memoranda by the National Resources Committee relating thereto.[1]

[211]

The study of the Chief of Engineers comprises 120½ pages. The first 63 pages consist of a description of the Mississippi River Basin and an historical review of the river and its tributaries with respect to navigation and flood control. The balance of the document reviews the present authorized plans for the control of floods in the Mississippi Basin and the basins of the tributaries of that river and submits, for consideration, certain modifications and enlargements thereof and additions thereto.

In response to a resolution of the Committee on Flood Control of the House of Representatives, dated February 10, 1937, the Chief of Engineers prepared a comprehensive flood-control plan for the Ohio and Lower Mississippi Rivers, estimated to cost approximately $850,000,000. This plan was forwarded by you to the Chairman of the Committee under date of April 28, 1937, and in your letter of transmittal you stated:

The report of the Chief of Engineers considers, of course, only one phase of the very large interlocking problem. For this reason it may be considered neither truly comprehensive nor effectively integrated. . . . In the light of all the circumstances attaching to this report, I am requesting that a further and complete study be made by all of the Government agencies involved, sitting together as a group to make recommendations for a complete picture. This report should be available to Congress by next January.

By your direction, the preparation of the report referred to in your letter to the Chairman of the House Flood Control Committee was undertaken by the National Resources Committee, with the cooperation of the Departments of War and Agriculture and other interested governmental agencies. At the same time the Chief of Engineers of the Army undertook the preparation of the document entitled "Information on Flood Control in the Mississippi River Basin." This document was submitted to you by the Secretary of War on January 8, 1938, and on January 17, 1938, it was referred by you to the National Resources Committee with the statement: "I think this should be coordinated with the work and recommendations of the National Resources Committee."

On March 10, 1938, you transmitted to Congress a report by the National Resources Committee entitled "Drainage Basin Problems and Prorgams, 1937 Revision," stating that: "In accordance with my message of August 13, 1937 (in returning without my approval Senate Joint Resolution 57), I am presenting herewith for your consideration a comprehensive national plan for the conservation and development of our water resources."

However, in the report of the National Resources Committee, under the heading "Foreword by the National Resources Committee," appears this statement:

Flood Control. The report recommends a program of investigations and construction for flood control and flood protection continuing many projects already authorized or under way. The interlocking problems presented by the Ohio and Mississippi Rivers, however, are so complex in character, so broad in scope, so inadequately explored as yet, and so far reaching in their relationships to various unsolved problems of national policy that it would be most unwise for the Congress to authorize at this time any additional general flood-control plan for them. We urge the early inauguration of the proposed comprehensive studies outlined on pages 72–75 of the report.

The National Resources Committee, in commenting on the January, 1938 study prepared by the Chief of Engineers, states that the data contained in the document appear to be drawn from a large reservoir of basic information, heretofore available only in part to its Water Resources Committee, that should be of great value in developing an over-all plan and program for the unified regulation and development of the Ohio and Lower Mississippi Rivers for all useful purposes; that the information demonstrates the need for review and revision of the flood-control plan submitted by the Chief of Engineers on April 6, 1937; that before an integrated plan and program may be formulated it will be necessary to correlate this information with other relevant material and to make additional investigations; and that such investigations would require *several years*. It is further stated that while requisite studies are being proceeded with on an experimental basis, extensive work of the type indicated requires additional allotments of funds to the Federal agencies concerned.

From the foregoing it would appear that the "Comprehensive Flood-Control Plan for Ohio and Lower Mississippi Rivers" of the Chief of Engineers, transmitted to the House Flood-Control Committee by your letter of April 28, 1937, has as yet been only superficially reviewed; that the preparation of an alternative plan by the National Resources Committee has not as yet been undertaken, and that that Committee is now calling to your attention the present status of the matter and pointing out the vastness of the undertaking and the need for additional funds. I assume that the Committee desires a directive from you that it proceed with the work and assurance that the necessary funds will be forthcoming. This, of course, is a matter of policy which you alone can decide. I may observe, however, that the statement by the Committee that the necessary investigations would require *several years* would seem to present some complication in view of the present temporary status of the Committee and the present lack of assurance that it will be made a permanent agency. Under these conditions I might suggest that you appoint a special committee to consider the Ohio and Lower Mississippi flood-control problem, composed of representatives of the Departments of War, Agriculture and Interior, the Federal Power Commission, and other interested agencies, including the National Resources Committee as long as it may remain in existence.

In the meantime, the House Flood-Control Committee is holding hearings, and has been for some time, preparatory to reporting out a new flood-control bill. I understand that it has gone rather thoroughly into the plan for the Ohio and Lower Mississippi Rivers contained in the report of the Chief of Engineers of April 6, 1937, which you transmitted to the Committee on April 28, 1937. This would seem to indicate that the Committee intends to take some action now with respect to these rivers. I do not believe that it could be induced to postpone such action for the several years which the National Resources Committee states would be required for it to further investigate the matter.[2]

D. W. Bell

[13:OF 79:TS]

[1] Sent to Roosevelt by Woodring with his letter of Jan. 8, 1938 (OF 25–N).
[2] Answered below.

776   Roosevelt to Daniel W. Bell, Acting Director, Bureau of the Budget

Washington, April 23, 1938

Memorandum for the Acting Director of the Budget: In regard to the flood control plans for Ohio and Lower Mississippi Rivers, I suggest that you hold a conference with representatives of the Departments of War, Agriculture and Interior, the Federal Power Commission and the National Resources Committee.

As a matter of policy I suggest the following:

(1) That the National Resources Committee undertake the study of and report on the large and permanent program even if, as the National Resources Committee states, this will require several years. Some organization must head up this permanent integrated investigation looking toward permanent integrate plans and the National Resources Committee should act in this coordinating capacity.

(2) In the meantime, there are plenty of projects in the Ohio and Lower Mississippi areas on which everybody can agree. These projects will actually cost more than we can afford to spend during the next two or three years. Therefore, at this meeting I suggest a report and recommendation, again headed up by National Resources Committee, approving such specific projects as will fit into the ultimate and permanent plan and policy.

F. D. R.

[13:OF 25–N:CT]

[WASHINGTON] *April 25, 1938*

MEMORANDUM FOR THE SECRETARY OF AGRICULTURE: I have given
a good deal of thought to the enclosed National Cooperative Reforestation Plan [1] and there are two points wherein I am not in agreement.

1. The plan mixes up wood-lot forestry with commercial forestry—
and that the two are very different problems is proved by the opinions
of a generation of foresters and by the distinctions made in state laws
between the two subjects. The enclosed plan is apparently meant to
work the same way for both the individual farmer who is trying to
make a living off anywhere from fifty to five hundred acres of land,
and a lumber company which rarely operates on units of less than ten
thousand acres—running from that acreage up to hundreds of
thousands.

It seems to me that the treatment of the wood-lot problem should
be looked at a good deal in the way we look at the problem of farm
tenancy—spending a good deal more of government funds than we ever
expect to get back. If this distinction is made publicly and with our
eyes open, it amounts to a gift of government money in the form of
labor, trees and supervision. On such a basis, if the government only
gets back $750 over a long period of years out of the $1,500 which it
expends in behalf of the Ozark farmer, I have little objection.

2. In the case of lumber companies, however, I see no reason why the
government should give them a subsidy any more than it gives a subsidy
to many other forms of private enterprise conducted by corporations or
the equivalent.

If the government is to help lumber companies by means of free labor,
free trees and free supervision, it should get back all of the money it costs
the government. And I think, indeed. that it should get back a low rate
of interest in addition.

May I suggest that the plan be restudied in the light of these suggestions.

Apparently there is no provision in this plan for cooperative forestry—
in other words taking a fairly good sized tract of, say ten to twenty thousand acres and handling the whole long-range operation through a cooperative association of the actual land owners themselves. [2]

F. D. R.

[13:OF 1–C:CT]

[1] See *ante,* 759.
[2] Answered *post,* 792.

778   ROOSEVELT TO GOVERNOR CLARENCE D. MARTIN, Olympia,
Washington

[WASHINGTON, *April 26, 1938*] [1]

DEAR GOVERNOR: I am ~~intensely~~ interested in your letter of March 31
and the accompanying map.[2]   It had been my definite conviction that
the establishment of the national park in the Olympic Peninsula would
promote State as well as national interests.   ~~I want you to know, however, that action in the Olympic matter which might unnecessarily curtail the economic advancement of the State of Washington has been and is farthest from my desire.~~

Views expressed in your letter will be given more careful and complete
consideration than I have yet been able to accord them, and at the first
opportunity I shall discuss the matter with the Senators and Representatives from your State, and with the members of my Cabinet most directly
concerned.

Thank you for so frankly telling me of your own position in the
matter.[3]

Sincerely,

[FRANKLIN D. ROOSEVELT]

[13:OF 6–P:CT:DRAFT]

[1] A supplied and approximate date.
[2] The map is not present.
[3] This draft was prepared by the Agriculture Department; the deletions were made
by Roosevelt.   Acting Secretary of Agriculture Wilson, in his letter to Roosevelt
enclosing the draft, April 26, 1938, said, "It occurs to me that the views expressed
by the Governor bear so definitely upon your own personal conclusions regarding the
proposed Olympic National Park that the enclosed draft may not, perhaps, be adequate under the circumstances."   An attached memorandum, Roosevelt to Wallace,
April 26, 1938, reads, "Will you speak to me about this at your convenience?"   The
letter was sent as revised, according to a notation on this memorandum.

779   ROOSEVELT TO CARL VROOMAN, Bloomington, Illinois

[WASHINGTON] *May 11, 1938*

MY DEAR CARL: This is in reply to your day letter of April twenty-
third, 1938, regarding application of the 1938 A. A. A. Farm Program
to your particular area.[1]

In carrying out the purposes of the Agricultural Adjustment Act of
1938, it is our duty to maintain a continued and stable supply of agricultural commodities from domestic production adequate to meet the consumer demand at prices fair to both producers and consumers.   The Act
directs us to approach this problem through national, State, county, and
farm allotments of acreage for several of the principal soil-depleting
crops.

As you know, the new farm Act prescribes formulas by which the national acreage allotments shall be determined and apportioned among the States, counties and farms. These allotments are determined and apportioned in accordance with a uniform procedure and should result in equitable treatment to all farmers.

I am advised by the Secretary of Agriculture that to increase these allotments of soil-depleting crops would tend to defeat the purposes of the farm Act. Farmers again would be faced with price collapse such as heretofore has penalized heavy production. In the case of crop failure, an increased acreage allotment of soil-depleting crops would not necessarily affect the situation favorably and actually might be detrimental to the welfare of the farmers.

It does not appear feasible, therefore, to make the changes you recommend. The farmer administrative representatives in the field appear to be opposed to any alteration of the acreage allotments now in effect.

May I suggest that the farmers you represent make a further study of the provisions of the 1938 A. A. A. Farm Program, bearing in mind its objectives. Farmers have an opportunity to participate in a program designed to meet both their current and future needs. I believe this fact will be recognized more generally as the program becomes better understood.

I appreciate your interest in these farm problems and shall be grateful for your continued leadership and encouragement in obtaining the greatest possible participation in the 1938 Farm Program.[2]

Very sincerely yours,

[FRANKLIN D. ROOSEVELT]

[APS] Do come & see me when you come to Washington

[13:OF I-K:CT]

---

[1] Vrooman said that the great majority of farmers in his area believed that twice as much land had been allotted to soil-building crops as was desirable (OF I-K). Vrooman was Assistant Secretary of Agriculture during the administration of President Wilson.

[2] Drafted by the Agriculture Department.

780   ROOSEVELT TO KENNETH A. REID, GENERAL MANAGER, IZAAK
       WALTON LEAGUE OF AMERICA, Chicago

WASHINGTON, *May 12, 1938*

MY DEAR MR. REID: This will acknowledge receipt of your letter of April 14, stating that the Izaak Walton League of America is supporting the Water Pollution Bill, H. R. 2711, and submitting suggestions relating to the prevention and abatement of water pollution.

I have read with interest your suggestion that Federal allotments made for the purpose of relieving unemployment might be made effective in reducing the loss the nation now suffers from stream pollution, and aid in accomplishing the primary purpose of the Water Pollution Bill. It is apparent that you have given careful thought to the protection of one of our greatest national resources.

As you know, I am vitally interested in the protection of our streams. I appreciate your thoughtfulness in calling my attention to your stand in connection with the Water Pollution Bill, and in submitting suggestions as to how its operation might be made more effective.[1]

Very sincerely,

[FRANKLIN D. ROOSEVELT]

[13:OF 114–A:CT]

[1](Drafted by the Interior Department.) The Izaak Walton League withdrew its support from this bill when its enforcement provisions were stricken out in conference. Reid said these changes actually encouraged pollution by making the act of polluting a condition of eligibility for Federal aid (Reid to Roosevelt, June 13, 1938, OF 114–A). The Sanitary Water Board of Pennsylvania took the same stand and urged that the bill be vetoed because it would lull the public to a false sense of security (P. G. Platt to Roosevelt, June 23, 1938, OF 114–A). See veto message, *post*, 799.

781   ROOSEVELT TO HARRY H. WOODRING, SECRETARY OF WAR

WASHINGTON, *May 17, 1938*

MEMORANDUM FOR THE SECRETARY OF WAR: In view of the enclosed report of the National Resources Committee, it seems to me that the War Department should advise the Committee that while the plan proposed by the Acting Chief of Engineers is probably in harmony with the best long-term water plan for the Southern California drainage area, nevertheless, because of lack of final surveys covering the whole subject, the Congress should not authorize or appropriate for the project at this session. Probably by next January a complete report can be made.

F. D. R.

[13:OF 132–C:CT]

782   [Enclosure] FREDERIC A. DELANO, CHAIRMAN, ADVISORY COMMITTEE TO THE NATIONAL RESOURCES COMMITTEE, TO ROOSEVELT

WASHINGTON, *May 13, 1938*

MY DEAR MR. PRESIDENT: In accordance with your request of May 10 [1] for a report and recommendation on the project for flood control of San Antonio and Chino Creeks in San Bernardino and Los Angeles Counties, California, the following statement has been prepared by our staff with the approval of Chairman Wolman of the Water Resources

Committee. In view of your request for an "immediate" report, this statement is submitted without waiting for reference to the members of the Water Committee or clearance by the members of the full National Resources Committee.

The Acting Chief of Engineers, in his memorandum of May 5, 1938, in effect recommends that the Congress authorize construction of a project along the lines described in the preliminary examination and survey, with the right of the Corps of Engineers to make such modifications as detailed investigations may suggest.

The parallel preliminary examination and survey by the Department of Agriculture for run-off and water flow retardation and soil erosion prevention which were authorized in the same act as the Army survey, are still in progress and the conclusions may not be available within a month or more. Since the problem in this part of Southern California is as much one of water conservation as of flood control, the report of the Department of Agriculture is of special importance.

In recent weeks an agreement has been reached among the State of California, the Corps of Engineers, and the Department of Agriculture for flood control surveys in Southern California. This project, however, has not yet been cleared through procedure outlined in that agreement, although the State of California has expressed special interest in the survey and in the project.

It is our conclusion that the plan proposed by the Acting Chief of Engineers is probably in harmony with the best long-term water plan for this drainage area, but that it may be subject to question on the score of economic justification and on adequacy of surveys. For its economic justification, both the estimated value of the flood loss prevented and the estimated increase in property values on account of such loss-prevention, are together claimed with possible duplication of amounts. The problem and the benefits are primarily intrastate. There is no indication whether less expensive techniques such as zoning for modified land use in areas of greatest risk may in any degree be applicable.

If it is your policy to encourage authorization by Congress of apparently useful projects in advance of completion of studies, we would, of course, see no objection to authorization of this project by the Congress at this time. However, we believe that allotments should certainly *not* be made for construction until detailed studies more fully support its economic justification as a Federal undertaking and until more complete agreement has been arrived at with reference to the most important engineering features of the project, among the Corps of Engineers, the Department of Agriculture, and the State of California.

Sincerely yours,

[FREDERIC A. DELANO]

[13:OF 132–C:CT]

¹ Roosevelt's memorandum (OF 132–C) reads, "For immediate report and recommendation." It is attached to a copy of Woodring's letter to Roosevelt of May 6, 1938, covering the report of the Acting Chief of Engineers of May 5, 1938, mentioned below. Apparently the report was not returned to the White House.

783   PRESS CONFERENCE, Executive Offices of the White House, May 20, 1938, 10:50 A. M.

[*Excerpt*] The President: I am sending out today to the Congress the message on phosphates, you will all be glad to know, since it is somewhat overdue.

It does call attention to the need of phosphates in the land and to some rather interesting figures in regard to the supply of phosphates in the world. We probably have the largest deposits of phosphate rock, phosphorous rock, of any other nation in the world, and the rest of the phosphates is only in three countries, Russia and French and British Colonies.

Science has been more and more coming to the conclusion that land runs out in most climates if it does not have the phosphates renewed in it. Of course the whole thing ties up with soil conservation because, if land runs out, farmers abandon it and thereupon erosion sets in. In other words, it is tied in with the general soil conservation problem.

In the United States, about seven or eight billion tons of phosphate rock that has been located, nearly all of it, the great bulk of it, is out in the Rocky Mountain states. About the only chemical phosphate that is being produced at the present time in this country comes from Florida and Tennessee and a very large portion of the Florida phosphate is exported. Actually, of the entire supply of phosphate rock, probably the Government owns today, on public land, something like three-quarters of it and it is a very important thing to get a national policy as to the present development, including export, and the future development of phosphate, in view of these rather simple figures.

If you want to add a human interest touch to any story you write, it was brought home to me when I was preparing this message—I haven't got it in the message—the fact that no life can be successfully produced without phosphate. Just as an example, that includes human life, animal life and plant life. If you produce a crop for human consumption that is produced on a field with very little phosphate in the soil, it means that the children who eat hominy or the oatmeal do not get enough phosphate and of course we all know that the lack of phosphates in children is the cause of rickets and things like that. It is the same way with animal life of all kinds. It does not maintain its standard unless it gets phosphates out of its food. If cows do not get enough phosphate in the grass they eat, their milk has got less phosphate than it would have otherwise. So you can go on and enlarge on that ad lib.

It really is a new thought for the American people that phosphate is necessary for all kinds of life, human, animal and plant and that is why it is of importance to this country for the next thousand years or so that we have a policy in regard to returning phosphate to the land.

Q: Mr. President, is it not the idea with respect to plant food to have a combination of phosphate and nitrates?

The President: Yes, and of course on the nitrate end of it—

Q: I was going to ask you about the nitrate side.

The President: That is the other side, Fred.[1] I am only a layman on this but the general idea is that when you plough under a cover crop in order to help bring the soil back, or when you put on the other types of fertilizer and manures, you do increase the nitrates but you increase the phosphates very little. When you plough a crop back, the bulk of the chemical is the nitrate end rather than the phosphate end, and the two are absolutely essential.

Q: Isn't the nitrate supply almost inexhaustible by reason of the power plants?

The President: We are not troubled by the nitrate supply. You can always bring the nitrate factor in the land back by ploughing crops under.

Q: Can you tell us what the recommendations are?

The President: The recommendation is that the Congress appoint a Joint Committee to make an immediate study and report back, with recommendations on policy, at the next session.

[13:PRESIDENT'S PRESS CONFERENCES:T]

[1] Fred Essary of the Baltimore *Sun*.

784 ROOSEVELT TO THE CONGRESS

THE WHITE HOUSE, *May 20, 1938*

To THE CONGRESS OF THE UNITED STATES: The soil of the United States faces a continuing loss of its productive capacity.

That is a challenging statement. It would seem, therefore, to be the part of wisdom for the Government and the people of the United States to adopt every possible method to stop this loss and begin to rebuild soil fertility.

We give the name of "soil conservation" to the problem as a whole; and we are already active in our efforts to retard and prevent soil erosion, and by the more intelligent use of land to build up its crop, its pasturage and its tree producing capacity.

As a result of the studies and tests of modern science it has come to be recognized that phosphorus is a necessary element in human, in animal and in plant nutrition. The phosphorus content of our land, following generations of cultivation, has greatly diminished. It needs replenishing. The necessity for wider use of phosphates and the conservation of our supplies of phosphates for future generations is, therefore, a matter of great public concern. We cannot place our agriculture upon a permanent basis unless we give it heed.

I cannot over-emphasize the importance of phosphorus not only to agriculture and soil conservation but also to the physical health and economic security of the people of the Nation. Many of our soil types are deficient in phosphorus, thus causing low yields and poor quality of crops and pastures.

Indeed, much of the present accelerated soil erosion in the United States has taken place, and is still taking place, on land that has either been abandoned or is ready to be abandoned because of a low productivity brought about by failure to maintain the fertilizing elements in the soil. In many cases the reclaiming of eroded land is largely a matter of stimulating plant growth such as legumes and grasses; but hand in hand with this we must also replenish the actual phosphorus content of the soil.

Recent estimates indicate that the removal of phosphorus from the soils of the United States by harvested crops, grazing, erosion, and leaching, greatly exceeds the addition of phosphorus to the soil through the means of fertilizers, animal manures and bedding, rainfall, irrigation and seeds.

It appears that even with a complete control of erosion, which obviously is impossible, a high level of productivity will not be maintained unless phosphorus is returned to the soil at a greater rate than is being done at present. Increases by the addition of phosphorus to the soil must be made largely, if not entirely, in the form of fertilizers which are derived principally from phosphate rock.

Therefore, the question of continuous and adequate supplies of phosphate rock directly concerns the national welfare.

The total known world supply of phosphate rock is estimated at 17.2 billion tons, of which 7.2 billion tons is located in the United States. Nearly all the remainder is controlled by Great Britain, France and Russia. The supply in the United States is distributed as follows: Florida 7.4%, Tennessee 1.4%, Western States (Idaho, Montana, Utah and Wyoming) 90.8%, and other States (Arkansas, Kentucky, South Carolina, and Virginia) 0.4%. The domestic production of phosphate rock amounted to 3,351,857 tons in 1936, drawn from Florida (78.3%), Tennessee (19.2%), and Idaho and Montana (2.5%). Exports of phosphate rock amounted to 1,208,951 tons, almost entirely from Florida, and consumption of phosphate rock for non-agricultural purposes totaled 352,275 tons.

Thus, it appears that of the total domestic production of phosphate rock only 53% was used for domestic agricultural purposes.

Owing to their location in relation to the principal fertilizer-consuming districts, the Florida and Tennessee deposits, which contain less than 10% of the nation's supply, are furnishing more than 97% of all the phosphate rock used for domestic agricultural purposes. Under present conditions, by far the greater portion of our phosphate requirements will continue to be drawn from the Florida and Tennessee deposits so long as these deposits last. When it is realized that the consumption of phosphatic fertilizer must be increased considerably if our soils are to be maintained reasonably near their present levels of fertility, which in many cases are far below the levels necessary for an efficient agriculture, it becomes apparent that the deposits of Florida and Tennessee will last but a comparatively short period.

It is hardly necessary to emphasize the desirability of conserving these deposits to the fullest extent for the benefit of agriculture in the East, the South and a considerable portion of the Middle West.

At the same time, serious attention should be given to the development of the Western phosphate deposits in order that they may be made to serve economically the widest possible territory. It is evident that our main reliance for an adequate supply of phosphate must eventually be placed on our Western deposits.

As of December 1, 1936, the Government owned 2,124,904 acres of proven and potential phosphate lands in Idaho, Montana, Utah and Wyoming, and 66,916 acres in Florida. The Government owns no extensive areas of phosphate land in other States. Although an exact estimate of the tonnage of phosphate rock on Government land is not available, the quantity in the Western reserve no doubt exceeds 5 billion tons. It appears that only a small portion of the Florida supply is on Government land.

I call your special attention to the interesting and valuable work of the Tennessee Valley Authority and the Department of Agriculture in devising new processes for treating phosphate rock and for using the new types of phosphate products. This work promises to make the great western deposits available to a large area of America.

These developments by themselves, however, will not lessen the drain on the comparatively small deposits in Tennessee and Florida because the methods of treatment can be used as well on these deposits as on those in the West. Inasmuch as the deposits in Tennessee and Florida are, and will continue to be, of vital importance to American agriculture, it is to the national interest that they be conserved to the fullest extent.

The disposition of our phosphate deposits should be regarded as a national concern. The situation appears to offer an opportunity for this nation to exercise foresight in the use of a great national resource heretofore almost unknown in our plans for the development of the nation.

I invite the especial attention of the Congress to the very large percentage of known phosphate rock which is on government owned land— probably three-quarters of the whole supply; and to the fact that the Eastern supply, while in private ownership, is today being exported in such quantities that when and if it is wholly depleted, Eastern farms will have to depend for their phosphate supply on the Far Western lands.

It is, therefore, high time for the Nation to adopt a national policy for the production and conservation of phosphates for the benefit of this and coming generations.

To the end that continuous and adequate supplies be insured, and that efficient forms of this key element, phosphorus, be available at the lowest cost throughout the country, I recommend that a joint committee of the Senate and of the House of Representatives be named to give study to the entire subject of phosphate resources, their use and service to American agriculture, and to make report to the next Congress.[1]

FRANKLIN D. ROOSEVELT

[W. H. PRESS RELEASES:M]

[1] The text of this message is made up of parts of one of two drafts prepared by the Agriculture Department, together with a number of paragraphs that appear, from their form and language, to have been composed by Roosevelt. Both drafts were reviewed by Chairman H. A. Morgan of the Tennessee Valley Authority (Le Cron to Durand, April 26 and 27, 1938, Speech File), but the one which Morgan favored was not used. (The final draft is present.) In the message as here printed paragraphs 7 to 15 and 17 to 18 are from the Agriculture Department draft. (Paragraph 9 was somewhat revised.)

By joint resolution of June 16, 1938 (52 *Stat.* 704), a joint Congressional committee was appointed to investigate the phosphate resources of 'the United States. Numerous hearings were held and a report was issued, *Phosphate Resources of the United States*, S. Doc. 21, 76th Cong., 1st sess. (Washington, 1939). This report is described in a note to the message as printed in Rosenman (ed.), *Public Papers*, VII, 345–350.

785   ROOSEVELT TO SENATOR ALBEN W. BARKLEY OF KENTUCKY

WASHINGTON, *May 25, 1938*

MEMORANDUM FOR SENATOR BARKLEY: The attached is tremendously important and there are several other objections to the Flood Control Bill which have been raised by the Budget, including a dangerous tax feature.

As the Bill stands now I should, of course, have to veto it.

I do not want to take this up with Copeland directly but will you do it?

F. D. R.

[13:OF 132–D:CT]

MEMORANDUM FOR THE PRESIDENT: The Flood Control Bill (H. R. 10618) which passed the House on May 19, 1938, and which is now pending before the Senate has far-reaching effects on the national power policy and program.

The bill authorizes 90 or more dam and reservoir projects, many of which have power possibilities. The amount of local contribution for such projects has been reduced, so that the Federal Government will bear in excess of 90% of the total cost of the projects, including the cost of land, easements and rights of way. However, in the case of only two projects (the Denison project on the Red River in Oklahoma and Texas, and the Bluestone project on the New River in West Virginia) does the bill provide for the acquisition of title by the United States in project lands and rights of way. By specifically requiring title to vest in the United States in these two cases, the bill by implication permits title to project lands and rights of way for all other dam and reservoir projects to be taken and held by local agencies. Thus, the bill can be given an interpretation which is diametrically opposite to the construction which the Federal Power Commission has consistently given to the Flood Control Act of 1936. For almost a year this Commission had advised against the ratification of the New England Flood Control Compacts on the ground that the provision in the compacts reserving title to the projects in the New England States is contrary to the provision of the Food Control Act of 1936 as well as the established national power policy. If the pending flood control bill is enacted without making clear that title to all dam and reservoir projects shall be in the United States, any future program of Federal ownership and operation of flood control-power projects will be seriously impeded, if not foreclosed.

Although the bill expressly recognizes the power possibilities of two projects, provision is made for the installation in any project of penstocks or other similar facilities adapted to possible future use in the development of hydroelectric power when approved by the Secretary of War upon the recommendation of the Chief of Engineers. The report of the House Committee on Flood Control in describing the dam and reservoir projects included in the program makes reference to provision for "permanent pools" in the reservoirs. The report intimates that such "permanent pools" will be utilized for recreation, possible wild life preserves, municipal water supply, and "other useful purposes."

The enactment of the bill in its present form would have the following effects upon the national power program:

(1) Title to projects constructed on many of the nation's water power sites on navigable rivers and their tributaries would be lost forever to the Federal Government; and

(2) Projects having power possibilities in addition to flood control may be constructed in such a way as to preclude the use of the project for joint purposes.

The attached amendment would: (1) expressly provide that title to lands, easements, and rights of way for all dam and reservoir projects shall be in the United States; and (2) authorize the construction of dam and reservoir projects for power in addition to flood control whenever in the judgment of the Federal Power Commission the project could be economically used for the development of hydroelectric power.[1]

CLYDE L. SEAVEY, Acting Chairman
OSWALD RYAN, General Counsel

[13:OF 132–D:TS]

[1] Roosevelt had before him at this time a memorandum on the bill prepared by Acting Director of the Budget Bell, May 23, 1938 (OF 132–C). Bell pointed out that with respect to the acquisition of land for floodways on the lower Mississippi, the bill provided, in event the Government retained ownership, for Federal payment of the state and local taxes on such property.

787   GOVERNOR FRANK MURPHY OF MICHIGAN TO ROOSEVELT

LANSING, MICHIGAN, *May 26, 1938*

DEAR MR. PRESIDENT: I am taking the liberty of presenting to you certain facts regarding the management of forest lands in Michigan, which was the subject of your letter to me of March 15, 1938, with the thought that they will be of interest to you.

The problem of proper management of forest lands is one in which this state is vitally interested.   It has been one of the major concerns of the Department of Conservation, and the University of Michigan and Michigan State College have also expended much time, thought, and effort toward its solution.

In your letter you pointed out that Michigan has 19,000,000 acres of land which might properly be classified as forest land.   This acreage may be itemized as follows:

3,500,000 acres—farm wood lots scattered throughout the state but located mostly in the southern farming district.   Under the Norris-Doxey law these will be brought to maximum production when enforcement funds are available.

5,000,000 acres—eventual state ownership (includes 2,400,000 acres now under active forest management by the state and the estimated increase resulting from the recent tax sale). The area replanted in the state forests during the past 15 years has exceeded that of any other state.

4,000,000 acres—eventual federal ownership (includes present federal lands of 1,500,000 acres and proposed purchases).

1,000,000 acres—private recreational areas such as those held by hunting and fishing clubs.

2,500,000 acres—cut-over and denuded land (submarginal and of same class as most state forest land but for one reason or another not in public ownership). This land has no immediate bearing on the question of government regulated cutting on private land. It does not support any material quantity of merchantable growth.

3,000,000 acres—privately owned merchantable timber held by a comparatively few large landholders.

Of this total of 19,000,000 acres of forest land, 16,000,000 acres are in the "fire zone" or northern Michigan wild land area. This land has been placed under intensive fire protection and fire losses have been held at a minimum. The remaining 3,000,000 acres include farm wood lots in the Southern Michigan farming district and potential forest lands in the same area that are not classed as wood lots because of insufficient growth.

Michigan has utilized every practical legal stimulus to maintain stability of private ownership of forest lands and to keep them in productive condition. The Farm Wood Lot Tax Law provides for tax exemption of the timber and only a nominal land valuation assessment. The Pearson Act, which applies to second growth timber and prescribes no acreage limit, provided a uniform tax rate of ten cents per acre per year which was later reduced to five cents. Although this act has been in force for twelve years, however, less than 100,000 acres have been registered under it.

Selective cutting has been advocated and is still being practiced by some private operators, but as yet no selective method or any other system of continuously productive management has been demonstrated conclusively to be financially practicable in the forest types of Michigan. Obviously private capital cannot hold or manage its timbered lands for the benefit of the public if no profit is realized on its investment. Until some workable method of conservative cutting is evolved which makes possible reasonably profitable operations, it seems that outright purchase by the state or federal government would be the only means of keeping the remaining merchantable stands in good productive condition. It is possible that a plan of selective cutting under government specifications with a mutual agreement for purchase of the residual forest by the governmental agency would prove feasible.

I wish to assure you that Michigan is heartily in accord with the objectives set forth in your message to the Congress and with your belief that the forest resources of the state should be so managed that they will contribute their proper share to the wealth and prosperity of our people. As you no doubt are aware, Michigan was represented at the conference of federal, state, and private forestry interests held in St. Paul, Minnesota, May 20 for the purpose of discussing this problem.[1]

Sincerely,

FRANK MURPHY

[13:OF 149:TS]

[1] Answered *post,* 809.

788   EBERT K. BURLEW, ACTING SECRETARY OF THE INTERIOR, TO ROOSEVELT

WASHINGTON, *May 27, 1938*

MY DEAR MR. PRESIDENT: The Wallgren Bill, H. R. 10024, to establish the Olympic National Park in the State of Washington, amended to exclude the corridors on the Hoh and Bogachiel Rivers and about 33,000 acres in the lower Bogachiel Valley, was passed by the House of Representatives on May 16 and has been referred to the Senate Public Lands and Surveys Committee. An amendment has been submitted by this Department to the Chairman of that Committee which would authorize the President to add to the proposed park any lands within the boundaries of the Olympic National Forest. The amendment reads as follows:

Provided, That the President may by proclamation add to the park any lands of the United States within the limits of the Olympic National Forest, including any lands therein that have been or may be acquired through donation or purchase, which he may determine to be desirable for national park purpose.

The Senate Public Lands and Surveys Committee has not yet had a hearing on the bill. The Chairman and the Senators from the State of Washington have expressed the opinion that the time before adjournment may be too limited to allow action on the bill.

If the park is to be established by this Congress, the Committee should be influenced to consider the bill promptly and the Senators from the State of Washington urged to further its passage on the floor of the Senate.

Sincerely yours,

E. K. BURLEW

[13:OF 6–P:TS]

[WASHINGTON, *May 27, 1938*] [1]

STE: Call up Schwellenback [*sic*] & Bone and tell them I hope they
will press for the passage of this bill—H. R. 10024 and ask if there is
anything I can do to help.[2]

FDR.

[13:OF 6–P:A]

[1] This memorandum was attached to the preceding letter and has been given the
same date. It is in Grace Tully's hand.
[2] Answered *post,* 791.

790   ROOSEVELT TO GEORGE G. BATTLE, New York City

WASHINGTON, *May 31, 1938*

MY DEAR MR. BATTLE: I have received your letter of May 14 voicing
your opposition to S. 3925, and H. R. 10489 which would authorize the
construction of a weir and tunnel in Yellowstone Lake for the purpose
of diverting its waters into a tributary of the Snake River.[1]

In creating the Yellowstone National Park in 1872, the Congress
provided that the Secretary of the Interior should make regulations "for
the preservation, from injury or spoliation, of all timber, mineral deposits,
natural curiosities, or wonders within said park, and their retention in
their natural condition."

During the past half century, certain groups have sought to have the
Congress sanction the use of the lands and waters of this park for commercial purposes. Conspicuous among such attempts have been efforts,
since 1919, to have either a part of the park eliminated, or its waters
diverted for the purpose of irrigating lands in the upper Snake River
Valley. After carefully examining such proposals, the Congress has
upheld, without any compromise, the policy enunciated in 1872.

You are assured that I am personally opposed to all measures which
would interfere with the preservation of the wonders of the Yellowstone
National Park in their natural condition.[2]

Very sincerely yours,

[FRANKLIN D. ROOSEVELT]

[13:OF 6–P:CT]

[1] Battle, a member of the legal firm of Battle, Levy, Fowler and Newman, said
that the proposed project would go far to destroy the beauty of Yellowstone Park
and would be most harmful to the entire national park system (OF 6–P).
[2] Drafted by the Interior Department.

791   Stephen T. Early, Secretary to the President, to Roosevelt

WASHINGTON, *June 2, 1938*

MEMORANDUM FOR THE PRESIDENT: I have talked, as requested, to Senators Schwellenbach and Bone. It so happens that Senator Adams is Chairman of the Public Lands and Surveys Committee which has this bill [1] in charge. He is, at the present time, in charge of the Relief Bill now before the Senate and, of course, that has the right of way for the time being.

Senators Bone and Schwellenbach think that if they could have five minutes with you, tomorrow, since they expect the Relief Bill to be disposed of tonight, it would help them materially in pressing for the passage of this bill, both from the publicity point of view and in negotiating with Senator Adams.

I hope you will be able to give them a five minute appointment tomorrow.

STEPHEN EARLY

[13:OF 6–P:T]

[1] The Olympic National Park Bill (H. R. 10024).

792   Henry A. Wallace, Secretary of Agriculture, to Roosevelt

WASHINGTON, *June 2, 1938*

DEAR MR. PRESIDENT: The enclosed National Cooperative Reforestation Plan has been re-studied in the light of the specific and helpful suggestions included in your memorandum of April 25.

I agree with you that the plan should provide for a decided difference in benefits as between farm-owned and non-farm-owned forest lands. I am sure, however, that you recognize the need, in the public interest, for any such plan to: (1) provide a *large* measure of constructive emergency work on liquidating or semi-liquidating projects; (2) increase opportunities for *permanent* employment, and for stabilizing it, by rehabilitating unproductive forest land and building up forest capital and growth over *large* areas now only partially productive; (3) develop *maximum* public benefits such as are inherent in flood and erosion control, recreation, etc.

To be efficient, any plan should also recognize that, in forested regions such as the South, the Northeast, and the Lake States, farm woodlands are inextricably intermingled with comercial timber holdings; that the two often are (and by force of circumstances must be) managed simultaneously, for similar purposes, and under comparable conditions; that in the public interest large ownerships, as well as small, should be made more productive; that because of certain additional costs inevitable with relief labor, it may be equitable to exclude interest; that in the interest of the social structure and of local governments, taxes on forest properties must be collectible.

Recognizing all these elements, and to make the differential in benefits as between farm-owned and non-farm-owned forest property more marked, the following is suggested *with respect to forest lands owned by others than bona fide farmers.*

1. The Government to recapture 100% of its expenditures, without interest.

2. To meet practical considerations the Government to include in its expenditures a nominal annual rental under a long-term lease, which in no case shall exceed the amount of local and State taxes on the land involved.

The leasing procedure is suggested primarily to avoid jeopardizing local taxes on forest land from which, under this plan, there will be little or no income to the owner over a considerable period of years; taxes on which local governments must depend, often in large part, for public services that must be rendered. Possibility of applying this plan to forests owned by communities, etc., is apparent, and recapture of 100% of Federal expenditures is indicated in such cases.

No provision was made in the original plan, and none has been made here, for associations of farmers to practice cooperative forestry. We have found by experience that a great deal of educational work is necessary before any such cooperative effort among farmers can be set up. I believe experience under the procedure here outlined will provide that education; that cooperative forestry among farmers will be a natural outgrowth of the plan, after it has been in operation.

Since you agree in principle with the original plan insofar as it has to do with forest lands owned by bona fide farmers, the changes suggested in this memorandum apply, as I have said, only with respect to forest lands owned by others than bona fide farmers. As the French have learned, a plan such as this offers the only apparent way of getting effective access to the private forests of the country. A process of purchase is expensive, and may well be too slow to be effective in the sound public policy of balancing our timber budget.

I am attaching a copy of a portion of the French "Audiffred Law," because it offers an interesting parallel to the suggestions here made.[1] I am also attaching a hypothetical case of 10,000 acres developed under the leasing basis.[2] Representatives of the Department's Forest Service will be glad to discuss this idea with you, with a view to initiating early action, in case you wish to have them do so.

Sincerely,

H. A. WALLACE

[13:PPF 1820:TS]

¹ Wallace enclosed a quotation from a work he cited as "G. Huffel's *Economie Forestiere* (I, 346 ff.)," on the "Audiffred Law" of July 2, 1913.

² A one-page statement entitled, "Operations and Cost Plan for Increasing the Productivity of a Forest Holding Belonging to a Forest Land Operator in Southern Arkansas."

793   ROBERT FECHNER, DIRECTOR, CIVILIAN CONSERVATION CORPS, TO ROOSEVELT

WASHINGTON, D. C., *June 6, 1938*

DEAR MR. PRESIDENT: Nearly a year has passed since the new Civilian Conservation Corps Act (Public No. 163—75th Congress—approved June 28, 1937) became a law. As you will recall, this law states that, "The Director shall have complete and final authority in the functioning of the Corps, including the allotment of funds to cooperating Federal departments and agencies . . ."

The experience gained from approximately a year's operation under the above Act, in addition to four and one-quarter years prior thereto, prompts the expression of the following statements with regard to the administration of the Civilian Conservation Corps. These statements are designed to clarify and execute more effectively the law passed by Congress and approved by you.

1. The unity of the Civilian Conservation Corps as an organization is essential to its success and must be maintained. The effectiveness and appeal of the Corps, both to the public and its immediate beneficiaries, would be largely lost if it were partitioned or if Departmental or Bureau objectives were placed on a parity with the objectives of the Corps as a whole.

2. Representatives of the Cabinet Officers on the Civilian Conservation Corps Advisory Council should feel free of obligation to any specific bureau within their departments, and should be responsible, within their departments, directly to their Cabinet Officers. These Advisory Council representatives have the dual responsibility of representing their departments and of working for the common good of the Civilian Conservation Corps as an organization.

3. Additional personal participation in this program by the Cabinet Officers involved is desirable. This participation might take the form of a quarterly meeting between the President, the Cabinet Officers of the cooperating agencies, and the Director of the Civilian Conservation Corps.

4. The following basic principles are essential to achieve the results contemplated by the Civilian Conservation Corps Act:

(a) By the very nature of the Civilian Conservation Corps, the Director does not desire to participate actively in what may be termed "operations functions." These functions he delegates to the cooperating agencies. Such delegation will continue.

(b) All matters of policy will be initiated by or approved by the Director.

(c) The Director will satisfy himself, through such methods as he may deem appropriate, that his policies are being administered and executed as approved. If violations are established, corrective action thereon shall be taken upon the request of the Director.

Your approval of the above statements is respectfully requested.

Sincerely yours,

ROBT. FECHNER

Approved: FRANKLIN D. ROOSEVELT, Oct 14 1938 [1]

[13:OF 268:TS:PHOTOSTAT]

[1] Roosevelt's oral approval was apparently given much earlier. See *post*, 817.

794   ROOSEVELT TO REPRESENTATIVE FRANK E. HOOK OF MICHIGAN

[WASHINGTON] *June 7, 1938*

MY DEAR CONGRESSMAN: I have your letter of May 23, 1938, with reference to your bill H. R. 9979, for acquiring lands in the Ottawa National Forest and other lands in Baraga, Gogebic, Houghton, Iron, and Ontonagon Counties, Michigan.[1]

Under our Budget procedure a proposed favorable report on this bill by the Secretary of Agriculture was submitted to the Acting Director of the Bureau of the Budget for advice as to the relation of the proposed legislation to my program. The Acting Director advised the Secretary to the effect that the proposal ran counter to my program in that it would authorize specific appropriations, totaling $10,000,000 for the acquisition of the lands in question. This was in accordance with my policy that the purchase of lands for additions to our national forests should properly be financed from annual appropriations made for such purpose, based upon estimates submitted in the annual Budget. Only in this way can the merit of projects of this character be considered in their proper relation to the merits of other projects of the same character, and all of these projects be then considered in their relation to the needs of the other Government activities that are presented for incorporation in the annual Budgets.

In making up my annual Budget, I must determine, under my financial program for the next year, just how much money can be allocated to the purchase of forest lands under the existing general authority of law providing for such purchases, and the building up of any considerable number of specific legislative commitments—for which your proposed legislation would serve as a precedent—would seriously interfere with the necessary flexibility of this procedure.

While existing law provides for the selection by the National Forest Reservation Commission of lands to be added to national forests, I would not object to special legislation *authorizing* the purchase of the particular lands in which you are interested, should the Congress deem this advisable, out of the regular annual appropriations for the acquisition of forest lands.

Sincerely yours,

[FRANKLIN D. ROOSEVELT]

[*Notation*:AS] DWB[2]

[13:OF 1–C:CT]

[1] Hook said (OF 1–C) that he understood that the Forest Service was in favor of the bill and that he could not understand why the Budget Bureau had declared it not in conformity with the President's program. The bill in question was introduced March 22, 1938, and referred to the House Committee on Agriculture, which took no action (*Cong. Rec.*, 75th Cong., 3d sess., 83:4, 3889).

[2] Acting Budget Director Daniel W. Bell, in whose agency this letter was drafted. With the draft is a memorandum, Bell to Roosevelt, June 1, 1938, on the subject of Hook's bill.

795   ROOSEVELT TO LOUIS B. DE KOVEN, New York City

[WASHINGTON] *June 8, 1938*

DEAR LOUIS: I have received your letter of May 22, enclosing a newspaper clipping regarding the bills recently introduced in the Congress to provide for the diversion of water from Yellowstone Lake to the Snake River in Idaho.[1]

Last fall, while I was visiting in Yellowstone National Park, I learned something of the plans of the Snake River Valley water-users which are now reflected in this proposed legislation. I find that among the various proposals made from time to time since 1884 to use Yellowstone Lake for industrial purposes, those of Idaho irrigation interests have been most conspicuous. The present proposal represents the fourth attempt to establish water rights for local Idaho irrigation purposes.

Congress has repeatedly upheld the policy written into the Act of 1872 establishing Yellowstone National Park, that the area shall be preserved in its natural condition, and I am opposed to any measure affecting the national park and monument system which would modify this vital and inviolable principle.[2]

Very sincerely yours,

[FRANKLIN D. ROOSEVELT]

[13:OF 6–P:CT]

[1] De Koven had asked Roosevelt to use his influence against the enactment of the proposed legislation (OF 6–P).
[2] Drafted by the Interior Department.

796   ROOSEVELT TO HARRY H. WOODRING, SECRETARY OF WAR, HENRY A. WALLACE, SECRETARY OF AGRICULTURE, AND HARRY L. HOPKINS, WORKS PROGRESS ADMINISTRATOR

WASHINGTON, *June 13, 1938*

MEMORANDUM . . . I have signed the bill making appropriations for civil functions administered by the War Department.[1] This includes for rivers and harbors and for flood control over $200,000,000, including $18,000,000 made available from Title I of the Emergency Relief Appropriation Act of 1938 (to be applied to rivers and harbors).

Furthermore, $7,000,000 of the appropriation for flood control is made available to the Secretary of Agriculture to survey soil erosion prevention and for soil erosion works.

Will you be good enough to appoint a committee representing War, Agriculture and WPA, to coordinate this work, giving special attention to the employment of as many people as possible from the relief rolls out of the more than $200,000,000 available, and giving special attention also to starting as much of the work during the coming sixty days as possible?

Where any possibility—even a remote possibility—of power development is concerned, I should like this committee of three to consult with the Federal Power Commission.

F. D. R.

[13:BUDGET BUREAU ENROLLED BILLS:CT]

[1] Act approved June 11,1938 (52 *Stat.* 642).

797   DANIEL W. BELL, ACTING DIRECTOR, BUREAU OF THE BUDGET, TO MARVIN H. McINTYRE, SECRETARY TO THE PRESIDENT

WASHINGTON, *June 23, 1938*

MY DEAR MR. McINTYRE: By your memorandum of June 16, 1938, you referred to me, by direction of the President, for advice as to whether there is any objection to its approval, the following bill: H. R. 10618, Authorizing the construction of certain public works on rivers and harbors for flood control, and for other purposes.

I have referred this bill to the Secretary of War, the Secretary of Agriculture, the Secretary of the Interior, the Chairman of the Federal Power Commission, and the Chairman of the National Resources Committee. I am transmitting herewith their reports, as follows: [1]

[235]

Secretary of War: Report dated June 21, 1938, giving a brief synopsis of the various sections of the bill and stating that "While the War Department has not favored each and every feature of this Act, nevertheless it considers that the Act as a whole is in the public interest and therefore recommends its approval."

Secretary of Agriculture: Report dated June 20, 1938, in which it is stated that "The principles of the provisions of H. R. 10618 in respect of the responsibilities of the Department of Agriculture, and specifically section 1, the first paragraph of section 2, and sections 5, 6, 7, 8, and 9, are considered in the public interest; it is therefore recommended that the bill be approved."

Secretary of the Interior: Report of the Acting Secretary, dated June 22, 1938, stating that his Department does not consider the bill to be wholly satisfactory legislation for the reason that it provides for assumption by the United States of the entire cost of lands, easements, and rights-of-way in connection with flood control dams and reservoirs, which would establish a precedent which might weaken the repayment policy of the Reclamation Law and tend to create a strong pressure for extension of Federal subsidization to reclamation projects; also, that flood control projects in any given drainage basin are an integral part of any sound program for such drainage basin and that the bill makes no provision for cooperation, except indirectly, and at the pleasure of the War Department, with agencies of the Department of the Interior which are concerned with the conservation of water.

Chairman, Federal Power Commission: Report of the Acting Chairman, dated June 21, 1938, recommending a favorable report to the President on the bill and stating that "In undertaking to pay 100% of the cost of dam and reservoir projects and in expressly reserving title to such projects in the United States the bill, in the Commission's opinion, offers a practical solution to the flood control problem of this country, and at the same time protects the Federal interest in the water power resources of the nation" and that "The additional expenditure of funds by the Federal Government made necessary by the assumption of the entire cost of certain of the flood control projects included in the bill, and the cost of additional investigations which will be undertaken by the Federal Power Commission will be offset many fold by the advantages to the entire nation which will flow from the prompt initiation of the projects thereby made possible."

Chairman, National Resources Committee: Report of the Vice Chairman, dated June 22, 1938, inclosing a memorandum on each section of the bill; stating that the bill is inimical to the public interest and should be vetoed for reasons stated; and inclosing a suggested draft of memorandum of disapproval.

Cost of the Bill

Facially, the bill authorizes $375,000,000 for carrying out the improvements provided for therein over the five-year period ending June 30, 1944, plus $11,500,000 for examinations and surveys, total $386,-500,000. However, the Secretary of War states that this amount will be insufficient to cover all the costs of lands and damages for previously authorized projects and that therefore the number of new projects instituted will have to be limited so that these costs can be met.

While the bill authorizes, facially, $386,500,000, it should be noted that with respect to certain of the authorizations going to make up that amount the bill provides that such authorizations are for the initiation and partial accomplishment of the plan. For example: The bill authorizes for the Ohio River Basin a total of $125,300,000 and states that such sum is for the initiation and partial accomplishment of the plan; same for Missouri River Basin, $9,000,000; same for White River Basin, $25,000,000; same for Arkansas River Basin, $21,000,000; and same for Willamette River Basin, $11,300,000. What the additional cost for completion of these plans may amount to is unknown at this time.

Potentially, the bill involves possible heavy future demands upon the Treasury in furtherance of other phases of water control and development and, by establishing the principle of reimbursing local agencies for expenditures made by them under previous laws in partial payment for flood protection, invites demands that this principle be extended to all previous flood control projects and to other projects and to other fields.

Recommendation

From a Budget standpoint, I am opposed to the bill for the following reasons:

1. It violates the principle of local responsibility in the cost of all flood control projects involving dams and reservoirs, which should be maintained in the interest of sound financial policy and of fundamental equity. This establishes a dangerous precedent and will inevitably lead to its application to other projects in other fields. Heretofore the President has steadfastly adhered to the principle of local cooperation.

2. It authorizes the appropriation from the general fund of the Treasury of the quite appreciable sum of $386,500,000 over a five-year period, 1939–1944, without providing any means for the raising of the additional revenue which will be required therefor, such expenditures not now being provided for in the present tax structure.

3. It superimposes upon existing unliquidated authorizations for flood control and protection, amounting to approximately $425,000,000, an additional $386,500,000.

I concur in the opinion of the National Resources Committee that the bill should not receive the approval of the President.

I recommend that before the President acts upon the bill that he confer with the Chairman of the National Resources Committee and the Chairman of the Water Resources Committee of the National Resources Committee.

Very truly yours,

D. W. BELL

[13:BUDGET BUREAU ENROLLED BILLS:TS]

798 [*Enclosure*] FREDERIC A. DELANO, VICE CHAIRMAN, NATIONAL RESOURCES COMMITTEE, TO DANIEL W. BELL

WASHINGTON, *June 22, 1938*

MY DEAR MR. BELL: In accordance with the request from the Bureau of the Budget, addressed to Chairman Ickes under date of June 17, 1938, I am transmitting to you herewith comments on HR–10618, a bill authorizing the construction of certain public works on rivers and harbors for flood control and other purposes. Owing to the absence of Chairman Ickes and the necessity for immediate reply, I am taking the liberty of forwarding these comments without the opportunity of having them reviewed by the members of the National Resources Committee.

HR–10618 is inimical to the public interest and should be vetoed.

(1) It approves plans for flood control which are in many instances inadequately studied, and in so doing provides that these plans may be modified at will by the Corps of Engineers and thereupon may be put into action without review by the Congress.

(2) It largely ignores the responsibility of local agencies to provide in equitable degree for their own protection from flood damage. In so doing, it not only assigns to the Federal Government a heavy burden which the latter should not be called upon to bear, but through establishment of a precedent, it also invites raids upon the Treasury in furtherance of other phases of water control and development for which the Congress has wisely not assumed responsibility in the past.

(3) It establishes the principle of reimbursing local agencies for expenditures made by them under earlier laws in partial payment for flood protection. Insistent demands that this pernicious principle be extended to other projects and to other fields would inevitably follow approval of the Bill.

(4) It largely ignores important corollary problems, and would not be likely to promote the unified control and development of the water resources of the river basins to which it relates.

(5) A flood control act should be drawn in consonance with a national water policy, and the present act includes certain advances to-

ward this objective. None the less, it is seriously defective in various particulars.

(6) The Bill redefines national policy, embracing so many important fields, with such haste, that it should not become law. The Bill abandons principles and procedures which have reduced to some degree the raids on the Treasury and substitutes for them no restraints on unlimited pressures from local groups. These controls are eliminated under the claim that their existence has prevented the construction of flood control works. The facts point to the contrary. Sufficient undertakings, adequately explored, are available for construction for three or four years in the future. They may tax the financial and technical resources of the Federal Government, without throwing the gates wide open for the inclusion of projects now inadequately studied and in some instances actually ill-advised.

(7) The Bill explicitly reenacts the resolution vetoed by the President on August 13, 1937. The principles which the earlier resolution embodies were pernicious in 1937 and are no less so today.

(8) A memorandum on each section of the Bill is attached herewith.[1]

Sincerely yours,

FREDERIC A. DELANO

[*Notation*:A:DELANO] Immediate

[13:BUDGET BUREAU ENROLLED BILLS:TS]

[1] Present, together with a draft veto message. The debate on H. R. 10618 (introduced May 12, 1938, by Representative Whittington of Mississippi) centered on certain basic issues of national policy rather than on particular projects: whether flood control dams should be designed for power generation; whether the Federal Government should assume the total cost of flood control works; whether the states, when forming compacts for joint creation of flood control works, should retain rights to possible future power generation; and the extent of the responsibility of the Army Engineers for flood control planning (*Cong. Rec.*, 75th Cong., 3d sess., 83:6, 6842, 7137–7174; 83:8, 8599–8601, 8601–8614, 8614–8626, 9288–9306, 9354–9355, 9365–9369, 9369–9391, 9394–9398).

Senator Norris (Nebr.) called the attention of the Senate to the President's veto of Senate Joint Resolution 57 in the previous session. He said he did not anticipate a veto but if there should be one it would be because the bill contained stipulations which would prevent the development of public power from the proposed dams, the proper handling of erosion and the proper handling of reforestation, or "for the reason that it will attempt to turn over to the Corps of Engineers of the United States Army the entire planning, investigation, and development of this problem of natural resources and their preservation" (*ibid.*, 83:8, 8610–8611).

Norris had urged that the Secretary of War be divested of the sole responsibility of deciding whether dams should include facilities permitting future power generation. Copeland (N. Y.) charged (in a memorandum inserted in the *Record*) that efforts, like Norris', to change the bill were being proposed for the purpose of justifying a veto if they were not accepted, and were being urged by those who hoped finally to secure passage of the Norris "seven-TVA" bill (H. R. 2555). Copeland said that adoption of H. R. 10618 would virtually preclude revival of the Norris bill (*ibid.*, 83:8, 8619). The bill was passed, and was approved June 28, 1938 (52 *Stat.* 1215). See statement by Roosevelt of June 29, 1938, *post*, 803.

THE WHITE HOUSE, *June 25, 1938*

MEMORANDUM OF DISAPPROVAL: I have withheld my approval of
H. R. 2711 "An Act To Create a Division of Water Pollution Control in
the United States Public Health Service, and for other purposes."

This bill authorizes the appropriation of $300,000 for administrative
expenses of the Division of Water Pollution Control $700,000 for ex-
penditure by State health authorities for the preparation of project
requests, and in addition, such amounts as may be necessary for loans and
grants-in-aid of States, municipalities, public bodies, or individuals to
carry out projects for treatment works to prevent water pollution.

I appreciate the importance of the results sought to be accomplished
by the legislation and I fully approve the establishment of a Division of
Water Pollution Control in the Public Health Service. This bill, however, provides for the direct presentation, through the Secretary of the
Treasury, of the recommendations of the Surgeon General for the authorization by Congress of specific projects to be carried on under the loan or
grant-in-aid provisions of the bill, without any opportunity for review by
the Chief Executive.

Thus, this bill provides for the legislative assumption of responsibilities
of the Executive branch, and, therefore, runs counter to the fundamental
concept of our budget system that the planning of work programs of
the Executive agencies and their presentation to Congress in the form
of estimates of appropriation is a duty imposed upon the Chief Executive and not one for exercise by the legislative branch.

I am convinced that appropriations for projects of this character
should be based upon estimates submitted in the annual Budget. Only
in this way can the merit of such projects be considered in their proper
relation to the merits of other projects of a similar nature, and all of these
projects be then considered in their relation to the needs of the other
Government activities that are presented for incorporation in the annual
Budgets.

FRANKLIN D. ROOSEVELT

[W. H. PRESS RELEASES : M]

800   ROOSEVELT TO RUDOLPH FORSTER, EXECUTIVE CLERK, WHITE
       HOUSE OFFICE

POUGHKEEPSIE, N. Y., *June 29, 1938, 1:22 p. m.*

[*Telegram*] MEMO FOR R. F.: Will you get from the Interior Department complete data in regard to the new Olympic National Park as set
up, together with maps?

Also, will you get the same thing separate from the Forest Service? [1]

F.D.R.

RV–C

[13:OF 6–P:T]

[1] See the two letters following.

801   EBERT K. BURLEW, ACTING SECRETARY OF THE INTERIOR, TO
        ROOSEVELT

[WASHINGTON, *June 29, 1938*] [1]

The Olympic National Park bill (H. R. 10024) was passed by the
75th Congress at 6:30 P. M. June 16.

As finally enacted the bill provides for a park of approximately 634,000
acres including the former Mount Olympus National Monument and
additional surrounding acreage as shown on the attached map. The
bill also provides that the President is authorized to add any lands
within the boundary of the Olympic National Forest and any lands that
may be acquired by the government by gift or purchase which he may
deem advisable to add to the park provided that the total area of the
park shall not exceed 898,292 acres. Provision is also made that the
President shall consult with the Governor of the State of Washington
and the Secretaries of Agriculture and Interior advising them of the
lands which he proposes to add to the park before issuing a proclamation; also that no lands shall be added to the 634,000 acre tract prior
to the expiration of a period of eight months from date of the approval
of the Act.

Briefly, the history of this piece of legislation is as follows: H. R.
10024, calling for 898,292 acres, was passed by the House on May 16.
On June 11 the Senate Public Lands and Surveys Committee recommended amendments to reduce the park to approximately 634,000
acres as proposed last year by the second Wallgren Bill, H. R. 4724,
and to authorize the President to add to the park any lands from the
Olympic National Forest and which might be acquired by the government through gift or purchase. The Senate approved the committee's
report on June 13. Unanimous consent to accept the Senate amendments was refused by the House on June 15, there being objection to
the provision to authorize the President to add to the park. The bill was
then sent to a conference committee who recommended that the authority to add be limited not to exceed 898,292 acres, and that any additions
could not be made until eight months after approval of the Act.

The House then approved the committee report at 11:30 A. M. June
16. Senator Bone objected to the conference report and the Senate
amended the bill to limit the total area of the park, after additions, to

[241]

898,292 acres. No specific recommendation regarding area to be added through Presidential Proclamation has as yet been made.[2]

E. K. B.

[13:OF 6–P:TS]

[1] A supplied date. This memorandum bears no address but an accompanying note refers to material from Acting Secretary Burlew.

[2] On approving the act on June 29, 1938 (52 *Stat.* 1241), Roosevelt issued a statement from Hyde Park in which he expressed special pleasure in signing the bill:

"In the future the new Olympic National Park may be extended in area by adding lands acquired by gift or purchase or additional lands from the Olympic National Forest . . . The establishment of this new national park will be of interest to everybody in the country. Its scenery and the remarkable tree growth are well worth seeing, and it is a worthy addition to the splendid national parks which have already been created in many parts of the country" (New York *Times,* June 30, 1938, p. 2).

No other form of this statement has been found. It is probable that it was made orally to reporters, for McIntyre, in reply to a request for a copy of the statement, said that no statement had been issued (McIntyre to Fred M. Packard, Emergency Conservation Committee, July 19, 1938, OF 6–P).

802   HENRY A. WALLACE, SECRETARY OF AGRICULTURE, TO ROOSEVELT

WASHINGTON, *June 29, 1938*

DEAR MR. PRESIDENT: Mr. Forster has asked that you be sent data regarding the Olympic National Park, Washington, presumably as contemplated by enrolled enactment H. R. 10024 now before you for signature.

The enclosed small map of the Olympic National Forest indicates by a heavy black line the boundaries originally described in H. R. 10024, by red hachures the area described in the Senate amendment, to which the House agreed and which therefore is described in the enrolled enactment, and by green hachure the area which, under the bill, will be subject to mineral development for an ensuing period of five years.

The records of this Department indicate that the Park as described in the enrolled enactment will embrace a total of 648,960 acres; of which 298,730 acres is within the existing National Monument and 350,230 acres consists of lands hitherto a part of the Olympic National Forest. It thus exceeds by 200,000 acres the area proposed for a Park status by Governor Martin. The maximum area to which the Park may be enlarged by action of the President is almost identical to the area described in H. R. 10024, prior to its final amendment.

As now described the Park will include 8½ billion board feet of timber of commercial species and quality, exclusive of the three billion feet within the existing National Monument. The finest examples of virgin tree growth characteristic of the region are included within its boundaries.

Sincerely,

H. A. WALLACE

[13:OF 6–P:TS]

[Hyde Park, *June 29, 1938*]

I have approved this bill with some reluctance. It authorizes but does not appropriate the money for a large number of public works on rivers and harbors, these authorizations being in addition to many other very large authorizations already on the statute books but for which money has not yet been appropriated.

It is unnecessary for me to emphasize the importance of carrying on a large and continuing program to eliminate floods, lessen soil erosion, continue reclamation, encourage reforestation and improve navigation.

Insofar as this bill provides for an improvement in jurisdictional control over the properties involved, and a more adequate control over consequential power developments, it is a definite step in the right direction.

It is not a step in the right direction in the set-up provided for general government planning.

I am in doubt as to the value of some of the projects provided for and it is unwise to place recommendations to the Congress solely in the hands of the Engineer Corps of the Army in some cases and of the Department of Agriculture in other cases.

Coordination of all such public works involves a wider survey and the examination of more national problems than any one bureau or department is qualified for.

In these respects future legislation will be vitally important, in order to give to the Congress and to the country a complete picture which takes all factors into consideration.

For the coming year, however, I shall try to obtain this coordination by asking for complete consultation between all groups and government agencies affected. In this way the whole of the problem can be made more clear. I have, however, approved the bill because it accomplishes a number of good things, with, however, the reservation that its deficiencies should be corrected as early as possible.[1]

[new york *Times*, june 30, 1938]

[1] This statement was not directed to the Congress, which had adjourned, but was issued as a matter of public information. Neither the news release nor other text has been found in the Roosevelt Library but because of the importance of the statement it has been reproduced as printed in the New York *Times* of June 30, 1938, p. 2.

804   DANIEL W. BELL, ACTING DIRECTOR, BUREAU OF THE BUDGET,
TO ROOSEVELT

WASHINGTON, *July 8, 1938*

MEMORANDUM FOR THE PRESIDENT: I have your memorandum of
July 5 transmitting two drafts of reply, one prepared by the Department
of Agriculture and one by the Department of the Interior, to the letter to
you of May 10, from Mr. Vernon W. Hunt, Attorney at Law, Suite 1211,
Pacific National Building, Los Angeles, California, in which memorandum you ask for my recommendation as to which one of these two drafts
you should sign.[1]   Mr. Hunt's letter indicates that he is interested in the
hunting and fishing resources of the Kings River Canyon area in California and that he thinks the interests of sportsmen like himself would be
better served by the continuance of this area in its present National
Forest status than by its transfer to a National Park status as has been
proposed at various times.

The most recent proposal to give to this area National Park status
was embodied in H. R. 10436 introduced (by request) on April 27,
1938, by Chairman DeRouen of the Public Lands Committee.[2]   The
proposed report on the bill by the Secretary of Agriculture strongly
opposed, and that of the Secretary of the Interior strongly favored,
the enactment of this measure.   I felt obliged, therefore, to advise the
two Secretaries that while there would be no objection to the submission
of their reports to the Chairman of the Committee, it was to be understood that no commitment would thereby be made with respect to the
relationship of the proposed legislation to your program.

I think the Forest Service concedes, as it would be obliged to concede, that the Kings River Canyon area is one of high National Park
character.   But so, for that matter, are various other areas now included
in National Forests, some of which, indeed, are of a higher National
Park standard than are certain of the existing National Parks.   The
Forest Service fears, therefore, as I see the situation, that the present
proposal will be only one of a series of proposals for the transfer to the
National Park Service of large areas of National Forest lands.   In order
to forestall such transfers, and because it recognizes the scenic and
recreational value of these areas, the Forest Service feels, I believe, that
it must take steps to develop such areas in somewhat the same way that
the Park Service has developed its National Park areas.   Since this
would result in a duplicated exercise of a function which the National
Park Service thinks it alone should perform, that Service is naturally
desirous of taking over these high standard National Forest areas whenever there is likelihood of their development by the Forest Service in
accordance with National Park Service standards.   That time approaches as to the Kings River area, because of the present construction
by the State of California of a highway that will have as its terminus

a canyon valley on the South Fork of the Kings River, one-half mile wide and twelve miles long, which has been compared, not unfavorably by some, with the valley of the Yosemite.

Because of the difficulties heretofore encountered in the efforts to secure reorganization authority which would permit the amalgamation of the Forest and Park Services under one head, and on account of the growing use of recreational facilities in this country, I think the time is coming for a larger development along National Park Service lines of certain areas of high scenic and recreational values that are to be found in a number of our existing National Forests. Until these possibilities are exhausted on lands that we already own, the purchase of lands for the establishment of National Parks can be criticized, it seems to me, as reflecting a somewhat inconsistent, and expensive, attitude on our part.

The Kings River area, which forms a part of three of our existing National Forests, is a good case in point, and while I do not know that all of the 415,000 acres proposed by H. R. 10436 for National Park status are necessary for that purpose, or that the proposed boundaries of the Park area have been properly drawn, I am inclined to the view that the most scenic and inspirational portion of this area should be placed under the jurisdiction of the National Park Service for development in accordance with its highest standards. There would be left adjacent lands in the National Forests that would be susceptible of recreational development by the Forest Service along somewhat more commercial lines, and without interference with its main forestry programs. It would not appear, moreover, that the Park Service proposal would unduly interfere with the development, at any rate with the early development, of the water resources of the region for power and irrigation purposes, since the sites of the only reservoirs considered practicable for any early construction are situated outside of the proposed Park boundaries.

As to the fishing and hunting utilization of the region, in which Mr. Hunt is interested, there would be fishing in both the Forest and Park areas, and while there would be hunting only in the Forest area, I am not sure that the protected Park area might not provide a larger continuous supply of game migrating to the Forest area than would be the case if hunting were permitted over the entire area.

In returning the drafts of letters to Mr. Hunt prepared by the Departments of Agriculture and Interior, I am attaching a suggested substitute form of letter prepared in my office.[3]

D. W. BELL

[13:OF 6–P:TS]

[1] Roosevelt's memorandum ("For recommendation as to which one I should sign"), with Hunt's letter and the drafts mentioned, are with the letter here printed. The

Interior Department draft noted the scenic character of the area and its unsuitability for the growing of economic timber crops, and urged support of the national park project. The Agriculture Department draft was noncommittal on the desirability of national park status for the area.

² The bill was referred to this committee but was not reported.

³ See *post*, 807.

805   SPEECH BY ROOSEVELT, Oklahoma City, July 9, 1938

[*Excerpt*] SENATOR THOMAS, GOVERNOR MARLAND, MR. MAYOR, MY FRIENDS OF OKLAHOMA: . . . Probably the most important long-range problem is something that affects all of us, whether we live in the city or the country, and that is the use of land and water. I was sorry this morning that I could not have stopped to view the Grand River Dam Project. It was due to the persistent effort of my old friend, Senator Thomas, and Senator Lee, that that particular project is definitely under way, and I might say the same thing about other projects on other watersheds of this State.

I think the Grand River project is a good illustration of the national aspect of water control, because it is a vital link in the still larger problem of the whole Valley of the Arkansas—a planning task—and some people laugh at planning—that starts far west in the Rocky Mountains, west of the Royal Gorge, and runs on down through Colorado and Kansas and Oklahoma and Arkansas to the Mississippi River itself and thence to the sea. The day will come, I hope, when every drop of water that flows into that great watershed, through all those states, will be controlled for the benefit of mankind, controlled for the growing of forests, for the prevention of soil erosion, for the irrigation of land, for the development of water power, for the ending of floods and the improvement of navigation.

A vision like that, my friends, will be of direct benefit to millions of our people, not only to the people of the territory through which that river flows but indirectly to the people on the Pacific Coast, on the Atlantic Seaboard, and in the deep South. And the price, the dollars and cents we pay for a great development of that kind, will return to the pocketbooks of the State manyfold. The same thing applies to the Red River and to the tributaries that flow into the other streams.[1]

[SPEECH FILE: T]

[1] The text of this excerpt is that of the stenographic transcript; this shows numerous departures from the reading copy (Speech File). The reading copy contains several last-minute additions and other changes in Roosevelt's hand, and is signed by him, "Franklin D. Roosevelt   Original reading copy." (A page from this is reproduced in facsimile, with the text of the entire speech, in Rosenman, ed., *Public Papers*, VII, 442–445.) With the reading copy is a copy of the mimeographed press release of the reading copy with Kannee's shorthand notes of the changes made when the speech was delivered. This was one of a number of speeches made by Roosevelt

in the course of a trip to the West Coast beginning July 7. He returned by sea on
the U. S. S. *Houston* and got back to Washington on August 12.

806   SPEECH BY ROOSEVELT, Amarillo, Texas, July 11, 1938

MY FRIENDS OF THE PANHANDLE AND YOU FROM NEIGHBORING CITIES
WHO HAVE BEEN GOOD ENOUGH TO COME HERE TODAY: . . . All this
shows what you can do in the Panhandle if you put your minds to it,[1]
and that is why I am very happy that you are putting your minds on
the subject of land and water. Everywhere you go in the United States
you find the problem of land and water, and the same thing is true
within any given state. For instance, in Texas here in Marvin Jones'
district most of the time the problem is to get water out of the land and
to keep the land from blowing away. Down in Austin the problem of
my friend, Congressman Lyndon Johnson, is to keep his land from
washing away—washing down the rivers and into the sea. And further down at San Antonio, where my friend, Congressman Maury
Maverick, represents a great city and its surrounding territory, the
problem of land use there is tied up with better housing and the needs
of a great municipality.

I wish that more people from the South and the East and the Middle
West could visit this Plains country. If they did you would hear less
talk about the great American desert, you would hear less ridicule of
our efforts to conserve water, to restore grazing lands and to plant trees.

Back in the East, in Washington and on the Hudson River I have
seen the top soil of the Panhandle and of Western Kansas and Nebraska borne by the high wind in the air eastward to the Atlantic Ocean
itself. I want that sight to come to end.

And it can be ended only by united national effort, backed up one
hundred per cent by you who live in this area, and you are giving us
that backing.

Money spent for the building of ponds and small lakes, for the
damming of rivers, for planting shelterbelts, for other forms of afforestation, for putting plough land back into grass, that is money well spent.
It pays to do it, not only for this generation but for the children who
will succeed to the land a few years hence.

People who are ignorant and people who think only in terms of the
moment scoff at our efforts and say—"Oh, let the next generation take
care of itself—if people out in the dry parts of the country cannot live
there let them move out and hand the land back to the Indians." But,
my friends, that is not your idea or mine. We seek permanently to
establish this part of the Nation as a fine and safe place which a large
number of Americans can call home.

[247]

Every year that passes we are learning more and more about the best use of land, about the conserving of our soil and the improvement of it by getting everything we can out of every drop of water that falls from the heavens and today is a good example of it. Back in the Allegheny Mountains many of the rivers are called "flash streams"—dry beds or rivulets most of the year—but raging torrents sweeping all before them when a cloudburst or heavy rain occurs. And you have flash streams here.

We are fortunate in Washington in having as Chairman of the Agricultural Committee of the House of Representatives a man who has a well-rounded knowledge of agricultural programs and problems in every part of the United States.[2] He and I have discussed many times the great objective of putting agriculture and cattle raising on a safe basis—giving assurance to those who engage in those pursuits that they will not be broke one year and flush the next. We need a greater permanency, a greater annual security for all who use the soil.

The farming and cattle raising population of the United States has no wish, no desire to be paid a subsidy or given a handout from the Federal Treasury. They have come to understand, and the rest of the country is learning too, that the agricultural program of the Administration is not a subsidy. It is divided into three simple parts.

The first part represents government assistance to help the individual farmer to use his land for those products for which it is best fitted, and to maintain and improve its fertility.

The second objective is, with the approval of those who raise crops, to prevent overproduction and low prices—and at the same time to provide against any shortage, in other words, to apply common sense business principles to the business of farming and cattle raising. And as a part of that second objective we seek to give to the farmers throughout the country as high a purchasing power for their labor as those who work in industry and other occupations.

The third effort of your Government is directed towards a great decrease in farm tenancy and towards the increase in farm ownership by those who till the soil. That includes the encouragement of small farms and of even smaller acreages for those who live near the cities and work in the cities, and who should by all the rules of common sense grow on a few acres around their homes a substantial part of their own family food supply.

You have given me a wonderful reception today in Amarillo, not counting the rain, and I am happy, I am happy indeed, to have been able to see this extraordinarily interesting and progressive part of the United States. I am grateful to you for your cooperation with your National Government, your cooperation in and understanding of all that we are trying to do in the National Administration to help those who are willing to help themselves, and you people will.

And so, my friends, I shall never forget this visit of mine to Amarillo. And I am coming back again. And I think this little shower we have had is a mighty good omen.[3]

[SPEECH FILE: T]

[1] Roosevelt had been talking about the 2500-piece band with which he had been greeted. The speech was given in Ellwood Park at about 6 P. M.
[2] Marvin Jones of the 18th Texas District.
[3] The text here printed is that of the stenographic transcript; this contains a number of departures from the reading copy (Speech File). The reading copy contains some half-dozen changes in Roosevelt's hand, and is signed by him, "Franklin D. Roosevelt (Original—delivered in a downpour)." (The pages of the speech show unmistakable evidence of a wetting.)

807   ROOSEVELT TO VERNON W. HUNT, Los Angeles

FORT WORTH, TEX., *July 11, 1938*

MY DEAR MR. HUNT: Reply to your letter of May 10 has been delayed pending the receipt from the Departments of Agriculture and Interior of information regarding the proposal to place in a National Park status a certain portion of the Kings River area in California that is now included in National Forests under the jurisdiction of the Forest Service.[1]

The proposal contemplates, I am advised, the transfer to the National Park Service of some 415,000 acres, representing the most scenic portion of the area, for development by that Service in accordance with its standards for the recreational utilization of National Park areas of this character.

While I do not know that all of the area proposed for a National Park status is necessary for that purpose, or that the proposed boundaries of the Park area have been properly drawn, I am inclined to think, from the information thus far supplied to me, and in the long view of the matter, that the proposal is not without a considerable degree of merit.

As to the utilization of the fishing and hunting resources of the region concerning which you have written me more particularly, there would be fishing in both the Forest and Park areas, and while there would be hunting only in the Forest area, I am not sure that in the long run the protected Park area might not provide a better supply of game that would migrate to the Forest area than would be the case were hunting permitted over the entire area.

What I have said above represents only a tentative conclusion on my part at this time, and I shall be glad to give the matter further consideration in the event of its presentation to me in the form of a request for legislative authority for the establishment of such a Park area.

In appreciation of the interest which prompted you to write me regarding this matter, I remain, Sincerely yours,

[FRANKLIN D. ROOSEVELT]

FJB:MLM 7/7/38 [2]

[*Notation*:AS] DWB

[13:OF 6–P:CT]

[1] Hunt, a Los Angeles attorney, opposed a national park in the Kings Canyon area because the highways that would then be built to make it accessible to tourists would ruin the hunting and fishing (OF 6–P).
[2] Drafted in the Budget Bureau, presumably by Frederick J. Bailey, chief of the Division of Research and Investigation.

808   ROOSEVELT TO HAROLD L. ICKES, CHAIRMAN, NATIONAL RESOURCES COMMITTEE

WASHINGTON [*July 15, 1938*]

MY DEAR MR. SECRETARY: In approving the Flood Control Bill (H. R. 10618) on June 29, 1938, I called attention to certain deficiencies in the legislation. I also expressed the hope that these would be corrected as early as possible. I stated further that I would ask for complete consultation among the government agencies affected with respect to the problems of water resources raised by the bill.

I should like to have the National Resources Committee continue its important and useful work in the water resources field. It is my understanding that the major agencies concerned already are represented on the Committee.

Sincerely yours,

[FRANKLIN D. ROOSEVELT]

[*Notation*:A] C. T. H.   Original in pouch 7/15 [1]

[13:OF 132–D:CT]

[1] Roosevelt was in Yosemite Park on this date. This is one of the letters that were returned to Washington for mailing. The initials are those of Clarence T. Hess, Chief of the Office of Records of the White House.

809   ROOSEVELT TO GOVERNOR FRANK MURPHY, Lansing, Michigan

SAN DIEGO, CAL., *July 16, 1938*

MY DEAR GOVERNOR: I read with much interest your letter of May twenty-sixth referring to previous correspondence regarding the forest land problem of the State of Michigan.

The facts you have submitted are of great interest. To me, Michigan has always been the outstanding example of the rise and fall of the lumber and other wood-using industries. Its colorful history in the lumber industry is well known. With the high productive capacity of the forest soils of the State, the migration of the wood-using industries was obviously unnecessary and we are now faced with the practical problem of bringing these lands back into production to support urban enterprises and to furnish permanent employment to the people.

Assuming that lands under public control, or to be brought under public control, will receive proper management, it appears obvious that the State and Federal government should develop a plan of action that would bring this about.

With regard to the commercial timberlands, containing merchantable timber, remaining in the State, it seems clear that some plan is justified that will prevent the further devastation of the forest lands of the State, which after devastation must be taken over by the public and rehabilitated at great cost. I understand that Michigan still has a considerable acreage of magnificent beech, birch and maple forest, of very high social and economic value, that is still being cut under a "cut-out and get-out" policy. It seems clear that this is so contrary to the public welfare of the people of the State that some definite action is justified. When the Joint Committee of the Congress investigates the forest land problem, it is hoped that it will be possible for your Conservation officials to give the Committee a clear-cut presentation of your situation in order that it may play its part in determining the course of Federal action.[1]

Very sincerely yours,

[FRANKLIN D. ROOSEVELT]

[13:OF 149:CT]

[1] Drafted by the Agriculture Department. Wallace, in his letter to Roosevelt of July 13, 1938, enclosing the draft, said that he thought the letter was "peculiarly appropriate" in view of the acute forest land problem in Michigan.

810 HAROLD L. ICKES, CHAIRMAN, NATIONAL RESOURCES COMMITTEE, TO ROOSEVELT

WASHINGTON, *July 28, 1938*

MY DEAR MR. PRESIDENT: The problem of abating water pollution in the United States has received increasing attention during the past four years, culminating in a water pollution bill which was passed by the last session of the Congress, but .which failed to receive your approval because of the proposed procedure for submission of projects to the Congress without review by the President and the Budget. In that respect, the bill was contrary to the recommendations of our special advisory committee on water pollution.

Because the problem is still pressing for solution and because the previous bill utilized many of the technical findings and recommendations of our special committee, I think that it would be helpful if the committee would review its earlier findings and bring them up-to-date, so that during the autumn we may have a complete picture of the water pollution situation in the United States, of the effectiveness of recent Federal and state activities in the abatement of water pollution, and of the current needs in that field.

I am requesting the committee to proceed with the preparation of such a statement, with a view to submitting it to you in advance of the next session of the Congress. The group includes representatives of the Public Health Service, Biological Survey, and all other interested Federal agencies.[1]

Sincerely yours,

[HAROLD L. ICKES]

[*Notation*:A] Original will go in pouch 8/1 to Panama
[13:OF 1092':CT]

[1] Answered *post*, 814.

811   ROOSEVELT TO GOVERNOR ELMER A. BENSON, St. Paul, Minnesota

[WASHINGTON] *August 12, 1938*

MY DEAR GOVERNOR: I am pleased to learn from your letter of July thirteenth that you are interested in the work of the Quetico-Superior Committee.[1] Its proposal to establish an international wilderness reserve makes a strong appeal. In the maintenance of such an area, I see lasting opportunities for recreational use by millions of Americans on both sides of the International Boundary. I believe, too, that the Committee's suggestion is a fine one that the area be established as a Peace Memorial. It would not only be a memorial to the men who gave their lives in the World War but would be a continuing living reminder of the peace between the United States and Canada.

Although it is true, as you stated in your letter, that the whole of the United States' portion of the proposed reserve is in Minnesota, I regard the proposed reserve as of national importance. Certainly, the interests of the citizens of Minnesota should be considered, but the interest of the Nation should not be disregarded. Minnesota should be represented on the Committee, but it is not clear to me that its representatives should predominate. I am informed that one member of the Committee has been a resident of Minnesota for more than twenty-five years. Of the other members, one resides in Chicago, a second in New York, and the remaining two, representing the Secretary of the Interior and the Secretary of Agriculture, in Washington. By virtue of my Executive Order of June thirtieth extending the existence of the Committee until 1942, these five members are continuing to serve.

It may be desirable, however, to increase the number of members to permit the addition of one or more of the men whom you have suggested. I have referred your letter to the Secretary of the Interior and the Secretary of Agriculture, upon whose joint initiative the Committee was established. As soon as I have received their comments upon your suggestion, I shall be glad to write you again.

Very sincerely yours,

[FRANKLIN D. ROOSEVELT]

[*Notation*: T] Draft of letter prepared by Secretary of the Interior. mdp [13:OF 1119:CT]

[1] Benson thought that some members of the committee should be residents of Minnesota and proposed several persons as having proper qualifications (OF 1119).

812   ROOSEVELT TO HAROLD L. ICKES, SECRETARY OF THE INTERIOR, AND HENRY A. WALLACE, SECRETARY OF AGRICULTURE

WASHINGTON, *August 15, 1938*

MEMORANDUM . . . Now that the Olympic National Park has been created by law, I should like to have the Interior Department and the Department of Agriculture set up an informal joint board with the following objectives:

(a) To work out the relationships and administration of the Olympic National Park and the surrounding national forest lands.

(b) The relationship of the national park and forest lands to State owned land in the vicinity.

(c) To work out the relationship of the national park and forest land to privately owned lands in the vicinity.

(d) To make informal recommendations to the President about March 1, 1939 as to what lands should be added to the Olympic National Park.[1]

F. D. R.

[13:OF 6–P:TS]

[1] A. E. Demaray, acting director of the National Park Service, in a letter to Acting Secretary of Interior Burlew of Aug: 23, 1938, said that it was his belief

that the formation of such a board would make it difficult, if not impossible, to add any lands to the park, "and, particularly, any of the lands with stands of the big trees." The Park Service had already made studies and was prepared to recommend the addition of certain lands. Local opposition in Washington State was aware of these studies and "would like nothing better than to forestall our recommendations by some such means as an interdepartmental board." On September 7, Ickes informed Wallace that Irving Brant would represent the Interior Department. On November 10, Wallace told Roosevelt that Ickes was evidently unwilling to participate in the appointment of the suggested joint board, and added that since the Forest Service would make no objections to existing or proposed Olympic Park boundaries, he would make no further effort toward setting up a board. (These letters are in OF 6–P.)

813   PRESS CONFERENCE, Hyde Park, August 23, 1938, 2 P. M.

[*Excerpt*] Q: Can you tell us about your talk this morning with Mr. Martin and Mr. Duffy, of Vermont? [1]

The President: The chief topic of conversation was—I don't know whether we can call it the "National Highway." It is the continuation of what we outlined four years ago, the development of President Hoover's Skyline Drive. President Hoover invented, in his administration, a great scenic highway from Washington, D. C., over a distance of seventy or eighty miles south into Virginia along the top of the Blue Ridge, and laid out a national policy which was to the effect that if the State would buy the land—the right of way—with a strip on each side so as to be a scenic parkway, then the Federal Government would build and maintain the highway on that land. Before I got to Washington most of the work, a very large part of the work, had been done on the Skyline Drive. We have been trying in the last five years to develop that idea for a highway extending from the Canadian line, at the north end of the Green Mountains, down through what really is the Blue Ridge all the way. For instance, the Berkshires correspond to the Blue Ridge and you go across through the Hudson Highlands, at West Point, Bear Mountain, and then get on down to the Delaware Water Gap, and then that same range extends down to just west of Harrisburg, through Gettysburg and Harper's Ferry—a little this side of Harper's Ferry, you know, where Braddock Heights is—it is really the nearest point to Washington—and then it goes on to Front Royal with the Skyline Drive and through Virginia and down to North Carolina, to the Great Smoky Park, and thence to Georgia, to the end of the Appalachian System, which is approximately Stone Mountain.

[13:PRESIDENT'S PRESS CONFERENCES:T]

[1] Fred C. Martin and Frank Duffy, prominent Vermont Democrats. Martin denied that the visit had political implications (New York *Times,* Aug. 28, 1938, IV, 7).

Hyde Park, N. Y., *August 29, 1938*

Memorandum for the Secretary of the Interior: Go ahead with the reconvening of the water pollution committee so as to have the report ready with a new bill by November fifteenth.[1]

F. D. R.

[13:OF 1092:CT]

[1] This is in reply to Ickes' letter of July 28, 1938, *ante,* 810.

815   Harold L. Ickes, Chairman, National Resources Committee, to Roosevelt

Washington, *Sept. 21, 1938*

My dear Mr. President: In accordance with your instructions, the National Resources Committee has made a special review of conditions in the Northern Great Plains, and I am forwarding herewith a report approved by all of the members of the Committee.[1]

I am also enclosing drafts of a release, memorandum and letters which are intended to implement the recommendations in the document.[2] If these drafts are agreeable to you, we should like to release the report through the Press Section of the Public Works Administration, as in previous cases, some time on or after September 26, and to arrange for circulation of the report to interested persons in the Great Plains Area.

If you are agreeable to making public the letters to the Governors, we shall be pleased to have a representative of the Committee confer with Mr. Early as to arrangements.

Sincerely yours,

Harold L. Ickes

[13:OF 2285:TS]

[1] *Rehabilitation in the Northern Great Plains. Preliminary Report of the Northern Great Plains Committee* (Washington, 1938).
[2] The drafts are present; see *post,* 821, 825, 826.

816   Roosevelt to Stephen T. Early, Secretary to the President

Washington, *September 22, 1938*

Memorandum for S. T. E.: Will you talk this over with Lowell Mellett and see how we can get out publicity throughout the States involved which will be more easily understood than this release,[1] and that [*sic*] we can accomplish much education if it is handled right? Before bringing it back to me, will you talk it over with the National Resources Committee and with the Secretary of Agriculture?

These letters to the Governors should be held up until our publicity is released here.

F. D. R.

[13:OF 2285:T]

¹ *Post,* 821.

817   MEMORANDUM BY HENRY M. KANNEE, ASSISTANT TO MARVIN H. MCINTYRE

WASHINGTON, *9/28/38*

MEMORANDUM FOR THE APPOINTMENT FILES: Miss Holbrook, Robert Fechner's secretary, called and asked for an appointment for Mr. Fechner to discuss his letter of June sixth to the President. She indicated that this letter had had the approval of the President but that no indication of it had been sent to them and Mr. Fechner was anxious to get the President's approval to his letter.

I spoke to Jim Rowe and he acquainted me with the situation, i. e., that all the departments concerned have objected strenuously to the President approving the procedure suggested by Mr. Fechner, and that hearings held by James Roosevelt had done nothing to change their opposition or create grounds upon which the President's approval could be based.

Accordingly, I informed Miss Holbrook that the exigencies of the international situation precluded the arranging of this appointment at this time—that the matter would have to remain in status quo until things had quieted down.

K.

[13:OF 268:T]

818   ROOSEVELT TO FERDINAND A. SILCOX, CHIEF, FOREST SERVICE

WASHINGTON, *September 30, 1938*

MEMORANDUM FOR HON. F. A. SILCOX: I understood sometime ago that Regional Forester Buck had said that road work would not be resumed in the Dosewallips Valley, Olympic Peninsula. Now I hear that it is to be resumed—in fact, that work is going on.

It seems to me that before any further work is done there should be general government agreement.

Will you let me know about it? ¹

F. D. R.

[13:OF 1–C:CT]

¹ This was inspired by a memorandum from Brant to Ickes, Sept. 22, 1938 (OF 1–C): "The Quinault people asked both the Park Service and the Forest Service to promise a road up the Quinault and down the Dosewallips, so that they would have direct connection with the Seattle tourist travel. The Park Service refused to make any promises. The Forest Service not only promised the road . . . but started to build it . . ." Silcox replied Oct. 4, 1938 (OF 1–C), that there was no work under way or planned on the Dosewallips road and that none would be done until after the park boundaries were settled.

819 ROOSEVELT TO NELSON C. BROWN, New York State College of Forestry, Syracuse University, Syracuse, New York

WASHINGTON, *October 1, 1938*

[*Telegram*] Have decided go Hyde Park tonight. Can you come for lunch tomorrow or Monday and we can plan next spring's plantings.¹

FRANKLIN D. ROOSEVELT

[13:PPF 38:CT]

¹ Brown had written Sept. 27, 1938 (PPF 38), that the trees in the Roosevelt plantations had "responded remarkably well to the excellent growing season," and had asked what lots were to be planted in 1939. He came to Hyde Park on Monday, October 3 (PPF 1–O).

820 PRESS CONFERENCE, Hyde Park, October 7, 1938, 10:45 A. M.

[*Excerpt*] The President: How is everybody? There is a release coming out from Washington on the detail and I won't give you that, but I do want to discuss with you the general subject of trying to end water pollution of streams. I have a book here today with PWA allotments for 113 additional sewage disposal projects in almost every part of the nation to end pollution in streams and lakes, where they are located, providing for $19,588,000 worth of construction of disposal plants, sewers and other means to clean up local streams and rivers in thirty states and Puerto Rico.

They started in five years ago to encourage communities to end the pollution of lakes and rivers and the work is progressing very well. Off the record, the City of Poughkeepsie is still dumping its sewage in within half a mile of where it is taking its water out.

Q: In the Nelson House?

The President: I said that was off the record.

Mr. Early: Drinking water, Mr. President, never involved anyone in the Nelson House.

The President: I don't blame them. I would not drink water in Poughkeepsie.

Q: Will the tide carry up that far?

The President: Sure. The tide carries water back and forth about six miles.

Q: That is another good reason.

The President: And none of these different allotments will continue sewage disposal into lakes and rivers. Since 1933 PWA loans, not counting what WPA has done, I approved have carried through approximately 500 sewage disposal plants at a total construction cost of over a billion and a quarter of dollars in five years. That is pretty good.

Mr. Early: But not including this?

The President: Not including this. The communities assessed themselves for over half this amount in order to become partners with the Federal Government in this valuable work. This water purification work is finally producing tangible results. It is a splendid beginning and efforts must be continued for the cleaning up of our rivers on a national scale . . .[1]

Q: Is there anything we can say on the record in the local press in connection with this ridding of the Hudson River of pollution? Of course it is a very vital thing right here in Poughkeepsie. In turning down this thing, there was a feeling that they should get some state aid on the question—I don't know—in addition to the federal aid, to aid communities in constructing these plants. I don't know whether there is—

The President: I don't know, frankly, I don't know any of the financial details at all except that for twenty-five years I have been talking to the people of Poughkeepsie about two subjects. The first was to quit dumping raw sewage into the Hudson River and, second, to get a decent supply of pure drinking water—not out of the Hudson River—which, during the whole of the twenty-five years has been a perfectly practical self-liquidating plan under the law—that is, getting the water—but nobody has done it.

Q: So there isn't anything you can say on the record?

The President: No, except that I have been trying to accomplish those two things and suggesting it for twenty-five years and perhaps it will be another twenty-five years before something is done.[2]

[13:PRESIDENT'S PRESS CONFERENCES:T]

[1] The part omitted is on another subject.
[2] In 1957 Poughkeepsie was still discharging its raw sewage into the Hudson River.

821 WHITE HOUSE PRESS RELEASE ON A REPORT OF THE
NORTHERN GREAT PLAINS COMMITTEE, October 7, 1938

Seven years of drought have disrupted the economy of the Northern Great Plains area and produced conditions which demand urgent rehabilitation measures according to a report of the Northern Great Plains Committee which has been transmitted to The President by the National Resources Committee.

The Northern Great Plains Committee, which included in its membership representatives of both Federal and State agencies, was appointed last Spring by the National Resources Committee, and its recommendations are being studied at the White House.

A statement of the problem which confronted the Committee and which concerns directly North and South Dakota, eastern Montana, northern Nebraska and northeastern Wyoming was made public today.

In brief, the Northern Great Plains Committee found that the prevailing system of land utilization in the region has failed and that tax delinquency, mortgages and dependence on relief are so widespread as to require immediate action.

In North Dakota, it was found that 70 percent of all farms are listed as tax delinquent, more than 75 percent of the farms in representative counties are mortgaged and approximately 35 percent of all people are on relief. The other sections studied also show conditions which threaten the economic stability of the areas concerned.

In its statement of the problem the Great Plains Committee said, in part:

The history of settlement and land use in the Northern Plains indicates clearly that another period of normal or supernormal rainfall, however desirable, would not alone insure stability. The plague of dry years would presently return; crop failures would follow bountiful harvests; despair would again replace optimism. The future of the region cannot be left safely to the unpredictable hazards of rainfall and the inadequate resources of individual farmers. The need of recognizing these facts and of acting in accordance with them has not been lessened by the generous rains of the earlier part of 1938.

Generous public assistance has prevented extreme human suffering in the Northern Plains during the recent years of drought and depression. Food, clothing, and fuel have been furnished to all in need. Relief employment has been afforded all certified applicants who were in towns and who were able to work. Farm Security Administration grants and loans, A. A. A. benefit payments, Farm Credit Administration loans, and other types of aid have been extended to farmers.

Though the activities noted have attained their special objectives and have minimized suffering, they have not contributed to the permanent rehabilitation of the area to the degree that now seems possible through coordinated effort. For example, some farmers have been enabled to stay on their farms and to continue cultivating land suited only to grazing. Relief labor naturally has been used chiefly for such projects as roads and schools. The people would be little better equipped on the whole to cope with a serious drought next year than they were in 1930. To the greatest degree possible, relief should hereafter promote permanent rehabilitation.

Many families—perhaps 20,000 in all—have given up the fight during the recent years of distress and have left the region. Most of the farmers hang on tenaciously with Federal aid, hoping that conditions will improve. Many have moved to the villages and few cities, where, with Federal assistance, they await opportunities in other regions or the wet year that would enable them to return to their farms and produce a big crop.

Large-scale evacuation of the Northern Plains, were it practicable, would not solve the basic problems of the region. Cheap land, the chance for speculative gain, the false promise of a few wet years, all these and more would lure new settlers likely to repeat the mistakes of earlier years with similar consequences. So far as can be foreseen, the economic and social life of the region must always depend largely on agriculture. A type of agriculture suited to the climate, topography, soils, and natural vegetation, involving in general larger operating units, a judicious combination of grazing and feed-crop production, and, so far as practicable, supplemental irrigation, should replace the cash-grain and small-scale stock rearing type in the many areas where the latter has failed and cannot succeed. Locally, irrigation projects of considerable size are possible. In short, rehabilitation and stabilization can come only through fundamental readjustments in land utilization. Immediate action for rehabilitation is essential; continued action through years will be needed.

Members of the Northern Great Plains Committee are as follows: Harlan H. Barrows, Chairman, University of Chicago; W. T. Brokaw, Director of Extension, University of Nebraska; J. P. Cain, Chairman, North Dakota State Planning Board; A. M. Eberle, Director of Extension, South Dakota State College; D. P. Fabrick, Chairman, Montana State Planning Board; Perry A. Fellows, Assistant Chief Engineer, Works Progress Administration; Lt. Colonel Philip B. Fleming, District Engineer, Corps of Engineers, St. Paul; Dan W. Greenburg, Director, Wyoming State Planning Board; W. W. McLaughlin, Office of Land Use Coordination, Department of Agriculture; John C. Page, Commissioner, Bureau of Reclamation; and Colonel Clarence J. Sturdevant, Division Engineer, Corps of Engineers, Kansas City, Missouri.[1]

[13:OF 2285:M]

[1] This press release is based on the draft sent by Ickes to Roosevelt on Sept. 21, 1938 (*ante,* 815), but is considerably briefer. With the release here printed is a one-page memorandum entitled, "General Material for Use of the President in Calling Attention to a Forthcoming Report on the Problem of the Northern Great Plains Area." It bears the notation, "For the President's Press Conference on Oct. 4." Roosevelt made only passing reference to the forthcoming report at that press conference.

822   JOHN H. BAKER, EXECUTIVE DIRECTOR, NATIONAL ASSOCIATION
       OF AUDUBON SOCIETIES, TO ROOSEVELT

NEW YORK, N. Y., *October 7, 1938*

Sheep Refuges in Arizona

DEAR MR. PRESIDENT: You have shown, we understand, a definite interest in the state of such refuges for the benefit of the Bighorn Sheep in the Southwestern States.

This Association initiated two years ago a Desert Bighorn Sheep Fellowship Research Project, and the findings resulting from that work are now available to the Federal bureaus that may be concerned with the problem of preservation and restoration of those fine game animals.

We have constantly urged the establishment of the Cabeza Prieta and the Kofa Mountain Refuges under the administration of the Biological Survey. Executive orders to effect such establishment have, we understand, been up to this time stalled through the necessity of gaining approval by the Department of Interior, inasmuch as public domain is involved. It now appears that the Interior Department has developed plans of its own, involving the administration of such wildlife areas by the Bureau of Grazing under the terms of the Taylor Grazing Act. Such a development would, it seems to us, hold forth little promise of favorable treatment of the Desert Bighorn Sheep or any other wildlife.

May we encourage you to sign now executive orders establishing the wildlife refuges in these areas under the jurisdiction of the Biological Survey?

We would appreciate it if this letter were not forwarded to either the Department of the Interior or the Department of Agriculture, both of which are already well acquainted with our views. Our concern is wholly as to the Sheep and we are not interested one way or another in any differences there may be between the bureaus or departments most concerned.

May we hope for your favorable consideration of this earnest request? [1]

Sincerely yours,

JOHN H. BAKER

[13:OF 378:TS]

[1] An attached memorandum, Roosevelt to McIntyre, Oct. 11, 1938, reads, "Do not show this letter to Agriculture or Interior but have a letter prepared in reply by both Departments." See *post*, 830.

823   DANIEL W. BELL, ACTING DIRECTOR, BUREAU OF THE BUDGET, TO ROOSEVELT

[WASHINGTON] *Oct. 14, 1938*

MEMORANDUM FOR THE PRESIDENT: Reference is made to the letter of June 6, 1938, addressed to you by Mr. Fechner, Director of the Civilian Conservation Corps, in which he sets forth and requests your approval of certain principles of administration in the operation of the corps.

These principles appear to be directly in line with the purpose expressed in the Act, approved June 28, 1937, which gives the Director complete and final authority in the functioning in the Corps, and which authority is desirable and necessary to meet changes in operating condiditions and the shifting of camps from the jurisdiction of one agency to another.

At the time the bill was drafted for the purpose of establishing the Corps, and which resulted in the Act of June 28, 1937, representatives of this office, together with Mr. Fechner and representatives of the Department of Agriculture and the Interior Department, spent some time in joint conference in the preparation of such draft and it was understood by all concerned that it was your desire that the Director of the Corps be given complete and final authority in carrying out its purposes, which authority appeared to be most desirable and necessary in view of some experiences that had been encountered prior to the enactment of the bill.

I therefore recommend that you approve the principles of authority and operation set forth in Mr. Fechner's letter. I assume that your endorsement on Mr. Fechner's letter will be preferable to a separate letter addressed to Mr. Fechner and I have not, therefore, prepared any separate draft.

In this connection, reference is made to previous communications between this office, yourself and Mr. Fechner on a closely related subject, as set forth in my memorandum to you of January 24, 1938, and your letter of the same date to Mr. Fechner, copies of which are attached.[1]

[DANIEL W. BELL]

VLA/OT 10/14/38
[*Notation*:A] O. K.   F. D. R.
[13:OF 268:CT]

[1] The memorandum and letter have not been found in the Roosevelt papers. They were, with the original of the memorandum here printed, presumably returned to the Budget Bureau.

824   ROOSEVELT TO W. ESPEY ALBIG, Wassaic, New York

HYDE PARK, NEW YORK, *October 18, 1938*

DEAR MR. ALBIG: Thank you for your letter of October fourth.[1] I am very glad to know of your interest in chestnut and about the several saplings which have escaped the blight. Apparently there is a great deal of interest in the vigorous and persistent re-sprouting of chestnut in many parts of the East. Several government, state, and private agencies are conducting experiments to introduce the Oriental chestnut. I have planted several of these trees on my place near Hyde Park, to determine how they will grow under those soil and climatic conditions. The Oriental strains apparently are resistant to the chestnut blight. Experiments in cross pollination of European and Oriental forms of chestnut with our own domestic variety are being attempted. It is likely that several years will pass before we shall determine definite results from some of these experiments. Meanwhile, we hope sincerely that these trees may develop an immunity to the blight.

Authorities at the Brooklyn Botanic Garden and the New York State College of Forestry, as well as several other agencies, are now working on the problem. The reported experiment at Dover, New Jersey, is certainly interesting. We shall know a little more about it after results of tests made have been determined. However, in view of the fact that so many agencies are already working on this problem, I doubt the advisability of having a special representative from the U. S. Forest Service assigned to work in Dutchess County, as the conditions found there are rather typical of conditions found in many parts of New England and the other eastern states.[2]

Thank you for your interesting letter, and with kind regards,

Very sincerely yours,

[FRANKLIN D. ROOSEVELT]

[13:PPF 38:CT]

[1] Albig reported on chestnut saplings he had found on his farm and suggested that the Forest Service look into the circumstances of their survival (PPF 38).

[2] Drafted by Nelson C. Brown. A similar letter (also drafted by Brown), dated Oct. 18, 1938, was sent to Gifford C.Ewing, Amenia, New York, in reply to his letter of Oct. 4, 1938 (PPF 38). Ewing suggested using Boy Scouts to collect chestnuts for planting.

825   ROOSEVELT TO CERTAIN FEDERAL AGENCIES

[WASHINGTON] *October 19, 1938*

MEMORANDUM TO FEDERAL AGENCIES CONCERNED WITH RELIEF, RE-HABILITATION, WATER DEVELOPMENT, OR LAND USE PROBLEMS IN THE NORTHERN GREAT PLAINS: As a result of my recent request that the National Resources Committee make a special review of conditions in the Northern Great Plains and advise me of policies and procedures which might be initiated promptly with a view to promoting the permanent rehabilitation of the area, the Committee has submitted a report directing attention to the desirability of undertaking various developments (including irrigation projects) and land-use readjustments of lasting benefit and of the desirability of using relief funds and relief labor in effectuating them to the greatest degree practicable.[1]

Please instruct appropriate officials of your organization in North Dakota, South Dakota, Montana, Wyoming, and Nebraska, as well as in Washington, to assist in all possible ways in carrying out the co-opera-tive rehabilitation program in the region. An appropriate committee of the National Resources Committee will act as a general co-ordinating agency, and each Federal department should provide for co-ordination of all relevant activities within its jurisdiction.[2]

[13:OF 2285:CT]

[1] *Rehabilitation in the Northern Great Plains* (Washington, 1938).
[2] Drafted by the National Resources Committee.

826 ROOSEVELT TO GOVERNOR ROBERT L. COCHRAN, Lincoln, Nebraska

WASHINGTON, *October 19, 1938*

MY DEAR GOVERNOR COCHRAN: I am sending you herewith a copy of a preliminary report by the Northern Great Plains Committee, entitled *Rehabilitation in the Northern Great Plains.* This Committee, which included in its membership representatives of both Federal and State agencies, was appointed at my request by the National Resources Committee to suggest measures, including specific changes in Federal procedure and policy affecting land and water conservation, which might be carried out promptly in order to promote the rehabilitation of the area.

The Committee's recommendations are of three classes from the standpoint of action necessary to effectuate them.

First, certain improvements in the activities of Federal agencies may be made under existing authorizations of the Congress. I approve the recommendations of the Committee in these particulars, and I have directed all executive departments and agencies to modify their procedures accordingly. The report outlines the character of rehabilitation work which will be undertaken by the Federal government during the fiscal year 1939.

Second, several proposed changes in policy may be made only under new authorization of the Congress. I hope that the suggestions of this nature may receive careful study by the Congress at its next session.

Third, the responsibility for a number of basic lines of constructive action rests largely or wholly with state and local agencies. I recommend that you review the proposals of this class, and I hope that you may carry out such of them as are appropriate to the conditions in your state. A large measure of responsibility for the success or failure of a rehabilitation program in the Northern Great Plains rests with the state and local governments.[1]

Sincerely yours,

[FRANKLIN D. ROOSEVELT]

[13:OF 2285:CT]

[1] (Drafted by the National Resources Committee.) The same letter was sent to the governors of North and South Dakota, Montana, Nebraska and Wyoming.

Roosevelt to Will Simons, Chairman, Idaho State
        Planning Board, Boise

[Washington] *October 25, 1938*

My dear Mr. Simons: The problems raised by the migration of farm families into Idaho and other States of the Northwest, to which you allude in your letter of October 6, and which are discussed in the report of the Pacific Northwest Regional Planning Commission on "Recent Migration in the Pacific Northwest," merit the consideration of all State and Federal agencies concerned with the development of a properly conceived land program in that area.[1]

In order to arrive a such a program, I am asking the National Resources Committee to form a joint committee, composed of State and Federal representatives operating in the area, along the lines of, and of course in close cooperation with, the Northern Great Plains Committee. The cooperation of the Federal agencies will, of course, be effected through their representation on this committee. I am confident that the States, through their State Planning Boards and the Pacific Northwest Regional Planning Commission, will also give full support.[2]

Very sincerely yours,

[Franklin D. Roosevelt]

[13:OF 834:CT]

[1] Simons called attention to the problem created by the migration of Great Plains farm families to Idaho and their settlement there on submarginal lands. He urged appointment of a committee under auspices of the National Resources Committee to deal with the problem (OF 834). The report mentioned (mimeographed) was issued in Portland, Oregon, in 1938.
[2] Drafted by the National Resources Committee.

Governor Lloyd C. Stark of Missouri to Roosevelt

Jefferson City, *October 28, 1938*

My dear Mr. President: A satisfactory solution has not yet been found to the situation confronting the rural population in the Ozark Region of southern Missouri. As you well know, the lumber industry is gone, much of the land has proven to be submarginal for crop agriculture, and there is little opportunity to absorb the surplus labor through industrial channels. Education, public health and living conditions are unsatisfactory.

One of the hopeful vehicles for improvement is with the National Forest program, inaugurated soon after the start of your first administration. More than a million acres of the three and one-half million acres included within the established purchase units have been bought and paid for but, as yet, the program has made no adequate provision for the ten thousand rural families living within the boundaries, or even for the more than four hundred families living on the land which has passed to Government ownership.

The Forest Service men are making an earnest, if wholly inadequate, study and start on rehabilitation in place of these families. I hope that sympathetic Budget consideration can be extended to this activity as a permanent feature of that Bureau. The rehabilitation of these tenants on public lands, through a combination of subsistence farming and cash income from work restoring the forest resources, seems to be the best and least costly way to proceed.[1]

Respectfully yours,

LLOYD C. STARK

[13:OF 149:TS]

[1] Answered *post*, 833.

829   ROOSEVELT TO REPRESENTATIVE MALCOLM C. TARVER OF GEORGIA

HYDE PARK, NEW YORK, *November 5, 1938*

MY DEAR MR. TARVER: On receipt of your telegram of October thirty-first,[1] I asked for a report from the Director of the Civilian Conservation Corps on what had been done and what could be done to assist in fighting forest fires on private lands.

It appears that the 1937 Act of Congress setting up the Civilian Conservation Corps authorizes and the present CCC policies provide that appropriate assistance may be given by CCC camps to supplement local forces in suppressing forest fires on privately owned lands provided that they are eligible under Clarke-McNary or other Acts of Congress and provided further that CCC assistance can practically be supplied in line with established procedures pertaining to protection of private forest lands.

I believe you will agree that an Executive Order could not enlarge present legal provisions to include private lands not now eligible under such Acts. I understand the situation in your section is critical due to dry weather and I want every possible aid rendered in preventing fire losses. I have, therefore, asked the Director of the Civilian Conservation Corps to request the National Park Service and the United States Forest Service to consult with you and investigate conditions you describe with the object in view of rendering whatever assistance may be possible under present legislation.[2]

Very sincerely yours,

[FRANKLIN D. ROOSEVELT]

CD

[13:OF 268:CT]

[1] Not found.
[2] Drafted by the Civilian Conservation Corps.

WASHINGTON, *November 10, 1938*

DEAR MR. PRESIDENT: In response to the request of Mr. McIntyre under date of October 14,[1] the following information is submitted concerning the proposed establishment of the Cabeza Prieta and Kofa Bighorn Refuges in the State of Arizona:

As the plans and policies of the Interior Department began to crystallize in the organization of the public domain into grazing districts in the thirteen western states included under the Taylor Grazing Act of 1934, this Department through the Bureau of Biological Survey proposed the establishment of hereditary ranges to safeguard the various species of native big game animals that were threatened with extinction or serious depletion in numbers. Of the twelve or fifteen major projects originally proposed three were located in the State of Arizona, including the two above mentioned. The third, the House Rock Valley project, was abandoned because of a conflict with plans for the enlargement of the Navajo Indian Reservation.

The Cabeza Prieta and Kofa projects, as originally recommended, comprised 3,400,000 acres and under date of April 23, 1936, this Department recommended their establishment as Game Ranges for the primary protection of desert bighorns or mountain sheep under the joint administration of the Departments of Agriculture and the Interior in accordance with plans previously formulated with the Interior Department for the handling of projects of that nature.[2] The plans of the Interior Department for the establishment of Arizona Grazing District No. 3, which included the proposed Cabeza Prieta and Kofa Bighorn areas, met with local opposition in the State and it was, therefore, decided not to establish the grazing district at that time, and, of course, the areas could not be established as Game Ranges without the organization of a grazing district. This Department was advised of this decision under date of December 7, 1936.[3]

This Department then decided to ask that these areas be established as straight wildlife refuges under its jurisdiction. Accordingly, the Orders were redrafted along that line and resubmitted to the Interior Department under date of January 25, 1937. After further consideration the Interior Department decided, with the approval of local interests, to establish Arizona Grazing District No. 3. The advice of Acting Secretary West under date of August 7, 1937 [4] had led this Department to believe that these areas would be established as Game Ranges, as requested in letters of April 23, 1936. This, however, failed to materialize.

There was much local interest in Arizona for the protection of the bighorns and after several conferences with representatives of the Gov-

[267]

ernor's office, the State Game and Fish Commission, State Land Commissioner, sportsmen's organizations, and the Arizona delegation in Congress, the boundaries of the proposed areas were curtailed to a maximum of approximately 1,675,000 acres. Proposed Executive Orders to establish these revised areas as straight refuges under the jurisdiction of this Department, in accordance with local sentiment, were resubmitted to the Interior Department in December 1937.[5] The Secretary of the Interior failed to approve and submit these Orders to the President for consideration. Under date of July 14, 1938,[6] this Department was advised by the Interior Department of its disapproval of the proposed refuges but that favorable consideration was being given to the establishment of Arizona Grazing District No. 3 (which was approved and published in the *Federal Register* under date of July 21, 1938). This Department was further advised that the proper safeguarding and propagation of the wildlife species could be adequately managed with facilities available in the Department of the Interior.

Feeling that the Bureau of Biological Survey has the primary responsibility on behalf of the Federal Government to develop and perpetuate the wildlife resources of the Nation, this Department, in a letter of April 12, 1938,[7] sought to reopen the question of establishing these areas as wildlife refuges. At the same time the Department offered to study the areas further for the purpose of eliminating any possible unnecessary tracts from the proposed refuges, should the Department of the Interior feel inclined to reconsider their establishment. No reply to this letter has been received.

There are attached for your further information copies of the correspondence between the Department of Agriculture and the Department of the Interior on this subject,[8] together with copies of the proposed Executive Orders for the establishment of the Cabeza Prieta and Kofa Bighorn Refuges; also copies of resolutions, informally brought to the attention of this Department, which were recently adopted by the Arizona Game Protective Association at its annual convention, October 1, 1938, and by a special "Big Horn" meeting of officials and interested citizens held at the State Capitol on October 3, 1938.[9]

This Department feels that the only satisfactory solution to this matter is the establishment of these areas as Bighorn Refuges under its administration in accordance with its recommendations of December 1937. The grazing within the revised boundaries of the proposed refuges is of so little consequence that it can well be handled under the regulations of this Department for the administration of National wildlife refuges. However, if you do not look with favor upon the proposition of turning these areas over to this Department for administration as straight refuges, then it is suggested that they be set up as "Game Ranges," as originally proposed, under the joint administration of the two Departments in accordance with the joint regulations adopted in February 1937, which appear in the special publication, S. R. A.–B. S. 86,[10] of the Biological Survey of this Department. The character of Executive Order covering the joint ranges is shown on page five of this publication.

If either of these suggestions meets with your approval and you so advise me, I shall be glad to prepare and submit for your further consideration drafts of appropriate Executive Orders in accordance with your decision.[11]

Respectfully,

H. A. WALLACE

[13:OF 378:TS]

[1] McIntyre's request for information (OF 378) was occasioned by Baker's letter to Roosevelt of Oct. 7, 1938, *ante*, 822.

[2] Tugwell to Ickes, April 23, 1936 (two letters), copies of which are enclosed with the letter here printed.

[3] Acting Secretary of Interior Walters to Wallace, enclosed.

[4] West to Wallace, enclosed.

[5] Acting Secretary of Agriculture Wilson to Ickes, Dec. 3, 1937, enclosed.

[6] Ickes to Wallace, enclosed.

[7] No letter of this date is with the enclosures. There is present a copy of a letter from Acting Secretary of Agriculture Gregg to Ickes, Aug. 12, 1938, on the subject in question.

[8] In addition to the letters cited above there are the following: Acting Secretary of Agriculture Wilson to Ickes, Dec. 14, 1936, and Wallace to Ickes, Jan. 25, 1937.

[9] Copies of the proposed executive orders are present; the resolutions are not.

[10] *Service and Regulatory Announcements of the Bureau of Biological Survey* (Washington, 1937).

[11] Wallace's letter, with its enclosures, was sent to Roosevelt to Ickes under cover of a memorandum, Nov. 14, 1938 (OF 378), reading, "For comment." See Ickes' reply, Dec. 15, 1938, *post*, 839.

831   MARVIN H. McINTYRE, SECRETARY TO THE PRESIDENT, TO JOHN H. BAKER, EXECUTIVE DIRECTOR, NATIONAL ASSOCIATION OF AUDUBON SOCIETIES, New York City

[WASHINGTON] *November 15, 1938*

MY DEAR MR. BAKER: I am very sorry that we have been so long in replying to your letter of October seventh to the President, with reference to the proposed establishment of the Kofa and Cabeza Prieta Bighorn Refuges in Arizona.

I am informed that proposals to establish game refuges have met with some dissatisfaction in Arizona for the principal reason that the withdrawal of large blocks of public domain in that State would interfere with its program of reclamation and development and would greatly aggravate the situation already existing; namely, that two-thirds of the State's area is controlled by Federal bureaus and that less than one-fourth is subject to taxation.

Earlier in the year of 1937, the Interior Department suggested to the Secretary of Agriculture that in view of these protests further consideration be given to the proposed withdrawals with a view to eliminating from the proposal lands under reclamation withdrawals in connection with the Colorado River development and the Gila Valley project. Subsequently, certain non-livestock interests in Arizona arrived at the conclusion that the including of any of this territory within a game range would be detrimental to their interests, but they expressed themselves as being in favor of much smaller game areas than had been originally proposed. This procedure, if followed, would, however, overlook the rights of livestock interests in the area. Further investigation by the Interior Department disclosed that the livestock interests were very eager to have the protection of a grazing district extended not only over the area now proposed as refuges but also over a much larger grazing area than was originally contemplated. Interviews with stockmen found sentiment in favor of bringing the lands under Federal administration, provided suitable protection was given to domestic livestock. Accordingly, an order establishing Arizona Grazing District No. 3, and embracing the lands under discussion, was signed by the Secretary on July 14, 1938.

Undoubtedly, large portions of this part of Arizona contain areas suitable to the welfare and protection of native bighorn and other wildlife species. On the whole, however, it would appear that the use of certain portions by wildlife is not in conflict with the interests of domestic livestock. The facilities of the Interior Department for the management of the area, both for the grazing of domestic livestock and game animals and for other uses such as mining, are adequate, and, under the Taylor Grazing Act, that Department is charged with the proper safeguarding and propagating of wildlife species inhabiting lands under its jurisdiction as well as with the preservation of the forage resources and the stabilization of the livestock industry.

The National Park Service maintains a wildlife division consisting of trained biologists and botanists whose services and advice on these matters are available to the Division of Grazing. The protection and welfare of native game species of the area are embodied in a plan that contemplates the cooperation of the Arizona Fish and Game Commission and the participation of that commission in the management of game, including all authority for establishing and collecting fees for harvesting surplus wildlife, if any, and its cooperation with the Interior Department in establishing as State game refuges such wildlife allotments as may be designated. In harmony with the program in this grazing district and of other districts, where necessary, I am informed that the Division of

Grazing will request and be guided by the technical advice of the National Park Service of the Department of the Interior.

Sincerely yours,

[MARVIN H. McINTYRE]

[13:OF 378:CT]

832   FREDERIC A. DELANO, ACTING CHAIRMAN, NATIONAL
RESOURCES COMMITTEE, TO ROOSEVELT

WASHINGTON, *November 15, 1938*

MY DEAR MR. PRESIDENT: In accordance with your request of August 29, I am transmitting herewith a draft revision of the Barkley-Vinson water pollution bill, together with a summary of the salient points in a report on "Water Pollution in the United States" which now is in preparation by our Special Advisory Committee on Water Pollution.[1] The report, which presents a comprehensive picture of the status of water pollution, will not be ready for transmission to you until the middle of December.

Although the draft revision of the Barkley-Vinson Bill has been prepared by a special advisory committee on which all interested Federal agencies are represented, and although the advice of the Acting Director of the Budget has been obtained, it has not been possible within the time allowed to obtain review by all members of the National Resources Committee. Our Advisory Committee has approved the statement of principles to guide new Federal legislation but has not passed upon the detailed sections of the bill. I therefore am submitting the bill to you informally, with the understanding that at a later time I shall transmit the report and the bill with the comments of the full Committee.

In the absence of Chairman Ickes, I am sending this letter so as to make this progress report available to you at the requested time.

Sincerely yours,

FREDERIC A. DELANO

[13:OF 1092:TS]

[1] The draft bill was sent by Roosevelt to Acting Director of the Budget Bell and was returned by Bell with his letter of Jan. 6, 1939, *post*, 845. The report was published; see *post*, 842.

833   ROOSEVELT TO GOVERNOR LLOYD C. STARK, Jefferson City,
Missouri

[WASHINGTON] *November 17, 1938*

MY DEAR GOVERNOR STARK: I am glad to have your letter of October 28, commending the National Forest program as a hopeful medium of permanent aid to the distressed populations of the Ozarks.

Exactly similar problems confront us in every forest region of the country where the originally abundant timber resource has been stripped from the land with little or no concern as to social or economic stability, and the lumbering industry has moved on to virgin territory. Such problems are acutely present not only in the Ozarks but also in the northern lake states and in the south.

The climb back to a sound and permanent forest land economy is unavoidably both long and difficult. I completely agree that the rehabilitation of our forest people in place should go hand in hand with restoration of the physical forest resources.

It has happily been possible to give tremendous impetus to the National Forest program over the past six years. Since 1933 about $55,000,000 has been used to purchase more than 13,000,000 acres of forest lands in critical areas, place them under administration and initiate the work of restoration. This has meant an advance in this brief period nearly three times as great as was made in the 21 years following initiation of the National Forest purchase program in 1911.

Purchase will continue, though necessarily at a slower pace. On the lands acquired restoration of forest wealth and rehabilitation of the social structure will be pressed forward as steadily as our means permit. Not alone the work of the Forest Service, but the various other programs of the Department of Agriculture in soil conservation and rural rehabilitation should and will be brought to bear increasingly toward a successful combination in these regions of small-farm operation and cash-income-producing employment in the woods and small wood-using industries.

Sincerely yours,

[FRANKLIN D. ROOSEVELT]

JES:MLM 11/12/38 [1]
[*Notation*:A] Copy of reply sent to Budget 11/17/38
[*Notation*:AS] DWB
[13:OF 149:CT]

[1] Drafted in the Budget Bureau, presumably by James E. Scott, an investigator.

834   HAROLD L. ICKES, CHAIRMAN, NATIONAL RESOURCES COMMITTEE, TO ROOSEVELT

WASHINGTON, *Dec. 1, 1938*

MY DEAR MR. PRESIDENT: From past experience we have found that a note from you is most helpful in securing the cooperation of Federal bureaus and outside agencies in the work of our various subcommittees.

We are launching a new effort to stimulate and coordinate land planning, and have persuaded Dr. W. I. Myers, former Governor of the Farm

Credit Administration, to serve as chairman of the Committee,[1] which is composed as follows:

Hon. Harry Slattery, Under Secretary, Department of the Interior

Hon. M. L. Wilson, Under Secretary, Department of Agriculture

Lee Muck, Director, Forestry Division, Office of Indian Affairs, Interior Department

Joel D. Wolfsohn, Assistant to the Commissioner, General Land Office, Interior Department

H. R. Tolley, Chief, Bureau of Agricultural Economics, Department of Agriculture

M. S. Eisenhower, Land Use Coordinator, Department of Agriculture

Carl L. Alsberg, Giannini Foundation, University of California

Charles C. Colby, University of Chicago, Chicago, Illinois

Philip H. Cornick, Institute of Public Administration, New York City

George S. Wehrwein, University of Wisconsin, Madison, Wisconsin

This committee has suggested a program of work involving decentralization of land planning, studies of basic data and techniques, a record of publicly owned land, and studies of fringe problems between city and country, crop land and forest, farm and range, etc.

It would be most encouraging and helpful to the work of the committee if you could see your way clear to approving a letter along the lines of the enclosed draft.[2]

Sincerely yours,

HAROLD L. ICKES

[13:OF 1092:TS]

[1] The Land Committee of the National Resources Committee.
[2] Sent as the letter printed below.

835   ROOSEVELT TO WILLIAM I. MYERS, CHAIRMAN, LAND COMMITTEE, NATIONAL RESOURCES COMMITTEE

WARM SPRINGS, GEORGIA, *December 3, 1938*

MY DEAR DR. MYERS: I am glad to hear that you have agreed to serve as chairman of the Land Committee of the National Resources Committee and that your committee proposes to make studies of some of the pressing land planning problems which need solution if we are to make the best use of our land resources.

The policy of the National Resources Committee to build from the ground up in all planning efforts will, I feel confident, provide your committee with strong support from local and State planning agencies, State Agricultural Advisory Councils, and other public and private organizations concerned with land planning.

Your committee can be helpful not only to the national administration but also to State and local governments through your projected study of publicly owned land, tax delinquency, and such other investigations as funds and the available services may permit. The problems of land use on the fringes of our cities and in the border zones between forest and farm, range and crop land can only be solved by joint effort of Federal, State, local and private agencies, such as those represented on your committee. From time to time, as may be appropriate, your committee, through the National Resources Committee, can help to coordinate plans and provide advice on current problems of land planning.

I am sure that you will have the hearty cooperation of all executive agencies of the Federal Government in your new work.[1]

Sincerely yours,

[FRANKLIN D. ROOSEVELT]

[13:OF 1092:CT]

[1] Drafted by the National Resources Committee.

836   ROOSEVELT TO HAROLD L. ICKES, SECRETARY OF THE INTERIOR

[WASHINGTON] *December 10, 1938*

MEMORANDUM FOR THE SECRETARY OF THE INTERIOR: I have read Mr. Irving Brant's report on the enlargement of the Olympic National Park with great interest.[1]

I am disturbed, however, by three matters which I realize we cannot accomplish under the recent Olympic National Park Bill.

The first of these relates to the preservation of the Pacific shore line. I should like to have legislation considered to accomplish this purpose.

Second, my authority does not extend to the acquisition of a strip down the length of the Bogachiel-Hoh Valleys or a strip down the Queets River Valley from the National Park to the ocean. I think it is of the utmost importance that such strips be made a part of the Olympic National Park.

Third, I think we should have legislation for the preservation of all the remaining timber in the Quinault River Valley, and, indeed, most of the timber in the Quinault Indian Reservation. At the present time Indians can and do sell their timber to lumber interests, and I have personally seen what amounts to criminal devastation without replanting on the Reservation. It would be necessary, of course, in fairness to the Indians, to buy their lands for their actual stumpage value, leaving them, of course, enough cleared land for crops, etc.

I suggest that you work on these three proposals and talk with the two Congressmen and the two Senators as soon as they arrive.

F. D. R.

[*Notation*:A] Report on table in the President's office.
[13:OF 6–P:CT]

[1] *Report on the Enlargement of the Olympic National Park* (Manteo, N. C., 1938). Twelve copies were printed.

837   ROOSEVELT TO MONSON MORRIS, PRESIDENT, AIKEN COUNTY
       FOREST PROTECTIVE ASSOCIATION, Aiken, South Carolina

[WASHINGTON] December 12, 1938

DEAR MONSON: I, of course, regret that you could not get to Columbia as it would have been a real pleasure to see you.[1]

I am glad you were able to attend the hearing of the Joint Congressional Committee at Jacksonville and to contribute something to their information. I suggested the formulation of this Committee because of my very keen interest in the forest land problem. It is my hope that the Committee will give consideration to the national implication of this problem and its relationship to social as well as economic development.

I was keenly interested in the newspaper cliping that accompanied your letter, as well as the suggested draft of a bill to provide for the management, including forestation, of forest and submarginal land.[2] I was particularly interested in this because I have given a good deal of personal consideration to an identical proposal made by the Forest Service. Their proposal had two objectives: The first to get a maximum acreage under good forestry management with the recapture of a portion, if not all, of the public expenditures; and the second, the integration of reforestation and afforestation activities with efforts to relieve unemployment and the farmer in the marginal or submarginal class.

I objected to the initial proposal of the Forest Service because it did not distinguish in its plan between farm woodland and commercial forest lands belonging to large lumber companies. I quote from a communication I forwarded to the Secretary of Agriculture covering this specific point.

The plan mixes up wood-lot forestry with commercial forestry and that the two are very different problems is proved by the opinions of a generation of foresters and by the distinctions made in state laws between the two subjects. The enclosed plan is apparently meant to work the same way for both the individual farmer who is trying to make a living off anywhere from fifty to five hundred acres of land, and a lumber company which rarely operates on units of less than ten thousand acres—running from that acreage up to hundreds of thousands.

It seems to me that the treatment of the wood-lot problem should be looked at a good deal in the way we look at the problem of farm tenancy—spending a good deal more of government funds than we ever expect to get back. If this distinction is made publicly and with our eyes open, it amounts to a gift of government money in the form of labor, trees and supervision. On such a basis, if the Government only gets back $750 over a long period of years out of the $1,500 which it expends in behalf of the Ozark farmer, I have little objection.

It is my understanding that the Forest Service has revised its proposal and I am asking them to forward to you a modern version of their plan with suggested legislation. They indicate that they believe the adoption of some such plan would be one of the greatest steps forward in forest conservation we have taken since the creation of the National Forests. It is to be hoped the Joint Committee will give the proposal thorough consideration.

I appreciate very much the suggestion you have made.

Mrs. Roosevelt and I will both look forward with pleasure to seeing you in the near future.[3]

Very sincerely yours,

[FRANKLIN D. ROOSEVELT]

[13:PPF 2637:CT]

[1] This is in reply to Morris' letter of Dec. 5, 1938 (PPF 2367).

[2] As described in the draft bill and in the clipping (from the Aiken, S. C., *Standard and Review* of Nov. 30, 1938), Morris' plan provided for the management by the Federal Government of private forest lands in the interest of improved timber production, watershed protection, erosion prevention and wildlife protection. Fifty per cent of the expense of such management would eventually be returned to the Government through the sale of forest products.

[3] Drafted by the Forest Service.

838   ROOSEVELT TO W. S. BROWN, DIRECTOR, STATE COOPERATIVE EXTENSION WORK IN AGRICULTURE AND HOME ECONOMICS, Athens, Georgia

[WASHINGTON] *December 13, 1938*

DEAR MR. BROWN: Thank you for your very kind letter of December tenth.[1] My farm at Warm Springs is hardly worthy of having experimental work done on it. .I am maintaining it in effect in behalf of the Georgia Warm Springs Foundation and most of the land is used for fodder for the cattle. Most of the land also has been terraced in conjunction with the work of the county agent.

In all probability the whole of the top of Pine Mountain ought to be planted in long-leaf pine. There is bound to be continuing erosion if the top of the mountain is used for crop or orchard purposes.

I believe that the Extension Service of the State of Georgia, in cases like this, work primarily for replanting with trees rather than for soil improvement.

Down in the neighboring valley, on the other hand, as in the case of the Pine Mountain Valley Settlement in Harris County, the principal effort should be made to control soil erosion.

Very sincerely yours,

[FRANKLIN D. ROOSEVELT]

[13:PPF 5744:CT]

[1] Brown wrote that the Georgia Extension Service was of the opinion that because of the topography and location of the Roosevelt Georgia farm, "a conservation plan for control of soil erosion would have a wide influence in that area" (PPF 5774).

839   HAROLD L. ICKES, SECRETARY OF THE INTERIOR, TO ROOSEVELT

WASHINGTON, *Dec. 15, 1938*

MY DEAR MR. PRESIDENT: I have received your memorandum of November 14[1] requesting my comment on the memorandum of November 10 of the Secretary of Agriculture relating to the establishing of the Cabeza Prieta and Kofa Bighorn Refuges in the State of Arizona.

In referring to the correspondence between the Department of Agriculture and this Department concerning these matters, the Secretary of Agriculture failed to mention the letter of the Acting Secretary of the Interior dated August 20, 1937. This letter made reference to the letter of August 7, 1937, referred to by the Secretary of Agriculture, and suggested that further consideration be given the proposed withdrawals with a view to eliminating from the Executive order particular areas the inclusion of which had caused serious objection on the part of certain interests in the State of Arizona. No reply to this letter has been received. This is the principal reason that the plans for the establishment of game ranges failed to materialize.

Thereafter, by the letters of December 3 and 6, 1937, the Department of Agriculture renewed its requests for the establishment of the Cabeza Prieta and Kofa Bighorn Refuges, but for somewhat reduced areas. As stated in my letter to the Secretary of Agriculture on July 14, 1938, a copy of which is attached with the record, these proposals excluded entirely the interests of the livestock users in the areas. Considerable sentiment developed locally, particularly among the livestock interests, opposing the establishment of the game refuges, and favoring the administration of the areas with provision for the grazing of domestic animals in certain areas. I am convinced that the Taylor Grazing Act provides a type of administration whereby all of the various resources in these areas can be protected adequately. Under such an administration, the conservation of wildlife can be taken care of adequately, and consideration may also be given to grazing and mining. The Secretary of Agriculture has stated that the Biological Survey is willing to regulate grazing and to permit mining if the refuges are established, but this would constitute merely the taking over of functions which have long been assigned to this Department.

The facilities of the Department of the Interior for the management of areas of the type under consideration for the grazing of both game animals and domestic livestock, as well as for other purposes, are adequate and available to undertake the job immediately.

I have already taken up the matter of cooperation with the Arizona Fish and Game Commission asking its assistance in making suitable provision for wildlife under section 9 of the Taylor Grazing Act. I have been advised by the chairman of the commission that the commission would be glad to consider such a proposal and that it would be taken up at a meeting early in December.

This Department has frequently acceded to requests of the Department of Agriculture for large areas of public land for various purposes. That does not mean, however, that all requests should be or can be complied with. The requests are so numerous and sometimes so unreasonable that were they granted in every instance in their entirety, there would soon be little public land remaining for the purposes for which it is now being used and conserved under the present public land laws. For example, the original request in this instance was for 3,400,000 acres of land.

The resolutions adopted by the Arizona Game Protective Association, a copy of which is attached to the memorandum of the Secretary of Agriculture, call for comment. In those resolutions, it is stated that were the areas turned over to the Biological Survey adequate provision would be made for grazing livestock which would not interfere with the primary purposes of the refuges and that 25 percent of all grazing fees collected for the grazing of livestock would go to the county or counties in which the refuges are located, the inference being that under grazing district administration these benefits will be lost to the local people. This, of course, is not true. Under grazing district administration as provided in the Taylor Grazing Act, 50 percent of all moneys collected is returned to the State to be expended as the legislature may direct for the benefit of the county or counties in which the district is located, and 25 percent of all fees collected when appropriated by Congress is made available to the Division of Grazing of this Department for the purchase and maintenance of range improvements. Furthermore, there is apparently no provision of law under which any part of the fees that might be collected by the Biological Survey for grazing on the proposed refuges could be returned to the county or counties in which the refuges were located.

In establishing Arizona Grazing District No. 3, I am confident that I was carrying out the provisions of the Taylor Grazing Act and fulfilling its conservation objectives, thereby protecting all interests whether they be Federal, State, or those of organizations or individuals.

Attached are a map showing the location of Arizona Grazing District No. 3, a copy of the Taylor Grazing Act as amended, and a copy of the letter of the Acting Secretary of the Interior of August 20, 1937.

The memorandum of November 10 of the Secretary of Agriculture is returned herewith.

Sincerely yours,

HAROLD L. ICKES

[13:OF 378:TS]

[1] (OF 378.) The letters mentioned below are enclosed with the one here printed, except those of Dec. 3 and 6, 1937, which were enclosed with Wallace's letter to Roosevelt of Nov. 10, 1938, *ante*, 830.

840   REPRESENTATIVE BRENT SPENCE OF KENTUCKY TO MARVIN H. McINTYRE, SECRETARY TO THE PRESIDENT

NEWPORT, KENTUCKY, *December 16, 1938*

DEAR MC: When I took advantage of your very kind invitation to accompany the President on his train when he was in my District and spoke at Latonia,[1] I talked with him about the problem that is probably of more interest to the people of the District I represent than any other legislative matter, viz: the elimination of stream pollution.

As you know the Ohio River is locked and dammed and in the summer time instead of a flowing stream we have a series of stagnant pools from which emanate foul odors. Into the pool, which extends from Coney Island about eight miles above Cincinnati to the Fernbank Dam about four miles below Cincinnati, flows the industrial waste and domestic sewage of 800,000 people and out of it comes our water supply.

We were all greatly interested in the enactment into law of the Barkley-Vinson Bill. The President told me he was also deeply interested in this matter but he informed me he vetoed the Bill because it did not conform to the ordinary budgetary requirements, and said he would approve a bill that would not contain the objectionable features of the other Bill.

It is my opinion the President's position is entirely meritorious. Those interested have jointly prepared the enclosed bill.[2] I trust it eliminates the features to which the President did not give his approval. However, if the President has any objection to this bill or he feels there should be any change made I would like to have his ideas and will certainly make the bill conform to his views.

If it is not too much trouble and if you think we can do so with propriety I wish you would submit the enclosed bill to the President.

While I am of the opinion the people I represent have a more vital interest in this matter than any others because of the peculiarly bad conditions that exist in the Ohio River at this point, the great majority of the people of Kentucky are deeply interested in it and it is also a matter of major national importance.

The City of Cincinnati, by reason of its large population and great financial ability, is able to construct filtration and chlorination plants to meet to a certain extent the situation but many of the cities on the Kentucky side of the river are small without great resources and are unable to give the river water the proper treatment, consequently it presents greater difficulties to the smaller towns than to the larger ones.

If you can give me the information requested as soon as possible, I assure you it will be greatly appreciated.[3]

With kindest regards and all good wishes, I am,

Sincerely yours,

BRENT SPENCE

[13:OF 114–A:TS]

[1] July 8, 1938, while en route to the Pacific Coast.
[2] "To create a Division of Water Pollution Control in the United States Public Health Service . . ." This is a draft of the bill introduced by Spence as H. R. 922 on Jan. 3, 1939, companion bill of S. 685, introduced by Senator Barkley on Jan. 16, 1939.
[3] An attached memorandum, Roosevelt to McIntyre, Dec. 21, 1938, reads, "Tell him I want to see him after the fifth of January about water pollution." See *post*, 845.

841   ERNEST C. OBERHOLTZER, EXECUTIVE SECRETARY, QUETICO-SUPERIOR COMMITTEE, TO ROOSEVELT

WASHINGTON, D. C., *December 21, 1938*

MY DEAR MR. PRESIDENT: The Quetico-Superior Committee, created by Executive Order in June, 1934, has now served for four and one-half years. It is the duty of the five members to facilitate early attainment of a vast wilderness sanctuary along the Border between Ontario and Minnesota.

Aside from its broader social aspects, the project will realize two of the main objectives of the present Administration—conservation of natural resources and closer relations with Canada. It has already gone far toward achievement. On October 13, the State Department addressed an inquiry through the Legation in Ottawa as to the disposition of the Canadians, thus initiating the final stage.

At this point Premier Hepburn of Ottawa enters the picture, as he does in the St. Lawrence Treaty. All the resources that are involved on the Canadian side belong to the Province of Ontario. Therefore, the consent of the Province is primary. The next step would be for the Province to enter into a contract with the Dominion, binding itself to fulfill the principles of the treaty.

Though no one can yet predict what Premier Hepburn's reactions will be, there are reasons to believe that his support can be won. His Minister of Lands and Forests, in a private discussion, has recently declared himself very favorable to the proposal. A reply should be received about the middle of January.

In addition to the uncertainty as to the Canadian reaction, the Quetico-Superior Committee is faced by one other serious difficulty. The Minnesota portion of the area is not yet sufficiently under Federal control to enable the Government to fulfill its portion of the proposed treaty. In July 1930, Congress passed the Shipstead-Nolan Act, which designates the area and forbids further exploitation of lakes and streams. The Act, however, is operative only to the extent that the Government owns adjacent lands. Eight and one-half years have passed and yet the Act has never been implemented by the necessary appropriation for the purchase of lands. A minimum fund of a million and a quarter dollars is urgently needed. This amount would not only insure sufficient control to prevent further serious desecration of the area but would go far toward persuading the Canadians of the seriousness of American intentions.

The project is not without opponents—some of the most powerful lumber and power interests in the country. Their misrepresentations and obstruction have hampered the Committee from the beginning. These interests resent public planning for the area and view a comprehensive forestry program of the character proposed, with commercial values yielding wherever intangible values are of greater public importance, as an unwarranted bar to private plans for exploitation.

The Committee feels that your first-hand knowledge of the problem at this time is vital to further progress and for the first time seeks a brief personal discussion. The Committee is naturally not in the best position to deal with the delicate Canadian problem. It also hesitates to introduce a bill to authorize a special appropriation of the necessary funds without knowing your attitude. If, either at a press conference or in some address, you would say a few words in support of the program, you would do more, we believe, than any other influence to resolve the difficulties on both sides.

Sincerely yours,

ERNEST C. OBERHOLTZER

[13:OF 1119:TS]

WASHINGTON, *December 22, 1938*

MY DEAR MR. DELANO: A constructive Federal policy for the abatement of water pollution is a social necessity. Such a policy is now lacking. It should be formulated promptly so that the great progress of the past six years under the public works and work relief programs in reducing objectionable pollution may continue undiminished.

The basic facts on which a judicial consideration of policy must rest are summarized in the report on "Water pollution in the United States," which we transmit herewith.[1] The report was prepared at the request of the President by our Special Advisory Committee on Water Pollution, a group representative of Federal and non-Federal agencies prominently concerned with water pollution. That committee reviewed its earlier reports,[2] collected and analyzed much new material, especially material relating to industrial waste, and consulted with many technicians having an interest in water pollution from the standpoint of public health, wildlife conservation, or industry. The resulting document is the first relatively complete statement of the status of water pollution in the United States and of suitable means of correcting the present unsatisfactory conditions. It recommends appropriate remedial action by the State and Federal governments.

We concur in the findings and recommendations of the Special Advisory Committee. In so doing, we call particular attention to the need for integrating the recommended abatement programs with drainage basin plans for the effective control and efficient use of water for all beneficial purposes.

We call attention also to the fact that the characteristics of surface waters are considered in this report only from the standpoint of deleterious pollution and its abatement. For the most part the transportation by streams of products of erosion, the siltation of water channels, and the like, did not come within the scope of the report.

Respectfully submitted,

ABEL WOLMAN, Chairman . . .[3]

[13:OF 1092:T]

---

[1] The report here enclosed was a mimeographed copy; this was submitted to Roosevelt by the National Resources Committee on Jan. 25, 1939 (*post*, 854), and by him sent to the Congress with his message of Feb. 15, 1939 (*post*, 868). There it was ordered printed as *Water Pollution in the United States. Third Report of the Special Advisory Committee on Water Pollution. Message from the President of the United States Transmitting a Report on Water Pollution in the United States*, 76th Cong., 1st sess., H. Doc. 155 (Washington, 1939).

[2] *Report on Water Pollution by the Special Advisory Committee on Water Pollution, July 1935* (Washington, 1935); *Second Report on Water Pollution . . . February 1937* (Washington, 1937).

* (This was also signed by the other eleven members of the committee.) The report was vigorously denounced by the Izaak Walton League as "an amazing document of half truths much more sympathetic toward the problems of industrial polluters than toward the inherent right of the public to pure streams" ("An Analysis of House Document 155, Water Pollution in the United States," undated news release, Izaak Walton League of America). The league denied the major premises of the Wolman report: that the discharge of untreated or partially treated wastes into streams (short of endangering public health) was a proper use of streams; that the cost to industry of treating industrial wastes was a public problem of greater public concern than the pollution of public waters; that the responsibility for devising pollution treatment techniques lay on the Government rather than on polluting industries; that pollution could be controlled satisfactorily by state agencies and interstate compacts; and that satisfactory progress was being made.

843   SENATOR CARL HAYDEN OF ARIZONA TO MARVIN H. McINTYRE,
       SECRETARY TO THE PRESIDENT

[WASHINGTON] *January 5, 1939*

MY DEAR MARVIN: I thank you for your note of December 28, transmitting the digests of reports by the National Resources Committee.[1] I thoroughly concur in what I heard the President say yesterday respecting the desirability of creating a permanent organization to carry on the work of that Committee and I am enclosing herewith copies of a bill which I have introduced to accomplish that purpose.[2]

Yours very sincerely,

CARL HAYDEN

[13:OF 1092:TS]

[1] OF 1092.
[2] In his annual message to Congress of Jan. 4, 1939, Roosevelt said: "To guard against opportunist appropriations, I have on several occasions addressed the Congress on the importance of permanent long-range planning. I hope, therefore, that following my recommendation of last year, a permanent agency will be set up and authorized to report on the urgency and desirability of the various types of government investment" (Rosenman, ed., *Public Papers*, VIII, 11). Hayden introduced his bill on January 4 but it was not reported from committee (*Cong. Rec.*, 76th Cong., 1st sess., 84: 1, 64). Two copies of the bill are present, "S. 19, A Bill to establish a National Resources Board."

844   ROBERT FECHNER, DIRECTOR, CIVILIAN CONSERVATION CORPS,
       TO ROOSEVELT

WASHINGTON, D. C., *January 6, 1939*

DEAR MR. PRESIDENT: You will recall my letter of June 6, 1938 which you approved on October 14, 1938. I attach copy for your ready reference.

If it meets with your approval I would like very much to have a conference with you and the four Cabinet Secretaries whose Departments participate in the work of the Civilian Conservation Corps. I think it would be desirable to inform the Secretaries of the amend-

[283]

ments to the present Civilian Conservation Corps legislation which, with your approval, will be submitted to Congress at an early date.

I would also like to discuss the desirability of having the federal agencies benefiting by the work of the CCC camps plan a program for the proper maintenance of this work. We have reached a point in our work on national parks and national forests where the tremendous amount of work already done cannot or is not being properly maintained by the regular personnel and funds of the National Park Service and the United States Forest Service. This makes it necessary for the Civilian Conservation Corps to expend a substantial part of its funds and personnel on this maintenance work. It is my understanding that you did not desire to have a condition of this kind develop.

I would also like to discuss with you and the Secretaries the problem of sending CCC companies from Eastern states to far Western states. There is constantly increasing pressure from state officials in the East and South to have all enrollees originating in those states retained there for work projects authorized under the law.

I also feel that there should be a clearer understanding of the responsibility of the Director to decide disciplinary cases in such unfortunate instances as the recent fatal forest fire in Pennsylvania in which eight enrollees were burned to death.

There may be other points that would be worthwhile to discuss. In almost six years I have never met the Secretaries jointly and have very seldom met any Secretary individually to discuss the affairs or the policy of the Corps. I am glad to state that the representatives appointed by the Secretaries to serve on my Advisory Council have rendered most excellent service and have given me splendid cooperation. I feel, however, that at least occasionally it would be worthwhile for me to meet with you and the Secretaries personally.

Sincerely yours,

ROBT. FECHNER

[*Notation*:A] Mac Arrange this conference some afternoon at two o'clock after Thurs. of this week. F.D.R. 1/9 [1]

[13:OF 268:TS]

[1] On January 16 Roosevelt conferred with Fechner, Ickes, Perkins, Wallace and Woodring (PPF 1–O).

845   DANIEL W. BELL, ACTING DIRECTOR, BUREAU OF THE BUDGET, TO ROOSEVELT

WASHINGTON, *Jan. 6, 1939*

MEMORANDUM FOR THE PRESIDENT: Your memorandum of November 18, 1938 transmitted to me the letter of November 15, 1938 addressed to you by Acting Chairman Delano of the National Resources Committee, together with a draft of a bill to establish in the Public Health Service a Division of Water Pollution Control and for other purposes, and a summary of a report of the Resources Committee on "Water Pollution in the United States."[1] In returning these papers to you I have indicated in red on the draft of bill certain revisions which, after conferring with Mr. Abel Wolman of the Water Resources Committee of the National Resources Committee, I think should be embodied in the bill. These suggested revisions do not affect adversely its basic purposes and are for the purpose partly of eliminating more or less objectionable features in the bill that was vetoed last year and partly for the purpose of perfecting the structure of the bill.

The draft as amended establishes a Division of Water Pollution Control in the Public Health Service, Treasury Department; establishes an advisory board consisting of 5 members from the Federal service and 5 members outside the service; provides for Federal aid in the form of grants-in-aid to States, municipalities, or other public bodies of not to exceed 30% of the cost of the project; provides for loans to States, etc., for a period of not to exceed 30 years with interest at 4%; provides for loans on a ten year basis with interest at 5% to persons, firms and corporations for construction of treatment works; requires the division to submit lists of projects to the Secretary of the Treasury, through the Surgeon General, subject to review by the National Resources Committee or other agency designated by the President; provides for the inclusion in the Budget of estimates of appropriation for grants-in-aid and loans in an amount of not to exceed $50,000,000 annually; authorizes the annual appropriation of necessary funds for administrative expenses and also authorizes an appropriation of $700,000 a year for ten years for the purpose of assisting the several States in the promotion, investigation, surveys and studies necessary in the prevention of water pollution, to be conducted by or under the direction of the respective state health authorities.

The bill also provides for the appointment of ten additional sanitary engineer officers in the regular corps of the Public Health Service, for the calling to active duty of 10 reserve engineer officers, and for the detail of employees from other Federal departments and agencies.

While I have not eliminated in my revision of the draft the section (Sec. 8) authorizing the appropriation of $700,000 for expenditure by the States for surveys, studies, etc., I question the appropriateness of including this section in the bill. It seems to me that the States should make provision for these surveys and studies out of their own funds.

If you are willing to approve the draft of bill, as revised in red, and will indicate whether or not Section 8 should be retained therein, I will be glad to prepare a letter for your signature addressed to Acting Chairman Delano advising him of the relation of the proposed legislation to your program.²

D. W. BELL

[13:OF 1092:TS]

¹ No copy of the November 18 memorandum is present. The draft bill, a twenty-seven-page typescript, is entitled: "An Act to provide Federal aid to states in the control of water pollution, to create a Division of Water Pollution Control in the United States Public Health Service, and for other purposes." It is dated Nov. 12, 1938, and is marked "Fourth Draft." This was introduced as the Barkley-Spence bill.
² An attached memorandum, McIntyre to Delano, Jan. 7, 1939, reads: "Attached is self-explanatory. The President asked me to refer it over to you for consideration of Mr. Bell's memorandum." See below.

846   FREDERIC A. DELANO, CHAIRMAN, ADVISORY COMMITTEE TO
THE NATIONAL RESOURCES COMMITTEE, TO ROOSEVELT

WASHINGTON, *January 10, 1939*

MY DEAR MR. PRESIDENT: I am returning Mr. Bell's memorandum of January 6, 1939, concerning the draft of a bill to establish a Division of Water Pollution Control in the Public Health Service which was referred to me for comment on January 7.

The revisions to which Mr. Bell refers are in harmony with the recommendations of our Water Resources Committee for a Federal pollution-abatement policy, and they improve the draft bill notably. Our Advisory Committee concurs in them.

Mr. Bell questions the desirability of the authorization (in Section 8) of annual appropriation of funds to be allocated among the States for investigations of water pollution and pollution abatement. In our opinion, such aid is a basic element in a sound Federal policy in this field. State and local agencies already are making substantial expenditures for investigations of the desired type, but their work should be expanded in order to provide a firmer and broader basis for planning and constructing pollution-abatement works, and for State enforcement activities. Expansion of studies in that field is needed urgently. From the Federal standpoint it would be of great value in building up a reservoir of meritorious public works projects and in providing essential data for comprehensive drainage basin plans.

Since most pollution problems are local in character they may be studied best by State agencies in cooperation with local and private agencies. However, the lack of adequate studies already has given rise to regrettable efforts to shift complete responsibility for such studies to the Federal Government. The Ohio Basin pollution study, now being made by the Public Health Service and Corps of Engineers at a cost of $500,000 under authority of the Rivers and Harbors Act of 1937, sets a precedent for numerous other Federal authorizations for similar work, wholly at Federal expense, if the State activities are not enlarged. Experience under the Social Security Act has demonstrated the stimulating effect which Federal allocations of the type proposed in Section 8 of the draft bill would have on the activities of state health authorities and related agencies. The proposed appropriation of $700,000 seems reasonable in amount, but we are not so much concerned with the exact amount as we are with the principle involved.

For all these reasons, our Advisory Committee recommends strongly in favor of retaining Section 8 in the draft bill.[1]

Sincerely yours,

FREDERIC A. DELANO

[13:OF 1092:TS]

[1] A copy of this letter was sent by Roosevelt to Acting Budget Director Bell under cover of a memorandum of Jan. 13, 1939 (OF 1092): "I think we are together on this now. Please prepare the necessary letter or letters, in accordance with your memorandum and Mr. Delano's." See Roosevelt's reply, *post,* 851.

847 MARVIN H. McINTYRE, SECRETARY TO THE PRESIDENT, TO ROOSEVELT

WASHINGTON, *1/10/39*

MEMORANDUM FOR THE PRESIDENT: Senator Bankhead called. Said that he wanted to call your attention to the fact that a Committee appointed under a Joint Resolution last Congress to make a complete study and a report on the whole Forestry problem, never functioned.[1]

McAdoo was Chairman and Pope was on the Committee.

Said that at a meeting yesterday he was elected Chairman and Fulmer Vice-Chairman and the Committee instructed them to arrange to talk to the President and find out if he wanted Congress to grant an extension beyond April so that the matter could be handled correctly.

I told him I thought you could see them the first of the week.

MHM

[*Notation*:A:LEHAND] Mac I'll see him the first of the week.[2]

[13:OF 149:T]

[1] Senate Concurrent Resolution 31, passed June 14, 1938 (52 *Stat.* 1452), provided for a committee of five senators and five members of the House to investigate the condition, ownership and management of the forest land of the United States "as it affects a balanced timber budget, watershed protection, and flood control and the other commodities and social and economic benefits which may be derived from such lands."

[2] Bankhead and Secretary of Agriculture Wallace saw Roosevelt on January 18 (PPF 1–O).

WASHINGTON, *Jan. 14, 1939*

MY DEAR MR. PRESIDENT: Following your inquiry of December 22 concerning Senator Donahey's interest in an Ohio Basin Planning Commission,[1] our Advisory Committee has reviewed the many organizations and efforts now engaged in planning work for the Ohio Valley. These efforts include:

1. The Ohio Valley Regional Planning Commission, composed of the chairmen of State Planning Boards in the area.

2. The Ohio Valley Water Sanitation Compact Commission, which has recently negotiated an interstate compact for abatement of pollution.

3. Special Pollution Committee, authorized by the Rivers & Harbors Act of 1937, for which you designated membership composed of Major General Julian L. Schley, Surgeon General Thomas Parran, and Mr. Abel Wolman of our Water Resources Committee.

4. A series of Drainage Basin Committees, organized by the National Resources Committee for cooperative study of water programs by local representation of Federal agencies and representatives of State and local interests.

5. The Ohio-Lower Mississippi Flood Control Subcommittee, set up at your request a year ago by our Water Resources Committee, which has made a series of studies and reports on flood control projects with special reference to their effect on the lower valley.

6. "INCOHIO," meaning Interstate Committee on the Ohio, organized by the Council of State Governments from the representatives of Commissions on Interstate Cooperation set up by the legislatures of the several States. At the last meeting of INCOHIO, on November 21, 1938, they proposed the organization of a joint "Planning Committee."

Our Advisory Committee suggests that this situation be brought to the attention of Senator Donahey and that effort be made through negotiation with all concerned to establish a simplified organization for planning work based on the experience and programs of regional offices of the National Resources Committee.

If this proposal meets with your approval, the Advisory Committee will be glad to take the matter up with Senator Donahey and arrange the proposed negotiations among all the organizations now active in planning for the Ohio Basin.

Sincerely yours,

HAROLD L. ICKES

[13:OF 1092:TS]

[1] In a letter of Dec. 21, 1938 (OF 1092), Donahey told Roosevelt that the latter's proposal for a study of flood control and water conservation in the Ohio Valley was

"splendid" and would meet with unanimous approval. This proposal was apparently made at a White House meeting on Dec. 12, 1938 (PPF 1–O). Roosevelt sent Donahey's letter to the National Resources Committee with a note (Dec. 22, 1938, OF 1092) reading: "I think that Senator Donahey would go along with a plan for an Ohio Basin Planning Commission of some kind. What do you think?"

849   ROOSEVELT TO HARCOURT A. MORGAN, CHAIRMAN, BOARD OF DIRECTORS, TENNESSEE VALLEY AUTHORITY, Knoxville

[WASHINGTON] *January 16, 1939*

MY DEAR MR. MORGAN: I am glad to have your letter of December 23 and the accompanying statement of the forest fire situation in the Tennessee Valley.[1]

You know, I am sure, that my active interest in the restoration, protection, and wise use of our forest resources long antedates my first term as President. It has happily been possible to give tremendous impetus to public action along these lines over the past six years. Through the National Forest purchase program more than 13,000,000 acres of forest lands in critical areas have been brought into Federal ownership, placed under sound administration, and pointed toward renewed productivity. Through the Civilian Conservation Corps and other work-relief agencies forest land protection and improvement have made great strides forward, and we have seen on a nation-wide scale a real public awakening to the opportunities for national wealth and social welfare which our forest lands afford.

Much remains to be done. The inadequate status of forest fire control, as you find it in the Tennessee Valley, is found also in other important forest regions. We are still exploiting our forest lands and denuding forest watersheds.

These and other facts impelled me to recommend to the Congress in a special message dated March 14, 1938, study by a joint committee of the entire forest-land problem of the United States. In my suggested agenda for such a committee, the adequacy and effectiveness of present activities in forest protection were given first priority.

Congress moved promptly to appoint this committee, known as the "Joint Committee on Forestry" and composed of five Senators and five Members of the House of Representatives. The committee is to report its findings not later than April 1, 1939. Several public hearings have been held in various sections of the country, and I assume that the results of the study will soon be available.

In view of the comprehensive action thus initiated and under way, I do not feel that I should inject at this time a special recommendation to the Congress dealing with a single phase of this many-sided problem. I understand that through a recent hearing in the South, conditions in that section have been described to the committee, but any additional representations which you might care to submit would doubtless be welcomed and carefully considered.

Sincerely yours,

[FRANKLIN D. ROOSEVELT]

JES/MLS 1/16/39 [2]

[*Notation*:AS] DWB

[13:OF 42:CT]

[1] Morgan pointed out that the major problem in forest fire protection was on private lands and urged greater protection through an increase of Clarke-McNary Act funds. The enclosure is a nine-page typescript, "Statement of Forest Fire Situation in the Tennessee Valley. Prepared by Tennessee Valley Authority, Forestry Relations Department, December 1, 1938" (OF 402).

[2] Drafted in the Budget Bureau, presumably by James E. Scott, an investigator.

850   HENRY A. WALLACE, SECRETARY OF AGRICULTURE, TO
       ROOSEVELT

WASHINGTON, *January 16, 1939*

DEAR MR. PRESIDENT: Last Friday you spoke of having heard the statement that the Forest Service was sponsoring a meeting at Sacramento today to protest the proposed creation of the Kings River Canyon National Park. I find that the meeting in question is one called by a committee of the Senate of the California Legislature to discuss a resolution introduced into that body by several State Senators memorializing the President and Congress against the creation of the park. The Regional Forester of the Forest Service at San Francisco was invited to be present or represented. I assume that others also have been asked to be present.

I am told that your instructions to the Forest Service to refrain from public opposition to the proposed park have been conveyed to the Regional Forester at San Francisco, and I have no reason to believe that they are being violated. Of course, you know, however, that for many years there has been widespread opposition to this movement, and the Forest Service is bound to be asked for facts and opinions which it cannot appropriately avoid supplying.[1]

Sincerely yours,

H. A. WALLACE

[13:OF 6–P:TS]

[1] On Jan. 21, 1939, Ickes wrote to Roosevelt (OF 6–P) that at this meeting the regional forester had opposed the establishment of the park. Roosevelt referred to this in a memorandum to Wallace and Silcox on Jan. 24, 1939 (OF 6–P), asking, "How long are the orders of the President, the Secretary of Agriculture and the Chief Forester to be disobeyed?"

851   Roosevelt to Frederic A. Delano, Chairman, Advisory
Committee to the National Resources Committee

[Washington] *January 17, 1939*

My dear Mr. Delano: I have your letter of January 10, 1939, with
further reference to the draft of bill to establish a Division of Water Pollution Control in the Public Health Service. The corrected draft of
bill which was referred to you with Mr. Bell's memorandum of January
6, 1939, is returned herewith, and you are advised that there would be
no objection to its presentation to Congress.[1]

Sincerely yours,

[Franklin D. Roosevelt]

WEM:MLM 1/16/39
[*Notation*:AS] DWB

[13:OF 1092:CT]

[1] Drafted in the Budget Bureau, presumably by William E. Mattingly, an investigator.

852   Roosevelt to Senator Vic Donahey of Ohio

[Washington] *January 18, 1939*

Dear Vic: I am enclosing a very interesting letter from the National
Resources Committee relating to Ohio Basin Planning.[1] I shall be glad
to talk with you about this at your convenience.[2]

Always sincerely,

[Franklin D. Roosevelt]

[13:OF 1092:CT]

[1] *Ante*, 848.
[2] Donahey replied Jan. 19, 1939 (OF 1092), that he felt something could be done
"along the lines of coordinating all of the present Federal agencies without destroying states rights."

853   Roosevelt to Henry A. Wallace, Secretary of
Agriculture

Washington, *January 25, 1939*

Memorandum for the Secretary of Agriculture: During the
Hoover Administration an attempt was made by certain large timber
interests to get the cutting rights on Admiralty Island, Alaska. It is my
recollection that you and I blocked this early in the Administration—
partly because it looked like a bad bargain and partly because Admiralty
Island has a wonderful growth of virgin timber and a wonderful growth
of very large bears on it.

Would you be good enough to let me know the situation today? Is there any thought of selling timber? If we decide that it should be preserved as a permanent wildlife virgin forest tract, how can we make such a status permanent? [1]

F. D. R.

[13:OF 378:CT]

[1] Answered *post,* 869.

854   THE NATIONAL RESOURCES COMMITTEE TO ROOSEVELT

WASHINGTON, Jan. 25, 1939

MY DEAR MR. PRESIDENT: We transmit herewith a comprehensive statement on the status of water pollution in the United States and on the technical, financial and administrative problems involved in water pollution abatement.

The report, prepared by the Special Advisory Committee on Water Pollution and approved by our Water Resources Committee, contains a revision and extension of material presented in the reports of March 22, 1937 and September 30, 1935, together with new analysis of the cost of a national pollution-abatement program.[1]

We are in agreement with the general recommendations of the Committee that new Federal legislation should provide for Federal financial and technical assistance in pollution-abatement and that construction activities for which financial aid is given should be planned as an integral part of a general public works program, and should be correlated with other activities affecting water use and control in the drainage basins concerned.

Sincerely yours,

HAROLD L. ICKES, Secretary of the Interior, Chairman
HARRY H. WOODRING, Secretary of War
H. A. WALLACE, Secretary of Agriculture
HARRY L. HOPKINS, Secretary of Commerce
FRANCES PERKINS, Secretary of Labor
F. C. HARRINGTON, Works Progress Administrator
FREDERIC A. DELANO
CHARLES E. MERRIAM
HENRY S. DENNISON
BEARDSLEY RUML

[13:OF 1092:TS]

[1] *Water Pollution in the United States. Third Report of the Special Advisory Committee on Water Pollution* (Washington, 1939).

855   ROOSEVELT TO HAROLD L. ICKES, SECRETARY OF THE INTERIOR

WASHINGTON, *January 26, 1939*

MEMORANDUM FOR THE SECRETARY OF THE INTERIOR: I enclose copy
of letter from the Secretary of Agriculture. I think well of the idea.
What do you think?

F. D. R.

[13:OF 6–P:CT]

856   [*Enclosure*] HENRY A. WALLACE, SECRETARY OF AGRICUL-
TURE, TO ROOSEVELT

WASHINGTON, *January 18, 1939*

DEAR MR. PRESIDENT: Each year proposals are made for the creation of new national parks or extension of existing park boundaries which
involve national forest land. Oftener than not these proposals raise
honest differences of opinion, both on the part of the public and between
the Department of the Interior and this Department. Sometimes these
differences have resulted in controversies which, I am sure, are embarrassing to you and which we would all like to avoid. Furthermore, these
controversies may easily becloud the fundamental considerations on
which decisions should be based.

Neither the Forest Service nor I wish to give any appearance of ob-
structing the proper development of the national park system. On the
other hand, proposals to remove from economic use large areas of land
which contain substantial values other than recreation obviously need
thoughtful consideration. Likewise, there are genuine questions concerning the form and agency of administration best suited for different
types of land possessing recreational value.

I would like to suggest that an impartial committee be created, composed of people in no way associated with either the Department of the
Interior or this Department. Such a committee might consist of four
members appointed by you, of whom two would be selected from nominees proposed by the Secretary of the Interior and an equal number
from nominees proposed by myself. The members thus appointed might
then agree upon a fifth man for chairman.

Within a reasonable period the Park Service would submit to this committee a list of all national forest areas which it feels should be established
as national parks or national monuments, while the Forest Service would
submit a list of converse proposals. The committee could then investigate each proposal on the ground, considering among other things the
economic, social, and aesthetic factors and the local sentiment. From
this investigation it would be possible to reach an impartial conclusion
much more basically sound than any derived from present procedures.

The Department of Agriculture would be willing to accept the findings of such a committee and thus do our part to avoid laying embarrassing controversial matters on your desk.[1]

Sincerely,

H. A. WALLACE

[13:OF 6–P:TS]

[1] No comment by Ickes on Wallace's suggestion has been found in the Roosevelt papers.

857 ROOSEVELT TO GOVERNOR CLARENCE D. MARTIN, Olympia, Washington

WASHINGTON, *January 26, 1939*

MY DEAR GOVERNOR MARTIN: I have received your letter of January 5 concerning the Olympic National Park.[1]

Since the studies being conducted at my direction are nearing completion, I believe it would be inadvisable to involve the National Resources Committee in this problem.

In accordance with the provisions of the Act establishing the Park, I shall, upon completion of those studies, set a date to consider here in Washington the findings and recommendations of the State of Washington, the Department of the Interior, and the Department of Agriculture, and I shall notify you when that date has been determined.[2]

Very sincerely yours,

[FRANKLIN D. ROOSEVELT]

[13:OF 6–P:CT]

[1] Martin urged that the question of the future size of the Olympic National Park be given to the National Resources Committee for study (OF 6–P).
[2] This letter was drafted by the Interior Department and approved by the Agriculture Department (Wallace to Roosevelt, Jan. 25, 1939, OF 6–P).

858 ROOSEVELT TO R. K. WICKSTRUM, PRESIDENT, ARIZONA GAME PROTECTIVE ASSOCIATION, Phoenix

WASHINGTON, *January 26, 1939*

MY DEAR MR. WICKSTRUM: I have received your telegram of January 8, urging the establishment of the Kofa and Cabeza Prieta Game Ranges under the administration of the Bureau of Biological Survey, Department of Agriculture.[1]

The administration of these areas has been given careful consideration and I believe the Executive Order, which I have just signed, will solve the problem. This order sets up a limited game range within the grazing district and protects the interests of prospectors as well as those of the

[294]

stockmen, while at the same time taking care of the matter of the preservation of the Big Horn sheep.[2]

Very sincerely,

[FRANKLIN D. ROOSEVELT]

[Notation: STAMPED] (Sgd) Burlew (Sgd) Ickes

[13:OF 378:CT]

[1] Wickstrum urged Roosevelt to give the preservation of the big horn sheep his first consideration (OF 378).
[2] (Drafted by the Interior Department.) Cabeza Prieta and Kofa Game Ranges were established by Executive Orders 8038 and 8039, both signed Jan. 25, 1939.

859　HAROLD L. ICKES, SECRETARY OF THE INTERIOR, TO ROOSEVELT

WASHINGTON, *January 26, 1939*

MY DEAR MR. PRESIDENT: Last Tuesday I discussed with you the possibility of creating a national park at Admiralty Island, Alaska. For your information, I enclose an editorial from the St. Louis *Star*, written by Irving Brant in 1932, and also a letter from him to me.[1] From an administrative point of view I am inclined to think that Admiralty Island could be included in the proposed enlargement of Glacier Bay in one national park, since Juneau is the natural center for both areas.

Sincerely yours,

HAROLD L. ICKES

[13:OF 378:TS]

[1] The editorial (dated by Brant November, 1932) commented upon charges brought by the New York Zoological Society that the Department of Agriculture had "virtually given away 5,000 square miles of virgin timber on two Alaskan Islands" to a San Francisco pulpwood manufacturer, and that every influence of the Government was being exerted to block an effort to have these islands made into a national park for the preservation of the Alaskan bears.

860　*[Enclosure]* IRVING BRANT TO HAROLD L. ICKES

[ST. LOUIS] *January 24, 1939*

[Excerpt] I talked with the manager of Crown-Zellerbach pulp operations last summer, sounding him out as to the company's present interest in Alaska, and he said that the idea of building pulp mills up there had been abandoned as unfeasible; that if any use was made of Alaska timber in the future it would be rafted to Puget Sound. That can hardly occur before Vancouver Island is stripped to pulp timber. Practically speaking, it eliminates Alaska from commercial consideration for many decades.

The people of Alaska have an implacable hostility to the grizzly bear, chiefly because it eats one salmon where human beings eat 100,000, and because it makes occasional raids around fox farms. The brown bear of Alaska can be protected on Admiralty Island, because it has range, food and cover permanently adequate. But if fox farms are allowed on the island, or if casual local lumbering develops, the slaughter now going on will turn into a ruthless war of extermination, as it is on the mainland in the neighborhood of all settlements. There is plenty of room on the mainland and on other islands for a hundred times as many fox farms as there are in Alaska, and for all the lumbering that ever will be needed, even if Alaska becomes a pulp mill center.

I think that the Glacier Bay National Monument ought to be enlarged, but I noticed in talking with one of the Forest Service staff about the recent withdrawal of Forest Service opposition to the enlargement that he persisted in speaking of it as a proposal to transform it into a national park. The thought behind that suggestion, I think, coming from that source is that if Glacier Bay were made a national park it would make it practically impossible to establish Admiralty Island as a national park. Admiralty Island contains something less than 2,000 square miles. Canada has established one national park in the far north, as a sanctuary for the wood bison, containing 20,000 square miles.

IRVING BRANT

[13:OF 378:TS]

861   ROOSEVELT   TO   HENRY   A.   WALLACE,   SECRETARY   OF   AGRICULTURE

WASHINGTON, *January 27, 1939*

MEMORANDUM FOR THE SECRETARY OF AGRICULTURE: Reverting to the subject of King's Canyon: I think you will find that three former Chief Foresters agreed that this area ought to have a national park status.

I think you will find that a grand Secretary of Agriculture, by the name of Henry C. Wallace, wrote on January 17, 1924, in reference to H. R. 4095, "to add certain lands to Sequoia National Park" the following: "The proposed enlargement of the park and the specific boundaries relating thereto are endorsed by this department." I think you will find that the area then proposed for addition to the Sequoia Park was even bigger than the area now proposed for the King's Canyon Park.[1]

F. D. R.

[13:OF 6–P:CT]

[1] The letter of Henry C. Wallace (father of Henry A.) was called to Roosevelt's attention by Ickes in a letter of Jan. 25, 1939 (OF 6–P).

WASHINGTON, *January 31, 1939*

MEMORANDUM FOR HON. F. A. SILCOX: Thank you for your memorandum in regard to the hurricane down timber in New England.[1]

1. I hope you will take up with WPA and CCC the continuation of the fire hazard work.

2. Will you be good enough to take up with Admiral Peoples, the Director of Procurement, the possibility of a plan under which the government would purchase its government lumber needs from such portion of the lumber as will most greatly fail to meet the government guarantee price? In other words, if we can buy for government use what might be called the "distress sale" lumber at the guarantee price, it will save the government's pocketbook in the long run. Also, in connection with this, the Procurement Division of the Treasury can probably increase the use of pine lumber and hardwood lumber from the New England area instead of using as much west coast lumber as we now use on the Atlantic Coast. It is true that the west coast lumber is clearer and more uniform and, therefore, easier to work with—but, on the other hand, the government uses a great deal of lumber for rough construction work where quality does not make much difference.

I do not know what the total volume of government purchases amounts to but I think it is substantial.

F. D. R.

[13:OF 149:CT]

[1] The New England hurricane of Sept. 21, 1938, left an estimated three billion feet of down timber. In the memorandum here referred to (Jan. 26, 1939, OF 149), Silcox advised against a plan proposed by Roosevelt that the Government buy the down timber and log it. He pointed out that approximately seven million dollars worth of logging equipment would be needed and, because of the great number of individual ownerships, hundreds of small lumber camps would have to be set up. He described aid being given by the Government through the Disaster Loan Corporation and the Farm Security Administration, and called attention to the fire hazard that would exist in the spring. The measures taken by the Government to alleviate hardship caused by the timber destruction are summarized in the *Report of the Chief of the Forest Service, 1939* (Washington, 1939), pp. 19–22.

863   ROOSEVELT TO GOVERNOR PRENTICE COOPER, Nashville, Tennessee

[WASHINGTON] *February 1, 1939*

MY DEAR GOVERNOR COOPER: Just before you took office Governor Browning sent me an experimental plan, proposed by your State Forester, to increase public forest holdings and remodel the Civilian Conservation Corps setup in Tennessee.[1]

When the Civilian Conservation Corps program began in 1933 the Forest Service advocated smaller camps, but I felt that 200-enrollee units, allocated to and under control of various specializing Federal agencies cooperating with each other and State authorities, would be the most economical and advantageous in the long run. I can see, however, that the proposal to break camps into smaller units for work purposes, and to spread their efforts most widely, has some advantages over the present arrangement.

But I want to point out that the proposed plan involves departures from standard practice for administering Civilian Conservation Corps camps. It would require revision and broadening of current legislation and present conservation policies in order to permit a wider range of work projects on private holdings. These things, and the effects on present functioning and respective interests of the various specializing agencies of the Departments of Interior and Agriculture, now responsible for conservation programs, will require thoughtful consideration and analysis before any decision on Mr. Hazard's plan can be made.

I have been gratified, as I am sure you have, by the smooth functioning of the Civilian Conservation Corps along present lines, and the favorable place it has won for itself. I hope, as you know, that the Civilian Conservation Corps will be placed on a permanent basis: that it may become a better vehicle than it has been, even, for unemployed young men and as an instrument to aid in developing and conserving natural resources.

Thank you for referring Hazard's plan to me. Copies of it have been sent to Mr. Fechner and to the Forest Service, and I assure you the plan will receive consideration in connection with future plans for the Corps.[2]

Very sincerely yours,

[FRANKLIN D. ROOSEVELT]

[13:OF 268:CT]

[1] State Forester J. O. Hazard's plan, "A Proposal for a State-Wide CCC Service for Tennessee," enclosed in Browning's letter to Roosevelt of Dec. 30, 1938, and a memorandum commenting on it by Silcox and Fechner, Jan. 30, 1939, are with the letter here printed. The plan proposed the establishment of 100 state forests of about 10,000 acres each, and of 100 Civilian Conservation Corps camps of 50 men each, to protect and develop all forests in the state, public and private. Fechner and Silcox agreed that the plan had many desirable features but pointed out that the state would have to be aided in acquiring the forest areas, more funds per capita would be needed to maintain the smaller camps, and Federal policy with respect to conservation work on private lands would have to be changed.

[2] Drafted jointly by the Forest Service and the Civilian Conservation Corps.

864   ROOSEVELT TO GOVERNOR W. LEE O'DANIEL, Austin, Texas

WASHINGTON, *February 4, 1939*

MY DEAR GOVERNOR O'DANIEL: As you may know, I am very much interested in the proposed Big Bend National Park in your State. I

have been hoping that this Park could be dedicated during my Administration. My advices are that this large and very interesting area
could be bought for a comparatively small sum—a sum that would be
insignificant in comparison with the economic returns that would flow
to the State of Texas after the creation of the Park. I regard the establishment of this Park as of great advantage, both to Texas and to the
Nation, from every point of view.

If the Texas Legislature at this session should see fit to make an appropriation for the acquisition of this land, it would be very gratifying
to me personally, and I am sure that it would win the general approval
of people everywhere.[1]

With personal regards, Sincerely yours,

[FRANKLIN D. ROOSEVELT]

[13:OF 6–P:CT]

[1] O'Daniel replied March 3, 1939 (OF 6–P), enclosing a copy of his message to the
Texas Legislature in which he urged acquisition of the area.

865   ROOSEVELT TO REPRESENTATIVE JOHN J. COCHRAN OF
       MISSOURI

[WASHINGTON] *February 7, 1939*

Personal

DEAR JACK: If you have a separate bill to cover White House assistants, would you think of putting the National Resources Committee under the name of "planning division" into the same bill? Otherwise I
fear it may get lost in the shuffle.[1]

Very sincerely yours,

F. D. R.

FDR:G

[13:OF 1092:CT]

[1] Cochran was chairman of the House Select Committee on Government Reorganization. An identical letter, Feb. 7, 1939, was sent by Roosevelt to Rep. Lindsay
C. Warren (N. C.), a member of Cochran's committee who was in charge of the
drafting of the Reorganization Bill. Warren replied Feb. 10, 1939 (OF 1092), that
there was "terrific opposition" to Roosevelt's proposal, and that while he had not
closed his mind to it, he believed inclusion of the National Resources Committee in
the Reorganization Bill would have an "adverse effect." Cochran's reply follows.

866   REPRESENTATIVE JOHN J. COCHRAN OF MISSOURI TO
       ROOSEVELT

WASHINGTON, D. C., *February 8, 1939*

MR. PRESIDENT: I have your personal note.[1] So far as I am concerned, I am 100 per cent in favor of the National Resources Committee.
I really think it would be a grave mistake if it is not made permanent.

[299]

Mr. Warren has been working on a bill and while we have discussed its contents, it is not in such shape that I have been able to get a copy. It so happens that I spoke to him in reference to the National Resources Committee and I regret to say that he fears, that if he included it in his bill, it might jeopardize the passage of the bill.

For your personal information, I will say, that he advised me that there is very strong opposition in the House to the National Resources Committee and it comes from the so-called powerful Rivers and Harbors Bloc. Why there should be opposition to the National Resources Committee, it is beyond me to understand. Certain interests have had a great deal to say in reference to Rivers and Harbors authorizations and appropriations. Organizations retain men in Washington during the entire period of Congress looking after their interests.

I will talk to Mr. Warren again in reference to this matter and see if I can induce him to follow your suggestion. While I will not tell him I received your letter, nevertheless, I did tell him when I discussed the National Resources Committee with him, that you were strongly in favor of including it in the general Re-Organization Bill.

With assurance of my high esteem, I am,

Sincerely yours,

JOHN J. COCHRAN

[13:OF 1092:TS]

[1] Above.

867   ROOSEVELT TO REPRESENTATIVE JOHN J. COCHRAN OF MISSOURI

WASHINGTON, *Feby 11/39*

MY DEAR MR. COCHRAN: I am sending you the enclosed "Progress Report" of the National Resources Committee because it is more than the usual annual statement of a Federal executive agency. This report reviews the problems and progress with which a planning agency has been concerned during the last five years. It demonstrates the usefulness of the kind of planning service which, as I have recommended to the Congress, should be provided as a permanent establishment within the Federal Government.

I hope that this report will be helpful to you and your colleagues on the Select Committee on Government Organization in the development and enactment of appropriate legislation to provide for continuation, correlation and decentralization of planning work.[1]

Sincerely yours,

[FRANKLIN D. ROOSEVELT]

[13:OF 1092:CT]

¹(Drafted by the National Resources Committee.) An identical letter, of the same date, was sent to Senator Byrnes (S. C.), chairman of the Senate Select Committee on Government Organization; no reply is present. Cochran replied Feb. 13, 1939 (OF 1092), that he would do everything he could to get his committee to agree to provide for the National Resources Committee under the name suggested in Roosevelt's letter of February 7.

868   ROOSEVELT TO THE CONGRESS

THE WHITE HOUSE, *February 15, 1939* ¹

To THE CONGRESS OF THE UNITED STATES: The last Congress recognized the national importance of pollution abatement in our streams and lakes by passing, during its closing days, an act providing for the creation of a Division of Water Pollution Control in the United States Public Health Service and for the establishment of a permanent system of Federal grants-in-aid and loans to assist in constructing pollution-abatement projects. Although fully subscribing to the general purposes of that act, I felt compelled to withhold my approval of it because of the method which it provided for the authorization of loans and grants-in-aid. It would have prevented the consideration of such appropriations as a part of the annual budget for all purposes. My reasons are set forth in detail in my memorandum of June 25, 1938. I hope that at this session the whole problem of water pollution may again receive your attention.

To facilitate study of the problem by the Congress, I am transmitting a report on "Water Pollution in the United States," which outlines the status of pollution, the cost of bringing about a reasonable degree of abatement, and the financial, technical, and administrative aspects of such a program. The document was prepared at my request by a special advisory committee of the National Resources Committee composed of representative experts from the departments of War, Treasury, the Interior, Agriculture and Commerce, and from private and state agencies.²

No quick and easy solution of these problems is in sight. The Committee estimates that an expenditure by public and private agencies of approximately two billion dollars over a period of ten to twenty years may be required to construct works necessary to abate the more objectionable pollution. Inasmuch as the needed works are chiefly treatment plants for municipal sewage and industrial waste, the responsibility for them rests primarily with municipal government and private industry. Much construction work is in progress. Many State agencies have forced remedial action where basic studies have shown it to be practicable.

Unprecedented advances in cleaning up our streams have been made possible by the public works and work-relief programs during the past six years. The report states that more progress has been made in abatement of municipal waste during that period than during the entire twenty-five years preceding, chiefly as a result of Federal financial stimulation. As in many other fields of conservation, great improvement in the Nation's basic assets of water has been incident to the fight against unemployment. If this construction work is to continue at a substantial rate, and if the necessary research, education, and enforcement activities are to be carried out most effectively, the Federal Government must lend financial support and technical stimulation.

It is my opinion that pending further experimentation with interstate and state enforcement activities, Federal participation in pollution-abatement should take the general form of establishing a central technical agency to promote and coordinate education, research, and enforcement. On the basis of recent experience, it should be supplemented by a system of Federal grants-in-aid and loans organized with due regard for the integrated use and control of water resources and for a balanced Federal program for public works of all types. The time is overdue for the Federal Government to take vigorous leadership along these lines.[3]

FRANKLIN D. ROOSEVELT

[W. H. PRESS RELEASES:M]

[1] Read in the Congress on Feb. 16, 1939.
[2] *Water Pollution in the United States. Third Report of the Special Advisory Committee on Water Pollution* (Washington, 1939).
[3] This message was based on a draft submitted by Ickes Feb. 9, 1939 (OF 1092). Roosevelt used it without change except for the dropping of a paragraph that called attention to the effect of polluted water on humans, industry and wildlife, and to the fact that no single type of treatment could be prescribed. With the draft is a note, Roosevelt to Early and Forster, Feb. 13, 1939, reading: "Will you go over and see if the proposed Messages to Congress are O. K. and, if so, I will send them up before I leave?" (On February 16 he left for Key West.)

Following the reading of the message in the Senate, Barkley (Ky.) noted that he had introduced a bill (S. 685) to do what the President proposed. He said that this was the same as the Vinson bill (H. R. 2711) which the President had vetoed in the previous session but with the objectionable feature omitted, and that this bill was now before the Senate Committee on Commerce. The companion bill, H. R. 922, introduced by Spence (Ky.), was before the House Committee on Rivers and Harbors. In the House the message was referred to the Committee of the Whole House (*Cong. Rec.*, 76th Cong., 1st sess., 84:2, 1484, 1495).

869   HENRY A. WALLACE, SECRETARY OF AGRICULTURE, TO ROOSEVELT

WASHINGTON, *February 23, 1939*

DEAR MR. PRESIDENT: With reference to your note to me, dated January 25, about the timber on Admiralty Island, Alaska, in the Tongass National Forest:

There have been no definite projects for the development of pulp and paper manufacturing in southeastern Alaska since the conditional awards, made in 1927, for a large sale in the vicinity of Ketchikan and another on Admiralty Island were both terminated on March 14, 1933, for failure to meet their conditions. Nothing is now in sight involving any timber cutting on Admiralty Island beyond occasional small sales of locally used fish-trap logs and the like.

Less than half of the 1,065,000 acres of Admiralty Island are heavily enough timbered to be considered for the possible growing and harvesting of successive timber crops. These timbered areas are mostly in a belt, broken in places and of varying width, around the island. The present stand has been estimated at 8,500,000,000 board feet, very largely hemlock and spruce. This is about 11 per cent of the timber volume in southeastern Alaska. The area is sufficient to supply, permanently, the wood needed to manufacture about 130,000 tons of newsprint annually.

The establishment of an industry of the size to make that much paper would give southeastern Alaska a needed increase in opportunities for employment amounting to about 1,000 wage earners in woods and mill operations. I have felt that it should be possible to use the present timber resource and timber productive capacity of most of the forest land, and at the same time preserve the wildlife and potential recreational resources of the island. Carefully thought out plans have been made for this integrated use of the land, so as to assure the perpetuation of the large Alaska brown bears. which are the outstanding wildlife on the island, and to provide for the maintenance of the forest recreational resources. A comprehensive management plan covering the bears is in effect to insure against depletion. Under this management the bear population is increasing. The preservation of recreational and wildlife values can be effected without forbidding the use of the major timber resources which, because of their accessibility and nearness to water power sites on the mainland, will be needed if there is to be established a permanent industry in this now sparsely inhabited region.

Under these circumstances, it has not seemed necessary or desirable to withdraw the timber on Admiralty Island permanently from direct economic use. However, the status described in the last sentence of your note could be given by my declaring it a wilderness area and also establishing a wildlife refuge there. If additional safeguard were considered necessary, national forest lands could be included under the bill recently introduced for national park lands which gives the President authority to designate wilderness areas among such lands by proclamation. We are at present contemplating a request to Congress that the bill should be amended to make this possible.

I understand Secretary Ickes may wish to propose National Park status for Admiralty Island, so it is planned to discuss that, along with other proposals for national parks, with the Interior Department under an arrangement agreed upon by Silcox with Secretary Ickes.

Sincerely,

H. A. WALLACE

[*Notation*:A:LEHAND] Sec Int   Please read & return
[13:OF 378:TS]

870   JAMES G. K. MCCLURE, PRESIDENT, AMERICAN FORESTRY ASSOCIATION, TO ROOSEVELT

WASHINGTON, DISTRICT OF COLUMBIA, *March 3, 1939*

DEAR MR. PRESIDENT: The jurisdictional conflicts which are characterizing the development and administration of the National Forests and National Parks have become a matter of deep concern to this Association because of their possible effect in preventing these two systems of federal reservations from rendering their greatest long-range service to the public.

The Association has been an ardent advocate of both systems since their inception. It holds that each has its definite place and purpose and that adjustments of policies and boundaries which changing conditions may suggest should be determined solely by broad public interest.

The present situation involving as it does frequent controversies between administrative agencies is due, we think, largely to the increased use of both systems for outdoor recreation. The result, however, is serving to confuse the primary objectives of the two systems and to jeopardize desirable processes of determining from time to time to the types of resource management that will yield largest public benefits. Furthermore, bureau hostility appears to have reached a point that leaves much to be desired in the way of necessary coordination of policies and administration.

The situation has been the subject of frequent discussion by the Directors of The American Forestry Association. They view it as one which makes urgently desirable a critical study of those federal lands adapted to primary management for parks, forests, forage and wildlife purposes in order to assure that these resources may be administered and developed along lines that will best meet local and national needs. To this end, our Board at its last meeting voted to appeal to you and to Congress for such a study.

It is believed that the situation would be most speedily and amicably met by having the proposed study made by a nongovernmental agency in order that no question of partiality might be raised. Such an agency naturally must be competent and must have public confidence. The Board believes that the National Academy of Sciences meets this requirement and it therefore suggests that it be asked to undertake such a study.

The Board further believes that it would be in the interest of long-range progress to set aside controversial questions involving boundaries and jurisdictions until the study in question is completed and recommendations are available. This belief is predicated on the fact the resources concerned would not thereby be jeopardized and that there is merit in awaiting impartial determination of issues involved.

Our view in respect to this situation is more fully set forth in the attached editorial published in the current issue of the Association's magazine, *American Forests*.[1] May I bespeak for the Board and for the Association your earnest and sympathetic consideration of their desire to suggest a helpful and constructive course of remedial action? [2]

Sincerely yours,

JAMES G. K. MCCLURE

[13:OF 149:TS]

[1] "The Forest-Park Conflict," in *American Forests*, 50 (March, 1939), 119; this urged a study of Government lands to determine what their proper use should be and thereby to end the jurisdictional disputes between the Forest Service and the National Park Service.

[2] Answered *post*, 872.

871   EBERT K. BURLEW, ACTING SECRETARY OF THE INTERIOR, AND
       HENRY A. WALLACE, SECRETARY OF AGRICULTURE, TO
       ROOSEVELT

WASHINGTON, *Mar. 6, 1939*

Through: The Bureau of the Budget, The Attorney General, Division of Federal Register

MY DEAR MR. PRESIDENT: We submit for your consideration a form of proclamation to enlarge the boundaries of Glacier Bay National Monument, Alaska, in accordance with the provisions of the Act of June 8, 1906 (34 *Stat.* 225).[1]

The proposed proclamation would enlarge Glacier Bay National Monument by approximately 904,960 acres, composed of public domain and national forest lands. The proposed extension of the boundaries of the monument is based upon comprehensive studies carried out since the monument was established in 1924, and it is designed to round out the area geologically and biologically, as well as from the standpoint of its administration.

During the period of contracted ice fields which preceded the last glacial advance about a century and a half ago, the forest in this section of Alaska extended from timberline to the water's edge. The tree species were chiefly hemlock and Sitka spruce, the same as the mature forests of today. This forest, which was at least 400 years old, finally

[305]

was overwhelmed and buried by ice and gravel during the last glacial advance and is now being uncovered by the retreat of the glaciers and by the erosive action of streams and waves.

In its retreat the ice is exposing two general types of land surface: (a) rock exposure, and (b) depositional accumulations. In some places gravel deposits have been built up by lateral drainage from the glaciers, forming extensive sheets of gravel in the low country and glacial terraces between the ice and the abutting mountains.

The vegetation of the area recently laid bare by the final retreat of the glaciers may be roughly marked off into three communities: (a) the pioneer community most recently vacated by the ice, characterized by a growth of certain mosses, perennial herbs and willows; (b) willow alder thickets occupying the slopes around the middle portion of the area to be added to the monument, and (c) a conifer forest along the shores of the bays and the ocean, characterized by a growth of hemlock and Sitka spruce. Because of the rapidity of vegetational change, these communities lack sharpness of definition.

The Fairweather Range of mountains included in the proposed extension of the monument contains magnificent scenery and features of outstanding geologic importance. The entire area to be added to the monument presents an exceptional opportunity for the study of glacial action and post-glacial ecology.

The attached folder contains photographs, maps and other data concerning the area being added to Glacier Bay National Monument.

The proposed proclamation is drafted subject to all valid existing rights. Therefore, any private rights within the area will not be affected if the boundaries are extended.

The issuance of the proclamation is respectfully recommended.[2]
Sincerely yours,

E. K. Burlew
H. A. Wallace

[13:of 6–b:ts]

[1] The American Antiquities Act.
[2] Issued April 18, 1939, as Executive Proclamation 2330 (53 *Stat.* 2534).

872   Roosevelt to James G. K. McClure, President, American Forestry Association, Washington

Washington, *March 11, 1939*

My dear Doctor McClure: Your letter of March 3 came duly to hand, and while I recognize the force of much that you say in your letter and in the printed article in the *American Forestry Magazine*,[1] I am not quite ready to take action at this moment. The subject of forestry has long interested me, and I agree with you that there seems to be a good deal of confusion of thought in dealing with the problem. It is already more than thirty years ago since, as a Nation, we became aware of the rapid spoliation of our forest reserves and saw the necessity for reforestation if for no other reason than restoring the lumber industry; but I confess that not much progress has been made in those thirty years, apparently because of a confusion of ideas. Forests are valuable to man in a number of different ways; for example, much of our natural terrain should not be tilled because of the nature of the soil, the heavy rainfall, the steepness of the bank; and yet this same terrain is admirably suited for the growing of trees. In recent years we have recognized this so truly that we have classed as *submarginal*, lands which are unsuited for tilling and the growth of annual crops, with the expectation of converting the submarginal land into forest or grazing areas. Although we have made a start in this direction, the total progress has not been large when compared with the area of the country as a whole.

European experience has clearly pointed out the way that forests operated in order to produce a sustained yield for lumbering or even for wood pulp should be managed, but here again, while this has been explained frequently, no great progress has been actually secured in our country.

On the other hand, we have also a totally different kind of forested areas, such as the forests of rare or exotic trees which it is desirable to preserve in their natural splendor because they may be classed among the wonders of nature. I refer, for example, to the Giant Sequoias in Southern California, to the Sugar Pines in the same general area, to the Redwood Forests of the California Coast, and to the Douglas Fir of the Columbia River region; not overlooking in the east the Swamp Cypress of the Carolinas and some of the rare semitropical trees of the Everglades Park in Florida. In the case of all these varieties, with the possible exception of the Douglas Fir, it is too much to expect that we can cut and renew these forests on a yield basis. Apparently, Congress has decided that the only way of preserving these marvelous trees is by including these stands in the National Parks.

There are still other kinds of forests which are of no great value for lumbering operations, nor even for wood pulp, but which have considerable charm in protecting wildlife, stream valleys, and affording recreation to tired humanity. A number of the States of the Union have appropriately regarded this class of forest reservations as more particularly their function. Forests of this kind rarely measure up to the standard of national parks, but we have, for example in New York State, the Adirondack forests, the Catskill forest reserve, and Bear Mountain Park, all of which are important forested recreational areas. Obviously, too, those States having large cities have every reason to create such reservations, and yet, in the interest of economy of management in those States, it is common to combine the management of forested recreational areas with non-forested playground facilities. This perhaps raises a question whether, if it is desirable in the States to combine under one management forests and other park areas, the same policy should not be followed by the Federal Government. One answer to this is the size of the problem and the fact that there is a wide difference between forests which exist in order to produce a lumber crop on a continuous yield basis and those forests which exist simply in order to preserve intact rare varieties of trees, trees which might become entirely extinct if they were not preserved.

Under all the circumstances, I agree with you that the whole subject requires further study, and I shall, perhaps, make a recommendation to the Congress on the matter. I cannot help thinking that a part of the confusion of ideas has been due to the fact that two separate bureaus of the Government have been competing with each other for public favor in the recreational field.[2]

Sincerely yours,

[FRANKLIN D. ROOSEVELT]

[*Notation*: A] Copy of President's reply to Dr. McClure sent to Mr. F. A. Delano—3/13/39. hm

[13:OF 149:CT]

[1] *American Forests* is meant; see McClure's letter, *ante*, 870.
[2] Drafted by the National Resources Committee.

873   ROOSEVELT TO NELSON C. BROWN, New York State College of Forestry, Syracuse University, Syracuse, New York

[WASHINGTON] *March 17, 1939*

DEAR NELSON: Thank you for yours of March thirteenth.[1] I am glad the planting will soon begin at Hyde Park, and I hope to be up there fairly early in April for a day or two.

That is an excellent preface. I have duly signed it and return it herewith. I am most anxious to see the little booklet.[2]

Always sincerely,

[FRANKLIN D. ROOSEVELT]

[13:PSF:HYDE PARK:CT]

[1] Brown said that the State College of Forestry was planning to plant 20,000 Norway spruce and 2,000 each of red pine, European larch and white pine (PSF: Hyde Park).
[2] A Forest Service pamphlet, *Community Forests* (Washington, 1939), prepared by Brown as a collaborator of the State Forestry Division of the Forest Service. The copy of the preface printed below as an enclosure was typed in the White House; apparently no changes were made in Brown's draft.

Community forests are an old and popularly accepted part of forest conservation.   They have helped for many years to reduce local taxes by yielding profitable timber crops.   They have also provided other benefits, such as watershed protection, outdoor recreation, shelter for bird and beast, and permanent jobs through the sustained production of cordwood, posts, telephone poles, railroad ties, Christmas trees, pulpwood, and logs for lumber.

I believe more of our communities could profit economically, socially, and spiritually by ownership and operation of their own forests close at home.   I am in favor of more and better community forests.   Development of such local forests would be an important step in the rebuilding of our natural resources and would provide additional outdoor playgrounds for the children of America.

I am very glad to endorse the Forest Service program to establish and maintain more community forests.

(Signed)   FRANKLIN D. ROOSEVELT

[*Notation*:A] Orig. returned to Professor Brown 3/17/39   hm
[13:PSF:HYDE PARK:T:COPY]

875   ROOSEVELT TO GOVERNOR CLARENCE D. MARTIN, Olympia, Washington

[WASHINGTON] *March 18, 1939*

MY DEAR GOVERNOR MARTIN: I have personally considered the subject matter of your letter of March first dealing with the effect on labor and industry of exporting high-grade Douglas fir peeler logs.[1]

I am very much in sympathy with the idea that exports of high-grade raw forest material of which our domestic supply is limited should not be encouraged.   The continued existence of wood-using industries on the Pacific Coast, particularly of the plywood industry, depends upon an adequate supply of high quality raw material in the form of standing timber—a supply which is all too limited.

It is hardly necessary for me to assure you that I am in favor of sound proposals that redound to the benefit of American labor and industry.   I am particularly impressed with the fact that organized labor is actively supporting the measures which have been proposed to protect its source or raw material upon which the payrolls of industry are built.[2]

Very sincerely yours,

[FRANKLIN D. ROOSEVELT]

[13:OF 446:CT]

¹ Martin urged support of legislation pending in Congress to prohibit the exportation of high-grade Douglas fir logs (OF 446).
² Drafted by the Agriculture Department.

876   ROOSEVELT TO SENATOR KEY PITTMAN OF NEVADA

[WASHINGTON] *March 21, 1939*

DEAR KEY: In regard to the Forestry Bureau, I have no hesitation in telling you that I have no thought of transferring them to the Interior Department.

I am meeting with a good deal of success in getting the public lands and forestry people to work together in such a way as to prevent duplication of work and render better service to the cattlemen. I think that working along this line for some time to come will produce results without any drastic change in organization.

Always sincerely yours,

[FRANKLIN D. ROOSEVELT]

P. S. This, of course, should not be used in any way until the Reorganization Bill is finally disposed of in both Houses and has been acted on by me! ¹

[13 : PSF : SENATE : CT]

¹ Pittman replied March 26, 1939 (PSF: Senate), that he was pleased to know that the Forest Service was not to be transferred. See *post,* 968 n.

877   ROOSEVELT TO MAYOR ANGELO J. ROSSI OF SAN FRANCISCO

WASHINGTON, *March 24, 1939*

MY DEAR MAYOR ROSSI: I appreciate your telegram of March 13, expressing your support of the proposed John Muir-Kings Canyon National Park.

It is my belief that this area merits national park status and I am happy to know that the project has your endorsement.¹

Very sincerely yours,

[FRANKLIN D. ROOSEVELT]

[*Notation*:A] Copy of reply sent to Mr. Ben Thompson, Nat. Park Service, Dept. of the Interior 3/25/39.   hm

[13:OF 6–P:CT]

¹ Rossi's telegram is with the letter here printed.

[Washington] *March 25, 1939*

Private

Dear Key: In regard to grazing in forests and public lands: It is my thought that the following can be attained by study and cooperation:

(a) Eliminate the undoubted overgrazing which exists in some places (by no means all) both in forests and on public lands.

(b) Where in a given area there is grazing in both forests and on public lands, especially some grazing in forests and winter grazing on public lands, the offices of the two services, if located in different places, should be put in the same place and under the same roof.

(c) Where Rangers from both services cover essentially the same territory, the range work should be consolidated, in some places the Forest Ranger acting for both Bureaus and in other cases the Public Lands Ranger working for both Bureaus.

(d) A greater uniformity in all paper work, purchases of supplies, maintenance of camps, etc., etc.

None of the above suggests in any way a change in functions.

I am sure you and I will be pleased by greater economy and efficiency, and, at the same time, that the cattlemen will also be pleased.

Always sincerely,

[Franklin D. Roosevelt]

[13:PSF:SENATE:CT]

879   Frederic A. Delano, Chairman, Advisory Committee to the National Resources Committee, to Roosevelt

Washington, *March 29, 1939*

Attention of: Mr. Rudolph Forster

Memorandum for the President: In our recent reviews of the reports of the Chief of Engineers on the Beaver-Mahoning project and the Clark Hill project[1] we have attempted to confine our comments to broad problems of national policy involved in those reports and to questions relating to water and land-use problems for which agencies other than the Corps of Engineers have a special responsibility. We have not attempted to evaluate the detailed engineering features of the project recommendations. Even so we have found that a period of approximately three weeks is required to consummate the necessary review. I believe that the reviews which have already been made demonstrate the desirability of taking this amount of time for consideration.

Realizing, however, that there is severe pressure to obtain early release of these and similar reports, I would appreciate having your advice on whether or not you wish to have us continue to follow the procedure described above.[2]

FREDERIC A. DELANO

[13:OF 1092:TS]

[1] The former proposal (never consummated) would have utilized the Beaver and Mahoning rivers to build a canal linking Lake Erie with the Ohio River, thus giving the Youngstown, Ohio, steel district water access to its iron ore and coal sources. The Clark Hill power dam was built on the Savannah River near Augusta, Georgia.
[2] An attached note, Roosevelt to Forster, April 4, 1939, reads, "Will you tell my Uncle that this procedure is O. K.?"

880   ROOSEVELT TO ERNEST F. COE, DIRECTOR, EVERGLADES NATIONAL PARK ASSOCIATION, Miami

WARM SPRINGS, GEORGIA, *April 1, 1939*

MY DEAR MR. COE: I appreciate your letter of February 17 and the enclosures concerning the proposed Everglades National Park.[1]

I consider the Everglades one of the foremost national park projects today. It is my hope that the State of Florida will take the necessary steps to make the State-owned lands within the proposed park area available for the project at an early date. I consider this action necessary to insure the further success of the project.[2]

Very sincerely yours,

[FRANKLIN D. ROOSEVELT]

[13:OF 6–P:CT]

[1] Enclosing press releases and reprints of articles about the proposed park and commenting on Roosevelt's continuing interest in it (OF 6–P).
[2] Drafted by the Interior Department.

881   ROOSEVELT TO LITHGOW OSBORNE, NEW YORK STATE CONSERVATION COMMISSIONER, Albany

WARM SPRINGS, GEORGIA, *April 3, 1939*

MY DEAR MR. OSBORNE: There can be no question but that completion of the forest survey, to which your letter of February twenty-eighth refers,[1] is essential if forest lands and their resources are to be managed so they may increase the basic wealth of the nation and help achieve sustained prosperity.

I recognize that this inventory, the first we have ever undertaken on a national scale, is no light task; that, once completed, it should be kept up to date. And I assure you that, when it comes before me, I shall give it sincere and sympathetic consideration.[2]

Very sincerely yours,

[FRANKLIN D. ROOSEVELT]

[13:OF 1–C:CT]

[1] Osborne urged support of S. 224, a bill to continue the national survey of forest resources authorized by the act of May 22, 1928 (OF 1-C). S. 224, introduced by Senator McNary (Ore.) on Jan. 4, 1939, was not acted upon (*Cong. Rec.,* 76th Cong., 1st sess., 84: 1, 68).

[2] Drafted by the Agriculture Department.

882   ROOSEVELT TO ROBERT FECHNER, DIRECTOR, CIVILIAN CONSERVATION CORPS

WARM SPRINGS, GA., *April 4, 1939*

MEMORANDUM FOR HON. ROBERT FECHNER: Thank you for your memorandum about Haiti.[1] Will you be good enough to have a talk with Secretary Wallace and Undersecretary Welles on the possibility of somehow helping the Haitian government to establish ten CCC camps under American direction?

These camps are needed for

(a) The improvement of roads and trails.
(b) The elimination of soil erosion.
(c) The encouragement of irrigation.
(d) Experiments in diversification of agriculture.

In view of the world overproduction of sugar, it would be a mistake to increase Haitian sugar, but it may be possible to grow other crops which could find an outside market.

I am sending copies of this memorandum to Secretary Wallace and Undersecretary Welles.

F. D. R.

[13:OF 162:CT]

[1] March 31, 1939 (OF 162), proposing a soil and forest conservation program for Haiti.

883   FREDERIC A. DELANO, CHAIRMAN, ADVISORY COMMITTEE TO THE NATIONAL RESOURCES COMMITTEE, TO ROOSEVELT

WASHINGTON, *April 11, 1939*

MY DEAR MR. PRESIDENT: I enclose herewith some papers which originated with a memorandum from Mr. Charles W. Eliot, Executive Officer of the National Resources Committee, to me and other members of the Advisory Committee,[1] which memorandum I passed on to Secretary Ickes for his consideration and which he now returns to me with the suggestion that I take it up with you.[2] I hesitate to do so, realizing that you are heavily pressed with various weighty matters; but in view of the attitude of my chief, I submit these papers to you for your kind consideration and for such action as you may wish to take or recommend.

Respectfully submitted,

FREDERIC A. DELANO

[13:OF 1092:TS]

¹ Printed below.

² Ickes urged Delano to see the President as soon as he could: "Only he can solve the riddle for you. Just what, if anything, he plans to do under the Reorganization Bill, I do not know. My own general impression is that you ought to press for definite legislation" (memorandum, April 11, 1939, OF 1092).

884 [*Enclosure*] CHARLES W. ELIOT, EXECUTIVE OFFICER, NATIONAL RESOURCES COMMITTEE, TO THE ADVISORY COMMITTEE

WASHINGTON, *April 5, 1939*

MEMORANDUM FOR THE ADVISORY COMMITTEE, MR. DELANO, DR. MERRIAM, MR. DENNISON,¹ MR. RUML: OUTLOOK ON STATUS AFTER JUNE 30, 1939: As you know, we have had three or four "strings to our bow" in meeting the problem of continuance of the Committee's activities after June 30. All of the strings are now taut. As I saw the plan of campaign, we had three or four lines of defense or attack as follows:

1. A bill to establish a permanent agency. As you know, Senator Hayden's amendment to the Byrnes Public Works Department bill has been reported to the Byrnes Committee by Chairman Ickes.² No action as yet has been taken. Rumors persist that Senator Byrnes intends to insist on action concerning his Public Works proposal before the Relief Appropriation for the next fiscal year is submitted to Congress. In the last few days there has been some doubt as to whether or not the Hayden Amendment will be attached to the Byrnes Bill or reported out as a separate measure. I have been unable to get any definite information on this score. In general, the situation in the Senate looks very favorable to action in favor of the Hayden Amendment or a modification of it. Since Senator Wagner's statement advocating the re-establishment of the Stabilization Board, there have been indications that Senator Hayden would be agreeable to including in his amendment provisions to meet Senator Wagner's point. It therefore looks as if we would have the combined support of Senators Hayden, Byrnes and Wagner in the Senate.

In the House, no bill has yet been submitted, and Senator Hayden has indicated that he wanted no action taken in the Senate until he could get some assurance from the House "managers" as to how the bill would be handled in the House. He has told one friend that he would make no move until he got assurance from the White House that the President would take some action with the House leaders to line up support. We know of no definite opposition to the bill in the House except the agitation among the so-called "River and Harbor bloc." That opposition was bolstered by the River and Harbor Congress which met here week before last.[3] In this connection, the action of the Resources Committee on the Beaver-Mahoning Project and further requests from the Chief of Engineers for quick reports on controversial projects has certainly not helped our standing with the River and Harbor people. We are being "put on the spot" by the Chief of Engineers through reference over here of all the most difficult projects. I have hoped that by emphasizing Senator Wagner's interest in employment stabilization and by talk concerning the Land Committee, Public Works Committee, etc., we could find some support in the House which would emphasize aspects of our work other than Water.

2. Presidential Order under the Reorganization Bill. While the recent Act would permit the President to issue an order combining various planning agencies in the Executive Office, there are grave doubts as to the wisdom of his doing so. In the first place, any such action would immediately kill the chances for a separate bill such as the Hayden Amendment and would put our fight not on the basis of constructive action with the support of influential members of the Senate, but instead it would be a defensive campaign to maintain the President's authority and prestige. After so much talk in both Houses about the economies to be achieved by the reorganization, I fear that any order establishing a new planning agency would be easily misinterpreted to the public by our opponents. In any event, an executive order would have to lie on the table of both Houses for 60 days, and we would not know where we stood for two full months. We would lose all that time and be awfully close to the deadline before we could get any appropriation started or make any moves in any other direction. For these reasons, I have personally concluded that it is better not to do anything about it under the Reorganization Bill.

3. Continuation under the Relief Appropriation in the same manner as last year. The Bureau of the Budget is already at work in preparation of the next Relief Bill for the fiscal year beginning July 1. The Bureau called up here day before yesterday to ask whether we stood by the original estimates submitted last fall. In view of Congressman Woodrum's declaration on the House floor last year, we will have a much more difficult fight on our hands to get continuation by this method this year. It is by no means impossible, but it is definitely going to be a tough fight.

[315]

4. Executive Order. I have always assumed that our Executive Order, based on the NIRA of 1933, continued in effect after June 30 anyway. I had hoped that under that, P. W. A. could give us allocations for administrative expenses in the same manner as the previous allotments for the Pecos Study and the Pacific Northwest.

In the last few days we have learned that a ruling by the Comptroller General cast some doubts on this possibility. The warrant for the allotment of the Pecos money was returned by the Comptroller General to the Treasury with a ruling to the effect that the Resources Committee automatically goes out of existence on June 30, and the money allotted from P. W. A. was good only until that date. The Treasury Department in a letter of March 17 agreed with the Comptroller General and changed the warrant without consulting either P. W. A. or the Resources Committee. They went further and agreed to change the previously approved warrant for the Pacific Northwest money to limit that also to June 30, 1939. I have protested to the Treasury against this action without consulting us, and, at Mr. Delano's suggestion, put the matter in the hands of the General Counsel for P. W. A., Mr. Farbach. I have asked Mr. Farbach for two things:

(1) An analysis of our situation concerning continuance under Executive Order and an interpretation of the action of Congress in the Relief Bill last year which "extended" the Committee to June 30, 1939.

Whatever we get on that score will be used presumably as an answer to the Comptroller General.

(2) I have asked Mr. Farbach for a proposal or alternative to the first which would set up the money for the Pecos and Pacific Northwest Study to June 30 "and thereafter for such other agency as the President may designate."

If we cannot get some such adjustment in the warrant, it seems to me we are definitely not justified in entering into agreements with the States of Texas, New Mexico and various Federal agencies for the Pecos Investigation. It cannot possibly be done short of at least two field seasons, and we would be starting something which we cannot finish unless we can get some such adjustment as I have suggested.

This action of the Comptroller General presumably does not affect the possibility of a new Executive Order establishing a new agency after June 30. That possibility is still to be explored.

In summary, the lines are taut, and we are engaged on all fronts, and as days slip by, I feel the responsibility for our hundred-odd full-time employees weighing more and more heavily on my mind.

Have you some suggestions? [4]

CHARLES W. ELIOT

[13:OF 1092:TS]

[1] Henry S. Dennison, president of the Dennison Manufacturing Co., Framingham, Massachusetts, was appointed to the Advisory Committee in 1935.

[2] Hayden's amendment was presumably his National Resources Board Bill (*ante,* 843). Byrnes introduced his bill on February 9 but it was not reported from committee (*Cong. Rec.,* 76th Cong., 1st sess., 84:2, 1275).

[3] The National Rivers and Harbors Congress met in Washington on March 23–24, 1939.

[4] See *post,* 889.

885   ANTHONY J. DIMOND, DELEGATE FROM ALASKA, TO
       ROOSEVELT

WASHINGTON, D. C., *April 11, 1939*

DEAR MR. PRESIDENT: Reports are continuously being circulated in Alaska to the effect that an attempt is being made to have Admiralty Island, situated in Southeastern Alaska, placed in a national park or a national monument in order to protect and preserve the bears which live on the Island.

While I wholeheartedly believe in conservation, the view that Admiralty Island ought to be placed in some such kind of reservation in order to protect the brown bears is conservation gone mad. Admiralty Island is now included in the Forest Reserve. The bears on the island are amply protected by the Alaska Game Law and the regulations thereunder which are enforced and obeyed. In fact, if anything, the bear population of the Island is now becoming too numerous. As you are aware, the game laws of Alaska are made by Congress, and the Alaska Game Commission, which enforces the laws, is an agency of the Bureau of Biological Survey in the Department of Agriculture. There is not even the remotest suggestion of the need of any change in existing conditions for the protection of the bears on Admiralty Island or elsewhere in Alaska.

Under present law Admiralty Island is open to prospecting and mining which does not interfere with the bears to the slightest extent. Anyone who knows anything about conditions with respect to Admiralty Island and will confine himself to the facts is bound to say the same thing, and that is that there is no more occasion to withdraw Admiralty Island into a national monument or national park than there is to build a trap to catch the aurora borealis. I earnestly hope that you will put a stop to all such foolishness.[1]

Sincerely yours,

A. J. DIMOND

[13:OF 378:TS]

[1] Answered *post,* 894.

WASHINGTON, *Apr. 14, 1939*

MEMORANDUM FOR THE PRESIDENT . . . PROPOSED QUETICO-SUPERIOR PARK OR WILDERNESS AREA: The Quetico-Superior Committee was created by Executive Order No. 6783 of June 30, 1934, and by Executive Order No. 7921, dated June 30, 1938, the life of the Committee was extended to June 30, 1942. Members of the Committee serve without compensation. The first Executive Order named three persons to serve on the Committee, and required the Secretaries of Interior and Agriculture each to designate one person to serve on the Committee.

The Quetico-Superior project, initiated in 1927, seeks the establishment of a wilderness sanctuary in the Rainy Lake and Pigeon River watersheds through which runs the international boundary line between Canada and the United States. A strong impetus toward the preservation of this area, situated about 500 miles northwest of Chicago and comprising roughly 15,000 square miles, or 9,600,000 acres of wilderness of great natural attraction was given when the Shipstead-Nolan Act of July 10, 1930 (46 *Stat.* 1020) withdrew from entry all public lands in a described area, and declared it to be the intention of Congress, with respect to the entire Quetico-Superior area in Minnesota, to protect the natural water levels, and wooded shores, islands and waterfalls. In 1933 a similar and even more comprehensive act was passed by the Minnesota legislature.

Approximately two-thirds of the Quetico-Superior area is within the Province of Ontario, Canada, and is owned almost in its entirety by the Provincial Government. Included within this area is the Quetico-Superior Provincial Park, of about 1,000,000 acres, adjoined on the international boundary by the Superior National Forest.

In its report made in February, 1938, the Committee reported that, "Its activities have served to reduce the main steps still to be taken to . . . Federal acquisition of the remainder of the area, and negotiation of a treaty with Canada."

Following your recent discussion of this matter with me, two members of the Committee have discussed with me a proposed draft of a bill, "To authorize an appropriation to carry out the purposes of the Act of July 10, 1930 (46 *Stat.* 1020) . . ." a copy of which is attached. This bill would authorize appropriations aggregating $2,500,000 as follows:

(1) $2,250,000 for the acquisition of lands within the Superior National Forest Purchase Unit.

(2) $200,000 for acquisition of lands to be added to the Grand Portage Indian Reservation.

(3) $50,000 (not more than $15,000 in any fiscal year) for the expenses of the Committee.

The items are discussed in the following paragraphs:

(1) Superior National Forest Purchase Unit: The private land to be purchased lies entirely within either the Superior National Forest as now proclaimed, or the Superior National Forest Purchase Unit already approved by the National Forest Reservation Commission. Within both of these areas the purchase of land is now in progress under the Authority contained in the Weeks Act of March 1, 1911, as amended. There are now 85 separate National Forest Purchase Units, located in 31 States and Puerto Rico. Their gross area approximates 52,000,000 acres, of which only 17,000,000 acres have been purchased to date. From 1911 to 1933 the Federal Government expended $25,200,000 in forwarding this program, acquiring some 8,000,000 acres. During the present administration the program has been given tremendous impetus, $46,000,000 having been made available during the period 1933 to 1937, and the acquired acreage more than doubled. The regular annual appropriation for this work for each of the fiscal years 1938 and 1939 was $3,000,000 and the 1940 Budget contemplates an appropriation of $2,000,000.

The widespread scope of the national forest program, the low financial returns to private ownership from lands of the character included in the purchase areas, the unsatisfactory social and economic situations, and the increasing urge for publicly-owned forest areas for purposes of recreation, as well as timber production, result in continual pressure for special appropriations to hasten Federal acquisition in many of these purchase areas. The endorsement of Section 1 of the proposed bill would be contrary to your established policy of disapproving specific legislative commitments for land purchase projects which would give a preferred status to such projects thereby interfering with the necessary flexibility now possible in purchasing lands for addition to our national forests. Furthermore, it is believed that the $2,250,000 would by no means complete the National Forest purchases in the Quetico-Superior area. It is admitted, however, that progress toward complete ownership in this area will be slow with national forest acquisition appropriations at their current level.

(2) Addition to Grand Portage Indian Reservation: The Chippewa Indians in Minnesota have organized under the Indian Reorganization Act of June 18, 1934 (48 *Stat.* 984). Section 5 of that act authorizes appropriations of not to exceed $2,000,000 annually for the purchase of lands for additions to Indian Reservations. While Budget estimates have not been submitted in any year for the full amount authorized, Congress generally has not approved the full amount of the Budget estimate. There have been several specific enactments in recent years authorizing land purchases for Indian benefit, but those enactments have involved tribes which failed to accept the Indian Reorganization Act. The ap-

proval of Section 2 could be cited as a precedent for other special cases. Specific legislative commitments for land acquisition for organized tribes would be as objectionable as such commitments for national forest land acquisition.

(3) Expenses of Quetico-Superior Committee: The Secretary of the Interior submitted an estimate in the amount of $15,000 to meet the expenses of the Quetico-Superior Committee for the fiscal year 1940. Two members of the Committee are Federal employees and their traveling and other expenses incidental to the work of the Committee are properly chargeable to annual appropriations available to their respective departments. The other three members of the Committee serve without compensation and I understand their expenses so far have been borne from personal or contributed funds. The $15,000 estimate contemplated a paid secretary for the Committee, clerical assistance, travel and other expenses. In the absence of specific legislative authority for such an appropriation, an estimate was not recommended for inclusion in the 1940 Budget.

(4) Interest of State Department: I have been informed that the State Department has been in correspondence with officials of the Canadian Government regarding the project. If the two Governments are agreeable to the project, and a treaty is desirable it is not believed that incomplete Federal ownership on our side of the border would operate as a bar to the negotiation of such a treaty. Its terms undoubtedly could be applied to all lands now Federally owned, and provision made for extending its coverage as additional lands are acquired.

The members of the Committee who called upon me sought information as to whether the proposed legislation, or any part thereof, would be in accord with your program. It seems to me that while the project appears to be a desirable one, there is no emergency to justify the approval of any part of the proposed legislation. The section authorizing the appropriation of funds for expenses of the Committee may be desirable. It has functioned for nearly five years, however, without direct appropriations for this purpose, and I doubt the advisability of providing funds now for a salaried secretary or other permanent employees.

In the circumstances I recommend that the proposed legislation be considered as not in accord with your program. May this office be informed by [sic] your wishes so that the members of the Committee who called upon me may be advised.

D. W. Bell

[Notation: AS] Harold Smith [1] I agree. FDR.
[13: OF 79: TS]

[1] Smith was sworn in as Director of the Budget on April 15, 1939.

WASHINGTON, D. C., *April 14, 1939*

DEAR MR. PRESIDENT: I was greatly interested in your brief statement at our conference on last Tuesday about the place of the Civilian Conservation Corps in any plans that you may decide on for a reorganization of Federal departments and agencies. I have been in full agreement with your views that a reorganization was undoubtedly greatly needed.

I have watched efforts that were made by individuals and groups while the reorganization bill was before Congress to have some particular agency removed from the possibility of its status being changed by the President in any reorganization plan that you might decide to be desirable. I have been entirely willing to leave the disposition of the Civilian Conservation Corps to your own judgment.

My own experience and the judgment of all of those who have been actively associated with me in setting up and carrying forward the work of the Corps is that unless its set-up is completely revamped, it could not be successfully operated except as an independent agency. Four Federal departments and one independent agency have had vitally important parts in the work of the Corps. After May first three departments and one agency will still carry on the work. If the Corps is put under the jurisdiction of one department or combined with other agencies to create a new agency, I do not believe the present set-up could function. I have discussed this situation at considerable length with all of those who have been closely associated with me in this work for the past six years. Their views were not official but expressed to me simply as individuals who knew the working of the Corps as thoroughly as I do. They join with me in expressing the hope that the Civilian Conservation Corps as now constituted will be continued and as an independent agency responsible directly to the President.

If, however, you decide that this cannot be done we are of the unanimous opinion that the Civilian Conservation Corps should be placed in a so-called "work group" rather than "a welfare group." Although welfare has been an important feature of the beneficial effects of the Corps we have constantly striven to realize the hope that you expressed in your first message to Congress in March 1933 when you asked for authority to set up this organization and stated that the Corps would engage in useful constructive work not competitive with existing industry but to develop and carry forward a comprehensive program of conservation. All of us have felt that this was one of the finest objectives toward which our efforts could be directed and we have constantly tried to instill that spirit into the enrollees as well as other Corps personnel.

I believe that the general popularity of the Corps is due in large measure to the belief of the general public that it has not been conducted as a welfare organization but has engaged in useful worthwhile work that was adding substantially to the wealth of the Nation. If the Corps is put into a group organization it will be necessary in our judgment to completely revise its set-up and method of operation. The Corps could be constituted as a self-contained work agency making its facilities available to other Federal departments or independent agencies whose activities had to do with some feature of a general conservation program. If this were done, it would be necessary in my opinion to wholly cut loose from the War Department, the Interior Department and the Agricultural Department. Any of these departments or other Federal agencies in cooperation with the states and their political subdivisions having conservation projects to be accomplished could apply to the Civilian Conservation Corps for its personnel and equipment to carry out work projects in line with the legislation under which the Corps is operating. If the proposed project were approved, the Corps would go in largely as would a contractor and perform the necessary work in strict accordance with the plans made by the department or agency.

Considerable expense would probably be involved in initially reorganizing the Corps but ultimately the cost of the Corps might be substantially reduced. If these drastic changes are made in the set-up of the Corps, it might be a proper time to revise the cash compensation now paid to the enrollees. At the present time each enrollee receives thirty dollars cash allowance per month of which not less than twenty-two dollars must be allotted to the enrollee's dependent family or deposited by the enrollee with the office of the Chief of Finance if he has no dependents. This might be changed to a cash allowance of ten, twelve or fifteen dollars per month, a substantial portion of which would have to be deposited to be paid to the enrollee on the completion of his period of enrollment. This would give the enrollee a definite sum of money when he returned to civil life.

I hope I may have the opportunity to discuss this matter with you before final decision is made and I have no doubt others closely associated with me in this work for the past several years would also appreciate an opportunity to be heard.[1]

Sincerely yours,

ROBT. FECHNER

[13:OF 268:TS]

[1] Reorganization Plan No. 1, effective July 1, 1939 (53 *Stat.* 1423), transferred the Civilian Conservation Corps to the Federal Security Administration.

888 Press Conference, State Dining Room of the White House, April 20, 1939, 9:10 P. M.

[*Excerpt*] The President: On conservation, somebody has asked about Federal water pollution legislation. I cannot answer it because there are two or three or four bills up there on the Hill. As far as I know, I have not read any of them and I do not know what is coming out. I am in favor of eliminating water pollution and that's all, I guess.[1]

[13:PRESIDENT'S PRESS CONFERENCES:T]

[1] This was Roosevelt's reply to one of a series of questions put to him at a special press conference arranged for 200 members of the American Society of Newspaper Editors.

889 Roosevelt to Frederic A. Delano, Chairman, Advisory Committee to the National Resources Committee

[Washington] *April 21, 1939*

My dear Mr. Delano: I have had very much in mind the problem presented in your letter of April 11, which accompanied the memorandum from Mr. Charles W. Eliot, the Executive Officer of the National Resources Committee, and also a memorandum initialed by Mr. Ickes.

I have had two conferences with Mr. Charles E. Merriam on this subject and hope to have another with him, and also with you, in the near future.[1]

Very sincerely yours,

[Franklin D. Roosevelt]

[*Notation*:AS] HDS [2]

[13:OF 1092:CT]

[1] This "subject" was the future of the National Resources Committee (see *ante*, 883). A bill, S. 19, to establish a permanent planning agency had been introduced by Senator Hayden (Ariz.) on Jan. 4, 1939, but was not reported from committee. Efforts to provide for one in the Reorganization Bill (H. R. 4425) were unsuccessful, but the 1939 Emergency Relief Appropriation Bill (H. J. Res. 326) appropriated $750,000 for the National Resources Committee for the ensuing fiscal year (to July 1, 1940). In the House an amendment by Representative Taber (N. Y.) to strike out the appropriation was defeated by a small margin; following this, Representative Ditter (Pa.) attacked the National Resources Committee as socialistic and as a New Deal propaganda agency. In the Senate, an amendment (proposed by Hayden) was adopted that changed the name of the National Resources Committee to the National Resources Planning Board, to be composed of the Federal Works Administrator and all of the department heads except State, Navy and Justice, with three other members to be appointed by the President (*Cong. Rec.,* 76th Cong., 1st sess., 84:1, 64; 84:7, 7162, 7341, 7349–7351, 7971–7972). The Hayden amendments are discussed in a letter of Delano to Roosevelt, June 17, 1939, enclosing a committee print (OF 1092);

the provision for a planning board made up in part of cabinet members was removed at the President's insistence when the bill went to conference (Watson to Roosevelt, June 29, and the latter's reply, June 30, 1939, OF 1092).

The Emergency Relief Appropriation Bill was approved June 30, 1939 (53 *Stat.* 927). By Reorganization Plan I, effective July 1, 1939, the newly established National Resources Planning Board was given the functions of the National Resources Committee and the Federal Employment Stabilization Board of the Commerce Department. This board, established in 1931, advised the President on employment cycles and cooperated with the public works agencies in laying out future work projects.

[2] Harold D. Smith, Director, Bureau of the Budget.

890   THE NATIONAL RESOURCES COMMITTEE TO ROOSEVELT

WASHINGTON, *Apr. 22, 1939*

MY DEAR MR. PRESIDENT: In February, 1938, Congressman John Luecke of Michigan urged you to appoint a committee to study the economic and social conditions of the cut-over area in northern Michigan with a view to making recommendations for its rehabilitation. At your request, the National Resources Committee proceeded with the organization of a regional committee comprising representatives of three States (Michigan, Wisconsin and Minnesota) and of the Federal agencies chiefly concerned, thus extending the scope of the inquiry to include the two other States in which similar problems exist. For several years the Federal Government and the States have contributed large sums for relief and security payments, ~~without any substantial improvement in basic conditions in the area.~~ For the wise *best* [1] use of such funds in the future a general program of rehabilitation was desired. Mr. Alfred Bettman, Regional Chairman for the National Resources Committee, was instrumental in perfecting the organization, and Mr. M. W. Torkelson of the Wisconsin State Planning Board, as Chairman of the Northern Lakes States Committee, has guided the preparation of a report on these problems.

We have the honor to transmit herewith the findings and recommendations of that committee. Credit is due to the leaders and to the educational institutions in the three States for the progress which they had made previously in analyzing and correcting their own problems. By promoting land classification studies, county zoning ordinances, State laws encouraging sustained forest yield management and similar measures, the local and State groups have gone far in the direction of a sound program for the rehabilitation of the region. The report reviews the progress to date, presents the major unsolved problems, and outlines a plan for constructive action by local, State and Federal agencies.

We agree in principle with the recommendations of the Committee as to the program necessary to restore the region, and urge their prompt consideration by the Congress and the State governments.

Sincerely yours,

HAROLD L. ICKES, Secretary of the Interior, Chairman
HARRY H. WOODRING, Secretary of War
H. A. WALLACE, Secretary of Agriculture
HARRY L. HOPKINS, Secretary of Commerce
FRANCES PERKINS, Secretary of Labor
F. C. HARRINGTON, Works Progress Administrator
FREDERIC A. DELANO
CHARLES E. MERRIAM
BEARDSLEY RUML
HENRY S. DENNISON

[13:OF 1092:TS]

[1] The reason for this last-minute change in language may be surmised but the circumstances of the revision are not explained. Presumably the letter was not retyped because it had already been signed and bound with the printed report it covered: *Regional Planning, Part VIII, Northern Lake States, May 1939, Report of the Northern Lakes States Regional Committee to the National Resources Committee* (Washington, 1939). With the changes indicated, the text of the letter as here printed is the same as that printed in the report (p. iii).

891   HAROLD L. ICKES, SECRETARY OF THE INTERIOR, TO ROOSEVELT

WASHINGTON, *Apr. 28, 1939*

MEMORANDUM FOR THE PRESIDENT: It has come to my attention that Commissioner Seavey of the Federal Power Commission has referred to the Bureau of the Budget a proposed letter to Congressman Elliott in which he stated the attitude of the Federal Power Commission on the bill to create the John Muir-Kings Canyon National Park in California.[1] It is reported that this communication urges that the legislation creating this park, now before the Public Lands Committee of the House of Representatives, be deferred until the Commission can make a detailed survey of the potential power possibilities for comparison with the value of the area as a national park.

Strong and aggressive opposition has existed to this proposal. This opposition has been successful in delaying the creation of this park for 50 years.[2] Previously, this opposition centered around the need of proper development of the Kings River for the irrigation of a million acres of highly developed land and the generation of power to be used primarily for pumping irrigation water. Studies by the Bureau of Reclamation and the Park Service have resulted in the coordination of the park plans with those of proponents of water conservation and power development, thus removing the only valid objection. The opposition has continued, however, with strong indications that local selfish interests have lost sight of the greatest public benefit.

A letter from the Federal Power Commission containing the recommendations which I understand are included in this draft of a letter would give much aid and support to the opposition and, I feel sure, would result in a further delay of this park proposal.

The area is now within a national forest and Secretary Wallace and Mr. Silcox have both publicly favored the creation of the park. I am confident that creation of this park would meet with your favor. For this reason, I believe the proposed letter should not be sent, and there is attached a brief statement to this effect for your signature to Mr. Seavey.[3] I strongly urge that this or a similar letter be sent to the Federal Power Commission.

HAROLD L. ICKES

[13:OF 6–P:TS]

[1] H. R. 3794, introduced by Representative Gearhart (Calif.), on Feb. 7, 1939 (*Cong. Rec.*, 76th Cong., 1st sess., 84:2, 1222).
[2] The first bill providing for the creation of a national park in this area was introduced in 1881 by Senator John F. Miller of California (*ibid.*, 84:9, 9439).
[3] Sent as the letter printed below.

892   ROOSEVELT TO CLYDE L. SEAVEY, ACTING CHAIRMAN, FEDERAL POWER COMMISSION

HYDE PARK, NEW YORK, *April 29, 1939*

DEAR MR. SEAVEY: I have seen the draft of the letter to Congressman Elliott of California which you prepared and referred to the Bureau of the Budget.[1] In this you recommend that action by the Congress on the bill proposing to establish the John Muir-Kings Canyon National Park in California be deferred until the Federal Power Commission more accurately can evaluate the potential power possibilities in comparison with the scenic and recreational values.

The creation of the John Muir-Kings Canyon National Park would protect a unique area in the High Sierra which is magnificently scenic. It has been shown that this area has no large economic value and that the potential water powers are of doubtful feasibility. Undoubtedly the many beautiful little lakes do afford opportunities for power production, but the inaccessibility of the lakes and the cost of constructing tunnels and power plants in so wild a region would make this area less attractive for power development than many others in California.

For these and other reasons, the creation of the Kings Canyon Park is favored by those best informed about this area. Two members of the cabinet, the Secretary of the Interior and the Secretary of Agriculture, have consistently urged the passage of this legislation, which has been the subject of consideration for nearly half a century.

The opposition to the bill seems to center in Congressman Elliott and a group who do not have the views of conservation of our natural resources which I most fervently support. It is feared that a letter such as you have drafted would give much help to this opposition.

There have been many indications that some of this opposition represents people with ulterior motives, who thus lose sight of the major benefit to the Nation. It would be, therefore, very unfortunate if by some act of the Federal Power Commission the bill failed of enactment, and I therefore request that the letter as drafted be not dispatched but that the Commission do whatever it can, conscientiously, to support the establishment of this park.[2]

Sincerely yours,

[FRANKLIN D. ROOSEVELT]

[13:OF 6–P:CT]

[1] Not present; presumably returned to the Budget Bureau.
[2] Drafted by the Interior Department.

893   TOM WALLACE, EDITOR, LOUISVILLE *Times*, TO MARVIN H. MCINTYRE, SECRETARY TO THE PRESIDENT

LOUISVILLE, KY., *May 2nd, 1939*

MY DEAR MARVIN: If you will get the record of the meeting between the President and the American Society of Newspaper Editors Thursday evening, April 20th, and read a question which the President referred to as a "conservation question," and to which he replied, you will see the background of this letter.[1]   But it is not necessary for you to go to that trouble.

Quite a group of ardent conservationists believe the Barkley-Spence water pollution bill lacks teeth, and that the Clark-Mundt bill should pass.[2]   We believe the President a good enough conservationist to be willing to listen to our argument.

I am asking you if you will ask if a committee could see the President for any number of minutes upon which he might decide, after May 6th, and as soon thereafter as might suit the President. The committee, tentatively, would include Dr. Henry Baldwin Ward, of the University of Illinois, and Preston Bradley, Chicago clergyman, both of whom you could run down in *Who's Who In America* if you don't know them.

If we could get a few minutes with the President would he prefer a small committee, say three, as against a committee of five?

I shall be much obliged if you will let me know if it would be possible for a date to be made, and how many should constitute the committee.[3]

Sincerely,

Tom Wallace

[13:OF 114-A:TS]

[1] *Ante,* 888.

[2] The Clark bill, S. 1691, "to prevent the pollution of the navigable waters of the United States," was introduced by Senator Clark (Mo.) on March 3, 1939, and referred to the Committee on Commerce. The Mundt bill, H. R. 4170, of the same title (and presumably the companion bill), was introduced by Representative Mundt (S. D.) on Feb. 15, 1939, and referred to the Committee on Harbors (*Cong. Rec.*, 76th Cong., 1st sess., 84:2, 1646, 2196). The effort to secure enactment of an effective anti-pollution bill is described *post,* 915, n.

[3] Answered *post,* 899.

894   Roosevelt to Anthony J. Dimond, Delegate from Alaska

Washington, *May 3, 1939*

My dear Mr. Dimond: I have received your letter of April 11, stating that reports are being circulated in Alaska to the effect that an attempt is being made to establish Admiralty Island as a national park or national monument for the protection of bears that live in that region.

It is my understanding that the Departments of Interior and Agriculture are considering the possibilities of Admiralty Island, along with other areas in Alaska, for addition to the national park and monument system. However, no recommendations have reached me.

I do not expect to approve any change in the administration of Alaska resources which might later prove adverse to the public interest.[1]

Very sincerely yours,

[Franklin D. Roosevelt]

[13:OF 378:T]

[1] (Drafted by the Interior Department.) Ickes, in his letter to Early of April 29, 1939, enclosing the draft, said that biologically Admiralty Island was one of the most remarkable areas of North America and that it should be given national monument status in order to preserve its timber and wildlife. He said that he expected to submit a form of proclamation to do this in a few days; whether he did so is not clear.

895   Roosevelt to Gertrude Ely, Bryn Mawr, Pennsylvania

[Washington] *May 3, 1939*

Dear Gertrude: Thank you for your note.[1] That Charleston paper, *The News and Courier,* represents everything that is reactionary in the South. It is the old row between the landed gentry and the field laborers, white and colored—only in this case the landed gentry are not South

Carolinians but are Northerners who have bought up the old places and use them for winter sojourns. A few of them, like Nick Roosevelt of Philadelphia, do a good job by raising cattle, etc., but most of them are distinctly rich absentee landlords. Most of the opposition to Santee-Cooper comes from them, aided and abetted by the anti-Administration Democrats.

As a matter of fact, it is perfectly reasonable to admit that the success of the Santee-Cooper project cannot be guaranteed. But the fact remains that it will develop power, it will prevent floods, and will, first and last, give a tremendous lot of work.

The complaint that it will kill all the ducks from Florida to Maine is silly. As an old-line professional ornithologist, I vouch for this!

The thing is not political any more than building a schoolhouse or a bridge or a Boulder Dam or a Grand Coulee is political—and the fact remains that the opposition comes 100% from every non-liberal element in the State of South Carolina.

It was approved four years ago—it is under way—it could not be stopped even if I wanted to—and I don't.

As ever yours,

[FRANKLIN D. ROOSEVELT]

[13:PPF 3154:CT]

[1] April 27, 1939 (PPF 3154), asking if the Santee-Cooper project could not be postponed until agreement could be reached between the Government and the people of the area on the estimated costs and benefits. A copy of the *News and Courier* of April 16, 1939, was enclosed; this carried a statement of the Santee-Cooper Landowners' Association opposing the project. Gertrude Ely was a close friend of the Roosevelts. She was active in Pennsylvania Democratic circles and in the League of Women Voters.

896   JAMES H. ROWE, JR., ADMINISTRATIVE ASSISTANT TO THE PRESIDENT, TO ROOSEVELT

WASHINGTON, *May 4, 1939*

MEMORANDUM FOR THE PRESIDENT . . . JOHN MUIR-KINGS CANYON PARK BILL: Chairman Seavey of the Power Commission talked to me today about his inability to reach a compromise with the Secretary of the Interior over the Kings Canyon Park Bill. I have also talked to Mr. Youngman, one of the advisors to the Secretary of the Interior, so that I feel that I state both views accurately.

On April 24th Seavey brought over a draft of a letter which he proposed to send to Congressman Elliott. The Park Service had told him you did not wish such a letter sent and he wished to check with you. On April 29th you replied asking him not to send the letter. (See attached file.)[1]

The Power Commission wishes to add to the Park Bill a provision permitting the development of power in the Park if it becomes necessary because of the demand for power in California. The Power Commission is willing to favor the Park Bill if the following amendment is added:

"Section 5. Power may be developed from the waters of the John Muir-King's Canyon National Park within said Park only by the United States or by the State of California or a duly authorized agency of either but with due regard for the scenic and recreational aspects of the Park, provided, that any such project shall be approved in advance of construction by the Secretary of the Interior and the Federal Power Commission."

Seavey is preparing a short memorandum tomorrow indicating there is a great deal of potential power, and feels *now* is the time to protect it.

The Secretary of the Interior is opposed to any amendment. He believes the development of power in such a remote region is uneconomic and unnecessary for a long time. The Power Commission at the present time has no jurisdiction over any National Park. The Secretary of the Interior does not believe it is necessary to make an exception in the case of Kings Canyon. If at some time in the distant future it becomes desirable to develop power, Congress can then authorize it.

The Secretary of the Interior is particularly opposed to the part of the proposed amendment that permits the State of California to develop power on federal property without compensation.

Seavey says that under the present Federal Power Act, States, as well as the federal government, are entitled to a preference over private utilities to develop power and points out that if this area is made into a Park, California will lose that right, unless it is provided for by the suggested amendment.

Seavey says that a situation may eventually develop whereby the State of California will be more public power-minded than the federal government and also points out that with the exception of the present Secretary, all Secretaries of the Interior have been opposed to public power development. I do not think he will recede on his point of view about including the State of California in the language.

There seem to be at least three possible courses for you to adopt:

(1) To accept the Seavey amendment.

(2) To recommend the passage of the Bill without amendment, making the situation like that in other National Parks, where Congress must authorize power development.

(3) To take a compromise position between the two and accept an amendment eliminating the State of California, thus limiting development to the federal agencies subject to the approval of the Secretary of the Interior and the Power Commission.

When I talked to Mr. Seavey I suggested that he and the Secretary might be able to work out this problem without consulting you. Since then, however, I have learned that personalities are involved and probably it will be difficult for them to work it out without your intervention.

JHR

Respectfully forwarded: EMW [2]

[13:OF 6–P:TS]

[1] Not present.
[2] Edwin M. Watson, Secretary to the President.

897   CLYDE L. SEAVEY, ACTING CHAIRMAN, FEDERAL POWER COMMISSION, TO JAMES H. ROWE, JR., ADMINISTRATIVE ASSISTANT TO THE PRESIDENT

[WASHINGTON] May 6, 1939

MEMORANDUM TO MR. JAMES ROWE . . . JOHN MUIR-KINGS CANYON NATIONAL PARK BILL (H. R. 3794):

1. The proposed National Park covers the upper water bearing region of the South and Middle Forks of Kings River, California.

2. The potential annual power development of these waters is estimated at 3,600,000,000 kilowatt-hours according to the report made by Mr. Ralph R. Randall, an engineer of the Federal Power Commission in 1930. This report is the most comprehensive of any official report published on this subject. Mr. Randall did not make extended detailed surveys of this territory but relied upon basic and extensive data from studies made by the Water and Power Department of the City of Los Angeles, also studies made by the State Engineer of California and other incidental sources of information. Mr. Randall made reconnaissance examination of the territory in order to be able to utilize properly the data above indicated.

3. If the full 3,600,000,000 kilowatt-hours were developed the value of such power at the conservation figure of 5 mills per kilowatt-hour would amount to $18,000,000 annually.

4. The Federal Power Commission's concern in this matter is its duties under the law to promote the most comprehensive development and utilization of the water-power resources of the nation and their development in the public interest with due regard for recreation. The Commission is in full agreement with the purpose of the Act to preserve the primeval features of the Kings River territory. Its chief concern is the possible unnecessary loss of a large block of power to future generations of consumers of electricity.

5. The engineers of this Commission believe that a comprehensive power development of the resources of this mountain area can be so

[331]

accomplished as not to affect its scenic grandeur. The greater portion of the high mountain lakes that can be used for storage are without littoral vegetation and can be raised without affecting their beauty. The reservoirs can be so operated that they will not be drawn down during the recreational season which is a comparatively short time in the summer season. Plants on the system can be so used in connection with Pine Flat and the lower plants as to permit operation of the upstream plants only after the recreational season.

6. My personal concern in this matter in addition to that as a member of this Commission is the future need of all of the possible development of hydro power in California. While California at the present time has an immense amount of cheap fuel in its oil and gas reserves this fuel is not inexhaustible and has only an estimated relatively short life. There are no resources of coal except a low grade lignite which experiments so far have shown cannot be used for cheap steam fuel, and California must eventually depend upon hydro power for cheap power to serve the potential and necessary requirements of the urban and farm territory in that State.

7. It is the belief of the Power Commission that if this potential power is to be preserved that it should be accomplished at the time of the passage of the bill creating the park, otherwise it would be extremely difficult to get any legislation through providing for this development with the hereditary opposition of the Park Service and the Secretary of the Interior in opposition to any use or development of waters in a National Park.

8. The Secretary of the Interior recently called me and asked if it were possible that an amendment might be offered to satisfy this Commission's objections to the bill. On behalf of the Commission I offered to cooperate with him in trying to prepare an amendment. This Commission offered for his consideration as an amendment a new section 5 to the bill which would provide that power might be developed from the water of the proposed park only by the United States or by the State of California or a duly authorized agent of either with due regard for the scenic and recreational aspects of the Park and provided that any such project or development should be approved in advance by the Secretary of the Interior and the Federal Power Commission. This, I am informed, was considered by the Secretary and the Park Service with the result that the Park Service opposed any amendment which would permit future development of power and that while the Secretary was not adverse to provisions permitting the United States to develop the power, he was opposed to allowing the State of California the right of development.

9. The reason the Federal Power Commission included the State of California in the proviso was because of the fact that the Federal Power Act now gives the State of California or any political subdivision preferential rights to develop this power or any other power in the State of

California. It is the belief of the Commission that all of the rights of the State of California should not be taken from it in relation to this substantial block of power which it is believed will be essential to the development of the State in the future. This Commission could have no objection to a provision that would permit the State of California or an agency there to develop power under the provisions of the Federal Power Act under which the Federal government would have the right of recapture and also to impose a charge if the power is developed by the State and sold to the public at a profit.

This Commission is willing to support the creation of the Park if an amendment to the proposed bill can be agreed upon which will preserve what we believe are policies fundamental to the larger interest of the public.

CLYDE L. SEAVEY

[13:OF 6–P:TS]

898   ROOSEVELT TO FERDINAND A. SILCOX, CHIEF, FOREST SERVICE

WASHINGTON, *May 8, 1939*

MEMORANDUM FOR CHIEF FORESTER SILCOX: How soon can we get out the bulletin on Community Forests? I am getting a good many requests for it.[1]

F. D. R.

[13:OF 149:CT]

[1] See *ante,* 873. Brown had asked Roosevelt to expedite the printing of the bulletin by the Agriculture Department in a letter of May 3, 1939 (OF 149). Silcox replied May 9 (OF 149), promising to get it printed as soon as possible.

899   EDWIN M. WATSON, SECRETARY TO THE PRESIDENT, TO TOM WALLACE, EDITOR, LOUISVILLE (KY.) *Times*

[WASHINGTON] *May 8, 1939*

MY DEAR MR. WALLACE: Reference is made to your letter of May second, addressed to Mr. McIntyre and referred to me in his absence.

I regret that it is not possible at this time to arrange the appointment you request. The President's schedule up to the end of June is so full that I have been compelled ot restrict his engagements to those of an official and inescapable nature. Of course this does not indicate any lack of interest on the President's part.

As you know, the President has always been in favor of any provision which will check water pollution and promote conservation. However, the merits of the two bills in question is really a matter for Congressional consideration and it is felt that it would be extremely helpful if your committee would discuss it with the appropriate committees of the Senate and House of Representatives.[1]

With all good wishes, Sincerely yours,

[EDWIN M. WATSON]

K/MDP

[13:OF 114–A:CT]

[1] The Barkley-Spence Water Pollution Bill and the Clark-Mundt Water Pollution Bill. Wallace replied May 12, 1939 (OF 114–A), "The conservationists will, of course, be sorry that it will be impossible for them to contact the President, but it is easy, of course, to understand that his schedule is quite full."

900   HAROLD L. ICKES, SECRETARY OF THE INTERIOR, TO ROOSEVELT

WASHINGTON, *May 9, 1939*

MY DEAR MR. PRESIDENT: The Interior Appropriation Bill for the fiscal year 1940 contains the following item:

Water Conservation and Utility Projects. For construction, in addition to labor and materials to be supplied by the Works Progress Administration, of water conservation and utilization projects, including acquisition of water rights, rights-of-way, and other interests in land, in the Great Plains and arid and semiarid areas of the United States, to be immediately available, $5,000,000, to be allocated by the President, in such amounts as he deems necessary, to such Federal departments, establishments, and other agencies as he may designate, and to be reimbursed to the United States by the water users on such projects in not to exceed 40 annual installments: Provided, That expenditures from Works Progress Administration funds shall be subject to such provisions with respect to reimbursability as the President may determine.

The language in the item was provided by the Bureau of the Budget and is in accord with the recommendations of the Northern Great Plains Committee, as set forth in its report to you, which you released for publication in October, 1938.

The comments on the floor of the House when the item was under discussion and the provisions in the item which provide for repayment by the water users in not to exceed forty annual installments (the same terms as contained in the Reclamation Act) indicate that the Bureau of Reclamation should take the lead in the planning and prosecution of the work. In addition, the Northern Great Plains Committee, in its report, proposed that the Bureau of Reclamation should be the principal construction agency, recommended that the engineering plans for all relatively large projects should be subject to approval by the Bureau, and stated that the appropriation of $5,000,000, if supplemented by aid from the Works Progress Administration, would permit construction of the greater part of the reclamation projects included in the report.

[334]

Therefore, I propose that the Secretary of the Interior, acting through the Bureau of Reclamation, shall administer the fund after the allotments have been made by you for specific projects. A separate report will be submitted to you for approval for each project to be undertaken. This report will include a brief description of the work to be done, an estimate of the construction cost, including the proportion to be performed by relief labor, a finding on the estimated amount that could be repaid by the beneficiaries without undue burden, and recommendations for participation in the construction and operation of the project by various Federal agencies. Preparation of the first of these reports will be initiated as soon as your approval of this plan and procedure is received.[1]

Sincerely,

HAROLD L. ICKES

[13:OF 6:TS]

[1] Answered June 14, 1939, *post*, 913.

901 HENRY A. WALLACE, SECRETARY OF AGRICULTURE, TO ROOSEVELT

[WASHINGTON] *May 9, 1939*

DEAR MR. PRESIDENT: In spite of the early criticism of the Shelterbelt Project, the Forest Service has planted approximately 126,000,000 trees in over 11,000 miles of shelterbelts on 20,000 Prairie-Plains farms during the past five years, and the work has been an outstanding success. The average survival to date has been about 65 percent, and growth up to 35 feet in four years is reported, with 4 to 8 feet per year rather common.

As now carried on, the farmer and the Federal Government contribute about equally to the ultimate cost of the shelterbelt establishment operation.

The farmer: (1) furnishes the planting site free; (2) furnishes fencing material to exclude livestock; (3) prepares the site for planting; (4) carries out neecssary rodent control work; (5) cultivates the trees for 3 to 5 years.

The Government: (1) furnishes technical supervision and coordinates the work between States; (2) furnishes the planting stock; (3) erects necessary fences; (4) furnishes rodent control materials; (5) plants the trees; (6) gives general supervision to cultivation work to assure adequacy and quality.

My investigations have shown the work is receiving a strong local accord.

I believe the undertaking has such merit, insofar as its farm and public benefit aspects are concerned, that it should be included in any permanent public works program that may be developed.

I wish to endorse the Project as it has been carried out, and recommend that Congress be asked to give it recognition by appropriating at least sufficient funds for the Department to carry the administrative and supervisory personnel and provide basic facilities needed on a year-long basis. The Project can then be expanded or contracted, according to the employment situation, with emergency funds.[1]

Respectfully,

[HENRY A. WALLACE]

[13:OF 1–C:CT]

[1] Answered below.

902   ROOSEVELT TO HENRY A. WALLACE, SECRETARY OF
       AGRICULTURE

WASHINGTON, *May 15, 1939*

MEMORANDUM FOR SECRETARY WALLACE: I am glad to know about the success of the Shelterbelt Project. What we need on it now is publicity—in Congress and throughout the country.

Will you make a special drive to get this. You can also get Lowell Mellett to help.[1]

F. D. R.

[13:OF 1–C:CT]

[1] Director of the Office of Government Reports.

903   HAROLD L. ICKES, SECRETARY OF THE INTERIOR, TO ROOSEVELT

WASHINGTON [*May 20, 1939*][1]

MY DEAR MR. PRESIDENT: With this letter I am enclosing in draft form a reorganization plan and a message of transmittal which I respectfully submit for your consideration under the Reorganization Act of 1939. The proposed plan would transfer from the Department of Agriculture to the Bureau of Reclamation in this Department the function of administering the water resources program provided for in the act of August 28, 1937 (50 *Stat.* 869).[2] For the reasons outlined in the proposed message of transmittal I believe this plan to be an appropriate and desirable one under the Reorganization Act, and recommend its adoption.[3]

Respectfully,

[HAROLD L. ICKES]

[13:OF 6–E:CT]

¹ This supplied date is that of the accompanying memorandum mentioned below.
² The Water Storage Facilities Act.
³ With the enclosures mentioned is a memorandum, Roosevelt to Budget Director Smith, May 20, 1939, reading, "To talk over with Louis Brownlow."

904   HAROLD L. ICKES, SECRETARY OF THE INTERIOR, TO ROOSEVELT

WASHINGTON, *May 22, 1939*

MY DEAR MR. PRESIDENT: With reference to the proposed John Muir-Kings Canyon National Park in California, and the difference between the attitudes of Mr. Seavey and myself toward the proposal, I have considered the memorandum from Mr. Seavey to Mr. Rowe of May 6, 1939, and the memorandum to you from Mr. Rowe of May 4, copies of which you transmitted to me.

I am deeply anxious that something additional be done. It would be most regrettable if the position of the Federal Power Commission, which I believe is not well taken, should block the creation of the National Park in the Kings Canyon area. There should be no necessity, in my opinion, of compromising the integrity of the National Park in an effort to open the way for a water power development at some distant future date, especially since everyone is agreed that this water power development is not needed now and is not likely to be needed in any calculable time. If and when an emergency develops in the power field in the area, it would seem to me that the Congress could be entrusted to weigh the needs of recreation and for power, and make its decision then on facts actually developed.

A letter has been prepared for your consideration, therefore, and I suggest that you send it to Mr. Seavey.¹ It answers the points raised in Mr. Seavey's memorandum of May 6, 1939.

Sincerely yours,

HAROLD L. ICKES

[13:OF 6–P:TS]

¹ Sent as the letter printed below.

905   ROOSEVELT TO CLYDE L. SEAVEY, ACTING CHAIRMAN, FEDERAL POWER COMMISSION

[WASHINGTON] *May 24, 1939*

MY DEAR MR. SEAVEY: Mr. Rowe has shown to me your memorandum of May sixth, relating to the John Muir-Kings Canyon National Park Bill (H. R. 3794).

The Ralph R. Randall report, made in 1930, in which the estimates are made of the water power and the cost of developing the power in the area which would be included in the park, seems to me scarcely adequate to support such firm conclusions as you make. I have heard no doubts raised as to general accuracy of the report with respect to the water power potentialities, but the cost estimates have been, and it seems to me justly so, seriously questioned. I understand Mr. Randall's field explorations consisted of eight days by pack horse and one day by airplane, which is hardly sufficient to provide a sound basis for making cost estimates. I understand Mr. Randall had available to him engineering data gathered by more thorough surveys by the City of Los Angeles and the State Engineer of California. It might be pointed out, however, that the City of Los Angeles, which gathered most of the data, rejected the area for water power development because of its conclusion that the costs would be too great, and that prior to the rejection of the area by the City, a private utility had also rejected the area on the same grounds.

In view of the scanty engineering information at hand, the figure of $18,000,000 given in your third paragraph as the conservative estimate of the annual value of the power, seems arbitrary. It might be much greater, but it also might be zero. The ruggedness and inaccessibility of the area, it would appear, might greatly reduce the value when actual costs are found.

The matter apparently is resolving into a problem of determining precisely how best the public interest can be served in the Kings River Canyon.

Despite the contention that power developments in the lakes of the uplands of Kings Canyon can be effected without damaging the scenic values of the area, it is difficult for me to see how this can be done. I am informed that this is a very wild region, with no roads. I believe the power development would contemplate tunnels, penstocks, dams, generating machinery, and other works. I am afraid I cannot agree that in constructing the necessary facilities the recreational values would not be diminished.

The time is far distant when this power will be needed. I understand there remains outside of the proposed boundaries of the Park, undeveloped water power equal to all the power now used in the region which would be served. Many things may occur between now and the time when the power latent in the uplands section may be needed. I cannot see how inclusion of the area in a National Park could prevent the development of power in the future, if and when it is needed. The Congress could not be foreclosed from acting then. Creation of the Park could prevent the development of the power in the distant future only if in the opinion of the majority of the people of that time the use of the area for recreation to the exclusion of power would best serve the public interest of that day.

Certainly the best interests of the public today will be served by creation of the National Park. The possibilities of future use of the energy resources will not be lost. If the public interest at a later date requires a change in the status of the area, no harm will have been done by the establishment now of the National Park for the service of the people of this and of the intervening generations.

I do not believe it would be good public policy to reserve for a state the right to enter a National Park. The precedent would be bad and the national interest in the park would be in constant jeopardy.[1]

Very sincerely yours,

[FRANKLIN D. ROOSEVELT]

[13:OF 6–P:CT]

[1] The Interior Department draft of this letter contained an additional paragraph which Roosevelt deleted. This referred to the Federal Power Commission's "duty to promote comprehensive development and utilization of the water power resources and their development in the public interest with due regard for recreation."

906   FREDERIC A. DELANO, CHAIRMAN, ADVISORY COMMITTEE TO THE NATIONAL RESOURCES COMMITTEE, TO ROOSEVELT

WASHINGTON, May 25, 1939

MY DEAR MR. PRESIDENT: Progress is being made along two fronts in the solution of the critical and interlocking problems of the Great Plains and the Pacific Northwest.

Although drought again threatens the Northern Great Plains, the co-ordination of Federal relief and rehabilitation activities is being improved through our Northern Great Plains Committee and the regional, state and county advisory groups of the Department of Agriculture. The Interior Department Appropriation Bill made available $5,000,000 for use, in addition to Works Progress Administration labor and materials, in constructing water conservation and utilization projects which are instrumental in developing economic havens of refuge for Great Plains farmers. Plans for administration of that fund are well advanced.[1]

Recent Weather Bureau reports show a rainfall deficiency from normal during the period March 1—May 23 of 56% in North Dakota, 48% in South Dakota, and 81% in Montana. This may be the setting for another serious drought in the Northern Plains this summer, although it is too early to forecast that condition with certainty. Drought undoubtedly would cause further restless migration of farmers within and out of the area. In any event a continuation of the migration from the Great Plains to the Pacific Northwest this year is to be expected in some degree—depending largely upon rainfall conditions. Approximately 25,000 families have migrated from the Great Plains states to the Pacific Northwest since 1930.

With migrants to the Northwest settling largely on low-grade land and with every available acre on Federal irrigation projects in that area used or claimed many times over, the problem of developing settlement and other economic opportunities in the Pacific Northwest is an acute one. Free public land no longer is available. The forest industry which is the main arch in the region's industrial structure has passed the period of maximum production. The present population movement, instead of quickening economic activities, may easily lead to expanding areas of poverty-ridden settlements and to a decline in living standards. Utilizing the Public Works Administration allotment which you made for that purpose on November 14, 1938 to supplement funds appropriated to various departments, a thorough appraisal of land and migration problems in the Pacific Northwest is now being made by the interested State and Federal agencies working through the National Resources Committee. The Departments of the Interior, Agriculture and War, the Public Works Administration, and the Works Progress Administration are joining in cooperative studies of lands suitable for settlement and of settlement problems, and in preparation of programs for public works construction and for legislative action. We expect two reports from that group:

1. An interim report by July 1, 1939 summarizing the present knowledge of the Pacific Northwest problems, and recommending remedial action which may be taken promptly by Federal and State agencies and at the next session of the Congress.

2. A final report recommending a long-term program of action relating to the plans and policies of Federal and State agencies concerned with migration, land settlement, reclamation, water conservation, employment and public works in the Pacific Northwest.

The futures of the Great Plains and the Northwest obviously are linked, and Federal activities in the two areas are being planned and better integrated.[2]

Sincerely yours,

FREDERIC A. DELANO

[13:OF 1092:TS]

---

[1] In a letter from Delano to Roosevelt of May 12, 1939 (OF 1092), on the disposition of this fund, Delano called attention to the Oct. 14, 1938, report of the Northern Great Plains Committee, which recommended that the construction of new irrigation projects should be by the Bureau of Reclamation or such other Federal agency as would be "best adapted to the work involved," that responsibility for the operation of completed projects should rest with the Department of Agriculture, and that the latter agency should also assume responsibility for establishing on the projects persons in need of resettlement. The report (a processed document) was issued as *Rehabilitation in the Northern Great Plains, Preliminary Report of the Northern Great Plains Committee* (Washington, 1938).

[2] An attached memorandum, Roosevelt to Watson, May 27, 1939, reads: "I want a meeting, next Wednesday or Thursday, for half an hour, with National Resources and Reclamation Commissioner Page and M. L. Wilson to talk over the subject of

this letter." Nothing, however, has been found in the Roosevelt papers to indicate that such a meeting was held.

907   M. O. RYAN, TEMPORARY SECRETARY, NORTH DAKOTA STATE PLANNING BOARD, TO ROOSEVELT

BISMARCK, NORTH DAKOTA, *May 29, 1939*

DEAR MR. PRESIDENT: Forgive the impertinence in writing you as Chief Executive, rather than some of the administrative branches of our Government. Only grave concern for a program which appears to be still in the making prompts us to do so.

Your Great Plains committee came to the troubled great plains area and made its investigation. They suggested water and soil conservation as means by which partial rehabilitation of this area might be accomplished out of current government disbursements. Then you personally appealed to the 1938 Congress for the ear-marking of $5,000,000 in relief monies to tackle some of these jobs in the Great Plains. Finally, you urged the present Congress to pass an authorization measure and to reappropriate that sum, without the $50,000 limitation per project. Up to this point, our entire northern Great Plains feels that you have understood our great need, and sought helpful legislation which would bring permanent benefits.

Now we understand that a three-man committee is to be established, representing Reclamation Bureau, WPA and the Department of Agriculture, and that this committee will recommend the various projects which are to be undertaken with this fund. We also understand that the existing WPA labor load is to be a determining factor in the selection of projects and project sites. At this point, Mr. President, we are very fearful that the full intent of the three-year long program may fall down.

For instance, let us cite a project on the Grand river, known as the Bowman-Haley project. For long years the federal government has held title to some river bottom land which would be flooded when and if a dam and reservoir were constructed for the irrigation of down-river lands. The area has long since been organized as an irrigation district, and can legally proceed on 24 hours' notice to bind the resident landowners to a contract with the Reclamation Bureau. The Bureau has long felt that if the dam and reservoir were constructed as a relief measure, the resulting irrigation project could be entirely self-liquidating. The War Department and the Reclamation Bureau have both surveyed the watershed, and could blueprint the construction from their offices. And yet, there are no cities in the area large enough to offer a labor load under WPA which would suffice.

Bowman County has received from March 1933, to September 1, 1938, total federal benefits of $2,973,675, representing $2,511 per family. The adjoining county of Adams, which would share in the benefits, has received, during the same period, $3,806,729 or $2,784 per family. Formerly two of the state's greatest livestock counties, they have been compelled to liquidate their entire livestock holdings because of the inability to grow feed crops during these drought years. The only way they can ever safely renew their livestock population is through the assured production of local feed reserves, and this could only be accomplished through irrigation in dry years.

More than 50 percent of the farmers in that locality are now clients of the Farm Security Administration, and are being subsidized in their daily operations. But they can't begin to rehabilitate themselves until they can balance their farm production through livestock, supplementing grains.

This three or four-year fight to develop a technique by which federal agencies can aid in the rehabilitation of some of these drought areas has had a definite objective. Now that objective could well be surrendered to an irrelevant regulation such as the existing WPA labor load. May we beg you to guard against sacrificing the workability and the practicality of the program by permitting the adoption of such regulations as would definitely prevent the accomplishment of the original objectives.

If the WPA labor load were not adequate, could a CCC camp, under the Reclamation Bureau, tackle the construction of such a dam? Or could farmers in the area, who are now under Farm Security Administration, be made eligible for assignment to the WPA, for the duration of this one project? Or could WPA labor, from surrounding cities and towns be imported and placed in concentration camps?

There are other similar projects in the western part of North and South Dakota, as well as Kansas and Nebraska. We believe that if this Great Plains program is set up in such a way as to care for the feasible projects in those areas that it need not increase the total federal spending in those sections, but that the funds so expended would do more to aid those communities in becoming again self-sustaining than any other type of federal spending which could be authorized.

Although written as a representative of the state planning board, the sense of this letter conveys the thought of our esteemed Governor, our state water conservation commission, and other state groups. We shall be honored if this appeal gains consideration.[1]

Respectfully,

M. O. RYAN

[13:OF 402:TS]

[1] Answered *post*, 916.

WASHINGTON, *May 31, 1939*

MY DEAR MR. BAKER: I have received your letter of May 8 concerning the disastrous effects of the recent fires in southern Florida and the
action that may be taken to restore the Everglades and to prevent recurrence of such catastrophes.[1]

The destruction of so much of the natural value of the Everglades has
distressed me. The action of the Florida legislature in making special
arrangements to cope with the situation is important, though not entirely
adequate. Appropriation of equal funds from Federal sources is now
under discussion in the Congress. Personally, I would like to see an
appropriation made for the study and development of methods that
may prevent the recurrence of these fires.

It would seem possible to restore water to the land in question.
How this may be done, however, is a complex matter, as legitimate
agricultural and other interests must be protected. Secretary Ickes has
asked the National Resources Committee to study the entire subject, and
to submit specific recommendations.

Thank you for bringing this matter to my attention. I am anxious to
do everything possible for the restoration of our wildlife.[2]

Very sincerely yours,

[FRANKLIN D. ROOSEVELT]

[13:OF 378:CT]

[1] Baker said (OF 378) that unwise drainage was responsible for the recent disastrous fires in the Everglades and urged that the artificial canals (such as the St.
Lucie, Hillsborough, Miami, North New River, and West Palm Beach) be provided
with sluice gates to maintain a controlled level of water at all seasons. Unless this
were done, there would be no point in creating an Everglades National Park.

[2] Drafted by the Agriculture Department.

909 THOMAS PARRAN, SURGEON GENERAL, PUBLIC HEALTH
SERVICE, TO ROOSEVELT

WASHINGTON, *June 1, 1939*

Through the Secretary of the Treasury.

MY DEAR MR. PRESIDENT: Reference is made to the pending stream
pollution legislation (S. 685) which has been passed by the Senate,
reported in the House with amendments, and designed to carry out the
recommendations in your message of February 16, 1939.[1]

I understand that considerable opposition has developed to the bill
on the part of two groups: (1) the economy bloc, and (2) the extreme
conservationists who want to federalize stream pollution control through

the Corps of Engineers, U. S. Army, with provisions for federal enforcement.

Senator Barkley's bill, S. 685, as now before the House, meets all of the objections cited in your veto message of June 25, 1938.

A copy of the bill now before the House, together with the report of the House Committee on Rivers and Harbors, is attached hereto.[2] I feel sure that a word from you at this time to those who guide the course of legislation in the House would do much toward securing favorable consideration of this important legislation.[3]

Sincerely yours,

THOMAS PARRAN

[13:OF 114–A:TS]

[1] Feb. 15, 1939, *ante,* 868.
[2] The report only is present: *Creating a Bureau of Water Pollution Control in the Public Health Service,* 76th Cong., 1st sess., H. R. Report No. 611 (Washington, 1939).
[3] Parran's letter was sent by Roosevelt to Budget Director Smith with a note, June 2, 1939, reading, "For preparation of reply."

910   JAMES H. ROWE, JR., ADMINISTRATIVE ASSISTANT TO THE PRESIDENT, TO EDWIN M. WATSON, SECRETARY TO THE PRESIDENT

WASHINGTON, *June 1, 1939*

MEMORANDUM FOR GENERAL WATSON . . . JOHN MUIR-KINGS CANYON NATIONAL PARK BILL: Attached is a memorandum from Chairman Seavey of the Federal Power Commission.

As you remember, Seavey and Secretary Ickes are arguing about this bill which proposes to make the area in question a national park. Seavey, while not opposed to the bill, wants an amendment retaining power rights for the federal government *and* the state of California.

Secretary Ickes prepared a letter for the President's signature refuting Seavey's arguments.[1] The present memorandum is an answer to the Secretary's memorandum.

The argument has now reached the technical stage about whether the power potentialities of the region are worth saving. The President should not be bothered with this technical disagreement.

The practical point involved is that several Congressmen opposed to the bill want a report from the Power Commission on the subject. Seavey wants to give them this report and Secretary Ickes does not want the Power Commission to do so. The President has practically told Seavey he does not want him to make any report, but it is my judgment he is likely to prove stubborn on this point.

Although there has been some animosity on both sides, it is my judgment that a compromise satisfactory to both could be reached if only they would sit down together.

Seavey is pressing for a release from the President so that he can make his report to Congress.

JHR

[13:of 6–p:ts]

¹ *Ante,* 905.

911   [*Enclosure*] CLYDE L. SEAVEY, ACTING CHAIRMAN, FEDERAL
         POWER COMMISSION, TO JAMES H. ROWE, JR.

June 1, 1939

MEMORANDUM FOR MR. JAMES ROWE . . . JOHN MUIR-KINGS CANYON NATIONAL PARK BILL (H. R. 3794): In accordance with my conversation with you last week I am submitting memorandum regarding the letter addressed to me from the White House under date of May 24th regarding the above bill.

In regard to the position taken, that the estimates of cost were not adequate, may I state that they were made by an engineer who was recognized as highly competent and was qualified in the matter of California hydraulic development. His estimates were checked and he was assisted by other engineers in the Federal service who were qualified and experienced. It might also be of interest for you to know that this engineer in his estimates for construction work in the inaccessible parts of the development increased several fold some of the estimates made by the Los Angeles engineers, in order to be on the safe side. It might be noted that the Los Angeles engineers are also noted for their ability in California hydraulic development, and have always had the reputation of being exceedingly accurate in their estimates. I am convinced that the estimate of $18,000,000 annually as the potential value of 3,600,000,000 kilowatts can be sustained.

I wish also to call your attention to the last sentence in the first main paragraph which reads as follows: "It might be pointed out, however, that the City of Los Angeles, which gathered most of the data, rejected the area for water power development because of its conclusion that the costs would be too great, and that prior to the rejection of the area by the City, a private utility had also rejected the area on the same grounds." In conjunction with this statement I wish to call your attention to the fact that recently in California there was released a transcribed address of the Secretary of the Interior in which he made a similar statement at the time he urged the people of California to actively support the bill now in Congress.

The applications of the City of Los Angeles, Projects Nos. 98 and 122, for development of this territory, and also the application of the San Joaquin Light and Power Corporation, Project No. 226, were considered by the Federal Power Commission at hearings in Fresno, California, in 1922, and action upon the same was taken by the Commission on June 15, 1923. In relation to the applications of the City of Los Angeles, the record of the Commission shows that the applications were rejected for the reason: ". . . it appearing that all of said developments are located in whole or in part within the proposed extension of the Sequoia National Park; and it further appearing that the applicant would not be prepared within a reasonable time to proceed with the construction of said project even if permit were granted; . . ." In relation to the application of the San Joaquin Light and Power Corporation, part of that application was for development on the main river and on the south fork outside of the area in which it was contemplated to extend the national park. The part of Project No. 226 within the proposed park area was rejected for the same reasons as those given in the instance of the City of Los Angeles. Nothing in the record indicates that applicants were stopped from proceeding because of excessive costs of the development.

In this connection I might state that in 1923 as President of the California Railroad Commission I discussed with President Wishon [1] of the San Joaquin Light and Power Corporation the matter of his power development program, and in that discussion he disclosed to me the facts of the rejection of the development on the south and middle forks of the Kings River, and indicated that he believed it was a feasible development except that he was concerned about the possibility of damages below because of the storage of flood water under the then riparian doctrine of the use of waters in California. It might be noted that since then California, by constitutional amendment, followed by decisions of the State Supreme Court, has adopted the doctrine of the beneficial use of water. Mr. Wishon also told me that he presumed that so long as the Secretary of the Interior was a member of the Federal Water Power Commission that it would be of no use for him to file additional applications for the development on the Kings River.

I believe in light of the facts as disclosed by the record of the Commission as stated above and the information given me by the President of the San Joaquin Light and Power Corporation that the quoted statement from the letter and the statement in the Secretary of the Interior's transcribed address are not in accordance with the facts.

In regard to the effect that this development might have upon the recreational values of this region, I simply wish to answer by a proposed slogan: "What the Swiss have done in the Alps of Switzerland, Californians can do in the Sierra of California if they have the opportunity."

CLYDE L. SEAVEY

[13:OF 6–P:TS]

[1] A. Emory Wishon.

Washington, *June 8, 1939*

My dear Senator Wheeler: I have received your letter of May 17, 1939, and the enclosed communication from the National Reclamation Association, proposing that the Bureau of Reclamation be placed in charge of the program of the Northern Great Plains Committee, which has been made possible by the $5,000,000 item in the Interior Appropriation Act.[1]

The plan which I have formulated will, I believe, meet with your approval. I shall place in the Bureau of Reclamation the responsibility for conducting investigations, preparing reports, submitting recommendations to me on definite projects, and directing the construction of the projects which I approve. The Department of Agriculture will work out the problems of repayment and resettlement, receiving such assistance from the Bureau of Reclamation as may be necessary.

I will make allocations to the Bureau of Reclamation from the $5,000,000 item and expect that the application of the Bureau of Reclamation to the Works Progress Administration for other funds will receive prompt approval. Relief labor will be used to the maximum extent. Payments for work accomplished by other Federal agencies will be made by transfer of funds from the allocation to the Bureau of Reclamation. This arrangement will provide flexibility in planning and in the execution of the work and will place the responsibility for the success of the undertaking in the Federal agency which has had the maximum experience in this line of endeavor. It is also in accord with the recommendations of the Northern Great Plains Committee, as contained in its report of October, 1938.[2]

Sincerely yours,

[Franklin D. Roosevelt]

[13:of 6–e:ct]

[1] F. O. Hagie, secretary-manager of the National Reclamation Association, to Wheeler, May 16, 1939. This and Wheeler's letter are present with the letter here printed.
[2] Drafted by the Interior Department.

913   Roosevelt to Harold L. Ickes, Secretary of the Interior

[Washington] *June 14, 1939*

My dear Mr. Secretary: In order to effectuate the purposes of the appropriation of $5,000,000 for water conservation and utility projects in the Interior Department Appropriation Act, 1940, about which you wrote me on May 9, I am requesting that the following procedure be adopted by the interested Federal departments and agencies:

[347]

1. Allocations from the $5,000,000 appropriation will be made for projects individually.

2. Recommendations for allocations will be prepared by the Department of the Interior in accordance with the general policies set forth in the report of the Northern Great Plains Committee, dated October 14, 1938, and will include the concurrence or views of the Department of Agriculture and the Works Progress Administration.

3. Each recommendation will include a description of the proposed project, an estimate of the total cost of the completed project, estimates of the work which can be performed by relief labor and of the reimbursable cost, and a statement of the proposed participation of each Federal Agency concerned together with the recommended amounts of funds to be allocated to each.

4. The Secretary of the Interior acting through the Bureau of Reclamation will be responsible for the construction of projects, except as may be otherwise recommended.

5. Recommendations will be transmitted to me through the Bureau of the Budget.

6. The National Resources Committee through its Northern Great Plains Committee will continue to coordinate these and related activities as directed in my memorandum of October 19, 1938.

I am forwarding copies of this letter to the Chairman of the National Resources Committee, the Secretary of Agriculture, and the Administrator of the Works Progress Administration for their information and guidance.

Sincerely yours,

[FRANKLIN D. ROOSEVELT]

[*Notation*:AS] HDS [1]

[13:OF 6–E:CT]

[1] Budget Director Harold D. Smith, in whose agency this letter was drafted.

914   HAROLD D. SMITH, DIRECTOR, BUREAU OF THE BUDGET, TO ROOSEVELT

WASHINGTON, *June 14, 1939*

MEMORANDUM FOR THE PRESIDENT: Reference is made to your memorandum of June 2, 1939, transmitting to me for preparation of reply, the attached letter from the Surgeon General of the Public Health Service,[1] with reference to S. 685, a bill to create a Division of Water Pollution Control in the United States Public Health Service and for other purposes.

The bill S. 685 does not conform, in certain more or less important respects, to the draft of bill which, after approval by you, was introduced in the House by Mr. Mansfield on February 20, 1939, as H. R. 4314. For example:

Section 5 (2) of S. 685 provides as to States, municipalities, or public bodies that no grant-in-aid shall be made in respect of any project of an amount in excess of 33⅓ per centum of the cost of labor, materials, etc., and is silent as to interest on or duration of loans, whereas Section 4 (2) of H. R. 4314 provides that no such grant-in-aid shall exceed 30 per centum, (3) that all loans made under this section shall be fully and adequately secured and shall have interest at the rate of 4 per cent per annum, and (4) each loan may be made for a period not exceeding 30 years.

Section 6 of H. R. 4314 provides that the Division of Water Pollution shall make estimates of the amount of money required for each year for various projects, showing the order of priority and cost of each, and also provides for review of these estimates by the National Resources Committee or such other agency as the President may designate. There is no such provision for review of the estimates in S. 685.

My principal objection to S. 685 is its underlying conception of an agency that would be able to by-pass the Bureau of the Budget, the Chief Executive, and the Appropriations Committees, by placing in the hands of legislative committees of Congress such detailed reports and recommendations regarding proposed projects and the cost thereof as would result in the enactment of legislation having the effect, as a practical matter, of an appropriation measure. This procedure would follow the procedure of the Corps of Engineers with respect to river and harbor projects, and would thus place the estimates of appropriations for water pollution projects on a more favored plane than that occupied by the ordinary estimates of appropriations for the departments and establishments.

I am wondering whether, in view of other legislation that should be disposed of during the short period remaining in the present session, you may not consider it advisable to postpone any further action on your part with respect to this water pollution legislation until the beginning cf the next session of Congress.

HAROLD D. SMITH

[13:OF 114-A:TS]

¹ *Ante,* 909.

915   ROOSEVELT TO HENRY MORGENTHAU, JR., SECRETARY OF THE
       TREASURY

[WASHINGTON] June 15, 1939

MY DEAR MR. SECRETARY: I have the letter of June 1, 1939, from Dr. Parran with reference to S. 685, a bill to create a division of water pollution control in the United States Public Health Service and for other purposes, in which he suggests that a word from me would do much toward securing favorable consideration of this legislation in the House of Representatives.

While S. 685 is not subject to all of the objections that were applicable to the bill H. R. 2711 of the 75th Congress which I declined to approve, it is still different in important respects from H. R. 4314 which had my approval before introduction in Congress.

A main objection to S. 685 is its underlying conception of an agency that would be able to by-pass the Bureau of the Budget, the Chief Executive, and the Appropriations Committees, by placing in the hands of legislative committees of Congress such detailed reports and recommendations regarding proposed projects and the cost thereof as would result in the enactment of legislation having the effect, as a practical matter, of an appropriation measure. This procedure would follow the procedure of the Corps of Engineers with respect to river and harbor projects, and would thus place the estimates of appropriations for water pollution projects on a more favored plane than that occupied by the ordinary estimates of appropriations for the departments and establishments.

I would prefer to see H. R. 4314 receive attention instead of S. 685.[1]

Sincerely yours,

[FRANKLIN D. ROOSEVELT]

[13:OF 114–A:CT]

[1] (Drafted by the Budget Bureau.) See veto message of June 25, 1938, ante, 799. H. R. 4314, introduced on Feb. 20, 1939, by Representative Mansfield (Texas), was not reported from committee. S. 685 was introduced by Senator Barkley (Ky.) on January 16. From his explanation of the bill it appears that Barkley was under the impression that the objections voiced by the President in his veto of H. R. 2711 had been met. In the Senate debate on April 27, however, Clark (Mo.) noted that Acting Secretary of War Johnson had reported to the chairman of the Senate Commerce Committee that the Budget Bureau had declared S. 685 not in accord with the President's program. Senator Clark moved adoption of his own bill, S. 1691, as an amendment (in the nature of a substitute) to the Barkley measure. S. 1691, similar to the Lonergan bill of the previous session, would have provided for the enforcement of anti-pollution measures through court action and would have established a division of water pollution control in the Corps of Engineers of the Army. It was vigorously supported by the Izaak Walton League and other conservationist organizations, which condemned the Barkley bill as ineffectual and harmful. Bills similar to the Clark measure, H. R. 4170 and H. R. 6723, were introduced in the House by Representative Mundt (S. D.), but neither was reported from committee. Clark's amendment was defeated. Senator Danaher (Conn.), who with Clark objected to that provision of S. 685 whereby Federal grants or loans for the construction of pollution-abatement facilities could be made to agencies, public or private, that had themselves caused pollution, then offered an amendment. This provided for action by the United States District Courts against the perpetrators of pollution nuisances. Senators Austin (Vt.) and Taft (Ohio) attacked the proposed amendment as impossible of enforcement and it was defeated. S. 685 was then passed by the Senate; in the House it was referred to the Committee on Rivers and Harbors. This committee reported the bill (much altered), but it was not acted upon during the session (Cong. Rec., 76th Cong., 1st sess., 84: 1, 355; 84: 2, 1446,

1645–1646, 1732–1733; 84: 5, 4842, 4848–4856, 4911–4931, 5089, 5408; 84: 14, 3345–3348).

916   ROOSEVELT TO M. O. RYAN, TEMPORARY SECRETARY, NORTH
       DAKOTA STATE PLANNING BOARD, Bismarck

WASHINGTON, *June 19, 1939*

MY DEAR MR. RYAN: I have received your letter of May 29, 1939, in which you discuss various phases of the program for partial rehabilitation of the Northern Great Plains through the building of Water Conservation projects, and express concern that the availability of local WPA labor may be the determining factor in the selection of projects.

A committee composed of representatives from the Works Progress Administration, Department of Agriculture, Bureau of Reclamation, and Northern Great Plains Committee of the Water Resources Committee, has been established primarily to coordinate the efforts of all agencies involved in this program. It will also review the data concerning each proposed project and submit recommendations for the use of the Bureau of Reclamation in the preparation of its recommendations to me.

Among the factors to be considered in the study of each project will be the engineering and economic feasibility and also the available labor on relief rolls. This latter factor is important but relief labor can be obtained from a wide area and assembled in construction camps. Farmers in the vicinity can be employed whenever practicable and, if the available labor supply is inadequate, the time for completing the project may be extended beyond the one-year period now contemplated for most projects.[1]

Sincerely yours,

[FRANKLIN D. ROOSEVELT]

[13:OF 402:CT]

[1] Drafted by the Interior Department.

917   ROOSEVELT TO HARRY H. WOODRING, SECRETARY OF WAR

WASHINGTON, *June 27, 1939*

MEMORANDUM FOR THE SECRETARY OF WAR: I approve the Whitney Dam (Brazos River) project, together with installation of power plant. The whole development of flood control storage, studies of power costs, etc., should be conducted in constant cooperation with the Federal Power Commission and the National Resources Committee.

Please advise the Congressional Committee of this.

F. D. R.

[13:OF 132–C:CT]

918   ROOSEVELT TO NELSON C. BROWN, New York State College
       of Forestry, Syracuse University, Syracuse, New York

[WASHINGTON] *June 29, 1939*

DEAR NELSON: Thank you for your letter.[1] I am glad you are going
abroad again on the seventh, and I am sure you will have a very successful trip.

The drought at Hyde Park is serious and during the past four days we
have been watering the trees—but I fear that unless we get some really
soaking rain in the next week, we are going to have a high percentage
of loss.

I look forward to seeing you when you get back.

Always sincerely,

[FRANKLIN D. ROOSEVELT]

[13:PPF 38:CT]

[1] June 27, 1939 (PPF 38), expressing concern over the newly planted trees on the
Roosevelt estate and saying that he was going to Europe to study community forest
development.

919   ROOSEVELT TO HENRY P. KENDALL, PRESIDENT, THE KENDALL
       COMPANY, Boston

[WASHINGTON] *June 30, 1939*

DEAR HARRY: Thank you for your letter of May thirty-first and for
the comprehensive picture you have drawn of the possibility of having
major forestry enterprises in the South make a large contribution to the
southern social and economic situation.[1] I believe the facts will bear
out the conclusions you have drawn and it only remains to develop a
comprehensive program that will get results in the form of increased
forest production on a permanent basis on the part of the farmers and
timberland owners of the southern States. You suggest a three-point
program, with which I am in thorough accord and to which I have
given real consideration.

You probably know that for many years the Department of Agriculture has been carrying on, through the Extension Service, an educational
campaign in an effort to develop forestry knowledge and a forestry con-
sciousness throughout the entire country. Perhaps the limitations on
these efforts have so circumscribed the results that they have been inadequate. Two years ago I approved the so-called Norris-Doxey Act
which provides for an expansion along this line and I have every hope
that with this expansion the educational needs of the situation will be
adequately met.

As a part of any educational program, effective demonstrations are,
as you suggest, a very vital tool to use. I am informed that the State
Extension Foresters, working with the Forest Service, State Forestry

agencies and the C. C. C., have developed a plan of establishing demonstration areas which is being put into effect generally throughout the East. Of necessity these demonstrations have to be established through arrangements with the owners of private forest lands and such contributions as you have made are extremely helpful. I am in thorough accord with your idea that this is a vital part of the entire program.

As you know, at my request, the Congress has appointed a Joint Committee to study the whole forest problem and to make recommendations to the Congress. It is my hope that this Committee will bring about recognition of the possibilities of a real national forest conservation program and make definite recommendations leading to its initiation. I am keenly interested in the subject and I hope that you will make an effort to see that the facts of the situation are pointed out to the Committee.

For a long time I have felt that the forest lands of the United States offered one of our largest opportunities to use surplus labor in the building up of our national wealth. I have given this matter a good deal of thought and study and recently reviewed a proposal of the Forest Service that involved the use of private forest lands under an arrangement that would assure the return of all or part of the public expenditures and at the same time encourage the private owners to carry on permanent forest enterprises.[2]

I am suggesting to the Forest Service that they inform you of this proposal and I know they will be interested in your reaction to it.[3]

Very sincerely yours,

[FRANKLIN D. ROOSEVELT]

WDH—MW

[13:PPF 2912:CT]

[1] In his letter (PPF 2912), Kendall, a prominent cotton manufacturer and a member of the Business Advisory Council of the Department of Commerce, described the problem created by the rapid population growth of the South and the declining importance to it of cotton culture. He proposed a program of forest restoration, to consist of education in forest conservation, demonstration plantings, and uniform state legislation to encourage proper silviculture.
[2] Roosevelt apparently here refers to the proposal made by Wallace in his letter of March 15, 1938, *ante,* 759.
[3] Drafted by the Agriculture Department. Hassett made some minor revisions in the draft.

920   MARGUERITE A. LeHAND, PRIVATE SECRETARY TO THE PRESIDENT, TO I. VAN METER, *Time,* New York City

[WASHINGTON] *July 15, 1939*

MY DEAR MR. VAN METER: I have shown your letter of June twenty-third to the President, with respect to the question as to who is entitled to the credit for the conception of the Civilian Conservation Corps.[1]

Basically the idea is one of conservation of forests and water and soil. No one alive today can claim to have originated the idea of conservation. True, it has become, in our generation, a more pressing need than ever before, as the tragic results of centuries of heedlessness and waste have piled up and become increasingly menacing. Modern wisdom and statesmanship is willing to spend public funds in the cause of conservation in order to prevent even greater and irreparable loss of public resources in the days to come.

Early in the President's political life, in the Senate of the State of New York in 1910–1913, he was interested in conservation. Later, as Governor, he took part in instituting a program of reforestation and soil conservation on a scale never before attempted in that State. Typical of his views in those days are several addresses printed in Chapter XX of Volume I of his presidential *Public Papers.* Others may be found in his gubernatorial *Public Papers,* for 1930 and 1931.

Reforestation was tied up in his program with the whole subject of proper land utilization. Forests were replanted on submarginal farm land, which was not longer serviceable for other crops and which had been purchased by the State for the purpose of planting vast areas of trees upon them.

As the depression of 1929 continued and deepened, and as the Federal Government continued to refuse to accept responsibility for feeding and clothing and sheltering the unemployed, it was in his opinion the duty of the respective States to take up the burden to the limit of their resources. Therefore, the State of New York, in his term as Governor, definitely assumed the responsibility of providing public work for the unemployed where possible and of providing the necessities of life to those for whom work could not be provided.

Essentially, the Civilian Conservation Corps idea is merely a combination of these two thoughts: (1) putting people to work with public funds, and (2) conserving forests, water and soil.

As he looks back upon the origin of his message to the Congress in the Spring of 1933 on unemployment relief in general, in which was included the proposal for the Civilian Conservation Corps, he cannot find that the idea of the Civilian Conservation Corps was taken from any one source. It was rather the obvious conflux of the desire for conservation and the need for finding useful work for unemployed young men. This type of work had the added advantage of not providing competition with private enterprise.

The details of the project as finally worked out were shaped and formulated with the object of meeting the necessity for quick action over as wide an area as possible. They were changed from time to time only as experience showed the way to improvement.

I trust this answers the question in your mind as to the "actual origin of the CCC." This letter is not to be published or quoted from.[2]

Very sincerely yours,

[MARGUERITE A. LEHAND]

[13:PPF 2265:CT]

[1] Van Meter referred to a statement in the magazine *Time* of Feb. 6, 1939, on the origin of the Civilian Conservation Corps, to which a reader had taken exception (PPF 2265).

[2] Drafted by Samuel I. Rosenman, Special Counsel to the President.

921   HENRY M. KANNEE, ASSISTANT TO MARVIN H. MCINTYRE, TO EDWIN M. WATSON, SECRETARY TO THE PRESIDENT

WASHINGTON, 7/18/39

MEMORANDUM FOR GENERAL WATSON: Mr. Monson Morris telephoned that he would like to have not more than five minutes this afternoon for:

Himself

Mr. Putnam, Pres. of the Farm Bureau [1]

Mr. Ogg of the Grange

Harry Kendall of Boston

Ovid Butler of the American Forestry Ass'n.

"We have now whipped the Fulmer Forestry Bill into shape. It contains many suggestions made by the President in his letters to me. We have one or two revisions on which we want to get his OK. After we get his approval, we are going to make a concerted effort to get the Bill through this session."

K.

[*Notation*:AS] What are The Pres.' wishes   EMW
He is awfully sorry but just cannot see Mr. Morris [EMW] [2]
I put them on to Sec Wallace   K

[13:OF 149:T]

[1] George M. Putnam.

[2] Watson's first note was directed to Roosevelt; his second to Kannee.

922   MONSON MORRIS, PRESIDENT, AIKEN COUNTY (S. C.) FOREST PROTECTIVE ASSOCIATION, AND HENRY P. KENDALL, PRESIDENT, THE KENDALL COMPANY, TO ROOSEVELT

WASHINGTON, D. C., *July 18, 1939*

DEAR MR. PRESIDENT: In accord with General Watson's suggestion, we transmit herewith request for the action we desired to discuss with you today.

[355]

You are familiar with the proposal of the Forest Service as endorsed by the Secretary of Agriculture covering a plan to lease and place in effect cooperative agreements with private forest landowners looking to the restoration of such lands and the creation of jobs through this process. This proposal has received wide endorsement and a bill (H. R. 800) has been introduced that would, in a very limited way, initiate operations. H. R. 800 has received consideration by members of the Farm Bureau, the Grange and others and they have suggested certain changes which we consider very much in the public interest. Specifically the changes suggested by the members of the Farm Bureau and the Grange involve a clearcut definition between farmer-owners and non-farm owners, as well as a democratic process of effectuating the act.

Consideration has been given to the bill as amended by Senator Walsh and endorsed by him. It would therefore be appreciated if you could suggest to Congressman Fulmer that his bill be amended to conform to the desires of the Farm Bureau and the Grange as indicated in the attached draft of the legislation as they propose it.

It would probably help passage in this session if Senator Walsh could receive some encouragement on the suggestion which he had made of endeavoring to secure the signatures of Senators Bankhead, LaFollette and Byrnes of South Carolina, with his own.[1]

Very sincerely,

MONSON MORRIS
HARRY KENDALL

[APS] Dear Franklin Mr Kendall and I have seen Congressman Fulmer and feel sure he will change his bill if you urge it. Sorry not to have seen you. MONSON MORRIS

Dear Mr President—This will carry out nationally just the ideas I expressed to you. HARRY KENDALL

[13:OF 149:TS]

[1] H. R. 800, "To authorize the Secretary of Agriculture to enter into cooperative agreements with farmers, with States, and with . . . political subdivisions of States to lease forest lands . . .", was introduced by Fulmer (S. C.) on Jan. 3, 1939, but was not reported from committee. Similar bills were introduced late in the session: H. R. 7271, by Fulmer, on July 18, and S. 2927, by Walsh (Mass.), Byrnes (S. C.), Brown (Mich.), and LaFollette (Wis.), on July 31. On Feb. 14, 1940, Fulmer reintroduced his bill as H. R. 8550. None of these was reported from committee (*Cong. Rec.*, 76th Cong., 1st sess., 84: 1, 31; 84: 9, 9460; 84: 10, 10460; 3d sess., 86: 2, 1674). The bills are described *post*, 1038.

923   Charles W. Eliot, Director, National Resources Planning Board, to Rudolph Forster, Executive Clerk, White House Office

Washington, *July 18, 1939*

Dear Mr. Forster: In accordance with our conversation this morning I am submitting the following notes concerning the "clearance" of the report on "Kings River and Tulare Lake" submitted to the Resources Planning Board [1] by the Chief of Engineers [2] on July 12 in accordance with the instructions of the President.

Upon checking up on agencies interested in the problem, our Water Resources Committee found that the Bureau of Reclamation has just completed its own separate report on the same problem, which we are told differs from the recommendations of the Army Engineers in respect to the design and cost of works and the allocation of costs among irrigation and flood control beneficiaries.

The report of the Reclamation Bureau has not been made available to us "in view of the President's instructions to keep it confidential until the conference on Wednesday." We understand informally that the conference referred to has been called by the President for tomorrow and includes Secretary Woodring and Secretary Ickes and is concerned primarily with the Kings River problem.

We believe that the President should know that this Kings River dispute between the Army Engineers and the Reclamation Bureau is only one of a number which have been referred to us in recent months. The proposed dam at Wagon Wheel Gap in the Upper Rio Grande Valley, the Cherry Creek Project in Colorado, and other projects involve similar issues. We have been working on these problems for several months through the Water Resources Committee on which all of the agencies concerned (Army, Interior, Agriculture, Power, Public Health, and Tennessee Valley Authority) are represented. A word from the President to the conference tomorrow, requesting these agencies to cooperate with the National Resources Planning Board in developing a system of joint investigation and joint reporting, would be most helpful.

We are glad to be of service in clarifying and suggesting solutions for these problems, and believe that with the President's interest and support, and given time for adequate study, we can make a useful contribution.

Sincerely yours,

Charles W. Eliot

[13:OF 1092:TS]

[1] The National Resources Planning Board replaced the National Resources Committee on July 1, 1939.
[2] Julian L. Schley.

WASHINGTON, *July 19, 1939*

MY DEAR MR. TAYLOR: On September 1, 1937, there was enacted into law a measure reasonably calculated to insure to the Eskimos and other natives of Alaska, a food supply in perpetuity by eliminating all non-native ownership of reindeer, by providing for the conservation of the range, and the protection of the herds.[1]

Basic to the humanitarian purposes of the Act is its authorization of an appropriation of $2,000,000 to purchase those herds now owned by non-natives. No appropriation has, however, been made, although the passage of the measure was preceded by prolonged consideration, and although the provisions of the Act have been supported by investigations subsequent to its passage made under the immediate direction of the Chairman of the House and Senate Committees on Appropriations.

I am deeply interested in the efforts of these people in their struggle to preserve for the future the only controllable food supply for which the tundra areas of Alaska are suitable. In the press of other matters, I hope the commitments of the Reindeer Act of 1937 may not be forgotten and that those who are dependent upon reindeer may be enabled by an adequate appropriation to regain full possession of the industry upon which their future depends, to protect their herds from the inroads of predators, to conserve the grazing areas, and otherwise to reap the full benefits of the reindeer industry.

It must be remembered that reindeer were imported to Alaska at the close of the last century to replace in some measure the indigenous food supply of the natives, which had been depleted by the expansion of American commerce and industry, and it seems only logical that we now should take the steps called for by the Reindeer Act.

I trust this matter will receive the earnest consideration of your Committee and of the Congress.[2]

Very sincerely yours,

[FRANKLIN D. ROOSEVELT]

[13:OF 3396:CT]

[1] 50 *Stat.* 900.

[2] This letter was drafted by the Interior Department. In his note to Roosevelt enclosing the draft, July 19, 1939, Ickes said that it had been prepared at the request of Representative Taylor. An appropriation of $795,000, in the form of an amendment to the Third Deficiency Bill (H. R. 7642), was debated by the House in Committee of the Whole on Aug. 2, 1939. This was opposed by Representatives Colmer (Miss.), Schafer (Wis.) and Taber (N. Y.), who argued that it was merely an attempt to give relief to unsuccessful speculators (the owners of the private reindeer herd), and was a socialistic effort to put the Government in business. Defenders of the appropriation, including Representatives Taylor (Col.), Faddis (Pa.),

and Alaskan Delegate Dimond, urged its adoption as an humanitarian measure and as a means of making the natives self-supporting. In the course of the debate Taylor read the President's letter into the *Record*. The amendment was adopted and was incorporated in the act as approved Aug. 9, 1939 (*Cong. Rec.*, 76th Cong., 1st sess., 84: 10, 10845–10850; 53 *Stat.* 1031).

925   HAROLD D. SMITH, DIRECTOR, BUREAU OF THE BUDGET, TO ROOSEVELT

WASHINGTON, *July 22, 1939*

MEMORANDUM FOR THE PRESIDENT: The First Assistant Secretary of the Interior [1] has referred to this office the attached draft of legislation to provide for the establishment of the Katahdin National Park in the State of Maine and proposed letter of transmittal to the Speaker of the House of Representatives.[2]

The proposed park would have an area of about 328,000 acres. There are numerous lakes and streams in the area. Mt. Katahdin, rising to an elevation of 5,200 feet, is the principal feature of the area, and is included in a State Park. The proposed legislation provides that the land required for the park shall be acquired by public or private donation rather than by the appropriation of public funds, and that upon establishment of the park, it shall be permanently reserved as a wilderness. Development of facilities and services for public convenience, including such roads as may be desirable, is to be restricted to that portion of the area not more than 800 feet above sea level. A provision is contained in the bill which would authorize the Secretary of the Interior, in his discretion, to eliminate the area in the State Park from the proposed national park.

The present Baxter State Park was donated to the State of Maine by former Governor Baxter. Recently Mr. Baxter has acquired additional lands within the proposed national park area and he has announced that these lands will be given to the State for State Park purposes. The Department advises that Mr. Baxter is not in favor of the inclusion of the State Park, or the additional lands acquired by him, in the proposed Katahdin National Park.[3]

On July 11, 1938, Acting Director Bell transmitted to you a proposed favorable report of the Secretary of the Interior to the Chairman of the House Committee on Public Lands, on H. R. 6599, 75th Congress, providing for the establishment of the Katahdin National Park,[4] and called attention to the fact that since Mount Katahdin was already adequately protected by being included in the Baxter State Park, there would seem to be no justification for the establishment of a national park, and requested instructions from you before advising the Secretary of the Interior as to the relation of the proposed legislation to your program. The files of this office fail to show that any instructions were received from you and no further action was taken by this office.

It seems to me that the Secretary of the Interior should be advised that the proposed legislation would not be in accord with your program; however, I shall await your instructions before communicating with him.

HAROLD D. SMITH

[*Notation*: AS] H.D.S. Not this year FDR

[13:OF 79:TS]

¹ Ebert K. Burlew.
² Neither is present.
³ Gifts by Baxter in 1939 enlarged the park to an area of 48,000 acres. See "Mount Katahdin Established as State Park," in *The Living Wilderness*, IV (March, 1939), 11–12.
⁴ The only transmittal letter from Bell answering this description is dated June 11, 1938 (OF 6–P), and this is apparently the one meant. A note attached to this letter, Roosevelt to Ickes, June 14, 1938, presumably referring to Ickes' report, reads, "Will you speak to me about this after your return?"

926   ROOSEVELT TO HARCOURT A. MORGAN, CHAIRMAN, BOARD OF DIRECTORS, TENNESSEE VALLEY AUTHORITY, Knoxville

WASHINGTON, *July 28, 1939*

MEMORANDUM FOR DR. HARCOURT A. MORGAN: That is an interesting study of the work of the Land-Grant Colleges.¹

It is my plan to stop in the TVA territory in November on my way to Warm Springs—and on this trip to avoid paying any attention whatsoever to the power development and to concentrate on fertilizer, forestation, soil erosion, transfer of population, standard of living, etc., etc. Will you and Jim and Dave² work on a trip of this kind, figuring that I could get to the northeastern end of the Valley one morning, spend the day, move by night to the southwestern end of the Valley and leave the second evening for Warm Springs?

I told Dave about this the other day.

F. D. R.

[13:OF 42:CT]

¹ Carleton R. Ball, *A Study of the Work of the Land-Grant Colleges in the Tennessee Valley Area in Cooperation with the Tennessee Valley Authority* (1939), enclosed in Morgan to Roosevelt, July 25, 1939 (OF 42): "The study describes the way in which the Authority's developments in the interest of soil conservation and control of water on the land have been translated into the varying farm programs of the people of the region . . ."
² James P. Pope and David E. Lilienthal were the other two members of the TVA Board of Directors.

927   Roosevelt to Harold D. Smith, Director, Bureau of the Budget

Washington, *July 28, 1939*

Memorandum for the Director of the Budget: I agree with the Secretary of the Interior.[1] Please have it carried out so that fur-bearing animals remain in the Department of the Interior.

You might find out if any Alaska bears are still supervised by (a) War Department (b) Department of Agriculture (c) Department of Commerce. They have all had jurisdiction over Alaska bears in the past and many embarrassing situations have been created by the mating of a bear belonging to one Department with another bear belonging to another Department.

F. D. R.

P.S. I don't think the Navy is involved but it may be. Check also on the Coast Guard. You never can tell!

[13:OF 1–F:CT]

[1] Ickes opposed a proposal of the American Fox and Fur Breeders Association that the functions of the fur-animal research of the Bureau of Biological Survey be returned to the Department of Agriculture (Ickes to Roosevelt, July 21, 1939, OF 378). The Bureau of Biological Survey and the Bureau of Fisheries (of the Commerce Department) were transferred to the Interior Department on July 1, 1939, under authority of Reorganization Plan II.

928   Roosevelt to the Congress

The White House, *July 31, 1939*

To the Congress of the United States: Exploitation of our resources has created many problems, but none more pressing than in those areas of the United States where a basic resource has been mismanaged and the principal industry has moved or waned, leaving the working population stranded.

The cut-over region in the northern part of the States of Michigan, Minnesota and Wisconsin was once the scene of a flourishing lumber industry. Today a large section of the population in that area depends for its very existence on public aids, work relief, and security payments. The large expenditures for these purposes in the area have enabled these people to survive, but could not provide a satisfactory permanent solution to their problem.

Members of Congress representing the region appealed some time ago for aid in developing a program to assist the people in the area to find a way of life that would provide opportunity and reasonable security. The problem is now to make the best use of the natural and human resources of the area.

Over a year ago the National Resources Committee began a study of the region, establishing large local committees in order to insure accurate representation and true understanding of the local point of view. Individual reports were prepared by groups representing the cut-over areas in the three States. From these individual reports a summarized version of what is thought to be a feasible program has been developed. This summary constitutes the most recent in the series of regional reports by the National Resources Committee and is entitled "Regional Planning, Part VIII—the Report of the Northern Lakes States Regional Committee."

I am asking that the National Resources Planning Board keep in touch with the regional committee, which sponsored this report, to assist the regional committee in promoting correlation of activities of Federal, State and local agencies concerned with bringing about the accomplishments desired. I commend the report to your careful study for whatever action may be appropriate.[1]

FRANKLIN D. ROOSEVELT

[W. H. PRESS RELEASES:M]

[1] In the Senate the message was referred to the Committee on Agriculture and Forestry; in the House, to the Committee of the Whole House (*Cong. Rec.*, 76th Cong., 1st sess., 84: 10, 10512, 10601).

---

929   HAROLD L. ICKES, SECRETARY OF THE INTERIOR, TO ROOSEVELT

MARION, VIRGINIA, *August 4, 1939*

[*Telegram*] THE PRESIDENT. Kings Canyon bill passed House in satisfactory form and has been reported favorably by public lands committee of Senate by unanimous vote. I would appreciate it very much if you would indicate to Senator Barkley that you would like to have this bill passed at this session. So far as I know there is little opposition, but it may not be possible to get it through by unanimous consent.[1]

ICKES

[*Notation*:A:TULLY] General Watson   Will you phone this to Barkley if they do not adjourn until tomorrow
[*Notation*:AS] too late   E.M.W.

[13:OF 6–P:T]

[1] The House Committee on Public Lands held hearings on H. R. 3794 from March 15 to April 6, 1939: *Establishing John Muir-Kings Canyon National Park, Hearings*, 76th Cong., 1st sess., on H. R. 3794 (Washington, 1939). The report of the committee is also printed, *Establishing Kings Canyon Wilderness National Park, Calif.*, H. Rept. 718, 76th Cong., 1st sess. (Washington, 1939). On July 18 the bill was taken up by the Committee of the Whole House. The debate was acrimon-

ious, with two members of the California delegation, Englebright and Elliott, vigorously opposing the bill. The former said that the future of the agricultural area served by the Kings River depended on cheap power and that creation of the park would preclude development of such power. To this, supporters of the bill, led by its sponsor, Gearhart (Calif.), replied that the Army Engineers and the Bureau of Reclamation agreed that all feasible reservoir sites were located outside the proposed park.

Elliott charged that the Forest Service, which had opposed a similar bill in the previous Congress, had changed its stand only because "pressure was brought to bear," and that a Federal Power Commission representative had feared to continue giving testimony adverse to the bill before the Public Lands Committee. Gearhart's defense of the bill was aided by Voorhis, also of California, who said that ". . . the most reasonable use for this area of surpassing scenic beauty . . . is that it should be converted into a national park."

The bill had been reported with the following amendment: "But nothing herein shall prevent the construction upon said lands of such works as may be recommended by the Chief of Army Engineers or the Bureau of Reclamation for the control of floods or for the use or conservation of water for irrigation or hydroelectric power in the areas adjacent or contiguous to said lands." Cochran (Mo.) moved to strike this out because it would set a dangerous precedent: parks should be parks and not areas of commercial exploitation. White (Idaho) supported the amendment and urged the members to "get away from this sentimental scheme to keep people from utilizing the natural resources of this country." The Cochran motion carried, however, and the bill was passed by the House.

In the Senate the bill was reported favorably (August 3) but was not acted upon until the third session. Brought up Feb. 19, 1940, it was passed the same day after speeches in opposition by Pittman (Nevada) and Ashurst (Ariz.) (*Cong. Rec.*, 76th Cong., 1st sess., 84: 9, 9434–9454, 9476; 3d sess., 86: 2, 1587–1592). The act was approved March 4, 1940 (54 *Stat.* 41). Details of the long struggle to bring Kings Canyon within the protection of the national park system may be found in Robert Shankland's *Steve Mather of the National Parks* (New York: Knopf, 1951), *passim*.

930   EDWIN M. WATSON, SECRETARY TO THE PRESIDENT, TO ANTHONY J. DIMOND, DELEGATE FROM ALASKA

WASHINGTON, *August 4, 1939*

MY DEAR MR. DIMOND: Receipt is acknowledged of your letter of July 7 enclosing a copy of a telegram to you from the United States Commissioner at Unalaska [1] protesting the proposed plan for reorganizing fox farming and the protection of wildlife in the Aleutian Islands Reservation.[2]

This matter is under consideration in the Department of the Interior. During the past three seasons, the Biological Survey has conducted investigations throughout the Aleutian Chain and has ascertained that the present system of utilizing practically all of the islands for the production of blue foxes is working to the great disadvantage of the bird colonies owing to the heavy drain on them as a source of food for the foxes. As you are no doubt aware, the lack of means for adequate supervision of this reservation has resulted in the development of unsatisfactory conditions, particularly from the standpoint of the natives and from that of

[363]

the wildlife resources of the area. The sea otter colonies that are gradually returning in the Aleutians are also an important factor to be taken into consideration.

The Biological Survey has now established resident supervision in the area, and with the cooperation of the Office of Indian Affairs, which has charge of the native interests, it is prepared to inaugurate and carry out efficient administration of the area.

The necessary amendments to existing regulations for carrying out the proposed plan have not as yet been adopted by the Department of the Interior, and I have every reason to feel that careful consideration will be given to any changes found necessary to accomplish the desired results.

It is deemed highly desirable to discontinue the practice of issuing individual permits to natives, and it is planned to revoke all such outstanding permits and, where the islands are not to be devoted exclusively to wildlife conservation, to reissue the permits to the native village or community of which the former permittee was a member. The many advantages that will accrue to the general benefit of the natives under this procedure are obvious. In the case of private individuals and interests, every possible consideration will be given to the protection of their investments. As you are doubtless aware, the fox farming industry in the Aleutians has been greatly over-capitalized, notwithstanding the provisions of regulations designed to prevent speculation. Moreover, this situation has reacted greatly to the disadvantage of the natives. It is contemplated that the close supervision which the Government is now prepared to exercise in the Aleutians will gradually eliminate this influence.

Where it is necessary to retire certain islands from fox farming for the protection of the colonies of birds or sea otters, every possible consideration will be given to the former permittees in the matter of trapping or capturing and removing their stock from the islands, and in granting permits for the use of other islands in lieu of those retired from fox farming. It was first thought that normally such transfers could be accomplished in about one year, but upon giving the matter further study, it is realized that more time will be necessary in specific instances to protect the investments of the owners. You have already called attention to a few cases that require particular consideration and I wish to assure you that every case will be given careful study with a view to protecting these private interests.

I am in accord with the general plan for improving conditions in the Aleutians and am reassured by the Secretary of the Interior and the Chief of the Biological Survey that the utmost attention will be given to individual cases before final decisions are reached with respect to the more important islands involved.

Since the Biological Survey and the Office of Indian Affairs are now in a position to keep the islands under constant observation and to continue studies and research on the various problems, there would seem to be no need for the appointment of a special committee to study the matter, as suggested by Commissioner Martin, before initiating action along the lines contemplated, with the considerable expense that would be involved in such a special investigation.

It will be appreciated if you will keep in close touch with the Chief of the Biological Survey and the Secretary of the Interior in working out the solutions to these problems.[3]

Sincerely yours,

[EDWIN M. WATSON]

[13:OF 378:CT]

[1] Jack Martin.
[2] OF 378.
[3] (Drafted by the Interior Department.) With this letter is a six-page memorandum dated July 14, 1939, on the safeguarding of the interests of the natives and the protection of the wildlife of the region prepared for the Secretary of the Interior by Director Ira N. Gabrielson of the Bureau of Biological Survey.

931   STATEMENT BY ROOSEVELT ON HIS VETO OF AN ACT AFFECTING THE GRAND CANYON NATIONAL MONUMENT

THE WHITE HOUSE, *August 7, 1939*

MEMORANDUM OF DISAPPROVAL: I have withheld approval of S. 6, entitled "An Act To return a portion of the Grand Canyon National Monument to the public domain."

I am constrained to veto this legislation, which proposes to return approximately 148,159 acres within the Monument to the public domain, because it appears that insufficient consideration has been given to the matter.

While appreciating the needs of the stockmen, and the desirability of affording them range facilities on the public domain when it can be done without unnecessary damage, I think that the stockmen will not be harmed by the delay necessary for full consideration of this subject. Grazing can be continued under special permits of the Department of the Interior while a further survey on the ground is being made of the lands proposed to be eliminated from the National Monument.

Before approving any measure which would eliminate lands from any national monument, I would want to receive a report from representatives of the National Park Service based upon a thorough investigation of the lands proposed for elimination from the Monument.

For the foregoing reasons, I am compelled to withhold my approval of the bill. I seek especially a report on the possibilities of this area for tree growth.[1]

FRANKLIN D. ROOSEVELT

[1] The National Park Service conducted an investigation of the area and recommended a reduction in size of the monument. The boundary was drawn to retain the heads of the side canyons, to retain the principal volcanic exhibits on the western boundary, to exclude private lands not likely to be acquired, and to exclude grazing lands not needed for monument purposes. The recommendation was approved by the President on Jan. 22, 1940 (Ickes to Roosevelt, Jan. 18, 1940, OF 928).

932   STATEMENT BY ROOSEVELT ON HIS VETO OF AN ACT AFFECTING THE SHENANDOAH NATIONAL PARK

THE WHITE HOUSE, *August 9, 1939*

MEMORANDUM OF DISAPPROVAL: I have withheld approval of S. J. Res. 160, providing for the maintenance for public use of certain highways in the Shenandoah National Park.

The primary objection to this legislation is that it would subordinate national parks standards to local considerations. National parks are created for the benefit of the nation as a whole, and for the preservation of specific areas in their natural condition, with a minimum of development. Such developments as may be required in national parks are undertaken for general public use, as distinguished from local use. The approval of S. J. Res. 160 would encourage local communities to request the opening of minor roads in national park areas solely for the purpose of conferring local benefits upon adjacent communities, and would establish a dangerous precedent. Both the Congress and the Executive agencies have in the past rejected similar attempts on the part of local interests to force construction of roads within the Yellowstone and other national parks. This proposed legislation for Shenandoah National Park would, therefore, be in direct conflict with an established precedent.

I am informed that these roads are in bad condition, and that they are narrow and have excessive grades and hairpin curves. It has been estimated that it would cost over one million dollars to put these roads in safe condition. In addition, their annual maintenance cost would be approximately $10,000.

The Act of the General Assembly of Virginia ceding to the United States exclusive jurisdiction over the Shenandoah National Park in the State of Virginia, approved March 22, 1928, exempted from that cession only the Lee Highway and Spotswood Trail, thereby indicating that these were to be the only roads to remain free from Federal regulation.

If it can be later shown that the opening of the roads in question would be to the benefit of the nation, that the large expenditures involved would be justified, and that a precedent contrary to national park policies would not be established thereby, the problem can then be solved administratively.

For the foregoing reasons, I am compelled to withhold my approval of the Joint resolution.[1]

FRANKLIN D. ROOSEVELT

[W.H. PRESS RELEASES:M]

[1] This resolution, introduced June 23, 1939, by Senators Byrd and Glass of Virginia, declared that the closing of the roads in the Shenandoah National Park had caused the people of Virginia "great injury and inconvenience" and noted that the area had, since colonial days, been traversed by public roads. It would have required the Interior Department to keep open and in a safe condition the Browns Gap Road and the Gordonsville-New Market Turnpike. There was no debate (*Cong. Rec.*, 76th Cong., 1st sess., 84: 7, 7761; 84: 10, 10664).

933   ROOSEVELT TO REPRESENTATIVE R. EWING THOMASON OF TEXAS, El Paso

HYDE PARK, NEW YORK, *August 9, 1939*

MY DEAR CONGRESSMAN THOMASON: I have been very glad to hear that you are active in the campaign in behalf of the "Big Bend National Park." I greatly hope that the acquisition of the necessary land will make it possible for the government very soon to establish it for the benefit of all of the people of the country.

I have heard so much of the wildness and the beauty of this still inaccessible corner of the United States and also of its important archeological remains that I very much hope that some day I shall be able to travel through it myself.

Furthermore, I feel sure that it will do much to strengthen the friendship and good neighborliness of the people of Mexico and the people of the United States.

Very sincerely yours,

[FRANKLIN D. ROOSEVELT]

FDR/DJ

[13:OF 6-P:CT]

934   STATEMENT BY ROOSEVELT ON HIS VETO OF AN ACT AFFECTING THE BOULDER DAM AREA

THE WHITE HOUSE, *August 10, 1939*

MEMORANDUM OF DISAPPROVAL: I am withholding my approval of S. 2, a bill, "authorizing the Secretary of the Interior to convey certain lands to the State of Nevada to be used for the purposes of a public park and recreation site and other public purposes."

This bill provides for the granting of more than 8,000 acres of Federally-owned land in the Boulder Dam-Lake Mead area to the State of Nevada. Eighty percent of this land is located within the boundaries of the Boulder Dam National Recreational Area, and the residue is immediately adjacent thereto. The entire tract is of national interest and value, both for the protection from pollution of the waters impounded in Lake Mead and for the enhancement of the recreational and scenic values created through the building of Boulder Dam.

Since the lands proposed to be conveyed are appurtenant to a project of national importance, their ownership and administration should be retained by the Federal Government. The transfer of control over these lands to a non-Federal agency necessarily would open the door to uses which might be at variance with the national interest in the Boulder Dam-Lake Mead region. All of the people of the United States have a paramount interest in Boulder Dam and its related facilities for water conservation and utilization. Likewise, they have a paramount interest in the outstanding recreational and scenic attractions of Lake Mead and the surrounding territory. The expenditure of Federal funds was the chief if not the only factor in producing these values, and the lands proposed to be conveyed are an integral part of them. In the light of these facts, I firmly believe the Boulder Dam-Lake Mead region in its entirety should continue to be administered uniformly by the Federal Government in the interest of the nation as a whole.

The area from which the proposed grant would be carved is endowed with many features that appear to make it worthy of consideration as a possible national park or monument site. Independently of this, the area is one which has been definitely set apart for Federal purposes and which is actively being used for these purposes. Not only is the control of Lake Mead essential to the operation of Boulder Dam, but also the recreational values of the region have attracted to the Lake thousands of visitors from all parts of the Union. The recreational use of this area is truly national in character. A grant of the reserved lands would consequently set an undesirable precedent for the grant of other public lands already in actual utilization by the Federal Government, as well as for the grant of lands which should be retained in Federal ownership because of their potential value to fill anticipated future needs. Were this grant to be made, involving as it does a region of national significance, the denial of other grants affecting lands reserved for national uses would be difficult.[1]

FRANKLIN D. ROOSEVELT

[W. H. PRESS RELEASES:M]

[368]

¹ Introduced by Senator Pittman (Nev.) on Jan. 4, 1939, this bill was unopposed in either House. In discussing it on June 13, Pittman said that the Secretary of the Interior had opposed its passage because he feared the proposed recreation area would cause pollution of the waters of Boulder Lake and that the area would be used for gambling and the sale of intoxicating drinks. This had been guarded against, Pittman said, by a committee amendment to the bill which imposed Interior Department regulations on the development of the area and provided for its return to Federal administration if these regulations were not observed (*Cong. Rec.*, 76th Cong., 1st sess., 84: 1, 64; 84: 7, 7072–7073).

935   ROOSEVELT TO SENATOR KEY PITTMAN OF NEVADA

HYDE PARK, NEW YORK, *August 10, 1939*

DEAR KEY: I feel very badly that I have to veto the Boulder Dam State Park Bill but I do so for the real reason that if we once start this policy we will have to go through with it with national parks, national monuments, national forests, etc. etc. I know of at least ten or twelve bills that will be introduced at the next session covering every section of the country and based on my signature of this bill of yours.

I know of your great interest in this particular state park and I would gladly sign the bill if I did not greatly fear the precedent created thereby.¹

F. D. R.

[13:OF 6–P:T:COPY]

¹ The White House copy of this letter has not been found; the text here printed is derived from a letter of Pittman to Roosevelt of Aug. 12, 1939 (OF 6–P).

936   HAROLD D. SMITH, DIRECTOR, BUREAU OF THE BUDGET, TO MARVIN H. McINTYRE, SECRETARY TO THE PRESIDENT

WASHINGTON, D. C., *Aug. 10, 1939*

MY DEAR MR. McINTYRE: On August 6, 1939, you advised me that S. 1802 "Authorizing construction of water conservation and utilization projects in the Great Plains and arid and semi-arid areas of the United States" had been received at the White House, and requested reports and recommendations as to the approval of the bill.

I have referred facsimiles of the enrolled enactment to the Department of Agriculture, the Department of the Interior, the Federal Works Agency and the National Resources Planning Board, and I am attaching their replies.¹

The purpose of this legislation is to authorize appropriations for the rehabilitation of both the people and the land in the "Dust Bowl" and in similar arid and semi-arid regions, through the construction of water conservation projects. In these areas of inadequate rainfall the water supply of flowing streams is limited in quantity and in many localities the conditions are such that the cost of irrigation works is too great to be financed by the water users themselves or to be fully repaid if construction were undertaken under the reclamation laws of the United States.

On June 14, 1938, the President transmitted to Congress an estimate for a direct appropriation in the amount of $5,000,000 for similar purposes. As passed by Congress the money was to come from the appropriation of $1,425,000,000 made available to the Works Progress Administration by Section 1 (1) of the Emergency Relief Appropriation Act of 1938, and a limit of $50,000 was established for expenditure for any one project. This limitation made the appropriation inoperative. On March 4, 1939, a similar estimate for a direct appropriation of $5,-000,000 was transmitted to Congress, and the appropriation was included in the Interior Department Appropriation Act, 1940. In the discussion of the estimate in Congress, emphasis was laid the non-existence of statutory authorization for the appropriation.

On June 14, 1939 the President addressed a letter to the Secretary of the Interior outlining the procedure to be adopted by the interested Federal agencies to effectuate the purpose of the appropriation. Copies of this communication were forwarded on the same day to the Chairman of the National Resources Committee, the Secretary of Agriculture and the Administrator of the Works Progress Administration.

The bill in its present form enacts a relatively permanent policy along lines which are now the subject of experimentation. That policy was recommended for the Northern Great Plains only and is being tested only in that area. As indicated in the attached letter of the National Resources Planning Board. this permanent authorization for all arid and semiarid states would appear to be somewhat premature. However, it undoubtedly would be easier to obtain desired amendments in a later session of Congress than to obtain the reenactment of the entire bill. Moreover, some of the objections raised to the bill in the attached letters are not to me particularly appealing.

On the whole, it seems to me that the considerations in favor of the approval of the bill outweigh the objectionable features; and I accordingly recommend approval of the bill.

I am enclosing for the attention of the President, for his consideration in connection with this bill, a letter to me on this subject from Secretary Ickes.

Very truly yours,

HAROLD D. SMITH

[*Notation*: AS] JHR ²
[*Notation*: A] Approved 8/11/39
[13: BUDGET BUREAU ENROLLED BILLS: TS]

¹ All the enclosures are printed below except a letter from Federal Works Administrator Carmody to Smith, Aug. 8, 1939. This merely stated that the Federal Works Administration had no objection to the proposed bill.

² James H. Rowe, Jr., Administrative Assistant to the President.

937 [*Enclosure 1*] CHARLES W. ELIOT, DIRECTOR, NATIONAL RESOURCES PLANNING BOARD, TO F. J. BAILEY, ASSISTANT DIRECTOR, BUREAU OF THE BUDGET

WASHINGTON, *Aug. 9, 1939*

MY DEAR MR. BAILEY: In the absence of the members of the Board, I am submitting the following comments by members of our staff. It must be clearly understood that in view of the necessity for haste, all statements submitted represent the views of those named and are in no sense an official action of the Board.

The enrolled enactment S–1802, to which you refer in your letter of August 7, would establish new irrigation policy on a basis having many strong as well as weak points.

The principal arguments against the enactment at this time are:

1. It fails to enact the integrated policy for irrigation development recommended by the Northern Great Plains Committee (report dated October 14, 1938) in that:

(a) No provision is made for the cooperation of the Department of Agriculture or other interested Federal agencies in project planning.

(b) The Department of Agriculture likewise is given no responsibility for determining reimbursable cost or for operating completed projects.

(c) Responsibility for allocation of funds is vested in the Secretary of the Interior rather than the President.

(d) No authority is given for the acquisition of agricultural land for re-sale or lease as a means to controlling and guiding project development.

2. It enacts a relatively permanent policy along lines which are now the subject of experiment for the first time under authority of the Interior Appropriation Act for 1940. That policy was recommended for the Northern Great Plains only, and it is being tested only in that area. In that respect this permanent authorization for all semiarid and arid states would appear to be premature.

3. No additional funds will be needed for this type of work until the fiscal year 1941.

The chief arguments in favor of the enactment are:

1. The deficiencies in the bill as passed by the Congress probably could be remedied at the next session.

2. It probably would be far easier to obtain those desired amendments than to re-enact an entire bill in the event that S-1802 were to be disapproved. Better half a loaf than none at all.

3. Enactment and approval at this session would make possible the consideration of a request for additional funds as a part of the regular budget-making procedure. Disapproval of the enactment would render the appropriation of additional funds exceedingly difficult until such time as permanent authorization of that type of work might be obtained.

4. Disapproval would have a disheartening effect upon those who have sought to effectuate the Northern Great Plains Committee recommendations.

The Department of the Interior advances the further argument that approval of the enactment would strengthen the Department's hand in dealing with threats of Department of Agriculture encroachment under the Water Facilities Act of 1937; if the limitation of $50,000 per project were to be removed in the Department of Agriculture appropriation bill, that department could construct projects of the type contemplated in S-1802 on such conditions of reimbursability as the Secretary of Agriculture might require.

Mr. Barrows, Chairman of our Northern Great Plains Committee, recommends approval of the bill even though it has the above-mentioned deficiencies. As previously noted the members of the Board have had no opportunity to take a position in the matter. Personally, I am inclined to recommend approval, with an accompanying statement by the President pointing out the deficiencies in the act and informing the Congress of his intention to request appropriate action at the next session to bring the authorization in line with an integrated water and land policy.

As a matter of record I am returning without comment your letter of August 1, 1939 transmitting a proposed report of the Secretary of Agriculture on S-1802 and HR-6613, before enactment.

Sincerely yours,

CHARLES W. ELIOT

[13:BUDGET BUREAU ENROLLED BILLS:TS]

938   [*Enclosure 2*] MILBURN L. WILSON, ACTING SECRETARY OF AGRICULTURE, TO HAROLD D. SMITH

WASHINGTON, *August 9, 1939*

DEAR MR. SMITH: This is in reply to Mr. Bailey's letter of August 8, asking for our comments on the enrolled enactment S. 1802, authorizing construction of water conservation and utilization projects in the Great Plains and arid and semiarid areas of the United States.

This bill is apparently an attempt to provide a permanent legislative basis for carrying into effect certain recommendations of the Northern

Great Plains Committee of the National Resources Planning Board. Those recommendations were transmitted to the President on October 4, 1938. The bill, however, falls far short of supplying the necessary legislative authority.

The Report of the Northern Great Plains Committee outlined a rehabilitation program for the Northern Great Plains to promote permanent improvement in the economic conditions of the area by coordinating the efforts of the various agencies working there. The recommendations of the Report proposed a new land development and irrigation policy designed to make a maximum use of funds spent for relief purposes in the areas concerned, including measures for better land use, rural rehabilitation, and coordinated planning and action on the part of the various Federal agencies. It was contemplated that all costs above reimbursable costs would be supplied from relief funds with preference given to areas of greater relief load.

The essence of the recommended program may be summarized in the following four points:

1. Detailed planning of the developmental program should be undertaken cooperatively by the various Federal agencies which will participate in construction, settlement, and guidance of settlers, and by local planning agencies; and the over-all planning program should be coordinated by the National Resources Planning Board.

2. Construction of new irrigation projects should be by the Bureau of Reclamation or such other Federal agency as may best be adapted to the work involved, the engineering plans for all relatively large projects to be subject to approval by the Bureau of Reclamation, and the plans for all projects to be subject to certification by the Department of Agriculture with respect to their agricultural soundness.

3. Responsibility for operation of completed projects should rest with the Department of Agriculture, and settlers should be required to repay the costs of construction and operation to the extent of their ability as determined jointly by the Bureau of Reclamation and the Department of Agriculture.

4. The Department of Agriculture should assume responsibility for acquisition of agricultural lands, for locating on the projects persons in need of resettlement, for collecting repayments, and for guiding settlers in matters of farm practice.

You will recall that the Department of the Interior, the Department of Agriculture, and the WPA are today under administrative regulations of the President cooperating effectively and successfully in the administration of the first few projects of this type to be undertaken in the Northern Great Plains in accordance with the recommendations of the Northern Great Plains Committee. This is being done under the $5,000,000 appropriation contained in the current Interior Department Appropriation Bill.

The enrolled bill S. 1802 does not, however, provide for the program summarized above. It does authorize the Secretary of the Interior to construct water conservation and utilization projects in the Great Plains and arid and semiarid areas of the United States. It does authorize the use of WPA and CCC labor and materials. It does not, however, provide for cooperation between the Departments of Agriculture, Interior, and other agencies in planning the general program or specific projects; it does not provide that the Department of Agriculture shall be responsible for certification of agricultural feasibility of proposed projects; it does not provide for operation of completed projects by the Department of Agriculture; it does not adequately provide for administration of the land acquisition and settlement phases of the projects, or for guiding settlers in matters of farm practice.

The Department of the Interior today has authority to construct large scale reclamation projects under the reclamation laws; the Department of Agriculture today has authority to construct small water facilities in the arid and semiarid areas in aid of proper land use. To bridge the gap between these two programs was a chief purpose of the Report of the Northern Great Plains Committee. S. 1802, as indicated above, falls far short of enabling that bridging to be accomplished. We are satisfied that it is no part of the intention of the Department of the Interior to attempt under the provisions of S. 1802 to duplicate the type of work carried on by the Department of Agriculture under the Water Facilities Act of 1937. The present problem, therefore, is to determine how the recommendations of the Northern Great Plains Committee may be best carried out.

If the President should decide to approve the bill, then at least the following steps would appear to be necessary:

1. The President may wish to issue appropriate administrative instructions to the various departments to provide for the necessary coordinated planning, execution and administration.

2. These administrative regulations of the President cannot, however, cure the defect of S. 1802, which arises from its omission to give express authority to the Department of Agriculture to cooperate in these projects or to receive part of the funds to be appropriated for effectuating its provisions. Therefore, a further necessary step is to seek appropriate amendment of S. 1802. The way in which S. 1802 needs to be amended to accomplish the purposes of the Northern Great Plains Committee Report is set forth in the Department's proposed report to the House Committee on Irrigation and Reclamation on the companion bill, H. R. 6613. This proposed report was sent by the Department to the Bureau of the Budget on July 26, 1939.

Sincerely,

M. L. WILSON

[13:BUDGET BUREAU ENROLLED BILLS:TS]

939 [*Enclosure 3*] Harold L. Ickes, Secretary of the Interior,
to Harold D. Smith

Washington, *August 8, 1939*

My dear Mr. Smith: In addition to the formal report on S. 1802, which is enclosed, I am writing you this special letter.

The Water Facilities Act which is the Act of August 28, 1937, 50 *Statutes at Large* 869, in effect set up in the Department of Agriculture another Bureau of Reclamation. My solicitor advised me at the time that by this Act broader powers were granted even than the Bureau of Reclamation has. This Act was slipped through the Congress. My own people were asleep at the switch or we would have had it objected to when it passed on the unanimous consent calendar. I strongly urged the President to veto this bill and, confidentially, he has told me since that it should have been vetoed. However, he signed it.

The author of that bill in the House was Congressman Marvin Jones, Chairman of the Committee on Agriculture. Recently he has told me that the Act was a mistake and, personally, he is in favor of the powers given to the Department of Agriculture under that Act being transferred to the Bureau of Reclamation. However, he did not want to antagonize Agriculture by espousing an amendment to S. 1802 that would have had this effect. Marvin Jones is not satisfied with the way the Water Facilities Act has worked out.

It is my purpose to suggest to the President that all powers under the Water Facilities Act be transferred to the Bureau of Reclamation under the Reorganization Act. Unless this is done there will continue in the Federal Government two bureaus endowed with substantially the same powers.

To come now to S. 1802. This Act was supported by Marvin Jones among others. If this bill becomes a law, as I have recommended, it will further tend to concentrate in this department the power that heretofore has been exercised by the Bureau of Reclamation. If this Act is vetoed it will serve to continue the uncertainty and confusion which have existed ever since the Water Facilities Act became a law.[1]

Sincerely yours,

Harold L. Ickes

[13:BUDGET BUREAU ENROLLED BILLS:TS]

[1] S. 1802 was introduced March 14, 1939, by Senator Wheeler (Mont.), passed by the Senate August 1 and by the House August 4. In the House the bill was amended by the removal of a section which called for cooperation of the Interior Department with the Agriculture Department and other Federal agencies in the construction, operation and maintenance of projects. The Senate accepted the House amendments on August 5 (*Cong. Rec.*, 76th Cong., 1st sess., 84: 3, 2689; 84: 9, 9464; 84: 10, 10670, 11109, 11144). The act was approved Aug. 11, 1939 (53 *Stat.* 1418); see statement of that date, *post*, 941.

THE WHITE HOUSE, *August 11, 1939*

MEMORANDUM OF DISAPPROVAL: I have withheld my approval of
H. R. 3959 "An Act to authorize the Secretary of the Interior to dispose
of recreational demonstration projects, and for other purposes." [1]

While the objective of this legislation is good, I am inclined to think
that certain safeguards should at least be studied at the next session of
the Congress.

It should probably be made more clear that equitable arrangements
with local communities taking over such recreational projects should involve the Federal Government in no legal or moral commitments.

There should probably be a provision allowing departments of the
government to take over for their purposes such projects as it seems desirable for the Interior Department to part with.

Probably the approval of the President should be given to any transfers
of these properties to local communities or other departments as this is
the general rule in similar cases.

(Signed) FRANKLIN D. ROOSEVELT

[W. H. PRESS RELEASES: M]

[1] Printed, *Cong. Rec.,* 76th Cong., 1st sess., 84: 10, 10905.

941   "STATEMENT BY THE PRESIDENT ON APPROVING S. 1802"

[WASHINGTON] *August 11, 1939*

"An Act authorizing construction of water conservation and utilization projects in the Great Plains and arid and semi-arid areas of the
United States."

This bill is better than no bill at all, though it has in it a number of
deficiencies and also ~~evidence~~ *experimentation* on a national scale ~~of~~ *in*
what is being done today in a rather limited area in the northwestern
drought area.

These deficiencies will be called to the attention of the Congress at
its next session.[1]

FRANKLIN D. ROOSEVELT

[13: BUDGET BUREAU ENROLLED BILLS: TS]

[1] The changes in this draft (presumably a Budget Bureau draft) are in Roosevelt's
hand. The statement was issued as a White House press release on Aug. 11, 1939.
See below.

HYDE PARK, N. Y., *August 11, 1939*

MEMORANDUM . . . I have signed S. 1802 and suggest that National Resources Planning Board and the Budget work out the necessary cooperation of all departments and agencies in order that Congress may be advised in January in regard to deficiencies in this bill.

F. D. R.

[13:OF 177:CTS]

943   ROOSEVELT TO JOHN H. BAKER, EXECUTIVE DIRECTOR, NATIONAL ASSOCIATION OF AUDUBON SOCIETIES, New York City

WASHINGTON, *August 12, 1939*

MY DEAR MR. BAKER: I am glad to have your letter [1] reporting the stalemate which has occurred with respect to the State of Florida's share of the funds necessary for joint study of the Everglades water supply situation by the Soil Conservation Service and the special fire district of the state.

It is my understanding that the Bureau of Biological Survey, the National Park Service, and the United States Geological Survey, each had a representative at the Okeechobee hearing and that these specialists are preparing a joint report to the Secretary of the Interior on the problem. As soon as the report has been received and reviewed, I will be in a position to take such action as may seem appropriate. I agree with you as to the urgency of action in this matter, and I will cooperate so far as possible in expediting this joint study.

The interest and cooperation of your organization in the early solution of the Everglades water supply problem is deeply appreciated by myself and all the Federal conservation groups with which you are working.[2]

Sincerely yours,

[FRANKLIN D. ROOSEVELT]

[13:OF 378:CT]

[1] July 28, 1939 (OF 378). Baker said that the adoption of a plan for the maintenance of a minimum water table in the Everglades was being delayed by the inaction of the governor, and that "any pressure that might be brought on Governor Cone to expedite his necessary action would be deeply appreciated."

[2] Drafted by the Interior Department.

944 ROOSEVELT TO SENATOR CHARLES W. TOBEY OF NEW
HAMPSHIRE

WASHINGTON [*August 24, 1939*]

MY DEAR SENATOR TOBEY: I have received your letter of August 4,
transmitting a copy of a letter from Mr. Thomas D. Cabot, President
of the Appalachian Mountain Club, concerning a rumor that I may be
asked to sign a proclamation placing the White Mountain National
Forest in New Hampshire under the jurisdiction of the National Park
Service as a national monument.[1]

The National Park Service and the Forest Service are making joint
studies in forest areas throughout the country which are important for
public recreational purposes. No recommendations have reached me,
although I expect to be advised well in advance of any changes contemplated. This is one of the surveys of national resources in which
I am greatly interested.

I shall not approve any changes in the national forests which are adverse to the public interest.[2]

Very sincerely yours,

[FRANKLIN D. ROOSEVELT]

[*Notation*:A] 8/24/39

[13:OF 1–C:CT]

[1] Cabot (Aug. 1, 1939, OF 1–C), said he believed the Appalachian Mountain
Club would oppose any change in the status of the White Mountain National Forest
because it would result in a large increase in expense of administration without
benefit to anyone.
[2] Drafted by the Interior Department.

945 SENATOR GEORGE W. NORRIS OF NEBRASKA TO ROOSEVELT

WAUPACA, WISCONSIN, *September 9, 1939*

MY DEAR MR. PRESIDENT: For some time, even before I left Washington, there came to my attention rumors of an indefinite nature that
the next order you issued under the Reorganization Act the TVA would
be placed under some other department of government or at least some
of its branches would be taken away from the TVA and placed under
other bureaus or departments. I paid but little attention to these rumors
because I took it for granted that the TVA Act, one of the marked operations of your Administration that had proved so successful, that had withstood the fire of criticism of the most malicious and unjust propaganda
ever instituted against any part of your Administration and had come
through unscathed, unblemished, purified, and fully justified, would not
be changed or modified by you. The rumors, however, have persisted,
and although I do not know of any I consider well founded, neverthe-

less they have caused me some worry, and while my fears may be ground-less, yet I have thought it best to write you concerning them.

I would never have supported the Reorganization bill, if I had had any idea or belief that the TVA was going to be modified in any way. From its very birth, it has been fought by the most powerful organized monopoly of human greed that has ever been put together by human hands. It has withstood these onslaughts, and has been victorious in the courts. History will show that it is one of the greatest and noblest of all the under-takings of your Administration. The law intended that it should be in-dependent of any department or any bureau of government. It was intended by this means to avoid the changes that might come about for partisan political reasons.

The board was to be appointed entirely upon merit, with an express stipulation that the members should profess a belief in the principles in-volved in the TVA Act, so that those who administered the law were to be selected entirely because of their ability to handle the subject matter covered by the law and therefore would not be handicapped or interfered with by Cabinet changes or by other officials who had been appointed for political reasons, other than the very merits of the Act itself.

Admittedly, it was a unique law. Politicians criticized it because it placed beyond their influence any possibility of interference which would disrupt or dismantle the organization set up under the law. Rumors of some agitation that have come to me indicate there is an attempt on the part of other departments to take over part of the work of the TVA. For instance, it is argued that some of the duties of TVA ought to be in the Department of Agriculture. That others ought to be in the De-partment of the Interior, while still others ought to be in the War Depart-ment, either directly under the heads of these departments, or under the heads of bureaus connected with the departments. It is argued, also, that the budget, as it applies to TVA, should go through one or more of the various departments. Any of these changes would injure, and if enough changes were made, would ruin the real objects of TVA.

The Act is based primarily upon the power of Congress to control navigation. Navigation is modified, increased, improved, and perfected by the control of flood waters. Flood water, if uncontrolled, would destroy navigation a great portion of the year. Part of the time, the water would be too high. At other times, the water would be too low. Therefore, the control of flood waters has a direct effect upon naviga-tion. These floods, in turn, are modified and controlled by erosion of the sloping hillsides of river valleys. If nothing is done to prevent erosion, the fertile soil of the valleys will be washed into the lakes made by the dams, filling them up, and, in time, rendering them useless.

This in the end would not only ruin navigation, but would also despoil the entire country of that fertility of the soil upon which, in the

[379]

last analysis, everything depends. Therefore, erosion is intimately connected with navigation and flood control. Reforestation of denuded lands is necessary to save and perpetuate the capacity of reservoirs to hold water. It would follow, if this is done, that the soil which would thus be perserved ultimately might become one of the greatest things to be accomplished and brought about through the carrying out of the TVA Act. The manufacture of fertilizer has a direct effect upon the preservation and reclamation of already denuded portions of the country. If, by fertilization, the necessary plants can be induced to grow, to impede the flow of water and hold it back long enough to prevent the filling up of the reservoirs, then fertilizer is directly connected with and under the jurisdiction of the Act. The fact that fertilizer accomplishes other things, also, does not detract from this, but only adds to it and makes it the more essential that it should not be interfered with.

The building of these dams makes it possible to generate large quantities of electric power. If this were not done, one of the valuable resources of Nature would be dissipated and wasted. It follows that this power generated at these dams, to prevent its monopolization by private monopoly, should be carried to a proper place of sale on transmission lines. The sale of this power is going to pay for more than one-half of the cost of constructing these dams. And because this electricity so developed goes into the homes of the people, bringing happiness and comfort where they were unknown before, this is another reason why the sale of this power should not be permitted to pass into the hands of monopolistic organizations based upon a desire only for human greed.

The money that must be appropriated by Congress must be based upon a combination of all these factors, as well as other factors which I have not mentioned. While the Act provides that the cost of these dams should be allocated to flood control, navigation, and power, yet it is an impossibility, mathematically, to draw a line where the division should be.

It would be ruinous if these different activities of the TVA were to be divided up among the various departments and bureaus of the government. Without any question, there would come a time when a quarrel would arise over the jurisdiction of these activities, as to who should control this particular activity, and who should control that. The Act places all of these powers and duties under the jurisdiction of a board whose members are appointed because of their ability to handle these intermingled powers and duties. If you undertake to separate them, to place them under other jurisdictions, you have taken the first step which will ultimately interfere with the success of the entire undertaking and, in time, bring the TVA to ruin. If any separation of these powers and duties is contemplated by friends of the undertaking, it will result in throwing into the lap of the enemies of TVA the very possibilities they have been trying to bring about.

In the recent congressional investigation, the minority, composed of the bitterest enemies the TVA has ever had, suggested some of these very things. They have given up the idea of fighting the TVA fairly upon reasons originally given. The courts at last have decided in favor of TVA in all these controverted issues. Now, the enemy is trying to "chisel"—to take away this power and that power, none of which can be taken away without injury to all. The object of the enemies of TVA now seems to be to try to divide up the duties of the TVA among various departments, bureaus, and offices, which will bring about conflicts and injurious quarrels and claims as to jurisdiction. The TVA has passed unscathed through the most tremendous opposition that has ever been presented against any activity of the government. It is successful in its work. It is working in perfect harmony with all the departments and bureaus of the government. It has won its cases in the Supreme Court of the United States. There is no jar or conflict anywhere in its organization. Its great problems are now coming to be realized and appreciated. The men in charge are selected for the particular duties of the office. The organization at the present time is one of the most harmonious, one of the most successful in the federal government.

Partisan politics has been excluded. It has been a hard, tedious, laborious fight, but it has succeeded, and it would be the height of folly now to curtail its activities in any particular. It could not be done without injury to the whole. It was established as an independent activity and it ought to remain so.

I hear claims made by enemies of TVA that the civil service laws applying to other departments ought to be extended to TVA. I have always been a believer in civil service, not because it is perfect, but because it is an improvement, a great improvement, over the old spoils' system. But it is not perfect, and the TVA Act undertook to set up a method of civil service superior to that of civil service law. In that respect, it has been successful. The TVA has a better civil service than any other department or bureau of the government today. It is the one civil service that comes more nearly being perfect, it seems to me, than any other that has ever been attempted or attained.

From the very beginning it seemed to me perfectly clear that if civil service laws applied fully to TVA, there would be grave danger of the enemies of that institution, paid by monopolistic private power companies, succeeding in getting into the civil service and, through it, into the organization, thus honeycombing TVA with its enemies. This has been attempted, but it has not succeeded. If the general Civil Service Act had applied to TVA, it would have succeeded in many particulars. But the TVA is acting in perfect harmony with the Civil Service Commission. Wherever the Civil Service Act can be applied, it is applied. It has been applied, and the most thorough investigation has vindicated TVA in its action. In respect to civil service, it stands out preeminently above anything ever put into force by the federal government.

The only thing to do now, it seems to me, is to let it alone. This organization, under your Administration, has reached the highest type of perfection ever attained. It should not be modified, and should not be changed.

Nothing in any investigation of any charges made against TVA has sustained any claim that there has been anything wrong in any particular. Politicians, friendly and unfriendly, have tried to have appointments made upon partisan political grounds. They have failed. Even those who have tried to get their friends into the organization have generally admitted that TVA is one place in the federal government where machine politics is absolutely excluded and kept out.

I dislike to burden you with this long letter, when you have so many official duties to which you must give attention, but I do beg of you that you take the time to read everything I have said. I do not want this shining light of your Administration to be blighted or dimmed. Let it stand, Mr. President. Let it go on. The fruits of its accomplishments will come, many of them, long after you and I have passed away. Already, it stands as a shining example of efficiency and of humanity. It has already brought its blessings to millions of our people, and, regardless of politics, those who have stood aloof, who are disinterested, when they have been fair and honest, have been moved to praise, and to congratulate you and the country upon the success of this great undertaking.[1]

Sincerely yours,

G. W. NORRIS

[13:OF 42:TS]

---

[1] With the letter here printed is a telegram from Norris to Roosevelt, Sept. 9, 1939, asking him to defer any action on the TVA until his letter had been received. An accompanying note from Budget Director Smith to White House Executive Clerk Rudolph Forster, Oct. 4, 1939, stated that the President had handed him the letter and telegram and that he was returning them "inasmuch as the matter mentioned therein has been taken care of."

946   "REPORT OF CONFERENCE OF NATIONAL RESOURCES PLAN-
         NING BOARD WITH THE PRESIDENT AT THE WHITE HOUSE"

WASHINGTON, *October 17, 1939, 11:40 a. m.*

Present: The President, Frederic A. Delano, Chairman, Charles E. Merriam, George F. Yantis

[*Excerpt*] The discussion was based on the letter to the President by Chairman Delano dated September 5, 1939, which letter enumerated projects.[1]

The President's first comment was a general one to the effect that he did not wish the Resources Planning Board or its members to participate as members of interdepartmental committees in view of the fact that it would be his plan to refer the reports of such committees and other agencies to the National Resources Planning Board, and that members of the Board should not be involved in the formation of reports which would be referred to the Board for consideration. He also stated that the new budget for the Executive Office would include the National Resources Planning Board and that this Executive budget would be presented as a unit.

The President then turned to the list of projects or studies enumerated in the letter, commencing on page 2 thereof. He read the headings of the first four items, to wit: "Public Works, Water Resources, Land Planning, and Minerals," and with a brief comment on the content of each proposed study as indicated in the letter, gave rather emphatic approval and clearance to each. No question was left as to whether or not he approved any one of the four items mentioned. Summing up the items, his general comment was "Grand!"

On Item 5, Science, his statement was somewhat different. He seemed particularly concerned that the NRPB coordinate its work in this field with the work of other departments or agencies of the Government which were undertaking similar or related work. He commented particularly on an elaborate study being developed or proposed in the field of aeronautics and referred to it as embracing a body of study which might have a much broader implication than the comparatively narrow field indicated, and seemed to be concerned that the work of the committee take cognizance of the study with a view to proper coordination and the fullest use of research facilities which were available. With these injunctions, he also cleared item 5.

As to Item 6, Energy Resources and Power Policy, he dwelt at some length on the interest, activity, operating and regulatory authority of the Department of the Interior in this field, especially as relates to oil, coal and water power; and indicated that overlapping or possible conflict between the two lines of study should be avoided; that much work would head up through the Department of the Interior and would come to the President through that Department, then back to the NRPB for over-all consideration and report.

It was suggested by the President that the study made by the Board should not be an elaborate and detailed one involving any large staff or great expenditure of money. It was stated to the President that as the plan relating to Energy Resources and Power Policy had developed in the committee, it indicated a limited study, with observance of studies in the field through a very small staff, probably Dr. Watkins; and that the plan proposed seemed exactly in line with the President's expressed wishes, in which suggestion he heartily concurred.[2]

GEORGE F. YANTIS

[13:OF 1092:T]

[1] In a letter to Roosevelt of Aug. 25, 1939 (OF 1092), the National Resources Planning Board said that it planned to continue the special studies of the National Resources Committee, including "the preparation of the six-year Program of Public Works, further efforts to formulate a National Water Policy, the inventory of publicly owned land and the formulation of a policy on public acquisition of land and tax delinquency problems, further studies of consumption habits, and continued analyses of the problems of full use of our resources . . ." In the September 5 letter (OF 1092) some revision of projects was made in light of the international crisis: river and harbor improvements were emphasized in water resources planning, and the possible effects of war on land use were emphasized in land planning.

[2] Omitted are discussions of projected studies of transportation, taxation and national income, relief and reemployment, and industrial-economic problems.

947   ROOSEVELT TO SENATOR KEY PITTMAN OF NEVADA

WASHINGTON, *November 16, 1939*

MY DEAR KEY: I have received your letters of August 12 and 14 explaining in detail your reaction to my veto of your Bill S. 2.[1] A study has been made of all the statements you have presented in favor of the bill, as well as those which have been made in opposition to it.

I feel confident that the reversal of my position would mean the establishment of a precedent which could be used effectively by selfish interests against the integrity of Federal reclamation and park areas throughout the country.

From the viewpoint of national use and usefulness, the Boulder Dam National Recreational Area is, I am convinced, in the same class with the national parks and national monuments. The creation of Lake Mead, through the construction of Boulder Dam, has resulted in great material benefits for nearby towns and, of course, for the contiguous States. It would appear that the State of Nevada is particularly fortunate in having a portion of such an unusual project within its border, a project which the Federal Government is developing in accordance with public requirements and from a national point of view.

Furthermore, the National Park Service plans to construct a road connecting the Hemingway Wash development area with the State WPA road, graded to the head of Las Vegas Wash. This road would serve as a lake shore scenic loop road. Visitors driving to the area from the West could come in over one highway, enjoy a lake shore scenic drive, and return by the other highway, or vice versa. The National Park Service also proposes to develop a small beach in Las Vegas Wash for the residents of the contiguous area. It appears to me that these proposed developments, which could be initiated under appropriations for the fiscal year 1941, would serve all the needs of the local people who have been pressing you for a State park.[2]

I appreciate and reciprocate the cordial spirit with which your letters were written and remain,

Very sincerely yours,

[FRANKLIN D. ROOSEVELT]

[13:OF 6–P:CT]

[1] In his letter of August 12 (OF 6–P), Pittman said that Congress should have been permitted to decide the issue, that in such arbitrary withdrawals from use of public land the Western states were discriminated against, and that the Secretary of the Interior had been arbitrary in recommending the veto. In his August 14 letter (OF 6–P), he reviewed the history of the vetoed bill, denied that any danger of pollution existed, and said that he knew of no bills of the sort mentioned by the President.

[2] (Drafted by the Interior Department.) Answered *post*, 950.

948 ROOSEVELT TO HENRY A. WALLACE, SECRETARY OF AGRICULTURE

[WASHINGTON, *November 16, 1939*]

SEC. AGRIC.: Item 80—in budget for '41.   Cooperative Distribution of Forest Planting Stock—$100,000.

Can I get for nothing trees for a bare hillside at Warm Springs—For the Warm Springs Foundation?[1]

F. D. R.

HM
[13:PPF 76:T:COPY]

[1] According to correspondence accompanying this memorandum, it appears that the Forest Service supplied the trees.

949 ROOSEVELT TO THE SOCIETY OF AMERICAN FORESTERS

[WASHINGTON] *November 18, 1939*

To THE SOCIETY OF AMERICAN FORESTERS: Natural resources such as soils, forests, and forage are sources of necessities of life, and of employment and income.   We have used these resources for three hundred years, but we have also thoughtlessly abused them.

The time has come when we must redouble our efforts to combat this abuse as definitely and as vigorously as we combat other insidious enemies within our borders.   Through united and democratic and vigorous action we must now build up our natural resources, and keep them continuously and fully productive.   For, basic in peace as well as in war, they are vital to the social and economic life of our people **and our Nation.**

As fellow foresters, and fellow members of the Society of American Foresters, you know that I have a deep and abiding interest in forest conservation. You know that when I first asked Congress to provide for the Civilian Conservation Corps I was convinced that forest lands offered one source of worthwhile work, noncompetitive with industry, for large numbers of our unemployed.

You know, too, that in March 1938 I recommended to the Congress an immediate study of the Nation's forest problem, and that Congress is now making such a study.[1] I still believe, as I said in that message, that the forest problem is part of the broad problem of modern agriculture, that it is common to every section of the country, and that definite action should be taken by an early Congress to solve it.

As a practical forester I feel that we may count on the Society of American Foresters, to whose members I extend cordial greetings, to help solve this problem in such a way that forest lands and forest resources will contribute their full share to social and economic structures of this country; to the security and stability of all our people; and to the internal as well as the external defenses of a great and truly democratic Nation.[2]

[13:PPF 1112:CT]

[1] *Ante,* 758.
[2] (Drafted by the Agriculture Department.) The Society of American Foresters was in convention in San Francisco.

950 SENATOR KEY PITTMAN OF NEVADA TO ROOSEVELT

WASHINGTON, D. C., *November 24, 1939*

MY DEAR MR. PRESIDENT: Upon my return to Washington today your letter of November 16th in further reply to my letters of August 12th and 14th was placed before me. I assume, of course, that the study that you refer to was made by the Park Service ...[1]

You urge that, "From the viewpoint of national use and usefulness, the Boulder Dam National Recreational Area is, I am convinced, in the same class with the national parks and national monuments." That raises a question of national policy that Congress has considered for many years and is even now more seriously considering. I do not have to argue to you that I am a conservationist, but for the record I reassert that I have actively supported in the Senate all conservation legislation. At one time the character of lands to be included in a national park was defined and definitely limited. Today through the wild stampede of the Park Service, it isn't a question of the character of the land or the scenery or the phenomena, but the area over which arbitrary bureaucratic authority can be exerted.

There are two kinds of conservation of public lands: namely, conservation without regard to use, and conservation with as full public use as is possible. National parks come into the first category; national forests within the second. Insofar as use by the public is concerned, there are far more opportunities offered in a national forest than there are in national parks.

The Boulder Canyon Reclamation Area is not, and never was intended as, a national park. The truth of it is that without authority of law, it's being administered by the Secretary of the Interior as a national park with all of the arbitrary restrictions appertaining to national parks.

There must be some limit to the creation of national parks for two reasons, if for no other. In the first place, the Government will not support them. And in the second place, there must be some taxable property left in a public land State.

From what I have stated, you must realize that it is my opinion that it's very doubtful whether Congress is going to appropriate the money necessary to carry out the development outlined by the Park Service at Mead Lake. I, of course, would like to see as full a development as possible of the recreation possibilities of Mead Lake. However, there are so many new parks, and so many Congressmen and Senators, that I think that the grabbing is going to be very difficult.

Of course, you haven't had an opportunity to study this question and I have been compelled to study it both on the ground and from the records. It is a matter totally insignificant in your administrative duties. It is a matter that may be of vital concern to me.

If you could only realize that this proposed State Park only takes in about 3 miles of a narrow gulch on the extreme edge of the Boulder Canyon Reclamation Area; that it is entirely off the route of travel by any boats on the Lake; that there is no reason for any boat carrying tourists or fishermen ever to go up this narrow Wash. There is nothing of scenic beauty in this neighborhood. About a fifth of the people of the State live adjacent to this little Wash. They desire to use it and improve it. The Park Service will have its hands full in attempting to handle the 250,000 people that go down to Hemingway Wash every year.

You will pardon me for stating that, in my opinion, I do not think there is any foundation for your statement in which you say: "I feel confident that the reversal of my position would mean the establishment of a precedent which could be used effectively by selfish interests against the integrity of Federal reclamation and park areas throughout the country." I do not think there is a similar situation in the United States. I know of no other case in which any State has asked the Federal Government to surrender any part of a national park for State park purposes. And yet we have passed many bills to grant public lands to States for State park purposes.

The whole truth about it is that your Secretary of the Interior, by reason of his character and disposition, would never consent that any jurisdiction should be taken away from him, and particularly through the efforts of the Senior Senator from Nevada.[2]

Sincerely yours,

KEY PITTMAN

[13:OF 6–P:TS]

[1] In the part here omitted, Pittman traced the course in the Congress of his bill to create a Nevada state park in the Boulder Dam National Recreational Area (S. 2), vetoed by Roosevelt on Aug. 10, 1939.

[2] Answered *post*, 954.

951　HAROLD L. ICKES, SECRETARY OF THE INTERIOR, TO ROOSEVELT

WASHINGTON, *December 7, 1939*

MY DEAR MR. PRESIDENT: You asked me to submit a statement on the proposed additions to Olympic National Park prior to the conference that you will hold on Saturday morning, and which I now understand Governor Martin will attend. I have asked Mr. Irving Brant, the man most familiar with this area, to prepare such a statement, and this I am enclosing. There is a summarized statement of about two and one-half pages and a more detailed one of greater length.[1]

Sincerely yours,

HAROLD L. ICKES

[13:OF 6–P:TS]

[1] The longer report mentioned in the covering letter is present. The conference of Dec. 9, 1939, was attended by Ickes, Wallace, Governor Clarence D. Martin of Washington, Benjamin H. Kizer, chairman of the Washington State Planning Council, and George F. Yantis of Washington, chairman of Region 9 of the National Resources Planning Board. Yantis, however, with Martin and Kizer, was present as a representative of the Washington lumber and pulp mill industries. Ickes says: "With maps before the President, we discussed the issues for all of an hour and a half. Henry Wallace was also there, but said nothing. I let Irving Brant carry the ball for Interior because he knows that area better than anyone in the National Park Service . . ." (*Ickes' Diary*, III, 86). No agreement was reached on park boundaries and Roosevelt asked that another meeting be held the next day (Sunday). He did not attend this meeting but Burlew reported on it in a letter of Dec. 12, 1939, *post*, 956.

WASHINGTON, D. C., *December 6, 1939*

MEMORANDUM FOR THE SECRETARY . . . ADDITIONS TO OLYMPIC NATIONAL PARK: Authorized size of park, 898,292 acres. Present size, 648,000 acres. Authorized additions, 250,292 acres.

Present recommended addition, 187,411 acres. Reserve for future addition of Queets corridor, ocean front and private holdings, 62,881 acres.

Recommended on west side of park (Bogachiel, Hoh, Queets), 50,625 acres. Attitude of State of Washington—opposed, because of timber value.

Recommended on north, east and south sides, 136,786 acres. Attitude of State of Washington—suggests addition of 233,320 acres, with reservation that present five-year period for prospecting and patenting mineral claims be extended to ten or fifteen years. (Note: Washington Conservation Director Fink has been giving newspaper interviews opposing Queets corridor and seashore strip, and probably thinks they are included. One of his arguments, that seashore park would prevent oil exploration, needs study for possible effect on land prices.)

Drawing the Boundaries—Additions are based on Brant-Tomlinson line of 1938, modified in 1939 to include slightly more in west, much less in east, thus creating a reserve for Queets corridor and seashore strip. Washington State people commonly speak of "Kittredge-Tiffany line," on account of a discussion of the Brant-Tomlinson line by Ross K. Tiffany (now deceased), secretary of Washington State Planning Council, and National Park Service Regional Director Kittredge, in 1938. They disagreed as to additions on west side, but jointly recommended increase elsewhere to 202,292 acres. Recommendation not agreed to by Secretary of the Interior.

On March 16, 1939, Tiffany wrote to Secretary of the Interior, opposing Bogachiel-Hoh Queets additions, and stating that "consent" of the State to additions elsewhere depended on additional protection for manganese mining.

On August 25, 1939, George F. Yantis, for State of Washington, reiterated Tiffany's objections to western additions, but accepted others without reservation.

Manganese—On October 6, 1939, Yantis wrote that "a new factor of importance has now developed. . . . It develops that in this area are large deposits of manganese," and these "highly important strategic minerals" should be left open for more than five years to location of claims.

Newness of the factor—same argument about manganese used to induce President Woodrow Wilson to cut down Mount Olympus National

Monument in 1915. Geological Survey has made two-year study of Olympic manganese. Findings in line with what was known before. Practically all manganiferous rocks inside proposed boundaries are of bementite, a silicate of manganese of no commercial value. Recent laboratory experiments show it can be extracted by roasting, leaching and electrolysis, but too expensive.

Bureau of Mines says vastly larger deposits of manganese carbonates in Montana and lowgrade manganese oxides in New Mexico can be worked more cheaply than bementite, if scarcity or price increase occurs. Two pockets of hausmannite (high grade manganese oxide) were found by Geological Survey in park area. One is a worked-out mine, both are on slopes above Lake Crescent which all parties want in park, both can be mined under prior rights. One-third of all manganese deposits recommended for further exploration lie in 93,000 acres not recommended by Secretary of the Interior, but proposed by State of Washington apparently to use up park acreage and block the Bogachiel-Hoh-Queets extensions.

State Lands—State owns 200,000 acres of pulp timber west of national forest and claims it is too small a unit for sustained yield lumbering, without Bogachiel-Hoh-Queets tracts. Actual purpose is to log federally owned saw timber in these valleys to subsidize a railroad to the State's pulp timber. When hemlock is at normal level, $7 to $8 per thousand, State timber cannot be marketed even with a subsidized railroad. When hemlock is stabilized at a price level that permits profitable logging, 200,000 acres form a large enough unit to amortize a logging railroad.

~~(When Queets corridor is added, easement for railroad and logging highways across it should be included in proclamation).~~

Pulp Timber Reserves—State claims all forest growing lands outside present park are needed to sustain present woodpulp industry. Not true. Hearings on first Wallgren bill showed Grays Harbor had pulp reserves for 500 years, Port Angeles for 70 years, at present mill capacity. Regrowth cycle of pulp timber is 50 years. Woodpulp industry on Peninsula limited by lack of fresh water for the sulphite process at saltwater harbors, not by lack of timber. Crown-Zellerbach Corporation wants to lumber Sitka spruces in national forest for whitener, but will soon shift anyway to chemical whitener because spruce is disappearing.

Forest Service report published in 1938 shows that Olympic Peninsula timber problem results from large-scale, clear-cutting of forests by high-lead methods since 1920.[1] Sixty-three per cent of Douglas fir forests cut 1920–1929 have totally failed to restock, compared with only 16 per cent that failed before 1920.

Parkways—Washington State suggests modified parkways along Bogachiel, Hoh and Queets rivers, with selective logging inside parkways and sustained-yield forestry in the forest on both sides. First trees cut would be the scenic giants for whose preservation the park is created. Cutting of these trees, individually, would destroy the "rain forest" of moss-hung maples. "Sustained-yield forestry" involves clearcutting of selected areas, and on the steep slopes of the Bogachiel and Hoh, it would wreck the valleys scenically and result in destructive erosion.

Recreational Value—State claims these western forests can't be used by public because underbrush is so dense that experienced woodsman can't penetrate it. This incorrectly applies to park areas what is true of "blowdowns" northwest of proposed additions. State submits timber-type maps to show timber in proposed western additions is similar to that immediately east. That is true of any dividing line; it takes no account of adequate amount, varying recreational uses by motorists (Hoh) and wilderness hikers (Bogachiel), or need to protect rivers and winter range of elk.

State claims from 8 to 15 miles of "rain forest" along these rivers is already in park. Figures obtained by classing as "rain forest" all land with precipitation above 120 inches, ignoring fact that rainfall increases with altitude but "rain forest" depends on heavy rainfall at low altitudes. Result is, State classes alpine meadows as "rain forest" and puts 12 miles of Bogachiel "rain forest" in park when in fact it is wholly outside.

IRVING BRANT

[13:OF 6–P:TS]

¹ Cf. *Report of the Chief of the Forest Service, 1938* (Washington, 1938).

953   ROOSEVELT TO SENATOR KEY PITTMAN OF NEVADA

WASHINGTON, *December 9, 1939*

MY DEAR KEY: Reference is made to your letter of November 9, concerning the protests from livestock operators in Nevada against alleged "evasion by Interior Department of Judicial determinations, and arbitrary and unreasonable action by the Secretary of the Interior." ¹ I have caused an inquiry to be made and find that the following are the circumstances out of which the protests apparently have arisen:

The Taylor Grazing Act was approved by me on June 28, 1934 (48 *Stat.* 1269). Section 1 of the act authorizes the Secretary of the Interior "in his discretion, by order to establish grazing districts or additions thereto and/or to modify the boundaries thereof * * *." Pursuant to this authorization Nevada Grazing District No. 1, in which it is assumed the protests to which you refer have arisen, was established by the Secretary of the Interior on April 8, 1935.

Section 2 of the act provides in part:

The Secretary of the Interior shall make provision for the protection, administration, regulation, and improvement of such grazing districts as may be created under the authority of the foregoing section, and he shall make such rules and regulations and establish such service, enter into such cooperative agreements, and do any and all things necessary to accomplish the purposes of this Act and to insure the objects of such grazing districts, namely, to regulate their occupancy and use, to preserve the land and its resources from destruction or unnecessary injury, to provide for the orderly use, improvement, and development of the range; * * * and any willful violation of the provisions of this Act or of such rules and regulations thereunder after actual notice thereof shall be punishable by a fine of not more than $500.

Section 3 provides in part:

That the Secretary of the Interior is hereby authorized to issue or cause to be issued permits to graze livestock on such grazing districts to such bona fide settlers, residents, and other stock owners as under his rules and regulations are entitled to participate in the use of the range, upon the payment annually of reasonable fees in each case to be fixed or determined from time to time * * * no permittee complying with the rules and regulations laid down by the Secretary of the Interior shall be denied the renewal of such permit, if such denial will impair the value of the grazing unit of the permittee, when such unit is pledged as security for any bona fide loan.

At the outset of the administration of the act it was realized that its purposes would be completely defeated by the immediate issuance of what might in effect be nonrevocable term permits, since it would be impossible immediately to accomplish the range survey program essential to the determination of the persons entitled to preferences under the act, and most applicants for grazing privileges presumably either had or would have occasion to pledge their grazing units as security for loans. Accordingly, F. R. Carpenter, who was then Director of Grazing, requested Solicitor Margold, of the Interior Department, to advise him whether temporary grazing licenses, rather than term permits, could be issued during the period necessary for the accumulation of the necessary factual information. The Solicitor replied that in his opinion the Secretary of the Interior had sufficient authority under the general provisions of section 2 of the act, quoted above, to pursue such a course. Temporary licenses thereupon were issued and are still being issued annually in 51 of the 53 grazing districts, the permit system having been inaugurated in one district in Colorado and authorized in one district in New Mexico. A nominal fee of 5 cents per animal unit month has been charged since 1936 for use of the range under these temporary licenses.

In June 1936 some 40 livestock operators in Nevada Grazing District No. 1 joined in a suit to restrain Regional Grazier L. R. Brooks, who is the local officer of the Grazing Service in charge of the State of Nevada, from collecting grazing fees, the contention being that the Secretary of the

Interior was authorized by the act to make a charge only for the term permits described in section 3. This suit was filed in the Nevada State court, no effort apparently having been made to test the validity of the rules in a suit against either the Secretary of the Interior or the Director of Grazing. The suit was removed to the Federal court but was remanded by Judge Yankwich on the ground of lack of jurisdiction in the Federal court, the fees of no individual plaintiff amounting to $3,000. *Dewar* v. *Brooks*, 16 Fed. Supp. 636.

The United States Attorney thereupon instituted an injunction suit in the Federal court in the name of the United States to restrain any further proceedings in the State court. On April 8, 1937, however, Judge Norcross dismissed this suit under section 265 of the Judicial Code (Tit. 28, U. S. Code, sec. 379). Judge Norcross further held that apart from the applicability of section 265, it could not be assumed that "the State Court will erroneously decide the question [whether the collection of fees is a valid exercise of power by the Secretary of the Interior] when presented to that Court." *United States* v. *Dewar*, 18 Fed. Supp. 981, 983. The United States Attorney recommended that no appeal be taken to the United States Circuit Court of Appeals and upon inquiry by the Attorney General the Acting Secretary of the Interior on June 7, 1937, concurred in this recommendation.

The State court suit thereupon proceeded in due course, final judgment being entered by default against the defendant regional grazier on April 20, 1939. The State court held that the Secretary of the Interior was not an indispensable party to the suit, notwithstanding that it is one to test the validity of administrative rules promulgated by him. This holding seems open to question, in view of numerous decisions to the contrary by Federal courts, including a decision rendered in December 1937 by the United States District Court for the District of Colorado in a similar suit to restrain the regional grazier from enforcing the grazing rules promulgated by the Secretary of the Interior (*Livingston* v. *Moore*, Equity No. 11063). In the *Livingston* case Judge Symes stated in part:

The defendant here is merely a subordinate official without authority to change them. This court is asked to make a construction of an act which may or may not be contrary to that already made by the Secretary. I don't think this can be done without the presence of the Secretary as a party.

The State court suit is now pending on appeal in the Nevada Supreme Court.

On February 14 the Acting Secretary of the Interior requested the Attorney General to institute suits in the United States District Court for the District of Nevada in the name of the United States against any plaintiffs in *Dewar* v. *Brooks* who were delinquent in the payment of grazing fees, some of the persons involved having paid all or part of their fees direct to the Government, notwithstanding their nominal participation in the litigation. An amount approximately equivalent to the delinquent fees had been deposited with the clerk of the State trial court as bond for the issuance of the temporary restraining order. This amount subsequently was returned to the parties upon the entry of the final judgment. The Attorney General directed the United States Attorney to institute such suits. Subsequently, at the request of the Director of Grazing the Secretary of the Interior directed the Division of Investigations to serve notices of violation on all persons found grazing in the district who were delinquent in the payment of their fees. This was done during the month of October and I am advised that on November 20 the United States Attorney filed bills of complaint, as directed by the Attorney General, against 39 persons.

Several factors seem clearly to negative any suggestion that the Interior Department has evaded judicial determinations or has taken arbitrary or unreasonable action. First, neither the Secretary of the Interior nor the Director of Grazing has been made a party defendant in any suit to test the validity of their rules, the injunction being directed only to the local officer in charge, who has taken no action to violate it. Furthermore, in view of the fact that the correctness of the holding of the State trial court appears to be open to doubt there is no assurance that the merits of this particular case will be passed upon either by the State supreme court or the United States Supreme Court. Secondly, to the extent that the persons involved are delinquent in the payment of their grazing fees they are deriving benefit from a range improvement program at the expense of their neighbors, since 75 percent of the fees collected is being expended for such purposes. Thirdly, the Government's insistence that the delinquent fees be paid operates as a measure of justice to the 20,000 other licensees who do pay for the use of Government property. Lastly, the delinquent fees which have been assessed under rules promulgated by the officer charged by the Congress with the administration of the act must be regarded as obligations owing the United States until a court of last resort has determined, in an appropriate proceeding to which that officer is a party, that such rules transcend the authority vested in him by the Congress.

It accordingly would appear that the course now being pursued by the Government is an appropriate one and not one of which the persons involved need complain, since they will be in a position to make the same contentions with more certainty that they will be passed upon in the suits which have just been instituted in the Federal court.[2]

Very sincerely,

[FRANKLIN D. ROOSEVELT]

[13:OF 633:CT]

[1] Pittman said that he had received numerous protests from Nevada livestock operators "against what they term evasion by Interior Department of Judicial de-

terminations, and arbitrary and unreasonable action by the Secretary of the Interior" (OF 633).

² Drafted by the Interior Department; Ickes' covering memorandum, Dec. 7, 1939, is with the letter here printed.

954   ROOSEVELT TO SENATOR KEY PITTMAN OF NEVADA

WASHINGTON, *December 9, 1939*

MY DEAR KEY: I have received your letter of November 24, written in response to my letter of November 16 concerning the Boulder Dam State Park bill.

It has been obvious for some time that you do not like my Secretary of the Interior, but I cannot agree with you as to his *character;* nor do I think this consideration should have any place in our discussion. As an executive officer in my Administration, the Secretary of the Interior has certain responsibilities to perform. He cannot function independently, but he is in effect the apex of a pyramid built by laws, precedents and the opinions of thousands of officers and employees living and dead. He cannot fail to follow the sound and proven policies and precedents of his Department without grave danger to himself and to the Government as a whole. I wish we could keep personalities out of our discussion, because I feel sure that the Secretary of the Interior would be just as opposed to the Hemingway Wash proposal if the Senior Senator from Illinois or any other State were involved. He feels the step you propose would be detrimental to national park policies.

My personal views—and I do not see how you can fail to concur in them—are that the Boulder Dam reservation because of its unique character is of National importance and it should be administered and developed accordingly. It is desirable that our extensive study of this subject should result in constructive measures. I should like to have you introduce a bill to establish permanently the Boulder Dam National Recreational Area, with provision that prospecting and mining, except in certain strategic areas, may be carried on under the mining and leasing laws of the United States, subject to such general regulations as may be prescribed by the Department of the Interior to protect the other values involved. Provision should be made, also, for the continuation of existing grazing privileges under permit.

Such a measure would provide the people of Nevada with the opportunities they seek in this reservation, and, at the same time, protect the national interests.[1]

Very sincerely yours,

[FRANKLIN D. ROOSEVELT]

[*Notation*: STAMPED] (Sgd) ICKES

[13 : OF 6–P : CT]

¹ Drafted by Ickes.

955   ROOSEVELT TO HENRY A. WALLACE, SECRETARY OF AGRI-
CULTURE, AND FERDINAND A. SILCOX, CHIEF, FOREST SERVICE

[WASHINGTON] *December 12, 1939*

[*Excerpt*] MEMORANDUM . . . From my own cursory observation I am inclined to believe that if the 50,000 acres west of the park [1] is included in the park, there will still be far more than enough pulp wood land left to sustain pulp wood mills on the average of capacity on which they have been running for the last five or ten years—probably enough to maintain them in perpetuity at full capacity.

One trouble with the pulp wood operations has been, as anybody can see with the naked eye, that many thousands of acres have been so completely denuded that reseeding has failed and erosion has started.

If the pulp wood companies will make their cut with proper consideration for reseeding, denudation will cease. At the same time there should be replanting of the present denuded areas. These denuded areas exist on private lands, on state lands, and I regret to say on some of the U. S. forest lands.

I feel certain that the Forest Service can let me have a report on this within a comparatively few days because you have all the necessary figures here in Washington, D. C.

F. D. R.

[13:OF 6–P:CT]

[1] The Olympic National Park.

956   EBERT K. BURLEW, ACTING SECRETARY OF THE INTERIOR, TO
ROOSEVELT

WASHINGTON, *December 12, 1939*

MY DEAR MR. PRESIDENT: Before leaving Washington, Secretary Ickes asked me to write you concerning the outcome of the week-end conference requested by you between representatives of the Governor of Washington, the Forest Service, and the National Park Service.

Mr. Kizer and Mr. Yantis, representing Governor Martin, reaffirmed their statement that they had no objection to the proposed additions on the north, east and south sides of the park. Asked whether, in view of the plan for a corridor down the Queets to the ocean, they would apply the same principle to the Queets addition, they stated that they would do so only on the basis of compromise for the exclusion of land in the Bogachiel-Hoh region. This was not satisfactory to the Department of the Interior, but it reduced the discussion to the Bogachiel-Hoh area alone.

It was the impression of Secretary Ickes at the conference with you on Saturday, that Governor Martin and his representatives chiefly desired to have the Bogachiel-Hoh area excluded in order to allay what they described as a state of alarm in the State of Washington over rumored plans for other national parks, or fear that this one would be too large. The Governor's representatives minimized the scenic value of the area and treated it as unnecessary to the park, but did not urge that it was economically vital to the life of the Olympic Peninsula; rather, there seemed to be tacit acceptance of your suggestions that it could be judged by the fact that it constituted about one-half of one percent of the total land area of the peninsula.

On the following day, however, Messrs. Kizer and Yantis laid heavy stress upon the possible need of this tract to sustain the woodpulp industry. As this matter was completely threshed out in the hearing on the first Wallgren bill (which included the Bogachiel-Hoh tract) before the House Committee on the Public Lands in 1936, I have asked that this phase be covered in a brief factual summary which accompanies this letter.

When the Governor's representatives urged, at the White House conference, that the Bogachiel area be kept out of the park because it is a small acreage which would not be missed, they actually testified to its economic unimportance, but not to its lack of value to the national park. The worth to a national park of a superb beauty spot does not depend upon its size any more than the scenic value of Yosemite Falls is measured by the width of Yosemite Creek.

The Bogachiel Valley, in the area recommended for addition, is more ardently championed for preservation by lovers of nature in the State of Washington, who are personally familiar with it, than any other region in or out of the park. Messrs. Kizer and Yantis at Saturday's White House conference claimed that the best portion of the Bogachiel "rain forest," for a distance of twelve miles up the main valley, and eight miles up the North Fork, is already in the park. At Sunday's conference they laid still heavier emphasis upon this claim, apparently resting the main weight of their position upon it. Today, therefore, Mr. Brant submitted their assertions to Irving M. Clark of Seattle, one of the leading citizens of Washington and past secretary of The Mountaineers, Inc. His reply is as follows:

I am personally familiar with the Bogachiel River valley from its source to the sea. Not one foot of its "rain forest" is inside the present national park. The "rain forest" begins at the western end of the national forest, extends up the valley for a distance of less than nine miles, and ends about half a mile east of the Flap Jack Guard Station, which is one mile outside the park boundary. The statement that the "rain forest" extends twelve miles inside the park is completely contrary to fact. The Bogachiel River at a point twelve miles east of the park boundary is a high mountain brook in open country where the snow is many feet deep in winter and lies on the ground until July. There is no "rain forest" at all on the North Fork of the Bogachiel. The entire Bogachiel "rain forest" lies within the proposed extension of the park.

[397]

Against this testimony, Messrs. Kizer and Yantis offer theoretical calculations prepared by Ross K. Tiffany of the Washington State Planning Council, admittedly based on rainfall and forest type maps, and supported by the anonymous testimony of "those who know the region best." Backing this, and heavily emphasized by Mr. Kizer, at the Sunday conference, is a lawyer's technicality. He said that when NPS Regional Director Kittredge of San Francisco, making his first visit to a new national park, discussed park boundaries with Mr. Tiffany, he signed a "statement of fact" which included this tabulation of "rain forest" based on rainfall maps. Incorrect statements of "fact" do not become true because one man accepts the statement made by another man, about conditions in a region which neither man had ever seen; nor does a report disapproved by a governmental department because the facts in it are erroneous have any weight in fixing policy.

Members of the staff do not question the sincerity of Mr. Tiffany. He no doubt thought that the "rain forest" was to be found wherever rainfall is heaviest, which is on the high mountain slopes, while as a matter of fact the "rain forest" is on the floors of narrow valleys which for several miles, combine heavy rainfall with low altitude.

Mr. Kittredge's own statement in the Seattle *Post-Intelligencer* of October 23, 1938 is as follows:

No one knows at the present time what the ultimate boundary of the Olympic Park will be, but it would be a catastrophe if that boundary should be so limited that the national park did not include a representative forest extending down into one of the river valleys such as the Bogachiel. In the Hoh and Bogachiel valleys we find the very finest of all the rain forest on the peninsula.

The economic welfare of the Olympic peninsula does not depend upon the logging of these 40,000 or 50,000 acres of scenic forest. The memorandum accompanying this letter shows that vastly more pulp acreage is available than is needed to sustain the woodpulp industry. If the 1,077,000 acres of standing pulp timber in Jefferson, Challam and Grays Harbor Counties, outside the park and the proposed extension, do not suffice for the pulp industry on a sustained-yield basis, they can be added to indefinitely from the hundreds of thousands of acres of cut-over lands. The fundamental truth about the timber difficulties of the State of Washington was stated in a letter to Governor Martin on September 9, 1938, from Mr. Tiffany of the Washington State Planning Council, who wrote:

Of course, our timber operators, or most of them, are in rather desperately bad circumstances. But is that a valid excuse why we should complacently permit them to strip the hills of their virgin forests and leave on hundreds of thousands of acres absolutely no beginning of a new forest crop?

Mr. Tiffany was describing the destruction needlessly resulting from wrong lumbering practices. In a narrow valley like that of the Bogachiel

River, flanked by steep mountains, the only lumbering possible is that which "strips the hills of their virgin forests," and even with the best efforts at reforestation, the forces of erosion will begin where the lumbermen leave off.

It is the recommendation of Secretary Ickes that the Bogachiel-Hoh and Queets tracts, as shown on the accompanying map, be added to the Olympic National Park along with the other areas to which no objections have been raised. In so doing the Secretary would express the opinion that these three are by far the most beautiful and most essential to the park of all the recommended additions. Their preservation has become a symbol to many people of the new spirit in government which led to the creation of this national park.[1]

Sincerely yours,

E. K. BURLEW

[13:OF 6–P:TS]

[1] Ickes devotes a paragraph to this conference in his *Diary*, III, 94. He said that Roosevelt told them that he expected to sign the proclamation enlarging the park before the end of the year.

957   [*Enclosure*] FRED J. OVERLY, ASSOCIATE FORESTER, NATIONAL PARK SERVICE, TO ARNO B. CAMMERER, DIRECTOR, NATIONAL PARK SERVICE

WASHINGTON, *December 12, 1939*

MEMORANDUM FOR THE DIRECTOR: With minor exceptions, the areas proposed for addition in the Bogachiel, Hoh and Queets Valleys were included in the first Wallgren bill (H. R. 7086), which was favorably reported by the House Committee on the Public Lands in 1936. In addition, that bill included the Sams River and Matheny Creek areas between the Queets and the Quinault, containing approximately 50,000 acres of practically a solid stand of pulp timber, now eliminated from the park.

The hearing before the House Committee on the Public Lands showed that even with this larger volume of pulp timber, the establishment of the park would not injure the pulp industry. The testimony of Forester W. H. Horning showed that in the area tributary to Grays Harbor and Port Angeles, economically available pulp timber amounted to 73,000,-000 cords. Annual consumption at capacity of the mills at Port Angeles and Grays Harbor is 400,000 cords per year. At this rate the standing pulpwood would last 183 years, not considering new growth.

Mr. Horning estimated that the amount of pulpwood tributary to Port Angeles ". . . without any consideration of new growth, is sufficient to last these mills 77 years . . ." and that the pulpwood tributary to Grays Harbor was sufficient to supply the existing mill for 500 years.

The dividing line between timber economically available to one place or the other is not a fixed one, and any demand for it would bring part of the Grays Harbor surplus into the Port Angeles area.

Any deviation from these 1936 findings concerning the timber on the west side of the peninsula which were based on the inventory phase of the Forest Survey by the Forest Service would increase the pulp reserves of the peninsula by the elimination from the park of the 50,-000 acres on Sams River and Matheny Creek.

The figures furnished by Mr. Yantis, that the region north and west of the park contains 18,666,000,000 board feet of pulp timber and the consumption in tributary mills is 447,000,000 a year, are misleading. The figure of total pulp timber for the limited area embraced is probably correct, but the consumption given is greater than the capacity consumption of all the mills on the Olympic Peninsula. In fact, it is more than half of the total consumption of all the pulp mills in Western Washington from the Columbia River to Canada, based upon the 1936 rate of production.

If pulp mills on Puget Sound are to be considered in connection with timber stands on the west side of the Olympic Peninsula, then all the sources of their timber supply must be considered, and that includes all of Northwestern Washington and Western British Columbia.

The statements made by the representatives of the Governor of the State of Washington at our Sunday conference, that the proposed additions on the Bogachiel and Hoh contain little large old-growth Douglas fir, and that Sitka spruce and large old-growth fir increase as one goes up these rivers inside the park, are contrary to fact. The Bogachiel and Hoh additions contain approximately 319,000,000 feet of large old-growth Douglas fir. Furthermore, the Douglas fir inside the park, on the Bogachiel, quickly changes to small old-growth. The lithographed forest type maps of the Forest Service do not distinguish between large and small old-growth fir, but they are distinct on the large scale type maps.

It should be noted that the estimates of competent foresters which show adequate pulp reserves for the regions tributary to the western part of the peninsula, take no account of regrowth, which under proper management would greatly increase the amount of available pulpwood.

When H. R. 10024 was before Congress, and included a Bogachiel tract running three miles farther west than the present proposed addition, although including slightly less acreage, Chief Forester Silcox was quoted as follows in the Port Angeles *Evening News* of April 8, 1938 in connection with the timber in that park proposal: ". . . Chief Forester Silcox said he believes removal of the timber from the public market will never have much effect on paper mill operations especially if the supply outside the park is properly managed to insure a sustaining yield. . . ."

FRED J. OVERLY

[13:OF 6–P:TS]

958   ROOSEVELT TO EBERT K. BURLEW, ACTING SECRETARY OF THE
       INTERIOR

WASHINGTON, *December 14, 1939*

MEMORANDUM FOR HON. E. K. BURLEW: In order to clear up the question of whether the Bogachiel area west of the present national park boundary should be added to the park, please telegraph to one of your park service men to take photographs in the valley floor.   I should like these photographs taken every half mile beginning at a point two or three miles east of the present national park west boundary and proceeding thence westward three or four miles into the new proposed addition.

This should prove whether a rain forest gets its name from rainfall or from the type of vegetation in a given area.

F. D. R.

[13:OF 6–P:CT]

959   HENRY A. WALLACE, SECRETARY OF AGRICULTURE, TO
       ROOSEVELT

WASHINGTON, *December 18, 1939*

DEAR MR. PRESIDENT: In response to your request at the recent conference in your office on the Olympic National Park extensions, the Forest Service has studied the possible effects of the proposed additional park withdrawals on the pulp timber sustained yield possibilities of the part of the peninsula most likely to be affected.

Although the mixed ownership and the present pattern of cross haul of raw material make it impossible to tie down a given area of timber to any one industrial center, it is reasonable to assume that the additional withdrawals would affect principally the dependent populations in the territory around Port Angeles and on Grays Harbor.

The peninsula timber outside the Park and proposed extensions, exclusive of those on the Queets, Hoh, and Bogachiel rivers, most logically tributary to these two centers lies in an area beginning at Sequim, east of Port Angeles, on the north side of the peninsula and extending thence around the west side and to a line running generally north from about Montesano on the south side.   Forest Service estimates of the pulp timber in all ownerships in the various working circles in this territory show a total of 50 million cords.   The present annual pulp mill requirements in this area, at Port Angeles and on Grays Harbor, are approximately 400,000 cords.

Our research shows that in this territory a 90-year rotation will produce the highest yield of pulp timber. On this basis, the existing stand of merchantable timber would last the existing mills 125 years, without considering volume added by new growth. Thus existing mills would have more than enough timber to assure sustained yield. This oversupply would thus permit an expansion of pulp mill capacity of 38 per cent. The oversupply of pulp timber lies chiefly toward the Grays Harbor end of the territory. Some such expansion is obviously called for in order to help replace the employment base now furnished by the waning lumber industry.

Complete attainment of the foregoing objective will, of course, depend upon cessation of the present shipments of part of the pulp timber cut in this area to mills elsewhere, or offsetting shipments from non-peninsula sources, which would probably be limited largely to the area south of Grays Harbor.

The proposed park withdrawals on the Queets, Hoh, and Bogachiel rivers contain approximately 3½ million cords of pulp timber. Removal of this quantity from the economic base would not, as the above figures show, and as you surmise in your memorandum of December 12, endanger the life of the existing mills. It would reduce the opportunity for expansion to 30 per cent. . . .

Respectfully,

H. A. WALLACE

[APS] Silcox was taken with a severe heart attack Wednesday evening and today has about a 50–50 chance of living.[1]

[13:OF 6–P:TS]

[1] Silcox died Dec. 20, 1939, of coronary thrombosis. Ickes said that he was not only an excellent head of the Forest Service but that he had a broad social and economic outlook. He said that he had planned to make Silcox an Under Secretary of Interior when the Forest Service was brought under the Interior Department (*Ickes' Diary*, III, 94).

960   ROOSEVELT TO GOVERNOR CLARENCE D. MARTIN, Olympia, Washington

WASHINGTON, *December 21, 1939*

MY DEAR GOVERNOR MARTIN: I have given attentive consideration to the matters we discussed at our consultation on additions to the Olympic National Park, and to the memoranda submitted afterwards by your representatives and by the Secretary of the Interior and the Secretary of Agriculture. Since there was agreement in principle between us as to all of the proposed extensions, and agreement in fact as to all but one of them, I have paid particular attention to the tract on the Bogachiel and Hoh Rivers, which formed the principal basis of our discussion.

After reading the letter written to me by your representatives, Mr. B. H. Kizer and Mr. George F. Yantis, dated December 10,[1] I requested the Secretary of Agriculture to have the Forest Service make a special study of the principal question raised in it: whether the additions proposed on the western side of the park are necessary to maintain the wood-pulp industry of the Olympic peninsula. The other question raised, whether the portion of the Bogachiel valley now in the park contains an adequate representation of "rain forest," I reserved for a personal inquiry.

The Secretary of Agriculture reported to me on December 18 that although it is impossible to tie down a given area of timber to any one industrial center, "it is reasonable to assume that additional withdrawals [for inclusion in the park] [2] would affect principally the dependent populations in the territory around Port Angeles and on Grays Harbor." The Forest Service study, he said, showed that with pulp timber placed on a 90 year rotation cycle, "the existing stand of merchantable timber would last the existing mills 125 years, without considering volume added by new growth. Thus existing mills would have more than enough timber to assure sustained yield."

After deducting the timber in the proposed additions to the park on the Queets, Hoh and Bogachiel Rivers, the Secretary of Agriculture informed me that it would be possible to expand the existing pulp industry by 30 per cent, with timber on a 90 year sustained yield cycle. When you were with me at the White House, we talked of a 40 year or 50 year cycle for pulp timber. If the shorter cycle should be found more advantageous than the more conservative figure used by the Forest Service, it would of course increase the surplus of pulp timber for existing mills.

Having satisfied myself that the proposed additions would not harm the established pulp [3] industries of the peninsula, I considered the conflict of testimony as to the location of the most striking "rain forest" in the Bogachiel Valley—whether it is in the present park or in the proposed addition. I directed that all available photographs taken in that valley be sent to the White House, arranged in geographical sequence. From a study of them, covering the valley for a length of twenty miles, I concluded that the location of a "rain forest" depends to a great extent upon the definition of it, but that, taking it to mean the conspicuous rooting of trees on fallen trees and stumps and the heavy growth of tree moss, the principal part of the Bogachiel "rain forest" is west of the

[403]

present park boundary. These characteristics diminish with the increase in altitude inside of the park. I was also impressed by the steepness of the mountain slopes bordering the Bogachiel and Hoh valleys, as revealed by airplane photographs; a self-evident handicap to lumbering by the methods that we discussed here.

I feel sure, from our discussion at the White House, that the same considerations which induce me to include the Bogachiel-Hoh and Queets tracts in the national park will make the action satisfactory to you, since the only question that arose related to the factual basis for a decision.

Turning now to the proposed parkway down the Queets River to the ocean and north along the ocean front, I take this occasion to repeat the substance of our discussion of the subject. I fully approve of your request that statutory provisions be made for highway and railroad transit across the Queets corridor, if the parkway is established, so that no harm may be done to state or private timber lands. I think that we are in full agreement as to the recreational value of this project to the people of Washington and visitors to the State.

In conclusion, let me repeat also what I said at our conference, to the effect that I have always looked upon the establishment of the Olympic National Park as part of a much broader program of planned use of the larger land area around it; a program in which the Federal and State governments would act together to preserve the timber lands as a never-failing source of sustenance for the people. Outside of the park this is primarily a question of timber management. It was plain at our conference that we see eye to eye on this matter, and I hope that some plan of action may soon be worked out.

Allow me to express my appreciation of your co-operative attitude, and to say once more that my conviction is that our government has done well to preserve this perpetual scenic memorial of the world's most remarkable forest growth. I am still looking forward to the visit, postponed from last summer, to the State of Washington and the Olympic Peninsula.

Sincerely yours,

(Signed) FRANKLIN D. ROOSEVELT

[13:OF 6–P:T:COPY]

[1] Not present.
[2] Brackets in original.
[3] This letter was drafted by the Interior Department and sent by Roosevelt to Wallace for review. Wallace made no change except to suggest the addition of the word "pulp," here underlined by Roosevelt. Commenting on the draft in his letter to Roosevelt of Dec. 28, 1939 (OF 6–P), Wallace said: "In order to avoid the possibility of someone challenging your statement because of the possible effect of the withdrawals on the diminishing sawmill industry, I would suggest inserting the word 'pulp' before the word 'industries' . . ."

WASHINGTON, *Dec. 21, 1939*

Through: Bureau of the Budget, The Attorney General, Division of the Federal Register.

MY DEAR MR. PRESIDENT: I enclose for your consideration a form of proclamation to extend the boundaries of Olympic National Park, Washington, pursuant to the provisions of the Act of June 29, 1938 (52 *Stat.* 1241).

The terms and conditions of section 5 of the Act have been fully complied with.

The issuance of the proposed proclamation will give protection to an additional forest area of gigantic trees on the western slope of the Olympic Mountains. It will include, also, mountainous areas of unusual scenic and recreational value. The primary purpose of the Olympic National Park is the preservation of this outstanding wilderness. The recommended extension will provide a more complete administrative and recreational unit.

Of the 187,411 acres involved, 6,188 acres are patented homestead entries and 1,395 acres are State land. The remaining 179,828 acres are public land. There is attached a map showing the recommended additions.

The proposed proclamation has been drafted subject to valid existing rights, and its issuance is respectfully recommended.[1]

Sincerely yours,

HAROLD L. ICKES

[13:OF 6–P:TS]

[1] Issued Jan. 2, 1940, as Proclamation 2379.

962 ROOSEVELT TO HAROLD L. ICKES, SECRETARY OF THE INTERIOR

[WASHINGTON] *December 21, 1939*

MEMORANDUM FOR THE SECRETARY OF THE INTERIOR: In view of the fact that the Grand Coulee Dam will be finished early in 1941, I believe it is time for us to plan for its use.

This use divides itself into two parts:

(a) Surplus power over and above power needs for pumping water into the Columbia Basin. This subject should be referred to the National Power Policy Committee. It affects, of course, the tie-in with Bonneville and with existing power consumer cooperatives, rural lines, etc., and it has a bearing on a possible third dam in the Columbia River, half way between Grand Coulee and Bonneville.

(b) The development of the Columbia Basin itself. I feel very strongly on this subject. I understand that it is believed by Reclamation Bureau that when water is provided, 80,000 families can be put on the land. If this estimate is correct it will mean approximately 20,000 other families who will be engaged in services : ·· as gasoline stations, small stores, transportation, local governmental operations, etc., etc. I hope the Government can lay down a definite policy that all lands will be open only to relief families or families which for many different reasons have abandoned their homes and fled to the coastal region or are now "adrift" in various parts of the country. In other words, I want to give first chance to the "Grapes of Wrath" families of the nation.

I realize that a percentage of these families are shiftless and that an even larger percentage of them are so ignorant of farm and home economics that without help they would make a failure on this new land.

The work of the rural rehabilitation and WPA colonization projects during the past seven years has demonstrated nevertheless that given supervision and instruction for a few years this condition of ignorance can, in most cases, be overcome. This entails in any planning a fairly large overhead covering supervision and instruction during the first few years. It envisages also a percentage of families who, no matter how much they are supervised and instructed, will fail to make good. Such families would, of course, have to be replaced by others who would make good.

All in all this is a tremendous subject and I call your attention to the definite possibility of planning in the Columbia Basin for certain local industries to supplement agriculture—decentralized industries which will fill purely local needs and not export their production beyond the Columbia Basin.

It is obvious from the history of Oregon and Washington apple growing, for example, that there has probably been too much apple production in that area. There is, using the same illustration, a growing improvement in apple production in the Appalachian section with the result that proportionately fewer Pacific Coast apples are sold in local eastern markets than formerly. The eastern and southern growers have at last begun to learn how to grade, pick and store their apples.

In the same way there is a tendency in the Far West to grow too many onions and similar specialized crops, thus creating too great dependence on eastern markets and too little diversification of crops.

The Columbia Basin project requires, therefore, a comprehensive agricultural and industrial economic survey. The Basin can eventually support 500,000 of our citizens, and I should like to have it so planned that opportunity for settlement will be given primarily to those families which are today in need.

Finally, the whole Basin should be planned with the thought of making the Basin economically self-supporting as far as possible. There is no reason, for instance, why the Basin should not make the equivalent of its whole shoe supply because hides are available close to the site. Certain woolen goods can be manufactured and it might be possible to work out small glass and crockery factories.

This part of the survey should, I think, be referred to the National Resources Committee, and I am sending a copy of this memorandum to Mr. Delano.[1]

F. D. R.

[13:OF 360:CT]

[1](The National Resources Planning Board is meant.) Ickes replied Jan. 19, 1940 (OF 360), describing the plans for the power and irrigation development of the area. He agreed that homesteads should be furnished for some of the people in "dire need" but said that the project was not big enough to be divided into farm plots for all those needing resettlement.

963　Roosevelt to Clyde L. Seavey, Chairman, Federal Power Commission

[Washington] *December 22, 1939*

Dear Clyde: You and Mrs. Seavey are perfectly grand to make that wonderful suggestion of giving me some sequoia gigantea trees to plant at Hyde Park and I would be thrilled except for the fact that I have a very grave fear that they would not grow.[1]

Three years ago I planted four or five of them and several specimens of other sequoia, of western yellow pine, and western cedar. All of them died during the winter though they were planted in a protected space. Also I raised several sequoia from seed and while they did beautifully in the greenhouse, they died when put out in the woods the following year. The only Pacific Coast trees that I have had any luck with at all are three or four cedars and a small growth of Douglas fir.

The only sequoia that I know of which has really survived is a tree at Syracuse, N. Y. It is, I think, at least fifty or sixty years old.

Just to make sure, I will check with Professor Nelson Brown at the State College of Forestry and get his opinion on the possibility of survival at Hyde Park.

My warm regards and a Merry Christmas to you both.

Very sincerely yours,

[Franklin D. Roosevelt]

FDR/TMB
[13:PPF 6391:CT]

[1] This refers to Seavey's letter of Dec. 21, 1939 (PPF 6391), concerning a gift of sequoias for planting on the grounds of the Roosevelt Library.

[*Excerpt*] The President: I signed a Proclamation today that won't mean anything to anybody except an engineer or surveyor from the Interior Department or Forestry. It is the Proclamation enlarging the Olympic National Park. I was given authority under the bill to add a certain number of acres to the Olympic National Park which, as originally set up, followed the lines of the old monument.[1]

We had a hearing, as you know, and the Governor came down.

Steve, hold this up for me. I can explain it in about a minute.

Everything in the middle in here was the old Park. There was no question at all about the areas on the north or on the east or on the south—these green areas to be added, or that.

The only question that arose was as to whether these two little green areas should be taken out of the National Forest and added to the Park. There, again, the question hinged on two matters of fact. Some of the people out there thought that by taking these two little green corners on the west into the Park, that we might jeopardize what they call the sustained yield of pulp wood to supply paper, the pulp mills up on Puget Sound and down here around Tacoma on the south, the Pacific side. The Forestry [*sic*] Service gave us a survey that showed that even if these two areas are added to the Park, there is enough pulp wood on the rotation principle, that is to say, cutting the trees when they are between forty and fifty years old, in this general area west of the Park to maintain all of the pulp mills on Puget Sound and on the Pacific, not only at their present rate of capacity but thirty per cent greater than they are running today. On the basis of that report there is no reason why these two corners—strips on the west—should not be added to the Park.

The other question was the question of what is a rain forest? The southern strip, going west, follows the valley of the Hoh River, a very beautiful scenic section with very steep hillsides, and the northern strip is the upper valley of the Bogachiel River—wait until I find the thing; I cannot spell it unless I read it; B-o-g-a-c-h-i-e-l—and there again we wanted to preserve for the public this thing called rain forest, which means original virgin timber, very large timber, that is covered with a mossy growth. Some people said that this rain forest existed east of that green area in the higher latitudes, getting up towards the top of the mountains, but we found that while there is just as much rain up there, you do not have the moss because you get up too high.

And so, on those two reasons, of finding of fact, we are including those two areas in the Park.

Q: Is there any particular reason for leaving that so-called corridor you have in there?

The President: Well, eventually those two valleys, the southern one, the valley down the Hoh, and the northern one, going up this way, and down the Bogachiel—eventually we want to extend that to the Pacific Ocean.

Q: Why isn't that strip in there?

The President: Because that is just the tops of mountains.

Mr. Early: You want your total acreage.

The President: Oh, this still leaves—this still leaves under the Act about 50,000 acres more that can be, in the future, taken into the Park. There won't be any action on that until we know what the use is going to be like—whether the public will go in.

[13: PRESIDENT'S PRESS CONFERENCES: T]

[1] Roosevelt added 187,411 acres to the park by Proclamation 2379, under authority of the act approved June 29, 1938 (52 *Stat.* 1241).

965   ROOSEVELT TO HARRY H. WOODRING, SECRETARY OF WAR

WASHINGTON, *January 3, 1940*

MEMORANDUM FOR THE SECRETARY OF WAR: In regard to flood control projects for the Cumberland River, please ask the Chief of Engineers to get in touch with the Tennessee Valley Authority, the Reclamation Service, the Department of Agriculture and the National Resources Committee,[1] in order to work out with them an outline of procedure for the treatment of the broad development of the Cumberland Basin with somewhat the same objectives as in the case of the Tennessee Basin.

In other words, all I want at this time is an informal discussion between these agencies and an informal report to me as to methods of approach.

While these gentlemen are discussing the future of the Cumberland watershed, I suggest they also discuss the future of the Arkansas and Red River watersheds, all the way from the Mississippi to their source. In the case of the Arkansas, this means consideration of the whole watershed up to the main divide of the Rocky Mountains in central Colorado.

F. D. R.

[13: OF 132: CT]

[1] Roosevelt meant the National Resources Planning Board. The National Resources Committee had been abolished on July 1, 1939.

[Washington] *January 10, 1940*

My dear Seavey: I wrote to Professor Nelson C. Brown at the New York State College of Forestry in Syracuse, and I am evidently wrong about the Sequoias. He says:

I think it would be worth trying. There is a Sequoia gigantea which has survived the extreme winters of Syracuse for the past six years, and your part of the Hudson Valley is very much warmer. If we selected a protected spot with a southern exposure, I think they would survive the winters there. There are several good sized trees about 30 to 40 feet high at Rye, N. Y., which I have personally seen.[1]

Professor Brown also suggests that the planting should be done next April—preferably small trees up to 2 feet tall—and the root systems kept moist in transit.

I know the exact spot to put them in—on the south side of the new Library, which will give them protection from the north and northwest.

It would be grand to have these trees and if they are put in this Spring, you and Mrs. Seavey must come up and see them.

Always sincerely,

[Franklin D. Roosevelt]

[13:PPF 6391:CT]

[1] In the letter here quoted (Jan. 2, 1940, PPF 38), Roosevelt's letter to Brown is referred to as of Dec. 22, 1939. No copy of it has been found.

967   Roosevelt to the Congress

The White House, *January 11, 1940*

To the Congress of the United States: The provision for the wise use and conservation of our national resources must necessarily be one of the primary responsibilities of the Federal Government at all times. Through research leading to the development of programs and recommendations, the National Resources Planning Board and its predecessors have been at work for the past six years in the interest of planning for resources conservation and use. This is democratic planning. It is decentralized; it is based on the wishes of the people who through their elected representatives decide what plans we will develop and follow; it is planning "from the ground up."

The accomplishments of the National Resources Committee in a large measure have been the results of cooperation with Federal and non-Federal planning groups. Today there are planning organizations by various names in many Federal agencies; there are also 43 State Planning Boards and hundreds of county and city planning groups. The continuance in operation of these democratic planning activities demonstrates the desire of our people for the utilization of long-range planning to conserve and develop our resources.

The functions and duties of the National Resources Committee, as you know, were transferred under Reorganization Plan No. 1 to the National Resources Planning Board in the Executive Office. The story of the Committee's work and a picture of the responsibilities that lie ahead of the National Resources Planning Board are presented in the Progress Report of the National Resources Committee, which I now transmit for the information of the Congress.[1]

Franklin D. Roosevelt

[W. H. PRESS RELEASES:M]

[1] *Progress Report, 1939, Statement of the Advisory Committee, National Resources Committee* (Washington, 1939). In addition to covering the work of the National Resources Committee for the fiscal year 1939, the report reviewed the activities and recommendations of the committee and its predecessors during the preceding six years. In the Senate the message and report were referred to the Committee on Public Lands and Surveys; in the House to the Committee of the Whole House (*Cong. Rec.*, 76th Cong., 3d sess., 86: 1, 269–270).

968   Roosevelt to Harold D. Smith, Director, Bureau of the Budget

Washington, January 13, 1940

Memorandum for Harold Smith: When you get back, will you go over this draft transmitting Plan III with Louis Brownlow and add to it the changes we talked of for taking several bureaus out of Interior and try to put it in final form for me. I would like to plan to send it to the Congress the end of this month.

F. D. R.

[*Notation*:A] President made no changes in draft which was used as working copy on message.[1]

[13:OF 285–C:T]

[1] No further reference to the removal of bureaus from the Interior Department has been found. This "Draft of Message for Transmitting Plan III" was prepared by the Budget Bureau and sent to Roosevelt by Budget Director Smith with a note dated Jan. 6, 1940 (OF 285–C). The draft provided for the transfer of the Forest Service to the Interior Department; about half of the eleven-page typescript was devoted to a justification of the proposed change. No part of this draft appears in the President's message to Congress of April 2, 1940, transmitting Plan III (printed in Rosenman, ed., *Public Papers*, IX, 112–123), and the message contained no mention of a Forest Service transfer.

[411]

THE WHITE HOUSE, *January 15, 1940*

TO THE CONGRESS OF THE UNITED STATES: So much publicity has been given by the press and in other ways to the power development feature of the work of the Tennessee Valley Authority that it is fair to assume that many of our citizens and even government officials hold a belief that the purpose of the Act creating the Authority was primarily the development of electric power.

It is perhaps time to call attention to this utter fallacy.

The original legislation, based on my recommendation to the Congress in 1933, was intended—in part as an experimental project—to raise the standards of life by increasing social and economic advantages in a given area, in this case the whole of the watershed which runs into the Tennessee River and including portions of many States.

Part of this objective meant the elimination of very large annual damage to life and property as a result of floods; and, therefore, it was planned to build a series of dams in the Tennessee River and on some of its many tributaries. The building of such dams would, it was figured, reduce property damage which had averaged $20,000,000 a year for a long time. The building of such dams would also make possible the production of a large amount of electric power and would also afford barge navigation for many hundreds of miles up the river.

Furthermore, the original objective of the law included many other things, such as the planting of water-retaining forests near the headwaters of the many rivers and streams, the terracing of farm hillsides, the building of small check-dams, the development of fertilizer, the diversification of crops and other soil building methods, the improvement of highways and other forms of transportation, the bringing in of small industries, the extension of rural electric lines, and many other similar activities.

In other words, it is time that people should understand that power development was only a part—and ultimately only a relatively small part—of a great social and economic experiment in one of our major watersheds.

From time to time I have transmitted to the Congress special reports from the Tennessee Valley Authority relating to special subjects in the progress of this great task. I am transmitting herewith the latest of these reports, a monograph on the "Recreation Development of the Tennessee River System." [1] This summarizes "the results that have been accomplished through certain experiments and demonstrations in this field and contains specific conclusions and recommendations with respect to additional legislation on this subject." It is coming to be realized more and more that in the improvement of our American civilization we cannot stop at hospitals and schools any more than we can confine ourselves to strictly economic subjects. Recreation in its broad sense is a definite factor in the improvement of the bodies and minds of our future citizens.

I hope that this report, which is only one of many which the Tennessee Valley Authority has made from time to time will dispel any erroneous impression that the Tennessee Valley Authority's work is concerned primarily with the mere development of electric power.[2]

FRANKLIN D. ROOSEVELT

[W. H. PRESS RELEASES: M]

[1] Printed under this title, with the message of the President, as House Document 565, 76 Cong., 3d sess. (Washington, 1940).
[2] Other texts of this message (Speech File) are two drafts: the first a carbon typescript; the second an edited ribbon copy of the first. The first draft bears the notation, in what appears to be Miss LeHand's writing, "Dictated Jan. 11/1940." The second draft has several revisions in Roosevelt's hand, including the insertion of "and even government officials" in the first paragraph, and the substitution of "terracing" for "contouring" in the fifth. In the Senate the message was referred to the Committee on Agriculture and Forestry; in the House, to the Committee on Military Affairs (*Cong. Rec.*, 76th Cong., 3d sess., 86:1, 325–326, 342–343).

970   ROOSEVELT TO GIFFORD PINCHOT, Washington

[WASHINGTON] *January 15, 1940*

DEAR GIFFORD: I have received the form letters and my general reaction to them is unfavorable because this sort of organized drive is just as much a special group effort as drives on the Congress or the President by separate Protestant denominations or individuals like Coughlin or the United States Chamber of Commerce or the Cattlemen's Associations or, for that matter, horrid things like the K. K. K. itself.[1]

I do not believe in group drives anyway because I think they have hurt the improvement of the general processes of administrative government and Congressional decisions.

Furthermore, to suggest that we should have two recreation departments doing practically identical work, one in the Department of Agriculture and the other in the Department of the Interior is wasteful and inefficient.

There are two schools of thought in regard to the two Departments concerned—one is that everything that grows should be in the Department of Agriculture and only inanimate things, like minerals and oils, should be in the Department of the Interior. If this were done the Department of Agriculture would be bigger than all the other Departments of the Government put together, both in personnel and in money spending, and the Department of the Interior would have two or three minor Bureaus in it only. One of the essentials of Government is to

[413]

prevent any one Department from becoming a tail that runs the Federal dog!

A more logical division goes back to the origin of both Departments. The Department of the Interior was organized primarily to take charge of Government owned land, and the Department of Agriculture was organized primarily to look over the needs of the private landowners of the United States.

Frankly, I am getting to the point of believing that logic favors the latter view. And, incidentally, the days have passed when any human being can say that the Department of Agriculture is wholly pure and honest and the Department of the Interior is utterly black and crooked.

Very sincerely yours,

[FRANKLIN D. ROOSEVELT]

[13:PSF:INTERIOR:CT]

[1] Pinchot had drafted a letter to Roosevelt opposing transfer of the Forest Service to the Interior Department and had sent mimeographed copies to faculty members of American forestry schools for signature. One hundred and thirty-nine signed letters and fourteen unsigned letters were returned to Pinchot; these were sent by him to Roosevelt with his covering letter of Jan. 13, 1940 (OF 1–C).

971   GIFFORD PINCHOT TO ROOSEVELT

WASHINGTON, D. C., *January 17, 1940*

DEAR FRANKLIN: Many thanks for your letter of January 15.

Here are some of the reasons why, as a matter of sound government organization, the Forest Service should not be transferred.

The Service was born, grew up, and for a long generation has done admirable work in the Department of Agriculture. There is no tenable claim that it could do better elsewhere, and no reason to expect that it could do as well.

The Forest Service is a research as well as an executive organization. This union of research and administration underlies the progress of forestry and the morale and efficiency of the Service. To separate the two would ruin the Service. This union is also the distinguishing characteristic of the Department of Agriculture.

The Service is in constant necessary cooperation with more than half of the twenty-odd other organizations in the Department, such as the Soil Conservation Service, the Bureaus of Agricultural Economics, Entomology, Plant Industry, etc., etc. That cooperation would be badly dislocated if the transfer were made.

The sentiment of the people most concerned is overwhelmingly opposed to the transfer. Users of the National Forests; experts in forestry in and out of the government service; the great national agricultural organizations and many others; the people of the Rocky Mountain and

Pacific coast states and their representatives in Senate and House, of both parties—all these are, in immense majority, vigorously opposed to the transfer and in favor of keeping the Service where it is.

Silcox did not believe that the Forest Service could continue to succeed if transferred to the Interior Department. I understand that he gave you his reasons.

The transfer is not a question of personalities, but of good permanent organization. Secretaries pass; the natural relations between lines of work do not. If Harold Ickes were in Agriculture and Henry Wallace in Interior, I would still be emphatically opposed to the proposed transfer.

To uproot the Service from its lifelong surroundings would do great injury to its morale, to its essential cooperation with other agricultural bureaus, to its relations with the users of the National Forests, and to public support. Only the strongest constructive reasons could justify it. So far as I know, such reasons do not exist.

It strikes me as particularly unfortunate that conservation should become a controversial issue just at this time when I believe it can be made the foundation of enduring peace between nations. This is what I have wanted to see you about. I enclose a memorandum on the subject.[1]

Faithfully yours,

GIFFORD PINCHOT

[APS] And I still want to see you about it.

[13:PSF:INTERIOR:TS]

[1] "A Plan for Permanent Peace Through International Cooperation in the Conservation and Distribution of Natural Resources," a nine-page typescript, signed by Pinchot and dated Jan. 17, 1940. Because its content is duplicated in Pinchot's several later memoranda on the same subject it is not printed here.

972 PRESS CONFERENCE, Executive Offices of the White House, January 19, 1940, 10:50 A. M.

[Excerpt] The President: Well, I will give you a very simple example on the National Resources Committee:[1] I am studying now—I won't give you a story on it at the present time because it is a darned good story by itself—but in the course of the next couple of years we are going to be able to throw open to settlement this very great region called the Columbia Basin, which is the old bed of the Columbia River. When Grand Coulee starts the pumps going, pumping the water up on the Columbia Basin—some of you have been there with me—it means irrigated land for, oh, as I remember the figure, about eighty thousand families and probably another twenty thousand families to run the services for those eighty thousand.

That is a population, eventually, of half a million people.

Now, what are we going to do? Let them come in like Topsy, first come, first served? Shall we take people who need to go there or people who do not need to go there? Are we going to let that half a million people go in for one special crop, like the Yakima Valley did, and produce more apples than we can possibly use? Are we going to turn the area over to sugar beets and add to our complicated sugar problem? Or, are we going to plan for this? Are we going to make it purely agricultural or will we plan to put local industries in there?

Those are things we do not know. How does the Government study a recommendation to the Congress? No one department of the Government has qualifications to make a complete study. It is economic, social, agricultural, et cetera and so on. There has to be some small Government agency to make studies of that kind, calling on other Government departments, calling on private industry, private agriculture, to help work out a plan. That is the National Resources Board and, actually, by this type of planning ahead for new things, we save the expenditure in the future of millions and millions of dollars that could be saved by preventing overlapping and by preventing the kind of economy in this region which would lose a hundred times the cost of running this small National Resources Committee.

[13 : PRESIDENT'S PRESS CONFERENCES : T]

[1] Roosevelt had referred to certain agencies as "money saving agencies" in connection with appropriation bills under consideration by Congress.

973   ROOSEVELT TO HAROLD L. ICKES, SECRETARY OF THE INTERIOR

WASHINGTON, *January 25, 1940*

MY DEAR MR. SECRETARY: I have received First Assistant Secretary Burlew's letter of January 9, 1940, concerning the proposed reorganization of the Civilian Conservation Corps.[1]

While I recognize that the proposal has for its purpose economy in operations and perhaps more efficient administration, it is my belief that the Corps should not lose its identity and that it should be continued as a policy making body with a Director responsible for its general functions.

I am particularly interested in many of the economies mentioned. It seems to me, however, that it would be possible to accomplish a number of these under the present organization. I am therefore asking the Director of the Bureau of the Budget to undertake a study of the Corps' activities in the near future in order to determine what savings can be made and if any practical advantages would result from the changes suggested in Mr. Burlew's letter.

Sincerely yours,

[FRANKLIN D. ROOSEVELT]

[*Notation*:A] Copy sent to Budget 1/25/40 hm
[*Notation*:AS] HDS [2]

[13:OF 268:CT]

[1] According to Burlew's letter (OF 268), his plan for reorganization of the Civilian Conservation Corps was prepared in accordance with a request of Roosevelt to Ickes. Burlew proposed to reduce CCC expenses by abolishing the Office of the Director, replacing this with a committee to be composed of one of the President's executive assistants and representatives of the Agriculture and Interior Departments, and by the withdrawal of the Army from the program.

[2] Budget Director Harold D. Smith, in whose agency this letter was drafted.

974   SENATOR GEORGE W. NORRIS OF NEBRASKA TO ROOSEVELT

WASHINGTON, D. C., *January 25, 1940*

MY DEAR MR. PRESIDENT: I am very sorry to learn that you have changed your mind and have decided to issue an order transferring the Forest Service from the Department of Agriculture to the Department of the Interior.

I shall not go into details, because at the conference which we recently held I expressed quite fully my ideas on the subject.[1]   I want to make one last suggestion and that is that the entire matter might be settled satisfactorily by making Mr. Ickes Secretary of War.

I appreciate the fact that Mr. Ickes' real interest is in conservation. In the War Department, he would have a wonderful opportunity to do a real service in carrying out your ideas of conservation. He possesses the peculiar qualities that fit him admirably for this work, and as I have pointed out to you several times the War Department through some of its agencies has not been in harmony with your own policy of conservation.   As I see it, there is no other person who could more satisfactorily perform this job than Mr. Ickes.[2]

Sincerely yours,

G. W. NORRIS

[13:PSF:INTERIOR:TS]

[1] Norris lunched with Roosevelt on Jan. 18, 1940 (PPF 1-O). On the next day, following the weekly Cabinet meeting, Ickes again urged on the President the need for haste in transferring the Forest Service to Interior. Roosevelt told him that Norris had informed him that to send the executive order to Congress then would "split his friends in two factions." However, on January 24 Ickes had lunch with Roosevelt and they, with Budget Director Smith, went over a draft of an executive order to effect the transfer (*Ickes' Diary*, III, 114, 118). What probably caused Roosevelt to change his mind was a telephone call from Senator Bankhead on

January 29 to the effect that an order to transfer the Forest Service would arouse "serious controversy" in the Senate and would probably be defeated (**Watson to** Roosevelt, Jan. 29, 1940, OF 1–C).

[2] An attached memorandum, Roosevelt to Ickes, Feb. 6, 1940, reads, "To read for your amusement and return for my files." Ickes, however, was not unreceptive to the idea: on May 24 he noted in his *Diary* (III, 181): "The President . . . has Fiorello LaGuardia in mind for Secretary of War. . . . I am not sure of this and, besides, I frankly admit that I would like to have it myself now."

975   ROOSEVELT TO EDWARD A. O'NEAL, PRESIDENT, AMERICAN FARM BUREAU FEDERATION, Chicago

[WASHINGTON] *February 1, 1940*

Personal

DEAR ED: I have not made a final decision on the proposed transfer of Forest Service to Interior but there are two points I want to make clear to you.

1. There is no thought of transferring farmers' wood lots which are in a very true sense, a crop. This function will remain in Agriculture and there is no farmer who grows trees as one of his crops who needs worry.

2. The other point is that ninety-eight percent of the Forest Service work relates to Federal government lands, a great part of it checker-boarded with very similar public lands which have always been under the Interior Department. There would be a great saving in putting both Services on these contiguous lands in the same department and, incidentally, the cattlemen would have to go to only one source for their grazing permits instead of two places, usually far apart, as they do today.[1]

Very sincerely yours,

[FRANKLIN D. ROOSEVELT]

FDR/TMB

[13:OF 1–C:CT]

[1] This was in reply to O'Neal's letter of Jan. 27, 1940 (OF 1–C), opposing a transfer of the Forest Service to the Interior Department and urging that the administration of grazing and reclamation be placed under Agriculture. O'Neal sent a copy of Roosevelt's letter to Wallace who in turn sent a copy of paragraph 2 to the Acting Chief of the Forest Service, Earle H. Clapp, without informing the latter of its source (Wallace to Roosevelt, Feb. 8, 1940, OF 1–C). Clapp replied with a lengthy memorandum (Feb. 8, 1940, OF 1–C), denying that "ninety-eight per cent of the Forest Service work" related to Federal lands. Wallace concluded his letter to the President by saying:

"I do so hope in these days of national stress with the great national campaign coming on that no matter what your decision we may do our utmost to promote a situation which will most harmoniously bring about the realization of the great ideals for which you stand. There is so much controversy in the world today I have been hoping that the minor things might be quieted down as much as possible."

WASHINGTON, *February 2, 1940*

MY DEAR MR. PRESIDENT: There seems to be a good deal of uncertainty and misunderstanding, particularly in the Northwest, with respect to our policies and purposes in connection with the Columbia Basin project, with especial reference to plans for irrigation at Grand Coulee Dam.   In this connection I enclose a memorandum that has just come to me from Commissioner Page of the Bureau of Reclamation.

You and I have discussed this problem informally from time to time and I have furnished you with various written reports.   The Bureau of Reclamation has been working on plans for some time, as I have advised you.   I strongly endorse Commissioner Page's suggestion of a personal conference with you, and if you desire to have such a conference, we will hold ourselves subject to your wishes in the matter.[1]

Sincerely yours,

HAROLD L. ICKES

[13:OF 360:TS]

---

[1] No appointment was arranged (Watson to Roberta Barrows, Feb. 9, 1940, OF 360).

---

977   *[Enclosure]* JOHN C. PAGE, COMMISSIONER, BUREAU OF RECLAMATION, TO HAROLD L. ICKES

WASHINGTON, *Jan. 30, 1940*

MEMORANDUM FOR THE SECRETARY: You are familiar with the planning survey of the Columbia Basin project area initiated by, and now in progress under the leadership of, the Bureau of Reclamation.   Prof. H. H. Barrows of Chicago University was appointed on the Bureau staff to actively supervise this survey.   Under the direct counsel of more than 100 persons particularly qualified in special fields involved in the development of this 1,200,000-acre project, a cooperative, coordinated outline of study is now actively in progress among 32 federal, state and local agencies, representing all types of interest in this vast undertaking.

Prominent among those participating are persons interested and experienced in all branches of agriculture; sociology; engineering, both in the construction and power fields; industrial practices; economics; geology; geography; climatology; transportation on highway, railroad and water; architecture; village and rural planning; and many others.

Progress and enthusiasm have been heartening, but recently a disquieting factor has appeared and many contributors are faltering, apparently pondering recent press statements attributed to the President. These seem to originate both from his statements supporting an appropriation for the National Resources Planning Board to undertake and complete the same type of survey as that already in progress for several months, and from correspondence emanating from the White House and from the National Resources Planning Board.

While your letter to the President dated January 19, 1940 [1] stated the present status of the Columbia Basin matters, there is some doubt that these facts received sufficient study at the White House properly to inform the President. In order to prevent situations arising which are almost sure to embarrass the White House, the National Resources Planning Board, and us, I recommend that you discuss the situation with the President to clarify the whole matter. If you think it advisable, perhaps Mr. Warne, who is handling the survey in our office, Professor Barrows, if he is available, and I should accompany you, as we are more familiar with the details and with the personnel involved. [2]

JOHN C. PAGE

[13:OF 360:TS]

[1] Describing Interior Department plans for the development of the area (OF 360).
[2] The Bureau of Reclamation published a report on the project, *Columbia Basin Joint Investigations, Character and Scope* (1941). The studies made and problems encountered led to the passage of the Columbia Basin Project Act of March 1, 1943 (57 *Stat.* 14), an amendment to the act of May 27, 1937 (see *ante,* 609 n.). The project is described in Charles McKinley, *Uncle Sam in the Pacific Northwest* (Berkeley: University of California, 1952), pp. 138–145.

978   HAROLD L. ICKES, SECRETARY OF THE INTERIOR, TO ROOSEVELT

WASHINGTON, *February 7, 1940*

MY DEAR MR. PRESIDENT: I had a long talk with George Norris on Monday about Forestry. I found that he has no objection to transferring Forestry to Interior, per se. He does not think that Agriculture has any greater claim on Forestry than Interior has. He volunteered that every Secretary of the Interior might not personally be a scoundrel any more than that every Secretary of Agriculture might be a man of outstanding rectitude and civic virtue. He said that if your order had gone up some time ago it would probably have caused little disturbance. He feels that to send it up now would bring out in the open a fight that is already smouldering and that it would affect adversely your chances for re-election. He said to me that he had already told you that he regarded your election for a third term as of paramount importance.

As you know, I agree with Senator Norris as to this. No more than Senator Norris would I want to urge or be a party to any act on your part that might make it more difficult for you to be re-elected if the people should decide that it was your duty to them to run again.

Moreover, I have a feeling that, as matters have developed with respect to Forestry, it will now mean a hard fight to transfer it. It could have been done easily at the last session. It could have been done without much trouble if the order had gone up, as we had planned, upon the convening of Congress for this session without any prior intimation that such an order was in prospect. But already protests by the hundreds, stimulated undoubtedly by Gifford Pinchot and the well-organized Forest lobby, are pouring in upon individual members of Congress. Word has just come to me from one Congressman that he has received a letter from Pinchot containing this language: "The Interior Department has no claim whatever upon the national forests. Ambition for power is no good reason for upsetting a layout that works superbly as it is."

The result is that, whereas last spring I felt every assurance that there would be no difficulty in transferring Forestry, and while I believed the same at the beginning of this session, I no longer possess any degree of confidence. Accordingly, I cannot conscientiously ask that you transfer Forestry.

However, unfortunately, Forestry has become a symbol to me. I have had one consistent ambition since I have been Secretary of the Interior, and that has been to be the head of a Department of Conservation, of which, necessarily, Forestry would be the keystone. I have not wanted merely to be *a* Secretary of the Interior; I have wanted to leave office with the satisfaction that I had accomplished something real and fundamental. I have told you frankly that, as this Department is now set up, it does not interest me.

So I have come to the reluctant conclusion that, as matters now stand, I cannot be true to myself nor measure up to the high standards that you have a right to expect of a man whom you have honored by making him a member of your Cabinet. Accordingly, I am resigning as Secretary of the Interior and, at your pleasure, I would like my resignation to take effect not later than the 29th of February.

You have highly honored me by naming and retaining me as a member of your Cabinet for practically seven years. Until last July 1, I thoroughly enjoyed my work. Although I now feel that I cannot go on, I want you to know how much I appreciate the many expressions of regard and confidence that I have had from you and what an inspiration it has been to work in such close cooperation with the man whom I regard as the outstanding statesman of his generation.

Sincerely yours,

HAROLD L. ICKES

[13:PSF:INTERIOR:TS]

979   Roosevelt to Harold L. Ickes, Secretary of the Interior

Washington, *February 8, 1940*

Memorandum for F. D. R.: On receipt of the attached,[1] I wrote longhand a memorandum to H. L. I. and gave it to him.

Memorandum for H. L. I.: You and I have been married "for better or worse" for too long to get a divorce or for you to break up the home. I continue to need you.

Affectionately,

F. D. R.

[13:PSF:INTERIOR:T]

[1] The preceding letter. Roosevelt wrote this memorandum to himself.

980   Harold L. Ickes, Secretary of the Interior, to Roosevelt

[Washington] *Feb'y. 8, 1940*

My dear Mr. President: You are a hard man to deal with, especially when anyone admires and loves you as I do. Your letter quite touched me.[1] I am yours to command to the extent of my ability; of my devotion there can be no doubt.

However, in all sincerity, I believe that the flank attack on Forestry that I suggested yesterday is the proper approach at this time. You cannot afford to be beaten on this issue and I am apprehensive. Least of all would I want to be even indirectly responsible for your defeat.

With deep affection,

Harold

[13:PSF:INTERIOR:AS]

[1] Above.

981   Frederic A. Delano, Chairman, National Resources Planning Board, to Roosevelt

Washington, D. C., *February 8, 1940*

Memorandum for The President: Since the Senate voted $710,-000 for the work of the National Resources Planning Board for the fiscal year beginning July 1, I have reviewed the wording of the Federal Employment Stabilization Act which would control our future operations under the amendment approved by the Senate. As far as I can see now we could continue practically all of our present activities under the authority of that Act.

The emphasis by the Senate on the Employment Stabilization Act will clarify our legal status and should help the House Committee to justify agreement in conference to our appropriation.

[422]

I am informed that the Rivers and Harbors and Flood Control groups in the House are active in opposition to any appropriation for our work. It has been suggested that if you could talk with Judge Mansfield and Judge Whittington it might be possible to dissipate the fog of misunderstanding as to the relations between the Corps of Engineers and your Resources Planning Board.

FREDERIC A. DELANO

[*Notation*:A] Place on President's desk

[13:OF 1092:TS]

982   ROOSEVELT TO REPRESENTATIVE WILLIAM M. WHITTINGTON OF MISSISSIPPI, CHAIRMAN, HOUSE COMMITTEE ON FLOOD CONTROL

[WASHINGTON] *February 14, 1940*

MY DEAR JUDGE WHITTINGTON: I am dictating this just as I leave to go on a little holiday to take the place of the one I missed last Summer.

It relates to the Senate vote for $710,000 for the work of the National Resources Planning Board for the coming fiscal year.

Lest there be any misunderstanding, I can assure you that the work of this National Resources Planning Board interferes in no way with the work of the Army Engineers. Furthermore, this has been stated in writing to the Secretary of War by the Acting Chief of Engineers, and there is no opposition on the part of the Army Engineers to the Coordination of various kinds of public works with the assistance of the National Resources Planning Board. In other words, there is understanding and harmony in the Executive Branch of the Government.

Finally, I am sure you will realize that under the Constitution the President is the responsible head of the Executive Branch of the Government. After a somewhat long experience as Governor for four years and as President for seven, I am very certain that the office of President of the United States requires expert assistance in coordination work through some agency such as the National Resources Planning Board. This fact applies not to me personally as President but to any President in the future who occupies the office.

Therefore, I appeal to you officially and personally to help me to retain the very valuable coordinating services of the National Resources Planning Board. This is a matter of good administration, and I hope that every member of your Committee and every member of the Congress will think of the problem of the Chief Executive in this light—regardless of party and regardless of any other interest. May I add that the functioning of the National Resources Planning Board on the appropriation inserted by the Senate will, in my judgment and in the interest of economy, save the taxpayers of the United States several times the amount of the appropriation.[1]

Very sincerely yours,

[FRANKLIN D. ROOSEVELT]

[13:OF 1092:CT]

[1] The 1941 Independent Offices Appropriation Bill (H. R. 7922) carried an appropriation of $1,000,000 for the National Resources Planning Board. This was eliminated by the House Appropriations Committee on the ground that the activities of the agency were not authorized by law (*Cong. Rec.*, 76th Cong., 3d sess., 1940, 86: 1, 380). Budget Director Smith then suggested to Roosevelt in a letter of Jan. 19, 1940 (OF 1092), that an attempt be made to have the item restored when the bill came before the Senate Appropriations Committee. Smith said that it was his understanding that if this were done no point of order could lie against the appropriation.

Roosevelt asked for restoration of the appropriation in a memorandum to Speaker of the House William Bankhead of Jan. 23, 1940 (OF 1092), pointing out that he had always approved estimates of appropriations for the legislative department and that the National Resources Planning Board was an integral part of the Office of the President. Copies of this memorandum were sent to Representatives Rayburn, Woodrum, Warren and Cochran and to Senators Byrnes and Glass. When an amendment appropriating $710,000 was reported by the Senate Committee on Appropriations on Feb. 6, 1940, Senator Clark (Mo.) asked what authority in law there was for the action. Byrnes explained that under the Reorganization Act there had been transferred to the National Resources Planning Board the functions of the Federal Employment Stabilization Board of the Department of Commerce and that the latter board had been set up by the act approved Feb. 10, 1931 (46 *Stat.* 1084). Clark then offered an amendment to restrict the appropriation to those functions formerly performed by the Stabilization Board (to advise the President on employment cycles and to coordinate public works planning). Clark's amendment was approved and an acrimonious debate ensued, led by Taft (Ohio), who argued that the work of the National Resources Planning Board was unnecessary, or, if necessary, was work that could be done as well or better by the executive departments or by the President's assistants. The appropriation was, however, approved by the Senate but by a margin of three votes only (*Cong. Rec.*, 86: 1, 1046–1059).

The letter to Whittington here printed was answered Feb. 16, 1940 (OF 1092). Whittington said that he would support the appropriation but not legislation for a permanent planning board. Letters similar to the one to Whittington were also sent by Roosevelt to Representative Mansfield (Texas), chairman of the House Committee on Rivers and Harbors, and to Representative Woodrum (Va.), chairman of the House Committee on Appropriations, both dated Feb. 14, 1940 (OF 1092). The letter to Woodrum was read into the *Congressional Record* during the House debate on the Planning Board amendment; this was agreed to by the House on April 18. The Independent Offices Appropriation Bill was approved April 18, 1940 (*Cong. Rec.*, 86: 4, 4450–4460; 86: 5, 4889; 54 *Stat.* 111).

983   ROOSEVELT TO THE NATIONAL RESOURCES PLANNING BOARD

WASHINGTON, *February 14, 1940*

MEMORANDUM FOR THE NATIONAL RESOURCES PLANNING BOARD:
Ten days ago a member of the Congress suggested to me that at the Coolidge Dam, the reservoir is not being filled as usual in winter and spring because the large number of check-dams higher up on the water-

shed allow seepage and evaporation to such an extent that the water does not follow its normal course into the reservoir.

This complaint may be the forerunner of similar complaints in different parts of the country and would constitute a rather definite attack on the "up-stream" theory of soil erosion, of prevention, rapid run-off and floods.

I do not take much stock in it but I think the Government should be prepared with an answer.

For example, there is need for study of just what happens to water held back by check-dams in the higher parts of the semiarid belt which runs from the Dakotas to Texas. I have always felt that the hold back of this water either by increased vegetation or by check-dams ought to raise the general water table and that in doing so, the water would gradually find its way toward the sea either underground (thus raising water tables further downstream) or by finding its way to the surface again.

I suggest that the National Resources Committee handle this study in consultation with the Department of Agriculture, the Soil Erosion Service,[1] the Bureau of Reclamation, etc. I enclose a letter from the Secretary of Agriculture in regard to the San Carlos Reservoir.[2]

F. D. R.[3]

[13:OF 1092:T]

[1] Soil Conservation Service.
[2] Wallace to Roosevelt, Feb. 13, 1940, in which Wallace reviewed the rainfall and water discharge records in the Gila River and Salt River watersheds. He concluded that the cause of the irrigation difficulty was inaccurate estimates of Gila River run-off made prior to the construction of the Coolidge Dam, and that "sooner or later we must give even more serious consideration to retarding run-off from abused, eroding lands. Otherwise we may expect to have vast areas, even whole watersheds, completely denuded of vegetation, resulting in highly accelerated run-off and erosion."
[3] Copies of this letter were sent to Ickes and Wallace.

984   HENRY A. WALLACE, SECRETARY OF AGRICULTURE, TO ROOSEVELT

WASHINGTON, *March 2, 1940*

DEAR MR. PRESIDENT: During our discussion on February 13,[1] you referred to the grazing situation on the National Forests. I want to supplement briefly what I said to you then.

Grazing by domestic livestock was an established use of most of the western and some of the southern National Forests before they were established. When the Department of Agriculture took over the National Forests in 1905, it found widespread overgrazing. To a large degree the use of the range was dependent on who could get there first or who could defend his occupancy most stoutly.

Range administration was undertaken at once. The privilege was continued for those most entitled to it. Prompt steps were taken toward the elimination of overgrazing. Naturally, this could not be accomplished overnight, but it was not many years before there was marked improvement. This improvement was due both to reduced numbers of stock and the introduction of a long list of good range use practices developed or sponsored by the Forest Service.

Things were going along nicely, and range conditions were steadily improving when the World War came along. Then under the urge by the Administration to produce more livestock products, temporary overstocking of many ranges was permitted. This reversed the beneficial trend.

After the War, reductions began again. By 1939, there had been a reduction of 40 per cent of the number of stock using the National Forests in 1918.

Meanwhile, along came the prolonged droughts. The deterioration of the range due to drought in many cases offset the reductions which were being made, and it was not possible to keep fully abreast of the needs for livestock reductions. As a result, we still have too many localized overgrazed areas. However, the program of reductions and other measures are being applied, and we expect to work our way steadily toward satisfactory stocking and good range conditions. Meanwhile, the greater part of the National Forest ranges is in good condition.

It is, of course, impossible to make reductions all at once or at too sharp a rate. The reason for this is that the use of the National Forest summer ranges is an indispensable part of one of the big means of livelihood in the National Forest regions. We have about 25,000 permittees on the National Forests. Their use is based on the ownership, or control, of about 4½ million acres of cultivated crop lands and 22 million acres of pasture lands, mostly adjacent to the National Forests. There is an investment of about $300,000,000 in livestock and ranches, which is related to National Forest use.

A significant feature of this use is the degree to which it furnishes a means of livelihood to small home owners; 83 per cent of the cattle and horse permits are granted to owners who are permitted to run less than 100 head each; 91 per cent of the sheep permits are for less than 2000 head each. Some of the reductions will fall on this class. These numbers are already so small that it is difficult, or impossible, to reduce them further without jeopardizing the integrity of the home maintenance enterprise. Nevertheless, overgrazing must be eliminated.

In addition to reductions in livestock numbers for the protection of the range itself, there have been substantial reductions to prevent damage to other resources or undue interference with the use of the other resources. Grazing use is simply one element in multiple use. The grazing often occurs on areas also bearing timber; the open areas are interspersed among the forests or in the upper reaches above timberline. So grazing must on occasion give way to recreation or wildlife, for example, or be excluded temporarily from areas restocking with young growth or permanently from some city watersheds.

I am sure you will be interested in glancing at the enclosed booklet, *Along the Beale Trail.*[2] This was issued by the Office of Indian Affairs in the Department of the Interior. Some of the National Forest pictures are in the neighborhood covered by Mrs. Greenaway's comment to you.[3] While we have a good many spots on the National Forests that do not look as well as those pictured in the booklet, there is no question that in general the National Forest ranges stand out as being in much better condition than most of those in private ownership and on the public domain. I can assure you that the Department is pursuing an aggressive policy in curing all the sore spots on the National Forest ranges.

I shall send you separate comments on the matter of accomplishing more coordination in policy with the Taylor Act administration, and the reduction of costs through cooperation.[4]

Sincerely yours,

H. A. WALLACE

[13:PSF:AGRICULTURE:TS]

[1] Wallace lunched with Roosevelt on this date (PPF 1–O).
[2] H. C. Lockett and Milton Snow, *Along the Beale Trail. A Photographic Account of Wasted Range Land, Based on the Diary of Lieutenant Edward F. Beale, 1857* (Washington, 1939).
[3] Not explained; Mrs. Isabella Greenway, congresswoman from Arizona (1935–37), may be meant.
[4] Writing to Roosevelt March 19, 1940 (PSF: Agriculture), Wallace enclosed "Suggestions for Coordinating Grazing Work in the Department of the Interior and the Department of Agriculture," a one-page memorandum. This proposed joint use, where possible, of headquarters, exchange of short-term personnel and of data, joint consideration of grazing applications and range research needs, and the settling of differences.

985   ROOSEVELT TO CLYDE L. SEAVEY, Washington, D. C.

[WASHINGTON] *March 4, 1940*

DEAR CLYDE: I was delighted to find your letter on my arrival at Pensacola.[1]

Will you be good enough to ask the California Nursery Company when they ship the trees, to send them to William Plog, care of Mrs. James Roosevelt, Hyde Park, Dutchess County, New York.

Meanwhile I will let Mr. Plog know just where to plant the trees. The larger trees I will put—half of them, near the new library, and the other five at the edge of our front lawn.

[427]

The smaller trees, I think, I will try on the east end of our place near my new cottage. I am thrilled at the thought of having them.

Always sincerely,

[FRANKLIN D. ROOSEVELT]

FDR/TMB

[13:PPF 6391:CT]

¹ From Feb. 15 to March 1, 1940, Roosevelt was aboard the U. S. S. *Tuscaloosa*, cruising in West Indian waters. Seavey's letter of Feb. 29, 1940 (PPF 6391), informed him that ten sequoia trees would be shipped from California about April 1.

986   WARD SHEPARD TO EDWIN M. WATSON, SECRETARY TO THE PRESIDENT

OAKTON, VA., *March 4, 1940*

MY DEAR GENERAL WATSON: About three weeks before his death, F. A. Silcox engaged me to help him prepare a legislative program to present to the Joint Congressional Committee on Forestry, and since then I have worked with the Committee, without official status, to try to lay the groundwork for an effective report to the Congress.

I am intimately familiar with the deep-seated conflict over policy within the Forest Service that thwarted Silcox and that is now thwarting the Joint Committee in their efforts to create a genuine forest policy. I have brought this chaotic situation forcibly to the attention of the Department of Agriculture, but it remains uncorrected. Regardless of whether the Forest Service is transferred to the Interior Department, this grave internal weakness must be cleared up before any progress can be made in forest conservation.

It will, in my opinion, be a grave public misfortune if the Joint Committee, appointed by the Congress on the recommendation of the President, should after two years' work be misled into submitting a weak report to Congress because of the serious inadequacy of the program recently submitted to it by the Acting Chief Forester—a program which Silcox had decisively rejected.

This matter is urgent because the Committee expires April 1st. It is also closely related to the appointment of a successor to Silcox. On the latter point, I have no specific candidate to propose, but rather the type of man needed to meet a critical situation. In addition I have drafted a specific and far-reaching plan of action to end destructive cutting of our forests which I think is of such national importance and so politically and fiscally feasible that it should be brought to the President's attention.¹ For this reason, I greatly desire an interview with the President on matters that cannot be well treated in writing. . . .

Sincerely yours,

WARD SHEPARD

[13:OF 1–C:TS]

[428]

987   HAROLD L. ICKES, SECRETARY OF THE INTERIOR, TO ROOSEVELT

WASHINGTON [*March 7, 1940*]

MY DEAR MR. PRESIDENT: I have read Secretary Wallace's letter to you of March 2 with a great deal of interest. After carefully considering all of the points made by the Secretary I cannot escape from the idea that he has failed to grasp the broad importance of the matter under discussion. It seems to me that under these circumstances it would be entirely proper to present to you my concept of this problem and how it can best be solved in the public's interest and under a long-time land use plan.

The act authorizing the establishment of the forest reserves was for the primary and avowed purpose of protecting the Nation's forest resources. Forest reserves, and later national forests, were established pursuant to the Act of June 4, 1897 (30 *Stat.* 11, 34, 36) *U.S.C.* Title 16, Section 475. In that Act this significant section occurs:

> No public forest reservation shall be established, except to improve and protect the forests within the reservation, or for the purpose of securing favorable conditions of water flows, and to effect a continuous supply of timber for the use and necessities of citizens of the United States; but it is not the purpose or intent of these provisions, or of the act providing for such reservations, to authorize the inclusion therein of lands more valuable for the minerals therein, or for agricultural purposes, than for forest purposes.[1]

The original reservations and forests were largely of the type contemplated under the law of 1897. In recent years the forests have been extended to embrace large areas of land clearly outside the purview of the act. These extensions of forest areas into the open or sparsely timbered range lands of the West have aggregated many millions of acres. These extensions, ostensibly made for watershed protection purposes when timber values were impossible to defend, in general constituted an invasion of areas of primary value for range purposes and the imposition of a timber or forest economy that has often been inimical to grazing or range use, and to the unbalancing of the local economy built and maintained by the livestock industry. Grazing use by the livestock industry of lands within forests has been permitted because denial of such use would have resulted in widespread disturbance of social and economic conditions in the western range areas. Such grazing use of the forests under sufferance is contrasted with legal recognition of grazing use on the Federal ranges under the Taylor Act. The security provided under the Taylor Act has such obvious advantages as to need no defense. Such security is essential to stabilization of the stock industry;

[429]

the development of a sound economy in the range territory and rehabilitation of the ranges.

Of the thousands of forest grazing users, only a small percentage is entirely dependent upon forest range for a livelihood. The great majority use forest ranges for only limited seasons each year. During the other seasons the stock are on private, leased, or Federal range lands.

The ranges being administered under the Taylor Grazing Act provide a part or all of the off-forest grazing by an estimated 75 percent of the forest users, while only approximately 25 percent of the Federal range users are dependent in any degree upon the national forests.

Of the thousands of forest users, many receive permits for only a portion of the stock they own and wish to graze. The Forest Service restricts numbers of stock and grazing use in accordance with climatic conditions and requires owners to find other ranges for any additional numbers of stock or for all stock during seasons or parts of seasons when climatic conditions are unfavorable. Other lands, therefore, carry and have carried the burden of the full numbers of stock owned. In the case of the Grazing Service, the size of permits or licenses truly reflects the actual size of the operations of the permittees or licensees. The apparently large number of small licensees or permittees using the national forest ranges is not a true picture of the size of operations or the classification of users as small or large.

The condition of forest ranges where they are admitted to be in good condition is due largely to the forced use of public domain and other range outside the national forests by stock that have been excluded or those that are kept off until the Forest Service decides that the forest range is ready for use.

Because of this restricted range policy of the Forest Service, forest ranges have been protected at the expense of public and private holdings and with little regard for the economic effect on owners who, having the stock on hand, must necessarily graze them somewhere while waiting to get onto [sic] the forests. This long established policy of the Forest Service is in definite contrast with that being followed by the Grazing Service for meeting the broad social and economic problems in the range country. The Forest Service is interested primarily in timber and forest products and such related uses of forest lands that do not interfere with forest growth. Forest administration has been directed along these lines regardless of the effect on the livestock industry. They have permitted vast areas of open range land to grow up into a jungle of small reproduction, excluding grazing, and yet in many of these same areas there is little or no opportunity ever to develop commercial timber stands.

The cumulative effect of 35 years of this type of administration is noticeable in hundreds of mountain valleys and rural communities. Social and economic values have been sacrificed to the growing of timber of no commercial worth and of no greater watershed protection value than would have been furnished by a good stand of grass and browse, the use of which would have permitted continuance of a livestock economy, production of taxes, income, and a livelihood for many persons directly and a very large number indirectly.

The Forest Service has in its past administration failed to give due consideration to proper use of private as well as public lands in its long-time planning. It has substituted an economy based primarily on timber production for the one evolved by trial and error methods of the western people over a long period of years.

The Forest Service alone among Federal agencies has heretofore failed to indicate a desire to recognize the desirability or significance of correlated management of all Federal lands and land resources. This applies especially to grazing lands and the forage resources. This attitude on the part of the Forest Service is in strong contrast to that of other bureaus of the Government where cooperative agreements have been executed authorizing the Grazing Service of the Interior Department to administer lands or act as a grazing adviser. Such agreements are in effect with the Soil Conservation Service and the Farm Security Administration of the Department of Agriculture, and with the Reclamation Service, the Biological Survey, the National Park Service, the Indian Service of the Department of the Interior, and even on areas under the control of the War and Navy Departments. Furthermore, the Grazing Service secured enactment of the Pierce Act which permits correlated use of privately owned, State, and county lands without affecting titles or tax rolls.

The Grazing Service of this Department, under the authority of the Taylor Grazing Act, is engaged in the administration of approximately 134,000,000 acres of grazing land in 10 western States. Interspersed with this area are upwards of 25,000,000 acres of national forest lands, *including entire "forests" in a number of instances, which are non-timbered grazing lands.* In close association with these areas are 40,-000,000 to 45,000,000 acres more of national forest land, the primary resource value of which is grazing. *The tree growth supported thereon is of minor or insignificant value as a source of commercial timber or a basis for operations that would provide a livelihood for some of our citizens.* This area within grazing districts and forests of more than 200,000,000 acres of public grazing land, together with nearly a like amount of privately owned farm, ranch, and range lands constitutes the backbone of the livestock industry and the general economy of these western States.

In my opinion the existing divided administration of the public grazing land is productive of waste and inefficiency, in a large measure is unsound and ineffective, and consequently is detrimental to the public interest. The proposal of Secretary Wallace to continue with only slight modification, this method of administration would provide but minor improvements at best, and would be unworkable in practice. The proposed situation would be comparable to two families attempting to use the same household facilities. Confusion and conflict would be inevitable.

This Department has given long and careful consideration to the question of properly conserving or providing for orderly use of the vast heritage embraced in our Federal lands and the resources thereon. I know how interested you are in trying to effect and put into action a long-time program of administration that will provide the greatest possible benefit, not only to the lands and the resources, but to the public that owns both and is entitled to an efficient and proper administration thereof.

I believe that a unified administration of the public grazing land is imperative to the accomplishment of your purpose. May I suggest, therefore, that the first step toward accomplishing this most desirable objective would be to determine the primary values of the lands in question and then to assign them to the respective agencies responsible for their proper administration. This would result in the transfer from the forests, to the grazing districts, under Section 13 of the Taylor Act, of administratively manageable areas approximating 25,000,000 acres of open non-commercial timberland of primary value for grazing purposes, and the transfer of any manageable units of lands supporting commercial timber stands from the grazing districts to the adjacent forests. For the remaining 40,000,000 or 45,000,000 acres of land of combined forest and grazing value, such areas could be administered under cooperative arrangements similar to those now in effect with other bureaus of this Government as heretofore mentioned.

Sincerely yours,

HAROLD L. ICKES

[*Notation*: A] 3/7/40

[13:PSF:INTERIOR:TS]

[1] Ickes' quotation is not precise: for "protect the forests" read *protect the forest;* for "to effect" read *to furnish;* for "minerals" read *mineral.*

988   WARD SHEPARD TO ROOSEVELT

OAKTON, VIRGINIA, *March 14, 1940*

DEAR MR. PRESIDENT: In response to your request last Friday,[1] I tried to get the full transcript of the program Mr. Clapp recommended to the Joint Committee, but the Committee has at present only one master corrected copy. I have therefore copied verbatim all the salient features of the voluminous recommendations, and send them herewith, together with an analysis of their basic principles. I hate to afflict you with more documents, but the enclosed, I think, are the minimum required for full understanding. I shall send you the original transcript, as soon as it is available.[2]

Respectfully,

WARD SHEPARD

[13:OF 1-C:TS]

[1] Shepard talked with Roosevelt at the White House on Friday, March 8, and left with him his outline of a proposed forestry act, "Outline of a Proposed Organic Act of Congress to Prevent Forest Degeneration and Destruction and to Preserve and Rebuild Forest Resources." Roosevelt sent the outline to Senator Bankhead with a note asking Bankhead to speak to him about it ("Memorandum for Senator Bankhead," March 11, 1940, OF 1-C).

[2] Acting Chief Forester Clapp's statement to the Joint Committee and the statements of the other Forest Service officers are printed in part 8 of *Forest Lands of the United States,* Hearings before the Joint Committee on Forestry, 75-76th Cong. . . . 1938-40 (Washington, 1939-40).

989   [*Enclosure*]

OAKTON, VIRGINIA, *March 14, 1940*

Analysis of the Private Forestry and Public Acquisition Program Presented by the Forest Service to the Joint Congressional Committee on Forestry

Introduction

This program, as presented by Acting Chief Forester Clapp and his associates on behalf of the Department of Agriculture, is nihilistic and defeatist in its basic assumptions, in its plan of execution, and in its costs. It aims, in general, at mere reproductive logging instead of selective cutting, and is thus based on a century's cutting cycle instead of a five or ten-year cutting cycle. It contains two distinct, inadequate, and irreconcilable plans of administration. It seeks to perpetuate, on a gigantic scale, the indefensible investment of large sums in the purchase of cut-over, wrecked forest lands. By failing to build on the immediate public and private profitableness of selective cutting, it places on industry, on farmers, on government, and on the agencies of credit the insoluble fiscal problem of attempting to rehabilitate a steadily degenerating and ultimately worthless forest growing stock. . . .

Before proceeding, I wish to give an accurate definition of what I mean by "selective cutting." I use this popular layman's term to cover weeding, thinning, stand improvement, and proper methods of reproductive cutting, such as the shelterwood system—all flexibly adapted to the diverse needs of different forest types and even allowing clear cutting where desirable; and flexible in intensity of application, dependent on local costs and returns. I exclude "high-grading"—i. e., cutting the best and leaving the worst.

There are two great advantages in selective cutting, thus defined. First, it is the only means of preserving the fecundity and energy of the forest as a living organism. Its violation inevitably leads to forest degeneration and annihilation by exhausting the vitality of nature. Second, it is the most profitable form of forest exploitation, since it greatly speeds up quantity and quality growth and permits a return cut every five to ten years, thus exorcising the layman's pet ghost that it takes a century to grow timber. This is the only fiscally possible basis of private and public investment and of any sound system of public and private credit. Mere "reproductive logging" (i. e., seed-trees) will bankrupt private investors, the banks that give them credit, and the program of public acquisition.

Silvicultural Defeatism

The Forest Service's plan does not provide for selective cutting, except as it may be voluntarily adopted here and there. The Forest Service did not even mention the word or any equivalent thereof in the entire course of its three days' prepared testimony. It omits selective cutting from the regulatory program, as shown by the following statement after the specific regulatory requirements:

Except within restricted limits indicated, they will not control species and mixtures of species, or silvicultural systems. . . . They will, however, take an important step in the right direction by stopping the further destruction or deterioration of the forests we now have.

The last sentence is entirely erroneous. Such requirements would permit natural reseeding, but they would in no wise halt the rapid process of degeneration that is going on everywhere by clear-cutting and high-grading. The prevention of these two latter practices is the very essence of the immediate problem, because 10 to 20 years more of this kind of cutting will so degenerate the remaining growing stock as to make it an impossible field of private investment and will transform it into a gigantic and fiscally insoluble problem of public rehabilitation.

The decision on this single point spells the difference between forest regeneration and virtual annihilation. The Forest Service is apparently proceeding on the assumption that the kindest way to dock a dog's tail is to cut it off an inch at a time. On the contrary, the few adventurous lumbermen who have tried real selective cutting have found it amazingly profitable. Wilson Compton has told me he regards selective cutting as the only salvation of the lumber industry. Frederick Weyerhaeuser told me he looked on Article X of the Lumber Code as the life buoy of the industry. And at the conclusion of my polite but drastic testimony before the Joint Committee, George Jewett (a leading member of the Weyerhaeuser family and Chairman of the Conservation Committee of the National Lumber Manufacturers Association) told me that he would accept my *whole* program on behalf of his Committee *if* the Joint Committee would accept it as a whole. Furthermore, most European regulation (including the Swedish) in practice puts the main emphasis on selective cutting as defined above, even though their capital growing stock never had deteriorated remotely to the present degenerate level of our own second growth forests.

The public acquisition program (presented by Mr. Kneipp) is based essentially on buying cut-over lands, as shown by the low average per acre price of a little over six dollars and the failure to present any articulate program of investing in lands with good growing stock. It is unfair to ask the people to invest large sums in buying, administering, and developing these essentially worthless wrecked properties, when there is abundant opportunity for developing rapidly self-liquidating investments by buying good growing stock over 25 years old, as my plan suggests.

The Forest Service proposes to allot only ten million dollars for state and community acquisition. In Germany, all the public forests are state or community forests and yield large revenues. So disproportionate a Federal share in the public forest program will intensify present political pressure for larger and larger handouts to the States and counties in lieu of taxes.

This acquisition program is a revamping of that in the "Copeland Report" of 1933, and, like that report, is based on the unsound assumption that industry can make no substantial contribution to the solution of the forest problem, as shown by Mr. Kneipp's comment: "Notwithstanding all hopeful developments, and the declared intentions of certain forest owners, the test of the adequacy of present plans of forest utilization is whether the cut-over lands will again be fully productive by the time the remainder of the existing timber supply is utilized."

This passage contains a subtle trap for the unwary reader, namely, *"present plans of forest utilization."* The duty of the Forest Service is to help the Committee create an adequate plan to prevent forest liquidation instead of proposing a gigantic nationalization of wrecked forests to hide its failure to create such a plan. This pessimism is indeed justified by this failure and by the weakness of the latest Forest Service program; but it is not justifiable in relation to a program based on the true economics of selective cutting. This acquisition program is another proof of the inability of the Forest Service to understand the fiscal problems at the root of the forest problem. Even worse, it is nihilistic in that it fatalistically accepts forest devastation as inevitable and insoluble and erects a gigantic and jerry-built structure of public ownership on the ghastly ruins of destructive forest exploitation.

These man-made deserts are on the march. In another single generation they will engulf vast areas of this continent. Who, in God's name, is going to furnish the billions of dollars required to rebuild them? The answer is, Nobody. They will remain desolate wastelands for centuries. They will be like the lifeless valley of the Tigris and Euphrates that once supported a mighty civilization, in which the only visible sign of life that my old friend Lowdermilk saw on a recent journey there was a lean and hungry wolf sitting on his haunches in the mournful ruins of the palace of some mighty king of Babylon. The only answer is to prevent the making of these deserts by saving the precious capital growing stock while there is still time to make it a profitable private and public investment.

Administrative Defeatism

The Forest Service program contains two separate, antagonistic, and irreconcilable administrative systems:

(1) The appointment of 850 county foresters to operate under the Agricultural Extension Service;

(2) A system of administrative districts, to be set up by the Forest Service in co-operation with the State foresters for the operation of the huge leasing system proposed in the Fulmer Bill.

The problem of replacing destructive liquidation with sustained yield management is not primarily an educational problem, but a complex problem of readjusting and reorganizing forest land use and the manufacture and marketing of forest products. It is in the order of magnitude and complexity of the agricultural adjustment and the soil conservation programs.

The Extension Service, though it has a place in this job, is not qualified to be the principal agency. If it were otherwise, why is it that such formidable phenomena as agricultural maladjustment and soil erosion escaped not only the active attention but largely even the perception of the Extension Service for many years, and forced this Administration to create the Agricultural Adjustment Administration, the Soil Conservation Service, and the Grazing Administration? And why is it that 16 years after the passage of the Clarke-McNary Act, the Extension Service has only 50 extension foresters out of a total technical personnel of over 9,000? The formidable problem of forest devastation can not be solved by lantern slide lectures and half-acre demonstrations, which is the modus operandi of the Extension Service.

The district concept of the Fulmer Bill is excellent so far as it goes, but it should go much further and be, not merely a device for leasing, but the fundamental unit for the concurrent solution of the whole range of forest problems involved in a given geographical unit. This is what my bill proposes. It fits in with the ranger district unit of National Forest administration, with the public domain grazing districts already organized on 134 million acres of land, and with the Soil Conservation districts adopted by 36 States and already organized or being organized on 220 million acres of land. The inherent soundness of this district approach is due to the fact that the problems of land use on the ground are interlocked and their solution must be an integral solution.

My plan utilizes the soil conservation districts for forest management on private forest lands important for erosion and flood control and establishes forest conservation districts in all other private forests. This, incidentally, is the only logical dividing line yet proposed for the division of functions between two forestry agencies, for it is a geographical, not an ownership division. My plan, therefore, merely completes the New Deal strategy for improved land management. But it goes further: it unifies soil conservation, forest conservation, upstream engineering, and conservation relief work under one operational concept, a unification that is vitally essential to solidify the splendid gains of the New Deal in these fields.

Now, Mr. Clapp, in the entire course of his voluminous testimony, did not mention the words "soil conservation district." I am loath to believe that so impressive a social phenomenon as this almost unmanageable pressure of the people for soil (and forest) conservation has entirely escaped his observation. I hope, therefore, that my inference is not unjust that he regards bureaucratic jurisdiction as being superior to the public good, and that he prefers to throw the forest problem into the hands of the administratively powerless and politically powerful Extension Service because that Service has frequently shared with him a burning zeal to thwart the triumphant progress of Hugh Bennett's work of sheer genius. Mr. Glenn Frank is an unhappy fellow traveler in the same direction in his Republican program.

As to leasing: Silcox made it clear that he thought of leasing in terms of a limited localized solution of the rural relief problem rather than a generalized and major solution of the entire forest problem. Zealots on his staff have transformed it into the latter, and this in turn is due to the pervasive lack of understanding in the Forest Service of the basic economic advantages of selective cutting. My plan permits a limited leasing, which with the definition of hazard reduction, gully control and upstream engineering on private lands as public works, and the provision of low interest conservation credit, will permit the handling of the rural relief problem without the Government embarking on a gigantic and expensive real estate operation.

Fiscal Defeatism

The Forest Service program is estimated ultimately to cost 17 billion dollars, which is conservative because it is based on rehabilitation and not on silviculture. I propose to finance the districts by a light tax on forest products and the acquisition program by self-liquidating bonds

[437]

for a program based on profitable silviculture. I do not pretend to pass on the immediate political feasibility or the exact form of these fiscal methods, but in principle they are indispensable in financing so large and profitable an undertaking.

Conclusion

The Forest Service program should, in my opinion, be quietly withdrawn "for further consideration"—and laid on the shelf. The New Deal has nothing to lose and everything to gain by working out a real solution that will be immensely popular, even among the better class of lumber barons. There is still time, as Senator Bankhead is requesting the extension of the Committee to February 1, 1941.

WARD SHEPARD

[13:OF 1–C:TS]

990   HENRY A. WALLACE, SECRETARY OF AGRICULTURE, TO ROOSEVELT

[WASHINGTON] *March 14, 1940*

DEAR MR. PRESIDENT: With regard to the Ward Shepard story, you will be interested in knowing that before the death of Silcox and after his death Shepard has had only a very indirect connection with the Forest Service. Some time before Silcox's death it had been worked out that Shepard would be hired on a consulting basis, and for a limited time, by the Bureau of Agricultural Economics. He was so serving at the time of Silcox's death and continued so to serve for a month or so, to the expiration of the time for which he was originally appointed. Any differences he might have had were wholly with the Bureau of Agricultural Economics and without any knowledge at all and only an indirect involvement on the part of the Forest Service itself.

The only way in which the Forest Service may have come even indirectly into the picture was in connection with a contemplated revision of a report prepared in the Forest Service for possible submission to the Joint Congressional Committee on Forestry, in which, among other duties, Shepard was to serve in an advisory capacity as a representative of the Bureau of Agricultural Economics. The complications growing out of Silcox's death on December 20, the preparation for oral presentations at the hearings of the Joint Committee beginning in mid-January and extending to mid-February, and the pressure of other work has made it impossible as yet for the Forest Service to go forward with such a revision.

Shepard's contention now is that after Silcox's death the Forest Service scuttled the Silcox program and then presented to the Joint Committee the so-called Clapp program which Shepard says Silcox had disapproved. The truth is that Silcox, Clapp and many others cooperated in preparing for the Joint Committee a single, broadly conceived program for a national forestry economy. All the records prove this. The only revision undertaken was one to make the whole document more simple, direct and persuasive. This revison was not completed prior to the Congressional hearings. Hence, the Forest Service testimony was wholly oral. During the hearings Shepard exerted considerable pressure on the Joint Committee to be heard. A member of the Committee asked Earle Clapp, who was in charge of the Forest Service presentations, for advice. Clapp urged that Shepard be heard; this was done and afforded Shepard a full opportunity to present his views.[1]

Shepard's ideas on forest policy are good, but not unique and not the last word by any means. They are shared by many who are not inclined to credit Shepard with their authorship. . . .

Sincerely yours,

[HENRY A. WALLACE]

[13:PSF:AGRICULTURE:CT]

[1] "Statement of Ward Shepard, Bureau of Agricultural Economics," in *Forest Lands of the United States,* Hearings before the Joint Committee on Forestry . . . 1940 (Washington, 1940), pp. 1845–1856.

991   HENRY A. WALLACE, SECRETARY OF AGRICULTURE, TO ROOSEVELT

WASHINGTON, *March 28, 1940*

DEAR MR. PRESIDENT: Last year I wrote you regarding the Prairie States Forestry Project (the Shelterbelt)[1] and recommended that Congress be asked to give it recognition by appropriating at least sufficient funds for the Department to carry the administrative and supervisory personnel and provide basic facilities needed on a year-long basis with the idea that the Project could then be contracted or expanded with emergency funds. No regular funds were provided in the 1941 Budget.

This program has become very popular with the farmers in the six Plains States in which it operates.[2] Newspaper comment through that region, and generally throughout the Nation, is now preponderantly favorable. Testimony before the Joint Congressional Committee on Forestry has been favorable. , During the past summer the Department of Agriculture coordinators for the northern and southern plains made independent investigations of the work and their reports substantiate the worthwhileness of this work and its favorable public acceptance. I am of the opinion that abrupt termination of the work at the end of the fiscal year would not be received favorably by the public.

The Project has been conducted wholly with WPA funds during the last four years. The increasing restrictions and limitations in the use of

[439]

WPA funds on work of this nature, requiring the application of exacting technical and scientific practices, have reached a critical point. Basically it is extremely difficult to reconcile satisfactorily a program primarily designed to relieve unemployment with a long-term program such as the Prairie States Forestry Project. Changes in regulations and uncertainties as to funds militate almost disastrously against effective handling of the work, having in mind the coordinated planning and action required on a project wherein nursery production must be under way and planting plans developed and cooperative agreements secured one to two years in advance of actual planting. Present man-month allowances for other than wages are entirely inadequate to provide necessary equipment and other minimum needs for a technical and widespread program of this character. The present 90–10 employment ratio coupled with the need to employ certain technical and other personnel on a year-long basis places an unhealthy pressure on the Project to employ labor in off-seasons or in less efficient ways and places a premium on volume rather than quality or work. The "freezing" of allotments by States prevents obviously necessary inter-state adjustments of work which develop months after allotments are made. Drought, hail, prevailing temperatures and other weather conditions affect nursery production, seed collection, and planting operations, and from an administrative standpoint, the continual loss of trained personnel—because of these obstacles to effective planning, prosecution of the work, and individual satisfaction in a job well done—is by no means the least serious factor. Relief from these and other restrictions is necessary if the work is to be continued.

Under date of March 18, I wrote the Director of the Budget briefly outlining the difficulties the Forest Service is encountering in continuing the project. I suggested that in view of the desirability of continuing the work in the Prairie-Plains States, some provision should be made to prevent the Project activities from becoming unworkable and that this could be done by including specific language in the Relief Act, recognizing the unique problems surrounding this work. I now understand that the Budget Bureau has not provided the necessary change in language in the Relief Bill.

Knowing of your interest in this work, I feel sure you will wish to know of the exact situation for in the event that no relief can be obtained from the existing conditions, we shall feel compelled to suggest that the Project be abandoned. I strongly endorse the work that has been carried on so far, I strongly urge that it be continued, and I recommend that the Budget Bureau be asked to give it recognition by the insertion of the attached specific language in the Relief Act.[3]

Respectfully,

H. A. WALLACE

[13:OF 1–C:TS]

[1] *Ante,* 901.
[2] A summary of the reports on the Prairie States Forestry Project from the state directors of the Office of Government Reports in the states in which the project was operating was sent to Roosevelt by Director Mellett of that office in a letter of April 19, 1940 (OF 149).
[3] Providing for an appropriation of $2,120,000.

992   Roosevelt to the National Resources Planning Board

Washington, *April 5, 1940*

Gentlemen: You have under way the drafting of proposed amendments to the Wheeler-Case Act, the Act of August 11, 1939 (53 *Stat.* 1418) entitled "An act authorizing construction of water conservation and utilization projects in the Great Plains and arid and semiarid areas of the United States." I wish that you would incorporate in your draft of bill appropriate amendments to the Water Facilities Act, the Act of August 28, 1937 (53 *Stat.* 869) entitled "An act to promote conservation in the arid and semiarid areas of the United States by aiding in the development of facilities for water storage and utilization, and for other purposes."

The authorities contained in the two existing acts are overlapping to a very considerable extent and involve the same subject matter. Indications of my views as to what would be the appropriate scope of the Water Facilities Act are contained in the statement I made in a memorandum for the Bureau of the Budget, at the time I approved that measure. A copy of my statement is enclosed for your information and convenience.[1]

Sincerely yours,

[Franklin D. Roosevelt]

[13:OF 177:CT]

[1] *Ante,* 686. The letter here printed was drafted by the Interior Department. In his letter to Roosevelt enclosing the draft, April 4, 1940, Ickes expressed concern over the fact that the Water Facilities Act authorized the Agriculture Department to engage in reclamation activities of a kind that had always been administered by the Reclamation Bureau. He noted that the House Appropriations Committee in its report on the pending Agriculture Department appropriation bill had "expressly omitted any provision for carrying out the purposes of the Water Facilities Act on the ground that the authority of the Act should be exercised by the Department of the Interior."

993   Ward Shepard to Roosevelt

Vienna, Virginia, *April 8, 1940*

Memorandum for The President: Senator Bankhead is referring my "Outline of an Organic Forestry Act" to Secretary Wallace with the request that it be considered by the Department Program Board, which is composed of Chiefs of all the action Bureaus. This was the procedure

Silcox had in mind when he asked me to help him draft the legislative program. This fits in with Mr. Wallace's present plan, as he asked Mr. Milton Eisenhower, Chairman of the Program Board, to draft new recommendations to the Joint Committee.

As Mr. Eisenhower, a highly intelligent and devoted official, has little forestry background, and as my outline Act, in its basic principles, embodies Silcox's broad approach and appeals to Senator Bankhead, Secretary Wallace, and Secretary Ickes, I have two definite steps to recommend:

(1) That it be taken as the starting point for the detailed drafting of a thorough-going organic forest law or code.

(2) That a competent drafting committee be set up to negotiate with the many Bureaus, Departments, and agencies concerned, so that the Act will represent an all-Government attack.

The latter point is illustrated by the fact that at least eight Bureaus in Agriculture are concerned, five in Interior, the CCC, the Treasury Department, the Reconstruction Finance Corporation, the Works Projects Administration, the National Resources Planning Board, and the National Forest Reservation Commission.

A drafting Committee could function either under the Joint Committee or under the National Resources Board. I rather lean to the latter, because it represents the President and is experienced, unbiassed, and successful in the art of coordination.

As Secretary Wallace said, with profound truth, to the Joint Committee: "In the light of the whole job, the accomplishments so far (the past 30 years) seem pitifully small." Let's lift this job out of the category of the pitiful and go after a vigorous, fundamental, and effective New Deal forest policy.

If you think the above procedure is desirable, and if your time permits, may I respectfully suggest that you have a brief conference with Senator Bankhead, Secretary Wallace, Secretary Ickes, Mr. Delano, and myself.[1]

Respectfully yours,

WARD SHEPARD

[13:OF 1–C:TS]

---

[1] Apparently Roosevelt did not act upon this suggestion.

994   FREDERIC A. DELANO, CHAIRMAN, NATIONAL RESOURCES PLANNING BOARD, TO ROOSEVELT

WASHINGTON, D. C., *Apr. 9, 1940*

MEMORANDUM FOR THE PRESIDENT . . . Progress report on investigation of land management and water use in the Gila Basin, Arizona and New Mexico.

We have discussed with the interested Federal agencies your memorandum of February 14, 1940 concerning the alleged effects of soil
conservation and other land-management practices in the Gila Basin
upon water use downstream, and have initiated a joint study by them of
the issues involved in that case and in similar areas.

Our discussions with groups such as the Department of Agriculture,
Department of the Interior, Corps of Engineers, Tennessee Valley Authority, and Federal Power Commission reveal four major problems
which are present in most arid and semiarid drainage areas:

1. What is the effect of land-management practices upstream upon
quantity and silt content of water available for irrigation and other
uses downstream?

2. What is the effect of major flood-control structures upon the flow
and quantity of water available for use downstream?

3. What are the relative economic priorities for use of the available
waters for improvement of grazing lands and downstream irrigation?

4. What should be the legal principles governing the allocation of
rights between users (there is almost no legal precedent for this determination at present)?

The agencies are joining in investigation of these issues in the Gila
Basin, and we are pressing for tentative findings for that area before
attempting to investigate the problem in detail in other sections of the
West. Having once tried unsuccessfully to formulate generalized statements for the entire country or major sections of it, we are convinced
that we can clarify thinking with respect to these problems best by building up a complete picture for sample areas. In basins such as the Gila
Basin the effect of vegetal cover may be very important, whereas in
other basins such as the Cheyenne Basin in South Dakota it seems
probable that vegetal cover influences are relatively unimportant.

Although the facts with respect to the Gila Basin land management
programs have been subjects of informal controversy since 1933, and
although such controversy has been discussed by field officials working
through our drainage basin committees, the past month has seen the first
formal discussions between the Departments of Agriculture and Interior
in which both sides have attempted to present their evidence and to
understand the plans and assumptions of the other side.

FREDERIC A. DELANO

[13:OF 1092:TS]

995   ROOSEVELT TO NELSON C. BROWN, New York State College of Forestry, Syracuse University, Syracuse, New York

[WASHINGTON] *April 10, 1940*

DEAR NELSON: Thank you for your telegram.[1] I spent two days at home and the frost will be out of the ground inside of a week. The fields to be planted have been cleared and are all ready. Let Linaka and Plog know when to expect the trees.[2] I understand they are coming in two or three batches so as not to have to lie around too long before being put in the ground.

I hope to be home again the first Sunday in May and perhaps you will run down sometime this Spring.

As ever yours,

[FRANKLIN D. ROOSEVELT]

[13:PPF 38:CT]

[1] April 8, 1940 (PPF 38), saying that weather conditions would prevent the shipping of trees to Hyde Park before April 18 or thereabouts. The shipment was to consist of 50,000 trees (Brown to Roosevelt, April 9, 1940, PPF 38).
[2] Russell W. Linaka was in charge of, among other things, Roosevelt's tree nurseries. William Plog was superintendent of the Roosevelt estate.

996   ROOSEVELT TO GOVERNOR BURNET R. MAYBANK, Columbia, South Carolina

[WASHINGTON] *April 12, 1940*

DEAR BURNIE: I am so thoroughly sold on the desirability of preserving the original strain of wild turkeys throughout the eastern seaboard that it occurs to me that your own Game Department could accomplish much at relatively low cost and without public funds either from the Federal Government or the State of South Carolina.

So many sportsmen and winter residents are in South Carolina from all over the United States—and so many of them are blessed with a few dollars to spare that I am reasonably certain that funds could be raised by an appeal to them. This fund should, of course, be expended by the Game Department of the State under perhaps an Advisory Committee made up of sportsmen. Even $100,000 would go a long way toward the propagation of wild turkeys in areas suited for them.

I am sure also that if you undertake something like this the Biological Survey would give you their wholehearted blessing and advisory assistance. And, incidentally, you can quote me as being wholeheartedly for such a proposal.[1]

Always sincerely,

[FRANKLIN D. ROOSEVELT]

[13:OF 378:CT]

¹ This was in reply to Maybank's letter of March 28, 1940 (OF 378), urging Roosevelt to support H. R. 6080, to establish a wild turkey refuge in South Carolina. The letter here printed accompanied another, formal, letter from Roosevelt to Maybank, of the same date. The latter letter, drafted in the Bureau of the Budget, informed Maybank that the proposed legislation would have to be postponed for financial reasons. The bill in question was not introduced.

997   ROOSEVELT TO IRVING BRANT, CONTRIBUTING EDITOR, ST. LOUIS *Star-Times*

WARM SPRINGS, GEORGIA, *April 25, 1940*

MY DEAR MR. BRANT: I regret that the very great press of business has prevented an earlier reply to your letter of March 6, 1940, relative to the Forest Service.¹

The views which you expressed concerning the feasibility of transferring the Forest Service to the Department of the Interior and your suggested utilization of the powers conferred by the Taylor Grazing Act were of definite interest. You may be certain that this material will receive proper consideration in any further analysis that may be made of this subject.

Sincerely yours,

[FRANKLIN D. ROOSEVELT]

[*Notation*: AS] HDS ²

[13: OF 1–C: CT]

¹ Brant proposed (OF 1–C) that some 30,000,000 acres of national forest lands primarily suitable for grazing be transferred from the Agriculture Department to the Interior Department under authority of the Taylor Grazing Act. He said that the political power of the Forest Service derived more from the stockmen's associations than from the lumbermen. With its grazing control limited to forested areas, "the Forest Service would be likely to stiffen its conservation policy, with a reduced tendency to sacrifice timber and watershed values in order to build up local influence with stockmen."

² Budget Director Harold D. Smith, in whose agency this letter was drafted.

998   HAROLD D. SMITH, DIRECTOR, BUREAU OF THE BUDGET, TO ROOSEVELT

WASHINGTON, D. C., *May 3, 1940*

MEMORANDUM FOR THE PRESIDENT: Reference is made to the attached letter addressed to you by the Secretary of Agriculture under date of March 28, 1940, urging the inclusion in the Emergency Relief Appropriation Act for the coming fiscal year of special authorizing language and an appropriation item of $2,120,000 to provide for continuation of the Prairie States Forestry Project (the Shelterbelt).

Possible courses of action with respect to this project have been considered with the Department of Agriculture and the Work Projects Administration, as follows:

1. Special language and appropriation item in the new Relief Act. It is believed that this course would almost certainly lead to pressures in Congress in behalf of a large number of other projects by special interest groups who may be able to present the case for such projects as appealingly as that for the Shelterbelt can be presented. Either a large increase in the total Relief Act appropriation, or a legislative breakdown of the total into numerous and frozen project items with resultant handicap to W. P. A. in administering the program would be the probable consequence.

The Congressional history of the Shelterbelt as a distinct budgetary item is unfavorable. The 1937 Department of Agriculture Appropriation Act provided $170,000 for this project with what amounted to a mandate for its liquidation. This $170,000 was not used. Instead of liquidating the project it was continued with W. P. A. financing. Again in the Budget for 1939 you approved the inclusion of an item of $1,000,-000 for the Shelterbelt, under the authority of the newly enacted Norris-Doxey Cooperative Farm Forestry Act. The item was rejected by Congress, the House Committee stating that "the proposed expenditure is not in accord with the purpose and intent of Congress" under the above Act.

Although, as indicated by the Secretary, more favorable public and Congressional sentiment with respect to the project has since developed, another submission as a special project in the Relief Act would incur serious risk of a rejection which would force an abrupt abandonment of the project on June 30 of this year.

These factors lead to my recommendation that the proposed course of special treatment in the Relief Act submission should not be adopted.

2. An allocation from the funds which will be appropriated in the Relief Act for the Rural Rehabilitation program of the Farm Security Administration. The Solicitor of the Department of Agriculture has rendered an opinion that such funds could not legally be used to provide the "sponsor contribution" for continuation of the project with W. P. A. labor.

3. Continuation as a Soil Conservation Service project. The regular appropriations of the Soil Conservation Service are legally available for the purposes of the project. In the 1941 Budget the S. C. S. estimates were sharply reduced. The Senate restored $1,700,000 of the cut, but this restored amount, if finally approved, is rather definitely earmarked by the Senate "for cooperation with Soil Conservation Districts," which are rapidly growing in number and area. The Department holds that, even with the restoration above indicated, its funds

for cooperation with these organized Districts will be extremely short, and that a revision of the program to provide a $250,000 to $350,000 sponsor contribution for the Shelterbelt would not only be disadvantageous to the Conservation District program, but would involve unfortunate Congressional reactions.

4. Can the Work Projects Administration legally authorize exemptions which would permit continuation of the work, strictly as a W. P. A. Federal Agency Project? As stated by the Secretary, the Shelterbelt project has been carried forward wholly with W. P. A. funds for the past four years. The Department feels that it cannot be continued on this basis without material relief from present restrictions as to non-labor expense, 90–10 employment ratio, freezing of allotments by States and other administrative features. I have presented the above question to the Work Projects Administration, and have been assured that essential exemptions can and will be allowed. Consequently, I recommend that the Work Projects Administration and the Department be requested to work out arrangements which will permit the work to be carried on through the fiscal year 1941, from Agriculture's share of the Federal Agency Project fund which the new Relief Act is expected to provide.

5. Action subsequent to Fiscal Year 1941. You will recall that the Department's regular estimates for 1941 included an item of $500,000 to provide administrative and supervisory personnel and basic facilities which would enable the Forest Service to carry on the Shelterbelt as a special project on a scale adapted to the availability each year of relief labor financed by W. P. A.

In deciding against inclusion of this item in the 1941 Budget, you indicated that as the feasibility and value of the shelterbelt plantings become more fully demonstrated, it should be possible to reduce the Federal contribution to the ordinary degree of cooperative action by inducing the affected States, local agencies and individuals to assume the major part in the long-term program.

The Department states that orderly liquidation of the project as a Federal activity could not be accomplished in less than two years. It believes that due to the wide range of technical requirements for success, the States would not continue the work as State WPA projects were the Forest Service to liquidate its set-up. The Secretary expresses the conviction that it is not time to relinquish operation of the project as a Federal activity and that the work constitutes an important phase of the agricultural program in the plains States.

While a way has been found to continue through 1941 on the present basis, I suggest that definite steps be taken toward changing the pattern of Federal participation to that indicated by the decision last fall against setting up the Shelterbelt as a distinct and permanent regular Budget item. Each of the six States involved has enacted legislation authorizing

Soil Conservation Districts. The Shelterbelt area is likely to be largely embraced within such Districts. The maintenance and operation of nurseries and the furnishing of technical advice and assistance in tree planting are clearly authorized by the act establishing the Soil Conservation Service and there is further cooperative authority under the Farm Forestry Act which also is largely administered by the Soil Conservation Service. Within the regular annual appropriations to that Service for soil conservation research and cooperative operations, it appears that the Department should find it possible to do its proper part in continuing desirable tree planting and maintenance in the plains States. In the attached proposed draft of your reply to the Secretary's letter of March 28,[1] this course is suggested. The proposed reply also has been referred to WPA and initialed to indicate concurrence of that agency as to the 1941 handling of the project.

HAROLD D. SMITH

[*Notation*:AS] H. D. S.   OK   FDR

[13:OF 79:TS]

[1] Sent as the letter following.

999   ROOSEVELT TO HENRY A. WALLACE, SECRETARY OF AGRICULTURE

[WASHINGTON, *May 6, 1940*]

MY DEAR MR. SECRETARY: Reference is made to your letter of March 28, 1940, urging the inclusion in the Emergency Relief Appropriation Act estimates for 1941 of special authorizing language and an item of $2,120,000 for the Prairie States Forestry Project (the Shelterbelt).

Such a course would, I feel, open the way to pressures in Congress in behalf of numerous other projects by special interest groups and lead to either an undue increase in the total appropriation or a breakdown of the total into numerous frozen project items with resultant handicapping of the Work Projects Administration in its conduct of the general work-relief program.

I am glad to tell you, however, that the Work Projects Administration has assured me that it will cooperate as fully as practicable in making arrangements which will permit continuation of the project during 1941 about as it is now operating. It will doubtless be necessary, because of sharply reduced Federal Agency Project funds, to reduce somewhat your present scale of tree plantings in the Prairie States and it is to be hoped that this reduction may in some measure be offset by the stimulation of greater local agency and individual effort which should grow out of successful demonstration work.

Looking beyond 1941, I have in mind that since the Prairie States Shelterbelt idea was born, the acts providing for soil conservation as a major national policy, for the establishment of the Soil Conservation Service and for cooperative farm forestry have been written into our statutes. I note too with very real gratification the rapid growth of Soil Conservation Districts in both number and area. Since the Shelterbelt region is quite likely to be largely included within such Districts and the planting of trees as a measure of soil and moisture conservation is definitely included in the scheme of cooperative action within these areas, I feel that the Department should be able to fulfill satisfactorily its responsibility for technical advice and material assistance under the general soil conservation and farm forestry programs, gradually inducing the States, local agencies and individual beneficiaries to assume the major part in the long-term plantation program.

For these reasons I do not feel that we should seek to give distinctive regular budget status to the Shelterbelt as a long-term Federal project in the six Prairie States, unless or until the approach herein indicated has been proved inadequate.

Sincerely yours,

[FRANKLIN D. ROOSEVELT]

[*Notation*:A] 5/6/40
[*Notation*:AS] HDS [1]
[13:OF 1–C:CT]

[1] Budget Director Harold D. Smith, in whose agency this letter was drafted.

1000   ROOSEVELT TO WILLIAM P. WHARTON, PRESIDENT, NATIONAL PARKS ASSOCIATION, Groton, Massachusetts

[WASHINGTON] *May 7, 1940*

Private and Confidential

DEAR POLLY: There seems to be real objection on the part of the Interior Department and the National Park Service to an endorsement of the National Parks Association by me in a formal and public letter.[1] Apparently the National Parks Association has opposed most of the accomplishments in national park work during the past few years.

In view of this I know you will understand if I hesitate to write a letter which could be construed as an endorsement.

I hope all goes well with you and that I shall see you this Summer.

As ever yours,

[FRANKLIN D. ROOSEVELT]

[13:PPF 1811:CT]

[1] Wharton had asked (April 24, 1940, PPF 1811) for a message from Roosevelt to be read at the annual meeting of the National Parks Association on May 9, 1940. Ickes recommended against sending such a message (May 3, 1940, PPF 1811), on

the ground that the Association had opposed the bills for the establishment of Olympic and Kings Canyon National Parks. He enclosed a press release issued by him on the subject in 1939 (the press release contains copies of Ickes' letters to Wharton of Feb. 9 and May 2, 1939, but is not itself dated). Ickes charged the National Parks Association with being a subsidiary of the American Forestry Association. Wharton replied to Roosevelt May 9, 1940 (PPF 1811), saying that he hoped to have an opportunity to explain the "unfortunate situation" which had arisen.

1001   ROOSEVELT TO HAROLD L. ICKES, SECRETARY OF THE INTERIOR

WASHINGTON, D. C., *May 8, 1940*

MEMORANDUM FOR THE SECRETARY OF THE INTERIOR: The question of the feasibility of settlement plans for the East Mesa area in the Lower Colorado River Basin, California, has come to my attention. I understand that work has begun on the construction of the irrigation works which will supply water to that section.

Would it not be desirable for the Bureau of Reclamation to initiate a comprehensive survey of that area comparable in form to the current Columbia Basin study? If an investigation is started I would like to have it organized with the advice of a committee representing the Departments of Agriculture, Interior and Labor, and the State Planning Board. The National Resources Planning Board is ready to arrange for the appointment of such a committee if and when that seems appropriate.

[FRANKLIN D. ROOSEVELT]

[*Notation*: T] Nat Resources Plan Bd GFWhite/hs FAD:DJ 5–8–40 [1]
[*Notation*: AS] FAD
[13: OF 834: CT]

[1] White, senior research technician of the NRPB, was presumably the drafter of this letter. "FAD" stands for Frederic A. Delano, Chairman of the NRPB.

1002   ROOSEVELT TO HAROLD L. ICKES, SECRETARY OF THE INTERIOR

[WASHINGTON] *May 29, 1940*

MY DEAR MR. SECRETARY: I have considered your letter of March 7, 1940,[1] concerning the reports by the Bureau of Reclamation and the Corps of Engineers on the Kings River project in California. I have had this question examined by the National Resources Planning Board.

It appears from an examination of the reports that they are in agreement, except as to questions of policy as follows:

1. Should the development of power be initiated as a part of the irrigation improvement, or should provision be made for future development under license by the Federal Power Commission?

2. Should the project be constructed by the Bureau of Reclamation or the Corps of Engineers?

3. Should the irrigation beneficiaries repay their share of the cost in a lump sum or by 40 annual payments?

4. Should the Federal Government or local interests operate the completed project. If operated by the Federal Government, by what agency?

With respect to these matters, it seems to me that the project is dominantly an irrigation undertaking and is suited to operation and maintenance under the reclamation law. It follows, therefore, that it should be constructed by the Bureau of Reclamation, and that the portion of the project cost to be charged to irrigation should be financed on the basis of the prevailing Federal policy of 40 annual payments by irrigation beneficiaries. The project should be maintained and operated by the Bureau of Reclamation, but operation for flood control should be in accordance with regulations prescribed by the Secretary of War.

While there would be no objection to legislation specifically authorizing this project in accordance with the foregoing outline of policy, I would not expect to approve estimates of appropriations for the immediate construction of it. The present international situation requires the postponement of projects that could be undertaken in normal times.

A copy of this letter is being transmitted to the Secretary of War for his information.[2]

Sincerely yours,

[FRANKLIN D. ROOSEVELT]

[*Notation*:AS] HDS [3]

[13:OF 402:CT]

[1] This letter was sent by Roosevelt to Budget Director Smith for preparation of reply with a note of March 30, 1940 (OF 402) reading, "Will you try to straighten this out and let me know the result?" Apparently Smith did not return Ickes' memorandum.
[2] The conflict in policies over development of the Kings River area water resources is treated in detail in Maass, *Muddy Waters*, pp. 208–259.
[3] Budget Director Harold D. Smith, in whose agency this letter was drafted.

1003   HAROLD D. SMITH, DIRECTOR, BUREAU OF THE BUDGET, TO ROOSEVELT

WASHINGTON, D. C., *June 1, 1940*

MEMORANDUM FOR THE PRESIDENT REGARDING THE WHEELER-CASE ACT FOR CONSTRUCTION OF WATER CONSERVATION AND UTILIZATION PROJECTS IN THE GREAT PLAINS AND ARID AND SEMIARID AREAS OF THE

WEST: In approving the Wheeler-Case bill last August, you indicated that the bill contained certain deficiencies which would be called to the attention of the Congress at its next session; and called upon the National Resources Planning Board and the Bureau of the Budget to prepare such a revision of the Act.[1]

The National Resources Planning Board appointed a sub-committee for the purpose, which included representatives of the Interior and Agriculture Departments, and the Work Projects Administration. This subcommittee finally reached an agreement upon all details of the proposed revision, except one, viz.: the Interior Department representatives insisted upon the insertion of a section restricting in certain respects Agriculture Department operations under its Water Facilities Act of August 28, 1937. The restrictions suggested by these representatives were: (1) not to exceed $50,000 of Federal money from whatever source derived should be expended on any one project; and (2) no project involving the irrigation of more than 500 acres of land or the surface storage of more than 500 acre-feet of water or a total cost of $5,000 should be undertaken unless and until the Secretary of the Interior found and certified to you that the project could not feasibly or practicably be undertaken under the Wheeler-Case Act or the Federal Reclamation Laws. The Agriculture Department representatives were not agreeable to either of these restrictions.

The National Resources Planning Board, in its proposed memorandum to you, under date of May 2, 1940,[2] did not resolve the final point of disagreement between Agriculture and Interior, but indicated that it would accept the judgment of the Bureau of the Budget with respect to the solution of that problem.

Since all of the agencies concerned are in agreement with respect to all of the details of the proposed revision of the Wheeler-Case Act other than the section relating to the Water Facilities Act, I recommend that I be authorized to advise the Secretaries of Agriculture and Interior that the proposed revision (with the Water Facilities Act section eliminated therefrom) would be in accord with your program, but that there would be no objection to the presentation by the Secretary of the Interior for the consideration of the appropriate Committees of Congress of his proposed amendments to the Water Facilities Act.[3]

HAROLD D. SMITH

[*Notation*:AS] H. D. S.   OK   FDR

[13:OF 79:TS]

---

[1] *Ante,* 941.

[2] This memorandum, signed by Delano, is enclosed with the letter here printed.

[3] Ickes urged amendment of the Water Facilities Act because it placed no fiscal limitations on the operations of the Agriculture Department with respect to water conservation projects. In a letter to the National Resources Planning Board and to the Budget Bureau of April 17, 1940 (OF 177), he said that ". . . sound policy

requires in general that any water conservation project which can measure up to the standards of the Federal Reclamation Laws or of the Wheeler-Case Act should be undertaken only pursuant to those laws."

1004 HAROLD L. ICKES, SECRETARY OF THE INTERIOR, TO EDWIN M. WATSON, SECRETARY TO THE PRESIDENT

WASHINGTON, 6/18/40

MEMO FOR GEN. WATSON: I showed this to the President and the President asks that you call Sen Barkley and say "What is the matter with the Mundt amendment? We are in favor of it."

SEC. ICKES

[Notations:AS] To phone Sen. Barkley EMW.

[13:OF 114–A:T]

1005 [Enclosure]

Memorandum on Water Pollution Control

For the past five years, the subject of stream pollution has been approached on one side by the Lonergan-Mundt-Clark type bill; on the other side by the Barkley Bill. The former was initiated by the conservationists who believe the public is entitled to clean streams in the name of sound economics, health, recreation, and common decency. The latter was initiated by the industrial polluters who find it more profitable, in the spirit of heedless self interest, to defile public resources for private gain.

The Barkley Bill (S–685), amended by the House to include the so-called Mundt Amendment, places a quarantine upon stream pollution by declaring *new* sources of pollution, unless approved by duly constituted authority, to be "against the policy of the United States, and a public and common nuisance." In a spirit of compromise, the proponents of the Mundt Bill have agreed to support S–685 with this simple amendment agreed to by all conservation organizations, the Public Health Service, the majority of State health agencies, and a countless number of civic groups. Only the industrial polluters remain adamant in opposition to the amended Bill now in conference committee. Continued opposition to the Mundt Amendment can be construed only as favoring expansion of exploitation of public resources for private gain. In the Mundt Bill, advocates of clean streams asked for a loaf; in the Barkley Bill they were offered a stone; in the Mundt Amendment to the Barkley Bill, they have accepted a small slice. Agreement to the House Amendment now rests almost entirely with Senator Barkley who has so far been steadfast in his opposition.

The utter futility of State control of the problem is well exemplified in Pennsylvania's recent abdication of duty when its sanitary water board announced that it planned to discard existing law and approach the problem by "reasonable, practicable, progressive steps rather than by action harmful [sic] affecting employment and increased taxation." [1]

[13:OF 114-A:T]

[1] This memorandum was prepared at Ickes' request by Philip G. Platt, president emeritus of the Pennsylvania Division of the Izaak Walton League of America, and was probably delivered to Roosevelt on June 14, 1940 (Platt to Morris L. Cooke, June 15, 1940, Group 40). The Barkley bill (S. 685), approved by the Senate in the previous year, was the same as the vetoed Barkley-Vinson bill of 1938, except that the objected-to feature of the latter bill—authorization of projects by Congress without prior Budget Bureau review—had been removed. (See *ante*, 915.) S. 685, referred by the House to its Rivers and Harbors Committee on May 3, 1939, was reported, extensively rewritten, a week later, but no further action was taken during the session. Changes made by the committee included removal of the provision for Federal grants for the construction of pollution-abatement facilities. The provision for loans to public bodies and to industries for this purpose was, however, retained.

Representative Spence (Ky.), introducer of the House companion bill to the Barkley bill (H. R. 922), said (on Feb. 29, 1940) that the changes made were in consequence of a White House conference attended by him, by Senator Barkley (Ky.), "the health authorities of the Government," representatives of the Reconstruction Finance Corporation and Representative Mansfield (Texas), chairman of the House Rivers and Harbors Committee (*Cong. Rec.*, 76th Cong., 1st sess., 84:5, 5089, 5408; 3d sess., 86:2, 2178–2187, 2187–2197). This conference took place on Jan. 25, 1940; it is referred to in a White House memorandum as having been called by Roosevelt to consider means of securing an appropriation for the bill "without breaking the budget" (Watson to Kannee, Jan. 19, 1940, OF 114-A).

S. 685 was taken up by the House on Feb. 29, 1940. Mundt and others who in previous sessions had backed realistic "Lonergan-type" anti-pollution measures (providing for action in the Federal courts against violators) denounced the Barkley bill as ineffective and harmful because it did nothing to prevent the further contamination of streams by new sources of pollution. Mundt did not, however, move the recommittment of S. 685 but instead offered as an amendment the enforcing clause of his own bill, H. R. 7971, introduced in the previous session as H. R. 6723. This would have barred the addition to navigable waters of new sources of pollution and provided for injunctive action through the Federal courts against agencies, public or private, that persisted in the illegal pollution of waters. Mundt's amendment was accepted by the House (March 1) and the bill was sent to the Senate. That body refused to accept the amendment and the bill went to conference. The conferees failing to agree, Representative Mansfield moved (July 9) that the House managers recede from insistence on the Mundt amendment. This reopened debate on the whole question and on a roll call vote the Mansfield motion was defeated 198–155. No further action was taken on S. 685. The 198 votes the anti-pollutionists were able to muster against the Mansfield motion represented the high tide of their effort to secure an effective anti-pollution law. Mundt and others introduced anti-pollution bills in succeeding Congresses of the Roosevelt administration but without result (*Cong. Rec.*, 76th Cong., 3d sess., 86:2, 2187–2197, 2207–2226; 86:3, 2421–2423, 2754; 86:9, 9347–9359). A copy of S. 685 as approved by the House is printed *ibid.*, 86:3, 2421–2422.

Roosevelt passed on to Barkley, for his information, pleas received by him from the National Association of Audubon Societies and from Morris L. Cooke for the enactment of the Mundt bill (Baker to LeHand, Jan. 13, 1940; Cooke to LeHand, May 1, 1940, OF 114-A). Other than this, and the intimation contained in the

Ickes memorandum here printed, no particular effort was apparently made by him to secure passage of the measure.

The general attitude of the conservation organizations on the Administration's position was expressed by Izaak Walton League President Otto C. Doering in a letter to FWA Administrator John M. Carmody, March 20, 1940 (OF 344):

"It has always seemed to the Izaak Walton League, and numerous other conservation organizations, more than passing strange that this liberal Administration concerned with the best interests of the great mass of our people should have allowed itself to be jockeyed into the position where they are actually supporting the pollution of our waters. The Barkley bill, as passed by the Senate, is certainly not an anti-pollution measure, but a smoke screen to permit the continuation of pollution."

1006   HAROLD L. ICKES, SECRETARY OF THE INTERIOR, TO ROOSEVELT

WASHINGTON, *June 24, 1940*

MEMORANDUM FOR THE PRESIDENT: Attached is the outline for the proposed Conference on Conservation which I discussed with you. I am suggesting that this Conference be conducted October 1–5, 1940, in Washington and that it be called *The President's Conference on Resources.*

The Committee and administrative set-up is submitted for your consideration and approval.

HAROLD L. ICKES

Approved:

[13:OF 4030:TS]

1007   [*Enclosure*]

Draft 6–17–40

Proposed President's Conference on Resources

Keynote: (a) Preparedness through conservation.

(b) Prudent use of natural resources in this emergency.

Subject: It is becoming increasingly evident that our vast resources must be carefully utilized and preserved to serve this Nation as staunch bulwarks of our economy and tranquility. A recapitulation of our present position and the recommendation of a framework of action which will make possible the continued enjoyment of our resources in this time of international strife, while at the same time defending and improving our economic and social condition in the face of external danger. Some of the aspects of this broad problem which might be considered are the extension and integration of power facilities and resources; the stabilization of fuel resources; the orderly development of petroleum supplies; the location and orderly development of strategic mineral deposits; the accumulation of stocks of critical minerals; the continued development of improved metallurgical processes; the careful expansion of agricultural production; the increase of lumber production upon a sustained yield basis; the extension of the sustained yield system in the lumber industry; the protection and orderly development of water supply; the extension of systematic land use, and similar subjects.[1]

[13:OF 4030:T]

[1] Ickes also enclosed drafts of a proposed conference program, a budget, plan of organization, and a list of persons to be invited. The memorandum and enclosures were sent by Roosevelt to Lowell Mellett, director of the Office of Government Reports, under cover of a memorandum of June 25, 1940 (OF 4030), asking, "Will you find out if this is O. K. with the Secretary of Agriculture and Mr. Delano before I sign it?" Mellett replied June 26, 1940 (OF 4030), that Wallace and Delano thought it inadvisable to hold such a conference during the campaign. Roosevelt then asked Mellett to take up the matter with Ickes, Wallace and Delano, and to "try to straighten it out" (June 27, 1940, OF 4030). Mellett reported to Roosevelt on Aug. 3, 1940 (OF 4030), that further discussions revealed that all concerned agreed that the proposed conference should not be held until after the election.

1008   HAROLD L. ICKES, SECRETARY OF THE INTERIOR, TO ROOSEVELT

WASHINGTON, *July 5, 1940*

MY DEAR MR. PRESIDENT: Under your Reorganization Order No. 4 you indicated your desire to send to Interior for administration that part of soil conservation which has to do with public lands. Obviously we can't do the job assigned to us without money enough to do it with. The Department of Agriculture has bitterly resisted the turning over to us of a fair share of the funds appropriated for soil conservation for this fiscal year. The Bureau of the Budget, although I think that some of the people there recognize the justness of our claims and realize the intransigence of Agriculture, has come through with the usual "compromise."

Before the first of July, when I was advised of the trend of the Budget, I wrote to Director Smith telling him that unless we could have enough money to do a decent job I would prefer that you retransfer this segment of soil conservation to Agriculture. We were not given the money that we were entitled to in my judgment, although I think that we were exceedingly reasonable in our demands, and so I have refrained from exercising any jurisdiction over any part of soil conservation. I cannot believe that it was your purpose to draw attention to the fact that our public lands are being neglected in the interest of privately owned lands as would be the case if I should take over this unit and draw upon Interior the inevitable criticism that would follow from a patent neglect of the public lands. I can see no distinction in principle between turning over public lands to private exploiters, as used to be the policy of Interior, and devoting public funds to the improvement of private lands to the exclusion of public lands as now seems to be the policy of Agriculture.[1]

Sincerely yours,

HAROLD L. ICKES

[13:OF I-R:TS]

[1] Answered *post*, 1010.

1009   ROOSEVELT TO WILLIAM R. WALLACE, CHAIRMAN, WATER
        STORAGE COMMISSION, Salt Lake City

WASHINGTON, *July 10, 1940*

MY DEAR MR. WALLACE: I have received your letter of June 21, concerning the proposal to establish a national recreational area within the region of the Colorado River Canyon, Southeastern Utah.[1]

I am familiar with the various proposals for further control of the Colorado River for public benefit, and I believe that the interests of the people of Utah, as well as of the general public, are being given full consideration in all the studies which the Federal Government is making in cooperation with your State. The national recreational area proposal does not ignore, evade or avoid any Utah rights or interests. On the contrary, all existing rights are recognized, and additional advantages for the local people are anticipated.

In view of the close working relationship already established between the Governor of your State, your representatives in the Congress, other leading people of Utah, and officials of the Department of the Interior and National Resources Planning Board, I do not see the need for additional organization for the protection of Utah interests. I am not informed of any problems that cannot be worked out under the organized Colorado River Drainage Basin studies for all purposes, which are being carried on jointly by local, State, and Federal groups.[2]

Very sincerely yours,

[FRANKLIN D. ROOSEVELT]

[13:OF 6-P:CT]

[1] Wallace said that the proposed national recreational area would forever prevent the region "from producing the greatest benefit to Utah and the nation," and he asked why the President and the governor of Utah should not together appoint a committee "to make a thorough analysis and agree upon a plan that would protect Utah in the enjoyment of its own resources and at the same time protect scenic wonders and develop great recreational areas" (OF 6-P).

[2] Drafted by the Interior Department. In his letter to Roosevelt of July 9, 1940, covering the draft, Acting Interior Secretary Burlew noted that in February Governor Blood and Representatives Robinson and Murdock of Utah had discussed the project with National Park Service officials and had expressed their satisfaction with it. A letter similar to the one here printed, also drafted by the Interior Department, was sent by Roosevelt to Senator Thomas of Utah, July 15, 1940, in response to his

letter of July 3, 1940 (OF 6-P). Thomas said that the Utah delegation had not been consulted in the matter. Roosevelt denied this and added: "This is true despite the fact that the Utah Congressional delegation has not supported the legislation to amend section 2 of the Act for the Preservation of American Antiquities, embodied in S. 3827 and H. R. 9351, which would provide the means for integrating recreational developments with other essential interests in the Colorado River Basin."

The amendment referred to would have authorized the President to create, by proclamation, national recreational areas on the unreserved and unappropriated lands of the United States when in his opinion such property contained outstanding scenic or other natural features and was "of value to the Nation for recreational, educational, or inspirational purposes." The legislation was not reported from committee (*Cong. Rec.*, 76th Cong., 3d sess., 86:4, 4400; 86:5, 4809). It is further described *post*, 1020.

1010   ROOSEVELT TO HAROLD L. ICKES, SECRETARY OF THE INTERIOR

[WASHINGTON] *July 13, 1940*

MY DEAR MR. SECRETARY: Your letters of June 6 [1] and June 27, addressed respectively to me and to the Director of the Bureau of the Budget, relative to the effectuation of Section 6 of Reorganization Plan IV providing for the transfer to your Department of soil conservation operations on lands within your jurisdiction, have had my careful consideration. Your letter of July 5, reiterating but not materially altering your views as presented in the earlier communications is also before me.

In determining upon this transfer I gave great weight to the fact that conservation of the basic resources of soil and water on the public land is, and always has been, a primary responsibility of every public land managing agency. It follows logically, I think, that all the forces, facilities and funds available for the application of the essential techniques on any given area of Federal land should be made available to and directly handled by the agency managing that land. While recognizing that this consolidation of responsibility and facilities with respect to Interior lands would require apportionment between Agriculture and Interior of appropriations hitherto wholly made to Agriculture, I anticipated that this could readily be worked out between the two Departments, subject, of course, to review by the Director of the Bureau of the Budget and to my final approval.

In order to facilitate the disposition of this matter, I have prepared the following interpretative statements in which the Attorney General concurs:

1. In determining the amounts to be transferred in accordance with Section 15 of Reorganization Plan IV, the Director of the Bureau of the Budget must proceed on the basis of the existing program, regardless of the fact that certain changes may appear to be desirable. Thus, it would not be proper for the Director to determine that the Department of Agriculture had not been devoting a sufficient portion of its available

[458]

funds to soil conservation activities and attempt to rectify this by allocating to the Department of the Interior a much larger sum than was expended on public lands during 1940 or was contemplated for expenditure during 1941. Any interpretation to the contrary would have to be premised on the assumption that a reorganization plan can be made the means for forcing an agency to make important changes in its operating program.

2. On the other hand, the transfers of funds must provide not only for direct expenditures but also for items of an overhead character, which are usually secured through central bureau or departmental facilities.

3. In addition to the necessary funds, personnel, and records, the Department of the Interior will, of course, receive all property used primarily in the administration of the transferred activities, or in lieu of such property a compensatory amount will be included in the transfer of funds.

4. Since research is a relatively nebulous term, it is impossible to set down precise standards for determining the extent, if any, to which the appropriation for "soil and moisture conservation and land use investigations" should be made available to the Department of the Interior. The wording of both the Plan and the accompanying message reflects my intention that the transfer should extend only to the application of soil conservation techniques to Interior Department lands and should not include the conduct of underlying research and planning. However, this does not preclude the transfer of any activities that, while financed out of the appropriation for investigations, are nevertheless an integral part of the conservation operations.

I feel sure that the Director of the Bureau of the Budget has carefully canvassed all the pertinent facts relative to the necessary appropriation transfers, and that the amounts of such transfers as finally determined are fully as large as could be justified under the letter and intent of the Reorganization Plan.

The proper apportionment of the total Federal effort in soil and moisture conservation as between public and private lands is, of course, a matter concerning which there may be wide and equally well-supported differences of judgment. In general, I feel that while Federal land management has failed at times and in some areas to give due emphasis to these primary responsibilities, the resultant problems are somewhat less acute, and the necessary correctives less costly than in the private crop land areas. Moreover, I have in mind that the particular appropriation items which have now been divided between the Departments of Agriculture and Interior by no means constitute the total of Federal expenditure for soil and moisture conservation on Federal lands. Soil conservation is fundamentally inherent in the work programs of the Grazing Service, the National Park Service, the Indian Service, the Forest Service

[459]

and other land-managing agencies, and in recent years large sums in addition to regular appropriations have been available to all these agencies for soil and moisture conservation activities.

I am entirely confident that the immediate and thoroughly beneficial effect of this feature of the Reorganization Plan, and the fund apportionment which I have approved thereunder will be a material strengthening of the splendid work in soil and moisture conservation which has been going forward on the public lands under your management since 1933.

I want to have a conference with you with the object of putting into the 1942 budget this Autumn a special item for soil reclamation on half dozen [sic] public land areas. I should like to have half dozen separate places, averaging say twenty-five square miles, each in places which are readily accessible to tourists and other visitors. In other words, I want to see what the Interior Department can do with the reclamation of such demonstration areas so that there can be a visual comparison between the reclaimed area and the adjacent non-reclaimed lands. You might have this study started so that we can talk about it before the budget is made up.

In regard to the present allocation, Harold Smith tells me that Interior will get $185,240 net more than the 1941 budget contemplated.[2]

Very sincerely yours,

[FRANKLIN D. ROOSEVELT]

[*Notation*: A] Copy of reply sent to Budget 7/15/40 hm

[13:OF 1–R:CT]

---

[1] OF 1–R. The June 27 letter is not present.

[2] Drafted by the Budget Bureau. Budget Director Smith, in his letter to Roosevelt of July 12, 1940 (OF 1–R), enclosing the draft, described in detail the procedure criticized by Ickes.

1011   ROOSEVELT TO EBERT K. BURLEW, FIRST ASSISTANT SECRETARY OF THE INTERIOR

[WASHINGTON] *August 12, 1940*

MEMORANDUM FOR HON. EBERT K. BURLEW: I have read with interest Regional Forester Arnold's report on the Vanderbilt place.[1]

I fully approve his suggestions that the place so far as open spaces, lawns, etc., are concerned should remain permanently in present condition.

Please tell Mr. Arnold, however, that in order to attain this there should be laid down a rule as follows: "When it is estimated that an existing tree has an estimated additional length of life of 25 years or less, another tree, preferably of the same variety, should be planted at once as close to the original tree as possible."

The reason for this is that we do not want to lose the general character of the present plantings and it is always possible that half a dozen key trees near the house might die almost simultaneously.

F. D. R.

[13:OF 6–P:CT]

[1] Regional Forester Fred H. Arnold's report was enclosed with Burlew's letter to Roosevelt of Aug. 3, 1940 (OF 6–P). The Vanderbilt estate was designated the Vanderbilt Mansion National Historic Site on Dec. 18, 1940.

1012   MILLER FREEMAN, WASHINGTON STATE PLANNING COUNCIL, TO ROOSEVELT

SEATTLE, *Aug. 22nd, 1940*

DEAR SIR: Your careful examination is requested of the enclosed letter from Secretary Ickes and my reply.

As a publisher of industrial journals, I have been for many years actively interested in the conservation and wise utilization of the resources of this region.

I am enclosing copy of letter you wrote me Sept. 6, 1932,[1] outlining your ideas on a national conservation program in which you said:

"This must be jointly a State and Federal concern, but with more effective encouragement from the Federal Government than it has had in the past."

Shortly after receipt of this letter I initiated the movement to create the Washington State Planning Council, which has now been in existence for more than six years. No planning body in the union has a finer record of achievement in a like period of time.

We certainly haven't had any encouragement whatever from Secretary Ickes.

The irony of all this is that while the Council has devoted itself so largely toward coordination of efforts of the State and Federal Government, it is the subject of condemnation and vilification by Mr. Ickes in language unworthy of a member of the Cabinet.

After you have examined the matter, I would be glad to hear your present views in the light of these developments by which it seems plain that the Secretary of the Interior entirely ignores State interests, and is attempting to arbitrarily enforce Federal Dictatorship. Do you support his position? If so, you might as well abolish the State Planning Boards, as their further continuance would be futile.

Yours respectfully,

MILLER FREEMAN

[13:OF 177:TS]

[1] *Ante,* 120.

1013 [*Enclosure 1*] HAROLD L. ICKES, SECRETARY OF THE INTERIOR, TO *The Mining World*, Seattle

WASHINGTON, *Aug. 7th, 1940*

GENTLEMEN: I have received a copy of the July issue of *Mining World*.

On page one of this issue I note that *Mining World* devotes itself to its field "without sectionalism, without sensationalism, and with scrupulous regard for accuracy." Thirty pages later I come to an article entitled "Conservation—Should it Serve—or Only Save?" which is composed chiefly of sectionalism, sensationalism, and inaccuracy.

I suggest that before you printed this obviously biased attack upon the Department of the Interior you might have attempted to ascertain the facts from any authorized representative of the Department. You might have asked the Washington State Planning Council to let you read the material presented by the National Park Service, which the Council buried in its files while giving publicity to a theme to which it was already committed. If you had made inquiry you would have found newsworthy facts.

You would have found that in the early stages of the study the Planning Council held seven public mass meetings to pass public judgment on a park proposal which had not been made, and in the light of facts which had not been ascertained. You would have found that after this park proposal had served its purpose in arousing public apprehension, the Council then broadened the scope of its study to include a general inventory of the resources and potentialities of five national forests in the Cascade Range, and concluded that since those five national forests, as a whole, had extensive resources and potentialities no area therein could be considered for national park status. The Council now cites the sentiment of the seven mass meetings as evidence of the soundness of its position.

Had you made inquiry, you would have found that the Planning Council asked the National Park Service for policy statements, which statements were supplied by Superintendent Tomlinson of Mount Rainier National Park and by the Director of the Service. The Council ignored these official statements of policy and used instead its own statement of National Park Service policies, even after the Park Service had notified the Council that the Council's statement was inadequate. The Council included in its report a national forest policy statement which was largely prepared by the Forest Service. Your readers would have been interested in knowing that I authorized the Park Service to state that if the study should result in recommending an area for park status that included important mineralized zones, I would be willing to recommend to the Congress that prospecting and mining be continued. That assurance was given in complete candor. How could it possibly be construed as a threat to mining? Yet, both the Council and your magazine played down my statement, and you informed your readers that this Department's "ambitions threaten to close important areas to prospecting and mining."

You also did your readers a disservice when you further elaborated the Planning Council's fantastic statements about H. R. 9351, a bill to amend the Antiquities Act. That bill contains no new authority for the President; it actually restricts existing authority. If the bill were passed, the reservations that the President would be authorized to establish under it would be less restrictive than the national monuments that he can now establish under the Antiquities Act. If the bill were passed, the President would no longer have authority to establish national monuments, which are closed to mining, closed to water conservation projects, and to hunting; under the amended act, he would have authority only to establish recreational areas, in which prospecting and mining, water conservation projects, hunting and grazing would be permitted. The purpose of the bill is to permit the recognition and to integrate the development of outstanding recreational resources with the development and use of certain other resources in the same areas. The bill rightly provides no authority for logging in such areas, because the management of timber producing lands is already the responsibility of established Federal agencies.

The authority that the President has to eliminate lands from national forests, and that you view with such alarm in connection with this bill, he has had for forty-three years. He has had, also, authority under the Antiquities Act to remove lands from national forests and to establish them as national monuments since 1906, or for thirty-four years. Those powers of the President exist whether this bill is enacted or not. The real question involved in the bill is a very simple one: do you want recreational reservations set up by Executive Order that are closed to prospecting and mining, water conservation projects, hunting, and grazing, or do you want them open to these activities?

There are undoubtedly areas in the High Cascades that are primarily recreational, and that cannot justifiably be classified as timber producing lands. Even the State Planning Council admits this in a modest statement tucked away on page fourteen of its report, where it says:

"In addition to its national parks, comprising more than 1,140,000 acres, Washington has 1,207,694 acres within the national forests of the Cascade Mountains dedicated by executive order primarily to recreational uses."

The purpose of the study, of course, was to determine how these and similar lands might best be used, but at no time could the Council bring itself to the collection and analysis of facts pertaining to the point because it was so captivated by its symphonic development of the multiple-use theme.

If you had taken the trouble to analyze for your readers the meaning of this term "multiple use," you would have found that it is a meaningless expression. It is definitive of nothing. Its conflicting promises are as subject to question as are the promises of any patent medicine that claims to cure all ills. What conflicts will be resolved by repeating multiple-use platitudes? Any land use may be said to be a multiple use or a single use, depending upon one's point of view, but whether land use is called multiple or single is of no consequence. The main problem in land planning is to determine the most profitable use or combination of uses to which an area may be put. If there is to be profitable management, the area must be devoted to its dominant use or uses, and the extent and kind of subordinate uses must be gauged accordingly.

How best can the great scenic areas of the Cascade Range be used? That is the problem that the Washington State Planning Council had before it when it undertook the Cascade Mountain Study, but its final report throws no light on the question. The broad generalities and fine-sounding assumptions between the report's imposing covers have very little to do with the case. We may as well face the unpleasant fact that the "study" was not a study at all. It was merely a smoke screen to cover a dilatory maneuver. It produced fifty-six pages of nothing new.

Mount Baker, Glacier Peak, Mount Adams, Mount Saint Helens, Mount Hood, and the scenic wilderness areas of the High Cascades are national recreational resources. They cannot profitably be considered as timber producing, or forestry, lands. They should in fact be established as National Recreational Areas, to be administered, like Boulder Dam National Recreational Area, by the one authorized recreational agency of the Federal Government. In this liberal type of recreational reservation, prospecting and mining, water conservation projects, and grazing should be permitted, and hunting in accordance with State and Federal laws.

For years the scenic resources of the Cascade Mountains have been subordinated under a land management system that did not dare to recognize one resource above another. Establishment of National Recreational Areas will liberate these outstanding resources, to the benefit of both the State and the Nation.

Sincerely yours,

(Signed) HAROLD L. ICKES

[13:OF 177:T:COPY]

[SEATTLE] *Aug. 20th, 1940*

DEAR MR. SECRETARY: We have your letter of August 7th in which you comment at some length upon the article headed "Conservation—Should it Serve, or Only Save?" in the July issue of *Mining World*.

We shall not reply to, nor resent, the charge of "sectionalism, sensationalism and inaccuracy" which you lay against this journal, but we do resent and resist your castigation of the Washington State Planning Council and the special advisory committee for its Cascade Mountains Study.

You typically attribute roguery to those who have the temerity honestly to disagree with you.

The writer of this letter has served as a member of the Washington State Planning Council from the time of its creation six years ago. It is a non-partisan, non-salaried body, composed of men of high character and intelligence—men far above the petty lack of principle which you imply.

You accuse the Council of having ignored an official statement of National Park Service policy which it requested. I wonder if you know this official statement of policy was received by the State Planning Council in exactly nine days less than six months after it had been formally requested. Moreover, the National Park Service statement omitted any reference to "national recreational areas," an element of its program to which you point in your letter.

For these reasons, the Council and its committee rejected the official statement of policy as inadequate and used its own well considered statement.

People of the West know that National Park Service policies are better expressed by present evidence and the record of historic fact than by statements composed to conform to current expediency.

You point out in your letter that you had given a pledge, hedged by conditions, that you would recommend to Congress that prospecting and mining be permitted in Cascade lands given national park status.

Frankly, the people of the West have no faith in such pledges, whether they be made by yourself or the National Park Service.

Still fresh in memory is such a pledge, given at the time the Rainier National Park was created, only to be rescinded later by obscure and unheralded legislation.

You quibble about portions of the Cascade Mountains national forests which "cannot justifiably be classed as timber producing lands," and overlook the evident desire of the National Park Service to escheat to itself vast regions which cannot justifiably be classed as possessing the unique characteristics for which national park treatment is desirable.

The Western states prefer that the enormous areas of the public domain within their borders be administered by the Forest Service rather than the National Park Service because the former has shown willingness to permit true public use of the public domain; to permit people to work, as well as play on it; to permit men to earn, as well as spend on it.

You say the term "multiple use" is a "meaningless expression . . . definitive of nothing." Perhaps that is true in Chicagoanese, but to us in the West, as applied to the public lands it means employment of those lands for the benefit of Americans just as fully as is consistent with sound conservation of their resources.

Conservation has been defined as meaning "wise use." We conceive wise use of the public lands to include logging of ripe timber on a sustained basis; prospecting and mining of mineral deposits; grazing in such manner as to preserve the pastures; utilization of water for power and irrigation; enjoyment of their recreational aspects in full measure.

To the West, wise use of the public domain does not mean its dedication solely to recreation, save for those rare portions whose character specially recommends such treatment.

We will stand on the conclusions of the Washington State Planning Council that the Cascade Mountains do not come within this category.

Mr. Ickes, we wonder if since becoming Secretary of the Interior you have read the Parable of the Talents and have considered Christ's view of hoarding, compared with utilization, expressed in this Parable?

You may remember that the "wicked and slothful servant" only saved the talent with which he had been entrusted; but the "good and Faithful servant" employed his talents and increased them—put them to "multiple use," if you will.

It seems to us that this parable applies to public servants and the public domain with singular directness.[1]

Very truly yours,

[MILLER FREEMAN]

[13:OF 177:T]

[1] See *post*, 1020.

1015   SPEECH BY ROOSEVELT AT THE CHICKAMAUGA DAM CELEBRATION, near Chattanooga, Tennessee, September 2, 1940

GOVERNOR COOPER, GOVERNOR RIVERS, MEMBERS OF THE SENATE AND OF THE HOUSE OF REPRESENTATIVES, CHAIRMAN MORGAN AND MEMBERS OF THE TENNESSEE VALLEY AUTHORITY, AND YOU, THE GOOD

PEOPLE OF TENNESSEE AND OF THE OTHER SIX STATES THAT ABUT THIS GREAT VALLEY: I am glad to come here today, especially because I took part in the laying of the cornerstone of this dam some years ago.

But when I first passed this place, after my election but before my inauguration as President, there flowed here, as most of us remember, a vagrant stream, a stream sometimes shallow and useless, sometimes turbulent and in flood, always dark with the soil that it had washed from the eroding hills. This Chickamauga Dam, the sixth in the series of mammoth structures built by the T. V. A. for the people of the United States, is helping to give to all of us human control of the watershed of the Tennessee River in order that it may serve in full the purposes of mankind.

This chain of man-made inland seas may well be named "The Great Lakes of the South." Through them we are celebrating the opening of a new artery of commerce, of new opportunities for recreation—I see all these new power boats right here almost at my feet as I speak—we celebrate the relief from the desolation of floods, we celebrate new low-cost energy which has begun to flow to the homes and farms and industries in seven American states.

This national holiday—September second, Labor Day—has been appropriately selected, because in the miracle that man has wrought, labor has played a vital role. In all of these seven years, in heat and in cold, men have drilled and blasted through solid rock, they poured ton after ton of concrete and they have moved mountains of earth. They have worked with the strength of their hands, and they have operated complicated machinery with every form of modern skill. Never once in these years, never once in this the biggest consolidated construction job ever undertaken directly by the national Government, never has there been a substantial interruption in the continuance of your labors. This Dam, all the dams built in this short space of years, stand as a monument to the productive partnership between management and labor, between citizens of all kinds working together in the public weal. Collective bargaining and efficiency have proceeded hand in hand. It is noteworthy that the splendid new agreement between organized labor and the Tennessee Valley Authority begins with the words "The public interest in an undertaking such as the TVA is paramount . . ."

It is appropriate, therefore, that we recognize this signal achievement on the day, Labor Day, when the whole Nation pays tribute to labor's contribution to the democracy that we are now preparing to defend. To all of you, therefore—all of you who have contributed to make these structures possible throughout this beautiful Valley of the Tennessee—to all of you I extend the Nation's thanks.

[467]

The only note of sorrow that can properly be sounded on a great day like this, perfect in its scenery, perfect in the crowd that has come here today, perfect in our weather, but the only note of sorrow that can be properly sounded lies in the misplaced emphasis that so many people have put on the objectives of the Government in building up this great Tennessee Valley project. It was at a press conference that I held at Warm Springs, down in Southwest Georgia, away back in January, 1933, after I had visited the Valley with that splendid fighting American, Senator George Norris of Nebraska—it was way back there, more than seven years ago, that I put his vision and my vision into words. For many years, in different parts of the Nation, I have been interested in what I had called, already in 1933, the problem of better land use, a problem that necessarily had to include existing facts relating to harmful land use.

In the Valley of the Tennessee River, therefore, I had come to consider the fact of devastating floods that had existed for many generations—floods that washed away houses and roads and factories, floods that took great toll of human life—floods that threatened the very security of Chattanooga itself and of many other communities on this river, on the Ohio River and even down in the lower reaches of the Mississippi.

I had studied the washing away of the wealth, the wealth of soil on the main stem of the river, on its many mountain tributaries, and up in the creeks and the hills in the higher valleys. I had seen water commerce impeded by shoals, by winding variable channels. I had understood the waste of potential hydroelectric energy.

Yes, I had seen forests denuded or burned—but worst of all, I had seen the splendid people living in parts of several states fighting against nature instead of fighting with nature.

Being of a practical turn of mind—some people say I am part Scotch and part Dutch and therefore ought to be—but being of a practical turn of mind I asked for figures relating to losses and figures to show the cost of stopping the losses.

My memory is that the engineers told me that from floods alone the average annual damage in the Tennessee Valley was about $25,000,000 a year; that the top soil carried to the sea by annual floods averaged another loss of $25,000,000 a year; that better farming and better forestry could produce at least $25,000,000 a year more; and, finally, that a saving of $25,000,000 could be made by providing for and insisting on cheaper electric rates and a wider distribution of power. In other words, the complete development of the objectives of the T. V. A. would save or, in other words, gain for the people of the watershed $100,000,000 a year.

And, on the other side of the ledger—the cost side—we would have to figure—I am going back to the figures of seven years ago that have proved pretty accurate—we would have to figure on a total final investment of about $500,000,000, including, of course, the taxes, the amortization of the amount spent through a series of years—and including, incidentally, no watered stock. That total sum of dollars was to be spent on three major benefits. The first related to the control of the water for better navigation, for the building of lakes, for the prevention of erosion, for the development of power. The second objective we had was the building back of soil fertility through research into phosphate fertilizer, the use of nitrate plant life and the diversification of crops, and the reforesting of millions of acres of land. The third objective was to improve the social and the economic life of these citizens and, incidentally, improve it with their cooperation—to plan with them for a greater diversification of human effort, to make a richer farm life, to add new industries to our towns and villages, to give employment, and to bring a larger return in cash every single year, a larger return of cash to the average of our families.

Today you and I are seeing the progress that we have made, the progress that we are still making, and, incidentally, the progress that we propose to continue to make. We have come very far along this particular road. In this Valley, as in the Nation, we do not propose to abandon the goal, the goal that is directly before our eyes, abandon it either by sitting down or by going back.

These fine changes that we see have not come by compulsion—for thousands of farmers and thousands of townspeople have met together in this common effort. They debated it and they discussed it. Participating in the processes of their own Government—State Government, local Government, Federal Government—they have altered the looks of their towns and their counties. They have added fertilizer to the soil. They have improved their industries. No farmer was forced to join this conservation movement. No workman was compelled to labor here under onerous conditions, or for less than a rightful wage. No citizen has lost a single one of these human liberties that we prize so highly in this democracy. And so that is a demonstration, a demonstration of what a democracy at work can do, of what a people uniting in a war against waste and insecurity can and propose to do.

There were, of course, and there are those who maintain that the development of the enterprise that lies largely in this State, the development of it, they say, is not a proper activity of Government. As for me, I glory in it as one of the great social and economic achievements of the United States.

Today, my friends, we are facing a time of peril unmatched in the history of the nations of all the world. And because we are undertaking the total defense of this Nation of ours, the Tennessee Valley region has assumed, in addition to its own domestic betterment, its share of responsibility for national defense.

Already, and several years ahead of our carefully planned schedule, we are creating new plants which of necessity will use more power. I am glad, indeed, that in spite of partisan opposition, the Congress of the United States has overwhelmingly voted the necessary funds. And that money is now at work.

New defense industries are more safe from attack in this region behind the mountains than if they were located on our more exposed borders. And, therefore, it is good for our safety to develop further and to use the natural resources and the man power of this region. In that development, let us always remember that we must and shall retain the great gains that have been made for human social security in recent years. We propose, indeed, not to retain them alone but to improve and extend them. Most assuredly we are determined neither to repeal them nor weaken them.

We understand too, we understand now what we did not understand back in 1917—in 1918—that the building up of Army and Navy equipment and the training of men to use it ought not to result in a waste of our natural resources, and at the same time ought not to break down the gains of labor or the maintenance of a living wage.

We are seeking the preparedness of America, not against, not against the threat of war or conquest alone, but in order that preparedness be built to assure American peace that rests on the well-being of the American people.

I, therefore, today, on this very happy occasion, dedicate this Dam and these lakes to the benefit of all the people, to the benefit of the prosperity that they have stimulated, the faith that they have justified, the hope that they have inspired, the hearts that they encourage—the total defense of the people of the United States of America.[1]

[RL RECORDINGS: 291, 292]

---

[1] This text is that of the radio broadcast transcription. (The time of the speech was 10 A. M.) Other texts (Speech File) are: (1) a draft prepared by David E. Lilienthal, vice chairman of the board of directors of the Tennessee Valley Authority, dated Aug. 27, 1940; (2) a draft, labeled "First Draft," dated Sept. 2, 1940, embodying in paraphrase part of the Lilienthal draft; (3) the reading copy, signed by Roosevelt; and (4) the stenographic transcript. The broadcast recording contains a number of last-minute changes not caught in the stenographic transcript, and the latter varies considerably in phrasing from the reading copy. The text as printed in Rosenman (ed.), *Public Papers*, IX, 359–364, combines elements of both reading copy and stenographic transcript; with it is a long note on the accomplishments of the Tennessee Valley Authority.

[*Excerpt*] SECRETARY ICKES, GOVERNOR HOEY, GOVERNOR COOPER AND OUR NEIGHBOR, GOVERNOR MAYBANK OF SOUTH CAROLINA, AND MY FRIENDS FROM ALL THE STATES : I have listened with attention and great interest to the thousands of varieties of plants and trees and fishes and animals that Governor Cooper told us about, but he failed to mention the hundreds of thousands of species of human animals that come to this Park.

Here in the Great Smokies, we have come together to dedicate these mountains, and streams, and forests, the thousands of them, to the service of the millions of American people. We are living under governments that are proving their devotion to National Parks. The Governors of North Carolina and of Tennessee have greatly helped us, and the Secretary of the Interior is so active that he has today ready for dedication a number of other great National Parks—like Kings Canyon in California and the Olympic National Park in the State of Washington, and Isle Royale up in Michigan and, over here, the Great Cavern of Tennessee— and soon, I hope, he'll have another one for us to dedicate, the Big Bend Park way down in Texas, close to the Mexican line.

Yes, around us, around us here, there are trees, trees that stood before our forefathers ever came to this continent; there are brooks that still run as clear as on the day the first pioneer cupped his hand and drank from them. In this Park, we shall conserve these trees, the pine, the red-bud, the dogwood, the azalea, and the rhododendron, we shall conserve the trout and the thrush for the happiness of the American people . . .[1]

In these centuries of American civilization, greatly blessed by the bounties of nature, we succeeded in attaining liberty in Government and liberty of the person. In the process, in the light of past history, we realize now that we committed excesses which we are today seeking to atone for.

We used up, we destroyed much of our natural heritage just because that heritage was so bountiful. We slashed our forests, we used our soils, we encouraged floods, we over-concentrated our wealth, we disregarded our unemployed—all of this so greatly that we were brought rather suddenly to face the fact that unless we gave thought to the lives of our children and grandchildren, they would no longer be able to live and to improve upon our American way of life.

So in these later years, we have tried sincerely and honestly to look ahead to the future years. We are at last definitely engaged in the task of conserving the bounties of nature, thinking in the terms of the whole of nature. We are trying at least to attain employment for all who would work and can work, and to provide a greater assurance of security. throughout life—throughout the life of the family.[2]

[RL RECORDINGS: 289, 290]

[1] Omitted are several paragraphs dealing with the world crisis.
[2] This text is that of the radio transcription. (The time of the speech was 4 P. M.) Other texts are two drafts, the reading copy, and the stenographic transcript, the first three bearing numerous revisions in Roosevelt's hand (Speech File). Roosevelt made a number of departures from his reading copy in delivering the speech; most of them appear in the stenographic transcript. The entire text is printed in Rosenman (ed.), *Public Papers*, IX, 370–375; this follows the stenographic transcript for the most part.

1017   HAROLD L. ICKES, SECRETARY OF THE INTERIOR, TO ROOSEVELT

WASHINGTON, *Sept. 4, 1940*

MEMORANDUM FOR THE PRESIDENT: The House Committee on Irrigation and Reclamation will hold hearings in the near future on H. R. 10122, a bill to amend the Wheeler-Case Act and the Water Facilities Act. In my report to the House Committee, I have recommended enactment of the proposed legislation because, if enacted, it will accomplish two principal objectives, namely:

1. It will make possible the prompt construction of water conservation and utilization projects with investigations, procedures and standards of feasibility substantially like those which have been proved to be practicable on Reclamation projects; and

2. It will concentrate in the Department of the Interior the construction of all irrigation projects or water facilities that are primarily for irrigation and will eliminate overlapping and inconsistent provisions of existing law.

My recollection is that you had the first objective in mind when, on the occasion of your approval of the Wheeler-Case Act, slightly over a year ago, you said, in part: "This bill is better than no bill at all, though it has in it a number of deficiencies . . ."[1] The second objective was the one I believe you had in mind, when you approved the Water Facilities Act, approximately three years ago. At that time, in a memorandum for the then Acting Director of the Budget, you said, in part:

Reclamation projects should not be undertaken. As I understand it, most of the projects will be for what are described as, "farm ponds." If I am right in this assumption, why should we not set a top limit on the construction of each. The Department of Agriculture should get in touch with PWA and other agencies which have been doing the same work in the past. . . .[2]

[472]

With respect to the amendments of the Wheeler-Case Act, the Department of Agriculture has made a number of recommendations to which I readily agree, without conceding their correctness in every respect. I do not agree, however, with the suggestion that the extent, if any, to which the Department of Agriculture might wish to participate in a given project should be the subject of a formal report to you by the Secretary of Agriculture and that you should be required to determine what departments and agencies are to participate in investigations and surveys of proposed projects. I concur with the view of Congressman Case and Senator Wheeler, the authors of this bill, that sound administration requires that, busy as you are, you should not be burdened with such determinations.

The Department of Agriculture would eliminate from the bill proposed by Congressman Case and Senator Wheeler the requirement of clearance through the Department of the Interior of proposed projects involving the storage or utilization of water for the irrigation of more than 500 acres of land, or the surface storage of more than 500 acre-feet of water, or a total cost exceeding $5,000. On the other hand, it has no objection to the amendment which would limit its authority for construction under the Water Facilities Act to projects involving an expenditure of not more than $50,000 of Federal funds, whether appropriated or allotted or both. It seems to me that the restrictions proposed in the bill are designed to assure that the projects constructed by the Department of Agriculture under the Water Facilities Act shall be, as you evidently intended they should be, "farm ponds." A "farm pond" big enough to store more than 500 acre-feet of water or costing up to $50,000 may perhaps deserve to be called a "lake." However, since the Department of Agriculture has agreed to the over-all limitation of $50,000, I think that the question, whether the other restrictions should be eliminated, may safely be left to the Committee.

I shall appreciate it, if you will note hereon whether my views coincide with yours and, if such is the case, whether I may so advise the Committee.[3]

[HAROLD L. ICKES]

THE WHITE HOUSE, August   , 1940.
Approved:

[13:OF 177:CT]

[1] *Ante,* 941.
[2] *Ante,* 686.
[3] An attached memorandum, Roosevelt to the Director of the Budget, Sept. 5, 1940, reads, "For recommendation." No reply has been found in the Roosevelt papers. The bill as approved Oct. 14, 1940 (54 *Stat.* 1119), retained the $50,000-per-project limitation Ickes requested but not the other.

1018   ROOSEVELT TO CLAUDE R. WICKARD, SECRETARY OF
        AGRICULTURE

WASHINGTON, *September 7, 1940*

MEMORANDUM FOR THE SECRETARY OF AGRICULTURE: Please ask
the Forest Service for comment on this statement by the Lumber Survey
Report. I doubt if there is any "approximate balance of timber growth
with timber use at the current rate" within the United States at the
present time.[1]

F. D. R.

[13:OF 149:CT]

[1] *Report of the Lumber Survey Committee to the Secretary of Commerce,* Aug. 15,
1940, by Wilson Compton and the other members of the committee, issued by the
Commerce Department.

1019   [*Enclosure*] LEON HENDERSON, ADVISORY COMMISSION TO
        THE COUNCIL OF NATIONAL DEFENSE, TO ROOSEVELT

WASHINGTON, D. C., *September 6, 1940*

MEMORANDUM . . . I told you yesterday that timber growth and
timber use were about in balance. My authority was the Lumber Survey
Report of August 15, 1940, to the Secretary of Commerce, which reads:

Recent published estimates of the U. S. Forest Service, following extensive study and survey, of the available timber supply in this country shows
approximate balance of timber growth with timber use at the current rate.
Forest Service estimates show effective timber growth as 9.6 billion cubic
feet, including 27.5 billion board feet of saw timber. Better forest fire protection, selective cutting and other gradually improved forest practices, are
slowly but constantly improving the balance between timber supply, timber
growth and timber use.

[LEON HENDERSON]

[13:OF 149:T]

1020   ROOSEVELT TO MILLER FREEMAN, PUBLISHER, *The Mining
        World,* Seattle

WASHINGTON, *September 19, 1940*

MY DEAR MR. FREEMAN: I have received your letter of August 22
with several enclosures concerning an article which you published, entitled, "Conservation—Should it Serve—or Only Save?"
Your article is a warning to your readers and "to all mining States"
that Secretary Ickes' "ambitions threaten to close important areas to
prospecting and mining." Your article also states that if a bill (H. R.

9351) to amend the Antiquities Act is enacted into law "it would be possible for the President of the United States, 'in his discretion,' to transfer virtually any or all of the [national forests in the Western States] [1] from National Forest to National Park status, removing them forever from prospecting, mining, or other use of their resources . . ." and that "the states concerned might never know of the contemplated action before it had been taken." Your article presents these warnings as the "findings and conclusions" of an unbiased study recently made by the Washington State Planning Council.

Secretary Ickes pointed out in replying to you that the Council, as a part of its study, held public hearings to pass judgment on a park proposal before the facts had been ascertained; that the Council requested material from the Department of the Interior and then refused to publish it, whereas it published copiously from other sources; and that, during the study, members of the Council spoke at public meetings against park status for any additional area in the Cascades. The Secretary further pointed out that he had given assurances that if important mineralized areas were recommended for park status, he would support appropriate legislative measures to permit the continuation of prospecting and mining, if a national park were established.

In replying to Secretary Ickes, you, as the founder and a charter member of the Washington State Planning Council, state that you ignored his pledges because, you state, the people of the West have no faith in his word, and, moreover, that they prefer that the public lands be administered by some other agency.

Perhaps the Secretary had these actions and expressions of attitude in mind when he called to your attention the fact that the study had not been objective.

The bill to amend the Antiquities Act, if enacted into law, would provide that the public reservations established by the President, under that authority, would be open to public water conservation projects, prospecting and mining, grazing, and hunting in accordance with State and Federal laws. The national monuments now established under the Antiquities Act are closed to such forms of exploitation. The amended Act would apply to those public lands that are primarily and outstandingly of recreational value. The more liberal reservations that would be established under the authority of the new Act would be National Recreational Areas, and not national parks or national monuments.

I fail to see wherein the enactment of this bill would threaten forestry lands. The President has had the authority to remove lands from the national forests since 1897, and there are more national forests today than ever before. From 1933 to 1939 the Forest Reservation Commission, of which Secretary Ickes is a member, has had net appropriations of more than $54,000,000 for the purchase of new national forest lands, or more than twice as much as had been allotted to the Commission in the 22 years of its existence prior to 1933. Since March 4, 1933, 12,540,223 acres of forest land have been approved for purchase by the Commission. From 1933 to 1936 alone, I allotted to the Commission for land acquisition $46,712,150 which has made possible the purchase of more than 11,000,000 acres of forest land.

I believe that my forest conservation record measures up in every respect to the policy that I stated to you in my letter of September 6, 1932.

In view of these facts I can see no reason why the findings and conclusions of the State Planning Council should be in the nature of a public warning against the Secretary of the Interior and against the President of the United States as enemies of sound public land administration.

This Administration has cooperated with and given more encouragement to resource-planning agencies than has ever been given in the history of this country. The Secretary of the Interior was giving such cooperation when he appointed a representative, at your request, to collaborate with you in the Cascade Mountains Study; he was cooperating when he submitted data to you, and when, in fact, he submitted the whole question of the Cascade recreational resources to a joint study. If resource-planning agencies are to retain the confidence that the people have placed in them, they must maintain the standard of objective study that the people have a right to expect.[2]

Very sincerely yours,

[FRANKLIN D. ROOSEVELT]

[13:OF 177:CT]

[1] Brackets in original.
[2] Drafted by Ickes.

1021   IRA N. GABRIELSON, DIRECTOR, FISH AND WILDLIFE SERVICE, TO HAROLD L. ICKES, SECRETARY OF THE INTERIOR

[WASHINGTON] *September 25, 1940*

MEMORANDUM FOR THE SECRETARY: Pursuant to my recent conversation with you, in regard to the need for additional land purchases to round out the national wildlife refuge system, I wish to take this opportunity to set forth in more detail the Service's appropriation needs for refuge purposes.

The Fish and Wildlife Service is responsible for the administration of 263 refuges, involving 13,635,365 acres of land. The refuges are divided roughly into two classes, namely, those for big game animals and those primarily for migratory waterfowl, although all refuges are for the benefit of wildlife generally. The refuge program has expanded from 104 refuges consisting of 6,085,542 acres in 1934 to the present 263 refuges involving 13,635,365 acres at the end of the fiscal year 1940. This timely expansion was made possible primarily through the allotment of emergency funds to the Biological Survey by the Resettlement Administration for the purchase of submarginal lands, and through a special appropriation of $1,000,000 for the purchase of refuge lands.

The Biological Survey was further fortunate in receiving funds and labor from the Works Progress Administration and the Civilian Conservation Corps for the development of the newly-acquired refuge lands, to make them suitable for the purpose for which they were intended, and to place them under administration. The increased acreage under administration has so increased the refuge maintenance requirements that the monies regularly appropriated for this purpose are insufficient to carry the load. It has, therefore, been necessary to supplement the refuge maintenance allotment by an increasing amount each year from the monies received through the sale of duck stamps. The duck stamp funds are the only monies now available to the Fish and Wildlife Service for the purchase of lands for the rounding out of the national wildlife refuge system for migratory waterfowl. The original purchase plan called for the acquisition of breeding areas in the northern part of the United States, the purchase of strategic feeding and resting grounds along each of the major flyways, and the acquisition of major concentration areas on the waterfowl wintering grounds in the southern part of the United States.

That part of the program calling for acquisition of the more important breeding grounds within the United States is well advanced. There are still many blanks to be filled in along the Atlantic and Pacific flyways, and several major wintering areas remain to be acquired before a thoroughly effective refuge system for migratory waterfowl will be complete, and our treaty obligations with Canada and Mexico, for the protection of migratory birds, will have been consummated. In addition to the new flyway and wintering area refuges remaining to be acquired, extensive purchases must be made to consolidate holdings within existing refuges to facilitate development and administration. Unless the adverse [sic] lands within existing refuges are acquired the cost of administration is greatly increased, and development for the maximum use of wildlife is often definitely limited. Because of the ever increasing amount of duck stamp monies required to supplement maintenance appropriations, the amount of money available for land purchase has reached a point where the national refuge plan for migratory waterfowl cannot be effectively and economically prosecuted.

In order to effectively carry on the land purchase program for migratory waterfowl, our budget estimates for 1942 include an increase of $625,000 for the maintenance and development of bird refuges, under Project 4. This increase is based on the amount of money that would otherwise have to be used from the 1942 duck stamp money for maintenance and development of existing refuges. It is proposed to use practically the entire duck stamp appropriation, exclusive of the 10% authorized by law for administration and enforcement, for the purchase of land to round out existing refuge holdings and to fill in the remaining gaps in the national refuge system.

None of the current appropriations for the Fish and Wildlife Service are available for the acquisition of additional big game refuge lands. At the present time the Service is administering 13 such refuges, totalling 6,595,997 acres. Within the exterior boundaries of most of these refuges are large acreages of adverse lands. These private holdings complicate and greatly increase the cost of administration of the refuges. In some instances the lands are required for the proper development of water for the animals. The concentrations of game on the big game refuges overflow onto the private lands, and often seriously reduce the carrying capacity of the range for livestock. In many instances the private landowners are anxious to sell their lands to the Government, and considerable Congressional pressure is often brought to bear, in an effort to have the Service relieve the private operators of lands within refuge boundaries which are adversely affected by concentrations of big game. It is hoped that this situation may be corrected through the annual appropriations of $125,000 for the purchase of the more urgently needed big game lands as opportunities may present themselves. This item is being included in the 1942 budget estimate.

(Sgd) IRA N. GABRIELSON

[13:OF 6–CC:T:COPY]

1022   PAUL H. APPLEBY, ACTING SECRETARY OF AGRICULTURE, TO
        ROOSEVELT

WASHINGTON, *September 28, 1940*

DEAR MR. PRESIDENT: The statement by the Lumber Survey Committee referred to in your memorandum of September 7, according to the Forest Service, does not present a complete picture of the forest growth-drain relationship.

There is in this country according to estimates by the Forest Service, an *effective* annual timber growth—growth that may reasonably be expected sometime to become available for cutting—of 9.6 billion cubic feet of which 27.5 billion board feet represents saw timber. There is, in addition, an ineffective growth—timber not accessible for cutting and in trees too poor to use—of 1.7 billion cubic feet which for all practical purposes may be disregarded so far as the growth-drain relationship is concerned.

The estimated total drain in 1936, which is considered to have been a year of subnormal consumption, was 13.5 billion cubic feet, including 47.8 board feet [1] of saw timber. Of this drain, 70 percent was in trees of saw-timber size and 30 percent was in trees of cordwood size.

Moreover, of this total drain, 11.4 billion cubic feet (42.4 billion board feet) was cut for use for all purposes and the balance was non-salvaged timber destroyed by fires, wind, disease, and insects. Saw-timber drain, it should be noted, includes not only trees of saw-timber size cut for lumber, but also saw-timber size trees cut for purposes other than lumber (poles, piling, crossties, veneer, pulpwood, etc.), and those destroyed by fire, disease, etc. Lumber alone accounts for only one-half of the timber consumed in the United States.

The situation is actually more critical than the foregoing figures indicate, because:

(1) The drain is unevenly distributed with reference to the growth so that the rate of timber depletion in some localities is much more rapid than for the United States as a whole. In these localities the timber resource upon which nearby communities are dependent is rapidly being depleted.

(2) More than one-third of the saw timber is economically unavailable because of inaccessibility, poor quality, or inferiority of species. Moreover, a large portion of the effective growth consists of relatively inferior species and small sized and generally low grade material, while the cut is in the accessible areas and comes largely from better grade old growth timber which is being cut much more rapidly than it is being replaced by new growth.

(3) The forest growing stock—stand of immature timber—has been reduced far below the quantity required to support permanently a rate of drain even as large as that of 1936. Forest Service estimates indicate that the growing stock in the East must be increased 40 to 50 percent in terms of board feet, and even more in terms of cubic feet in order to maintain this rate of drain. To accomplish this it will be necessary to cut considerably less than the current growth for many years to come. In the West taken as a whole, the growing stock generally, has not been so seriously depleted, but in certain localities, as for example, in western Washington, the situation is critical.

(4) Finally, we should not be satisfied with the rate of consumption in 1936. Domestic use of wood has been considerably greater in the past and should be again, provided it is available in suitable qualities and at reasonable cost. One important potential increase in wood use of the immediate future is to relieve the existing housing shortage and repair and modernize or replace homes for millions of people who now live under incredibly unsatisfactory conditions. Other potential construction requirements and the steady increase in pulp production and

other forms of wood products are additional indications of a growing need for timber. The Forest Service visualizes a domestic consumption within the next few decades, considering existing uses only, of possibly 15.6 billion cubic feet, of which 51 billion board feet would be saw timber. Considering also probable new uses, inevitable losses from natural causes, exports to the extent that other countries are able and willing to buy, and a reasonable safety factor, it is estimated that a growth of 21.4 billion cubic feet, including 68 billion board feet of saw timber, would be a reasonable basis for a sound national program of forestry.

In a nutshell, the growth-drain relationship in our forests is this: In a time of subnormal use, and when forestry efforts of the country are making a larger contribution than they ever have before, we are cutting or destroying our second growth forests about as fast as they grow, and are steadily reducing the volume of old growth forests in which the major part of our current saw timber drain is taking place.

Very sincerely yours,

PAUL H. APPLEBY

[13:OF 149:TS]

[1] "Billion board feet" is meant.

1023 ROOSEVELT TO GOVERNOR JOHN MOSES, Bismarck, North Dakota

[WASHINGTON] *November 1, 1940*

DEAR GOVERNOR MOSES: I want to thank you for your kind commendations of the general agricultural policies of my Administration and your particular references to the Prairie States Forestry Project carried on by the Forest Service of the Department of Agriculture.[1]

We, too, have been pleased with the success farmers have had, with the help of the Forest Service and the Work Projects Administration, in establishing shelterbelt plantings and with the interest people in the Plains have shown in properly caring for them. We hope this work can be continued.

As you undoubtedly know, the project is now financed entirely with emergency funds. Congress has not provided funds specifically to carry on the work. The Work Projects Administration has supported the project generously, making special provisions from year to year to carry it on.

The Department of Agriculture now is studying methods of further stabilizing the Prairie States Forestry Project within the framework of the general land use policy for the Plains area. I hope these studies will result in placing the project on a firmer footing.

I feel, as you do, that we have made a good start toward working out a solution to the problem of stabilizing agriculture in the Plains area, yet there is still much that remains to be done—much that can be done only through close cooperation among local, State and Federal government agencies.

Very sincerely yours,

[FRANKLIN D. ROOSEVELT]

[13:OF 149:CT]

¹ In a letter of Oct. 1, 1940 (OF 149), Moses said that he was convinced that the Shelterbelt project offered important benefits to the farmers of his state and that he hoped that the work would be continued.

1024   CLAUDE R. WICKARD, SECRETARY OF AGRICULTURE, TO ROOSEVELT

WASHINGTON, *November 4, 1940*

DEAR MR. PRESIDENT: Shortly before Henry Wallace resigned you spoke to him about the possibility of developing the pattern of the Shelterbelt planting more along the lines of your original suggestion. Since then, at his request, I have been conducting some detailed inquiries, and I am now ready to report.

I think I understand and share your wish to have a pattern that will give very vivid effect to the planting—make entrance into the Shelterbelt a clear and sharp contrast, create an extensive national monument of trees in a treeless country. I shall first report, therefore, what has been done, and give the reasons why. Then I shall make a few suggestions.

The larger of the two attached maps prepared by the Forest Service shows the extent to which shelterbelts have been concentrated to date.¹ Planting has been carried on in some 200 counties in the six project states. However, almost 65% or 9,000 miles of the 14,146 miles planted is concentrated in 52 of these counties comprising 30% of the project area. The small map illustrates the pattern of shelterbelts already planted in Davison County, South Dakota, as well as the potential primary and intermediate belts and is representative of the concentration areas as a whole.

Study of the maps will show the factors that detract from the full monumental effect you originally had in mind. Plantings vary in intensity so that the traveler comes slowly—not suddenly—to realize that he is in the Belt. The contrast is not, at most of the border points, as marked as you had hoped. The rows of trees, insofar as they are complete, largely run parallel rather than at right angles to the roads, because the major highways are east-west roads.

[481]

Yet the plan of shelterbelt planting as actually being developed has already made a monumental showing which will be even greater as additionl areas are planted and as the trees become larger. It is safe to say that a very large majority of the people of the prairie region has accepted the program and are intensely interested in its development. During the past summer several forestry field day picnics were held the largest of these being at Neligh, Nebraska, on June 16, when twelve to fifteen thousand people turned out and viewed the results of the shelterbelt planting in that locality. This is perhaps the largest gathering that has ever attended a function of this type anywhere in the United States.

Many excellent concentration areas are being developed, and a continuously greater degree of concentration will be obtained each year that the project continues as new belts are added in the present concentration areas. It is planned that from ½ to ⅔ of next spring's planting, estimated at about 3,000 miles, will be concentrated in the same counties in which planting to date has largely been confined. Greater concentration is being hindered by the following two principal reasons:

1. With the operation of the project under W. P. A. regulations the question of available relief labor becomes serious. In many instances, particularly in the northern states, all local labor of this type available to the project is being used, and it has been found impracticable to transport labor long distances. This makes it necessary to operate in many scattered localities.

2. In the southern states, the percentage of transient tenant farmers is high. It is therefore difficult to obtain a greater degree of essential cooperation on the part of landowners than is now being received. This is also true in the northern states but to a lesser extent. This transient tenancy problem will no doubt be an important factor in limiting the degree of concentration that can ultimately be obtained, although the establishment of shelterbelts is doubtless helping to stabilize occupancy.

The original plan for arrangement of shelterbelts contemplated continuous belts one or more miles apart, running north and south from the Canadian boundary into the northern portion of Texas. After the initiation of the project, investigations revealed that for the most part the prevailing and most destructive winds were from the northerly and southerly directions. Therefore, as a general rule, it seemed that better protection from winter storms as well as from the hot dry summer winds could be obtained by east and west belts, supplemented by north and south belts. The investigative findings on wind directions were supported by experience statements from farmers. If due to the local terrain or other factors, the evidence on the ground indicated that the greatest protection could be realized by north and south orientation, the belts were so oriented.

Each farm is considered as a unit and the shelterbelts are located where they will best serve the farmer and at the same time tie in with a systematic community plan of development. Unbroken belts of great length have not proved practicable due to the occurrence of large areas of soils on which successful planting is not feasible.

To capitalize fully on what has been done, and yet to move as far as possible toward the effect you originally had in mind, I have a suggested program to offer:

(1) To continue to concentrate in the counties of present concentration until these are fully planted but to give priority within these counties to finishing all the straight planting lines that parallel and adjoin Federal highways or main passenger railway lines. In other words, to place major emphasis on the planting of east-west strips of trees along Federal highways and main railway lines, until all those strips which can be planted are completed in the counties of present concentration.

(2) Then to extend the same treatment in other counties in the Belt area—that is, in the counties where planting has been less concentrated, to place major emphasis again on planting along Federal highways and main railway lines in these counties until these straight strips are likewise completed. In carrying on this part of the program, priority should be given first to counties that will fill in the gaps from north to south between the present counties of intensive planting, so that as early as possible there will be an unbroken north-south line, at least one county wide, of intensively planted counties.

(3) When the above program is completed, planting should continue in the intensively planted counties to fill in all straight lines of planting more distant from the highways and railways, and finally

(4) The same completion of the program in counties in which planting is not now concentrated.

To do what is involved in items (1) and (2), which would give maximum monumental effect with least planting, would involve 21,000 miles of additional planting, 227,000,000 trees, and $14,000,000. This includes planting along some 2,500 miles of highways and railways and means stepping up this phase of the program to five times the present rate of accomplishment. It contemplates doing the roadside planting as part of the general program unless the cost per mile is to be very greatly increased.

In the light of the experience to date, I wonder whether the plan of shelterbelt planting as described satisfactorily meets what you had in mind.

Respectfully,

CLAUDE R. WICKARD

[13:OF 149:TS]

[1] One map is present, "Shelterbelt Planting Area. Prairie States Forestry Project." It is dated 1940.

1025   ROOSEVELT TO WILLIAM PLOG, SUPERINTENDENT, ROOSEVELT
        HYDE PARK ESTATE

WASHINGTON, *November 25, 1940*

MEMORANDUM FOR MR. PLOG: Please put out those chestnuts north of the farm lane next to the woods directly north of the wood-pile and put a little wire fence around them to keep the cows and the deer out.[1]

F. D. R.

FDR/TMB
[13:PPF 7102:CT]

---

[1] The chestnut seedlings, gift of Dr. Herman Baruch (brother of Bernard), were planted as directed, in the woods east of the Post Road, but did not survive.

1026   ROOSEVELT TO GOVERNOR W. LEE O'DANIEL, Austin, Texas

U. S. S. "TUSCALOOSA," AT SEA, *December 11, 1940*[1]

MY DEAR GOVERNOR O'DANIEL: Your letter outlining your program of planning for the development of Texas resources is deeply appreciated.[2] We need the cooperation of your State in our national efforts to plan for the best use of all our resources in building better communities and a more prosperous nation.

As you know, the National Resources Planning Board carries on this task nationally in my own Executive Office. I am glad to observe that you are creating a similar organization in your Executive Department. I am sure that you will find such a body extremely useful to you in your daily task of dealing with all the problems of the development of your State—the use of its land and water, its mineral and fuel resources, its agriculture and industry, the education of its youth, the transportation of its commodities, and the problems of the health, recreation and welfare of its people. Your State resources agency can be the center where the work on these special problems throughout the State, in the universities, private and business organizations and government agencies, is brought together and related for you in terms of its long-range significance.

I have found that a legislative charter outlining in broad terms the work of this new type of governmental agency is important in getting adequate appropriations for it. Our Federal experience with names for such an agency is also significant. I tried my own hand at it and suggested *National Resources* to include human, economic, and scientific resources as well as natural resources. The word "planning" was dropped from the name in 1934, but has since come back in—it is a much misunderstood word but still the best available.

The National Resources Planning Board and its regional office in Dallas stand ready to help you in this work in any way that we can. With the assistance of your agency, our State and national programs for the best use of our resources will go forward in close cooperation.[3]

Sincerely yours,

[FRANKLIN D. ROOSEVELT]

[*Notation*:AS] Copy of reply sent to Hon. F. A. Delano 12/13/40 hm [13:OF 1092:CT]

[1] On December 4 Roosevelt boarded the cruiser U. S. S. *Tuscaloosa* at Miami for an inspection of American naval bases on British owned islands in the Caribbean. He returned to Washington on December 15.

[2] Nov. 26, 1940 (OF 1092), describing the natural resources planning agency established in the executive department of the state government and offering its cooperation with the National Resources Planning Board.

[3] Drafted by the National Resources Planning Board.

1027   ROOSEVELT TO REPRESENTATIVE A. WILLIS ROBERTSON OF
        VIRGINIA, CHAIRMAN, HOUSE SELECT COMMITTEE ON
        CONSERVATION OF WILDLIFE RESOURCES

WASHINGTON, D. C., *December 16, 1940*

MY DEAR MR. ROBERTSON: I am grateful to you for your letter of November 29 with which you sent me a copy of the Committee hearings for 1939 and 1940.[1] It is with great satisfaction that I note the rapid strides made in the field of wildlife conservation during the past two years. Being an outdoor enthusiast myself, I am well aware of the importance of conserving this valuable natural resource. Particularly in times of stress, such as these, relaxation in the out of doors is an important asset to the morale of the Nation. I take this opportunity, also, to congratulate your Committee on the splendid work it is doing for wildlife conservation. I look forward to receiving your next report and trust that the achievements in the next few years will be as significant as they have been during the last decade.[2]

Sincerely yours,

[FRANKLIN D. ROOSEVELT]

[*Notation*:AS] Copy of reply sent to Interior 12/17/40 hm [13:OF 378:CT]

[1] *Hearings*, House Select Committee on Conservation of Wildlife Resources, 76th Cong., 1st sess. 1939 (Washington, 1939); *Hearings . . .*, 76th Cong., 3d sess., 1940 (Washington, 1940). In his covering letter (OF 378), Robertson said: "It is generally agreed that under your leadership more progress in the conservation field, and especially that of wildlife conservation, has been made during the past seven years than in any similar period of the Nation's history."

[2] Drafted by the Interior Department.

1028   ROOSEVELT TO FAIRFIELD OSBORN, PRESIDENT, NEW YORK
ZOOLOGICAL SOCIETY, New York City

WASHINGTON, *December 26, 1940*

MY DEAR MR. OSBORN: I have received your letter of December 12,
quoting the resolution of December 10 of the New York Zoological Society, in which it is requested that I designate a special board to consider
defense plans relating to the continued conservation of wild animal life
and other natural resources.[1]

The respective Federal Departments charged with responsibilities
for the conservation of our natural resources are currently informed of
the military needs affecting those resources under the national defense
program.   I am glad to have your suggestion.   However, I do not believe that the Departments are in need at this time of coordination by a
special board, as they are fully aware of the vital need to protect the
natural resources against all ill-considered action.   I am glad to inform
you that there is no authority to permit the cutting of timber on Govern-
ment-owned lands within the Olympic National Park.[2]

Sincerely yours,

[FRANKLIN D. ROOSEVELT]

[*Notation*: STAMPED] (sgd) Burlew

[13: OF 378: CT]

[1] OF 378.
[2] Drafted by the Interior Department.

1029   ROOSEVELT TO SENATOR GEORGE W. NORRIS OF NEBRASKA

[WASHINGTON] *January 3, 1941*

DEAR GEORGE: I had hoped to talk to Secretary Wickard and Secretary Ickes before replying to your letter of December 13.[1] The rush of
other business has prevented me from doing so and now Secretary Ickes
is out of town.

Agriculture and Interior deal with many problems that cut across
department lines. Grazing, reclamation, conservation, rehabilitation,
forestation, and other needs of western people require the services of
numerous agencies in the two Departments. As soon as I can, I wish
to explore ways in which all these services might best be coordinated.

I assure you, Senator, that I appreciate your writing me frankly as
you did.[2]

Very sincerely yours,

[FRANKLIN D. ROOSEVELT]

[13: OF I–C: CT]

[1] Norris wrote in opposition to transfer of the Forest Service to the Interior Department. He said that the sentiment of the country, especially in the West, was against such a transfer, and since it would be of no benefit, he could see no reason why the President should take such a step.

[2] Norris' letter was sent to Ickes and Wickard for preparation of reply; the reply here printed was drafted by Wickard after he had talked with Ickes (Wickard to Watson, Dec. 31, 1940, OF 1–C).

Part IV

The Third Term: 1941-1945

The Third Term: 1941-1945

1030 PRESS CONFERENCE, Executive Offices of the White House, February 4, 1941, 4:20 P. M.

[*Excerpt*] Q: Any change in Bonneville Power status? I understand when that agency was set up it was independent; then it was put under the Secretary of the Interior; and I heard on the Pacific Coast the other day that the War Department would take it over. Is there any truth in that?

The President: No, certainly not in that. I will tell you what may have given rise to it. It had nothing to do with the War Department— merely development of the whole idea. That started six or seven years ago. If the TVA worked out as a watershed development for the benefit of the people who lived in the watershed—mind you, this has nothing to do with any one specific thing, because it covers so many things; it is not just power or navigation or irrigation or flood control or planting trees or building check dams, but it relates to the general welfare of the people who live in that district, with all those component things that go with human life; and the general feeling back there was that if it worked we might extend the idea of the economic and social development of an entire watershed in other places. And at that time—it's awfully old stuff, but it has come to a head again, and we talked it over; and I think if you will go back in the old Press Conference Reports you will find that somewhere back there I suggested that if it worked in one place, we could try to work it out in other watersheds.[1]

We didn't want to undertake too large an area, and at that time we rather thought that the Arkansas Watershed was a proper and logical one to try, because the Arkansas River runs all the way from the Mississippi clear back to the middle of the State of Colorado, up through past Pueblo, where they had those bad floods, and away on back through the Royal Gorge; and from Colorado it runs down through the Arkansas area at the eastern slope of the Rockies and flows out to the dust bowl area of eastern Colorado and over into Kansas; and from Kansas over

[491]

into Oklahoma, and then on down to lower Arkansas, in the south end of the State of Arkansas; so that you have all kinds of problems, not just one but eight or ten entirely separate problems in that one watershed, where they grow all kinds of produce from cotton to cattle.

Away back—I guess it was '34—we talked about the Arkansas Valley as being a proper one to take up this general idea in, and then because we went ahead on certain public works out in the Northwest they got the idea we would extend the plan to the Northwest. We talked about a Columbia River Watershed plan because it was relatively a small area. That would include the watershed that runs into Puget Sound.

Both of those projects are being discussed on the Hill at the present time—the idea of setting up some sort of authority to cover each of those places, but certainly not to put any one thing under the War Department, because that would be just power. This goes much further than power.

[13: PRESIDENT'S PRESS CONFERENCES: T]

¹ Cf. ante, 587.

1031   HAROLD D. SMITH, DIRECTOR, BUREAU OF THE BUDGET, TO
        ROOSEVELT

[WASHINGTON] *Feb. 7, 1941*

MEMORANDUM FOR THE PRESIDENT: The Bureau of the Budget soon will be obliged to review various bills to create regional development authorities. Major legislative proposals of this character are the following:

1. The Columbia River Power Administration bill has been reintroduced by Representatives Hill and Smith, but it is being revised by the Interior Department in the light of comments from other Federal agencies.¹

2. The Arkansas Valley Authority bill has been introduced by Representative Ellis and Senator Miller.

3. Central Valley of California Authority bills are reported to be under preparation both by Mr. Lilienthal and by the Interior Department working separately.

The Federal Power Commission, Department of Agriculture, Treasury Department, and other interested Federal agencies, are being or will be called upon for reports to Congress on these bills.

Basic changes in government organization, and in Federal fiscal and planning policy, are involved in the proposed bills. Whatever action may be taken with respect to these three drainage areas is likely to become a pattern for similar proposals in other drainage areas.

I assume that you would like to develop a unified administration policy toward these proposals without committing yourself at this time as to the details of regional authority duties and organization.   If this is correct, would you consider it in order for the Bureau of the Budget and the National Resources Planning Board to take the lead in bringing together the views of the agencies named above, in analyzing the various proposals, and in referring to you the major issues of policy?   The agencies would not, of course, be advised as to the relationship of their proposals to your program until after you had reviewed a report on the issues involved.

[HAROLD D. SMITH]

[13:OF 402:CT]

¹ Although consideration of power resources as such is outside the scope of these volumes, this and certain similar letters have been included because they show Roosevelt's ideas on the regional concept of resource conservation.

1032   ROOSEVELT TO HAROLD D. SMITH, DIRECTOR, BUREAU OF THE BUDGET

WASHINGTON, *February 11, 1941*

MEMORANDUM FOR THE DIRECTOR OF THE BUDGET: Yes.¹ I wish Budget and National Resources would reconcile these various regional authorities.

I sent the Columbia River bill to Fred Delano today.

F. D. R.

[13:OF 402:CT]

¹ This is in reply to the preceding letter.

1033   ROOSEVELT TO ANTHONY J. DIMOND, DELEGATE FROM ALASKA

[WASHINGTON] *February 20, 1941*

MY DEAR MR. DIMOND: I have received your letter of February 6, informing me that a proposal to add Admiralty Island, Alaska, to the Glacier Bay National Monument may soon be presented for my consideration.¹

Interest in Admiralty Island has broadened during recent years because early attention was directed primarily to the potential commercial importance of its timber, and it became necessary to identify the other resources of the island with equal clarity in order to insure their appropriate conservation together with that of the timber.   With its extraordinary concentration of bear species, and its other scientific and scenic interests, Admiralty Island is considered a particularly significant area both scientifically and recreationally.

As Alaska's development gains momentum, and as sound forestry practices are more widely accepted throughout our country, it is possible that the other values of Admiralty Island may exceed its timber value. I state that not as a prediction but as a possibility. In view of such a possibility, I believe that we should approach Alaska's problems with an open mind, attempting to do only that which will be best for Alaska's development.

I appreciate having the information contained in your letter.[2]

Sincerely yours,

[FRANKLIN D. ROOSEVELT]

[13:OF 928:CT]

[1] Dimond objected to this proposal for a variety of reasons: Admiralty Island was sixty miles distant from the nearest boundary of Glacier Bay National Monument, the Indians of the island would be unable to pursue their traditional occupations of hunting and fishing, prospecting and hunting would be barred, and timber would not be available for the future Alaskan pulpwood industry (OF 928).
[2] Drafted by the Interior Department.

1034   ROOSEVELT TO HAROLD L. ICKES, SECRETARY OF THE INTERIOR

WASHINGTON, *February 21, 1941*

MEMORANDUM FOR THE SECRETARY OF THE INTERIOR: I have read with interest Director Gabrielson's memorandum to you of February seventh.[1] I wholly approve the thought that Wildlife should be conserved during the present period of stress, but I do not think any separate organization need be set up at this time toward this end.

I think that for the present the Fish & Wildlife Service should detail a representative to act as liaison officer with the War Department, the Navy Department and the Office for Production Management. It should be the duty of this representative to keep informed from day to day as to any plans for or operation of camps or other military or naval services, together with the operation of any plants, factories, etc., which would seem to be damaging to fish or wildlife.

In case such conditions are found by this liaison officer, the Director of the Fish and Wildlife Service should report to you as Secretary of the Interior and you should take it up with the offending agency.

F.D.R.

[13:OF 6–CC:CT]

[1] Gabrielson referred to the services in World War I of biologists of the Bureau of Biological Survey in controlling rodents in service camps and elsewhere (OF 6–CC). He suggested that the Fish and Wildlife Service be placed in a position "to recommend courses of action in the use of lands on which wildlife is important," and thus guard against damage to wildlife.

WASHINGTON, *April 4, 1941*

MY DEAR MR. PRESIDENT: Mr. Ward Shepard may have sent you a copy of this memorandum, but on the chance that he has not done so, I am sending you the enclosed.

Sincerely yours,

HAROLD L. ICKES

[13:OF 149:TS]

1036 [*Enclosure*] WARD SHEPARD, PRINCIPAL PLANNING SPECIAL-IST, INDIAN FIELD SERVICE, TO HAROLD L. ICKES

WASHINGTON, *Mar. 27, 1941*

(*Through Commissioner Collier*)

MEMORANDUM FOR THE SECRETARY: The Congressional Joint Committee on Forestry has just sent its final report to the printer.[1] Unfortunately no copies are obtainable. This report, though containing some good recommendations, is as a whole a weak compromise between sharply conflicting views within the Committee. It is so far short of what ought to be expected of this Administration that I bring the matter to your attention in the hope that you may, if you think proper, inform the President.

I mention only two main points, as all the other recommendations, except a forest leasing plan, are of subordinate importance.

1. The Committee fails to make an effective proposal on the all-important subject of public regulation of private forests. It recommends that the States adopt *minimum* regulations, and that if they fail to do so within five years, the Secretary of Agriculture *may* withdraw funds for fire protection and other forestry cooperation. As that Department has spent years in trying to spur the States to cooperate with it, that threat is pretty innocuous. This proposal closely fits the strategy of the lumbermen in opposing effective Federal intervention against forest devastation, for they can hamstring effective State legislation. Moreover, "minimum" regulations mean seed-tree logging instead of selective cutting; and as I emphasized to you and to the President last spring, selective cutting is the only possible economic basis for private forestry.

2. The Committee's recommendation on public forest purchase is woefully weak. It merely recommends some increase in present appropriations, which means that forest purchase, proceeding at a snail's pace, can make little contribution to saving our remaining forest capital.

Following my exposition last spring to you, the President, Senator Bankhead, and Secretary Wallace, of the confusion and weakness of the Forest Service recommendations to the Joint Committee, the Department of Agriculture emerged from its lethargy and drafted two important bills, which embrace the most important basic principles I urged:

(1) Federal cooperation with States in drafting and enforcing forest regulatory laws, with the alternative of direct Federal regulation if the States fail to cooperate or prefer Federal regulation.

(2) Selective cutting instead of seed-tree logging as the basis of regulation.

(3) A large public forest purchase program of well-stocked instead of devastated forests, through credit instead of annual appropriations, with a sinking fund from National Forest receipts.

These bills (H. R. 3850 and H. R. 3793, copies enclosed) should, in the public interest, supplant the Committee's recommendations on regulation and acquisition.[2]   It is unfortunate the Committee did not consult the responsible Department heads before it submitted its report.   But there is a far more important reason justifying renewed Executive leadership.   The President has asked Congress to authorize the National Resources Board to formulate a post-war program of public works employment, with emphasis on natural resources.   Adequate forest regulatory, leasing, and acquisition legislation, if adopted *now,* would give time to create a great framework for a rural works program that could absorb hundreds of thousands of men in constructive, publicly profitable work. We ought to take advantage of the gigantic creative energy that will be released by the defense effort to formulate an over-all program of natural resource reconstruction worthy of our national powers.

WARD SHEPARD

P.S.   Since writing the above, I have obtained the enclosed excerpt of Recommendations from the Committee's report.[3]

[13:OF 149:TS]

---

[1] *Forest Lands of the United States.   Report of the Joint Committee on Forestry . . . to Study and Make Investigation of the Present and Prospective Situation with Respect to the Forest Land of the United States . . .* 77th Cong., 1st sess., S. Doc. 32 (Washington, 1941); hereinafter cited as *Forest Lands of the United States.*

[2] H. R. 3793 was introduced by Hook (Mich.) on March 4, 1941, H. R. 3850 by Pierce (Ore.) on March 6, 1941.   Neither was reported (*Cong. Rec.,* 77th Cong., 1st sess., 87:2, 1784, 1945).   See Ickes to Roosevelt, March 2, 1942, *post,* 1078.

[3] Not present.   The joint committee report was sent by Roosevelt to Wickard with a note of April 7, 1941 (OF 149), "Please check on this report and let me have your views."

1037　CLAUDE R. WICKARD, SECRETARY OF AGRICULTURE, TO
　　　　ROOSEVELT

WASHINGTON, *April 5, 1941*

DEAR MR. PRESIDENT: In April 1937 Mr. Fechner informed Interior and Agriculture that you felt too much CCC effort had gone into recreational developments—with special reference to State Parks—and that more reforestation, erosion control and reclamation work should be done.

At that time there were 2,000 camps—20¾% being on park areas, 46½% on forestry, 23½% on erosion control and farm drainage and 4% on reclamation and grazing work. As camps are allocated today 19% are on national, state, county and municipal park areas, 40% on forestry, 26% on erosion control and farm drainage and 10% on reclamation and grazing work.

The CCC program now faces reduction from 1,500 to 1,365 camps on July 1 to meet indicated Budget requirements. In addition we are transferring camps to military defense and Case-Wheeler work. This calls for shutting down between 120 and 160 of Agriculture's forestry and erosion control camps (before their work is completed in many instances) and leaves fewer camps thereafter for types of work on which in 1937 you felt greater emphasis should be placed.

Naturally, I do not wish to open this question direct with the Federal Security Agency, the Department of the Interior, or any other agency. This would only be embarrassing to me and would accomplish nothing. So, because of the situation now existing, I am merely calling the matter to your attention for such action as you think appropriate.[1]

Respectfully,

CLAUDE R. WICKARD

[13:OF 268:TS]

[1] Answered *post,* 1041.

1038　HAROLD D. SMITH, DIRECTOR, BUREAU OF THE BUDGET, TO
　　　　ROOSEVELT

WASHINGTON, D. C., *Apr. 10, 1941*

MEMORANDUM FOR THE PRESIDENT: I am in receipt of a letter from Chairman Fulmer of the House Committee on Agriculture under date of March 28, 1941, requesting early and favorable clearance of a report by Agriculture on his bill, H. R. 969: "To authorize the Secretary of Agriculture to enter into cooperative agreements or leases with farmers and the owners of forest lands in order to provide for their management in accordance with proper forestry practices, and for other purposes."

Chairman Fulmer enclosed with his letter a copy of a letter written by you on December 12, 1938 to Mr. Monson Morris at Aiken, South Carolina . . .[1]

The Joint Committee on Forestry, appointed pursuant to your special message to Congress of March 14, 1938, and of which Representative Fulmer was Vice Chairman, submitted its report on March 24, 1941,[2] and there is included in its recommendations a proposal for legislation to provide for leases and cooperative agreements with private forest land owners, communities, institutions and States. The Committee sets forth the following principles on which to base such a program:

(a) Entering into a lease or a cooperative agreement on a voluntary basis.

(b) Retention of title by the owner. Owners would pay the taxes, but in case of lease would receive a nominal annual rental not to exceed the average annual tax for the 5 years preceding the lease. In the case of cooperative agreement, the owner would have the privilege of handling the rehabilitation work himself with Federal financial cooperation.

(c) The Federal Government should be reimbursed for its costs from the use of the land and sale of its products on a 50–50 basis for properties of less than 500 acres, and on a 100 percent basis above 500 acres.

(d) The administration should be done under the States in cooperation with and the approval of the Secretary of Agriculture.

(e) The President should be authorized to allocate to the Secretary of Agriculture such sums from relief, public works, or similar appropriations as may be needed, in addition to regular appropriations to effectuate the plan.

In the 76th Congress, Mr. Fulmer introduced H. R. 7271 and Senators Walsh, Byrnes, Brown and La Follette S. 2927, which were substantially the same as Mr. Fulmer's H. R. 969, now under consideration. On the basis of the earlier bills the proposals were thoroughly studied by this office, and I advised the Secretary of Agriculture under date of December 29, 1939 that "the enactment of this legislation would not be in accord with the program of the President."[3]

The Secretary's proposed report on H. R. 969 was received here March 27, 1941 and, upon determination that the new bill presents no new major features, I again advised the Secretary, on April 1, that its enactment would not be in accord with your program.

While at that time this office had no knowledge of your aforementioned letter to Mr. Monson Morris, and although Mr. Fulmer may hold our advice on H. R. 969 as inconsistent therewith, I am still of the opinion that you would not wish to approve this legislation.

H. R. 969 retains the mixture of woodlot management and commercial forestry to which you objected in your letter to Mr. Morris. It embraces all forest land except that in Federal ownership, including 24,000,000 acres of State, county, municipal and institutional forest and 341,000,000 acres of private land.

Of the 341,000,000 acres of private forests and woodlots, some 203,000,000 acres are commercial forest in approximately 1,000,000 ownerships. Of these 1,000,000 ownerships 1,700 are of 5,000 acres or more, aggregating 68,000,000 acres, and including 316 of 50,000 acres or more, 140 of 100,000 acres or more, and 51 of 200,000 acres or more. This leaves some 998,300 commercial ownerships aggregating 135,000,000 acres, or an average of 136 acres each.

Woodlots are found on some 3,000,000 farms and aggregate 138,-000,000 acres, the average farm woodlot thus comprising 46 acres.

The bill makes all of these ownerships eligible for participation in the program, subject to the organization of effective and economical administrative units. The Federal Government would pay the property taxes and the expenses of management, and would be entitled to recover, from uses of the land and sale of products, all of its tax outlay, 50% of its operating expenses on the first 500 acres of each cooperating ownership, and 100% of such expenses on any area above 500 acres of any ownership.

There is no satisfactory basis for predicting the ultimate extent of participation in such a program. Probably most of the non-Federal public forests and the larger commercial forests, except where intermingled with national forests, would remain under present systems of management. Among the 3,000,000 farm woodlot owners and the nearly 1,000,000 small commercial forest land owners there are doubtless some who would not voluntarily entrust the management of their property to the Government, and many more whose properties could not be grouped with others in practical administrative units. To the majority of such owners, however, the program should be highly attractive, and administrative measures for extension of the plan so as to include them could be devised.

On the basis of an average annual tax rate of 20 cents per acre, and annual expense of management of 15 cents per acre (Forest Service estimates), and assuming recovery of the tax outlay and 50% of the management expense (there would be few participating ownerships above 500 acres), the net Government subsidy would be 7½ cents per acre. From another angle, each acre leased would require an annual Federal appropriation of 35 cents, with a possible recovery of 27½ cents. Maximum participation might reach 200,000,000 acres, requiring annual appropriation of $70,000,000, with possible recovery of $55,000,000, and minimum subsidy of $15,000,000.

The Department of Agriculture feels that the measure should be comprehensively amended before enactment, and will shortly submit through this office a draft of amendments providing, among other things:

1. Simplification of administrative set-up.

2. Full recovery of Government costs from use of lands and sales of products on participating ownerships of more than 200 acres.

3. A straight leasing plan, giving the Government all rights of possession, with cooperative agreements eliminated.

With your approval, I propose to advise Chairman Fulmer that H. R. 969 was held as not in accord with your program because of—

1. The apparent need for revision to eliminate the mixture of woodlot management and commercial forestry.

2. Your desire to avoid further important additions to the regular budget while the necessity for extraordinary national defense expenditures continues.

In the judgment of this office, the soundness of this forest-land-leasing plan is not sufficiently clear to warrant its early adoption as a major action program, even if confined strictly to farm woodlots.

The estimates of necessary Government outlay are believed to be too low; those of the amounts likely to be recovered, extremely high.

If participation in the plan is confined to ownerships where revenues from sale of products may reasonably be expected to meet Government repayment requirements within any reasonable period, the social value of the plan will be very small.

If the plan is generally applied to reach even a majority of the farm woodlots, the Government subsidy will be much larger than has been indicated.

In practical effect the plan means adding to the national forest system the acres leased. Such additions might ultimately total 200,000,000 acres.

Private initiative and responsibility for management of the woodlot portions of our farms would disappear.

The prospects for profitable employment in woods work are over-emphasized in view of present and probable future market limitations.

The plan is but one feature of a very comprehensive forestry program recommended by the Joint Committee on Forestry, the adoption of which will require heavy additional Federal appropriations. This plan is of relatively low priority in the general program. Fully effective fire control should be the first objective.

Present major agricultural action programs already bring numerous units of the Department in frequent, direct contact with farmers. Excessive organization is a frequent complaint. The Soil Conservation Service and Extension Service have both legislative authority and funds for service to farmers in woodlot management. AAA pays benefits for proper woodlot management practices. The Farm Security Administration serves its clients with all-round farm management planning. It is suggested that the Forest Service should not get into farm management.

I would recommend that if any leasing plan is to be made operative, it should first have a five-year test period on an experimental scale.

HAROLD D. SMITH

[13:OF 149:TS]

¹ The Director of the Budget here quoted this letter in full. It is printed *ante*, 837.
² *Forest Lands of the United States* (Washington, 1941).
³ None of these bills was reported from committee.

1039   ROOSEVELT TO HAROLD D. SMITH, DIRECTOR, BUREAU OF THE BUDGET

[WASHINGTON] *April 11, 1941*

MEMORANDUM FOR THE DIRECTOR OF THE BUDGET: Here is "the law and the profits" in regard to privately owned timber:

1. Everybody should draw a line between the man and the corporation which owns land and uses it primarily for farming, and the man or corporation which owns land and uses it primarily for growing or raising or cutting trees. It is essential to accentuate the word "use." In effect, and as a matter of Government assistance, this can be attained by acreage limitation. For example, not one-tenth of one per cent of the farmers of the nation own more than one hundred acres of forest land—and most of them own, I suppose, an average of twenty or twenty-five acres.

2. The reason that what is known as woodlot forestry has never worked is that the farmer does not know how to dispose of his timber. Nobody has ever told him how. That is the duty of the federal and state governments—even to some method of agreeing to take his timber at the current market price. This would involve taking the lumber in the log because the woodlot forestry farmer, who has a small acreage, cannot afford and has no facilities for cutting his logs into boards or square lumber, nor does he know how to dispose of his smaller stuff.

3. Another wholly different class is the commercial, private lumber company or the company which buys stumpage on fairly large tracts and lumbers this stumpage.

4. Those individuals or companies are not farmers. They are lumbermen. They should not get any Government subsidy because they are primarily in the lumber business. They should receive all kinds of advice on fire-prevention, re-seeding, re-planting, etc., and they might be given a drawback or benefit up to a small amount if they can conform to our reforestation methods as laid down by the Government.

In regard to H. R. 969, there is no such thing as a mixture of woodlot management and commercial forestry.

If you want further instruction on growing trees and selling them, come and talk with me!

F. D. R.

[13:OF 149:CT]

1040   ROOSEVELT TO HAROLD L. ICKES, SECRETARY OF THE
        INTERIOR

[WASHINGTON] *April 16, 1941*

MY DEAR MR. SECRETARY: I doubt the proper availability of present appropriations for a study of the migratory course of seals from and to the Pribilof Islands, and their food habits while en route, referred to in your letter of March 7, 1941.[1]

In view of the need of the State Department for such data, this study seems advisable. Probably an early supplemental appropriation would provide funds sufficiently soon to effectively carry on the work for the first year. I am of the opinion, however, that a boat of the tuna clipper type could be purchased at a cost of not more than $200,000.

Sincerely yours,

[FRANKLIN D. ROOSEVELT]

[*Notation*:AS] HDS [2]

[13:OF 6–CC:CT]

[1] To protect the fur-seal resources of the United States, Ickes recommended an allotment of $394,055 for the study in question, this sum to be made available from current appropriations (OF 6–CC). Ickes estimated the cost of a suitable vessel at $300,000. Roosevelt asked Budget Director Smith to prepare a reply (March 10, 1941, OF 6–CC), and added: "This seems advisable in view of the need of the State Department for the information. You might ask Navy and Maritime Commission whether a tuna boat cannot be bought for a good deal less than $300,000."

[2] Budget Director Harold D. Smith, in whose agency this letter was drafted.

1041   ROOSEVELT TO CLAUDE R. WICKARD, SECRETARY OF
        AGRICULTURE

[WASHINGTON, *May 2, 1941*]

MY DEAR MR. SECRETARY: I have your letter of April 5th calling my attention to the apportionment of camps for the various types of work carried on by the Civilian Conservation Corps.

Reduction in the number of camps as provided in the 1942 budget, the assignment of camps for work on military reservations and the further development of training of enrollees as provided in Section 38 of the 1941 Emergency Relief Appropriations Act will necessarily reduce the amount of work that may be devoted to conservation projects.

As reductions are made in the number of camps available for conservation work, I agree that selection should be made in favor of the most effective type of projects, with respect to both training of enrollees and value of conservation work done. I am sure that the Federal Security Administrator and the Director of the Civilian Conservation Corps will give full consideration to these factors in any apportionment of camps between the cooperating agencies.

Sincerely yours,

[FRANKLIN D. ROOSEVELT]

[*Notation*:A] 5/2/41

[*Notation*:AS] HDS ¹

[13:OF 268:CT]

¹ Budget Director Harold D. Smith, in whose agency this letter was drafted. Smith, in his letter to Roosevelt enclosing the draft, April 30, 1942 (OF 268), said that the Agriculture Department "should realize that during this emergency period they cannot expect to continue conservation and other programs on the scale which has been in effect during the past few years."

1042   ROOSEVELT TO HENRY L. STIMSON, SECRETARY OF WAR

WASHINGTON, *May 5, 1941*

MY DEAR MR. SECRETARY: Recalling the discussion at the recent cabinet meeting, I believe it wise to record for reference the decision made with respect to the interests of the Corps of Engineers and of the Bureau of Reclamation in proposed developments on the Kings River and on the Kern River in California.

The Kings River and the Kern River projects are dominantly irrigation projects and as such they should be built at the appropriate time by the Department of the Interior through its Bureau of Reclamation rather than by the War Department through the Corps of Engineers. My letter to the Secretary of the Interior of May 29, 1940, which is published in Part 2 of House Document 631, 76th Congress, 3d Session, clearly stated my decision on the policy which should be applied to the Kings River project.¹   This decision is applicable to the Kern River project as well.   I do not consider it wise to authorize these projects, or any project dominantly for irrigation, for construction by the Corps of Engineers.

I am writing to Chairman Whittington of the Flood Control Committee of the House of Representatives to inform him on this matter.² By thus clearing doubts which may have persisted with respect to the scope of the fields of operation of the two outstanding construction agencies of the Government it is my hope that unnecessary duplication of work will be avoided and that potential sources of friction will be eliminated.

Copies of this letter are being sent to the Secretary of the Interior, to the Director of the Bureau of the Budget, and to the Chairman of the National Resources Planning Board for their information.³

Sincerely yours,

[FRANKLIN D. ROOSEVELT]

[13:OF 402:CT]

¹ *Ante,* 1002.
² Printed below.
³ (Drafted by the Interior Department.) Stimson replied May 15, 1941 (OF 402), that all War Department activities in the field of civil works were "initiated and conducted in strict accordance with specific Congressional directives." He said that he had submitted reports to Congress on the Kings and Kern River projects in compliance with section 6 of the 1936 Flood Control Act and would take no further action in the matter.

1043   ROOSEVELT TO REPRESENTATIVE WILLIAM M. WHITTINGTON
        OF MISSISSIPPI, CHAIRMAN, HOUSE FLOOD CONTROL
        COMMITTEE

WASHINGTON, *May 5, 1941*

MY DEAR MR. WHITTINGTON: On May 29, 1940, I wrote to the Secretary of the Interior with respect to the Kings River project in California. That letter is included in Part 2, House Document No. 631, 76th Congress, 3d Session.¹ Since your committee is again considering the Kings River development and also is considering a similar development on the Kern River in California, I want to call to your attention a part of that letter as follows:

It appears from an examination of the reports [by the Corps of Engineers and the Bureau of Reclamation] ² that they are in agreement, except as to questions of policy as follows:

1. Should the development of power be initiated as a part of the irrigation improvement, or should provision be made for future development under license by the Federal Power Commission?

2. Should the project be constructed by the Bureau of Reclamation or the Corps of Engineers?

3. Should the irrigation beneficiaries repay their share of the cost in a lump sum or by 40 annual payments?

4. Should the Federal Government or local interests operate the completed project? If operated by the Federal Government, by what agency?

With respect to these matters, it seems to me that the project is dominantly an irrigation undertaking and is suited to operation and maintenance under the reclamation law. It follows, therefore, that it should be constructed by the Bureau of Reclamation, and that the portion of the project cost to be charged to irrigation should be financed on the basis of the prevailing Federal policy of 40 annual payments by irrigation beneficiaries. The project should be maintained and operated by the Bureau of Reclamation, but operation for flood control should be in accordance with regulations prescribed by the Secretary of War.

That was written with respect to the Kings River project in 1940. Good administration continues to demand that projects which are dominantly for irrigation should be constructed by the Bureau of Reclamation, Department of the Interior, and not by the Corps of Engineers, War Department. The Kings River project is authorized for construction by the Bureau of Reclamation at this time. The proposed project on the Kern River, which also has been under consideration by your committee, is dominantly an irrigation project. If found wholly feasible from economic and engineering points of view by the studies that are now in progress, the Kern River project may be authorized for construction by the Bureau of Reclamation. Neither of these projects, therefore, should be authorized for construction by the Corps of Engineers. To do so would only lead to needless confusion.

A good rule for the Congress to apply in considering these water projects, in my opinion, would be that the dominant interest should determine which agency should build and which should operate the project. Projects in which flood control or navigation clearly dominates are those in which the interest of the Corps of Engineers is superior and projects in which irrigation and related conservation uses dominate fall into the legitimate field of the Bureau of Reclamation.[3]

Sincerely yours,

[FRANKLIN D. ROOSEVELT]

[13:OF 402:CT]

[1] *Kings River Project in California; Letter from the Secretary of the Interior Transmitting Pursuant to Law, a Report of the Bureau of Reclamation, Department of the Interior, Dated January 23, 1940, on an Investigation of the Kings River Project in California* (Washington, 1940).
[2] Brackets in original.
[3] Drafted by the Interior Department.

1044   ROOSEVELT TO HAROLD L. ICKES, SECRETARY OF THE INTERIOR

WASHINGTON, *May 6, 1941*

MEMORANDUM FOR THE SECRETARY OF THE INTERIOR: I wholly approve the plans of Dr. Gabrielson for the Okefenokee Swamp.[1] It is, in my judgment, especially important that in this rehabilitation of the Swamp no species of fauna or flora that is not indigenous to the swamp be allowed there. You will remember that I had a bit of a controversy over this seven or eight years ago.

In regard to the timing of this, I think the expenditure should wait until the international situation clears up. In the meantime, every effort should be made to prevent fires, but new work should be delayed.

F. D. R.

[13:OF 6–CC:CT]

[1] Gabrielson, director of the Fish and Wildlife Service, had recommended measures to ensure fire protection, reforestation, restoration of wildlife plant food and cover, stabilization of the water level of the swamp, and maintenance of the major part of the swamp as a wildlife sanctuary (Gabrielson to Ickes, April 29, 1941, enclosed in Ickes to Roosevelt, May 3, 1941, OF 1–F).

WASHINGTON, *May 12, 1941*

DEAR MR. PRESIDENT: This is in answer to your request of April 7 [1] for my opinion of the report of the Joint Congressional Committee on forestry.[2]

I am in general agreement as to some of the defects of the report as outlined in the memorandum transmitted by Secretary Ickes.[3] And it seems to me, for the reasons given as well as for those which follow, that the situation is one which can be satisfactorily salvaged only through your personal leadership.

I believe that an appraisal of the report and recommendations can best be made by indicating the extent to which they measure up to desirable objectives.

The ultimate objective of any really satisfactory Federal forest program should be the establishment and maintenance of a nation-wide forest economy in the broadest and most inclusive sense.

That the Committee recognizes this is indicated by the following quotation from its letter of transmittal to Congress: "The time is ripe for the establishment of a real forest economy in this country which, as an important segment of the broad agricultural economy, will put to constructive use one-third of our total land area."

Many of our most critical rural problem areas—most of our worst rural slums—are in depleted forest regions, and the process of creating others is still going on. The establishment of a sound, enduring forest economy can help to solve existing social problems and prevent others.

The Committee recognizes the condition, the cause, and also, somewhat weakly, the solution.

From the ownership standpoint, the major problem in American forestry today centers in privately owned lands. Private ownership has in the main failed to recognize and to redeem its social responsibilities and its natural resource responsibilities.

The Committee clearly recognizes the problem of private ownership, but does not as clearly recognize the failure of private ownership.

Only two forms of attack on the private forest land problem afford positive assurance that the public interest in these forests will be safeguarded.

The *first* of these forms is public regulation of forest practices. This is the most difficult job that has ever been faced in American forestry, and will require for successful consummation the full backing and, I believe, the full strength and authority of the Federal government.

While the Committee, for the first time in the history of Congress, recognizes—and unanimously—the necessity to apply the principle of public regulation to forests, the plan proposed has serious structural weaknesses which in my judgment will jeopardize its success, and which are as likely to set the forestry movement back as to insure its progress.

For example: The plan turns the job of regulation over to the States, with Federal financial cooperation and approval of standards. The chief Federal penalty for failure of the States to act is the mandatory withdrawal of funds for regulation and for fire protection. Thus, in effect, the State must agree to put public regulation into effect in order to receive Federal funds for fire protection. In some States strong industrial interests control the State machinery, and these are ordinarily hostile to regulation of forest practices. Control by industrialists is most likely to be exercised adversely in heavily forested States where the need for regulation is greatest, and in such States the result in the end might well be neither fire protection nor regulation.

Congressman Pierce's bill H. R. 3850 follows closely in its provisions the plan for public regulation recommended to the Committee by the Department.[4] The general principle which it follows is to afford the States a chance to try regulation with Federal financial and other cooperation, but to have the Federal Government take over the job if the States fail. My judgment is that this bill represents the minimum of Federal participation which will insure successful regulation. Congressman Pierce has also introduced another probably more desirable but less easily attainable bill, H. R. 3849, which provides for straight Federal regulation.

If public regulation is to succeed, it is essential also that various forms of public stimulation and aid and cooperation such as protection, extension education, credits, aid to small owner cooperatives, public leasing for development, research, etc., be coupled with it.

The Committee has recognized the need for public cooperation in a fairly comprehensive way, although there is considerable room for improvement as to details.

The second form of attack is public ownership. This, as stated in our recommendations to the Committee, requires large-scale public acquisition, and the high-grade administration of the forest lands acquired as well as those already in public ownership. For financial, among other reasons, a large share of this job will have to be assumed by the Federal Government.

The Committee's recommendations on Federal acquisition are weak, more or less conflicting, and altogether inadequate.

In short, the Committee's report is weakest on the two most important forms of attack on the major forest problem of private ownership and the social maladjustments that have resulted from forest-land abuse; and most satisfactory on other important but less essential forms of action.

In these and in a number of other respects, which I will not attempt to cover here, the report and recommendations of the Committee fall short of the recommendations the Department made to the Committee a year ago, and also fall short of what is necessary to attain the "forest economy" objective set by the Committee itself.

This analysis hits only the high spots. Since the report of the Committee became available we have been studying it intensively to form an opinion as to the extent to which the Administration can and should go beyond it to safeguard the public interest.

In the immediate future I hope to give you more specific recommendations, and will also give you a more complete analysis if you desire it. My recommendations will use the recommendations of the Committee as a starting point and will represent my own judgment of the position which the Administration should take. Unless we are satisfied to temporize, I believe that we must go considerably beyond the Committee recommendations. I am convinced that the Administration has an opportunity here—and the obligation also—for outstanding leadership. One aspect of the situation gives me real concern. I want to see a really comprehensive forest program on the statute books; we can not afford to pass up this opportunity.

I sincerely hope, therefore, that it will be possible for you to endorse the legislation necessary to carry out the plan that I shall propose to you, so that the stage will be set for meeting post-war requirements and even war requirements as they arise. In the latter field I may want to recommend some emergency legislation. The drafting of the legislation is now nearly complete.

The fact that the Committee has submitted its report obviously raises questions of strategy in advocating something more comprehensive. Something can be gained by liberal interpretations of Committee recommendations. Furthermore, despite various weaknesses in its recommendations, the Committee has not recommended *against* anything. I think that some of the more liberal members of the Committee will welcome the opportunity to go farther than the compromises necessarily reached in submitting a unanimous report. A complicating factor is an informal request from Senator Bankhead, the Chairman of the Joint Committee, for help in drafting a bill that will hew closely to the line in carrying out the recommendations of the Committee. In complying with the request, which we must do promptly, the difficulty will be to avoid the impression that the draft has Departmental and Administration support and thus to advance a partly satisfactory measure when we really want something more far-reaching.[5]

You of course appreciate better than anyone else that full Administration endorsement and backing offers the only hope of obtaining Congressional action on any broad program, and particularly a program that contains controversial provisions such as public regulation. Such endorsement should, I believe, be with the understanding that the program, if enacted into law, will be financed if and as funds become available.

Respectfully yours,

CLAUDE R. WICKARD

[13:OF 149:TS]

[1] OF 149.

[2] *Forest Lands of the United States* (Washington, 1941).

[3] *Ante,* 1036.

[4] This bill, and the one mentioned below, both entitled, "To Provide for the Conservation and Proper Use of Private Forest Lands . . .," were introduced by Rep. Walter M. Pierce (Ore.) on March 6, 1941, and were both referred to the Committee on Agriculture. Neither was reported from committee (*Cong. Rec.,* 77th Cong., 1st sess., 87:2, 1945).

[5] Bankhead introduced S. 2043, "A bill to effectuate the recommendation of the Joint Congressional Committee on Forestry . . .," on Nov. 13, 1941. It was not reported from committee (*Cong. Rec.,* 77th Cong., 1st sess., 87:8, 8812).

1046   ROOSEVELT TO CLAUDE R. WICKARD, SECRETARY OF AGRICULTURE

[WASHINGTON] *May 14, 1941*

MEMORANDUM FOR SECRETARY WICKARD: Thanks for yours of May 12th in regard to the forestry report. I agree with you and Ickes that the recommendations are on the whole pitifully weak.

Furthermore, I cannot go along with any proposal which calls for any form of financial matching with any State Government. The poorer States which need the most done in them will give the least matching support.

Just thirty years ago I undertook in the State of New York to encourage owners of farm wood lots to improve their wood lots under State direction, and to receive in return a form of tax rebate during the growing period of new timber. It was all very attractive and was hailed as the greatest step ever taken in this country. In the course of the next ten years I think that seven or possibly eight farmers in the State took advantage of it.[1]

The Forestry people in the Federal Government—Agriculture and Interior—and in the State Governments, have never been willing to differentiate between wooded land used primarily for lumber and lumber profits as the major crop, and wooded land which is a purely secondary consideration to the owner, who uses the rest of his land for strictly agricultural purposes.

I am inclined to think that there must be a wholly new approach to the general problem—an approach wholly Federal in its scope, just as much as Farm Security and Soil Conservation are already on a Federal status.

My suggestion is that the Secretary of Agriculture and the Secretary of the Interior each appoint one representative from the outside—not a professional forester—to go into this whole subject and make a report to both of you within two or three months. These two gentlemen can eliminate from their conference any reference to departmental or inter-departmental control in Washington, D. C. That is a different subject.

F. D. R.

Copy to Secretary Ickes

[13:OF 149:CT]

[1] See *ante*, 17 n. Forty-three parcels of land totaling 1279 acres were brought under the act referred to (and supplementary legislation enacted in 1916) between 1912 and 1919. The original law placed a maximum valuation on forested lands providing the owners adopted certain conservation practices; local assessors, however, defeated the purpose of the act by increasing valuations on the non-forested part of an owner's holdings (New York State Conservation Commission, *Annual Report, 1919*, Albany, 1920, pp. 164–166). Further legislation along this line was enacted in 1926; see the *Reports* of the Conservation Commission for this year *et seq.*

1047   ROOSEVELT TO SENATOR HOMER T. BONE OF WASHINGTON

WASHINGTON, *May 29, 1941*

MY DEAR HOMER: Since our last conversation about the Columbia River power bill, I have considered the matter at greater length. I think that it is imperative that Congress establish at this session a permanent administration for the federally owned developments on the Columbia River. I am willing to send up a bill for this purpose as an administration measure but I believe that it would be preferable if you and Senator McNary would introduce and assume the task of securing the enactment of this legislation. I know that you have thought a lot about this matter and that we agree on most of the essential points that are necessary to give the Northwest a federal authority that will vigorously prosecute the region's interests and at the same time discharge the responsibilities that the Federal Government has assumed on the Columbia River.

I believe that the following points are particularly important:

1. The Authority should be headed by a single administrator responsible to the Secretary of the Interior. As you know, the Secretary has set up in the Interior Department a new Division of Power which reports directly to him and is independent of any other bureaus or offices of the Department.[1]

2. The Authority should be responsible for the orderly marketing of available power and should encourage the development of suitable industries based on the resources of the Northwest.

3. The Authority should be responsible for the management and amortization of the Government's investment in the power facilities in a businesslike manner.

4. The Authority should be in a position to aid the public agencies of the region in effecting acquisitions of private utility properties quickly and economically.

5. The Authority should follow the present Bonneville policy of seeking the widest possible distribution of its power at the lowest possible rates, and to this end it should require that the resale of its power be at such rates and under such conditions as will assure these benefits to the people of the region.

I am writing Senator McNary to ask him to join you in this effort.[2]

Sincerely yours,

[FRANKLIN D. ROOSEVELT] [3]

[*Notation*: A] Copy of this letter sent to Mr. F. J. Bailey, Bureau of the Budget. 6/17/41   hm

[13:OF 4296:CT]

[1] Ickes not only wanted the administrators of the proposed regional authorities to be responsible to him but wanted to appoint them. His efforts to secure acceptance of this idea are described in his *Diary*, III, 440–442, 448, 501–502, 524.

[2] May 29, 1941 (OF 4296).

[3] This letter was drafted by the Interior Department.

1048   ROOSEVELT TO SENATOR GEORGE W. NORRIS OF NEBRASKA

Washington, *May 29, 1941*

MY DEAR GEORGE: I have today written Senators Bone and McNary asking that they get together and assume the task of putting through in this Session a bill for the permanent administration of the federally constructed developments on the Columbia River. I am enclosing copies of these letters for your information.[1]

You and I have been together on so many power problems that I very much want to get your help on this matter. I do not ask you to assume the responsibility for the passage of such legislation, but I do want you to manifest your interest in this effort and to give whatever time and attention you feel that you can spare. At least, if you feel that for any reason you cannot actively participate in the fight to consolidate and promote this great development, I hope that we will be able to proceed with the assurance that we have your sympathy and good wishes.

I hope that you will agree in general with the points that I have outlined in my letters to Bone and McNary as being essential to any legislation that is passed for these projects. I know that you may differ to some extent with me about the desirability of the form of organization that I have suggested, but I think that if I can give you the picture as I see it you may find yourself in agreement with me.

In the first place, I want you to know that I share with you a desire to see eventually in this country a series of regional conservation developments that will be responsible for the husbandry of the water and other natural resources of their respective areas. These authorities should avail themselves of a great deal of local advice and participation, but they should also discharge the Federal Government's responsibility for the conservation and use of the resources of our Nation. In my opinion these authorities should pool their experience in a major Federal department that will be responsible for conservation, and that department should iron out inter-regional problems and should give them over-all guidance with respect to policy. This type of coordination is particularly important, as you know, in respect of developments in the western states where the reclamation program is, and for many years has been, of great political and social importance.

That is the long-term picture. The present job is to establish regional agencies in those sections where we have major Federal developments, and to put these agencies on a sound basis. I believe that the TVA is already well established and I would not propose to change its status in any way. In the Northwest, however, there is a tremendous public power movement that has been seeking to put local administrative units into the power business through the purchase of the private facilities in the area. This effort has been hamstrung by tremendous opposition. In my opinion these local people will need the strength and prestige of the Federal Government to effectuate their desires. The people with whom they are dealing are not local people. The process of negotiation is tedious and expensive; as is also the process of condemnation. The substitution of one negotiating agent for entire systems will result in substantial savings. It is my hope that it will be possible to set up a strong public power area in the Northwest so that local people will be distributing the power that is sold to them by the Federal authority. When this partnership has been firmly established it will be impossible for any less progressive administration seriously to impair the work that we have done.

You know the tremendous job that we have before us. If I must personally supervise the many authorities that you and I feel should be created, I am sure that I would need to ask that their creation be postponed. But to postpone would probably be to lose any chance of accomplishing what we can now accomplish if we are diligent and work together. However, from both the immediate and from the long-run point of view, I believe that these agencies should be tied together in a Federal department. This department should also have jurisdiction over activities in the field of reclamation and the development of mineral resources.

The Secretary of the Interior has established a Division of Power that is giving over-all guidance to the Bonneville Power Administration and to the power end of the Reclamation Bureau projects. This Division reports only to the Secretary and is independent of any other bureau or officer of the Department. With this Division, the Department of the Interior becomes the logical bridge between these regional agencies and the Executive.

I hope that you can see your way to be again at my side in this effort.[2]

Sincerely yours,

[FRANKLIN D. ROOSEVELT]

[13:OF 4296:CT]

[1] The letter to Bone is printed above; the one to McNary (May 29, 1941, OF 4296), is similar.
[2] Drafted by the Interior Department.

1049   SENATOR GEORGE W. NORRIS OF NEBRASKA TO ROOSEVELT

WASHINGTON, D. C., *June 7, 1941*

MY DEAR MR. PRESIDENT: I am in receipt of your letter of May 29 and have read it, together with the enclosures, being copies of letters you have written to Senators McNary and Bone, with a great deal of interest.[1]

Part of the first requisite you set forth in both of these letters is as follows: "The Authority should be headed by a single administrator responsible to the Secretary of the Interior."

With this statement I cannot agree. It is contrary to the fundamental theory upon which legislation of this character should be based. It is contrary to what I have always believed was your own philosophy. In my many conversations and conferences with you on the power question during the time you have been President, and in the correspondence I had with you while you were Governor of New York and before you became President, never once, as I remember it now, did you ever advance that kind of a philosophy.

In my judgment, if any Governmental authority is set up for the control of the great power properties on the Columbia River, eventually failure will come if the authority set up becomes a part of any Department of Government. If the authority becomes a Bureau of any Department, it will in time become a football of politics. It will degenerate into a political machine and will ultimately prove to be a stupendous failure.

Please understand I am not making any criticism of Mr. Ickes, the present Secretary of the Interior. I am not thinking of men—I am thinking of an authority which, if properly set up by law, will be an efficiently managed and great industrial development long after you and the Secretary have passed from the political stage. You know—you must know—that members of a Cabinet—the heads of the Departments in every administration, under any political party, are selected for their various offices mainly on political grounds. This has been the custom for many years and I presume it will always be the custom. A Secretary of the Interior is not selected because of his views on public power. He has thousands of other duties to perform. They are Nation-wide and they cover a multitudinous number of other things. It is impossible for a Secretary of the Interior to give any concrete consideration to the proper control and management of great developments like the Grand Coulee and Bonneville projects.

An administrator, selected and responsible to a Secretary of the Interior, will be, in fact, a "hired man." Primarily his conduct of the duties of his office must be satisfactory to a Secretary of the Interior. The Secretary may remove him at any time. After a study on the ground, he will not be free to act and to follow his judgment because he knows that his boss in Washington can, at any time, change any important conclusion he may reach and, if he desires, remove him from office entirely. The administrator will, therefore, be doing his work with a sword hanging over his head by a thread. It would be natural for him to always bear in mind that the first thing he should do would be to please his boss and, by so doing, make his job secure.

During your administration, you have seen the workings of the Tennessee Valley Authority. It has been a great success. History will show that it is one of the dominating accomplishments of your administration. It is now demonstrating its value to the people of the whole Nation. One of the great things responsible for its success is the independent nature of the machinery set up by the Tennessee Valley Authority Act. It is operated by a Board of three. I concede that the number on the Board is not fundamental. Men will differ as to how large the Board should be. Some want seven, some would have five, some believe three would be better, and some men, just as honest and as intelligent, think it should be managed by one man.

Under the law, no member of the Board can be appointed unless he believes in the theory of the law itself. It is then made impossible for politics to enter into the appointment of inferior officials or into their promotion, demotion, or removal.

I was told a year or so ago by the General Manager of the Tennessee Valley Authority that he would not have retained his office for thirty days if it had not been for the protection of that part of the law. When the law was first passed, thousands of people of high standing all over the United States, in politics and public life, were seeking to get jobs for their friends. Senators and Members of the House of Representatives were recommending appointments by the thousands and, yet, the Board adhered to the law and every applicant for a position had to pass through the regular channels. An investigation was made of each applicant and no consideration was given to politics. This General Manager told me if it had not been for this provision of the Tennessee Valley Authority Act, no human being could have stood up under the political pressure, from powerful sources, to give positions to aspiring friends.

This Authority is taking up all the time of three able men in giving effect to the law and, as far as I know, no difficulty of a political nature has ever arisen except from those in high standing who have recommended various appointments. These people sometimes became very angry because their recommendations were not accepted as the final qualifications of an applicant. At the present time, this trouble has, to a very great extent, disappeared because politicians and others have learned that the intent of the law is being enforced and adhered to.

I do not understand, Mr. President, why you have changed your attitude, because I really believe it is a change. I do not understand why, when we have tried a method which has been such a success, you should now turn aside and try a new experiment which will, in my judgment, eventually throw the whole thing into the abyss of partisan politics and make the Act which you have already set up a virtual political pie-counter. If we enact a law such as you have suggested, the private power companies of the Nation will be united, through their various and secret methods of manipulation, in attempting to control the appointment of every Secretary of the Interior in the future—no matter what party may be in power. As you know, they will not give their real reasons for being interested in this office and it will not become known until after the appointment is made that what they have in view is to deal a death blow to the public ownership of power and the preservation of the natural resources of our country.

No man knows better than you do, from your experience during the past eight years, of the methods and means by which this unseen power creeps into the very avenues of government and undertakes to rob the people of their rightful heritage in the development of our natural resources.

If the control of the authority to be set up on the Columbia River is to be vested in a Board, regardless of the number on the Board, they will be picked because of their ability and their knowledge of power and navigation. They will be entirely nonpartisan—they will be selected with reference to their fitness for the particular position they are to fill and they should be independent of any Cabinet official. They will be on the ground and competent to deal with the various questions of administration and development which arise. It should not be necessary that they receive instructions from a Cabinet official, or even from a President, every time they intend to take a step toward improvement and development.

I am greatly disturbed and distressed at the announcement of your attitude on this question. It comes as a shock—like a thunderbolt from a clear sky. I am not so presumptuous as to think that I have the power to change your attitude no matter what I may do. I am practically helpless. You, of course, understand that I have no ambitions of any kind. I realize that I am nearly at the end of my public service, and that I can probably do nothing, but it is one of the sorrowful thoughts of my life to think that, as I am about to pass out of the arena, I should realize that one of my most cherished hopes has been thwarted by the most outstanding advocate of the preservation of our natural resources it has ever been my pleasure to know.[2]

Very truly yours,

G. W. NORRIS

[13:OF 4296:TS]

[1] The Bone and Norris letters are printed above; the letter to McNary, May 29, 1941 (OF 4296), is similar to the one to Bone.
[2] This was sent to Ickes by Roosevelt "For preparation of reply for my signature" (June 14, 1941, OF 4296). Ickes replied June 19, 1941 (OF 4296), that he did not think a reply was advisable as it seemed fruitless to prolong the discussion: "I am sorry that Senator Norris apparently feels that the TVA setup is the last word in sound administrative practice. The only conclusion that one can reach from a logical development of his position is that the present departmental system in the Executive branch of the Government should be replaced entirely by a multitude of independent agencies." No reply was made.

1050   ROOSEVELT TO THE NAVAJO PEOPLE

WASHINGTON, *June 19, 1941*

TO THE NAVAJO PEOPLE: Many months ago the Navajo Tribal Council addressed a resolution to me which pledged the support and loyalty of the Navajo people to our country.

I now take occasion in these days of world crisis to address you. I am concerned about the need for protecting your lands from erosion. I am concerned that some of your leaders do not understand that to protect your lands you must reduce the number of your sheep, and goats, and horses, sufficiently to permit the grass to grow thickly and stop erosion.

If our nation is to remain strong, our land and forests and waters must be protected and cared for. Especially must we protect our soil, for without soil no nation can endure.

One of the most important objectives of this nation is the protection of its soil and other natural resources. Your Government, through the Civilian Conservation Corps, the Soil Conservation Service, the Office of Indian Affairs and other agencies, has conducted an extensive program for the protection of these resources. This program is under way on the Navajo lands, as well as on lands throughout the nation.

I know that protection of your land will not be easy for all the Navajo people. Many of you must sell some of your animals, or move them to ranges away from the reservation. I know also that the Government must help by building projects which will bring water to your land so that you can grow food for your increasing population. The Government is building these projects. The great Fruitland and Hogback irrigation projects are examples. The Many Farms project which was authorized this year is another. And the Government is making surveys on the Little Colorado and San Juan rivers to find other opportunities to bring water to your lands.

The Government is planning for your future, but you must accept your share of the work, and make your share of the sacrifices. You must work with your Government. You must abide by the laws and regulations. You must follow the leadership of the Tribal Council which is the elected voice of the Navajo people.

By doing these things, you will remain strong and will defend the way of democracy.[1]

[FRANKLIN D. ROOSEVELT]

Through Mr. J. C. Morgan, Chairman, Navajo Tribal Council

[13:OF 296:CT]

[1] Drafted by the Interior Department. In his letter to Roosevelt enclosing the draft, June 18, 1941 (OF 296), Ickes said that the Navajo Tribe had voted to enforce the conservation regulations promulgated by the Interior Department for the Navajo Reservation but that a minority group within the tribe was urging opposition. He urged that the letter be sent to reassure the Navajos.

1051   ROOSEVELT TO CLAUDE R. WICKARD, SECRETARY OF AGRICULTURE

WASHINGTON, *June 26, 1941*

MEMORANDUM FOR HON. CLAUDE R. WICKARD: Will you please bring this to me next week some time and let me talk with you about the whole matter?

What would you think of your having a preliminary talk with Ickes about the whole subject? You and he have never locked horns on the problem. Then all three of us could go over it together.

F. D. R.

[13:OF 1:T]

WASHINGTON, *June 18, 1941*

DEAR MR. PRESIDENT: I have studied with interest your memorandum of May 14 in which you suggest that Secretary Ickes and I each appoint a representative outside the professional forestry field to prepare in the next two or three months a report on the forestry problem.

Finding the right man is not easy. If the job you have primarily in mind is a recommendation on regulation of privately-owned forest lands, and if the men had the time, I would suggest either Judge Rosenman or John Boettiger. Both men qualify as laymen, both have displayed a keen interest in forest policy, and I respect their judgment.

If it is your particular thought that the men to be designated should help us to strengthen our programs for wooded land owned by people whose interest in lumber and lumber profits is of secondary importance, rather than to review the whole forestry program, I suggest Al Stedman, Washington Correspondent of the St. Paul *Pioneer Press and Dispatch*. Al is personally a New Dealer, and personally well informed and deeply interested in farm forestry. He has good judgment, too.

There is a third alternative in the type of job the two appointees could do that I have been turning over in my mind. Would it not be a good plan to charge the two men with the task of studying our proposals to the committee, the suggestions of the Department of the Interior, and the recommendations of the Joint Committee, formulating them into an over-all report to aid you in preparing a message of recommendations to the Congress? I like this idea better the more I think of it.

Your thoughts and mine are identical in regard to proposals that call for State matching of funds. I don't like the matching principle. For the most part, the Federal Government doesn't get value received for money used in that way. Especially is this true where local, short-time self-interest is not identical with the Federal interest. In something like fire protection it works fairly well. In our recommendations to the committee, we saw to it that the matching principle entered into our proposals in only a minor way. It was limited to the pretty generally successful fire protection program on private and State forest lands, expansion of the program of distributing forest planting stock at about cost; expansion of the present system of farm forest education; and broadening of the Fulmer Act to include Federal aid in purchasing community as well as State forests. The remaining 90 percent is a straight Federal program; no part of it that goes to the root of Federal concern is based on the principle of matching funds, although in five of the twelve other parts the States are invited to contribute what they can afford.

It seems to me our problem is one of political judgment. How can we get the most favorable legislation when prevailing sentiment on the Hill is against public regulation? The Department favors straight Federal regulation. Our effort with the committee was to get it to come out as strongly for regulation as it could be persuaded to come; and for strategical reasons we suggested a program under which the States would be given a chance to do the job with Federal aid, with the Department of Agriculture authorized to take over if any State failed to tackle it. Even this was too much for the committee. What course shall we now pursue? Shall we ask the Congress for straight Federal regulation; or shall we, from considerations of States' relations and the sentiment on the Hill, stick with the present plan of asking for Federal regulation only on condition that the States fail to do the job? We have bills of both types prepared. One complicating factor is that Senator Bankhead has asked us to help him prepare a bill that hews to the line laid down by the Committee.

If we go directly after straight Federal regulation, what will be the effect on the Congress? If we ignore the Joint Committee's report I fear the reaction may be decidedly adverse. Somehow we must induce the Congress to modify and strengthen the report of its own committee, so that we can count on help from within the Committee itself. Several members, Pierce for example, are eager to take stronger action than their signatures on the report would indicate.

In this connection you may find it worthwhile to go over the attached summary of our recommendations to the Joint Committee, which we have drawn up in an omnibus bill.[1] In the event you are particularly interested in the farm forestry angle, you will find provisions for aiding cooperatives of small operators; technical assistance in woodland management along the lines of approach followed by the Soil Conservation Service; a public leasing and development provision; a credit program geared to the needs of small owners; and a practical educational program to help such people with their woods management and marketing problems.

In your reply I would be very pleased if, in addition to indicating your choice from among the names I have suggested, you would clarify for me whether you want these two men (1) to survey the entire forestry field, (2) to restrict their study to the problems of the owner whose timber is a secondary interest, or (3) to proceed along the lines of the third alternative I have suggested.

Respectfully yours,   CLAUDE R. WICKARD

[13:OF 1:TS]

---

[1] A typescript, "Digest of Department of Agriculture's Recommendations for a Forest Legislative Program."

WASHINGTON, *July 5, 1941*

MY DEAR MR. PRESIDENT: I have given careful consideration to your memorandum of May 14, directed to Secretary Wickard, a copy of which was sent to me, in which you suggest that the Secretary of Agriculture and the Secretary of the Interior each appoint one representative from the outside to study the forest situation in the United States with a view to submitting a report thereon.

Under date of March 14, 1938, you sent a message to the Congress recommending an immediate investigation of the forest situation in the United States. This message led to the approval by Congress on June 13, 1938, of Concurrent Resolution No. 31 which established a Joint Congressional Committee on Forestry. The Committee conducted hearings throughout the United States and accumulated a voluminous record covering the forest situation. The report of the Committee was submitted to the Congress on March 24, and as I have heretofore indicated, it does not offer a complete solution of the forest problem.[1] It appears, therefore, that a further investigation of the situation with a view to providing more definite and complete recommendations is desirable. In my judgment such a study could be pursued most effectively in cooperation with the former members of the Joint Congressional Committee on Forestry, many of whom are no doubt in a position to furnish valuable information which is not necessarily a part of the official report.

In the event that you still feel that the Secretary of Agriculture and I should proceed in accordance with the suggestion contained in your memorandum of May 14, I shall be pleased to confer with Secretary Wickard and work out the details essential to the formulation of a more conclusive supplemental report on the forest situation of the Nation.

Sincerely yours,

HAROLD L. ICKES

[13:OF 149:TS]

[1] *Forest Lands of the United States* (Washington, 1941).

1054   ROOSEVELT TO HAROLD L. ICKES, SECRETARY OF THE INTERIOR

[WASHINGTON] *July 8, 1941*

DEAR HAROLD: I have yours of July fifth in regard to a further study of the forest situation, and I should be delighted if you and Wickard will work out the details for the formulation of a more conclusive supplemental report.

Of course, as you know, and as I have told Claude, all my earlier studies have been confirmed by later thinking in regard to the ultimate responsibility.

The true division between the Department of Agriculture and the Department of the Interior is that Agriculture deals primarily with private citizens and their lands and the products thereof; whereas Interior ought to deal primarily with nationally owned land and the products thereof.

Taking up the case of Forestry for example. The ridiculous interlocking and over-lapping of jurisdiction between the public lands, the national parks, the national monuments and the national forests can only be ended eventually by putting all national lands under the Department of the Interior.

That means, however, that the Department of Agriculture should still retain two of its existing forestry functions: First, the different scientific bureaus relating to tree diseases of all kinds, tree breeding and experimentation, and the development of lumber uses. Second, the relationship between the Government and all owners of private lands on which trees are grown and on which trees should be protected.

These private lands range from the large private lumber holdings and, most important of all, the hundreds of thousands of individual private owners who have woodlots. It is primarily the latter who need immediate help, but who have had no help to speak of in the past from the Forestry Service.

It is my thought, for example, that the average owner of a small piece of timberland, which is not his primary business, ought to look to Agriculture for ways and means of marketing his timber. Today, as a matter of practice, he does not get any help at all.

That would put the relationship of the Department of Agriculture, in regard to trees, on exactly the same basis as the relationship of the Department of Agriculture to wheat or cotton or soil conservation or any other problem that directly affects the individual landowner.

That also would put into the Department of the Interior all national forests, the greater part of which can be used commercially by the Government for many years to come. When lumber becomes available from these national forests it is entirely probable that the cutting and marketing of lumber from these national forests could be absorbed, not by private industry, but by Government itself—federal, state and local.

It seems to me that this line of demarcation would greatly simplify the whole problem of forestry.

I am sending a copy of this to Claude with the hope that it will give you and him a basis of discussion.[1]

Always sincerely,

[Franklin D. Roosevelt]

[13:OF 149:CT]

[1] Ickes replied July 16, 1941 (OF 149), that he would "confer promptly with Secretary Wickard and work out with him a practical plan for a further consideration of the forest situation of the Nation and the reorganization of Federal forest administration."

WASHINGTON, D. C., *July 31, 1941*

MEMORANDUM FOR THE PRESIDENT: Proposed legislation relating to the control of water pollution again is the subject of reports to Congress from the interested departments.   The bill in question is S. 1121, introduced by Senator Gillette.[1]

This bill conforms to the recommendations in your message of February 15, 1939, insofar as it provides for the establishment of a division within the Public Health Service definitely charged with promoting research, plans, education, and other State and local measures for pollution abatement.   An annual appropriation of $250,000 is authorized. The bill partially meets the objections which you raised in disapproving the first water pollution bill in 1938, by requiring that plans for new pollution-abatement works must be cleared with the Federal Works Agency and your office before going to Congress.   It departs from your earlier recommendations by (1) establishing district water boards, (2) requiring that standards of water purity be fixed in each district, and (3) permitting Federal injunction proceedings against violators.   It also omits earlier provisions for loans and grants for construction of remedial works, and relies instead upon the availability of Reconstruction Finance Corporation loans.   You may remember that the regulatory features of this type of legislation have been the chief points of controversy in past.

Federal Security Agency is proposing to endorse the bill.   Agriculture approves the bill in general.   War takes a non-committal attitude, but calls attention to the facts that the Corps of Engineers now exercises certain regulatory powers over pollution of navigable waters, and that the current Ohio River Pollution Survey is intended to lead to the proposal of remedial legislation.

The staff of the National Resources Planning Board considers the provisions with respect to district water boards unduly cumbersome, and also agrees with this office in thinking that the need for Federal assumption of regulatory authority over water pollution is not urgent at this time.   Discussion with the Board's staff indicates, however, that the proposed planning work, while not essential to the continuation of the studies already in progress, might be useful in connection with the development of the program of post-emergency public works contemplated by the Board.

If you favor the enactment of some type of pollution-abatement legislation at this session, I shall be glad to work out with the Federal Security Agency a revision of S. 1121, which would eliminate the regulatory features and provide for planning work on a modest scale.   However, a more satisfactory solution might be to defer any legislation of this type at this time; and if you agree with this latter position, I will advise the interested departments that enactment of legislation of this character would not be in accord with your program during the present emergency.

HAROLD D. SMITH

[*Notation*:AS] H. D. S. *Defer* FDR

[13:OF 114–A:TS]

¹ S. 1121, "A Bill to create a Division of Water Pollution Control in the United States Public Health Service, and for other purposes," was introduced March 17, 1941, and referred to the Committee on Commerce. No further action was taken. The bill is adequately described in the letter here printed.

1056   CLAUDE R. WICKARD, SECRETARY OF AGRICULTURE, TO ROOSEVELT

WASHINGTON, *August 11, 1941*

DEAR MR. PRESIDENT: I had prepared but had not sent you a brief memorandum on urgently needed forestry legislation when I found that Secretary Ickes and I could jointly suggest to you the committee which I mentioned in a separate letter to you today. If you appoint this committee, perhaps it could take as its first task the formulation of an emergency legislative program. Certainly there is no time to lose if we are going to check the accelerated destructive cutting that is now under way. So I am sending my memorandum to you, thinking that you may care to give it to a committee if you appoint one now, or that you may pass on its merits if you do not go ahead with the committee idea.

Respectfully yours,

CLAUDE R. WICKARD

[13:OF 149:TS]

1057   [*Enclosure*] CLAUDE R. WICKARD TO ROOSEVELT

WASHINGTON, *August 11, 1941*

MEMORANDUM ON URGENTLY NEEDED FORESTRY LEGISLATION: I have become convinced that much will be lost unless we get an Administration measure on forestry—particularly on public regulation of present destructive cutting—introduced into Congress and enacted in the immediate future.

The principal reasons for this are:

1. Many weeks ago Senator Bankhead asked us informally to prepare a bill to carry out precisely what his Joint Committee recommended. The bill has long been ready and we cannot put him off much longer. Obviously if he, as Chairman of the Joint Committee, introduces his

[523]

own bill—something far short of what is needed—and pushes it as he plans, the fat will be in the fire.

Much the same considerations hold for Vice Chairman Fulmer, who is reported to be preparing a bill to carry out his own interpretation of the Committee recommendations.

2. Defense demands have led to greatly increased cutting all over the United States, and promise in the near future to rise measurably near to the peak of 35 years ago. Most of it is destructive. Most of our worst rural slums are already in depleted forest regions and make up nearly one-fourth of our total land area. In spite of everything else we can do, I believe that they will remain rural slums until the forest is restored. Even during the war period we ought as a minimum to stop further destruction.

An emergency legislative program along the right lines should be shaped up within the next several weeks.

It should recognize as the outstanding forest problem the lands now in private ownership. It should recognize also, to quote your own words, that "States, communities, and private capital can do much * * * but have, on the whole, accomplished little * * * it seems obviously necessary to fall back on the last defensive line—Federal leadership and Federal action."

It should place major emphasis on measures which will give positive assurance of (a) reasonably good treatment of all forest lands now privately owned, and (b) help in the solution of the social problems, now almost nation-wide, which have grown out of the destruction of our forests. The only two measures that carry such assurance are public regulation and greatly increased public ownership.

It should make nation-wide public regulation of forest practices on privately-owned lands a wholly Federal activity.

It should in general make all new measures a straight Federal responsibility, avoiding any hard and fast State matching requirements which would handicap the poorer States, but allow contributions where the circumstances seem to justify them.

It should adhere to the matching principle in a few long-established activities such as protection against fire, where they have worked out fairly well, and where an attempt to change now would stir up opposition which might defeat more important measures.

It should include special provisions to help owners of farm woodlots and other small holdings.

I am very much afraid that we will see the adoption of unsatisfactory legislation if we do not act promptly.

CRW

[13:OF 149:TS]

WASHINGTON, *August 12, 1941*

DEAR MR. PRESIDENT: In accordance with your recent suggestion to
us, we join in recommending that you ask Judge Rosenman, John
Boettiger, Jim Rowe, Al Stedman, and Tom Wallace to serve as a
special committee, advisory to you, on national forest policy and national forest legislation.

We hope that this committee will begin its work promptly and complete its task within a reasonably short time.   It seems to us that the
committee should study the broad social, economic, and physical problems involved and then recommend to you:

A comprehensive forest policy for the United States.

Action, educational, research, and service programs for the fields
of (a) Federal forestry, (b) industrial forestry, (c) farm forestry.

An improved Federal legislative program for all types of forest activity.

The committee, in order to have a specific purpose for its work,
might take as its principal objective the preparation of a brief but
comprehensive statement which you could use in submitting recommendations to the present session of Congress.   A logical starting point,
but only a starting point, would be the report which the Joint Congressional Committee on Forestry submitted to the Senate and House.
This would lead very well to your indicating in a covering message to
the Congress what modifications you desire in the Joint Congressional
Committee's recommendations.

This suggestion in no way implies that the special committee should
not consider critically matters that do not come within the scope of a
legislative program, but it occurs to us that the Joint Congressional
Committee might be offended if your advisory group considered Federal forest policies and needed legislation wholly independent of the
Joint Congressional Committee's conclusions.   In line with your letter of May 14 and in accord with our own view of its feasible function, the committee would not go into jurisdictional or governmental-
reorganization questions.

You will recall that you suggested to us a two-man committee of nongovernmental, non-technical men.   We are recommending five because we believe they have among them what no two men would likely
possess, namely, the essential understanding of public administration,
broad Federal policy, forest policy, Federal-State-local-private relationships, possible alternative methods of Federal action, the political
possibilities, fiscal problems, and the specific needs in farm forestry,
industrial forestry, and Federally-managed forestry.

To give the committee any help it might wish to have, each of us will if you wish designate a liaison representative who would be available to the committee at all times. The Assistant to the Secretary of the Interior in charge of Land Utilization and the Land Use Co-ordinator of the Department of Agriculture are both Departmental staff officers and are not directly engaged in supervising forest activities. The former, Lee Muck, is a technically-trained forester and the latter, Milton S. Eisenhower, is not but this seems to us to be immaterial. In addition, the two of us will gladly spend as much time with the committee as seems desirable.

If this arrangement appeals to you, we hope that you personally will ask Judge Rosenman, John Boettiger, Jim Rowe, A. D. Stedman (St. Paul *Pioneer Press*), and Tom Wallace (Editor of the Louisville *Times*) to undertake the task at once.

Respectfully yours,

HAROLD L. ICKES
CLAUDE R. WICKARD

[13:OF 149:TS]

1059   ROOSEVELT TO CLAUDE R. WICKARD, SECRETARY OF AGRICULTURE

WASHINGTON, *September 3, 1941*

MEMORANDUM FOR THE SECRETARY OF AGRICULTURE: I hear that the Forest Service is about to give to a lumber company the right to cut timber on the Morse Creek watershed of the Mt. Olympic National Park.[1]

Please hold this up until cleared by me, and let me see on the map just where the proposed cutting is to be.

F. D. R.

[13:OF 1–C:CT]

[1] Ickes had so reported in a letter to Roosevelt of Aug. 27, 1941 (OF 1–C). Acting Secretary of Agriculture Grover B. Hill replied Sept. 6, 1941, that no sale of national forest timber was contemplated (OF 1–C).

1060   HAROLD D. SMITH, DIRECTOR, BUREAU OF THE BUDGET, TO ROOSEVELT

WASHINGTON, D. C., *Sept. 20, 1941*

MEMORANDUM FOR THE PRESIDENT . . . PROPOSED COLUMBIA POWER AUTHORITY: In accordance with your directions of February 11, 1941, this office, in cooperation with the National Resources Planning Board, has studied the pending legislative proposals to establish additional regional authorities. The proposals have been analyzed in relation to regional needs, and the informal views of the Departments of the Interior and Agriculture, and the Federal Power Commission have been obtained. In view of the prospect for early hearings on this subject by the House Rivers and Harbors Committee, and of Secretary Ickes' desire to speed action on the proposed Pacific Northwest legislation, I am presenting the matter to you at this time in order to obtain your views on the basic features of the legislation.

Two major types of legislative proposals. Two major types of proposals are before the Congress. One type of bill—notably, the Arkansas Valley Authority bill and Congressman Rankin's regional authority bill—would establish independent authorities, patterned after the Tennessee Valley Authority, with power to plan and conduct experiments with respect to all phases of resources development, and to construct and operate all types of water and soil conservation works. The other type of bill—represented by the bills introduced by Senator Bone and Congressman Hill—would establish regional agencies with the primary function of planning, constructing or acquiring, and operating electric power facilities.

Functions of proposed regional agencies. The two types of legislative proposals are alike in providing for publicly-operated power development on a regional scale. The suggested agencies for the Pacific Northwest would be empowered to prepare regional plans for power generation and transmission, and to investigate methods of promoting the wider use of electricity. They would be authorized to acquire private power systems, to construct transmission lines, and, with the approval of the Congress, to construct new generating facilities. They also would be able to acquire private distribution facilities for resale to public agencies. Power rates would be as low as possible, and contracts for sale of wholesale power would provide for control of resale rates.

The proposed agencies similar to the Tennessee Valley Authority, would have all of these functions, and, in addition, would be charged with the planning of broad programs of water control, land use, recreation, and industrial development, and with sponsoring whatever research is necessary for those purposes. They would be authorized to construct any desirable water-control project or land-improvement measure, to operate such works, and to regulate private construction of water-control works.

Public power marketing is the primary function of the agencies proposed for the Pacific Northwest. Integrated regional development is the central concern of the Arkansas Valley Authority proposal.

Administration of proposed regional agencies. The power-marketing proposals contemplate a quasi-corporate agency exercising relatively

wide discretion in the issuance of bonds, acquisition and management of properties, and the promotion of power use. The bill favored by Secretary Ickes would provide for an administrator responsible to the Secretary of the Interior, and operating with the aid of an advisory board representative of the region. Although subject to civil service law, the regional agency would be free from the legal supervision of the Attorney General, and from auditing by the Comptroller General. Senator Bone's recent bill would hold to the same functions and financial organization, but would adopt the Tennessee Valley Authority form of administration.

Both the Bone bill and the Arkansas Valley Authority bill provide for a three-man board reporting directly to the President. Both would exempt the agency from civil service, from supervision by the Attorney General, and from auditing by the Comptroller General. All of the proposals make provision for repayment of the full Federal investment in power facilities, and, at the same time, allow considerable flexibility in the day-by-day operations of the agency in the field.

Power marketing urgently needed. The rapidly mounting number of Federal dams having sizeable power facilities and the prospect for even greater enlargement of such facilities under the Federal Power Commission's emergency power program, make it desirable to begin the organization of Federal power-marketing agencies in several regions as soon as practicable; but it is not believed that there is the same clear need at this time for developing in these areas the Tennessee Valley Authority type of agency.

Reasons for deferring complete Tennessee Valley Authority type of authority. While the United States still is far from having, even for the Tennessee Valley, the comprehensive plans and operating programs that ultimately will be necessary for full and effective resources development, our planning work has made fair progress on a national scale. In order to replace with thorough regional plans the single-purpose plans of individual agencies, such as the Bureau of Reclamation, Corps of Engineers, and Department of Agriculture, it will be necessary to strengthen the present planning work. This will involve funds for planning and correlation, as well as detailed guidance by the National Resources Planning Board. Both would be provided under the draft of legislation for the "shelf" of public-works projects which you recommended to Senator Wagner on June 6, 1941.[1] It is not believed, furthermore, that the conduct of desirable research and construction activities in these areas is necessarily contingent upon the establishment there of additional regional authorities such as the Tennessee Valley Authority.

While I am inclined to believe that sooner or later we must be prepared to reorganize certain Federal agencies on a national scale in order to obtain unified operation of the many projected reservoirs and other water-control works, I do not think that we are yet ready to take that step, nor that it is an immediately important one.

Regional agencies vs. national departments. The issue underlying all of this discussion of regional authorities is whether the authority for a given region should carry out all of the work involved in the conservation of the national resources of that region, or should concentrate upon a particular phase or phases of the whole conservation program for the region, leaving to the other agencies of government functionally concerned therewith, the conduct of the work to be performed under the other phases of the conservation program. Whatever the merits of a complete subdivision of the United States into regions of the Tennessee Valley Authority type, it is not believed that the time has yet arrived for such a fundamental reorganization of the structure of the Executive Branch.

Accordingly, it is recommended that regional planning and research be stimulated through the agencies already available for this purpose, including, in particular, the National Resources Planning Board, and that, for the present, any new authority should be established for the purpose of concentrating on the power-marketing job.

Pacific Northwest legislation. In the light of what has been said above, and of your letters of May 29, 1941, to Senators Bone, McNary, and Norris,[2] the Pacific Northwest legislation has been discussed with representatives of the Secretary of the Interior. Our discussions have revealed agreement on general objectives, and have centered on obtaining an effective administrative organization. As a result of these discussions there has been prepared by this office a draft of bill which, while not meeting the Interior Department views in every respect, does represent, it is believed, a reasonable compromise of conflicting views and would establish a workable and useful agency.

In addition to its grant of full authority for carrying on power-marketing activities, the draft of bill provides for:

(a) An administrator who, while appointed by and responsible to the Secretary of the Interior on major issues of policy and program, would enjoy much wider latitude in supervising the day-by-day operations of the Authority than does the average bureau chief;

(b) A board of five (including the administrator, and with three members from the region) that would review, and submit recommendations to the Secretary of the Interior on, (1) the development plan for the region; (2) the acquisition of private utility systems; (3) the construction of new generating facilities; and (4) the schedules of power rates;

(c) Administration under the provisions of the civil service laws, a commercial type of auditing by the Comptroller General upon a liberalized basis, and legal representation by the Attorney General;

(d) A well-defined method of correlating the Authority's plans and programs with those of other regional or national agencies through the National Resources Planning Board and the Budget; and

(e) Charging the power consumers only for their proper share of project costs, and not for any part of the costs properly chargeable to irrigation or other project purposes.

If you agree with the major provisions of the draft of bill, as listed above, I will take up this draft with the Secretary of the Interior and the National Resources Planning Board, with the object of working out the minor details of the bill, and of then advising the Secretary of the Interior and the other interested Federal agencies that enactment of the legislation in that adjusted form would be in accord with your program.

Legislation affecting other regions. In this formative stage of Federal power marketing, no single type of administration should be adopted rigidly; there should be latitude for experimental departure from the Pacific Northwest model. From time to time, as additional authority proposals are presented, they will be submitted to you for review before advising the interested agencies as to their relationship to your program.[3]

HAROLD D. SMITH

[13:OF 4296:TS]

[1] No communication of this date has been found.
[2] The letters to Bone and Norris are printed *ante*, 1047, 1048; the letter to McNary (OF 4296) is the same as the one to Bone.
[3] Answered *post*, 1062.

1061   ROOSEVELT TO LEVERETT BRADLEY, Lakeville, Connecticut

WASHINGTON, *September 23, 1941*

DEAR LEVERETT: This will acknowledge the receipt of your note of August 30 suggesting the use of Mount Desert Island, Acadia National Park, as a base for memorials to people of national stature and as a rendezvous for conferences of international character.[1]

Many plaques and other types of memorials have been proposed for placement in the national park areas during the past decade. The merits of the suggestions which have been made to have such memorials erected are appreciated and understood. They are foreign, however, to the purposes for which the national parks are established, namely, to conserve the scenery and the natural and historic objects and the wildlife therein, and to provide for the enjoyment of the same in such manner and by such means as will leave them unimpaired for the enjoyment of future generations.

The use of Acadia National Park as a rendezvous for conferences of international character would entail precautionary measures which would restrict the use of the area by the public and would be inconsistent with its status as a national park.

The shipboard meeting to which you refer took place hundreds of miles from Mount Desert Island.

I have read with interest the statement of your views on Mount Desert Island, which was printed in November, 1940.[2]

Sincerely yours,

[FRANKLIN D. ROOSEVELT]

[13:OF 6–P:CT]

[1] Bradley also suggested that the Atlantic Charter meeting held off Argentia had added significance to the proposed memorial (OF 6–P).
[2] Not identified. This reply was drafted by the Interior Department.

1062   ROOSEVELT TO HAROLD D. SMITH, DIRECTOR, BUREAU OF THE BUDGET

[WASHINGTON] *September 26, 1941*

MEMORANDUM FOR THE DIRECTOR OF THE BUDGET: Regarding your memorandum of September twentieth relating to regional authorities, I am inclined to think:

1. That as between the two major types of legislative proposals there should be regional authorities covering the entire nation, in accordance with the outline which I drew up four or five years ago.[1] I think that each authority should not only plan, contract, acquire and operate electric power facilities, but should also plan and conduct experiments with respect to all phases of resources development. This is essentially what the TVA does under the TVA Act.

2. I think that the head of each agency should be a member of two separate central committees in Washington—one of these committees to function as to planning under the National Resources Board, and the other (with possibly the same membership) should act as an operating advisory committee to the Department of the Interior.

3. In regard to administration of the proposed regional agencies, I am inclined to favor the one man administrator for each authority, though I would be willing to accept a three man board if the Congress should so determine.

4. In actual operation it is, of course, contrary to common sense that each authority should report directly to the President. We have successfully cut down the number of outside agencies reporting to the President, with the result that the Presidency can still be handled by one man if he works ten or twelve hours a day!

It is my thought that a method can be worked out by which each authority will report to the President through the Secretary of the Interior on all operating matters, the Secretary of the Interior to decide ordinary questions with, of course, the right of the authority to appeal to the President in exceptional cases. This leaves the authority as a self-governing organization in practically all of its work.

At the same time the authority in its planning for future development should report to the National Resources Board, get their approval of plans, if possible, and have them come to the President through the Director of the Budget.

Finally, the plans should also be submitted to the Federal Power Commission for the recommendation of the latter only.

I have not time to go into the other matters on the proposed legislation but I think that from the above, you and the Secretary of the Interior, the National Resources Board and the Federal Power Commission can work something out.

F. D. R.

[13:OF 4296:CT]

[1] *Ante,* 636.

1063   ROOSEVELT TO NELSON C. BROWN, New York State College
of Forestry, Syracuse University, Syracuse, New York

[WASHINGTON] *October 7, 1941*

DEAR NELSON: Thank you for yours of October first.[1] I think you are right about trying some balsam, spruce and some Canadian white spruce, so will you go ahead and see if you can get some good transplants for next Spring planting? I would suggest putting the twenty per cent balsam into a different location. As you remember, there is a ditch which runs through the east end of the three lots along the Post Road. East of this long ditch there are about four acres of open land. It is good soil, as proved by the existing plantation at the east end of the north lot.

The forty per cent of Canadian white spruce and the forty per cent of Norway spruce can go into the east end of the Linaka lot and the lot east of that.

I am delighted that you are having the signs prepared. The trees look well and I think that we have about 95% survival of what was put out last Spring—an excellent record.

I do hope you are all well again and that I shall see you soon.

Always sincerely,

[FRANKLIN D. ROOSEVELT]

[13:PPF 38:CT]

[1] Reporting on two visits to Roosevelt's tree plantations in Hyde Park.

Washington, D. C., *October 23, 1941*

My dear Mr. President: May I respectfully call to your attention
HR 2685 to permit mining within the Organ Pipe Cactus National
Monument, which passed the House on October 15, following the
passage of an identical bill (S 260) in the Senate on May 23, 1941?

Our Association would like to request you to veto the Bill. We opposed its passage by Congress and we believe that if it becomes the law
of the land it will not only involve unnecessary damage to the National
Monument but that it will be an exceedingly bad precedent. This
seems to be a clear case of public policy as against doubtful private gain.
We take pleasure in presenting the reasons for the stand we have
taken:

(1) The Monument was created by your Executive Order on April
13, 1937, as authorized by the National Antiquities Act of 1906. It
contains 330,687 acres—a little more than a third of the size of the
Joshua Tree National Monument and about a sixth of Death Valley
National Monument in California. The lines were drawn very carefully to exclude known commercial mineral areas. Your Executive
Order was designed to set up adequate protection to the area. Existing grazing rights were to continue only during the lives of the present
holders of permits and after that the area was to be free from grazing
of domestic animals. It was fully expected that in time the National
Park Service would be in a position to give the Organ Pipe Cactus National Monument that complete protection from non-conforming uses
which the area deserves. Under the act passed by Congress the area
would be forever open to prospecting and mining. Congress having
once delegated to the President the authority to create National Monuments, it seems illogical that it should pass measures to break down
the protection so authorized.

(2) The protection of the ground surface and the plant and animal
life in desert areas is a much more difficult and delicate process than the
protection of forested lands. In the vast desert areas of the Southwest
only a few places have been selected to receive the special care which
the National Park Service is prepared to give in order to conserve the
entire biotic life of the area. Thanks to your Executive Order, the
Organ Pipe Cactus National Monument is one of these precious possessions of the people.

(3) It is the opinion of eminent geologists who have examined the
region that although the area has been subject to prospecting for nearly
two centuries no profitable mines have been discovered and operated
within the present Monument. It seems doubtful whether in all this
time any mining effort in the whole Monument has ever paid operating

costs for more than a brief time, if at all. To permit further digging, and the presence of roving prospectors who would gather the scarce wood for fire, graze their domestic animals and shoot wild life, seems to involve useless sacrifice for the very doubtful chance that profitable minerals might be found.

(4) We believe that it would be an unfortunate precedent which would tempt other small pressure groups to try to secure concessions in other National Parks and National Monuments. In the discussions on the floor of the House it was argued that this would not create a precedent and yet to support this action five so-called previous precedents were cited. Of these only one involved permission for mining in an area already set up as a National Monument. One of the five was the Olympic National Park which was created by Congress in an Act which permitted, in a specified part of the Park the continuance of the location, entry and patent of mines for a period of five years.[1] More than three of the five years has already elapsed. After June 29, 1943, no more mining will be allowed in the Park under the present law. That would leave only four areas in the National Parks and Monuments in which mining would be permitted. In 1931 Congress passed a law which prohibited prospecting, development or utilization of mineral resources in National Parks and Monuments in which such operations had been permitted, including Grand Canyon and Mount Rainier, and greatly limited mining operations in Mount McKinley National Park in Alaska.[2] In the interests of conservation it has been the declared policy of the National Park Service to try to retire these precedents rather than to increase them.

We hope, Mr. President, that you will exercise your veto for this measure, in the interest of sound conservation of National Parks and Monuments from adverse uses and particularly to protect the National Monuments created by Executive Order from being opened up to commercial uses through Acts of Congress.[3]

Respectfully submitted,

HORACE M. ALBRIGHT

[Notation:A] Bill Signed 10/27/41
[13:OF 928:TS]

[1] Act approved June 29, 1938 (52 Stat. 1241).
[2] Act approved Jan. 26, 1931 (46 Stat. 1043).
[3] There was little debate in the House on H. R. 2675, and none in the Senate on S. 260. Representative Murdock (Ariz.), who introduced the House bill, replied to charges by conservationists that the bill would create an undesirable precedent by saying that the precedent had already been established in the opening to mining of Glacier Bay National Monument by the act of June 22, 1936 (49 Stat. 1817). The Senate bill, introduced by Hayden (Ariz.), was the one enacted. Roosevelt approved it without comment on Oct. 27, 1941 (Cong. Rec., 77th Cong., 1st sess., 87:1, 53, 303; 87:4, 4622–4623; 55 Stat. 745). The letter here printed is the only protest against the bill found in the Roosevelt papers.

1065 SAMUEL I. ROSENMAN, SPECIAL COUNSEL TO THE PRESIDENT, TO ROOSEVELT

NEW YORK, N. Y., *October 31, 1941*

DEAR MR. PRESIDENT: I find in my files the enclosed correspondence with respect to a proposed subcommittee on National Forest Policy.

You will recall at the time I mentioned it to you, and after a short talk, you said to forget about it. I am sending this to you, however, as they belong in the White House files.[1]

Yours very sincerely,

SAM

[13:OF 149:TS]

[1] This correspondence, all of it having to do with the establishment of a national forest policy, was sent by Roosevelt to Rosenman with a memorandum of Sept. 1, 1941 (OF 149), asking him to speak to him about it. The correspondence consisted of a note from Ickes to Roosevelt, Aug. 4, 1941, enclosing a memorandum, Lee Muck to Ickes, July 29, 1941 (OF 149); Wickard to Roosevelt, Aug. 11, 1941, and Ickes and Wickard to Roosevelt, Aug. 12, 1941, *ante*, 1056, 1058.

1066 ROOSEVELT TO CLAUDE R. WICKARD, SECRETARY OF AGRICULTURE

HYDE PARK, N. Y., *November 3, 1941*

MEMORANDUM FOR THE SECRETARY OF AGRICULTURE: I understand that there are now some 1,600 local community forests established in some thirty states. Also that the idea is spreading to the South, which is all to the good.

I hope the Forest Service will push these. They are not large but are very important from the educational angle and it is a matter which might not receive the attention it deserves.[1]

F. D. R.

[13:PPF 38:CT]

[1] Nelson Brown had written to Roosevelt Oct. 30, 1941 (PPF 38), on the growing interest in community forests. He did not believe that the Forest Service was giving as much attention to community forests as it should and he suggested that a note to Wickard "might push them along." Wickard replied *post*, 1068.

1067 HAROLD D. SMITH, DIRECTOR, BUREAU OF THE BUDGET, TO ROOSEVELT

WASHINGTON, D. C., *Nov. 6, 1941*

MEMORANDUM FOR THE PRESIDENT: On March 28, 1940, in response to his request that tree planting in the Plains States be given distinctive recognition as a Federal project in the Budget, you advised the Secretary of Agriculture that arrangements would be made to continue this work during the fiscal year 1941 on approximately the same basis as it had been previously conducted, . . .[1]

On a question of interpretation in connection with the foregoing, I further advised the Secretary on May 28, 1940, as follows:

. . . It will undoubtedly be necessary for many years that the Department furnish leadership, technical advice and material assistance to insure continued progress. The course outlined by the President, as I understand it, does not contemplate termination of such aids; but rather that they should be extended to the farmers of the Prairie States, in reasonable measure, under the authority of and through the programs launched by the acts providing for soil conservation as a material policy, establishing the Soil Conservation Service, and promoting cooperative farm forestry.

The work was continued through the fiscal year 1941 through WPA funds and facilities and the Department made no move toward merging it with the other work of the Soil Conservation Service in the Plains area.

In its estimates for 1942 the Department sought an increase item of $250,000 to provide a regular appropriation base for this work, again seeking to give it a distinctive status as the "Prairie States Forestry Project." This increase item was considered with you and denied, and the Department was again urged to take steps toward incorporation of the work in the general Soil Conservation Service program. However, at the instance of Senator Norris an item of $300,000 was included in the 1942 Agriculture Appropriation Act specifically to provide the Forest Service with funds for maintenance in the Plains States of its planning, executive and supervisory organization to continue this tree-planting activity with WPA labor. The work is going forward during the current fiscal year under the above provisions. Since inception of the work in 1935, over 17,000 miles of shelterbelts 5 to 10 rows wide on over 27,000 farms have been planted. Over 95% of these plantings are being maintained by the farmers. The plantings of 1935, 1936, 1937 and 1938 are already providing valuable protection to soil and crops and otherwise contributing to the welfare of the farmers and farm communities.

In the estimates for the fiscal year 1943 the Department sought to have provided again in the Cooperative Farm Forestry appropriation the item of $300,000 provided in 1942 by the Norris amendment. I have advised the Secretary that in the light of the policy outlined in your letter of May 6, 1940, we would feel compelled to eliminate this item from the 1943 Budget.

On the other hand, the Department recently sought through a supplemental estimate also under the Cooperative Farm Forestry appropriation an item of $300,000 to enable the Department to intensify service to farm woodlot owners, particularly in the South where increased demands for timber and pulpwood are resulting in heavy and haphazard cutting of such woodlots. This office felt and still feels that this estimate was exceptionally meritorious, and upon our recommendation you submitted it to Congress where unfortunately it was rejected.

With the foregoing in mind, I told the Secretary that we would recommend continuing in the 1943 Budget the $300,000 provided under this head through the Norris 1942 amendment if the Department would move to carry out the policy stated in your letter of May 6, 1940, transferring the tree planting in the Plains States from the Forest Service to the Soil Conservation Service, and thereby initiating a gradual transition in the management of the work, which ultimately would change it from a special project to one of normal soil conservation, cooperation with the Soil Conservation Districts, and service to farmers outside such districts, and thus permit a gradual shifting of the forces and facilities provided by this $300,000 to the very real need for intensified service to farmers in other regions in the management of their woodlots.

The act creating the Soil Conservation Service specifically contemplated tree planting as a feature of the Soil Conservation program. The desired planting is done on farms. In the Soil Conservation Service the Department has an action agency, the program of which is designed to reach every individual farm, to plan, aid in initiating, and cooperate in maintaining the best possible soil conservation practice on these farms, including tree planting and culture wherever trees are suited to the need and possible to grow. That Service is well organized, active in the Plains States, and achieving highly creditable results. In the Bureau of Plant Industry, the Department has a research bureau quite well prepared to advise the action agency as to useable tree species, where and how to grow them.

The Forest Service takes legitimate pride in its accomplishments in tree planting in the Plains States and it is quite understandably reluctant to leave the field to another organization. Nevertheless, its presence in the Plains area inevitably leads to duplication and overlapping of function, which are already noticeable and must become more intensive and expensive as the Soil Conservation Service program develops. The Soil Conservation Service already has a major part in the farm woodlot work of the Department and it is the most logical unit to absorb all such activity, particularly in the Plains area.

The Department has never taken strong exception to this view but has attached great importance to the timing of such a change and has been hesitant on this account.

In a memorandum to me, under date of October 31, Secretary Wickard has now agreed to our proposal with respect to the 1943 Budget and the transfer from Forest Service to Soil Conservation Service of the farm woodlot work. He wishes you to have in mind, however, "that

[537]

the Forest Service made the shelterbelt a success when no one else was willing to become associated with it," and also Senator Norris' long and deep interest in the work. As indicated in the foregoing, there is no thought whatever of taking from the Forest Service the credit justly due that Service for initiating this work under very difficult conditions and carrying it forward aggressively, efficiently, and successfully. The adoption of the Soil Conservation Act and the rapid development of the Soil Conservation Service under the authority of that act have, however, vastly changed the situation prevalent when tree planting in the Plains States was initiated as a Federal activity and the soundness of the position taken by you in your letter to the Secretary on May 6, 1940 is being increasingly demonstrated.

It is not unlikely that Senator Norris will call you concerning this program and possibly protest any change. I am confident that you may safely assure the Senator that the action thus taken will in no way interfere with the progress of tree planting in the Plains area, that the Soil Conservation Service is fully qualified to move steadily ahead in this work, that the interests of economical and efficient over-all management of the Department of Agriculture's programs will be well served by the change, and that as another important result, funds now available to the Department will be increasingly released for greater and urgently needed service to farmers in the management, harvesting and sale of material from woodlots already existing.

HAROLD D. SMITH

[*Notation*:AS] HDS OK FDR
[13:OF 79:TS]

¹ March 28 was the date of Wallace's letter; May 6, of Roosevelt's reply. Smith went on to quote paragraph four of the reply, *ante,* 999.

1068   CLAUDE R. WICKARD, SECRETARY OF AGRICULTURE, TO ROOSEVELT

WASHINGTON, *November 12, 1941*

DEAR MR. PRESIDENT: I have your memorandum of November 3, about community forests in which you indicate a special interest in this development in the South. ˙A tabulation showing the number and total acreage of community forests by States is enclosed. My understanding is that the development in the Southern States is very recent.

As you know, Professor Nelson Brown of Syracuse University was employed by the Forest Service during the year 1937, made a rather extensive examination of the community forest situation, and finished his work with the preparation of a publication entitled *Community Forests.*¹

After Professor Brown's return to Syracuse, the Forest Service placed another man on this work, who after two years had to be transferred to the Southwest because of his health.

Since that time two or three men have given part time to the community forest campaign. They have tried to stimulate interest in community forests through written information, suggestions for State legislation, film strips, radio programs, and by keeping interested agencies and individuals currently posted on progress.

I am inclined to believe that the interest shown in the community forest movement is such that it warrants the assignment of a full-time man to the project, and arrangements will be made by the Forest Service to do this.

Respectfully,

CLAUDE R. WICKARD

[13:PPF 38:TS]

¹ This pamphlet, issued by the Department of Agriculture (Washington, 1939), contains a preface signed by Roosevelt.

1069   SENATOR JOHN H. BANKHEAD OF ALABAMA TO ROOSEVELT

JASPER, ALA., *Nov. 19, 1941, 6:40 p. m.*

[*Telegram*] THE PRESIDENT: I beg to call to your attention the great importance of securing the passage of the Senate bill now pending in the House authorizing the continuance of the Federal administration of the soil conservation program. That program was approved in the platform of both major political parties last year. Unless the bill is passed by January first, the existing organization must be abandoned and all appropriations distributed to the several states for administration. The Senate bill has been pending in the House for several months. I suggest you take this subject up with your House leaders with the view of getting definite action before the end of this year. See Public Number 170, 75th Congress, Chapter 395, first Session.¹

J. H. BANKHEAD

[13:OF 2891:T]

¹ By the act of June 28, 1937 (50 *Stat.* 329), the time for the transfer to the states of the administration of the Soil Conservation and Domestic Allotment Act was advanced to Jan. 1, 1942. By 1941 only a minority of the states had enacted the necessary enabling legislation. The Administration considered it imperative to keep the program under Federal management and on Jan. 27, 1941, Senator Bankhead introduced the bill (S. 588) referred to in his telegram. This would have given the Secretary of Agriculture "permanent authority" to administer the act. The bill, amended by the House to continue Federal administration through 1946 rather than for an indefinite time, was passed as the act approved Dec. 26, 1941 (*Cong. Rec.*, 77th Cong., 1st sess., 87:1, 310; 87:4, 4111–4114; 87:9, 9578–9597; 55 *Stat. 860*).

WASHINGTON, *November 27, 1941*

MY DEAR MR. PRESIDENT: It would seem that, with respect to public lands, including National Parks and Monuments, Wildlife Refuges, etc., the jurisdiction of this Department is rapidly being restricted to a futile ex post facto protest so far as the Army is concerned. The War Department picks out lands for invasion without reference to the use to which they are devoted, without considering whether there are equally suitable sites for bomb ranges, recreational buildings, etc., and without consulting with this Department. Then when we protest we find that "plans are too far advanced to change." Some time ago, in our effort to work out matters harmoniously with the Army, we appointed a liaison man representing the Fish & Wildlife Division, but this liaison man does his "liaisoning" in solitary state.

With great respect, but also with emphasis, I protest against the assumption by the War Department, or rather the Generals thereof, of the right to invade Parks, National Monuments or Wildlife Refuges at their will. Of course, I would willingly surrender our most precious land area if turning it over to the Army were necessary in order to defeat Hitler and if there were no substitute area.

We have tried to accommodate ourselves to the desires of the Army. We have cheerfully yielded possession and agreed to the use of lands where there was a showing of necessity, but there are instances in which areas taken for bomb ranges, etc. do not serve the purpose of the Army any better than adjacent lands where historical values would not be destroyed and where wildlife would not be endangered.

Recently, I protested the invasion by the Army of the Colonial National Historical Park in Virginia. You referred my letter to the Secretary of War and he replied to you under date of October 29.[1] A copy of his letter to you I am annexing for your convenience. In it, Secretary Stimson said, among other things: "Apparently the Secretary of the Interior wrote this letter without having full information at his disposal."

The enclosed memorandum from Director Drury of the National Park Service shows that if Secretary Stimson had full information at his disposal, some of it, at least, was misinformation.[2] According to Director Drury, the Army, without consulting this Department, proceeded to take over, for its own purposes, land within the jurisdiction of this Department. Upon objection by us, the War Department, without consultation with this Department, obtained a lease of property for a recreation building adjoining land which has been designated as a National Historical Site. The lot upon which the recreation building is being built is not owned by the Government, *"but it is located* *within the boundary of the area established by the Congress as **Colonial National Historical Park**."*

Apparently the Army is proceeding to develop a bombing range in a location that will seriously defeat the purpose of a Wildlife Refuge and perhaps result in the extermination of the rare trumpeter swan which you and I have been at such pains to preserve. As to this, I shall send you a memorandum later.

In the meantime, I beg of you that this Department be at least consulted before the Army takes unto itself any more lands within the jurisdiction of this Department, especially if they are lands within National Parks, National Monuments or Wildlife Refuges. It is utterly discouraging to have a body of men who don't care about the sort of thing that this Department is charged with fostering and protecting, march in and take possession just as Hitler marched in and took possession of the small democracies of Europe.

I have tried to meet this issue in an orderly manner. I have observed all of the proprieties. I am appealing to you who alone can make the Army aware that it is not operating this Department under martial law.

Sincerely yours,

Harold L. Ickes

[13:OF 6–P:TS]

[1] Ickes' letter to Roosevelt, Oct. 18, 1941, and Stimson's letter are present (OF 6–P).

[2] The enclosure, Newton B. Drury to Ickes, Nov. 19, 1941, is present. Drury succeeded Cammerer as National Park Service director on Aug. 20, 1940.

1071   Roosevelt to Henry L. Stimson, Secretary of War

Washington, *November 28, 1941*

Memorandum for the Secretary of War: Considering the size of the United States, I think that Irving Brant is correct.[1] Please tell Major General Adams or whoever is in charge of this business that Henry Lake, Utah, must immediately be struck from the Army planning list for any purposes. The verdict is for the Trumpeter Swan and against the Army. The Army must find a different nesting place!

F. D. R.

[*Notation*:AS] Necessary orders have been issued. JWM [2]

[13:OF 378:T]

[1] Brant, in a letter to Roosevelt of Nov. 25, 1941 (OF 378), had protested the selection, by Major General E. S. Adams, of an artillery range site at Henry Lake, Utah. Brant said that this was likely to result in the extermination of the trumpeter swan because Henry Lake was "the solitary unprotected point on the short flyway of the swans between Yellowstone National Park and the Red Rocks Lake Wildlife Refuge which was established for their benefit."

[2] Presumably John W. Martyn, administrative assistant to the Secretary of War.

[WASHINGTON] *December 1, 1941*

DEAR HARRY: I want to avoid all possible crossing of wires with the Interior Department in regard to the Army use of public lands.[1]   I wish you would have a talk with Secretary Ickes in regard to this, in order to get some sort of clearance with the Interior Department before Army plans are finally made for the occupation or use of public lands.[2]

Always sincerely,

[FRANKLIN D. ROOSEVELT]

[13:OF 6–P:CT]

[1] See *ante,* 1070.

[2] Stimson replied Dec. 2, 1941 (OF 378), that he had halted Army plans to use Henry Lake, but that it had been planned to use the area for the training of mountain troops only in event of a further increase of such units.

1073   ROOSEVELT TO KENNETH A. REID, EXECUTIVE SECRETARY, IZAAK WALTON LEAGUE OF AMERICA, Chicago

[WASHINGTON] *December 3, 1941*

MY DEAR MR. REID: I am pleased to have your letter of November twelfth expressing your interest and that of the Izaak Walton League in various matters pertaining to the abatement of water pollution by industrial wastes and domestic sewage.[1]

I am sure you are aware of my continued interest in the protection of our streams and lakes from the harmful effects of undue amounts of polluting materials.   I appreciate the need for the application of corrective measures and to this end Federal assistance is being given to the construction of sewage treatment plants where added contributions of polluting material are resulting from the defense program.

The entire problem is one, however, in which cooperation of Federal and State authorities is most essential for a permanent solution of this problem.   I am sure that you will find the Federal Government willing to cooperate with State and local agencies where there is a disposition on the part of the local people to provide proper sewage treatment facilities.

The national defense program has required the careful distribution of various chemicals and materials, some of which are used for sanitation purposes including the treatment of public water supplies and sewage and industrial wastes.   I am advised that essential materials for such purposes are being made equally available to the defense program and to civil authorities charged with operating sanitation facilities.   It is hoped, therefore, that there need be no concern regarding a shortage of these essential chemicals for sanitation purposes.

The interest of the Izaak Walton League in these matters, and as expressed in your communication, is sincerely appreciated.[2]

Very sincerely yours,

[FRANKLIN D. ROOSEVELT]

CD

[13:OF 114–A:CT]

[1] Reid wrote (OF 114–A) in approval of Roosevelt's letter to Federal Security Administrator McNutt of Oct. 17, 1941, in which McNutt was directed to investigate the reported breakdown of the water and sewage systems in Philadelphia. (The letter to McNutt has not been found in the Roosevelt papers; it was published in the New York *Times,* Oct. 18, 1941, p. 10.)

[2] Drafted by the Federal Security Agency.

1074   CLAUDE R. WICKARD, SECRETARY OF AGRICULTURE, TO ROOSEVELT

[WASHINGTON] *December 26, 1941*

DEAR MR. PRESIDENT: I feel that I can no longer delay bringing to your attention the fact that we urgently need war legislation on some phases of forestry.

One need is for Federal regulation to stop the destructive cutting of privately owned forests.   Thus increased war demands for timber could be met without impairing the productivity of the forests.   Another is authority to extend and intensify fire protection, without which regulation cannot be effective.   Authority to keep abreast of supply, demand, price and related factors should be broadened so that we can anticipate and provide against bottlenecks.   To avoid direct appropriations for the purpose, authority is needed for RFC loans which can be used for the time being to acquire certain forest lands in order to prevent the repetition of such things as the spruce debacle of World War I in the Pacific Northwest.   Provision is urgent for a marketing service for farmers, who through ignorance or lack of sales facilities are permitting clear cutting nearly everywhere at ridiculously inadequate prices.

The war has intensified these needs, which as you know have long been with us.

The best way to get the legislation we need is to capitalize on the opportunity provided by Senator Bankhead's introduction of a bill to carry out the recommendations of the Joint Congressional Committee on Forestry.   The Senator apparently intends to press for enactment. Some of the provisions of his bill are satisfactory; others are not.   It should be amended to meet war needs, to strengthen the weak parts, to provide for direct Federal action wherever feasible and to eliminate mandatory matching of funds by the States.   Altogether, this should give us well-rounded legislation for both war and post-war requirements.

[543]

I urge that you authorize me to work this out with Congress along the lines indicated.[1]

Respectfully yours,

[CLAUDE R. WICKARD]

[13:OF 149:CT]

[1] Bankhead introduced two forestry bills on Nov. 13, 1941: S. 2043, "A bill to effectuate the recommendation of the Joint Congressional Committee on Forestry . . ." and S. 2044, "A bill to authorize the Secretary of Agriculture to enter into lease agreements with farmers in order to provide for the management of their forest lands and the marketing of their forest products in accordance with proper forestry and marketing practices." Neither was reported from committee (*Cong. Rec.*, 77th Cong., 1st sess., 87: 8, 8812).

1075   ROOSEVELT TO CLAUDE R. WICKARD, SECRETARY OF AGRICULTURE

WASHINGTON, *December 29, 1941*

MEMORANDUM FOR THE SECRETARY OF AGRICULTURE: Yes, go ahead and try to work this out with Senator Bankhead.[1] It is essential, however, to cut out the portions of the bill which would create subsidies to tree owners. If we start that we shall never get away from it.

F. D. R.

[13:OF 149:CT]

[1] See above.

1076   HAROLD L. ICKES, SECRETARY OF THE INTERIOR, TO ROOSEVELT

WASHINGTON, *January 17, 1942*

MY DEAR MR. PRESIDENT: In these times few people have the vision to think of the future even if a small effort will result in mighty gains for later generations. You have that vision, and since you are the only one who can do anything to save the wonderful Porcupine Mountain area, I hope that you will read this letter of Irving Brant's.

Sincerely yours,

(sgd) HAROLD L. ICKES

[13:OF 149:T:COPY]

1077   [*Enclosure*] IRVING BRANT TO HAROLD L. ICKES

WASHINGTON, D. C., *January 14, 1942*

DEAR MR. SECRETARY: The campaign to save Porcupine Mountain in northern Michigan is at a critical stage. This forest—the last area of virgin northern hardwoods in the country and long desired as a national park—is being lumbered at the rate of 100,000 feet a day. The lumbering railroad, just built, runs directly into the most beautiful area which will therefore be almost the first cut. In this region as a whole the nature of the soil, loose sand, means that this kind of lumbering will produce a desert.

Congressman Hook's bill authorizes an RFC loan to acquire 165,-000 acres, most of which would be selectively logged by the Forest Service to repay the loan. The Forest Service has promised that a scenic portion would be preserved from cutting by departmental order. The Hook bill is getting nowhere. Its author is shuttled between Jesse Jones and the Budget Director, the latter being hostile.

I should like to see the Hook bill passed to stop the cutting, but in the longer view it is unsound because it combines two desirable but incompatible objectives. An RFC loan on the commercial area would be a sound investment to stop the destructive lumbering. But if selective logging is relied on to finance both what is logged and what is not logged, it will result in logging all but a trifling part of the scenic area whose inviolate protection is the chief aim of the whole movement.

General Motors owns about 37,000 acres out of the 165,000 covered by the Hook bill, including most of the scenic area. It owns nearly all of Porcupine Mountain itself, and alternate sections along the beautiful Presque Isle River and other streams to the west, immediately threatened with lumbering. General Motors is doing no lumbering, but plans it in the future.

I think that General Motors should be asked by the President to give this land to the government for a national park, as a good will token return for what it is getting out of the government in defense contracts. It is valuable land. When a stand of hardwoods is so fine that it is worth being made into a national park it has high commercial value. But it is an invisible drop in the bucket of General Motors' war supply profits.

If this gift were made, it would then be sound financial policy to make an RFC loan for sustained yield lumbering in the surrounding area, and this part of Michigan would be saved from the ruin now facing it. The small purchases needed to solidify the park could be made out of this loan, without jeopardizing its repayment.

Unless action comes soon, the lumber company will destroy the scenic values of the district by cutting its alternate sections. Then General Motors will cut, and the country will be a blighted wasteland of rolling sand.[1]

Sincerely yours,

(sgd) IRVING BRANT

[13:OF 149:T:COPY]

[1] Brant's and Ickes' letters were sent by Roosevelt to Budget Director Smith with a note, Jan. 20, 1942, reading: "For preparation of reply. I think that Ickes and Irving Brant are right. We ought to save this virgin timber." See below.

WASHINGTON, *March 2, 1942*

MY DEAR MR. PRESIDENT: Attached are your memorandum of February 13, 1942, with Director Harold D. Smith's memorandum of February 4, 1942, and the preceding correspondence concerning the desirability of preserving an adequate portion of the virgin forest and other scenic and recreational features of the Porcupine Mountains area in northern Michigan.[1]

Director Smith proposes an RFC loan of $27,800,000 for a period of 60 years, to purchase 1,300,000 acres of forest in northern Michigan and Wisconsin for forestry purposes. This proposal is essentially similar to the Hook-Brown bills (H. R. 3793 and S. 1131) in the present Congress.[2] Of the total of 1,300,000 acres proposed to be purchased, 250,000 acres are covered with virgin forest, of which 30,000 acres would be set apart by the Secretary of Agriculture to be preserved in their natural condition for park purposes. Director Smith states that it is "very questionable that either economic or social justification can be found" for setting aside any larger portion of these lands for park purposes.[3]

Many economists and conservationists will disagree with Director Smith's view of the case.

Some indication of the comparative revenue-producing value of national parks and national forests may be found in the fact that in administration, protection, and maintenance for a recently computed five-year period, the Park Service was 42 percent self-supporting whereas the Forest Service, on a comparable basis, was only 27 percent self-supporting. A greater contrast may be seen in the fact that the average annual revenues of the Teton National Forests from 1934 to 1938 inclusive were only $13,860 whereas the average annual revenues from Yellowstone National Park for the same years were $314,272. Teton National Forest and Yellowstone National Park are contiguous reservations and are roughly of comparable size.

From the conservation angle, there is no national park readily accessible to the large populations of the Middle Western industrial centers. An adequate national park in the Porcupine Mountains region would serve an enormous number of people, but the park would have to be large enough to give them ample outdoor space. Thirty thousand acres in scattered tracts would be hopelessly inadequate. Moreover, national forest management is not a substitute for a national park. People do not enjoy logged off lands as much as they do an unspoiled primeval forest.

I am in sympathy with Director Smith's proposal that the purchase of critical forested areas be financed by an RFC loan at this time, and all of the areas mentioned in his letter are of interest to this Department also,[4] but I believe that the proposition will be much sounder if the outstanding recreational lands are managed for park purposes by the National Park Service of this Department and the timber-producing lands are managed for timber production purposes by the Forest Service, as I have consistently advocated.

I suggest, therefore, that you request the Secretaries of Agriculture and the Interior to consider the Hook-Brown bills, and similar proposals, and agree upon measures that both Departments can support, for submission through the Bureau of the Budget for your consideration.[5] Sincerely yours,

HAROLD L. ICKES

[13:OF 79:TS]

[1] Roosevelt's memorandum to Ickes of Feb. 13, 1942 (OF 149), covering the correspondence mentioned, reads: "What do you think? Please return papers for my files." Smith's memorandum of Feb. 4, 1942 (OF 149), is a detailed analysis of the financial problem involved in the purchase by the Agriculture Department of the Porcupine Mountain forest by means of a Reconstruction Finance Corporation loan. The "preceding correspondence" is Ickes' letter and enclosure, above.

[2] The Hook-Brown bill would have authorized the Reconstruction Finance Corporation to lend to the Agriculture Department $30,000,000 for the purchase of 1,500,000 acres of hemlock-hardwood forests in northern Michigan and Wisconsin, such lands to be administered as national forests or as state forests under cooperative arrangements. The bill authorized the establishment of sustained-yield units comprising national forest and private lands, or national forest lands exclusively, within which national forest timber could be sold without competitive bidding. The House bill was introduced on March 4, and the Senate bill on March 17, 1941, but neither was reported from committee (*Cong. Rec.*, 77th Cong., 1st sess., 87:2, 1784, 2278).

[3] In this connection Smith said: "It is . . . very questionable that either economic or social justification can be found for locking against reasonable use any larger portion of these lands. On the whole they are hardly of National Park quality. In many places it has been repeatedly demonstrated that carefully managed timber utilization is not wholly incompatible with preservation of aesthetic values."

[4] Smith referred to other "critical areas" in the national pattern of forest-land ownership: the Cascade Mountain area, the California redwood forests, and the Quetico-Superior forest in Minnesota.

[5] An attached memorandum, Roosevelt to Smith, March 5, 1942, reads: "Will you talk this over with the Secretary of Agriculture and the Secretary of the Interior and let me have a report?"

1079   ROOSEVELT TO SENATOR ELBERT D. THOMAS OF UTAH, CHAIRMAN, SENATE COMMITTEE ON EDUCATION AND LABOR

[WASHINGTON] *March 16, 1942*

DEAR ELBERT: You are dead right about the danger of forest fires on the Pacific Coast.[1]   It is obvious that many of them will be deliberately set on fire if the Japs attack there—and even if they do not attack there. I don't think people realize that both the CCC and the NYA are doing essential war work and that if they are abolished some machinery will have to be started to take their places—and probably at a net increased cost.

I have just sent Kenneth a letter, of which I enclose a copy.[2]

Always sincerely,

[FRANKLIN D. ROOSEVELT]

[13:OF 268:CT]

[1] Thomas, writing March 13, 1942 (OF 268), said that the McKellar bill (S. 2295), to abolish the Civilian Conservation Corps and the National Youth Administration, was before his committee, but that he was opposed to the bill, believing that the western forests needed more rather than less protection.

[2] See below.

1080   ROOSEVELT   TO   SENATOR   KENNETH   MCKELLAR   OF   TENNESSEE

[WASHINGTON] *March 16, 1942*

DEAR KENNETH: I hope you will come down and talk with me before anything more is done about S. 2295, which in effect provides for terminating the CCC and the NYA.

At the present time both of these organizations are engaged mostly on essential war work.

Just for example, we cannot afford to let the national forests go without fire protection. I am much worried about deliberate attempts to set our West Coast forests (and others too) on fire this Spring and Summer.

Similarly in NYA the bulk of their work is training workers for munitions plants. This work has to be done by somebody. If we set up wholly new machinery it will cost the Government more.

I hope you will run down and give me your ideas.[1]

Always sincerely,

[FRANKLIN D. ROOSEVELT]

[13:OF 268:CT]

[1] This bill, introduced by McKellar Feb. 23, 1942, was not reported (*Cong. Rec.,* 77th Cong., 2d sess., 88: 2, 1509). McKellar replied March 17, 1942 (OF 268), that he would be glad to discuss the matter at any time; he saw the President on March 21 (PPF 1-O).

1081   ROOSEVELT TO HAROLD D. SMITH, DIRECTOR, BUREAU OF THE BUDGET

WASHINGTON, *March 17, 1942*

MEMORANDUM FOR THE DIRECTOR OF THE BUDGET: I approve your recommendations of March 14th in regard to C. C. C.[1] The consolidation of it with N. Y. A. should be by executive order and not by the legislative route.

In regard to C. C. C., I would keep a skeleton organization going here in Washington with two or three definite orders.

(a) Take boys under twenty, giving preference to those who need physical rehabilitaiton in order to fit them for service in the army.

(b) Confine the C. C. C. work to forest fire prevention and looking after the bare maintenance of a number of national monuments or historic sites where they are now used.

In regard to N. Y. A., you might talk over the situation with Aubrey Williams—confine their work almost exclusively to the defense training program.

F. D. R.

[13:OF 268:CT]

---

[1] Smith recommended against legislation to consolidate the Civilian Conservation Corps and the National Youth Administration because, he said, ". . . this legislation looks more and more like a youth program for the post-war period, and I feel definitely that it will be murdered if presented to Congress at this time" (OF 268).

1082   WAYNE COY, ACTING DIRECTOR, BUREAU OF THE BUDGET, TO ROOSEVELT

WASHINGTON, D. C., May 16, 1942

MEMORANDUM FOR THE PRESIDENT: . . . On December 26, 1941 Secretary Wickard wrote you expressing the view that new forestry legislation is urgently needed. On December 29 you advised him to go ahead and try to work it out on the basis of Senator Bankhead's bill, S. 2043, which is designed to carry into effect the recommendations made last Spring by the Joint Congressional Committee on Forestry. You further advised that creation of subsidies to tree owners should be avoided, that action programs should be wholly Federal with "matching" requirements eliminated, and that special consideration should be given to farm woodlot owners.

Agriculture now wishes to report to the Senate upon the Bankhead bill by presenting a redraft covering the whole field of needs in forestry as envisioned by the present leadership of the Forest Service. During the past few months this proposed legislation has been thoroughly and jointly studied by representatives of Secretary Wickard and the Forest Service with members of my staff whose experience in and intimate familiarity with the forestry movement of this country extends back over 30 years. Upon this basis the principal legislative proposals of the Department and my recommendations with regard to each are presented as follows:

1. Federal Regulation of Forest Practices on Private Lands. The Secretary of Agriculture would be authorized to classify all privately-owned land in each State as either forest or nonforest land and through

a system of National and local advisory boards, with the Forest Service as the action agency, determine the area of forest land on which operating practices would be regulated, formulate rules of practice, place these rules in effect, and enforce compliance. All "small woodlots the forest products of which are wholly or almost wholly (1) used by the owner for domestic nonindustrial purposes, (2) not marketed in commerce" would be exempted from regulation. This would exempt many but not necessarily all farm woodlots.

The views of foresters and other qualified persons, whose interest in the better management of our forest resources is undoubtedly sincere, as to the necessity for and desirability of public regulation of forest practices, are widely divergent.

Few would deny the principle that the State should, if necessary, utilize its police power to keep forest land productive. Forest practices on private lands which would go beyond this minimum that legislation can reasonably be expected to bring about will be adopted when and only when private owners are convinced that such practices will pay. Many, perhaps most owners, have not been as open to conviction on the point of profit possibilities as they might have been, and foresters generally have been less active in determining the profit possibilities of refined forest practices than in urging their adoption.

The State foresters generally are opposed to Federal regulation. The American Forestry Association favors regulation, where found necessary, by the States rather than the Federal Government. This Association also has strongly urged that the highly controversial issue of forest regulation should be set aside until the war is won. The professional Society of American Foresters endorses public regulation to the extent necessary in any local situation but appears to lean toward State rather than Federal control. Forest industrial interests would, of course, fight vigorously this regulatory proposal.

This office believes that the need for public regulation and particularly Federal regulation of private forest practices has not been convincingly demonstrated. In general the protection of our forest resources and the application of sound practices in the management of these resources are making steady consistent progress each year. Despite the tremendous drain on our forests, arising from the current war, the danger of a timber shortage in the United States is steadily passing. I believe that with reasonable intensification of protection and cooperative action along the lines of research, education, technical advice and assistance, our public and private efforts will insure a growth of timber much more than sufficient to supply all consumption requirements. The economic problem of forestry in the United States is more likely to be one of markets than one of production. The introduction of legislation providing for Federal regulation in this field will certainly arouse a major controversy and would be particularly untimely now when unity of effort is so essential. The cost of a regulatory system such as is now proposed cannot be exactly determined but first year cost would probably not be less than $3,000,000 and this figure would undoubtedly increase year by year.

I recommend that the proposal for Federal regulation of forest practices on private lands be held as not at this time in accord with your program. *OK* [1]

2. Intensified Cooperative Forest Fire Protection. Under the Clarke-McNary Act of 1924 annual appropriations of not to exceed $2,500,000 are authorized for the cooperative Federal-State-private system of forest fire protection on State and private lands. The Department proposes an increase in the annual authorization to $9,000,000 and would eliminate the present requirement that State and private expenditure equal the Federal contribution.

This cooperative protection program which had its inception even before the enactment of the Clarke-McNary law has made steady and most gratifying progress for over 30 years. There remains the need for intensifying and expanding the program to the point of complete coverage. While I readily agree that a "matching" requirement may and frequently does seriously interfere with effective action in desirable programs, the present system of cooperative effort is in this instance thoroughly and successfully established, and a waiver of the matching requirement for the future might result merely in the assumption by the Federal Government of a greater proportionate share in the total program, rather than in the desirable more complete coverage.

I recommend your approval of the proposed increase in appropriation authorization and retention of the "matching" provision. *OK*

3. Cooperative Farm Forestry. Annual appropriations up to $2,500,000 would be authorized for intensified technical advice and assistance to farmers in connection with their woodlots. No matching of Federal expenditures would be required.

Your approval is recommended. *Approve "a very inexpensive program based on the County Agent system."*

4. Insect and Disease Control. The Secretary would be authorized directly or in cooperation with States and private owners to make surveys and undertake action programs designed to control or suppress forest insect pests and tree diseases, with appropriations in such amounts as Congress might from time to time determine to be necessary. No matching of expenditures would be required. The aim would be to discover and treat diseases and infestations in their incipient stages, thus reducing the necessity for large appropriations for eradication or suppression such as we are now forced to make in the white pine blister rust, Dutch elm disease, and similar programs. The annual cost aside from that of

eradication or suppressing diseases or insects which might still get out of
hand would approximate perhaps $500,000.

Your approval is recommended. *No appro during war*

5. Forest Management and Utilization Extension. The Secretary
would be authorized to expand and intensify the furnishing of technical
advice and assistance to nonfarm forest land. Without any clear-cut
basic legislative authorization the Forest Service now engages in this
work with the commercial forest owners to a very minor degree. This
office believes that if such work were reasonably intensified and effectively carried on very excellent results would follow. In fact it is believed that through such a program regulation would become less and
less necessary.

Appropriations for this purpose would be authorized in such amounts
as Congress might from time to time determine to be necessary.

Your approval is recommended. *OK*

6. Sustained Yield Management Units. The Secretary would be
authorized to organize units consisting of intermingled or adjacent National forest and private timber lands for sustained yield management, or
to designate such units consisting wholly of National forest lands.
Within such units he would be authorized to sell National forest stumpage
without competitive bidding. There are many cases where only through
such a plan will it be possible to bring about sustained yield management
and insure the permanent economic and social welfare of communities
dependent upon the forest resources. No new special appropriations
would be necessary, the legislation providing that the work done under
this head be chargeable to the regular Department appropriations.
Additional costs would probably not exceed $50,000 per annum.

Your approval is recommended. *OK*

7. Forest Credit. Long and short term credit would be provided
through Farm Credit Administration facilities with specialist personnel.
Loans to cooperatives would be authorized for terms up to 20 years for
general operating purposes.

It is believed that the proposed strengthening of the Federal forest
credit facilities would be very beneficial particularly with respect to the
farm woodlot owners and other small owners of commercial forest
properties.

Your approval is recommended. *OK*

8. Forest Cooperatives. The legislation would definitely promote the
establishment of cooperatives which would result in greatly improved
management and utilization of small forest holdings.

Your approval is recommended. *OK Forest Land-Leases—not in
accord see previous files.*

9. Forest Insurance. The Federal Crop Insurance Act [2] would be
amended to provide for insuring growing forests against loss of damage

[552]

by fire, disease, or other natural causes in accordance with sound insurance practices, the premiums of such insurance to be computed and payable in cash. Federal crop insurance met with severe criticism in Congress this Spring and the future of the wheat and cotton insurance programs now in operation is most uncertain. I believe these programs might be further jeopardized if an attempt were made at this time to expand the field of coverage. Furthermore it is not believed that there is as yet any sound actuarial basis for forest insurance.

I recommend that the forest insurance proposal be held not in accord with your program. *OK*

10. Forest Survey. The Secretary would be authorized to complete and keep current the nation-wide survey of forest resources launched by the McSweeney-McNary Act of 1928 with annual appropriations in such amounts as found necessary.

Your approval is recommended. *OK*

11. Community Forests. The new legislation would broaden the authority provided in the Fulmer Act of 1935 to aid States and other local governmental units in acquiring and managing forest lands, with authority for appropriations aggregating $10,000,000, not to exceed $2,500,000 in any one year.

Theoretically the Federal expenditures in this program would be reimbursed through revenues derived by the States or local governmental units from the forest lands so acquired. On two occasions you have submitted estimates to Congress to make operative the very similar plan authorized by the original Fulmer act. These estimates were rejected by Congress. This office regards the proposed plan as not at all likely to be self-liquidating and generally unsound.

I recommend disapproval of this proposal. *OK*

12. National Forest Planting. At present the annual expenditures for nursery and planting operations under the regular National Forest appropriations are limited to $400,000. The new legislation would remove this limitation.

I recommend your approval. *OK*

13. Financial Contribution in Lieu of Taxes to Local Governments. "Conservation lands" would be defined as (1) National forests, and (2) lands held under Title III of the Bankhead-Jones Farm Tenant Act. The legislation would authorize the payment to the States of 25 percent of the gross receipts from timber sales on such lands, but not exceeding ¾ percent per annum of the value of the timber on such lands, plus 25 percent of all other receipts from such lands and an additional sum if necessary to make the annual return to the State equal to ¾ of 1 percent of the cost of the lands.

Various plans are now in effect for payment to the States in lieu of taxes on lands acquired by the Federal Government. While the plan now proposed for the National forest and Bankhead-Jones lands is not specifically objectionable, if new legislation of this sort is to be enacted it should be sufficiently comprehensive to cover all forms of nonurban Federal land acquisition and harmonize the different formulas now in effect.

I recommend your approval if amended as above suggested. *OK*

14. National Forest Acquisition. Federal acquisition of critical areas of privately-owned forest lands bearing commercial stands of timber would be authorized until 1960 through use of Reconstruction Finance Corporation loans limited, at any one time, to $250,000,000. This program is designed to be self-liquidating over a long term of years, the revenues from the lands so purchased to be used for repaying the RFC loans with interest at 3 percent. In the event that such revenues were insufficient to repay any loan within 60 years from the date thereof the Treasury would make up the deficit from funds not otherwise obligated.

This authorization would make widely applicable the plan proposed in the Hook bill, H. R. 3793, to provide for acquisition of the Porcupine Mountain area and adjacent lands in the Michigan peninsula.

Your approval is recommended. *OK*

WAYNE COY

[13:OF 79:TS]

---

[1] This and the succeeding italicized notations were made by Budget Director Smith in the course of a review of the memorandum with Roosevelt at the White House on May 13, according to an attached note, Coy to Roosevelt, May 16, 1942.
[2] Title V of the Agricultural Adjustment Act of 1938 (52 *Stat.* 72).

1083   ROOSEVELT TO HAROLD D. SMITH, DIRECTOR, AND WAYNE COY, ASSISTANT DIRECTOR, BUREAU OF THE BUDGET

WASHINGTON, *May 19, 1942*

MEMORANDUM . . . In regard to forestry legislation, I think that at this time, and until the war is over, the following policy should be followed without any further action on the part of the Federal Government:

1. There should be no Federal legislation providing for Federal regulation of forestry practices on private lands.

2. In regard to the problem of the farmer's wood lot within slightly larger areas, while regulation should not be started we ought to start a very inexpensive program based on the county agent system, with the objective of instruction and advice to the farmer on his tree crops in the same way as we now give it to the farmer on his annual agricultural crop production.

The need for this has come to me very forcibly during the past year. I know of very many cases where timber cruisers have gone to farmers and have offered them a price far below market value for special types of trees. The farmer has been glad to get the cash and has not known how to find out what the real value of his trees is. For instance, in Georgia I know of a number of farmers who have sold their trees on the stump for 50% of the stumpage value. The same thing has been true in Dutchess County where many people have sold excellent timber for $8.00 a thousand, when they could have got $16.00 a thousand. Furthermore, the farm wood lot stumpage sales have in most cases contained no provision for the removal of tops or for the preservation of the other trees. Slash operations have been the rule rather than the exception.

I should like to have the Department of Agriculture study this subject with the objective of providing three things for the average farm wood lot owner:

(a) The real value of the timber

(b) The safeguarding of the removal of the timber

(c) What types of trees he should encourage and what types he should get rid of.

Finally, I am inclined to think that through the county agent system it might be possible to get even a part time agent who knows enough about the subject to start a policy, which I hope will later become general, and which ultimately can be handled by forester experts.

I approve your recommendation in regard to fire protection.

Your paragraph No. 3 is covered at the beginning of this letter.

I do not believe that in time of war we can afford to increase appropriations for insect and disease control.

I approve your paragraphs Nos. 5, 6, 7, 8, 9, 10, 11, 12, 13 and 14.

F. D. R.

[13:OF 149:TS]

1084   ROOSEVELT TO HAROLD L. ICKES, SECRETARY OF THE INTERIOR, AND CLAUDE R. WICKARD, SECRETARY OF AGRICULTURE

WASHINGTON, June 1, 1942

MEMORANDUM . . . Can you get together and present a united front in regard to the acquisition of the Porcupine Mountain area? I understand a large part of it is owned by General Motors. How about an effort to get them to deed all their acreage on the basis of their getting lumber out of it by the selective cutting process, spaced over a number of years in the post-war period? That would insure the right kind of cutting—and General Motors ought to be very liberal with the Government.

[555]

I am told that we ought to have 150,000 acres and that a large portion of this has already been lumbered and should be treated as a reforestation project. Also, I am inclined to think that 50,000 acres in the heart of it should be kept as a National Monument or National Park—in its original condition without cutting.

What do you think? [1]

F. D. R.

[13:OF 149:CT]

[1] Ickes replied (June 10, 1942) that National Park Service Director Drury would visit the area and that a conference would then be held with the Agriculture Department. Wickard replied (June 26, 1942) that this procedure was satisfactory, and writing again on July 22, said that the two departments had agreed on amendments to the pending bills H. R. 3793 and S. 1131 (OF 149).

1085   ROOSEVELT TO HAROLD L. ICKES, SECRETARY OF THE INTERIOR

WASHINGTON, *June 8, 1942*

MEMORANDUM FOR THE SECRETARY OF THE INTERIOR: I have signed H. R. 2685 authorizing the disposal of recreational demonstration projects—by turning them over to States under certain conditions.[1]

I think the authority granted is good but I hope that you will be guided by certain circumstances which are important from the long range point of view. I suggest a few of these:

(a) I do not think we should give up those recreational areas which lie along any possible through parkway. I have in mind the Catoctin recreational area which would undoubtedly be traversed by any expansion of the Skyline Drive through Maryland and Pennsylvania to connect with Bear Mountain Park and the Berkshires.

(b) I do not think we should give up any recreational area which at a later period could be greatly extended into a national monument or a national park.

(c) Very strict supervision by the Interior Department over state or local management should be established in order to assure adequate upkeep and improvement.

(d) We should encourage States to adopt laws similar to the New York laws under which a very large number of State parks have been created for scenic and recreational purposes.

(e) I think we should encourage the payment of a small fee for the use of these areas so as to get back as much as possible of the cost of upkeep. The New York State parks, large and small, are very nearly all on a paying basis.

F. D. R.

[13:BUDGET BUREAU ENROLLED BILLS:CT]

¹ Approved June 6, 1942 (56 *Stat.* 326), H. R. 2685 authorized the Secretary of the Interior, with the approval of the President, to convey or lease without charge certain of the Federal recreational demonstration projects to the states or their political subdivisions, and provided also that certain of the projects might be added to existing national parks and monuments. An earlier bill to accomplish these purposes had been vetoed (see *ante,* 940).

1086   ROOSEVELT TO HAROLD D. SMITH, DIRECTOR, BUREAU OF THE
        BUDGET

[WASHINGTON] *June 17, 1942*

MEMORANDUM FOR THE DIRECTOR OF THE BUDGET: I wish you would make it clear, on my behalf, to the Appropriations Committee in the Senate that the elimination of the CCC will call for a wholly separate appropriation to take its place in two of the CCC activities.

The first is the need for forest fire protection, especially on the Pacific Coast and back as far as the Rockies, where we must guard against Japanese incendiary bombs and incendiary fires during the dry season. This is an essential for our national future.

The second is the building of roads and other facilities for camps. These have to be built by someone and I shall have to ask for a special appropriation to let the work out by contract instead of having it done by the CCC.

Make it clear that the abolishing of the CCC saves the nation no money.¹

F.D.R.

[13:OF 268:CT]

¹ The Civilian Conservation Corps had at this time 158 camps working on military reservations, 42 more camps were about to be assigned to similar work, and 150 camps were to be assigned to forest protection. CCC Director McEntee estimated that to do this indispensable work with other labor would cost $125,000,000. Since the CCC budget called for $80,000,000, abolishing the agency would cost the Government $45,000,000 (McEntee to McIntyre, June 16, 1942, OF 268).

1087   ROOSEVELT TO SENATOR HENRIK SHIPSTEAD OF MINNESOTA

WASHINGTON, *July 30, 1942*

MY DEAR SENATOR SHIPSTEAD: I thank you for bringing to my attention the letter addressed to you by Mr. Al Belair, Secretary, Allied Sportsmen, Inc., of Minnesota, under date of July 12, 1942. Mr. Belair's letter is returned, as requested.¹

The Quetico-Superior Committee, created by me in 1934, has recommended the establishment of an international reserve in the Quetico-Superior Area. It has also recommended that the administration of

[557]

this Area, both within the United States and Canada, be left in the agencies which now exercise it, but that the two Nations join in a treaty which would permanently assure harmonious administration. Through the Secretary of State, I have informally indicated to the Dominion Government my approval of the Committee's recommendations. It appears from that Government's response that the negotiation of a treaty should be deferred until the conclusion of peace. In the meantime the Quetico-Superior Committee has received assurances from officials of the Ontario Government that lumbering within the proposed reserve will be carried on, in so far as possible, so that the recreational opportunities and the natural beauty of the area will not be destroyed. You may assure Mr. Belair that on the Minnesota side of the border the Indian Service of the Department of the Interior and the Forest Service of the Department of Agriculture are actively cooperating with the Quetico-Superior Committee and are pursuing the same objectives.

Although Mr. Belair does not refer to the attitude of the State of Minnesota, I assume that his desire to have Federal protection for this area immediately assured by treaty arises from a change in policy of the Minnesota Department of Conservation. Until recently the program for Federal acquisition of this border area apparently had the approval of that Department. The State Conservation Commission in 1935 invited Federal acquisition of certain areas outside of the Superior National Forest. This action followed express approval of the program by Governor Floyd Olson. More recently, however, the State Department of Conservation, presumably with Governor Stassen's approval, has indicated a hostility to the extension of Federal control. I believe that the whole of the Quetico-Superior Area should be under Federal administration, for the project is of national interest.[2]

Sincerely yours,

[FRANKLIN D. ROOSEVELT]

[13:OF 1119:CT]

[1] A copy is with Shipstead's covering letter of July 15, 1942 (OF 1119). Belair, on behalf of Allied Sportsmen, Inc., of Minnesota, urged the immediate conclusion of a treaty with Canada to assure the future preservation of the Quetico-Superior region as a wilderness area.

[2] (Drafted by the Interior Department.) The existence of the Quetico-Superior Committee was extended for another four-year term by Executive Order 9213, issued Aug. 4, 1942. Ickes reviewed the committee's progress in a letter to Roosevelt of June 23, 1942 (OF 1119). In 1948, under the Thye-Blatnik Act of June 22, 1948 (62 *Stat.* 568), Congress authorized expenditures up to $500,000 for the condemnation and purchase of lands in the area threatened with exploitation by hotel and resort owners. On Dec. 17, 1949, President Truman issued Executive Order 10092 barring air traffic over the "Roadless Areas" reserved for canoe travel. The legality of the executive order was challenged in the courts but was upheld: see Russell P. Andrews, *Wilderness Sanctuary* (ICP Case Series: Number 13, revised, Swarthmore, Pa., 1954).

1088   HAROLD L. ICKES, SECRETARY OF THE INTERIOR, TO
        ROOSEVELT

WASHINGTON, *September 29, 1942*

MY DEAR MR. PRESIDENT: The enclosed memorandum, which has
been summarized by Under Secretary Fortas, will answer at least in part
some of the questions that you asked about lumber at a recent Cabinet
meeting.

Sincerely yours,

HAROLD L. ICKES

[13:OF 446:TS]

1089   [*Enclosure*] ABE FORTAS, UNDER SECRETARY OF THE
        INTERIOR, TO HAROLD L. ICKES

WASHINGTON, *September 24, 1942*

MEMORANDUM FOR THE SECRETARY: I have made a "brief" abstract
of Mr. Muck's memorandum [1] for you:

The timber supply and mill capacity are adequate to meet the present
unprecedented demand for lumber.   However, the skilled labor, and in
some areas the unskilled labor, available to convert standing timber into
logs and lumber is inadequate.

The national lumber requirements for the year 1942 have been estimated by the war agencies at about 29 billion feet B. M.   This is about
10 percent above last year's lumber consumption.

Lumber production is currently running about 8 percent below last
year, and during the second quarter of 1942 consumption exceeded production by approximately 13 percent.   Accordingly, lumber stocks at
the mill are being rapidly depleted.   Action will be needed to hold mill
and woods labor, to lift the embargo on Canadian logs, and to secure
sufficient logging machinery and parts, particularly tires, to maintain
maximum operating efficiency.

The danger of over cutting is not yet serious except with respect to
certain species of which there is a limited volume available in the United
States.   This is particularly true of spruce in the Pacific Northwest.

Canada, our major source of softwood lumber imports, has directed
the allocation of 75 percent of the production of coastal lumber mills in
the province of British Columbia to fill Canadian, United Kingdom and
British Columbia requirements.   The United States, which formerly
took 50 percent of this production, has accordingly been limited to half
that amount.

This Department has set a production goal of approximately one
billion feet B. M. of timber from the Oregon and California Revested
lands and from Indian lands for the year 1942.   During the fiscal year

[559]

1942, a total volume of 456,131,000 feet B. M. having a value of more than a million dollars was cut from the O. and C. forests. The volume of timber cut and marketed during the year 1941 was 383 million feet B. M., reflecting a production increase for the year 1942 of approximately 75 million feet B. M.

One hundred and ninety-five new timber sale contracts were completed covering the O. and C. lands during the fiscal year 1942, involving 482,271,000 feet B. M., for which the purchasers agreed to pay a total of $1,356,820.

The sale of timber from Indian forests was also increased during the fiscal year 1942 and the income received was substantially increased by reason of the advance in stumpage prices which occurred. It is expected that the volume depleted during this period will approximate 600 million feet B. M. and that the value received will be in the neighborhood of $2,000,000.

This increase in lumber production on Department lands has been conducted in full accordance with the Department's conservation policies and the legal requirements with respect to the application of the principles of sustained yield forest management.

As a result of action by this Department, plans have crystallized for the development of the large supply of spruce in Alaska and the opening up of State lands on the Olympic peninsula. It has been predicted that approximately 60 million feet B. M. of Alaska spruce could be made available during the year 1942. However, it appears that a volume of not over 10 million feet can be delivered from Alaska during the current year.

Based on figures now available, it has been estimated that the requirements of the United Kingdom for Sitka spruce for the period July 1, 1942, to December 31, 1942, will be approximately 12,367,000 feet B. M., and that production during this same period for the United Kingdom in the United States will be approximately 5,352,000 feet B. M. Estimates of requirements for the United States for the period July 1, 1942, to December 31, 1942, have now been placed by the War Production Board at 9,500,000 feet B. M., and potential production for that period for the United States has been estimated at 8,000,000 feet B. M.

In view of the impending serious shortage in the supply of spruce, there is every reason to believe that opinion demanding the cutting of the spruce timber in the Olympic National Park will become more and more manifest. There is no denying the fact that this timber is accessible and that it could be placed on the market in a comparatively short period of time. The question as to whether it should be developed in the interest of the war is one of national policy which in my judgment should receive your careful consideration.

The forest protecton program of the Department was greatly strengthened early in the year 1941 by reason of its connection with the Facility Security Program of the Office of Civilian Defense, and the close cooperative relationships established with the Forest Service of the Department of Agriculture and State and private protection agencies. Protection programs were effected upon the enactment of the Sixth Supplemental National Defense Appropriation Act for 1942–43 which appropriated $812,000 for the protection of forest, brush, and grass lands under the jurisdiction of this Department and $800,000 for the protection of mineral resources and facilities, including petroleum, An additional appropriation of $95,900 for the protection of forests was contained in the Interior Appropriation Act 1943, thus making a grand total of $907,900 in addition to the regular funds appropriated to the land-management agencies of the Department for protection purposes. For the first time in the history of the Department a comparatively adequate plan of protection for the resources under its jurisdiction is in effect.

ABE FORTAS

[13:OF 446:TS]

¹ Lee Muck was an assistant to Secretary Ickes. His memorandum to the latter, Sept. 18, 1942, is present.

1090   CLAUDE R. WICKARD, SECRETARY OF AGRICULTURE, TO ROOSEVELT

WASHINGTON, October 12, 1942

DEAR MR. PRESIDENT: At a recent Cabinet meeting you raised questions (1) about the relationship between the drain on our forests from cutting and other causes and forest growth, and (2) whether the amount of destructive cutting had increased.

Your reference to an adverse 4 to 1 drain-growth ratio of some years ago and a present 2 to 1 ratio applies to the larger timber—that of sawtimber size.

Actually the estimates, both of which were made by the Department, are not comparable. One among several reasons for this is the fact that the first represents the best approximation which could be made some 20 years ago from very meager data. The second is based mainly on our Nation-wide forest survey, which has now covered approximately half of our forest area.

Forest growth has not increased by any such amount as the two estimates indicate. Growth has increased from a gradual expansion in fire protection and from better practices by some forest owners. But this has largely been offset by a continuation of bad cutting practices.

Recently, with the tremendous lumber demands which have characterized World War II, destructive cutting has increased. I am appalled at the reports which are reaching me of its extent and severity. Ninety-five percent of our cutting is on private land. Probably not over 20 percent of present private land cutting is with any conscious intent to maintain forest productivity. More than at any time in the past the land is being skinned of everything big enough to make a 2 x 4 or a piece of car blocking. This is particularly true in our second growth eastern forests and on the smaller holdings.

Incidentally, the ratio of drain to growth is much higher than average in the larger high-quality saw-timber material. This is where we are now having special difficulty in meeting our requirements—for example, in spruce and birch for airplanes, Port Orford cedar for separators in storage batteries, oak for ship timbers, and Douglas fir for plywood and ship decking. In fact, we are having great difficulty in maintaining the production of lumber in general. One of the main reasons is the depletion of forest resources in many areas due to destructive cutting practices in the past.

I am convinced that we can meet war requirements for forest products without destroying the young growth upon which continuing productivity depends. Destructive cutting is not necessary to maintain output.

Destructive cutting now is going to hurt us in the post-war period in meeting civilian demands, in supplying jobs, in progress toward curing sore spots in our social and economic system caused by bad forest practices.

I believe that the whole problem of meeting war requirements and at the same time maintaining the productivity of our forests unimpaired can be met much more wisely. In the near future I want to suggest ways and means for doing this.

Respectfully,

CLAUDE R. WICKARD

[13:OF 149:TS]

1091   HAROLD D. SMITH, DIRECTOR, BUREAU OF THE BUDGET, TO
        ROOSEVELT

WASHINGTON, D. C., *Oct. 28, 1942*

MEMORANDUM FOR THE PRESIDENT: Reference is made to your memorandum of March 5, 1942, addressed to me,[1] transmitting a letter from the Secretary of the Interior dated March 2, 1942, with respect to the acquisition and preservation of the Porcupine Mountains and to the request contained in your memorandum that I talk this matter over with the Secretary of Agriculture and the Secretary of the Interior and give you a report thereon.

This office has been endeavoring for many months to get an agreement between Agriculture and Interior on this proposal and we have just received a report on the subject from the Secretary of the Interior in which he concurs in the views and recommendations of the Secretary of Agriculture as to the principal objectives and features of the legislation.

There are, however, still two points of disagreement between Agriculture and Interior, namely, first, the Department of Agriculture recommends that the bills pending on the subject be amended by substituting the Commodity Credit Corporation for the Reconstruction Finance Corporation as a source of funds with which to acquire the property, on the premise that it would be more appropriate to finance this project as an agricultural project from funds of the Commodity Credit Corporation. The Interior Department does not agree with this conclusion and points out that financing through the Reconstruction Finance Corporation would be more appropriate. This office concurs in the position taken by the Interior Department on this phase of the proposal. Second, the Department of Agriculture recommends that the legislation be amended so as to provide that determinations with respect to the area and limitations of the Porcupine Mountains National Monument, proposed to be established by the bill, be determined jointly by the Secretary of Agriculture and the Secretary of the Interior, subject to the approval of the President. Interior Department is of the opinion that such a determination should be left to that Department.

While this office is not opposing the establishment of such a Monument, it proposes to advise each Department that there would be no objection to the submission of their proposed reports to the respective Congressional committees and leave to the Congress the determination as to the conditions and limitations that should be imposed with respect to the establishment of the Monument.

As you are aware, considerable pressure is being brought about in Congressional sources for the clearance of the reports of Agriculture and Interior on this proposed legislation and unless you inform me to the contrary, I will advise the Department of Agriculture that its recommendation with respect to the amendment hereinabove referred to regarding the source of funds to be used for the acquisition of property, would not be in accord with your program, and advise each of the Departments that with this exception, there would be no objection to the submission of their respective reports to the Committee, notwithstanding the fact that there was a lack of agreement between them as to the conditions and limitations that should be observed in the establishment of the Monument.

HAROLD D. SMITH

[*Notation*:AS] OK   FDR

[13:OF 149:TS]

¹ OF 79.

1092   CLAUDE R. WICKARD, SECRETARY OF AGRICULTURE, TO ROOSEVELT

WASHINGTON, *October 29, 1942*

DEAR MR. PRESIDENT: At a recent Cabinet Meeting you asked me to prepare for your consideration a program to increase lumber production and to decrease destructive cutting practices. I forwarded my proposal under date of October 23.

At the time of your request I told you that we had been discussing such a program with WPB for several months, but had been unable to obtain definite encouragement until very recently when Don Nelson ¹ told me that WPB was going to change its attitude.

I am now convinced that WPB does not intend to approve an effective program of this nature, because I have received another letter which makes reservations, and calls for further negotiations.

I am enclosing a chronological record of our unsuccessful efforts to work out a program with WPB. . . .

Sincerely yours,

CLAUDE R. WICKARD

[13:OF 446:TS]

¹ Donald M. Nelson, Chairman of the War Production Board.

1093   [*Enclosure*]

The Proposed Forest Products Program of the Dept. of Agriculture

Progress

1942

June 5   Secretary discussed the proposal with the President and then with Donald Nelson.

June 15   The Secretary wrote to Donald Nelson suggesting that an agency in the Forest Service collaborate with WPB to stimulate production of lumber and other forest products, using Commodity Credit Corporation funds.

June 26   As a result a conference was held by representatives of WPB and Forest Service.   Nathan [1] asked for specific plan and illustrative examples of its operation.

July 7   The above requested "General Plan—Illustrative Examples," and a proposed Memo of Understanding, D of A and WPB, reviewed in conference by the WPB representatives Alexander [2] and others and Forest Service people.

July 15   Six copies of revised General Plan, Illustrative Examples, and proposed Memo of Understanding, WPB and Department of Agriculture, sent WPB at its request for "WPB staff consideration" prior formal consideration by Mr. Nelson and Secretary Wickard.

August 7   Further conference with WPB representatives on above material.

August 11   Further conference with WPB representatives on above material.

August 26   Secretary formally transmitted above material to Nelson for final action.

August 27   Acknowledgement received from Nelson with suggestion that additional conference be held.

Sept. 9   WPB officials Alexander and Upson [3] held the "conference" with Forest Service representatives.

Sept. 10   All the above material revised slightly in accordance with conference agreements of September 9, sent WPB for final action.

Sept. 23   Secretary Wickard wrote Mr. Nelson again asking if any way in which he might help expedite action on proposed Forest Products Program.

Oct. 8   At Cabinet meeting, Nelson speaking to the Secretary, deplored delay in acting on the proposal.

Oct. 22   Reply from WPB (Nelson).   Agreed "it would be desirable to have CCC in a position to finance"—small sawmills, etc. However, the proposal "should be modified" (concerning points on which full agreement reached with WPB representatives previously, i. e., non-"interference" with Central Procurement and non-"interference" with WPB).   Nelson's Assistants—Alexander and Upson—directed to be "available to your staff to consummate such an arrangement." [4]

[13:OF 446:T]

[1] Robert R. Nathan, chairman of the Planning Committee of the War Production Board.
[2] Ben Alexander, an assistant to Nelson, was president of Masonite Corporation.
[3] Arthur T. Upson, chief of the Lumber and Lumber Products Branch of the WPB Bureau of Industry.
[4] An attached memorandum, Roosevelt to Rosenman, Nov. 2, 1942, reads: "Can you get at the bottom of this and try to work it out?"

1094   ROOSEVELT TO FREDERIC A. DELANO, CHAIRMAN, NATIONAL
        RESOURCES PLANNING BOARD

[WASHINGTON] *November 6, 1942*

DEAR UNCLE FRED: Ever so many thanks for that mighty interesting report about the Arkansas Valley. I most certainly want to send it to Congress as a suggestion for a large post-war planned operation.[1]

Affectionately,

[FRANKLIN D. ROOSEVELT]

[13:OF 1092:CT]

[1] National Resources Planning Board, *Regional Planning, Part XII, Arkansas Valley, Preliminary Report* (October, 1942), sent by Delano with a letter of Nov. 4, 1942 (OF 1092). In this letter Delano referred to a talk by Roosevelt to the board, "soon after the T. V. A. got going," on the possibilities of the development of the Arkansas Valley.

1095   ROOSEVELT TO GOVERNOR ARTHUR B. LANGLIE, Olympia,
        Washington

[WASHINGTON] *November 20, 1942*

DEAR GOVERNOR: I am very happy to have the report on forestry by your Forest Advisory Committee.[1]

I do hope that while we are in the war we can prevent unnecessary waste and, if the war ends while I am still here, I hope to call a conference of the State Executives on the whole subject of commercial forestry, including commercially using forests on State or Federal forest lands.

It has long been my thought that we are confronted with two problems. First, year by year we are cutting more lumber in the United States than the annual growth. Therefore, with each succeeding year, lumber becomes scarcer. Second, we are coming into an era when lumber will be used more and more as a fiber with which to make composition materials of all kinds. That means a greater demand. We have not solved that problem yet, by a long way.

Very sincerely yours,

[FRANKLIN D. ROOSEVELT]

FDR/TMB

[13:OF 149:CT]

[1] *Let's Keep Washington Forests Growing* (Forest Advisory Committee: Olympia, 1942).

WASHINGTON, *Dec. 21, 1942*

MY DEAR MR. PRESIDENT: On September 29, I submitted to you two
memoranda on the lumber situation generally and airplane spruce conditions in particular. Since that time, this Department has given consideration to the availability of and the need for cutting Sitka spruce on
lands under our jurisdiction in western Washington.

The lands in question, known as the Queets Corridor and the Ocean
Strip, were acquired with a view to ultimate incorporation in the Olympic
National Park pursuant to Executive Order No. 6343 of October 18,
1933, under the National Industrial Recovery Act. They have not
yet been given a national park status. I am advised that with your approval timber may be sold from such lands (Act of June 16, 1933, 48
Stat. 195, 202, Title II, sec. 203).

There is no doubt that there is an acute shortage of logs for the
manufacture of airplane stock in the Grays Harbor and Puget Sound
areas. A substantial amount of Sitka spruce that could be removed
without serious impairment of scenic and recreational values, is available within the Queets Corridor area. This Department has been
zealously devoted to the maintenance of primitive conditions in national park and monument areas, but the critical shortage of timber for
airplane production for war purposes compels me to suggest a temporary deviation from that policy.

I accordingly request that you authorize me to sell, for war purposes,
spruce and Douglas fir timber on the Queets Corridor and Ocean Strip
lands in accordance with the principles of selective logging.

Sincerely yours,

[HAROLD L. ICKES]

THE WHITE HOUSE, December 24, 1942.
APPROVED:

[13:OF 446:CT]

1097   HAROLD L. ICKES, SECRETARY OF THE INTERIOR, TO
ROOSEVELT

WASHINGTON, *January 16, 1943*

MY DEAR MR. PRESIDENT: I enclose a memorandum with respect
to your desire to set up the proposed Porcupine Mountains National
Monument in Michigan. We, of course, are willing to introduce legislation but you will note that even if such a bill should pass, it would not
include some of the area. Director Drury makes the suggestion to me
that I may wish to confer with General Knudsen [1] to ascertain whether

the General Motors Corporation would be willing to donate certain lands. I know General Knudsen so slightly that I have no reason to believe that anything that I might say would be influential. Moreover, I wonder whether he could speak now for General Motors. I suspect that you could designate someone else to do it with a better chance of results, unless, of course, you feel like doing it yourself.

Considering the fact that Senator Brown and Congressman Hook were both defeated in November, I shall await instructions from you before proceeding further.[2]

Sincerely yours,

HAROLD L. ICKES

[13:OF 149:TS]

[1] William S. Knudsen (1879–1948), former president of General Motors Corporation, was at this time director of production for the War Department on the War Production Board.

[2] Senator Prentiss M. Brown and Rep. Frank E. Hook of Michigan, sponsors of the Hook-Brown bill, mentioned in the enclosure.

1098   [*Enclosure*] NEWTON B. DRURY, DIRECTOR, NATIONAL PARK SERVICE, TO HAROLD L. ICKES

CHICAGO, *January 8, 1943*

MEMORANDUM FOR THE SECRETARY: This is to call to your attention the status of the proposed Porcupine Mountains National Monument, Michigan, which the President approved in principle when you submitted to him the letter of January 14, 1942 from Mr. Irving Brant [1] (copies attached).

On June 1, 1942 (copies attached) the President requested the Department of Agriculture and the Department of the Interior "to get together" on the acquisition of the area. This, you will recall was done through field conferences and by agreeing upon a suggested amendment of the Hook-Brown bill, which amendment would have authorized the establishment of a national monument comprising 45,000 acres.

The Department of Agriculture, however, did not submit a final report upon the bill because that Department wanted the purchase program to be financed by the Commodity Credit Corporation, whereas the Bureau of the Budget wanted the program financed by the Reconstruction Finance Corporation, as originally written in the bill.

Due to the defeat of Senator Brown and Congressman Hook, and drawing my inference from informal conferences with representatives of the Department of Agriculture, I believe it is doubtful that the so-called Hook-Brown bill will be reintroduced in the present session of Congress. The forest is being logged so rapidly that there is little hope of saving anything unless we act in the near future. One of the suggestions in

Mr. Brant's letter was that General Motors Corporation might be interested in donating its lands within the proposed monument area (see attached map).[2]   General Motors holdings do not include all the land that would be necessary for the proposed monument, but the Corporation owns an important part of the remaining virgin forest.   The donation of these lands might pave the way for obtaining additional lands either by donation or through an appropriation by Congress.

It is suggested that you may wish to confer with Mr. Knudsen to ascertain whether General Motors Corporation would be willing to donate the lands.

There is attached a copy of *Planning and Civic Comment* for July, 1942, on pages 30–33 of which there are pictures of the Porcupine Mountains forest.[3]

NEWTON B. DRURY

[13:OF 149:TS]

[1] *Ante,* 1077.
[2] Present, as is the publication mentioned below.
[3] No action was taken by the Federal Government but in 1944 Michigan established the Porcupine Mountains State Park in the area.   This comprises about 50,000 acres.

1099   ROOSEVELT TO FREDERIC A. DELANO, CHAIRMAN, NATIONAL
RESOURCES PLANNING BOARD

[WASHINGTON] *February 22, 1943*

DEAR UNCLE FRED: I am much upset over the Congressional attitude toward the National Resources Planning Board.   The need for such studying and planning as your Board is doing is so obvious that I am very hopeful that the Senate will restore the appropriation.

I know that you and your staff can and will present a strong argument to the Senate Appropriations Committee for the full amount of $1,400,000 as requested for the Board in the Budget estimates.

Congressman Cannon's reply to my letter to him of February sixteenth is attached for your information.[1]

Very sincerely yours,

[FRANKLIN D. ROOSEVELT]

MHM/J

[13:OF 1092:CT]

[1](Drafted by McIntyre.)   The Budget Bureau estimate for the National Resources Planning Board was dropped from the 1944 Independent Offices Appropriation Bill (H. R. 1762) by the House Appropriations Committee, of which Cannon (Mo.) was chairman.   Roosevelt's letter to Cannon of February 16 was a request that the item be restored (OF 1092).   Cannon replied Feb. 19, 1943 (OF 1092), that he thought it better strategy to try to get the appropriation restored in the Senate since the House committee was hostile.   In the meantime, on February 17, an attempt was

made in the House to secure favorable action. Representative Magnuson (Wash.) proposed an amendment to appropriate $415,000 for a "National Resources Planning Council" but a point of order made by Dirksen (Ill.) that there was no legal authorization for such an appropriation was upheld (*Cong. Rec.,* 78th Cong., 1st sess., 89: 1, 1072). Roosevelt again requested an NRPB appropriation in identical letters to Representative Cannon and to Senator Glass, chairman of the Senate Appropriations Committee, both dated March 24, 1943 (OF 1092). The Senate, on May 27, 1943, approved an appropriation of $200,000, following a lengthy debate in which Taft (Ohio), Tydings (Md.) and Byrd (Va.) attacked the NRPB and its predecessors as being unauthorized, useless and dangerous. The House refused to accept the Senate action, however, and the Independent Offices Act as approved June 26, 1943, provided for the abolition of the National Resources Planning Board as of Aug. 31, 1943 (*Cong. Rec.,* 89: 4, 4942–4966; 89: 5, 6044–6045; 57 *Stat.* 169).

1100   HAROLD L. ICKES, SECRETARY OF THE INTERIOR, TO EDWIN M. WATSON, SECRETARY TO THE PRESIDENT

WASHINGTON, *February 27, 1943*

DEAR "PA": This is what I was telephoning to you about yesterday:

For some fifteen years John D. Rockefeller, Jr., has been offering to give, without cost, approximately 32,000 acres of land to the Government. This land will not cost the Government a cent. No strings are attached to the offer except that the land be used either as a park or a national monument. It is intended that the land should be included in the Teton Mountains National Park, or be set up with adjoining United States forestry land as a national monument.

This land has cost Mr. Rockefeller about $1,500,000. He has been paying taxes on it of $11,000 a year while waiting for the Government to say either "yes" or "no" to his offer. He is now almost 70 years old, and, with the heavy additional taxes that he will be called upon to pay, he wants to get his affairs in order. Before Christmas he wrote to me, and the day before Christmas itself, he called on me to explain that he could not continue to offer this land to the Government later than February 28, next. I promised to take it up with the President, having in mind suggesing to the President the setting up of a national monument, which can be done under the law.

There should be no publicity on this. My own view is that the President ought to set up a national monument before we lose an offer that will never be made again. We need this land, not only to round out our park holdings in the Grand Teton area, including Jackson Lake, but also because much of this land would afford winter feed for elk and deer, thousands of which are without sufficient forage during the winter.

Naturally, I am anxious to move. We have the Executive Order all drawn and it has been submitted to Director Smith of the Budget. I have Director Smith's authority to say that he is in favor of setting up

this monument and doing it now.   I hope for an early appointment with
the President on this matter.[1]

Sincerely yours,

[HAROLD L. ICKES]

[13:OF 6–P:CT:PHOTOSTAT]

[1] Ickes had lunch with the President on March 12; the proclamation creating the
Jackson Hole National Monument (No. 2578) was issued March 15, 1943. Rockefeller wrote to Roosevelt on March 17, 1943 (OF 6–P), that in establishing the
monument he had "made possible the preservation for all time of the most uniquely
beautiful and dramatic of all the areas set aside for national park purposes."

1101   ROOSEVELT TO GOVERNOR ARTHUR B. LANGLIE, Olympia,
        Washington

WASHINGTON, *March 15, 1943*

MY DEAR GOVERNOR LANGLIE: I am prepared to issue a proclamation adding to the Olympic National Park, approximately 20,600 acres
of the area known as the Morse Creek Watershed, which is within the
boundaries of the Olympic National Forest.   A copy of the proclamation is enclosed.

Section 5 of the act establishing Olympic National Park, approved
June 29, 1938 (52 *Stat.* 1241, 1242, 16 *U. S. C.* sec. 255), provides
that "before issuing any such proclamation, the President shall consult
with the Governor of the State of Washington, the Secretary of the Interior and the Secretary of Agriculture and advise them of the lands
which he proposes to add to such park, and shall afford them a reasonable opportunity to consult with and communicate to him their views
with respect to the addition of such lands to such park."

The proposed addition is desirable to simplify administration of the
park, and to place a scenic area under the most suitable land classification.   Permanent protection of the forest in this watershed is essential
to the water supply for the City of Port Angeles.

Regional Director Tomlinson of the National Park Service and
Superintendent Macy of Olympic National Park have maps showing in detail the land involved, and will be glad to confer with you at
your convenience, if you so desire.

I shall be pleased to have you communicate your views to me concerning this proposed extension.[1]

Sincerely yours,

[FRANKLIN D. ROOSEVELT]

[13:OF 6–P:CT]

[1] (Drafted by the Interior Department.)   The addition included the greater part
of Mount Angeles on the northern boundary of the park and a lake of the same
name.   It also gave the National Park Service control over the route from Port

[571]

Angeles to the park. Governor Langlie replied March 25, 1943 (OF 6–P), offering no objection to the proposed enlargement. This was effected by Proclamation 2587, issued May 29, 1943.

1102   HAROLD L. ICKES, SECRETARY OF THE INTERIOR, TO ROOSEVELT

WASHINGTON, *March 29, 1943*

MEMORANDUM FOR THE PRESIDENT: I have your memorandum of March 13 requesting my consideration of the letter of March 2 from Mr. Irving Brant concerning the Olympic National Park situation with special reference to the relationship of the Park timber to the war program.[1]

Mr. Brant has offered the following suggestions:

1. That action be expedited looking to the incorporation of the Morse Creek Watershed in the Olympic National Park.

2. That you direct a memorandum to me requesting that timber cutting in the Park be not approved until after consultation with you.

3. That lumber production for military purposes be put on the same basis as other critical materials without regard to the cost of production.

4. That consideration be given to the effect of the Canadian embargo on the export of logs to the United States.

An Executive Order providing for the transfer of the Morse Creek Watershed from the Olympic National Forest to the Olympic National Park is now in process.

With respect to the second suggestion, it is my judgment that the proposed memorandum to me is unnecessary since the development of the resources within the Park proper is specifically prohibited by the Act of August 25, 1916 (39 *Stat.* 535)[2] and could not be authorized without legislation or action by you under authority of the War Powers of the President.

The suggestion that the development of timber for war purposes be authorized without regard to the cost of production has been met in part by the War Production Board in cooperation with the Public Roads Administration, and machinery has been established providing for the construction of access roads to inaccessible tracts of timber as well as to undeveloped mineral deposits. I doubt if anything further can be done in this direction unless the Federal Government goes into the logging business in the States as it has done in Alaska—a policy which I would hesitate to advocate at this time in view of the existing shortage of men and equipment in the lumber industry.

Mr. Brant's fourth proposal concerning the Canadian embargo on the exportation of high-grade logs to the United States is deserving of most careful consideration. British Columbia has very extensive resources and, until within the past two years, large volumes of logs have been exported to the mills in the State of Washington. In like manner British Columbia mills have drawn upon Washington log supplies and this interchange of materials between the two countries has operated to stabilize industry and employment. However, the placing of an embargo upon the exportation of logs from British Columbia has disrupted the interchange of logs and seriously upset conditions in the lumber industry in the Pacific Northwest.

In a letter dated September 1, 1942, from the Under Secretary of War to the Secretary of State, it was suggested that steps be taken by the Department of State to prevail upon the Canadian authorities to remove the log export embargo in effect in order that critical war demands might be met. I am not informed as to what steps were taken by the State Department but I am advised that the log embargo is still in effect with respect to the exportation of high-grade spruce and fir logs.

Under date of October 7, 1942, the War Production Board called a meeting on this question at which the Canadian Timber Controller was present. The Controller took the position that the Canadian industry could not spare any of its logs for export to the United States. This position was challenged by the War Department's representative who submitted for the record a memorandum dated October 6, 1942, over the signature of Colonel Clifford V. Morgan, Chief of the Materials Branch.[3] A copy of this memorandum is attached.

A consideration of the facts set forth in the War Department's memorandum has convinced me that it would be inadvisable to initiate action which would authorize the cutting of timber in the Olympic National Park until this Canadian embargo question is disposed of and until every other source of aircraft timber supply has been exhausted.

The Department fully recognizes the unfavorable balance which exists between the supply of and demand for aircraft lumber and is keeping in constant touch with developments. The situation is such that it may ultimately be advisable to make some of the spruce timber in the Olympic National Park available in the interest of victory. If such proves to be the case, I will submit proper recommendations to you for consideration.

Mr. Brant's letter is returned herewith.

HAROLD L. ICKES

[13:OF 6–P:TS]

[1] Roosevelt's memorandum, covering Brant's letter (OF 6–P), reads, "Will you be good enough to send me a memorandum on this?" Brant called attention to the fact that the Queets corridor, technically not in the park, had been opened to lumbering but that only one bid had been made for the lumber. Nearby state-owned timber drew no bids at all, "except for one tract." Brant said that this showed the speciousness of the argument that park timber was needed for war purposes.

[2] The act establishing the National Park Service.

[3] Of the Services of Supply. The memorandum is present.

WASHINGTON, *April 10, 1943*

MEMORANDUM FOR THE SECRETARY OF THE INTERIOR: Are we doing anything about this Calaveras Sequoia Grove?   If not, can we? [1]

F.D.R.

[13:OF 149:T]

[1] With this memorandum is a pamphlet, *Protect the South Calaveras Sequoia Grove,* by Irving Brant, published by the Emergency Conservation Committee, 734 Lexington Ave., New York (undated); see Ickes' rely, below.

1104   HAROLD L. ICKES, SECRETARY OF THE INTERIOR, TO
        ROOSEVELT

WASHINGTON, *Apr. 30, 1943*

MY DEAR MR. PRESIDENT: The Calaveras groves of Sequoia gigantea, referred to in your memorandum of April 10, should be preserved. The North Grove has been acquired by the State of California and the South Grove is included in the State's park program.

The Director of the National Park Service spent much time over a period of some 20 years in helping to work out the Calaveras project.[1] The attached map shows the present status of the two groves.   The North Grove State Park embraces 1,951 acres.   It cost $275,000, of which the State provided one-half.   The South Grove contains an area of 1,500 acres and can be acquired at an estimated cost of $250,000. The acquisition of this area is included in the present program of the California State Park Commission.

It is my judgment that these two groves should be a part of the California State Park System, since representative stands of Sequoia gigantea are already a part of the national park system.   There are two courses which might be pursued, namely, (1) to encourage the State of California to acquire the lands, and (2) to amend existing legislation (45 *Stat.* 428) which provides for the transfer of certain forest lands to the State of California for park purposes; thus making it possible for the Federal Government to acquire the South Grove by exchange or purchase for transfer to the State when it is prepared to reimburse the Federal Government for the property.

The National Park Service is very much interested in this project and Director Drury expects to confer with the State Park Commissioners thereon in the near future.   While the acquisition of the lands by the Federal Government would be a Forest Service undertaking, the National Park Service is in a position to assist in working out the details of the proposal.[2]

Sincerely yours,

HAROLD L. ICKES

[13:OF 149:TS]

[1] Before his appointment as National Park Service director in 1940, Drury was secretary of the Save-the-Redwoods League and executive secretary of the California State Park Commission.

[2] A copy of Ickes' letter was sent by Roosevelt by Brant (May 10, 1943, OF 149), with the hope that he would "take it up further with the Secretary." California acquired South Grove in 1954 through the efforts of many people and organizations, including the Save-the-Redwoods League and John D. Rockefeller, Jr., who gave $1,000,000 towards purchase of the forest. With an area deeded by the Federal Government in 1952 the state park now forms a preserve of over 5,000 acres.

1105   "STATEMENT MADE BY THE PRESIDENT UPON SIGNING S. 649, TO CONSENT TO THE REPUBLICAN RIVER COMPACT"

WASHINGTON, *May 26, 1943*

I am signing the Republican River Compact bill because I believe it offers a sound solution to problems of water allocation and utilization on that stream. The procedure prescribed by the bill for the exercise of the powers of the Federal Government would not be entirely satisfactory in all circumstances but the prospects in fact for the exercise of such powers in the Republican basin are not great. For streams where conditions are otherwise and there appears to be a possible need for Federal comprehensive multiple purpose development or where opportunities for important electric power projects are present, I believe the Republican River Compact should not serve as a precedent. In such cases the compact and the legislation should more adequately reflect a recognition of the responsibilities and prerogatives of the Federal Government.[1]

FRANKLIN D. ROOSEVELT

[13:OF 635:TS]

[1] The compact between Colorado, Kansas and Nebraska authorized by this bill (approved May 26, 1943) was intended to provide for the most efficient use and equitable distribution of the waters of the Republican River basin, and "to promote joint action by the States and the United States in the efficient use of water and the control of destructive floods" (57 *Stat.* 86). A similar act passed the preceding year had been vetoed because it sought to withdraw Federal jurisdiction from the waters of the basin (Budget Director Smith to McIntyre, March 31, 1942, Budget Bureau Enrolled Bills; *Cong. Rec.*, 77th Cong., 2d sess., 88: 3285–3286).

1106   ROOSEVELT TO MARVIN H. McINTYRE, SECRETARY TO THE
        PRESIDENT

WASHINGTON, *June 10, 1943*

MEMORANDUM FOR MAC: Will you ask Mr. E. I. Kotok to let us have
a report on this? Will you tell him I am adverse to opening up the
Skagit to any lumbering? [1]

F. D. R.

[*Notation*:A] MHM did do   6/10/43

[13:OF 446:T]

[1] This refers to a letter from Roy S. Leonard to McIntyre, June 7, 1943 (OF 466),
saying that the Forest Service proposed to permit the lumbering of the Skagit River
area. Leonard was a Seattle public utilities man working in Washington for the
War Production Board; Kotok was assistant chief of the Forest Service. See below.

1107   LYLE F. WATTS, CHIEF, FOREST SERVICE, TO ROOSEVELT

WASHINGTON, *June 18, 1943*

SUBJECT: PROPOSED NATIONAL FOREST TIMBER SALE SOUTHWEST
OF NEWHALEM, WASHINGTON, IN THE DRAINAGE OF THE SKAGIT RIVER:
Action on this proposed sale has been suspended pending decision by
you. The facts are:

1. The timber is urgently needed in the war effort. Of the estimated total of about 30 million board feet of logs to be cut, 24 million
will be Douglas fir. An unusually large proportion will be high-grade
logs suitable for conversion into veneers, pontoon lumber, ship decking,
long ship timbers, airplane lumber and other urgently needed materials.
Such areas are now scarce in the Puget Sound territory. The western
log and lumber administrator of WPB has emphasized the need for the
logs from this sale in meeting present deficiencies in production.

2. The logs can be put on railroad cars at Newhalem with an unusually short truck haul, and therefore with relatively small consumption of
strategic materials such as rubber and steel.

3. The sale area does not include any area used by tourists or recrea-
tionists based on the City of Seattle development at or above Newhalem.

4. Plans for the sale have been approved by Mr. Hoffman, Superintendent of the Seattle City Light Department, and by Mr. Kemoe, in
charge of the City Light Skagit Tours.

5. The sale area is chiefly in the drainage of Newhalem Creek which
enters the Skagit River from the south below Newhalem. This part
of the area is not visible from the road or the railroad which follow the
north side of the Skagit to Newhalem.

6. All that part of the sale area in the Skagit River bottom is across the river from the road and railroad. All of it and all of the area in Newhalem Creek suitable for that treatment is to be logged selectively, leaving virtually an unbroken crown cover. A light cut is to be made of about 30 percent of the stand volume in the largest and most mature trees.

7. The applicant (the North Bend Timber Company) has a trained, efficient crew, consisting in large part of local residents. It is just finishing cutting on another nearby area. If this crew is disbanded, the assembly and training of a new crew will be almost impossible under current conditions of shortage of skilled logging labor in the Northwest. The applicant Company has no other area of good quality timber in which to continue its operations.

I earnestly recommend that the suspension of action on the making of this sale be lifted, with the full understanding that the Forest Service has definite responsibility for so administering the sale as to protect the scenic and recreational values of the vicinity.

Very early action is essential if the continuous output of urgently needed high-grade logs by the applicant Company is not to be disrupted.

No sales in the Skagit River drainage above Newhalem are even under consideration.[1]

LYLE F. WATTS

[13:OF 446:TS]

[1] In an accompanying memorandum to Roosevelt of June 19, 1943, McIntyre summarized Watts' memorandum and said: "I am sending it up instead of holding it because Mr. Watts points out that it is a matter in which a speedy decision should be made." See below.

1108   ROOSEVELT TO MARVIN H. McINTYRE, SECRETARY TO THE PRESIDENT

WASHINGTON, *June 24, 1943*

MEMORANDUM FOR MAC: Will you tell the Chief Forester to let it proceed? [1]

F. D. R.

[*Notation*:A] MHM did do 6/24/43
[13:OF 446:T]

[1] This refers to the preceding memorandum.

WASHINGTON, *July 21, 1943*

MY DEAR MR. PRESIDENT: Irving Brant, who knows more about the
lumber situation in Olympic National Park than anyone in my acquaint-
ance, has written me a letter that I am sure will interest you.

Sincerely yours,

HAROLD L. ICKES

[13:OF 6–P:TS]

1110   [*Enclosure*] IRVING BRANT TO HAROLD L. ICKES

CHICAGO, ILLINOIS, *July 7, 1943*

DEAR MR. SECRETARY: Newton Drury has shown me his proposed
report on Sitka spruce in the Olympic National Park.   While I understand from him that they outline concessions to which he is opposed, but
which he fears may become necessary later, I can't help feeling that this
is a time for an "offensive defensive" rather than the charting of a line
of retreat.   Also, I feel that the matter involves some new dangers to the
entire park and monument system.

The only reason assigned for opening the park to lumbering is a shortage of manpower in the lumber camps.   It is therefore argued that
available lumberjacks should be used in the timber easiest of access,
which is said to be in the park.   There is no actual shortage of timber
outside, and a call for bids for some state-owned timber actually produced not one bidder.

Why is there a shortage of lumberjacks?   Because they have been
lured into shipyards and airplane factories by higher wages, or have been
drafted.   The argument for opening the national park to lumbering
therefore comes down to this: That all future generations, as well as we
ourselves, should be deprived of the scenic and recreational and scientific
value of these big trees and rain forests, because we haven't sense enough
to send a few hundred men back into the work for which they are trained.
That's about as monstrous a failure of democracy as I ever heard of.

You and I both know, of course, that the real drive behind this call
for lumbering is the desire of timber interests at Gray's Harbor and
elsewhere to exploit and despoil; also that the lumber decisions of the
War Production Board are being made by people who have never been
sympathetic toward the park.   . . . Neither the War Department nor
the Manpower Commission, left to itself, will lift a finger to send lumberjacks back into the woods, for the purpose of saving this park from ruin.

They will act only if the President orders them to, and probably only if he issues the orders two or three times. I don't see how he can refrain from acting if he understands that the cutting is absolutely needless, and that the area threatened with destruction is the portion of the park which he has always been most anxious to preserve—the Hoh, Bogachiel and Queets River Valleys. The unhappy results of the cutting in the Queets corridor is enough to show what the devastation will be, even under the most carefully supervised cutting.

I note what Mr. Drury says about eliminating these river valleys from the park if they are to be lumbered, and agree with him in theory but would go somewhat farther than he did (in conversation) in pointing to the danger found in any method of elimination. He is unquestionably right in saying that Congress should not be asked to make an elimination—that would set all the hounds of the Northwest converging on Washington. I think it would be a great misfortune to have even a legal ruling that the President has power to make such an elimination by proclamation. Based, as it apparently would be, on a distinction between the status of land placed in a park by Congress, and by the President under authority derived from Congress, it would not be limited to war power (which would be equal in relation to both classes of land), but would unsettle all the national monuments in the country. The Wallgren Bill [1] was worded so that it would not give sanction to the action of President Wilson in cutting down the Mt. Olympus National Monument during the first World War. It would be far better, in my opinion, to leave a despoiled area in the park than to open other areas to despoliation by the influence of pressure groups upon future Presidents.

But it will be a crime and a dereliction if a manpower shortage which can be remedied by one positive order is allowed to ruin these last scenic forests of the Northwest. It is not a case of putting these forests ahead of the lives of soldiers. If any soldiers die because of a shortage of lumber, the fault will lie upon those who drafted the lumberjacks out of the woods, or allowed them to shift to higher paid war jobs which could be done by men and women without their training. [2]

Sincerely yours,

IRVING BRANT

[13:OF 6–P:TS:PHOTOSTAT]

[1] The Olympic National Park Act of 1938.

[2] Roosevelt sent Brant's letter to Forest Service Chief Watts with a memorandum of July 23, 1943 (OF 6–P), reading, "For your information and please return for my files." Watts returned the letter with thanks for having had the opportunity to see it (Watts to Roosevelt, July 24, 1943, OF 6–P).

IIII   ROOSEVELT TO FREDERIC A. DELANO, Newburgh, New York

[WASHINGTON] *August 31, 1943*

DEAR UNCLE FRED: Congress may have abolished the National Resources Planning Board, but it can't stop the good work of planning
to which you have given so many years of hard work. By the way your
report on the "Unfinished Business of Planning" reads, it looks as if you
had really succeeded in making planning popular in business and in
states and cities.[1]   The work of the Board may not have pleased some
members of Congress, but it certainly seems to have convinced the country of the need for a lot more planning.

I am writing to your colleagues today to give them a personal word
of thanks for all they have done, but the principal thanks go to you as the
Chairman and responsible leader of the organization and movement.[2]
I hope you feel the satisfaction in what you have accomplished which
the work so obviously justifies.   It has been a grand job and grand fun
in the doing.[3]

Very sincerely yours,

[FRANKLIN D. ROOSEVELT]

WDH–MMS
[13:OF 1092:CT]

[1] This report is a typed memorandum, dated Aug. 24, 1943, enclosed with a letter
of the same date to Roosevelt from the National Resources Planning Board (OF
1092).   Only one paragraph of the ten-page report dealt with land, water and
energy resources; this noted that planning in connection with such resources could
be continued through interdepartmental committees but that these had not been
"uniformly or conspicuously successful for a variety of reasons, including the clash
of overlapping operating agencies."
[2] Copies of Roosevelt's letters to the other two members of the NRPB, George F.
Yantis and Charles E. Merriam, Aug. 31, 1943, are with the letter here printed.
[3] Drafted by William D. Hassett, Secretary to the President.

III2   ROOSEVELT TO CLAUDE R. WICKARD, SECRETARY OF AGRI-
        CULTURE

WASHINGTON, *September 8, 1943*

MEMORANDUM FOR THE SECRETARY OF AGRICULTURE: I am glad to
have your excellent report about the Farm Woodland Marketing Program.[1]   The real outcome of this, which is primarily a war measure,
should be to have attached to every county agent a forester—or perhaps
one forester to several counties.   This depends, of course, on the locality.

The point is that the average county farm agent knows nothing about
trees and it is too much to expect that county farm agents will ever add
this to their curriculum.   Such a local forest agent would not only give
advice in regard to planting trees and selling trees, but would also have a
big effect in the State Legislatures for the building up of state tree
nurseries.

[580]

We need state tree nurseries. For example, in a certain state I can
buy small tulip poplars for $4.00 a thousand from the state nursery, and
the best price I can get is $12.00 a thousand from a private nursery.

F. D. R.

[13:OF 1–C:CT]

[1] This report is a letter from Wickard to Roosevelt, Sept. 4, 1943 (OF 1–C),
enclosing copies of letters and reports of woodlot owners. With funds formerly used
for the Shelterbelt program, the Forest Service was providing a farm forestry service
"on a basis of getting for the seller a fair price for his product and for the buyer an
additional source of raw material to be harvested under good cutting practices."

1113   TOAST BY THE PRESIDENT TO KING ABDUL AZIZ IBN SAUD OF
SAUDI ARABIA, September 30, 1943

[*Excerpt*] I was telling His Royal Highness,[1] at supper, that I knew
that one of their problems in Arabia was an insufficiency of water in
many places, and also of not enough trees. And I was telling him of
what we in our younger years used to call the Great American Desert, a
strip running from the North in our own country, to the South where
there was very little water, and where there were very few trees.

I was telling him that some years ago we had undertaken a certain
project known as Shelter Belt, but since the outbreak of the war it has
been going only sporadically, yet the people out there have seen what it
has already done in many parts of the West. And I might just as well
tell the Congress of the United States now that I am going to revive it,
if I live long enough. It's a very excellent thing. Something like that
should be known and experimented with, and practised at, in many
parts of the world.

I use that just as an illustration, because Arabia is a land of great resources—agricultural and surface resources, and sub-surface resources.
And I want to assure their Royal Highnesses both, that the United States
is not a nation which seeks to exploit any other nation, no matter what
its size.

I wish much that the father of these gentlemen could come himself. I
hope some day he will be able to come over here, just as I hope that some
day I myself can go and visit him in Arabia. . . .

And so I should like to propose the health of the King of Arabia, wishing much that he could be with us tonight.[2]

[SPEECH FILE:T]

[1] Amir Feisal, son of Ibn Saud; Ibn Saud was not present. The occasion was a
White House dinner in honor of Amir Feisal, Minister of Foreign Affairs of Saudi
Arabia.
[2] For the entire toast, see Rosenman (ed), *Public Papers*, XII, 417–418.

WASHINGTON, *January 14, 1944*

My DEAR SENATOR McCLELLAN: I am very much interested in your bill, S. 1519, relating to the construction and operation of water control and utilization projects in the basins of the Arkansas and White Rivers.[1] Enactment of the bill would be an important forward step in effectuation of the policy of multiple purpose development of our great river basins and the prudent conservation of our vast public resources.

I feel certain that the people whose homes are in the basins of the Arkansas and White Rivers and the soldiers who will want to return to the area and to work and make homes there would be deeply grateful if the Congress were to pass S. 1519. The benefits that they would derive from a well coordinated program for the prevention and control of floods, the improvement of navigation, the disposition of low-cost electric power and the irrigation of fertile lands would be of incalculable value. I am particularly pleased that the direct and more tangible benefits from power and irrigation would be made available in accordance with the sound principles of public benefit that the Congress has previously laid down.[2]

Sincerely yours,

[FRANKLIN D. ROOSEVELT]

[13:OF 4283:CT]

[1] S. 1519 would have placed the construction and operation of navigation and flood control projects in the Arkansas and White River basins under the Secretary of War. Power not needed for operation of the projects would be sold and distributed by the Secretary of the Interior, who would also be permitted to construct and operate irrigation works in connection with such projects. The letter here printed was drafted by Ickes. In his covering letter to Roosevelt (Dec. 6, 1943, OF 4283), Ickes said that the bill was "designed primarily to implement the carrying out of water control and utilization programs in the basins through existing executive departments and agencies, as distinguished from special agencies or authorities." He also said that while he realized that the bill was not as comprehensive in setting a pattern of regional development "as you and I would prefer," he believed its enactment would be an important step forward. S. 1519 (a copy is with Ickes' letter to Roosevelt) was introduced Nov. 9, 1943, and referred to the Senate Committee on Commerce, but no further action on it was taken (*Cong. Rec.*, 78th Cong., 1st sess., 89: 7, 9393–9394).

[2] McClellan replied Jan. 22, 1944 (OF 4283), inviting further help in getting the legislation he had introduced.

1115   ROOSEVELT TO STEPHEN T. EARLY, SECRETARY TO THE PRESIDENT

WASHINGTON, *January 31, 1944*

MEMORANDUM FOR STEVE: Do you think I should see Bennett and tell him that I think what he is doing is all to the good but not send him any written communication?   I do want to tell him about some ideas I have anyway, outside of this.

F. D. R.

[*Notation*: AS] The President: Respectfully suggest that Pa make the appointment for purposes outlined above.   S. E.[1]

[13: OF 1–R: T]

---

[1] Morris Cooke had suggested that Roosevelt write to Hugh H. Bennett, chief of the Soil Conservation Service, to congratulate him on the great progress he had made in securing the cooperation of farmers in adopting contour plowing and other soil conservation practices (undated draft by Cooke, OF 1–R). According to a notation on the draft, no letter was sent nor was an appointment arranged. ("Pa" was Presidential Secretary Edwin M. Watson.)

1116   ROOSEVELT TO REPRESENTATIVE WILLIAM M. WHITTINGTON OF MISSISSIPPI, CHAIRMAN, HOUSE COMMITTEE ON FLOOD CONTROL

WASHINGTON, February 7, 1944

MY DEAR MR. WHITTINGTON: Over two years ago, on May 5, 1941, I wrote to you about the Kings River project and the Kern River project in California.   Your committee was then considering the authorization of both of these projects for development by the Corps of Engineers under the jurisdiction of the Secretary of War.

The Schedule of Hearings on the Flood Control Bill of 1944 indicates that proposals for authorizing these projects as undertakings of the Corps of Engineers will be considered again on February 9, 1944. I shall appreciate it if you will read this letter into the record at that time.

In my letter of May 5, 1941, I said, in part: "Good administration continues to demand that projects which are dominantly for irrigation should be constructed by the Bureau of Reclamation, Department of the Interior, and not by the Corps of Engineers, War Department. The Kings River project is authorized for construction by the Bureau of Reclamation at this time.   The proposed project on the Kern River . . . is dominantly an irrigation project. . . . Neither of these projects, therefore, should be authorized for construction by the Corps of Engineers.   To do so would only lead to needless confusion."   That letter is applicable today.

These projects should be constructed by the Bureau of Reclamation and that portion of their cost to be charged to irrigation should be financed on the basis of the prevailing Federal policy of 40 annual payments by irrigation beneficiaries.   These projects should be maintained and operated by the Bureau of Reclamation, but operation for flood control should be in accordance with regulations prescribed by the Secretary of War.

In my letter of May 5, 1941, I suggested that a sound policy in connection with these water projects would consist of selecting the construction agency by determining the dominant interest. Projects in which navigation or flood control clearly dominate are those in which the interest of the Corps of Engineers is superior and should be so recognized. On the other hand, projects in which irrigation and related conservation dominate are those in which the interest of the Bureau of Reclamation in the Department of the Interior is paramount and should be so recognized. No matter which agency builds a multiple-purpose structure involving in even a minor way the interests of the other, the agency with the responsibility for that particular interest should administer it in accordance with its authorizing legislation and general policies. For example, the Bureau of Reclamation in the Department of the Interior should administer, under the Reclamation laws and its general policies, those irrigation benefits and phases of projects built by the Corps of Engineers. These suggestions are, to my mind, even more pertinent today. For today we gird for peace. Confusion over jurisdiction ought not to be allowed to disrupt the great preparations now being made for postwar construction of vital public works.[1]

Sincerely yours,

[FRANKLIN D. ROOSEVELT]

[13:OF 402:CT]

[1](Drafted by the Interior Department.) Whittington replied Feb. 17, 1944 (OF 402), that the testimony at the hearings held by the House Flood Control Committee on Feb. 9, 1944, showed "conclusively" that flood control was the dominant interest in the Kings and Kern Rivers projects, that there were no Federal reclamation projects along these rivers, and that no public lands were involved. Testimony at these and earlier hearings of this committee is printed, *Flood-control Plans and New Projects, 1943 and 1944,* Hearings, 78th Cong., 1st sess., on H. R. 4485 . . . May 13, 1943 (Washington, 1944).

1117   ROOSEVELT TO KING ABDUL AZIZ IBN SAUD OF SAUDI ARABIA

[WASHINGTON] *February 10, 1944*

MY DEAR KING IBN SAUD: Because I have been laid up with the "flu" since the New Year I have not had an opportunity before this to thank you for that very interesting set of stamps of Saudi Arabia which you sent to me through Colorel Hoskins.[1] They have given me a great deal of pleasure and I have had much relaxation in putting them into my stamp album of Saudi Arabia.

It is my lasting regret that I was unable, because of the short time at my disposal, to see you on my trip to Cairo and to Teheran. However, I flew across the northwestern corner of your Kingdom on my way to and from Iran and I saw enough to make me wish that you and I could meet. My avocation, as you probably know, is the increase in water supply and in reforesting vacant land. I feel sure that the Kingdom of Saudi Arabia has a great future before it if more agricultural land can be provided through irrigation and through the growing of trees to hold the soil and increase the water supply.

It was good to see your two sons before I left Washington and I hope much that they were satisfied with what they saw in the United States. As they have undoubtedly told you, this Nation is in full production of munitions and other supplies for the carrying on of the war to a successful conclusion.

It is, of course, possible that I may visit the Near East again for conferences and if that happens I count on seeing you. There are many things I want to talk with you about.[2]

In the meantime, I send you my high regards and best wishes and I am,

Most sincerely yours,

[FRANKLIN D. ROOSEVELT]

[13:PPF 7960:CT]

[1] Harold B. Hoskins, in 1944–45 successively special assistant to the American ambassador in Iran and counselor for economic affairs at American diplomatic missions in Saudi Arabia and other Near Eastern countries.

[2] Ibn Saud replied April 1, 1944 (PPF 7960), expressing pleasure at the possibility of a visit from Roosevelt but making no comment on the latter's ideas on water conservation in Arabia.

1118   "STATEMENT BY THE PRESIDENT UPON SIGNING H. R. 2580 TO CONSENT TO THE BELLE FOURCHE RIVER BASIN COMPACT"

[WASHINGTON, *February 26, 1944*]

In signing the Belle Fourche River Basin Compact bill, I find it necessary to call attention, as I did last May in the case of the Republican River Compact bill,[1] to the restrictions imposed upon the use of water by the United States. The procedure prescribed by the bill for the exercise of the powers of the Federal Government would not be entirely satisfactory in all circumstances but the prospects in fact for the exercise of such powers in the Belle Fourche basin are not great. For streams where conditions are otherwise and there appears to be a possible need for Federal comprehensive multiple purpose development or where opportunities for important electric power projects are present, I believe the Belle Fourche River Compact should not serve as a precedent. In such cases the compact and the legislation should more adequately reflect a recognition of the responsibilities and prerogatives of the Federal Government.[2]

[*Notation:*AS] OK FDR

[*Notation:*A] 2–26–44

[*Notation:*A] Statement given to Press Febr. 28, 1944

[13:BUDGET BUREAU ENROLLED BILLS:T]

[1] *Ante,* 1105.

[2] This compact was entered into by South Dakota and Wyoming to secure for themselves the most efficient use of the waters of the Belle Fourche basin. Under the bill assenting to the compact (58 *Stat.* 94), the Federal Government agreed that the beneficial use of the waters of the basin was of "paramount importance" to the development of the basin itself, and that no Federal use of the waters would be made that would interfere with such paramount interest until after consultation of all the Federal and state agencies concerned. The issuance by the President of a statement having the purport of the one here printed was recommended by the Federal Power Commission and the Interior Department. Budget Director Smith did not think such a declaration necessary because article I of the compact declared that neither the states nor the Congress conceded that the agreement established any precedent with respect to any other interstate stream. However, he submitted a draft statement which was issued as the one here printed (Olds to Smith, Feb. 18, 1944; Fortas to Smith, Feb. 21, 1944; Smith to Latta, Feb. 23, 1944, Budget Bureau Enrolled Bills). This was issued as a press release Feb. 28, 1944.

1119   ROOSEVELT TO JAMES M. BARNES, ADMINISTRATIVE ASSIST-
        ANT TO THE PRESIDENT

WASHINGTON, *March 6, 1944*

MEMORANDUM FOR HON. JAMES M. BARNES: Before I send this, I wish you would have a talk with Secretary Ickes. Frankly, I am inclined to think that the Bureau of Reclamation should handle this because the waters concerned are not only inland waters, but do not even run into the sea. They run into a lake and thence disappear into thin air by evaporation.[1]

F. D. R.

[13:OF 402:CT]

[1] This refers to the letter following. Barnes replied (March 7, 1944, OF 402) that he had talked with Ickes and that he was in "perfect accord" with the signing of the letter.

1120   ROOSEVELT TO REPRESENTATIVE WILLIAM M. WHITTINGTON
        OF MISSISSIPPI, CHAIRMAN, HOUSE COMMITTEE ON FLOOD
        CONTROL

WASHINGTON, *March 7, 1944*

MY DEAR MR. WHITTINGTON: I have received your letter of February 17, 1944, in which you discuss the proposed Kern River, California, multiple-purpose project.[1] It may well be, as you state in your letter, that, when the structure proposed by the Chief of Engineers is considered alone, the benefits are predominantly flood control. However, I feel that neither the Kern River project nor the Kings River project can properly be viewed without regard to the development of the Central Valley of California as a whole.

It seems to me that the multiple-purpose projects proposed by the Chief of Engineers on the Kings and Kern Rivers are only two elements in a basin-wide plan for the development and use of the water resources in the Great Central Valley of California, and that the primary and dominant objective of that plan, especially in the southern part of the valley, is the provision of water supplies for domestic, municipal, industrial and irrigation uses. It would appear that, if any such plan is to be successful, the operation of all units of the plan should be fully coordinated on a regional basis. Such coordination, insofar as the projects undertaken by the Federal Government are concerned, can best be obtained by a single agency constructing, operating and maintaining the multiple-purpose elements of the plan, particularly those projects involving water conservation. Since the Congress has already authorized the construction and operation by the Bureau of Reclamation of certain multiple-purpose elements of the Central Valley plan involving water conservation, from the standpoint of good Federal administration it would follow that the Bureau of Reclamation should also be authorized to construct and operate the other multiple-purpose elements, such as the projects proposed on the Kings and Kern Rivers by the Chief of Engineers, with appropriate care exercised, of course, to observe the existing local irrigation rights established by usage, decrees, and agreements.

I know that you will understand that my expression of views arises from my desire to obtain what I believe to be the best method of Federal participation in the over-all plan for the development of the Central Valley, and not from any intention of interfering with the proper consideration of this matter by the Congress.[2]

Sincerely yours,

[Franklin D. Roosevelt]

RWH:FJB:CDC:ED 2/25/44

[Notation:AS] Copy of this letter sent to Mr. Hartley, Bureau of the Budget 3/8/44   hm

[13:OF 402:CT]

[1] OF 402.
[2] Drafted by the Interior Department.

1121   ROOSEVELT TO HENRY A. WALLACE, VICE PRESIDENT OF
        THE UNITED STATES

[WASHINGTON] *March 14, 1944*

DEAR HENRY: Thank you much for letting me see Watts' memorandum about the Redwood and the Sequoia. I have tried raising the Sequoia from seed in the greenhouse. I have tried it in two locations at Hyde Park but it has died the first winter or the second winter.

Also, I have twice tried Sequoias and Redwoods sent to me from the Coast, planting them immediately in sheltered good soil. Nearly all the trees died the first or second year except one outside my window in the new Library grounds and, after surviving for three winters, it died this past spring. I do not think it is possible to make them grow in the East—with one possible exception. As you know, the rainfall in the Great Smoky Mountain Park, or a little south thereof, is the highest in the East and I am going to get the Park Service to try planting them there in several correct locations.

As ever yours,

F. D. R.

[13:OF 6–P:CT]

1122   ROOSEVELT TO HAROLD L. ICKES, SECRETARY OF THE
        INTERIOR

WASHINGTON, *March 14, 1944*

MEMORANDUM FOR THE SECRETARY OF THE INTERIOR: Please read Chief Watts' memorandum to the Vice President and my letter to the V.P.[1] Will you go ahead and get the Park Service to plant some Sequoias and Redwoods in or near the Great Smoky Mountain National Park where there is more rainfall than any other part of the East? These trees are easy to raise from seed and grow fast, but they should be put out in their permanent location within a year. The location should be protected from winds and, at the same time, the soil should be as rich and deep as possible. There are many such places in the Smokies.[2]

F. D. R.

[13:OF 6–P:CT]

[1] See above.
[2] Ickes replied April 3, 1944 (OF 6–P), that he had asked the National Park Service to try to grow some of the trees referred to in the Great Smokies but that he was doubtful of the success of the experiment.

Washington 25, D. C., *Mar. 29, 1944*

My dear Mr. Latta: On March 24, 1944, you advised this office that S. 250, "To promote sustained-yield forest management in order thereby (a) to stabilize communities, forest industries, employment, and taxable forest wealth; (b) to assure a continuous and ample supply of forest products; and (c) to secure the benefits of forests in regulation of water supply and stream flow, prevention of soil erosion, amelioration of climate, and preservation of wildlife," had been received at the White House, and requested reports and recommendations as to the approval of the bill.

It is the purpose of the bill to give the Secretary of Agriculture and the Secretary of the Interior with respect to Federal forest lands under their respective jurisdictions, and intermingled and nearby private forest lands, discretionary authority—

(1) to establish cooperative sustained-yield units for the purpose of coordinated sustained-yield management of the public, and inter-related private forest lands;

(2) to enter into cooperative agreements with willing forest land owners within such units, under which, in consideration of the assured privilege of purchasing Government timber and of other benefits to them from coordinated management, they will manage their land in strict accordance with requirements as to the rate, manner, and time of cutting prescribed by the Secretary; and

(3) to establish sustained-yield units of exclusively Federal forest land where necessary in order to maintain dependent communities, and within such units to sell timber without competition at not less than appraised value to responsible purchasers established in such communities.

As a safeguard the bill provides for a public hearing before any sustained-yield unit is established or any cooperative agreement is consummated, and also that a hearing shall be held upon the request of any person having a reasonable interest before a sale of timber is made without competition.

A facsimile of the enrolled enactment has been referred to the Departments of War, Agriculture, and Interior, and the Federal Power Commission, and their replies, either recommending approval of the bill or interposing no objection to its approval, are attached.[1]

The bill authorizes appropriations for the purpose of carrying out its provisions in an annual amount of not to exceed $150,000 for the Department of Agriculture, and $50,000 for the Department of the Interior, which amounts would be in addition to funds made available for the management of lands under the jurisdiction of the respective Departments and under existing provisions of law.

I recommend that the bill be approved.[2]

Very truly yours,

HAROLD D. SMITH

[*Notation*:A] Approved 3/29/44

[13:BUDGET BUREAU ENROLLED BILLS:TS]

[1] These are all dated March 25, 1944. The Agriculture and Interior Departments recommended approval.

[2] S. 250 was approved March 29, 1944 (58 *Stat.* 132). This bill, introduced by Senator McNary (Ore.) on Jan. 11, 1943, had as its precursor the act of Aug. 28, 1937 (50 *Stat.* 874), which provided for sustained yield timberland management on Interior Department lands in the revested Oregon and California Railroad and reconveyed Coos Bay Wagon Road grant lands in Oregon. By establishing sustained yield forests areas the Government hoped to interrupt the process whereby forest communities became extinct in consequence of the long established practice of "cut and get out." S. 250 was intended to enable the owner of private forest land to adopt sustained yield practices by enlarging his cutting area through the opportunity to buy, noncompetitively, adjacent National Forest timber. In return he agreed to adopt Forest Service approved cutting practices on his own lands. The bill also provided for the noncompetitive sale of timber from National Forest areas to processors whose operations were vital to the life of the communities in those areas. Forest Service Chief Watts said that the law was a "major step towards obtaining the maximum benefits from the national-forest system for support of timber-dependent communities" but he noted that "great caution" would be required in its application to make sure that the long-term arrangements between the Government and private owners were clearly in the public interest (*Report of the Chief of the Forest Service, 1944,* p. 14). An account of the enactment of the legislation may be found in the diary of the forester David T. Mason, *Forests for the Future* (Rodney C. Loehr, ed.), p. 232 *et seq.*

1124   ROOSEVELT TO REPRESENTATIVE SAM RAYBURN OF TEXAS, SPEAKER OF THE HOUSE OF REPRESENTATIVES

WASHINGTON 25, D. C., *June 2, 1944*

MY DEAR SAM: The Rules Committee on the House has reported out a rule permitting the early consideration of H. R. 2241, a bill introduced by Representative Frank A. Barrett, of Wyoming, to abolish the Jackson Hole National Monument, and it is anticipated that the bill will come up for a vote in the House next week. This bill should be defeated or, if that is not possible, it should be recommitted to the Public Lands Committee.

Jackson Hole is one of the most scenic areas in the country and a wintering ground for the southern Yellowstone elk herd, the largest elk herd in the United States. About 15 years ago, after conferring with Wyoming State officials, with members of the Wyoming Delegation in Congress, and with the then Secretary of the Interior, Mr. John D. Rockefeller, Jr. purchased about 34,000 acres of land in Jackson Hole at a cost of

$1,500,000, to donate to the Federal Government for a national park. The park project would have been consummated years ago if suitable arrangement had been made to compensate the county for the loss of taxes when Mr. Rockefeller's lands are conveyed to the Federal Government and are removed from the local tax rolls.

Last year, to avoid losing Mr. Rockefeller's gift and to carry out the commitments made to him during the administrations of Presidents Coolidge and Hoover, I established the Jackson Hole National Monument, under the authority of the Act of June 8, 1906 (34 *Stat.* 225), known as the Antiquities Act. This Act had been used for this purpose many times before. Five Republican Presidents and one Democratic President before me have established a total of 71 national monuments under the authority of this Act, many of them larger than the Jackson Hole National Monument.

The Federal lands and the lands which Mr. Rockefeller bought to give to the public comprise more than 92 percent of the area within the monument boundaries, and the proclamation was issued subject to all valid existing rights. This applies to Federal lands and to the remaining 8 percent of state and private lands.

The establishment of the monument leaves some problems unsolved, such as the tax question. I would favor the enactment of some suitable bill to authorize the sharing of a reasonable portion of national park entrance fees with the counties in which the national parks and monuments are situated. Many other Federal land administering agencies now have this authority.[1]

Sincerely yours,

[FRANKLIN D. ROOSEVELT]

[13:OF 928:CT]

[1] Drafted by the Interior Department. In his letter to Roosevelt enclosing the draft, June 1, 1944 (OF 928), Ickes said that he had pointed out to Rockefeller's representatives that H. R. 2241 was not a partisan measure since establishment of the national monument was in fulfillment of commitments made during Coolidge's administration, and that he had asked them to "line up" the Republicans to vote against the bill.

1125   GIFFORD PINCHOT TO ROOSEVELT

WASHINGTON 6, D. C., *August 29, 1944*

DEAR MR. PRESIDENT: As previously arranged,[1] I enclose for your consideration a suggested draft of a letter to Allied Governments proposing a Conference on the conservation of natural resources as a necessary requirement for permanent peace.

If the course there outlined should meet with your approval, then I would like further to suggest:

That a Committee on Arrangements be appointed by the President to draw up a tentative program for the Conference; to prepare a suggested plan for an inventory of the known natural resources of the world; and otherwise to make ready for the sessions of the Conference.

That the Committee be authorized by the President to ask for and receive the full cooperation of all Government Departments and other Government organizations.

That a Secretary and such other assistants as may be required be assigned to the Committee from experienced persons already in the Government service.

That the Committee be authorized to invite and receive the friendly cooperation of experts not in the service of the Government.

If desired, I would be glad to prepare and submit for your approval a list of competent persons for appointment to the proposed Committee.

Faithfully yours,

GIFFORD PINCHOT

[13:OF 5637:TS]

[1] Pinchot was at the White House on June 29, 1944 (PPF 1-O). He referred to this in a letter to Roosevelt of July 29, 1944 (PPF 289): "When I had the pleasure of making . . . a short statement concerning conservation and permanent peace, you were good enough to express yourself, in general terms, as favorably impressed. It was agreed that I should prepare a plan and submit it to you in something over three weeks."

1126   [*Enclosure*] PROPOSAL FOR AN INTERNATIONAL CONFERENCE ON CONSERVATION

August 29, 1944

No worthier task confronts the world than to make future wars impossible. That can be done only by removing the incentives to war; by putting an end to the causes which drive nations to aggression.

Since human history began, the commonest cause of war has been the demand for land. Under whatever name, land means natural resources. And natural resources—forests and waters, soils and minerals are the material foundations of human security and progress. Without them we cannot live.

The conservation of natural resources means the planned and orderly use of all the earth produces for the greatest good of the greatest number for the longest time. It is the basic material problem of mankind.

Conservation as a policy is universally accepted as sound. The United Nations, through the Atlantic Charter and the Lend Lease Agreements, have declared for fair access to needed raw materials for all the peoples of the world.

If the commonest of all causes of war is the demand for land, for natural resources on which to live and grow strong, then permanent peace is impossible until general plenty, through the conservation of natural resources and fair access by the Nations of the world to necessary resources, is assured.

The conservation policy was first formulated in the United States nearly forty years ago. In 1908 President Theodore Roosevelt, on the valid ground that "The people of the whole world are interested in the natural resources of the whole world, benefited by their conservation, and injured by their destruction," sent to 58 Nations invitations for a world conference on the conservation of natural resources, to be held in the Peace Palace at The Hague. Thirty of the Nations, including Great Britain, France, Germany, Canada, and Mexico, had accepted when a change of administration defeated the plan.

The movement for international conservation thus begun has recently been given strong support. In 1940 the Eighth American Scientific Congress, representing all the Nations of the Americas, by unanimous vote declared that:

"International cooperation to inventory, conserve, and wisely utilize natural resources to the mutual advantage of all Nations might well remove one of the most dangerous obstacles to a just and permanent world peace."

In 1941 the British Association for the Advancement of Science, in preparing a plan for an International Resources Office, declared that: "Unless we apply our ordered intelligence to this question, the sequence of crisis and war will continue with ever more disastrous results."

We cannot safely ignore any course that may assist in abolishing war. Therefore I believe that it would be wise for the United Nations, through their appointed delegates, to meet and consider the conservation of natural resources, and fair access to them among the Nations, as a vital step toward permanent peace.

Accordingly, I have the honor to invite the Government of to take part in a Conference of the United Nations, to be held in the City of Washington, beginning on the   of   , to consider this question, and to formulate a plan for securing to mankind the blessings of enduring peace.

Such a Conference might well consider: An inventory of the natural resources of the world; a set of principles for the conservation of resources and fair access to them in the interest of permanent peace; conservation and fair access in the recovery and reconstruction of Nations; and such other related questions as the Conference might decide to take up.

If a majority of the United Nations accept this invitation, the Government of the United States is prepared to draw up and submit to the Conference tentative agenda for its approval or modification, together with available supporting data.

Open discussion should bring to light the principles upon which all Nations can agree for conserving and distributing the natural resources of the earth, to the great end of human welfare through general plenty and permanent peace.

Without world-wide conservation, lasting peace is impossible. And permanent peace is the hope of the world.

[13:OF 5637:T]

1127   ROOSEVELT TO JEAN SHERWOOD HARPER, Swarthmore, Pennsylvania

WASHINGTON, *September 13, 1944*

MY DEAR JEAN: Upon receipt of your letter of August 21 [1] I made inquiry through the Secretary of the Interior in regard to oil operations in the vicinity of the Okefenokee Wildlife Refuge. I understand that some prospecting has been carried on west of the area and that some of the Department officials have been consulted with reference to a possibility of drilling on the refuge. There is no intention of leasing the Okefenokee for oil exploration. I have directed the Fish and Wildlife Service to maintain this area in its untouched, pristine condition and they are making every possible effort to comply with my direction.[2]

Sincerely yours,

[FRANKLIN D. ROOSEVELT]

[*Notation*:AS] Copy of this reply sent to Interior 9/14/44   hms

[13:OF 378:CT]

[1] Expressing concern at the possibility that the Government might grant oil leases in the Okefenokee (OF 378).
[2] Drafted by the Interior Department.

1128   ROOSEVELT TO THE CONGRESS

THE WHITE HOUSE, *September 21, 1944*

TO THE CONGRESS OF THE UNITED STATES: I enclose a copy of a resolution adopted by all but one of the Missouri River States, represented in a recent meeting of their Governors and the members of the Missouri River States Committee.[1] In general, the resolution asks for executive and legislative action toward procuring a single, coordinated plan for the development of the Missouri River basin "for the greatest benefit of its citizens both present and future, and for the greatest benefit to the United States."

As the Congress knows, I have for many years advocated the establishment of separate Authorities to deal with the development of certain river basins where several States were involved. The general functions and purposes of the Tennessee Valley Authority might well serve as a pattern for similar developments of other river basins. The Tennessee Valley Authority was charged by the Congress with the development of practically all of the factors which are important in establishing better living standards and a better life for the people throughout that great watershed.

The benefits which have resulted in the Tennessee River Valley include flood prevention, irrigation, increased electric power for farms and shops and homes and industries, better transportation on land and water, reforestation and conservation of natural resources, the encouragement of small businesses and the growth and expansion of new businesses, development and wide-spread use of fertilizers and improved agricultural methods, better education and recreational facilities—and many kindred improvements which go to make for increased security and greater human happiness.

The Congress has at all times retained the final authority over the Tennessee Valley Authority, for the Authority comes before the Congress each year to obtain appropriations to continue its work and carry out its plans.

I have heretofore suggested the creation of a similar Authority for the development of the Arkansas River watershed from the Mississippi all the way west to its source in Colorado.

I have also suggested the creation of an Authority to render a similar service in the Columbia River watershed, including the States of Washington, Oregon, Idaho and Montana.

I now make a similar recommendation for the Missouri River basin.

The resolution very properly asks that the legislation dealing with matters relating to the waters of the Missouri River basin recognize that it is dealing with one river and one problem; and points out the necessity of a comprehensive development of the Missouri River, indicating that there can be no piecemeal legislative program. The resolution asks that "the Congress should recognize now the problem in its entirety as it affects the people of the Missouri basin and their economic destiny and that of the United States."

I am in hearty accord with these principles. I hope that the Congress will give careful and early consideration to the creation of this federal authority to consider the problem in its entirety, remembering always that any appropriations to carry out any plan are and will be within the complete control of the Congress, and that the interest of each of the States in the basin will, of course, be given full consideration. I am sure that none of the States in the Tennessee River basin have lost any of their rights because of the creation of the Authority in that valley.

May I also ask that renewed consideration be given to a study of the Arkansas and Columbia River basins? The fact has been established that such legislation can do much to promote the welfare of the great mass of citizens who live there—as well as their fellow citizens throughout the United States.

I need hardly point out to the Congress, in addition, how helpful this legislation will be in the creation of employment and in the stimulation of industry, business, and agriculture throughout the areas involved, in the days which will follow the end of the war.[2]

FRANKLIN D. ROOSEVELT

[W.H. PRESS RELEASES : M]

[1] "Resolution of the Missouri River States Committee to Secure a Basin-Wide Development Plan," sent to Roosevelt by Governor Merrell Q. Sharpe of South Dakota, chairman of the Missouri River States Committee, Aug. 21, 1944 (OF 1516). (Sharpe's covering letter was submitted to the Congress with the resolution.)
[2] This message is based on an undated draft bearing numerous additions and deletions in the hand of Samuel I. Rosenman, Special Counsel to the President (OF 1516). A copy of the revised draft was sent by Roosevelt to Budget Director Smith with a memorandum of Sept. 1, 1944 (OF 1516) reading, "The enclosed is merely a first draft. What do you think?" Smith sent back a completely different draft, undated, but endorsed as having been received at the White House on Sept. 20, 1944 (OF 1516). This draft made no mention of the resolution of the Missouri River States Committee nor did it refer to the example of the Tennessee Valley Authority. Instead of urging the creation of a TVA-type of authority for the Missouri valley, it recommended "the establishment of a temporary, engineering commission . . . which would be charged with the duty of preparing and presenting to the Congress through the President, after taking into account the plans that are presently being proposed, an integrated and comprehensive plan for the development of the water and land resources of the Missouri Valley."
No change, however, was made in the White House draft except for the insertion of the word "irrigation" in the first sentence of the third paragraph. This single addition, in Roosevelt's hand, appears on an undated teletype copy of the message headed, "To Miss Tully: Draft submitted to Budget Sept. 1. 2nd draft" (OF 1516). (From Sept. 9–21, 1944, Roosevelt was at the Quebec Conference and at Hyde Park.) In the Senate the message was referred to the Committee on Agriculture and Forestry, and in the House to the Committee on Rivers and Harbors (Cong. Rec., 78th Cong., 2d sess., 90: 6, 8065, 8108).

1129   ROOSEVELT TO REPRESENTATIVE BRENT SPENCE OF KENTUCKY

[WASHINGTON] *October 12, 1944*

DEAR MR. SPENCE: I have your letter of September 27, 1944,[1] regarding water pollution control in the Ohio River valley area and know of your deep interest in this whole subject.

My views regarding the need for water pollution abatement, as expressed in my message to the Congress, February 15, 1939, are, I believe, well known to you. More recently, the emergency conditions of the defense and war programs have prevented the undertaking of any active water pollution control program. Nevertheless, the importance of this field of conservation to the public health, industry, and other activities has not diminished but has rather been increased by the war production program. We can all agree, I am sure, that both the Federal and State governments should be working toward the development for post-war application of a program for water pollution control which would recognize the interests and responsibilities of the various public and private organizations concerned.

Please be assured of my continued sympathetic interest in this problem.[2]

Sincerely yours,

[Franklin D. Roosevelt]

[13:OF 114–A:CT]

[1] Spence said that the people of the Ohio Valley were greatly interested in the control of water pollution and that he would like to have Roosevelt's views on, the matter (OF 114–A).
[2] Drafted by the Federal Security Agency. FSA Administrator McNutt, writing to Hassett Oct. 10, 1944 (OF 114–A), enclosing the draft, said: "As you doubtless know, this whole question of stream pollution has been under consideration in Congress for a number of years and there is now more or less agreement on the type of bill that would be suitable. This Agency has had conferences with the Director of the Bureau of the Budget and I feel that the attached draft expresses in general terms the view of the Administration on this important matter."

1130   O. S. Warden, President, National Reclamation Association, to Roosevelt

Washington 4, D. C., *October 12, 1944*

Dear Mr. President: Your personal support of reclamation as a national policy in the development of comfortable farm homes throughout the western half of the United States has been continually helpful during all of the nine years that I have been President of the National Reclamation Association.

I am writing this letter because some confusion of understanding has followed your message to Congress, transmitted on September 21, 1944, in which it was stated that you were in "hearty accord" with the principles adopted and with the over-all plan urged to bring about a complete development of the land and water resources of the great Missouri Basin, as approved at a session of the Missouri River Nine States Committee, meeting at Omaha, Nebraska on August 6, 1944. This plan included irrigation, the incidental production of power, flood control, assistance to navigation and other industrial and domestic uses of the available water.

For the furtherance of this development proposal the Missouri River States Committee, at the close of a two day consideration, approved three important findings:

(1) That there must be an over-all unified plan for development of this Missouri Basin.

(2) The President and the Congress were urged to authorize and direct the United States Army Engineers and the United States Bureau of Reclamation to bring before the Congress such a plan of coordinated engineering.

(3) That whatever unified plan might be agreed upon nothing should be done that would adversely affect the use of water for the irrigation of land of the upstream states in carrying forward this basin-wide development.

Permit me to suggest that in the preparation of your message to Congress, transmitted under date of September 21, 1944, you quite definitely approve finding number (1). You appear to favor a modification of finding number (2). There is some confusion and friendly concern lest you may have overlooked the importance of number (3). This matter could be quite completely cleared up now by a statement that however the desirable unified proposal in question may be carried out, nothing should be done to adversely affect the use of water for irrigation in the upstream states.

I feel sure that this must be your present attitude because of your personal support of reclamation running through the years as mentioned at the beginning of this letter. Furthermore, this thought on my part is emphasized as I recall your letter of February 7, 1944 to Chairman Mansfield of the Rivers and Harbors Committee of the House of Representatives. I believe there have been other like communications declaring that the beneficial use of water in the upper basin should not be affected by the proposed lower basin improvements.

Please accept my assurance of wishing to be helpful, and thanks for such consideration as you think an important subject now before the Congress merits at this time.[1]

Most respectfully yours,

O. S. WARDEN

[13:OF 1516:TS]

[1] This letter and a draft of a suggested reply (composed by Warden) were brought to the White House by Postmaster General Frank C. Walker (Rosenman to Roosevelt, Oct. 21, 1944, OF 1516). Extensively revised by Rosenman, Warden's draft was sent as the letter printed below. An accompanying memorandum by Early, undated, presumably addressed to his secretary, reads: "Phone Mr. Warden in the the morning. Tell him I am going to tell the Press at 10:30 about the P's letter. Ask him if he cares to release it textually to the Press."

1131   ROOSEVELT TO O. S. WARDEN, PRESIDENT, NATIONAL RECLAMATION ASSOCIATION, WASHINGTON

[WASHINGTON] *October 23, 1944*

DEAR MR. WARDEN: I have read with interest your letter of October twelfth last directing attention to the possibility of some confusion in the minds of those who may not have followed the record of the present administration with respect to reclamation.

We have continually encouraged and favored support for such development of the land and water resources of the western states as would most benefit each region affected and the country as a whole. I think that record is clear. It has always been progressive. Whatever agency carries through a unified plan in the development of a watershed, such as is now under consideration for the Missouri River Basin, it should be so done as not to affect adversely the use of water for irrigation in the upstream states.[1]

Very sincerely yours,

[FRANKLIN D. ROOSEVELT]

[13:OF 1516:CT]

[1] Drafted by Warden; see preceding note.

1132   ROOSEVELT TO GIFFORD PINCHOT, Washington

[WASHINGTON] *October 24, 1944*

Dear Gifford: Remember that I have not forgotten that conservation is a basis of permanent peace, and I have sent the enclosed to Cordell Hull.[1] I think something will happen soon.

You must, of course, be on the American Delegation.

This blankety blank campaign is nearly over.[2]

My best to you, As ever yours,

[FRANKLIN D. ROOSEVELT]

[13:OF 5637:CT]

[1] The letter following.
[2] Pinchot replied Oct. 31, 1944 (OF 5637), that he would be delighted to be on the American delegation of the proposed conference.

1133   ROOSEVELT TO CORDELL HULL, SECRETARY OF STATE

[WASHINGTON] *October 24, 1944*

MY DEAR MR. SECRETARY: In our meetings with other nations I have a feeling that too little attention is being paid to the subject of the conservation and use of natural resources.

I am surprised that the world knows so little about itself.

Conservation is a basis of permanent peace. Many different kinds of natural resources are being wasted; other kinds are being ignored; still other kinds can be put to more practical use for humanity if more is known about them. Some nations are deeply interested in the subject of conservation and use and other nations are not at all interested.

Many nations have been denuded of trees, for example, and therefore find it extremely difficult to live on eroded lands. Many nations know practically nothing of their mineral resources. Many nations do not use their water resources. Some nations are not interested in development of irrigation. Some nations have done little to explore the scientific use of what they have.

It occurs to me, therefore, that even before the United Nations meet for the comprehensive program which has been proposed, it could do no harm—and it might do much good—for us to hold a meeting in the United States of all of the united and associated nations for what is really the first step toward conservation and use of natural resources—i. e., a gathering for the purpose of a world-wide study of the whole subject.

The machinery at least could be put into effect to carry it through.

I repeat again that I am more and more convinced that conservation is a basis of permanent peace.

Would you let me have your thought on this?

I think the time is ripe.[1]

Always sincerely,

[FRANKLIN D. ROOSEVELT]

[13:OF 5637:CT]

[1] Acknowledged by Stettinius, Nov. 2, 1944 (OF 5637), saying that the suggestion was "under active consideration"; answered by him *post*, 1137.

1134   ROOSEVELT TO GOVERNOR MERRELL Q. SHARPE, Pierre, South Dakota

[WASHINGTON] *October 24, 1944*

DEAR GOVERNOR SHARPE: Mr. Hassett has called my attention to your letter of September 28 with its enclosure.[1] I appreciate having your views concerning my message recommending a Missouri Valley Authority and have carefully considered your suggestion that the flood control bill be promptly passed with the understanding that, if Congress finally creates an Authority, that agency could take over flood control projects in the Missouri basin.

The answer to your proposal seems to me implicit in your statement before the Senate Subcommittee on Irrigation and Reclamation. There you point out that the "diversities of interest and divisions of opinion throughout the basin and within the several states themselves tend to assert themselves more and more as the several plans for basin development are presented." You further offer it as your view "that none of the divergent interests or localities should ever be given any permanently dominant position over the others, but that at all times one general coordinated plan of development and control should be followed. . . ."

I concur heartily in this view. In fact, it is precisely that reasoning which led me to recommend a Missouri Valley Authority. For more than ten years the Tennessee Valley Authority has been successfully demonstrating that the way to harmonize diverse interests and assure a coordinated plan for full utilization of the resources of a great river is to place the entire responsibility in a single agency created for that purpose. It has also shown that such an agency, located in the valley, can identify itself with the region which it serves and so assure the greatest possible state and local participation in the program.

This is in contrast with an approach to comprehensive river basin development through several agencies sponsoring omnibus bills to authorize special purpose projects in many river basins. Such an approach tends to foster centralization in Washington and, at the same time, to accentuate diversities of interest which attach themselves to particular bills and to the agencies authorized to undertake projects with which they are directly concerned.

So, while I agree with you on the urgency of the flood control program for the Missouri basin, I feel that the surest way to expedite it is to unify the development of the Missouri River and its tributaries for flood control, irrigation, navigation, power and other beneficial purposes under a single authority. In view of the fact that the several plans for the basin are still in preliminary stages, prompt action on the necessary legislation should entail no delay in the initiation of essential projects.

I appreciate your active leadership on behalf of a single comprehensive plan satisfactory to all interests in the basin.[2]

Very sincerely yours,

[FRANKLIN D. ROOSEVELT]

[13:OF 1516:CT]

[1] Sharpe to Hassett, Sept. 28, 1944 (OF 1516), enclosing, "Statement of M. Q. Sharpe before United States Senate Sub-Committee Relating to Bureau of Reclamation Plan for Missouri River Development," dated Sept. 22, 1944 (mimeographed).
[2] This letter was drafted by Leland Olds, vice chairman of the Federal Power Commission. In his letter to Roosevelt enclosing the draft, Oct. 21, 1944 (OF 1516), Olds said, in part: "Public support of the TVA pattern has been steadily rising. No attempt to achieve the same results through a make-shift wedding of specialized federal agencies can be more than partially successful."

1135 ROOSEVELT TO PRESIDENT MANUEL AVILA CAMACHO OF MEXICO

[WASHINGTON] *October 24, 1944*

MY DEAR MR. PRESIDENT: I want to inform you of the acceptance by the United States Government from the State of Texas on June 12, 1944, of the deed to the land for the Big Bend National Park, a project in which I believe that you are particularly interested, as I have been for a number of years.

In giving the land to the Nation the people of Texas have achieved high distinction in the park and recreation field. The new area contains over 700,000 acres. The southern border follows the International Boundary formed by the Rio Grande for a distance of more than 100 miles.

In the United States we think of the Big Bend region in terms of its international significance and hope that the Mexican people look forward in the same spirit to the establishment of an adjoining national park in the States of Chihuahua and Coahuila. These adjoining parks would form an area which would be a meeting ground for the people of both countries, exemplifying their cultural resources and advancement, and inspiring further mutually beneficial progress in recreation and science and the industries related thereto. I have followed the progress of the conversations between the representatives of our respective Governments regarding the establishment of international parks, and I do not believe that this undertaking in the Big Bend will be complete until the entire park area in this region on both sides of the Rio Grande forms one great international park.

Accordingly, I would appreciate your views regarding my hope that early in the postwar period such a park, formed of suitable areas on each side of the boundary in the Big Bend region, might be dedicated and that it might mark the initiation of a joint program of park development for the benefit and enjoyment of our peoples.[1]

As ever yours,

[FRANKLIN D. ROOSEVELT]

[13:OF 6–P:CT]

[1] (Drafted by the Department of State.) President Camacho replied Nov. 30, 1944 (OF 6–P), that the Mexican section of the park would be developed as soon as possible.

1136   SPEECH BY ROOSEVELT, Clarksburg, West Virginia, October 29, 1944

MY FRIENDS: This being Sunday, the Governor,[1] in cooperating with me in keeping politics out of it, says that he is not even going to introduce me.

I have been here before, and it is a great comfort to come on a Sunday in a campaign year, because on Sundays my life is made much more comfortable by not having to think about politics. Unfortunately, I do have to think about the war, because every day, including Sundays, dispatches come to me, on the train even, to tell me of the progress of our boys in Europe and in the Pacific and in the Philippines. I can't get rid of that.

So coming up through the State today, I have been looking out of the window, and I think there is a subject that is a good subject for Sunday, because I remember the line in the poem, "Only God can make a tree." And one of the things that people have to realize all over the United States, and I think especially in West Virginia, I don't see the trees I ought to see. That is something that we in this this country have fallen down on. We have been using up natural resources that we ought to have replaced. I know we can't replace coal—it will be a long time before all the coal is gone—but trees constitute something that we can replace.

We have to think not just of an annual crop, not just something that we can eat the next year, but we have to think of a longer crop, something that takes years to grow, but which in the long run is going to do more good for our children and for our grandchildren than if we leave the hills bare.

I remember a story, and it is taken out of Germany. There was a town there—I don't know what has happened in the last twenty years—but this is back when I used to be in grade school in Germany [2]—and I used to bicycle. And we came to a town, and outside of it there was a great forest. And the interesting thing to me, as a boy even, was that the people in that town didn't have to pay taxes. They were supported by their own forest.

Way back in the time of Louis something of France—some king—the French king was approaching this town with a large army. And the prince of the time asked the townspeople to come out to defend their principality, and he promised them that if they would keep the invader out of the town, out of the principality, he would give them the forest.

The burghers turned out. They repulsed the French king. And very soon the prince made good. He gave the forest to the town. And for over two hundred years that town in Germany had to pay no taxes. Everybody made money, because they had no taxes. In other words, it was a forest on an annual yield basis. They cut down perhaps 70 percent of what they could get out of that year's mature crop. And every year they planted new trees. And every year the proceeds from that forest paid the equivalent of taxes.

Now that is true more and more in this country. There are more and more municipalities that are reforesting their watersheds, putting trees on the top of their hills, preventing the erosion of soil. They are not on a self-sustaining basis because it has only been started within the last ten or fifteen years. And yet while only God can make a tree, we have to do a little bit to help ourselves.

I think that all of us sort of look at our lives in terms of ourselves, and yet your children, your grandchildren, your great-grandchildren, your great-great-grandchildren—some of them will be living right around here, right around where the population is today. Perhaps the old house—perhaps a better, new house. And more and more we Christians are going to think about those grandchildren and great-grandchildren. It doesn't amount to very much, this cost of planting trees, and yet the hillsides of West Virginia of our grandparents' day were much more wonderful than they are now. It's largely a deforested State. And I believe that from the point of view of the beauties of nature, from the point of view of all that trees can be, and from the point of view of your own grandchildren's pocketbooks, the small number of cents, the small number of dollars that go into reforestation are going to come back a thousand-fold.

Up where I live, in the country on the Hudson River, my family had—when I was a boy—five or six hundred acres. It wasn't valuable land. And my own father, in the old days, would go in every year and cut the family needs in the way of timber.

When I was a small boy, I realized that there was waste going on; and when I went to the State Senate as a young man, somebody appointed me to the Conservation Commission.[3] Some parts of upstate New York were being eroded, a lot of topsoil was running away, we were getting more floods than we had ever had in the old days.

And just as an experiment, I started planting a few acres each year on rundown land. I tried to pasture some skinny cows on it. And at the same time, I went into the old woods and cleaned out no'count trees, trees that were undergrown or would never amount to anything, crooked trees, rotten trees.

Well, the answer was this. When the last war came on, the old woods had some perfectly splendid trees, because I had cleaned them out, cleaned out the poor stuff. And during that war I made 4 thousand dollars, just by cutting out the mature trees. And I kept on every year. And in the winter-time, when the men weren't doing much, cleaning them out. And the trees grew.

And a quarter of a century later, there came this war. I think I co-operated with the Almighty, because I think trees were made to grow. Oh, yes, they are useful as mine timbers. I know that. But there are a lot of places in this State where there isn't any mine timber being cut out.

And in this war, back home, I cut last year—and this is not very Christian—over 4 thousand dollars' worth net of oak trees, to make into submarine chasers and landing craft and other implements of war. And I am doing it again this year.

And I hope that this use of wood for growing, for all kinds of modern inventions, plastics, and so forth, I hope that when I am able to cut some more trees, twenty or twenty-five years from now—it may not be me, it may be one of the boys—we will be able to use them at a profit not for building mine chasers or landing craft, but for turning them into some human use.

And I believe that in this country—not this State only, but a great many more—that we in the next few years, when peace comes, will be able to devote more thought to making our country more useful—every acre of it.

I remember eight years ago, I think it was, out in the west, we knew that there were great floods and a dry belt in there. We knew, also, that trees bring water and avoid floods. And so we started one of those "crackpot" things, for which I have been criticized, a thing called the shelter belt, to keep the high winds away, to hold the moisture in the soil. And the result is that that shelter belt—not much ran downhill—a great success has been made of it. And the farmers are getting more crops and better crops out there on the prairies in the lee of these rows of trees.

Forestry pays from the practical point of view. I have proved that. And so I hope—I hope to live long enough to see West Virginia with more trees in it. I hope to live to see the day when this generation will be thinking not just of themselves but also of the children and the grandchildren.

And so I had a happy day this morning in looking out at this wonderful scenery, but I couldn't take my eyes off those bare hilltops. I couldn't take my thoughts off the fact that this generation, and especially the previous generation, have been thinking of themselves and not of the future.

And so some day I hope to come back, and I hope to see a great forestry program for the whole of the State. Nearly all of it needs it. I hope to come back and be able to say, "I stopped, once upon a time, in Clarksburg, on a Sunday morning, and just avoided politics and talked to the people in Clarksburg, and they must have heard me all over the State, because they started planting trees."

And so I think my Sunday sermon is just about over. It has been good to see you, and I really do hope that I will come back here, one of these days soon.[4]

Thanks.

They say up here it's a good sermon.

[SPEECH FILE: T]

[1] Matthew M. Neely.

[2] In the course of a trip to Europe in the spring and summer of 1891, Roosevelt for a time attended the *Volkschule* at Bad Nauheim.

[3] The Forest, Fish and Game Committee of the New York State Senate is meant.

[4] This speech (delivered at 12:10 P. M.) was extemporaneous. The text here printed is that of the stenographic transcript; some of the more awkward locutions were edited (presumably by Early) in the version given to the press (cf. New York *Times,* Oct. 30, 1944, p. 11). (One of these revisions is interesting: in the twelfth

paragraph Roosevelt used the colloquial phrase "no 'count," a term certainly under-
standable to his audience. This became, in the press release, "no-account.") There
is present (Speech File) a draft labeled "Address of the President at Clarksburg,
W. Va., October 29, 1944. First Draft." The authorship of this draft, which deals
entirely with freedom of conscience, has not been determined. No part of it was used
by Roosevelt.

1137   EDWARD R. STETTINIUS, JR., ACTING SECRETARY OF STATE,
        TO ROOSEVELT

WASHINGTON, *November 10, 1944*

MEMORANDUM FOR THE PRESIDENT: Proposed Conference on Conservation and Natural Resources: Further reference is made to your letter
of October 24, 1944, suggesting the possibility of calling a conference of
the United and Associated Nations on the conservation and use of natural resources. There can be little doubt that, as you suggest, the development of effective international cooperation in stimulating the adoption of sound national conservation policy on a world-wide basis, in
promoting joint measures of attack upon common problems, and in enlarging our knowledge of the natural resource basis from which the
peoples of the earth derive their living, might make a significant contribution to the solution of the problem of maintaining world peace.

There are, however, a number of considerations which I should like to
bring to your attention that appear to me to make less urgent the need
for a special international conference on conservation at this time. These
considerations are set forth in the attached enclosure. Beginning with
the projected Food and Agriculture Organization of the United Nations
which grew out of the Hot Springs Conference, and extending through
to the Economic and Social Council of the general international organization, our post-war economic policy planning has given and will continue
to give a place of high importance to questions of conservation of natural
resources.

I have considerable doubt as to the desirability of a separate international conference in the near future centering its attention exclusively
on conservation. It seems to me unlikely that most of the governments
of the world will find themselves able to reach any firm views on the important problems of conservation in the absence of a clearer view than
they now have on the prospects for production and trade and of the
nature and extent of international collaboration therein.

I shall of course be glad to discuss this with you further if you should
so desire.

E. R. STETTINIUS, JR.

[13:OF 5637:TS]

1. In the years to come we shall be faced with a wide variety of situations pertaining to particular natural resources. In some of them, we shall be faced, for a few years at least, with continuing shortages in comparison with war and reconstruction needs. In others, we shall soon be faced with troublesome problems of surplus production and surplus capacity. I should be much inclined to doubt whether we should be able to reach significant international agreement on conservation programs without simultaneously considering the prospects for the orderly development and marketing of these resources. If this view is correct, it sets conservation as one part, and a very important part, of the total problem of international collaboration in the wisest use of the world's productive resources. This is the pattern which we have been attempting to follow to date.

2. The conservation and development of agricultural resources was one of the subjects discussed at the United Nations Conference on Food and Agriculture at Hot Springs, and Article I of the draft Constitution of the Food and Agriculture Organization of the United Nations specifically provides that the Organization "shall promote and, where appropriate, shall recommend national and international action with regard to . . . the conservation of natural resources and the adoption of improved methods of agricultural production." Under the terms of the proposed Constitution of the Food and Agriculture Organization, the scope of its activities covers fisheries and forestry, as well as agriculture proper. Arrangements are therefore well under way whereby provision will be made for the handling on an international basis of conservation problems in the fields of agriculture, fisheries and forestry.

3. The orderly development of world petroleum resources for the needs of international trade is a basic objective of the Anglo-American Petroleum Agreement now pending before the Congress and is similarly contemplated as an objective of the broader international agreement which is envisaged by the Anglo-American Agreement.

4. The preparation of the American program on other aspects of international post-war economic policy is, as you know, already far advanced. Part of this program is a proposal for an appropriate international organization to facilitate study and discussion of international commodity programs and to aid in the negotiation and operation of particular international commodity arrangements. In this preparatory work, for example, it has been recognized that conservation is an important element to be considered in connection with international commodity arrangements. For the reasons which I have set forth in paragraph number one above, I believe that it would be preferable to

introduce the problems of conservation as a part of the coming international discussions in the field of commercial policy and commodity problems, rather than to treat it separately from, and in advance of these negotiations.

5. To the extent that the foregoing steps would still leave need for special international machinery to deal with problems of conservation, the Economic and Social Council of the proposed general international organization might well be assigned this as one of its first and urgent tasks. This would safeguard against the possibility of creating too much international machinery with possibly overlapping fields of jurisdiction. The powers of the Economic and Social Council and its liaison with the Security Council will put this body in an excellent position to see the economic, social, and political ramifications of the entire problems of resource utilization in proper perspective. It can be expected to stimulate and supplement the activities of international agencies with specified responsibilities in its field.

[13:OF 5637:T]

1139   PRESS CONFERENCE, Executive Offices of the White House, November 14, 1944, 4:10 P. M.

[*Excerpt*] Q: Mr. President, Senator Overton says that the Missouri Valley Authority proposal would be dead, in his opinion, if the Corps of Engineers and the Bureau of Reclamation plan, which he favors, is adopted. Would you care to comment on the acceptability of that plan as a substitute?

The President: I am not really sufficiently in touch with the plans. I couldn't—I couldn't even tell you what is in them exactly.

The problem is this, in the Mississippi Valley. Like other watersheds that contain a good many States, there are always problems between—two kinds. The first is the problem of the States themselves. Each State wants everything, and the say in everything affecting, of course, their own State, but affecting incidentally the whole flow of the river from the top to the bottom, passing through a number of other States. Well, that is something that has to be reconciled.

In the Tennessee watershed, for example, there were, I think, seven States that were affected by the T. V. A., and there was a lot of feeling that they were going to give up some kind of a right; and that was a good many years ago, and it has been in operation for quite a while, and there isn't one of those States today that feels that they have been—that State has been unfairly treated. It has been done for the benefit of all the States, and in proportion to the flow of the water, and the mileage, and the character of the land in the whole Valley.

[608]

Well, there has been a feeling out there in the Missouri Valley, that there are two parts, the parts further back at the head of the streams—tributaries—of the Missouri, and the parts tha are lower down and that are affected by floods and other things. And they think that by some other method they will be able to agree, but it's always been terribly hard to get them to agree, unless there is some—what might be called a central authority to—to make the final decision.

Of course, they ought to be heard the whole length of the Missouri, which covers a tremendous territory, but somebody's—there ought to be somebody—it's a question of speed—getting things done. So they would hear them all, and bring them together, and talk things over, and make a final decision.

Then the second part of it relates to a thing that goes way, way back. Who is to build the dam, the Department of the Interior or the War Department? Well, that is purely a jurisdictional thing, and it has never worried me very much. They each have a corps of dam builders, and they are very good. They built some very, very good dams. Some of them were built by the War Department engineers and some by the Reclamation Bureau.

Of course, the theory—that goes way, way back to 1860 something—is that irrigation was always turned over to the Interior Department to do, but that navigation was turned over to the Army engineers to do. Well, I don't—I don't much care who—who does the actual dam building. It probably is a good thing to have two different dam building authorities—agencies—in the Government, because you get a certain amount of competition between two Government agencies.

Well, there is—as it worked out, they are both pretty good. They are both awfully cocky about the good dams they build. Well, that's fine. That's all to the good. They will both bring in a plan on the same dam, which is part of it navigational in its purpose and part irrigational. And we get plans from both, and then decide which one will do it. Well, that's not bad. There's very little waste as between—in the competition between the two Departments. I would say you would save money, on the whole. But that is a purely jurisdictional thing within the Government construction work.

Of course, the only real example that we have got in operations on a big scale is the T. V. A., and the people down there in all the seven States like it, and it seems to be working. There is no local dispute over the T. V. A. so far, because it has been fair as between the different States. So I don't—I can't tell you in that one particular case about the Missouri, because I am not sufficiently up to date on these different—these different bills.

I still think there ought to be a Missouri Valley Authority. There are an awful lot of States—an awful lot of territory.

And of course, I hope that there will be an authority, for instance, for the Arkansas river. Well, people there—in the East don't—don't visualize it. The Arkansas river rises right on the Continental Divide in western Colorado, and it already has become—has become a menace—floods—by the time it gets down to southeastern Colorado. Pueblo is on the Arkansas river. Well, Pueblo is way out in Colorado. And then it goes—meanders down through a lot of States before it gets down to Arkansas and Louisiana to the Mississippi river. It's an ideal thing to put under an authority.

Same way, we have talked about a Columbia river authority and some people talked about an Ohio river authority, so that I have drawn the thing out on a sheet of paper so many times I can do it in my sleep. A map of the United States—well, I divide it up roughly into seven different regions, one of them being the main stem of the Mississippi river itself, because that has been a separate entity for all time. There is the barge line on the—on the Mississippi, and it is more of a unit than any other river, just a narrow strip from the top end of the country to the southern end of the country.

And I hope that in time we will get seven different authorities, each one with a separate general location.

For instance, a good example, the Cumberland river, which starts up in—what?—northern Kentucky and wanders down into Tennessee. And it's almost parallel with the Tennessee, and actually as it gets west, just before the Ohio goes into the Mississippi, it turns north and goes into the Mississippi [1] within ten or fifteen miles of where the Tennessee goes in. And yet it is an entirely different watershed. Well, in all probability, affecting in general terms the same States, it ought to be part of the—of the Tennessee—Tennessee Valley Authority, to save time and trouble. And the construction work of the T. V. A., of course, will be completed pretty soon. I think it's fair to take on another valley basin.

When you come to the other problems, the little rivers to the south of it, like—what?—Tombigbee, which starts across a little watershed about 150 feet high and about 25 miles from the Tennessee—and the Tennessee, of course, running at that point northwest to the Tombigbee and due south to the Gulf of Mexico—well, there are half a dozen Tombigbees in that—in the Gulf section. Probably, they should be put into a separate authority, including rivers in Texas.

But it is awfully hard, because there is so much feeling, that no one State wants to join up with another State in the general policy or management of running a great watershed project. Mind you, it isn't only water power. That is one of the—one of the lesser things, on the whole.

[13:PRESIDENT'S PRESS CONFERENCES:T]

¹ The Ohio is meant.

1140   HAROLD D. SMITH, DIRECTOR, BUREAU OF THE BUDGET, TO ROOSEVELT

WASHINGTON, D. C., *Nov. 16, 1944*

MEMORANDUM FOR THE PRESIDENT: There are now before the Congress, for its consideration in connection with pending legislation and with your message of September 21 calling for a Missouri Valley Authority, two reports setting up engineering plans for the development of the waters of the Missouri River. The one of the Chief of Engineers, U. S. Army, submitted by the Secretary of War, is published as House Document 475, 78th Congress,¹ the other of the Bureau of Reclamation, submitted by the Secretary of the Interior, is published as Senate Document 191, 78th Congress.² The two reports are in part in conflict.

On October 16 and 17, in accordance with instructions of their bureau chiefs, representatives of the Corps of Engineers and of the Bureau of Reclamation met at Omaha, Nebraska, to develop a technical reconciliation of the engineering plans presented in the two reports. Such a reconciliation has been developed and at my request has been submitted to the Bureau of the Budget.³

Members of Congress and of the press are aware that this reconciliation report has been prepared and that it has been sent to the Bureau of the Budget. It can be anticipated that if this report is not otherwise made available to Congress, members thereof will call upon the departments for its submission.

This reconciliation now results in there being offered by the two agencies, the Bureau of Reclamation and the Corps of Engineers, a single coordinated plan for the development of the waters of the Missouri River. Such a plan would need to be developed ultimately under your proposal that the Congress create a Missouri Valley Authority. I recommend that you transmit this report to the Congress with the attached letters which I have prepared.⁴

HAROLD D. SMITH

[13:OF 1516:TS]

¹ *Missouri River Basin, Letter Submitting Report on Review of Reports on Missouri River for Flood Control Along the Main Stem from Sioux City, Iowa, to the Mouth* (Washington, 1944).
² *Conservation, Control, and Use of Water Resources of the Missouri River Basin* . . . (Washington, 1944).
³ This report of reconciliation, signed by Chief of Engineers Eugene Reybold for the War Department, and by Commissioner of Reclamation Harry W. Bashore for

the Interior Department, to the Secretaries of War and Interior, Oct. 25, 1944, is present (OF 1516). It encloses, "Joint Report of Representatives of Bureau of Reclamation and Corps of Engineers on Plans for Development of the Missouri River Basin," to the Chief of Engineers and the Commissioner of Reclamation, Oct. 17, 1944.

⁴ Identical letters to the Speaker of the House and the President of the Senate; see *post*, 1143.

1141   ROOSEVELT TO HAROLD D. SMITH, DIRECTOR, BUREAU OF THE BUDGET

WASHINGTON, *November 22, 1944*

MEMORANDUM FOR THE DIRECTOR OF THE BUDGET: Jonathan Daniels tells me that the pending Flood Control Bill will jeopardize the possibility of the creation of the Missouri Valley Authority and other similar projects.¹

Will you make a study and let me know?

F. D. R.

[*Notation*: T] Memorandum in re the Flood Control Bill, H. R. 4485, a copy of the bill being attached.

[13:OF 132:CT]

¹ Daniels wrote to Roosevelt Nov. 20, 1944 (OF 132), that the policy of the bill as stated in its preamble was antagonistic to his program of river development through regional authorities based on the TVA plan.

1142   ROOSEVELT TO EDWARD R. STETTINIUS, JR., UNDER SECRE-TARY OF STATE

WASHINGTON, *November 22, 1944*

MEMORANDUM FOR THE UNDER SECRETARY OF STATE: I am not satisfied with the Department's attitude on a Conservation Conference. Whoever wrote the memorandum for you ¹ has just failed to grasp the real need of finding out more about the world's resources and what we can do to improve them.

Just for example, take the case of Persia (Iran). The greater part of it, i. e., the North, used to be a forested country. Today it is utterly bare with a few cattle and a few very poor crops in the small valleys. The people are destitute. Anyone who knows forestry would say that an immediate program of tree planting is the only hope for the Persia of the future. The population is abject—poverty stricken—filthy. Very little water means that something drastic must be done and it will take several hundred years to accomplish it.

But it is a big country and there is plenty of labor. Persia has no resources to buy our products.

Very little is actually known about it, but I am sure there are enormous possibilities.

Lots of countries are like this.

My thought is that we should call a Conference to which each of the United and Affiliated Nations would send one representative. Most of them are poor. One man from each country is enough. The countries that wanted to send somebody could have them meet here in a more or less secluded spot and we would get world information which is now lacking, and in a short period of time we could begin a program to build up non-buying nations into good customers.

When I say a short space of time, I mean a hundred years but that is short in these times.

Will you let me have this memorandum back and also the letter from Governor Pinchot? [2]

F. D. R.

[13:OF 5637:TS]

[1] *Ante,* 1137.
[2] *Ante,* 1125. Answered *post,* 1145.

1143   ROOSEVELT TO REPRESENTATIVE SAM RAYBURN OF TEXAS, SPEAKER OF THE HOUSE OF REPRESENTATIVES

WASHINGTON, *November 27, 1944*

SIR: On September 21, 1944, I sent a message to the Congress recommending the creation of a Missouri Valley Authority that would be charged with the duty of preparing and carrying out a single coordinated plan for the development of the Missouri River Basin for the greatest benefit of its citizens, both present and future, and for the greatest benefit to the United States. At that time there was under consideration by the Congress two reports, the one presented by the Corps of Engineers, the other by the Bureau of Reclamation, which, while presenting comprehensive plans for the development of the Missouri River, were in conflict in many details. The two bureaus have reconciled the technical differences in these two reports and have prepared a joint recommendation which, in conjunction with the two reports, constitutes a basic plan for the development and control of the waters of the Missouri River.

This joint plan represents a beginning in the solution of the problems of the Missouri Valley. But it is only a beginning, for other important matters not within the scope of this joint report bear very materially upon the entire region. As a practical matter, most of these cannot be dealt with by conference and agreement among the ten states directly involved working with separate Federal agencies, for the delay in getting action would be too great to bring about the objectives important to the economy of the entire region. A single authority, such as the Tennessee Valley Authority, over the entire region would provide an adequate mechanism for the adjustment of the interests of the states and for the planning and development of the entire valley.

I am transmitting herewith a copy of that report of reconciliation together with accompanying papers. I now recommend that the plans of the two bureaus, published in House Document 475, 78th Congress, and Senate Document 191, 78th Congress, as modified in accordance with the recommendations of this joint report, be authorized as a basic engineering plan to be developed and administered by a Missouri Valley Authority, such as I have already recommended in my message of September 21.[1]

Sincerely yours,

[FRANKLIN D. ROOSEVELT]

[*Notation*: A] Copy of this letter sent to Budget
[*Notation*: AS] HDS [2]
[13:OF 1516:CT]

[1] This letter was read in the House on Nov. 28, 1944, and referred to the Committee on Rivers and Harbors. The same letter, addressed to the President of the Senate, was read in the Senate on the same day and referred to the Committee on Commerce (*Cong. Rec.*, 78th Cong., 2d sess., 90: 6, 8479–8491, 8504).
[2] Budget Director Harold D. Smith, in whose agency this letter was drafted.

1144   JAMES G. PATTON, PRESIDENT, NATIONAL FARMERS UNION, TO ROOSEVELT

WASHINGTON 4, D. C., *December 7, 1944*

DEAR MR. PRESIDENT: What people like about the TVA idea is that it has decentralized government back to the people themselves. National policies have been applied without adulteration, but they have been adapted to fit the realities of the region, states, and localities.

As one of our Rocky Mountain members has put it, we want to know at all times whom to go to, whom to blame or credit for policies and actions that hurt or help—and we want to get to them without having to travel half way across the continent to do it.

As we go into the historic fight to apply this new principle of government—perhaps the greatest proven discovery of your administration—I wish you would, if you feel you can do so, write me a brief message making explicit and unequivocal your support for the central idea of TVA, viz., *genuine decentralization to the region without the intervention of any department, agency, coordinating board or commission, with responsibility direct to the Office of the President and the Congress.*

Frankly, we fear that, in the midst of the debate over the MVA bill this winter, the issue may be confused by a superficially plausible argu-

ment that, to ease the burden on the President or on some other pretext, coordination of various regional authorities should be assigned either to Interior or some new agency.

In our view, coordination if it means anything, means control, and control of administration in Washington means the destruction of decentralization, the key to TVA's success. Unless the MVA, and any other regional authorities proposed, retain this essential characteristic, neither our organization nor people generally will be interested in supporting it.

At present, necessary fiscal and budgetary coordination is being attended to by your Bureau of the Budget and can be continued there, and broad general policies are coordinated by the Congress, as they should be.

Your assurance on this central issue of genuine, unequivocal, all-out decentralization with respect to MVA and similar authorities for the Columbia, Arkansas, and other river valleys will be of immense help in the weeks and months to come. I hope you will give that word now. With it in hand, we can be well on the way toward success in making TVA the pilot operation for the Nation.[1]

Respectfully yours,

JIM PATTON

[APS] Mr President: Ickes is certainly muddying up the whole basic T. V. A. concept. JIM

[13:OF 1516:TS]

[1] A copy of this letter, with the postscript omitted, was sent by Roosevelt to Ickes with a memorandum dated Dec. 11, 1944 (OF 1516), reading, "Please read and return. I am inclined to believe that he is right." Ickes reacted violently in a lengthy letter of Dec. 18, 1944 (OF 1516). After restating his position on the administration of regional conservation authorities, he charged that the Missouri Valley Authority bill would lead to the destruction of the Interior Department. He said that the problems confronting the development of the Missouri Valley's resources were far more varied and complex than those of the Tennessee Valley, and that the TVA method was unsuited to the former region.

1145   EDWARD R. STETTINIUS, JR., UNDER SECRETARY OF STATE, TO ROOSEVELT

WASHINGTON, *December 16, 1944*

MEMORANDUM FOR THE PRESIDENT . . . PROPOSED CONFERENCE ON CONSERVATION AND NATURAL RESOURCES: Your memorandum of November 22 makes it clear that we had previously misunderstood this proposal. We had been thinking of it in terms of a "full-dress" international conference and we had questioned its advisability during the war. We had had in mind the difficulty in getting facts from countries still the scene of hostilities, and possible duplication of the conservation work of some of the other conferences.

My suggestion would be that we start now finding out more about the world's resources and what we can do to improve them, on an experimental basis, in areas where the necessary information can be obtained during the war. These would include the Near and Middle East, Africa, and this hemisphere.

Subject to your approval, a meeting could be called in North Africa for the Near and Middle East and Africa. A similar one could be held in this hemisphere under the auspices of the Inter-American Economic and Financial Committee or the Pan American Union. A good start, even during the war, could thus be made on these areas about most of which existing data is very inadequate. Then, after hostilities cease, we could complete the job by gathering the requisite information on Europe and the Far East.

The next time we are together, perhaps we can discuss this further. The memorandum and the letter from Governor Pinchot are returned herewith, as you requested.[1]

E. R. Stettinius, Jr.

[13:OF 5637:TS]

[1] *Ante,* 1142, 1125.

1146   Harold L. Ickes, Secretary of the Interior, to Harold
D. Smith, Director, Bureau of the Budget

Washington 25, D. C., Dec. 22, 1944

My dear Mr. Smith: This Department has been requested to report on enrolled bill H. R. 2241, entitled "An Act to abolish the Jackson Hole National Monument as created by Presidential Proclamation Numbered 2578, dated March 15, 1943." [1]

I recommend that the President withhold his approval from H. R. 2241 for the reasons stated in the attached draft of a proposed memorandum of disapproval.[2] In addition, the abolishment of the Jackson Hole National Monument would make impossible the acceptance of the offer to the Federal Government by John D. Rockefeller, Jr., of 32, 117 acres of strategic land within the monument, a gift to the people of the United States which cost him approximately one and one-half million dollars.

The Proclamation of March 15, 1943, issued pursuant to the Antiquities Act of June 8, 1906 (34 *Stat.* 225), which established the Jackson Hole National Monument, merely reserved the Federal lands within the monument boundaries from all forms of appropriation under the public land laws, subject to prior existing rights, and provided for their administration as a national monument. The owners of private lands within the limits of the monument retain their ownership and are entitled to the full use and enjoyment of their property to the same extent as private landowners elsewhere.

Soon after the creation of Jackson Hole National Monument by the President I issued a policy statement outlining the principles to be followed in its administration. A copy of that statement is enclosed.[3] Since then I have repeatedly indicated that I would be willing to support legislation that would extend the force of law to the policies expressed in that statement. Nor would I object to the enactment of legislation which, in addition to providing for the continuance of existing leases, permits and licenses during the lifetime of the present holders and the members of their immediate families, would provide for the continuation of grazing privileges on Federal lands within the monument until such time as the lands to which these privileges are now appurtenant had been acquired by the Federal Government. Provisions to this effect were contained in H. R. 5469 introduced by Chairman Peterson of the House Public Lands Committee on November 16.

In all fairness it must be admitted that a serious tax problem will confront the people of Teton County, Wyoming, if and when the Rockefeller holdings are acquired by the United States. In order to overcome the objection that the local tax structure would be jeopardized as a result of the removal of these lands from the tax rolls, I have gone on record as favoring the enactment of legislation which would permit some part of the revenues inuring to the Federal Government from national parks and monuments to be turned over to Teton County. Appropriate provisions to this end were also contained in H. R. 5469.

I appeared before the House Committee on the Public Lands and the Senate Committee on Public Lands and Surveys when H. R. 2241 was before them for consideration. In my statements to those Committees I took great pains to outline the true facts involved and to explain the misrepresentations and misunderstandings which the proponents of H. R. 2241 have intentionally and widely circulated, not only through the press, but also in the course of the hearing and debates on this measure. For your information I am enclosing copies of my statements to the Committees.[4]

Sincerely yours,

HAROLD L. ICKES

[13 : BUDGET BUREAU ENROLLED BILLS : TS]

[1] H. R. 2241 was debated at length in the House on Dec. 8 and 11, 1943. Its supporters made much of the argument that in establishing the monument by proclamation the President had usurped the powers of Congress. They charged that the area was not worthy of monument status, that its residents would be unjustly deprived of their homes, and that the monument was not wanted by Wyoming. Most of the western representatives supported the bill; however, Outland (Calif.), in a long and obviously carefully prepared statement, said that the manner of the preservation of the area (whether by park or monument) was immaterial: the important thing was to preserve it while it retained its wilderness character. The bill was approved

by the House on Dec. 11 and by the Senate on Dec. 19, 1944 (*Cong. Rec.*, 78th Cong., 2d sess., 90: 17, 9090–9095, 9183–9186, 9804). With passage of the bill, supporters of the monument asked for a veto; its opponents urged approval.

² Ickes' draft is present; concerning it see *post,* 1148 n.

³ "Statement of Policy Concerning Administration of Jackson Hole National Monument, Wyoming," a one-page mimeographed document issued by the Secretary of the Interior on April 8, 1943.

⁴ "Statement of the Secretary of the Interior Before the House Public Lands Committee, June 1, 1943"; "Statement of Harold L. Ickes, Secretary of the Interior, Before the Senate Committee on Public Lands and Surveys, on H. R. 2241, A Bill to Abolish the Jackson Hole National Monument, Friday, December 15, 1944." (These are mimeographed documents.) The House Committee hearings are printed: *To Abolish the Jackson Hole National Monument, Wyoming,* Hearings, 78th Cong., 1st sess., on H. R. 2241, May 19–June 9, 1943 (Washington, 1943).

1147   STATEMENT BY ROOSEVELT ON SIGNING THE 1944 FLOOD CONTROL BILL

[WASHINGTON] *December 23, 1944*

I have signed, on December 22, 1944, the Flood Control Bill, H. R. 4485. It appears to me that, in general, this legislation is a step forward in the development of our national water resources and power policies. The plan of calling upon states affected by proposed projects for their views is a desirable one, but, of course, the establishment of such a procedure should not be interpreted by anyone as an abrogation by the Federal Government of any part of its powers over navigable waters. Authorization of the projects listed in the bill will augment the backlog of public works available for prompt initiation, if necessary, in the post-war period.

I note, however, that the bill authorizes for construction by the Corps of Engineers and the Bureau of Reclamation those improvements in the Missouri River Basin which, on November 27, 1944, I recommended be developed and administered by a Missouri Valley Authority. My approval of this bill is given with the distinct understanding that it is not to be interpreted as jeopardizing in any way the creation of a Missouri Valley Authority, the establishment of which should receive the early consideration of the next Congress.

I consider the projects authorized by the bill to be primarily for post-war construction, and, until the current wars are terminated, I do not intend to submit estimates of appropriation or approve allocations of funds for any project that does not have an important and direct value to the winning of the war.¹

FRANKLIN D. ROOSEVELT

[W. H. PRESS RELEASES: M]

¹ This was drafted by the Budget Bureau. A slightly different version, signed by Roosevelt, is present (Budget Bureau Enrolled Bills); in this the first sentence reads, "I have today signed the Flood Control Bill, H. R. 4485." A much longer Interior Department draft is also present; with this is a memorandum, Rosenman to Roose-

velt, Dec. 22, 1944, recommending that the Budget Bureau draft be issued. The Interior Department draft noted that the new law provided for "participation by the states and other agencies in the work of the Army Engineers," and gave "assurance that the views of affected states and agencies on proposed works" should be presented to Congress in an orderly manner. It noted that the Secretary of the Interior was given authority to make sure that electric power developed under the act would be disposed of in the public interest, and that reclamation uses of water from Army dams and reservoirs were placed under that official. The Interior Department draft also reviewed the Reclamation Bureau-Army Engineers dispute over the administration of the Central Valley of California projects and pointed out that the new law incorporated the policies urged by the Interior Department.

1148   ROOSEVELT TO THE CONGRESS

THE WHITE HOUSE, *December 29, 1944*

MEMORANDUM OF DISAPPROVAL: I have withheld my approval from H. R. 2241, "To abolish the Jackson Hole National Monument as created by Presidential Proclamation Numbered 2578, dated March 15, 1943."

The effect of this bill would be to deprive the people of the United States of the benefits of an area of national significance from the standpoint of naturalistic, historic, scientific and recreational values. The Jackson Hole National Monument as established by Proclamation Numbered 2578 constitutes an outstanding example of a valley formed by block-faulting and glacial action, and has as significant a story to tell of these great forces of nature as has the Grand Canyon to reveal of erosive processes. It also constitutes a breeding and feeding ground for rare types of birds and animal life. For many years it was a celebrated rendezvous of trappers and Indians; very few areas of the West preserve as many frontier associations. In addition, it provides the necessary foreground for the great mountain peaks in the adjoining Grand Teton National Park, and in its scenic and geologic characteristics forms an integral part of the whole Grand Teton region.

In issuing the proclamation creating the Jackson Hole National Monument, I followed precedents repeatedly established by my predecessors, beginning with President Theodore Roosevelt, in exercising the authority conferred by section 2 of the Antiquities Act approved by the Congress on June 8, 1906 (34 *Stat.* 225). Eighty-two national monuments have been established by Presidents of the United States of both political parties. Seven of these monuments are larger than the Jackson Hole National Monument. There are few official acts of the President of the United States, in the field of conservation or in any other phase of Government, so amply supported by precedent, as is the proclamation establishing Jackson Hole National Monument. In the light of the legislative history of the Antiquities Act of June 8, 1906, and the interpretation placed thereon by the Supreme Court of the United States in *Cameron* v. *United States* (252 U. S. 450), I am convinced that Jackson

[619]

Hole is an "object of historic or scientific interest" within the meaning of that Act. Therefore, I cannot assent to the position taken by the proponents of H. R. 2241 that the monument reserve should be annulled on the ground that there was no authority for its creation.

The proclamation establishing the Jackson Hole National Monument reserved only the Federal lands within appropriately designated boundaries, and was issued subject to all valid existing rights. As in the case of many other Federal reservations, certain private and State lands are also within the boundaries designated in the proclamation. These lands, which comprise a small fraction of the total acreage, are not affected in any way by the proclamation. They are still in private and State ownership and the rights of the owners are the same as they were before the proclamation was issued. No lands have been or can be confiscated; no citizens have been or can be dispossessed. Moreover, private property and incomes within the monument boundaries remain subject to taxation by the State and county to the same extent as they were before the monument was established.

Soon after Jackson Hole National Monument was created, the Secretary of the Interior issued a policy statement setting forth definite principles to govern the administration of the Federal lands within the monument. This statement provides for the continuance of all permits issued by the Forest Service or other Federal agencies for the use of lands now within the national monument during the lifetime of the present holders and the members of their immediate families. In this statement the Secretary recognized existing grazing privileges on monument lands and existing stock driveway privileges, and declared that cattlemen desiring in the spring and fall to drive their cattle across monument lands, between their respective ranches and the summer ranges, would be permitted to do so as a matter of settled administrative policy.

I recognize the seriousness of the tax problem that might be produced in Teton County, Wyoming, were those lands within the monument boundaries which have been acquired by private interests, for ultimate incorporation in the monument, to be removed from the tax rolls at a time when fully equivalent revenues have not as yet accrued to the County through the development of the tourist attractions of the region. I would be sympathetic to the enactment of legislation whereby revenues derived by the Federal Government from the National Park and Monument system could be used to off-set, on an equitable basis, any loss of taxes due to the Federal acquisition, by donation or purchase, of private lands within the monument. I would also be sympathetic to the enactment of legislation that would incorporate into law the administrative policies with respect to the private utilization of Federal lands within the monument to which I have already referred. Among other things, such legislation might provide assurance for private landholders within the monument who now have grazing privileges on Federal lands that these privileges will be continued to them, and to their heirs and assigns, so long as the lands to which these privileges are appurtenant remain in private ownership.

In the establishment of the Jackson Hole National Monument consideration was given to the interests of the people of the United States as a whole in order that the area might be preserved and made available to our citizens for the realization of its highest values, including its scenery, its scientific interest, its wildlife and its history. I believe that whatever reasonable objections may exist to the continuance of the monument can be overcome without depriving this area of the protection to which it is justly entitled under the Antiquities Act of June 8, 1906, and under the other laws relating to national monuments. Therefore, it would seem to me that the proper remedy in this situation is not the undoing of what has been done, but the making of such adjustments as may be appropriate to meet the local conditions.

For these reasons I feel that it is my duty to withhold approval from H. R. 2241.[1]

FRANKLIN D. ROOSEVELT

[W. H. PRESS RELEASES : M]

[1] This memorandum of disapproval was drafted by the Budget Bureau. It is the same as the draft that Ickes sent to the Budget Bureau in his letter of Dec. 22, 1944 (*ante*, 1146), except for the omission of a paragraph which followed paragraph two of the statement as here printed. This omitted portion called attention to the eighty-two national monuments that had been created by Presidents of both parties since the approval of the American Antiquities Act of June 8, 1906 (34 *Stat.* 225). With the Budget Bureau draft is a memorandum, Rosenman to Roosevelt, Dec. 27, 1944, referring to H. R. 2241, "I concur in the recommendation that this bill be vetoed, and recommend that the memorandum of disapproval prepared by the Budget Bureau be signed."

Senator O'Mahoney of Wyoming, leader of the Senate group supporting the bill, wrote to Roosevelt at length on Dec. 22, 1944 (OF 928). He urged that the bill be approved on the principal ground that the creation of the monument was an injustice to those landowners in the area who had not sold their land to Rockefeller. Hassett replied Dec. 30, 1944 (OF 928), that while the President regretted that he could not accede to O'Mahoney's wishes, he felt sure that his decision, "reached after most careful consideration," would merit his respect. Of the thirty-some letters in the Roosevelt Library concerning the act (OF 928), about a third (mostly from western governors) urged its approval, while the remainder (mostly from heads of conservation organizations) urged its veto. In 1950 Jackson Hole National Monument became part of Grand Teton National Park.

1149   ROOSEVELT TO EDWARD R. STETTINIUS, JR., SECRETARY OF STATE

WASHINGTON, January 2, 1945

MEMORANDUM FOR THE SECRETARY OF STATE: It is perfectly all right for Joe Grew to act as President of "The Save-the-Redwoods League" but I think it important to get the idea abroad that some long-time conservationists are interested. For example, Gifford Pinchot, who is undoubtedly our No. 1 conservationist, should be in this thing.[1]

F. D. R.

[13:OF 5666:CT]

[1] Stettinius, in a memoranlum to Roosevelt of Dec. 27, 1944 (OF 5666), asked if it would be proper for Grew to head a campaign for funds to establish a "National Tribute Grove" to honor the men and women of the armed forces of World War II.

1150 ROOSEVELT TO GEORGE SEHLMEYER, MASTER, CALIFORNIA STATE GRANGE, Sacramento

[WASHINGTON] January 8, 1945

MY DEAR MR. SEHLMEYER: Secretary Ickes has told me of his conversation with you regarding your proposal for establishing a Central Valley Authority, about which you wired me on October 5.[1] I am hopeful that this area may be included in legislation for establishing River Basin agencies.

I have repeatedly urged that additional projects in the Central Valley such as the Kings and Kern River developments be undertaken by the Reclamation Bureau in order to achieve orderly unified administration under the Reclamation Laws. Moreover, effective coordination of these multiple-purpose water conservation projects with the other local activities of the Department of the Interior, such as the mineral development work of the Bureau of Mines and the program for fish and wildlife conservation, is essential to a proper resource program of the basin.

I favor the establishment of regional agencies for the handling of Federal responsibilities in the field of conservation. However, legislation creating such an agency for the Central Valley or for any other region where the irrigation of arid lands is a major concern should include the most careful consideration of this phase of water conservation and should carry forward the sound traditions of the Reclamation Laws.[2]

Very sincerely yours,

[FRANKLIN D. ROOSEVELT]

JHL

[Notation:AS] Copy of this reply sent to Interior 1/9/45. hms

[13:OF 402:CT]

[1] Sehlmeyer said that the position of the California State Grange was that the complex problems of the Central Valley project could best be solved by a regional administration, and that the Grange feared that pending legislation in Congress would result in competition among Federal agencies in developing the project (OF 402).

[2] (Drafted by the Interior Department.) On the failure to resolve the Central Valley dispute, see Maass, <i>Muddy Waters</i>, pp. 252–259.

ROOSEVELT TO HAROLD L. ICKES, SECRETARY OF THE
            INTERIOR

[WASHINGTON] *January 8, 1945*

DEAR HAROLD: Before I answer Patton's letter about the Missouri Valley and other Authorities,[1] I wish you would give consideration to two problems which tie in with the whole subject.

The first is the preservation of State's rights and the Authority method seems to have done this very well in the case of TVA—McKellar being the only dissenter. The other matter relates to the Interior Department. What you say is perfectly true in the sense that no President ought to have to manage or settle the problems of seven or eight different Authorities.

On the other hand, TVA's great success has been the fact that it has been, in practice, autonomous and people in the Tennessee watershed can get decisions and actions from Knoxville instead of having to come to Washington. How can we arrange things so that this will continue but that at the same time, Interior will have a large say and a final say in things like grazing, irrigation, etc. etc.?

This, of course, would be more true in places like the Missouri Valley than in an Authority over the Eastern Seaboard Valleys, for example.[2]

F. D. R.

[13:OF 1516:CT]

[1] *Ante,* 1144.
[2] Ickes replied Jan. 15, 1945 (OF 1516), that he believed in "regional agencies administered in the region by officials who have jurisdiction to make final decisions." He described a plan which he favored: this contemplated a number of regional agencies, to be coordinated by a River Basin Planning Board, headed by the Secretary of the Interior. This board would "develop general national plans and programs for river basin development," and the Secretary of the Interior would be empowered to supervise the activities of the various regional authorities. Ickes said that he had drafted a bill embodying these proposals for introduction in Congress if Roosevelt approved, and he enclosed a draft reply to Patton which argued: (1) a drive for several regional authorities would be more successful than for one; (2) with "a multiplicity of such authorities" a central agency was necessary; and (3) this agency should be the Interior Department. Ickes' proposed letter was not sent. Patton wrote to Roosevelt again on March 28, 1945 (OF 1516), charging that Ickes' campaign to gain control of all valley authorities was threatening to block affirmative action on the Missouri Valley Authority bill.

1152   ROOSEVELT TO GIFFORD PINCHOT, Washington

WASHINGTON, *January 16, 1945*

MEMORANDUM FOR HON. GIFFORD PINCHOT: I have been so busy over the new year that this is the first chance I have had to send you

Stettinius' memorandum to me.[1] What do you think of these area conferences?

F. D. R.

[13: OF 5637: CT]

[1] *Ante*, 1145.

Part V

The Fourth Term: 1945

The Fourth Term: 1945

WASHINGTON 6, D. C., *January 21, 1945*

DEAR MR. PRESIDENT: When you told me at luncheon on Friday that you are going to take up the proposed Conference on conservation as a basis of permanent peace with Churchill and Stalin, I saw great things ahead and was more delighted than I can easily say.[1]   In view of that decision, would it be a good plan to make for you a rough preliminary list of subjects to be considered and get together some applicable facts about natural resources?

If you think it might be helpful, shall I go ahead, quietly and informally, and of course without publicity, and ask a few Government experts for needed assistance?   For I am very far from knowing it all.

Another matter.   I am deeply pleased and very grateful that you are willing to send a message to the Forest Service on its Fortieth Birthday. It is to be read on the afternoon of February first, on which day, forty years ago, Theodore Roosevelt signed the bill.   I hope the enclosed draft may be of use.[2]

Warmest good wishes to you and yours from Leila and me, and a safe and successful journey.

Yours as always,

GIFFORD PINCHOT

[*Notation*:A:TULLY] OK to prepare

[13:OF 1–C:TS]

[1] There is no record of Pinchot having lunched at the White House on the preceding Friday (January 19).   He may have seen Roosevelt on Friday, January 12, at Hyde Park.   The President left for the Crimea Conference on Jan. 22, 1945.   See below.

[2] Pinchot here referred to the passage of the act transferring the forest reserves from the Interior Department to the Agriculture Department, approved Feb. 1, 1905 (33 *Stat.* 628).   The enclosed draft was revised by Roosevelt and sent as a letter of congratulations to Forest Service Chief Lyle F. Watts, Feb. 1, 1945 (OF 1–C).

WASHINGTON 6, D. C., *January 22, 1945*

DEAR MR. PRESIDENT: Here is the brief preliminary statement on the proposed Conservation Conference about which Mrs. Boettiger spoke to me yesterday.[1] I hope it will answer your purpose.

I have intentionally avoided detail, first because you yourself don't need it, and also because the more detail, the more chance there might be for dissent from others.

During your absence I am going ahead to prepare a much more detailed plan for the proposed Conference, as I understand from Mrs. Boettiger you wish me to do.   Much material has already been collected by individuals, by certain Nations, and by the League of Nations.   I shall need to consult a number of experts, some in the Government service.   I take it I have your permission to do so.

Every good wish to you, and every success on your epoch-making journey.

Yours as always,

GIFFORD PINCHOT

[13:OF 5637:TS]

[1] This is embodied in the longer statement enclosed by Pinchot in his letter to Roosevelt of March 28, 1945, *post*, 1165.

1155   ROOSEVELT TO HENRY L. STIMSON, SECRETARY OF WAR

[WASHINGTON] *Jan. 31, 1945*

MY DEAR MR. SECRETARY: On December 22, 1944, I gave my approval to Public Law 534 authorizing the construction of certain public works on rivers and harbors for flood control and for other purposes. This bill authorizes the appropriation of $955,500,000 to your Department for surveys and for the construction of the public works authorized therein.   As I stated when I signed the bill, I consider the projects authorized to be primarily for post-war construction, and until the current wars are terminated I do not intend to submit estimates of appropriation or approve allocations of funds for any project that does not have an important and direct value to the winning of these wars.   Moreever, some of these projects have lower economic priority than others. Also there are features, I think, of some of these projects that will require adjustment before initiation of programs for their construction.   I wish, therefore, that you defer making any allocation of funds or request for appropriations either for construction or for the preparation of necessary plans, specifications, and preliminary work for any of these projects, until they are taken up with the Director of the Bureau of the Budget for Executive Office approval.

I think that all of us concerned with rivers and harbors and conservation of water resources recognize today that one river is one problem. No longer can we make a practice of treating each consideration as an isolated problem. Rather, the whole must be considered. I think that your Department has had for some years now full authority to make continuing surveys for flood control, navigation, and hydroelectric power development on practically all of the major streams of the Nation, and it seems to me that these individual flood control surveys might well be consolidated in comprehensive basin studies. Furthermore, other agencies of government concerned with water resource control and development are making surveys on the streams of the country. It seems to me that when more than one agency is concerned with development of a river basin, the best composite judgment of the executive branch shall be made available for consideration, and all the agencies concerned should work together and make reports, through the Bureau of the Budget, to me and to the Congress, jointly setting forth recommendations as to what physical works are needed for the development of the basin.

I wish you would have your Department proceed to follow out these suggestions in order that, with the least possible delay, work can go forward in full towards the preparation of necessary plans and specifications for this part of the backlog of public works for post-war construction.

Sincerely yours,

[FRANKLIN D. ROOSEVELT]

[*Notation*:AS] HDS [1]

[13:OF 635:CT]

[1] Budget Director Harold D. Smith, in whose agency this letter was drafted. In his memorandum to Roosevelt of Jan. 23, 1945 (OF 635), enclosing the draft, Smith said he thought the time had come to stop making piecemeal surveys of parts of the country's rivers. "We should consider each river basin as a whole and, in fact, should coordinate the surveys of the various agencies while they are being made." Stimson replied to Roosevelt Feb. 27, 1945 (OF 635), that he would comply with the President's wishes. With respect to the need for considering river basins as entities and for getting the "best composite judgment of the agencies concerned," Stimson said the Corps of Engineers had been doing this for several years.

1156   SAMUEL I. ROSENMAN, SPECIAL COUNSEL TO THE PRESIDENT, AND JONATHAN DANIELS, ADMINISTRATIVE ASSISTANT TO THE PRESIDENT, TO ROOSEVELT

WASHINGTON, *February 7, 1945*

MEMORANDUM FOR THE PRESIDENT: In your absence we have talked with David Lilienthal about the questions involved in the proposed extension of the TVA idea to other regions. At our request he has prepared a long memorandum, a summary of which is attached.[1] We are impressed with the points he makes and hope very much that no plans or decisions in this field will be made by you until we have had an opportunity to discuss it with you further.   Also, we hope that you can find time to discuss the matter with Lilienthal after your return.

SIR
JD

[13:OF 1516:TS]

¹ The longer memorandum has not been found in the Roosevelt papers.

1157   [*Enclosure*] DAVID E. LILIENTHAL, CHAIRMAN, TENNESSEE VALLEY AUTHORITY, TO SAMUEL I. ROSENMAN AND JOHATHAN DANIELS

[WASHINGTON, *February 7, 1945*]

This is a summary of a memorandum to you, prepared at your request and discussed with you February 6, 1945, plus reference to a few additional points developed in the course of our yesterday's discussion.

1. The effective way to secure legislation providing for additional regional agencies like TVA, as recommended by the President in his message to the Congress of September 21, 1944, is at this stage to concentrate on a Missouri Valley Authority (MVA).

The legislative phase, even for one more regional agency, will take a considerable period at best.   To press, simultaneously, for a number of "TVA's" at this point will endanger the early prospects of action on the one that has the best chance.   That one is probably MVA, because of strong and increasing support and understanding of the idea within that region.   This kind of priority attention will not discourage the continued growth of local support for such agencies in other regions— such as Arkansas Valley, Columbia Valley, and perhaps the Central Valley in California.   On the contrary.

2. The vitality in the TVA idea lies in the decentralization of its administration, the fixing of responsibility in a Board making its decisions in the field.   That is what the people want.   That is why the Tennessee Valley people fight for TVA.   It is the feature about TVA most widely discussed.   To suggest that an MVA should not be independent like TVA but should be made subordinate to the Department of Interior would be interpreted by advocates of an MVA as a repudiation of the essential characteristic of the regional development they are so vigorously supporting.   The only people now supporting MVA would fall away.   The loss of this support would spell defeat for any regional agencies.

3. Advocates of MVA have studied the TVA.   They understand that on this point there can be no compromise.   They realize that TVA's decentralized methods of administration rest squarely on the independ-

ence of its Board. The characteristics are not separable. When it is suggested that regional authorities may make their decisions in the field while at the same time reporting to the Secretary of the Interior for the purposes of "coordination" they recognize that such administrative "coordination" is a denial of the power to decide in the field. "Coordination" of operating decisions is control of those decisions. Under a regional agency like TVA coordination takes place in the field, not in Washington. Problems are settled where they arise, not referred up through bureaucratic levels.

4. The creation of an independent MVA need not result in an unreasonable burden on the President. In fact, properly organized, an MVA should be from the beginning as TVA has been in its maturity, a device to lessen the administrative burdens inevitably connected with the development of a region's resources.

An analysis of the problems on which TVA has been required to consult the President reveals that many of them would not be repeated. Today, on the part of Congress, other government officials, and the people there is wide understanding that under the TVA plan responsibility is fixed in the Board. That understanding provides a climate which tends to reduce all the requirements for the personal attention of the President and together with a perfected statute will eliminate almost all the problems which had to be considered by the White House in the early years of TVA.

[13:OF 1516:T]

1158   MORRIS L. COOKE TO ROOSEVELT

WASHINGTON 5, D. C., *February 15, 1945*

MY DEAR MR. PRESIDENT: In connection with an inquiry as to actual results which can be credited to the Great Plains Report (1936 Drought Report) I have run across some very exciting data about the much maligned "tree belt." As originally proposed, the line was theoretically to run generally north and south. Actually the direction of the plantings is generally east and west—to face prevailing local winds. The distance between the Canadian border and the southern end is approximately 2,000 miles but the tree belt sections, if placed end to end, would now run 100,000 miles. Rows of ten are a prevailing standard. 65 percent of the trees planted are in "excellent" condition and only 5 percent are poorly. Much of this area never did have trees. Now that 250,000 acres have been so successfully planted the people have plans for an additional two million acres. They like trees and now know they can have them. Many new varieties have been successfully tried. All these statements should be checked.

In view of the way this suggestion was originally received it occurs to me that you may care to secure "through channels" a report on accomplishments and prospects of the tree belt. Some airplane views would lighten the story. I would be glad to help if needed.[1]

Yours very sincerely,

MORRIS L. COOKE

[13:QF 149:TS]

[1] Answered *post*, 1160.

1159   PRESS CONFERENCE, Aboard the U. S. S. *Quincy*, February 23, 1945, 12:15 P.M.

[*Excerpt*] [1] The President: We can look as far ahead as humanity believes in this sort of thing. The United Nations will evolve into the best method ever devised for stopping war, and it will also be the beginning of something else to go with it.

Last year I flew to Teheran—across Persia. Persia probably is the poorest country in the world. In the early days, Persia was a pretty well wooded country. The Turks cut down all the woods. It has been a woodless country since. Niney-seven or eight percent of the people of Persia are tenants. Only one or two percent of the whole nation owns land or property. The only part they live in in Persia is in river bottoms.

Really, the people of Persia have no money. They can barely get enough to eat. The soil is all eroded—boulders where there should be fields. There's no rainfall, because it hasn't got absolutely any moisture; sun can't draw any out of the land, and the moisture in the land runs off in a few hours time. Persia has no purchasing power in the world except for certain things God gave it, like oil. It is neither sustaining nor has it any money to buy things.

Of course, the obvious thing for Persia to do is to improve its own country. Reforestation is the best hope, and the nation then might sustain itself, its whole standard of civilization would be a great deal higher. They could make more things than it could sell, buy many things it could not make.

The same thing is true about Iraq, Arabia, Lebanon, Syria, Palestine and Turkey. They've got no purchasing power to do anything with. Their only purchasing instrument is oil. Their people are not educated, do not get enough to eat, cannot cope with health problems. We talked quite a lot about this at the conference.[2]

Now, of course, all that is tied up more or less with peace. A country that isn't moving forward with civilization is always more of a potential war danger than a country that is making progress.

[632]

I even talked to Ibn Saud about that—mentioned the fact that I was a tree farmer.

One of his sons—I don't remember which one—was very much impressed, expressed his amazement. He said, "I am a farmer too."

Ibn Saud said, "I am too old to be a farmer. I would be much interested to try it, if I wasn't too old to take it up."

Take the Arabian, for instance. If you want to start a farm, you might build a dam, or start a pond or lake, but it would all evaporate overnight, the air is so dry. But there is plenty of water lying fifty or sixty feet below the ground. Now, if you can keep it below the ground to prevent evaporation, and put in pumps run by oil, you can get it out of the ground and do your irrigating at a very low cost.

This is just an example of how to do the same thing from a different angle.

Q: Wouldn't that be a long-time proposition?

The President: Growing trees is a long-time proposition.

Q: Do you mean that the conference looked ahead over a great many years?

The President: Sure, we are looking at the human race, which we hope won't end in fifty years.

[13:PRESIDENT'S PRESS CONFERENCES:T]

[1] This press conference took place while the *Quincy* was en route from Algiers to Newport News. The President had been asked if the United Nations could be the foundation for world peace for more than the immediate generation. Newspapermen present were Merriman Smith, Douglas Cornell and Robert G. Nixon.

[2] Cf. statement by Roosevelt at the fourth plenary meeting of the Yalta Conference, in the State Department's *Foreign Relations of the United States, Diplomatic Papers. The Conferences at Malta and Yalta, 1945* (Washington, 1955), pp. 715–716.

1160   ROOSEVELT TO MORRIS L. COOKE, Washington

WASHINGTON, *February 26, 1945*

MEMORANDUM FOR MORRIS L. COOKE: I have received yours of February 15th in the middle of the Atlantic. It would be fine if you will work up something for me to use as a statement in regard to the tree belt. This can be done in two ways. First, by something in about 3,000 words, and the other a more complete report with pictures.[1]

F. D. R.

[13:OF 149:CT]

[1] Cooke replied March 13, 1945 (OF 149), that he would have the report prepared as requested.

THE WHITE HOUSE, *March 2, 1945*

To THE CONGRESS OF THE UNITED STATES: I transmit herewith for the information of the Congress a copy of a communication from the Chairman of the Tennessee Valley Authority submitting a report entitled "A Report on the Physiographic, Economic, and Other Relationships Between the Tennessee and Cumberland Rivers and Between Their Drainage Areas." [1]   This report was prepared at my request under the authority vested in the Board of Directors of the Tennessee Valley Authority by section 22 of the Tennessee Valley Authority Act and Executive Order No. 6161 issued pursuant thereto.

The report points out the similarity and inter-relationship between the problems of development of the resources of the Cumberland and Tennessee Valleys.

I have heretofore recommended to the Congress the enactment of legislation to bring the Cumberland River and its tributaries within the scope of the Tennessee Valley Authority Act.   I take this opportunity to urge again that the Congress give consideration to the enactment of such legislation.[2]

FRANKLIN D. ROOSEVELT

[W. H. PRESS RELEASES: M]

[1] Published under this title as House Document 107, 79th Cong., 1st sess. (Washington, 1945).

[2] Read in the Congress March 2, 1945, this message was referred by the Senate to the Committee on Agriculture and Forestry and by the House to the Committee on Military Affairs (*Cong. Rec.*, 79th Cong., 1st sess., 91: 2, 1639, 1672).

On the same date as this message, Roosevelt paid his final tribute to TVA in a letter to Representative Estes Kefauver (OF 42), who had urged reappointment of Lilienthal as TVA chairman:

"You and I can remember when TVA was denounced as one of this administration's wild ideas.   It does not seem wild now even to many of those who damned it most loudly at first.   But it is, as it was, a great American idea.   It is still disturbing, of course, to old advocates of the exploitation of resources without much concern for people beside them.   It still disturbs, too, those who do not understand the meaning of TVA as an instrument by which big government need not be absentee government."

1162   DEAN ACHESON, ACTING SECRETARY OF STATE, TO ROOSEVELT

WASHINGTON, *March 19, 1945*

MEMORANDUM FOR THE PRESIDENT: Subject: Proposed Memorandum for Governor Pinchot.   You requested the Secretary to prepare for your signature a memorandum for Governor Pinchot suggesting that it would be unwise to have a separate International Conference on the subject of Conservation of Resources.

I am attaching a proposed memorandum along the lines outlined to me by the Secretary.

DEAN ACHESON

[13:OF 5637:TS:PHOTOSTAT]

1163 [*Enclosure*]

MEMORANDUM FOR GOVERNOR PINCHOT . . . CONSERVATION CONFERENCE: I refer to our previous talks on this subject.

There is no question that conservation of natural resources, including the rehabilitation of agricultural areas that have been denuded for one reason or another, and the planned use of the world's subsoil resources, is of the greatest importance for the future well being of the world. Also there is no question that international collaboration in this field is needed.

We would not want to have a separate international organization to recommend plans and projects with respect to conservation except subordinate to, and related to, the Economic and Social Council of the proposed United Nations Organization. There are, however, other organizations for which plans have been made and which would also come under the Economic and Social Council; and these other organizations would of necessity have some interest in the field of conservation. I refer particularly to the Food and Agriculture Organization, to the International Bank for Reconstruction and Development (which would, under certain circumstances, make funds available for conservation programs), and to the organization which would facilitate the study and discussion of international commodity programs and would aid in the negotiation and operation of commodity arrangements.

Thus, as you see, there are organizational problems involved which have not yet been fully worked out but many of which will, we hope, be settled at San Francisco. Until they have been worked out, I think we should delay the convocation of a conservation conference.

Meanwhile, however, I have this whole problem most urgently in mind and I shall include a recommendation about it in my message to the San Francisco Conference.

I shall want your advice on this matter after the San Francisco Conference, when we will be able to know better what immediate steps we want to take.

[13:OF 5637:T:PHOTOSTAT]

WASHINGTON, *March 23, 1945*

MEMORANDUM FOR THE PRESIDENT: Anna tells me you wish to be reminded about the world conservation plan in which Governor Pinchot is interested.   Anna also said you were not very pleased with the memorandum ~~on the suggestion~~ from the State Department and that you mentioned you would like Gov. Pinchot and Mr. Hugh H. Bennett, Chief of Soil Conservation Service, to get together and work out something pretty concrete.   After this has been done, you said you wanted it taken up with someone in the State Department who understands and is sympathetic to the idea.

Do you wish one of us to get in touch with Gov. Pinchot, explain to him that you are extremely busy but suggest that he get in touch with Bennett and even tell him that you were not satisfied with the State Department's working out of this matter? [1]

G. G. T.

[*Notation*:A:TULLY] OK
[13:OF 5637:T]

---

[1] Acting Secretary of State Grew took up the Pinchot proposal with Roosevelt following the Cabinet meeting of March 23, 1945. Grew asked him if he wished to discuss the matter or postpone it. "The President said to hold it over as it was not urgent" (memorandum of conversation by Grew, March 23, 1945, State Department, 800.508/3–2345).

1165   GIFFORD PINCHOT TO ROOSEVELT

WASHINGTON 6, D. C., *March 28, 1945*

DEAR MR. PRESIDENT: Before your brilliantly successful visit to Yalta, you were good enough to agree that a rough plan for a World Conference on Conservation as a Basis of Permanent Peace should be worked out during your absence.   Here it is.

T. R. introduced conservation to America.   Nothing could be more fitting than that you, who have already done so much for conservation on this continent, should crown your good work by rendering the same great service to the rest of mankind.

If you decide to call such a Conference, you will guide all Nations toward the intelligent use of the earth for the general good of men, and you will make to the movement for permanent peace the most enduring contribution of all.

The proposed meeting would assist powerfully in attaining the objectives of the Bretton Woods and Dumbarton Oaks Conferences.   It is intended to fit easily into the pattern of the coming international organization.

At your direction, I saw Secretary Wickard. He expressed agreement. Without exception, the Government experts I consulted approved holding the conference.

There will be objections, of course, but the thing can be done.

Every good wish to you, Faithfully yours,

GIFFORD PINCHOT

[13:OF 5637:TS:PHOTOSTAT]

1166   [*Enclosure*]

Table of Suggestions for the Conference

1. Statement of the case as a Preamble to the Invitation to the Conference.

2. Invitation to all peace-loving Nations, to be prepared by the Department of State.

3. Outline Order of Business.

4. Committee on Agenda.

5. Draft of Possible Conclusions.

6. Draft of Possible Recommendations.

7. Possible preliminary action at San Francisco.

A. Preamble to Invitation

Since human history began, the commonest cause of war has been the demand for land. Under whatever name, land means natural resources. And natural resources—forests and waters, soils and minerals—are the material foundations of human security and progress. Without them we cannot live.

Because the commonest of all causes of war is the demand for land, permanent peace is impossible until, through the conservation of natural resources and fair access by the Nations to raw materials they require, general plenty is assured.

No Nation is self-sufficient in all the natural resources its safety and prosperity require. As industrialization increases, so does the demand for more and more varied natural resources and the raw materials they yield.

The greater the demand for natural resources, the greater the mutual interdependence of Nations, and the more pressing the need for international coöperation in world-wide conservation and fair access as indispensable for permanent peace.

Conservation as a policy is universally accepted as sound, and rightly so. For the conservation of natural resources means the planned and orderly use of all that the earth produces for the greatest good of the greatest number for the longest time. It is therefore the basic material problem of mankind.

The conservation problem is concerned not only with the natural resources of the earth. Rightly understood, it includes also the relation of these resources and of their abundance or scarcity to the distribution of peoples over the earth, to the strength or weakness of Nations, to their leaning towards war or towards peace, and to the misery or prosperity, the constant dread or confident security, of their inhabitants.

In 1908 President Theodore Roosevelt, on the valid ground that "The people of the whole world are interested in the natural resources of the whole world, benefited by their conservation, and injured by their destruction" sent to 58 Nations invitations for a World Conference on the Conservation of Natural Resources, to be held in the Peace Palace at The Hague. Thirty of the Nations had accepted when change of Administration defeated the plan.

Although all intermediate attempts failed, the movement for international conservation thus begun in 1908 has recently been given strong support. In 1940 the Eighth American Scientific Congress, representing all the Nations of the Americas, by unanimous vote declared that:

1. Throughout human history the exhaustion of these resources and the need for a new supply have been among the greatest causes of war.

2. International coöperation to inventory, conserve, and wisely utilize natural resources to the mutual advantage of all Nations might well remove one of the most dangerous obstacles to a just and permanent world peace.

In 1941 the British Association for the Advancement of Science, in preparing a plan for an International Resources Office, declared that: "Unless we apply our ordered intelligence to this question, the sequence of crisis and war will continue with ever more disastrous results."

The United Nations took a long step towards lasting peace when, through the Atlantic Charter and the Lend Lease agreements, they declared for fair access to needed raw materials for all the peoples of the world. Yet war is still an instrument of national policy for safeguarding natural resources and for securing them from other Nations.

No more vital task confronts the world than to make future wars impossible. We cannot safely ignore any means that promises to assist in bringing lasting peace.

It would be wise, therefore, for the United Nations, through their appointed delegates, to meet and consider the conservation of natural resources and fair access to raw materials between the Nations as vital steps toward unbroken plenty and permanent peace.

Such a Conference might well consider:

1. An International Organization to promote the conservation of natural resources and fair access to necessary raw materials by all Nations.

2. An inventory of the natural resources of the earth.

3. A set of principles for the conservation of natural resources.

4. A set of principles for securing fair access to necessary raw materials by all Nations.

5. Conservation and fair access in postwar rehabilitation and reconstruction.

6. Such other factors of continuous plenty and permanent peace as the Conference might decide to take up.

The information necessary as a basis for such consideration undoubtedly exists here, and could be assembled without undue delay.

Open discussion by an International Conference should bring to light the principles upon which all Nations can agree for conserving and distributing the natural resources of the earth, to the great end of human welfare through general plenty and lasting peace.

Conservation is a basis of permanent peace. Without world-wide conservation, steadfast peace is impossible. And peace is the hope of the world.

B. Invitation to the Conference to be Prepared by the Department of State

If a majority of the Governments of the United Nations accept this invitation, the Government of the United States is prepared to assemble in advance existing data which the Conference might require, and to draw up and submit to the Conference tentative Agenda for its modification or approval.

C. Outline Order of Business

Address of Welcome: The President of the United States
Subject: Conservation is a Basis of Permanent Peace
Responses by Representatives of Other Countries
Organization of the Conference including appointment of Committees and Staff.

Proceedings

To be organized under the Chief Topics of Forests, Waters, Lands, Minerals, and People.

I. Sectional Sessions to consider the principles of conservation and fair access in relation to each of the five Chief Topics.

II. Plenary Sessions to consider general questions relating to two or more of the Chief Topics, such as:

1. Past Wars for Resources
2. An Inventory of Natural Resources
3. Fair Access to Natural Resources
4. Conservation and Human Welfare

5. Conservation and Full Employment
6. International Financing and Resource Development
7. Migration and Resettlement
8. Stockpiling for War and Peace
9. World-wide Conservation and World Peace
10. Whither Mankind?
11. Recommendations and conclusions of the Conference

The Conference might well be held in the City of Washington in late October, 1945, and be preceded by one or more excursions to the best American examples of conservation applied to Forests, Waters, Lands, Minerals, and People.

If sight-seeing can be included, New York Harbor, Niagara, TVA, an irrigation project, a National Forest, Grand Coulee or Boulder Dam, the Bohemian Grove, Yosemite and the Big Trees, and the Grand Canyon are suggested.

D. Committee on Agenda

A Committee, of nine or more members appointed by the President as soon as practicable, to include representatives of each of the Chief Topics and a representative from the Department of State, and authorized:

1. To prepare and arrange for detailed Agenda for the Sectional and Plenary Sessions.

2. To supervise the collection of material necessary or useful in the deliberations of the Conference.

3. To lay out and manage excursions.

4. To promote coöperation with, and secure necessary assistance from existing organizations in the Government, and in other ways to forward the work of the Conference.

E. Draft of Possible Conclusions

The conservation of natural resources being the planned and orderly use of all that the earth produces for the greatest good of the greatest number for the longest time, the Conference might conclude that:

1. Natural resources are the material foundations of human welfare.

2. No Nation is self-sufficient in all natural resources essential to the safety and prosperity of its people.

3. Without adequate supplies and effective use of necessary natural resources full employment and good living are impossible.

4. The commonest incentive to war has been and still is the desire for land and the natural resources it supplies.

5. The welfare of every Nation depends on fair access to natural resources which it lacks.

6. "The people of the whole world are interested in the natural resources of the whole world, benefited by their conservation, and injured by their destruction."

7. A knowledge of the natural resources of the world is indispensable for using them wisely in the general interest of all peoples.

8. "International coöperation in conserving, utilizing, and distributing natural resources to the mutual advantage of all Nations might well remove one of the most dangerous of all obstacles to a just and permanent world peace."

9. World-wide practice of conservation by wise use and fair access to necessary resources are indispensable bases of continuous plenty and permanent peace.

F. Possible Recommendations

The establishment of an International Conservation Office, whose duty it would be, in coöperation with the United Nations and their appropriate subdivisions:

1. To promote world-wide conservation of natural and human resources to the end of freedom from want and freedom from fear—of better living and permanent peace.

2. To advance the practice of fair access by all Nations.

3. To make, revise, and maintain world inventories of natural resources.

4. To promote international exchange of information concerning supplies on hand, new uses, and probable shortages, of natural resources.

5. To take note of possible disagreements between Nations based on the lack of natural resources, and to recommend means of avoiding them.

6. To cooperate with national organizations concerned with the conservation of natural resources.

7. To make available information useful in the relocation of peoples.

8. To assist in the development, distribution, and especially the conservation, of natural resources throughout the world.

9. To make provision for future Conferences at appropriate intervals.

G. Dr. Lewis L. Lorwin of the FEA [1] has suggested an addition to Chapter I of the Dumbarton Oaks Proposals, entitled "Purposes of the United Nations."

Dr. Lorwin's suggestion is as follows:

4. To encourage international coöperation in the conservation of natural and human resources to the mutual advantage of all Nations in order to maintain and develop the human and material foundations of permanent plenty and enduring peace.

Such an addition would round out and strengthen the statement of Purposes of the General International Organization, and would powerfully advance the cause of conservation among the Nations.

[13:OF 5637:T:PHOTOSTAT]

[1] Foreign Economic Administration.

1167   ROOSEVELT TO ELSA TOEPFER, PRESIDENT, WOMAN'S
       CONSERVATION LEAGUE OF AMERICA, Milwaukee

[WASHINGTON] *April 2, 1945*

MY DEAR MRS. TOEPFER: Because of my long-standing interest in forestry your two letters of February ninth, one to Mrs. Roosevelt and the other to me, were held for my attention while I was away.[1]   I have pretty deep convictions that our forests can and should be handled so that they will contribute much more adequately to our national welfare. Forests protect watersheds that are vital for power, irrigation, and flood control.   They provide outdoor recreation for millions of people.   Productive forests add to our national wealth and support permanent industries.   They mean jobs and payrolls for hundreds of thousands of workers and opportunities for other thousands in professional, personal and public services.

I recognize the facts set forth in the resolution of the Woman's Conservation League of America.   Abuses of our forest resources should be stopped.

The Secretary of Agriculture and the Forest Service have outlined a comprehensive forest program for the Nation.   This program includes the substance of your proposal: sufficient public control of cutting on private lands to prevent abuse and provide for adequate timber growth. It also includes additional aids to farmers and other private timber growers, an increase in public ownership of forest land unsuitable for private ownership, and public work to improve and develop the forests.

I should like to see all phases of such a program go forward at the earliest practical date.   However, viewing the situation in its entirety, I doubt if it would be practical or desirable at this time to single out destructive cutting for action by executive order.   It is important that we find permanent solutions.   That calls for legislative action.

Last year Congress passed and I signed several important forestry measures.   One opens the way for cooperative sustained-yield management of federal forest land and nearby private land.   Another increases the authorization for cooperation with the States in fire protection on the 430 million acres of State and private forest land.   Still another gives authority for completing the Nation-wide forest survey and keeping it up to date.   These measures, I think, show that Congress is deeply interested in forest conservation.[2]

I realize, of course, that the demands of war have aggravated an already serious forest situation.   At the same time, we have been repeatedly reminded of how vital to the war effort lumber and other forest products are.   I am sure that heavy demands upon our timber resources will continue when peace comes.   We shall have to meet pent-up

[642]

civilian needs and we may be asked to help reconstruct war-torn areas abroad. In this we must not lose sight of conservation objectives.

I want you to know that I appreciate your active interest in this subject. Groups such as yours can be of tremendous help in making people aware of the problem. Public discussion of the forest situation and its relation to human welfare will create a firm foundation for a fully effective national program of action.[3]

Very sincerely yours,

[FRANKLIN D. ROOSEVELT]

[13:OF 149:CT]

[1] In both letters (OF 149) Mrs. Toepfer urged that the President use his powers "as authorized by Congress" to prevent forest devastation through improper logging practices. She enclosed copies of a resolution of the Woman's Conservation League of America, Inc., to this effect; this was adopted at a meeting in Milwaukee on Jan. 19, 1945.

[2] The Sustained-Yield Forest Management Act, approved March 29, 1944; the act to amend the Clarke-McNary Act of 1924, approved May 5, 1944; and the act to amend the National Forest Survey Act of 1924, approved May 31, 1944 (58 *Stat.* 132, 216, 265).

[3] Drafted by the Agriculture Department.

1168   ROOSEVELT TO HENRY L. STIMSON, SECRETARY OF WAR, AND MAJOR GENERAL EUGENE REYBOLD, CHIEF OF ENGINEERS, UNITED STATES ARMY

WASHINGTON, *April 9, 1945*

MEMORANDUM . . . Will you talk with the Chairman of the Federal Power Commission [1] so as to get things planned uniformly on the Missouri River Valley Authority situation? Also, it would be a good idea if all of you would talk with Congressman Cochran.

F. D. R.

[*Notation*:T] Ltr of 3/21/45 to the President from Rep. John J. Cochran; in connection with the preparation of plans by the Interior Dept. re the development of the Missouri River Valley projects, it would be helpful to get a favorable expression from the Chief of Engineers of the Army and the Secretary of the Interior. Ltr sent to the Sec. of War.

[13:OF 1516:CT]

[1] Basil Manly.

1169   ROOSEVELT TO MORRIS L. COOKE, Washington

WASHINGTON, *April 9, 1945*

MEMORANDUM FOR MORRIS L. COOKE: Thank you much for the copy of the article.[1] I like it but it is too dull. Can you send me some human interest stuff to put into it—one story on what tree planting is doing for a given community; another on what it is doing for a typical family. And I need a little more material on what tree planting is doing to enable families to improve their yield in crops.

Things of that kind would help.

F. D. R.

[13:OF 149:CT]

¹ A 2000-word memorandum on the Shelterbelt prepared by Elmer A. Starch of the Lincoln, Nebraska, Office of the Bureau of Agricultural Economics, sent by Cooke April 6, 1945 (OF 149).

1170   GIFFORD PINCHOT TO ROOSEVELT

WASHINGTON 6, D. C., *April 10, 1945*

DEAR MR. PRESIDENT: You will be glad to know, I am sure, that the possibility of a conflict between the World Conference on Conservation and the Food and Agriculture Commission, concerning which Wickard sent for me, seems to have vanished. I had a talk with Pearson,¹ head of the latter, who assured me that he could see no reason for such a conflict.

May I say how much I hope that you will have time to glance at the plan I sent you (on March 28th) before San Francisco, where perhaps some action should be taken.²

Every good wish to you.

Faithfully yours,

GIFFORD PINCHOT

[13:OF 177:TS]

¹ L. B. Pearson, chairman of the United Nations Interim Commission on Food and Agriculture.
² Pinchot also wrote to Grace Tully on April 10 (OF 177), asking if his plan had been received. See below.

1171   WILLIAM L. CLAYTON, ASSISTANT SECRETARY OF STATE FOR ECONOMIC AFFAIRS, TO EDWARD R. STETTINIUS, JR., SECRETARY OF STATE

[WASHINGTON] *April 17, 1945*

GOVERNOR PINCHOT'S PROPOSAL FOR A CONSERVATION CONFERENCE: I understand that you are soon to meet with Governor Pinchot to discuss his proposal for a world conference on "Conservation as a Basis of Permanent Peace." This is a matter in which President Roosevelt took a personal interest and on which there is a background of correspondence between the Department and the White House. The chronology is as follows:

(1) On three previous occasions we commented at President Roosevelt's request on Governor Pinchot's proposal. Departmental memoranda, dated November 10, 1944, December 16, 1944, and March 19, 1945 (copies attached), were prepared and submitted to the White House.

(2) The memorandum of November 10 was adverse to the Pinchot proposal as we understood it. It was received unfavorably by President Roosevelt.

(3) The December 16 memorandum suggested a mild and partial acceptance of Governor Pinchot's proposals in the form of informal regional conferences on questions of conservation. It was received by the White House without comment.

(4) The March 19 memorandum was prepared upon the basis of your conversation with President Roosevelt and Secretary Wickard on March 16, and incorporated remarks along the lines of Secretary Wickard's comments which, when made orally, had apparently been well received by President Roosevelt. Our memorandum, however, was returned with the notation that he did not want to forward it to Governor Pinchot. It is not clear whether he disapproved the substance or merely wanted to handle the matter orally.

(5) All three of these previous memoranda were prepared without benefit of any detailed statement by Governor Pinchot of what his proposal specifically contemplated. We now have in hand a copy of what Governor Pinchot calls his "rough outline" for the kind of conference under discussion.[1] It confirms our early misgivings. The suggested agenda and "possible recommendations" and "possible conclusions" all indicate a coverage of discussion that would overlap at almost every turn with the functions of the Food and Agriculture Organization, with the subject matter of the World Trade Conference which you announced in your Chicago speech, with the responsibilities of whatever organization may be established under the Economic and Social Council to deal with international commodity arrangements and related matters, and with such Article VII conversations with individual governments as may be held in the next year or so.

(6) Governor Pinchot and President Roosevelt apparently had the impression that other government agencies were unanimous in support of the Pinchot proposal and that only the State Department was reluctant to give its approval. This impression is not borne out by information received from contacts at working levels. I recommend that before you see Governor Pinchot you discuss the conservation conference proposal with Secretary Wickard and with Mr. Howard Tolley, United States representative on the United Nations Interim Commission on Food and Agriculture.

(7) An attached memorandum contains in summary form the principal points which have been developed in the Department previously on this subject, and some further comments relating specifically to Governor Pinchot's outline proposal.

I recommend that in discussing this matter with Governor Pinchot the Department go no further in the way of encouraging the Governor than a promise to bring his proposal before the Executive Committee on Economic Foreign Policy for its consideration.

W. L. C.

ITP: JALOFTUS:DLW
[*Notations*:AS] B. F. H.   JAL
[13:OF 5637:TS:PHOTOSTAT]

¹ *Ante*, 1166.

1172   [*Enclosure*]

Proposed Conservation Conference

April 17, 1945

It is recognized that the principles and practice of sound conservation of natural resources are of primary importance to nations and that a considerable measure of international collaboration with respect to conservation can be fruitful.   There are, however, several considerations militating against the advisability of an early convocation of a separate conference to deal specifically with the question of conservation.

(1) Such a conference would necessarily be designed either (a) to facilitate the collection of information about natural resources and their utilization, or (b) to propose measures for a collaborative approach to problems of conservation.

(2) It is unnecessary to convoke a world conference in order to facilitate the collection of information.   Indeed this can better be done by technicians in the various countries of the world communicating with one another when necessary through normal channels.   It would be obviously undesirable to convoke any conference in the near future which is not absolutely necessary for the purpose intended.

(3) It is unlikely that nations could agree at the present time on measures of collaborative action with respect to conservation problems until some area of agreement has been blocked out with respect to larger problems of trade and commodity arrangements.   To convoke at the present time a conservation conference which could not agree upon useful and constructive decisions would prejudice the benefits that might be anticipated from the convocation of a conservation conference at some later date when the general international economic and commodity situation might be clearer.

(4) The topics uppermost in the thinking of Governor Pinchot have to do with the general subjects of soil conservation and reforestation. These topics fall clearly within the sphere of the Food and Agriculture Organization of the United Nations, whose Constitution specifically provides that it (the Food and Agriculture Organization) "shall promote and, where appropriate, shall recommend national and international action with respect to . . . (c) the conservation of natural resources" and "shall collect, analyze, interpret, and disseminate information relating to nutrition, food and agriculture." It also appears, both from the text of the Constitution of the Food and Agriculture Organization and from the first report by the Interim Commission on Food and Agriculture, that the responsibilities of the Food and Agriculture Organization extend to problems of conservation with respect to fisheries and forestry.

(5) The U. S. program with respect to international commodity agreements (which was approved by the White House) recognizes that conservation is an important element to be considered in connection with international commodity arrangements. Therefore, many issues connected with the general problem of conservation will necessarily arise in the forthcoming trade and employment conference, which would cover the general topics of commercial policy, commodity arrangements, cartels, international aspects of domestic full employment programs, and international organizations related to these matters.

(6) President Roosevelt is understood to have already recognized that any organization which might come into being to deal with conservation problems should be subordinate to the Economic and Social Council of the United Nations Organization. It will be recalled that Secretary Wickard emphasized this point when he spoke with President Roosevelt on March 16.

(7) Therefore, the course which the Department should pursue (and this should be explained to Governor Pinchot) is to examine the situation in the light of the arrangements concluded at San Francisco, and to examine the functions and responsibilities of the Economic and Social Council, and of the various organizations subordinate to it. In the light of this investigation it should be possible a little later in the year to determine the extent to which problems of conservation will be provided for on an international basis and what supplemetary mechanisms of international consultation and collaboration should be sought.[1]

ITP:JALOFTUS:REJ
[*Notation*:AS] JAL
[13:OF 5637:T:PHOTOSTAT]

[1] Following President Roosevelt's death on April 12, 1945, Pinchot tried to interest Harry Hopkins in the proposed conference. Writing to Hopkins on May 1, 1945,

Pinchot referred to Roosevelt's statement that he "intended to take this matter up with Churchill and Stalin," and to the plan that he had delivered to the President after his return from Yalta. He asked for an interview. Hopkins replied May 10, 1945, that his illness prevented him from "going into the conservation plan." He suggested that Pinchot talk with President Truman and Averell Harriman about it, and that in the State Department he would find Clayton "sympathetic and understanding." Pinchot replied May 15, 1945, that he had written President Truman and would try to get in touch with Clayton. (This correspondence is in the Harry L. Hopkins Papers in the Roosevelt Library.)

Index

Index

American Game Conference, 214
American Institute of Chemical Engineers, 198
American Legion, 78
American Museum of Natural History, 27 n.; FDR a member, 10 n.; Theodore Roosevelt memorial at, proposed, 53; FDR's speech at (ment.), 458 n.
American Nature Association, 399, 450; criticizes Taylor Grazing Act, 442; supports Lonergan Water Pollution Bill, 568
American Ornithologists' Union, FDR a member, 10, 30
American Planning and Civic Association, 457 n.; opposes mining in monument, 1064
American Scientific Congress, 1126, 1166
American Society of Newspaper Editors, FDR's statement to, on water pollution, 888 (text), 893
American Tree Association, 118 n., 417
American Wildlife Institute, 668, 690
America's Cup Races, FDR at, 294 n.
Anderson, F. A., letter of, 93
Androscoggin River, 485
Anglo-American Petroleum Agreement, 1138
Animal Industry, Bureau of, 569, 712
Anthony, Harold E., 634
Antiquities Act, see American Antiquities Act
Antonio Creek, 782
Appalachian Mountain Club, 101; opposes a White Mountains national park, 944
Appalachian Mountains, Skyline Drive, 400, 813; apple growing, 962
Appalachian Park, proposed, 79
Appalachian Parkway, proposed, 699, 704, 749
Appalachian Trail, 64, 289, 649
Appanoose (Iowa), 545
Appleby, Paul H., letters of, 225, 396, 1022
Arabia, FDR's views on, 1113, 1159
Arch Hurley Reclamation Act (1937), 656
Argentia, 1061 n.
Arizona, public lands and game refuges in, 657, 822, 830–831, 839; and Gila Basin project, 994
Arizona, University of, 622
Arizona-Colorado River Commission, 672 n.
Arizona Game Protective Association, favors game ranges, 830, 839, 858
Arizona State Game and Fish Commission, and game ranges, 830–831, 839

Arizona State Legislature, opposes game ranges, 657, 672
Arkansas, 517; proposed national forest purchases in, 140, 169; water conservation and flood control program for, 202, 279 n., 662, 1030, 1139; wildfowl sanctuary in, 265; reforestation plan for, 761; phosphate deposits, 784
Arkansas, University of, 106
Arkansas River, 333, 529, 565; development of watershed, 192, 196, 205, 207, 209, 636, 805, 965, 1030, 1094, 1144; control of, 485, 618, 797
Arkansas Valley Authority, proposed, 203, 587, 1128, 1139, 1157; bill to establish, 1031, 1060.
Arkansas-White River Watershed Bill (1943), 1114
Army, 136; helps establish CCC, 134, 135 n.; to establish Alaska air station, 451; misuse of public lands by, 1070–1071. See also Army Engineer Corps; War, Secretary of; War Department
Army Engineer Corps, 702, 1060; Arkansas River survey by, proposed, 192; control of stream pollution by, 215, 846, 909, 1055; river development plan, 278; reports on Ohio-Mississippi flood control, 604, 610–611, 613–614, 618, 775; and flood control planning, 607, 612, 662, 666, 674, 698, 706, 781–782, 786, 798, 803, 914–915, 1155 n.; to be on water resources committee, 665; and planning agencies, 884, 923, 981, 994; Kings Canyon reservoir report, 929 n.; to aid Cumberland Basin development, 965; opposes Reclamation on Kings River project, 1002, 1042–1043, 1116, 1120; Missouri River plan, 1130, 1139–1140, 1143, 1168. See also War, Secretary of; War Department
Army Engineer Corps, Chief of, Edward M. Markham, 502 n., 607; memorandum to, 520; flood control report, 604, 610, 618–619
Army Engineer Corps, Chief of, Julian L. Schley, 698, 923; on Special Pollution Committee, 848
Army Engineer Corps, Chief of, Eugene Reybold, memorandum to, 1168; Missouri Valley flood control plan, 1140
Arnold, Fred H., 1011
Ashbrook, William A., letter to, 430
Asheville (N. C.), 217, 704
Ash Sheep Company, 269

tional parks, 455, 503, 860; and Quetico-Superior project, 538, 751, 765, 841, 886, 1087; St. Lawrence Waterway treaty with, 637; embargoes timber, 1089, 1102

Cannon, Clarence, letter to, 394; and Shelterbelt, 490, 514 n.; views of, on Planning Board appropriation, 1099 n.

Capper, Arthur, 546; asks for drought investigation, 344

Capper-Cramton Memorial Parkway Act (1930), 248

Caraway, Hattie W., letter to, 612; introduces flood control resolution, 655 n.

Carey, Robert D., 495 n.; opposes Recreational Area Bill, 223 n., 363, 370

Carl Schurz Memorial Foundation, 150, 151, 160

Carmody, John M., 936 n., 1005 n.

Carpenter, Farrington R., 315, 953

Carpenter, Terry M., 137

Carter, C. E., 517 n.

Carter, E. E., 133 n.

Cascade Mountains, forests of, 1013, 1014, 1020, 1078 n.

Case, Francis, 1017

Case-Wheeler Act, *see* Wheeler-Case Water Conservation Act

Casper-Alcova Project, 167

Casper (Wyo.), 167 n.

Cates, Dudley, 166 n.

Catoctin Recreational Area, 1085

Catskill Park, conservation and development, 16, 82, 85, 91, 92, 122, 419, 872. *See also* New York State Forest Preserve

Central Northwest Regional Planning Commission, 560

Central Oregon Grazing Project, 429

Central Statistical Board, 502

Central Valley Authority, proposed, 1031, 1150, 1157

Central Valley Reclamation Project, 271, 437; authorized, 432

Chamberlain, Joseph P., letter to, 23

Chamber of Commerce, U. S., 47, 970

Chapel Corners (N. Y.) Grange, 52, 56

Chapman, C. S., 228

Chapman, H. H., 712

Chapman, Oscar L., 315

Charleston (S. C.) *News and Courier*, 895

Chattanooga (Tenn.), 1015

Chemistry and Soils, Bureau of, 569

Cherry Creek Reclamation Project, 923

Chesapeake and Ohio Canal, proposed for park, 241, 247–249

Chesapeake Bay, 738 n.

Chesapeake Bay Authority, 438

Cheyenne Bottoms Refuge, 190

Cheyenne River, 994

Chicago, University of, 977

Chicago (Ill.), 155, 710, 886, 893, 1171; FDR's acceptance speech at, 109 (text), 113

Chickamauga Dam, FDR's dedication speech at (text), 1015

Chihuahua (Mexico), 1135

Childress (Texas), 177

China, soil erosion in, 16, 78, 268, 419

Chino Creek, 782

Chippewa Indians, 886

Chirchillige, Deshna Clak (?), 347

Chokoluski (Fla.), 59

Churchill, Winston, and proposed conservation conference, 1153, 1172 n.

Cimarron River, 192

Cincinnati (Ohio), 437; pollutes Ohio River, 840

Citron, William M., letter to, 345

Civilian Conservation Corps, 93 n., 142, 163, 165, 178, 179, 555, 580 n., 639, 652, 949, 1050, 1093; origin and establishment, 62 n., 119, 129–136, 139, 180, 496, 920; *work of:* in forestry, 129 n., 131 n., 132, 135, 140, 143, 183, 321, 383, 419, 561, 566, 758, 919–920, 1037, in forest fire protection, 244, 829, 862, 1079, 1081, in parks, 248, 286, 320–321, 526, in soil conservation, 331, 332, 419, 464, 542, 546, in Okefenokee Swamp, 634, 731, on private lands, 654, 675, 681, 717, 722, on irrigation projects, 728, for TVA, 748, 756, 849, in Haiti, 882, in drought areas, 907, 938, in development of wildlife refuges, 1021; appropriations, 135, 218, 236, 486; location of camps, 146, 161, 169, 192, 325; camps, visited by FDR, 168; organization and administration, 219, 417, 435, 483, 566–567, 586, 606, 887, 973; praised by FDR, 296, 419, 771; praised by foresters, 312; reduced in size, 435, 474, 486, 489, 1037, 1041; accomplishments, 566; states asked to help maintain, 586; permanent establishment recommended, 606; Presidential letters drafted by, 756, 829, 863; and other agencies, 793, 817, 823, 844; new Tennessee program for, proposed, 863; transferred to Federal Security Administration, 887 n.; efforts to abolish, 1079–1080, 1086 *See also* Emergency Conservation Work; Emergency Conservation Work Act

Civilian Conservation Corps, Director of, *Robert Fechner*, 180 n., 435, 489, 586 n., 606 n., 863, 1037; letters and memoranda of, 179, 566, 675, 717, 793, 844, 887; letters and memoranda to, 146, 218, 296, 320, 486, 567, 654, 681, 718, 771, 882; and CCC organization, 146 n., 168 n., 321, 325, 474, 817, 823; Presidential letters drafted by, 435, 586; at drought conferences, 544–548

Civilian Conservation Corps, Director of, *James J. McEntee*, 1041; memorandum to, 722, drafts CCC bill, 606 n.

Civilian Conservation Corps Act (1937), 606; interpretation, 793, 823

Civil Service, 414; TVA not under, 945

Clapp, Earle H., 228, 484, 975 n.; memorandum of, 485; presents Forest Service program to Congress, 986, 988, 989, 990

Clapp, Gordon R., 1049 n.

Clark, Bennett Champ, attends drought conference, 544; introduces stream pollution bill, 915 n.; questions Planning Board appropriation, 982 n.

Clark, George Rogers, 517

Clark, Irving M., urges larger Olympic National Park, 750, 956

Clark Hill Project, 499, 879

Clark-Mundt Water Pollution Bill (1939), 893, 899, 915

Clarke-McNary Forest Act (1924), 125, 160, 217, 240, 675, 829, 849 n., 989; and forest land purchase areas, 140; amendments, 149, 1167; and Shelterbelt, 171, 291; appropriations for, 244, 1082

Clarksburg (W. Va.), FDR's speech at (text), 1136

Clayton, William L., memorandum of, 1171

Clinton Hollow (N. Y.), 694

Coahuila (Mexico), 1135

Cochran, John J., letter of, 866; letters to, 865, 867; introduces Reorganization Bill, 581 n.; supports Kings Canyon Park Bill, 929 n.; and Missouri Valley Authority, 1168

Cochran, Robert L., 589 n.; letters to, 541, 826; at drought conference, 548

Cocoanut Grove (Fla.), 59

Coe, Ernest F., letter to, 880

Coffman, John D., 136 n.

Cohen, Benjamin V., letter of, 753

Coil, E. Johnston, 444 n.

Colby, Charles C., 834

Cole, H. W., 228

Coleman, F. W., 163

Coleman, J. F., letter to, 34

Collier, Barron, 434

Collier, John, 347 n., 1036; proposes U. S. purchase of Everglades, 434

Collier and Son Company, 174, 234

Collingwood, G. H., 228; urges study of Swedish forestry, 178

Colmer, William M., 924 n.

Colonial National Historical Park, 1070

Colorado, 192, 565, 746, 768, 1009 n., 1030, 1139; grazing, 223, 953; water conservation, 421, 449, 560, 1105 n.; dust storms, 452; reforestation of, needed, 548

Colorado-Big Thompson Reclamation Project, effect of, on Rocky Mountain National Park, 643, 724–725, 768; legislation for, 644, 648, 658

Colorado River, 203, 237 n., 437; Boulder Dam and, 427; regional authority for, suggested, 636; reclamation and recreation projects on, 672, 831, 1001, 1009

Colton, Don B., introduces grazing bill, 227 n., 569

Columbia County (N. Y.), 2, 694; wildlife preserve in, proposed, 70

Columbia River Authority, proposals for, 141, 196, 202–203, 209, 237 n., 309, 333, 636, 706, 976, 1030–1032, 1047–1049, 1060, 1128, 1139, 1144, 1157

Columbia River Basin, development of, 39, 286, 437, 701, 962, 977, 1001

Columbia River Basin Land Speculation Act (1937), 609

Columbia River Power Administration Bill (1941), 1031, 1032, 1047

Columbia University Law School, 2

Commerce, Department of, 197, 225 n., 281, 595, 868, 919 n., 927 n.; authority of, 220 n.; to study recreational area programs, 523; reports on timber resources, 1019

Commerce, Secretary of, *Daniel C. Roper*, memorandum to, 386; on National Resources Board, 281

Commerce, Secretary of, *Harry L. Hopkins*, letters of, 854, 890

Committee on National Land Problems, described, 236 n.; abolished, 281

Committee on Water Flow, 226; appointed, 222 n.; report, 237, 254

Commodity Credit Corporation, and purchase of Porcupine Mountain, 1091, 1098; and timber production, 1093

Community forests, 873 n., 898, 918 n.; FDR's interest in, 78, 646, 874, 1066, 1068, 1136; Federal aid for, 762, 1082

Dairy Industry, Bureau of, 569
Dallas (Texas), 1026
Danaher, John A., 915 n.
Daniels, Jonathan, memorandum of, 1156; memorandum to, 1157; criticizes 1944 Flood Control Bill, 1141
Dannecker, K., 217
Darling, Jay N., see Biological Survey, Chief of Bureau of
Dasher, Charles L., 387, 428
Davey, Martin L., letter to, 586
Davis, Chester, 431
Davis, Henry P., 668
Davis, Vernon G., telegram of, 657; letter to, 672
Davis-Elkins College, 561 n.
Davison County (S. D.), 1024
Death Valley National Monument, 1064; mining in, 480 n.
Decatur (Ala.), 126 n.
De Koven, Louis B., letter to, 795
Delano, Frederic A., 178, 247, 421 n., 494 n., 562, 574 n., 613, 698, 725, 730 n., 747, 749, 845, 1001, 1003 n., 1042; letters and memoranda of, 248, 437, 498, 555, 575, 655, 696, 755, 782, 798, 832, 846, 854, 879, 883, 890, 906, 981, 994; letters and memoranda to, 457, 499–500, 551, 663, 697, 842, 851, 884, 889, 942, 1094, 1099, 1111; and CCC, 180 n.; on National Resources Board, 281; and water resource planning, 371, 574 n.; and national resources board bill, 466 n.; opposed to Big Thompson project, 725; suggests public works revolving fund, 766; at National Resources Planning Board conference, 946; and forestry program, 993; opposes conference on resources, 1007 n.
Delano, Warren, uncle of FDR, 10 n.
Delaware River, 237 n.
Delaware Water Gap, 813
Demaray, A. E., memorandum of, 363; and Olympic National Park enlargement, 812 n.
Democratic National Convention (1932), FDR's acceptance speech at, 109
Democratic Party, and conservation, 32 n., 40, 43, 63, 66, 71; and recovery program, 131
Dempsey, John J., 336 n.; introduces Soil Conservation Bill, 349 n.
Denison Dam, 499, 786
Dennison, Henry S., letters of, 854, 890; memorandum to, 884
Denver (Colo.), 643
Dern, George H., see War, Secretary of

Dern-Lonergan Conference on Water Pollution, 773
De Rouen, René L., 700 n.; sponsors Kings Canyon National Park Bill, 804
Deschutes County (Ore.), 418, 429
Deschutes Project, 728
Desert Bighorn Sheep Fellowship Research Project, 822
Des Moines (Iowa), drought conferences at, 544–548
Detroit (Mich.), 678
Devils Lake, shrinking of, 292–293
Dewar v. Brooks, 953
Dickerson, U. S. S., 487, 488, 489
Dickinson, L. J., 545
Dill, Clarence C., letter of, 203; letters and memorandum to, 141, 196, 209; to be consulted on regional authorities, 202
Dimond, Anthony J., letters of, 471, 885; letters to, 480, 740, 894, 930, 1033; favors mining in Glacier Bay Monument, 451, 503; urges Alaskan reindeer appropriation, 924 n.
Dingell, John D., introduces sewage disposal resolution, 507 n., 678
Dirksen, Everett M., opposes: Colorado-Big Thompson Project, 658 n., National Resources Planning Board, 1099 n.
Dismal Swamp, 285
Ditter, J. William, 889 n.
Dix, John A., 9 n., 25; and conservation of natural resources, 2 n., 21 n.
Dodge, Thomas H., 347
Dodge, Walton, 546
Dodge City (Kans.), 565
Doering, Otto C., 1005 n.
Donahey, Vic, letter to, 852; approves FDR's Ohio Valley plan, 848
Donnelly, Margaret, 183 n.
Dosewallips River, 818
Doughton, Robert L., 466 n.
Douglas, Lewis W., see Budget, Director of the Bureau of
Dover (N. J.), 824
Doxey, Wall, introduces forestry legislation, 512, 630 n.
Drainage Basin Problems and Programs, prepared by National Resources Committee, 549, 560, 575, 660; sent to Congress, 584, 757, 775; revised, 655, 671, 696; analysis, 715, 719–721
Drainage Policy and Projects, 460
Drainage projects, operated by CCC, 131 n., 566, 675, 717–718, 722, 728 n.; 1037; coordination of, 323, 460–462

[663]

Englebright, Harry L., and national parks, 621, 929
Entomology, Bureau of, 971
Erie Marshes, 250
Eskimos, 924
Euphrates River, 989
Europe, forestry in, 151, 226, 239, 350, 646; climate, 583
Everglades, FDR's cruise in, 54; national park proposed in, 55, 235, 880; and Federal wildlife program, 250, 434; water resources, 943, 908
Everglades National Park Association, 880
Evison, Herbert, 219
Ewing, Gifford C., 824 n.
Executive Committee on Economic Foreign Policy, 1171

Fabrick, D. P., 821
Faddis, Charles I., criticizes Vinson Water Pollution Bill, 601 n.; opposes Alaskan reindeer appropriation, 924 n.
Fahnestock Memorial Park, 704; wildlife preserve proposed in, 69
Fairchild, Fred W., 160
Fairweather Range, 871
Farbach, Carl F., 884
Farley, James A., 180 n.
Farm Credit Administration, and forest credits problem, 356, 379–380, 423, 713; aids drought area, 821
Farmers' National Grain Corporation, 712
Farm Loan Board, 244
Farm Security Administration, 1046; in Great Plains, 821, 907; funds, barred for Shelterbelt, 998. *See also* Rural Resettlement Administration
Farm Woodland Marketing Program, 1112
Fechner, Robert, *see* Civilian Conservation Corps, Director of
Federal Aid Road Act (1916), 688
Federal Aid to Wildlife Restoration Bill, *see* Pitman-Robertson Wildlife Act
Federal Crop Insurance Act (1938), 1082
Federal Emergency Administration of Public Works, 236 n.
Federal Emergency Relief Acts, *see* Emergency Relief Appropriation Acts
Federal Emergency Relief Administration, 368; establishment, 132; *actions, authority and policy of, with respect to:* national land problems, 236 n., 290, 412, wildlife refuges, 273, soil

conservation, 332 n., dust storms, 344, recreational area programs, 523; funds, proposed for Shelterbelt, 291, 295; Presidential letter drafted by, 344
Federal Emergency Relief Administrator, *Harry L. Hopkins,* 230, 264, 323 n.; letters of, 272–273; on National Resources Board, 281
Federal Employment Stabilization Act (1931), 981, 982 n.
Federal Employment Stabilization Board, 889 n., 982 n.
Federal Farm Banks, 160
Federal Farm Mortgage Corporation Act (1934), 379
Federal Forest Bank, proposed, 151, 160
Federal Forest Council, proposed, 160 n.
Federal Highways Act (1921), 555
Federal Land Banks, 356, 380
Federal Power Commission, 1134 n.; *actions, authority and policies of, with respect to:* Columbia Basin project, 141, land and water planning, 487, 618, 655, 660, 666, flood control, 614, 775, 776, 796, 797, Kings Canyon National Park, 891–892, 896–897, 904–905, 910, 929 n., Whitney Dam, 917, Gila Basin investigation, 994, Kings River project, 1002, Belle Fourche River Basin Compact, 1118, Sustained Yield Forestry Bill, 1123, Missouri River authority, 1168; and proposed regional authorities, 626, 1031, 1060, 1062; on Water Resources Committee, 923
Federal Power Commission, Acting Chairman of, *Claude L. Draper,* 655 n.
Federal Power Commission, Acting Chairman of, *Clyde L. Seavey,* memoranda of, 786, 897, 911; letters to, 892, 905, (chairman) 963, 966, 985; favors power development in Kings Canyon, 891, 896, 904, 910
Federal Security Agency, CCC under, 887 n., 1037; to endorse Gillette Water Pollution Bill, 1055; Presidential letters drafted by, 1073, 1129
Federal Security Agency, Administrator of, *Paul V. McNutt,* decides distribution of CCC camps, 1041; investigates Philadelphia water, 1073 n.; submits pollution bill, 1129 n.
Federal Surplus Relief Corporation, buys submarginal land, 230; to aid in resettlement, 281
Federal Water Power Act (1921), 369 n.
Federal Water Power Commission, 911

Forest Advisory Committee, *see* National Recovery Administration Lumber Code

Forest Conservation Code, *see* National Recovery Administration Lumber Code

Forest credit, 242; and NRA Lumber Code, 160, 228, 244; financing and legislation, 260, 356, 373–374, 379–380, 397, 415, 422–423, 713, 1082; FDR's views of, 419, 428

Forest fire control, *in:* New York, 8, 11, 17 n., 102, 103, 419, California, 303, Idaho, 433, Michigan, 763, 787, Tennessee Valley, 849, New England, 862, Everglades, 943, Okefenokee Swamp, 1044, Pacific Coast, 1079–1080, 1086; through CCC, 110, 114, 120, 130, 133, 135, 286, 296 n., 566, 675, 1079, 1086; through Clarke-McNary Act, 149; under NRA Lumber Code, proposed, 151, 160, 186, 228, 242–244, 260; Forest Service plan for, 153; legislation for, 254, 307, 758, 1045, 1057, 1082, 1167

Forest Manager, 217

Forest Preserve, *see* New York State Forest Preserve

Forest Ranger Camp, FDR helps establish, 62 n.

Forestry, 210, 255, 426, 496, 881; FDR's personal interest in, 2 n., 37–38, 48–49, 52–53, 56–57, 65, 67–68, 72–73, 76, 88–89, 99–100, 116, 128, 182, 256, 313, 339, 342, 381, 410, 419, 558 n., 596, 632, 639, 646, 653, 707, 709, 711, 819, 824, 837, 872, 918, 920, 948, 985, 995, 1011, 1025, 1063, 1117, 1121–1122, 1136; *practice of, in:* Europe, 16, 48, 178, 239, 1136, New York, 21, 25, 77, 80–85, 87, 91–92, 94–95, 97, 106–107, 268, 354, 419, 579, drought areas, 173, 527, 544, Oregon, 512, 522, Washington, 710, 770, 1095, South, 739, 919, Quetico-Superior area, 751, 841, Michigan, 787, 809, 1084, Haiti, 882; problems of, on farm woodlands, 17, 51, 54, 149, 226, 515–516, 628, 774, 777, 787, 792, 837, 975, 1038–1039, 1046, 1052, 1057, 1058, 1067, 1082, 1083, 1112, 1167; importance of, in flood control, 34, 254, 484, 487, 492, 497, 518, 612, 636; FDR's writings on, 62, 78, 90; FDR's plan for employment through, 109–115, 117, 119, 121, 123–124, 127, 129 n., 130, 131, 135, 949; establishment of a national policy for, 125, 153, 226, 758, 988–990, 1058,

1065, 1095; Federal aid to, on private lands, 133, 135, 149, 153, 186, 217, 307, 419, 545, 566, 675, 758–763, 767, 772 n., 1045, 1082, 1123; under TVA, 137, 926, 969, 1015; on submarginal land, 167, 236, 281; and water resources, 207, 254, 626 n.; profession of, 313, 350, 548; and pulp and paper industry, 395, 404–405, 708, 730; Resettlement Administration and, 412 n.; Joint Congressional Committee study of, 837, 847, 849, 919, 993, 1036, 1045, 1046, 1052, 1074, 1082; Agriculture-Interior joint control of, 872, 1054; wartime program for, 1056–1057, 1074, 1083; need for, in Arabia and Iran, 1117, 1142, 1159; and the United Nations, 1138, 1172

Forestry, Joint Congressional Committee on, 986, 993, 1053, 1057, 1082; work and status, 837, 847, 849; Forest Service program presented to, 990; Shelterbelt program presented to, 991; report, 1036, 1038, 1045–1046, 1052, 1058, 1074

Forest Service, 11 n., 78, 113, 160, 193, 290, 362, 370, 405, 479, 518, 519, 551, 618, 630 n., 665, 670 n., 712, 750, 762, 807, 833, 1018, 1089; provides work in California, 119 n.; *actions, authority and policy of, with respect to:* control of lumbering, 153–154, 164 n., 229, Shelterbelt, 176, 291, 514, 537, 600, 1023–1024, 1067, timberland taxation, 244, forest credit legislation, 253, 356, 380, 731, national forestry program, 260, 1167, Taylor Grazing Act and grazing lands management, 305, 539–540, 569, 876, 878, 984, 987, 1014, wildlife problem, 318, 645, CCC, 331, 756, 844, 863, recreational area program, 363, 523, Copeland Flood Control Bill, 499, Great Plains forest experiment station, 589, enlargement of Olympic National Park, 700, 800, 812 n., 956, 959–960, 964, Olympic Peninsula lumbering practices, 710, 955, Quetico-Superior area, 741, 1087, private forest management, 759, 919, 988–990, establishment of Kings Canyon National Park, 804, 850, 929 n., chestnut blight, 824, development of national park system, 856, enlargement of Glacier Bay National Monument, 860, community forests, 873 n., 874, 1066, 1068, forest demonstration areas, 919, forest recreation, 944, soil conservation, 1010, lumbering of Olympic National Forest, 1059, 1106 n., 1107, Porcupine Mountain, 1077; asked to abandon "timber famine propaganda," 186; proposed transfer of, to Interior, 274 n., 301, 876, 968 n., 970–971, 974–975, 978, 980, 997, 1029 n.; *reports and studies by, on:* silting of California reservoir, 303, forests as a means of flood control, 484, 485, forest fire problem, 829, timber supply, 1019, 1022; Presidential letters drafted by, 342, 446, 530, 538, 767, 837, 863; constructs forest roads in Idaho, 555; work of, in West Virginia, 561; prepares forest legislation, 772, 1082; furnishes trees for Warm Springs, 948 n.; forestry program, criticized, 986, 988–989, 1036; public opinion of, 1014; revenues, 1078; unable to stop destructive lumbering, 1092–1093; provides farm forestry service, 1112 n.; fortieth anniversary, 1153

Forest Service, Forester of, *Robert Y. Stuart,* 152, 158, 160–162, 166; letters and memoranda of, 138–140, 148, 159, 163, 171–172; memoranda to, 170, 173; helps establish CCC, 133 n., 136 n.; opposes national forests in South Carolina, 156 n.; reports on Shelterbelt, 177 n.; proposes study of European forestry, 178; death, 244 n.

Forest Service, Chief of, *Ferdinand A. Silcox,* 275, 291, 308, 322, 382, 468, 537 n., 850 n., 993; letter and memorandum of, 276, 623; letters and memoranda to, 350, 446, 818, 862, 898, 955; statement by, on Lumber Code conference, 244; appointment, 244 n.; requests Shelterbelt funds, 301 n., 477; *position of, on:* forest credit legislation, 380 n., 713, transfer of national forests to Olympic National Park, 467, enlargement of Yosemite National Park, 479, Copeland Flood Control Bill, 499, Olympic National Park boundaries, 750, 769, Aiken County (S. C.) reforestation plan, 767 n., Government logging of down timber, 862 n., enlarged CCC in Tennessee, 863 n., proposed Kings Canyon National Park, 891, Olympic Peninsula pulp industry, 957; quotes FDR on forest credit legislation, 396; to head wildlife conference committee, 445; title changed, 446 n.; and Up-Stream Engineering Conference, 518–519, 623; reports on western

range, 540; to report on southern paper industry, 708; death, 959 n.; forest program of, 986, 989–990

Forest Service, Chief of, *Lyle F. Watts,* 1110 n., 1121, 1122; memorandum of, 1107; supports McNary bill, 1123 n.

Forster, Rudolph, 281 n., 460, 500, 574 n., 575, 636 n., 802, 879, 945 n.; letter and messages to, 284, 800, 923

Fortas, Abe, 1088; memorandum of, 1089

Fort Glen (N. Y.), 67

Fort Hoyle, 738

Fort Jefferson National Monument, proposed extension of, 727, 736

Four-H Clubs of America, 623

Fowler, C. W., 509

Fowler, Frederick H., 529

France, 646, 784, 1126; reforestation in, 48, 114

Frank, Glenn, 989; letter to, 563

Franklin D. Roosevelt Conservation Camps, 62 n.

Frawley, James J., 8

Freeman, Miller, letters of, 1012, 1014; letters to, 120, 1020

Fremont (Nebr.), FDR's speech at (text), 426

French Lick (Ind.), FDR's speech at (ment.), 81 n., 476

Fresno (Calif.), 911

Friedsam Act (N. Y.), 91

Front Royal (Va.), 813

Fruitland Irrigation Project, 1050

Fulmer, Hampton P., introduces forestry legislation, 1038, 1057; on Congressional Forestry Committee, 847

Fulmer Forest-Leasing Bill, (1939), legislative history, 921–922; (1940), criticized, 989, 1038; discussed by FDR, 1039

Fulmer State Forest Act (1935), 512; legislative history, 351, 353, 356, 382, 440, 1082; appropriations for, disapproved, 376, 383–384, 390; FDR approves, 530; acquisition of forest lands under, 566, 989

Future Farmers of America, 623

Future of the Great Plains, 571, n., 685; summary, 577; sent to Congress, 588

Gabrielson, Ira N., *see* Biological Survey, Chief of Bureau of

Game Refuge Bill (1925), 60

Game refuges, 181; allotments for, 189, 250, 265, 273, 368, 495, 557, 561; Beck plan for, 189–190; and Wildlife Refuge Bill, 220–221; extent of, 220

Harriman, Averell, 1172 n.
Harrington, Francis C., 529 n., 554; letters of, 714, 854, 890; letter to, 716; on Great Plains Committee, 577
Harrisburg (Pa.), 813
Harrison, J. E., 622
Hart Mountain Antelope Refuge, establishment, 391, 442, 448, 450; funds for, 409
Hartley, —, 1121
Harvard University, 563; FDR student at, 2
Harvey's Weekly, 39
Harz Mountains, 226
Hassett, William D., 668, 1129 n., 1134, 1148 n.; letter to, 557; letters, messages and speeches drafted by, 459 n., 517 n., 771 n., 1111
Hawaii, Territory of, 702; FDR's visit to, 286
Hawes, Harry B., 221
Hawk, Wilbur C., 453
Hayden, Carl, letter of, 843; letter to, 624; confers with FDR on Taylor Grazing Bill, 245 n.; urges enlargement of Saguaro National Monument, 622, introduces planning agency bill, 843, 884, 889 n.
Hazard, James O., letters of, 111, 114; letters to, 112, 118; forest purchase plan of, 863
Headwaters Control and Use, 623
Heath, Ferry K., 197 n.
Heatley, Rebe E., letter to, 508
Hebard Lumber Company, 642
Hedges, Cornelius, originator of national park idea, 286, 457
Heiberg, Sven, 182
Helena (Mont.), 641
Hemingway Wash, Nevada-U. S. dispute over, 947, 950, 954
Henderson, Leon, memorandum of, 1019
Henry Lake, Army use of, 1071–1072
Hepburn, Mitchell F., 841
Herkimer County (N. Y.), 82
Herkimer (N. Y.), 78
Herring, Clyde L., at drought conference, 541, 545
Herty, Charles H., 262 n.
Hess, Clarence T., 428 n., 808 n.
Hetch Hetchy Canyon Reservoir Act (1913), 31–32
Hewitt, Charles J., 91
Hibbard, Benjamin H., 569
Hickerson, H. M., letter to, 50
Hicks, John R., letter to, 381
Hiester, B. U., letter to, 87
High, Stanley, memorandum to, 511

Hill, Grover B., 1059 n.
Hill, Knute, introduces Columbia River Authority Bill, 1031, 1060
Hill, L. S., 545
Hill, Lister, 137
Hill, Sam B., letter to, 412
Hitler, Adolf, 1070
Hochfelder, —, 180 n.
Hoe, Robert, 67
Hoey, Clyde R., 1016
Hoffman, —, 1107
Hogback Project, 1050
Hoh River Tract, proposed inclusion of, in Olympic National Park, 788, 836, 952, 956–960, 964; threatened with lumbering, 1110
Holbrook, —, 817
Hollingsworth and Whitney Company, 395
Hollis, Henry F., 38 n.
Home Owners Loan Act (1933), 379
Homestead Law, *see* Stock-Raising Homestead Act
Homestead laws, 540
Honolulu, FDR visits, 282 n.
Hood, Robert, 297
Hook, Frank E., letter to, 794; introduces Porcupine Mountains bill, 1077; election defeat, 1097–1098
Hook Michigan-Wisconsin Forest Conservation Bill (1941), legislative history, 1036, 1078, 1082
Hoover, Herbert, 94 n., 1124; attacks FDR's farm policies, 456; Skyline Drive begun under, 813
Hoover Dam, *see* Boulder Dam
Hopkins, Arthur S., letter of, 90; letter to, 100; advises FDR on forest purchases, 89
Hopkins, Harry L., heads state relief agency, 93 n.; views of, on, world conservation conference, 1171 n. *See also* Commerce, Secretary of; Works Progress Administrator
Horner, Henry, 517
Horning, W. H., and Olympic National Park, 467, 957
Hoskins, Harold B., 1117
Hot Springs (Va.), 1137, 1138
Houghton, A. S., letters of, 18, 26; letters to, 19, 28; arranges for Pinchot speech, 12
Houghton County (Mich.), 794
House Rock Valley Bighorn Refuge, proposed, 830
Houston, David F., 569; letter to, 38
Houston, U. S. S., FDR's trips on, 282 n., 284, 427 n.

[671]

Kent Public Lands Bill (1916), 569
Kentucky, 840, 1139; land survey in, proposed, 83; proposed national forest purchases in, 140; phosphate deposits, 784
Kern River Project, Reclamation Bureau-Army Engineers' dispute over, 1042–1043, 1116, 1120, 1150; FDR's views on, 1119. *See also* King's River Project
Kemoe, —, 1107
Key, W. S., 547
Key West (Fla.), 736, 868
Kilmer, Grace C., letter to, 63
King, Ed., 547
King, William H., opposes removal of soil conservation activities from Interior, 349 n.; opposes Copeland National Resources Board Bill, 494 n.
Kings Canyon National Park, 55 n., 1016; *establishment of, favored by:* Budget Bureau, 804, FDR, 807, 861, 877; *establishment of, opposed by:* California group, 850, National Parks Association, 1000; future power generation within, debated, 891–892, 896–897, 904–905, 910–911; legislation establishing, 891 n., 929
Kings River Project, Reclamation Bureau-Army Engineers' dispute over, 923, 1002, 1042–1043, 1116, 1120; and proposed Central Valley Authority, 1150
Kirkland, Burt P., 160, 228
Kittredge, Frank A., and Olympic National Park, 952, 956
Kizer, Benjamin H., and Olympic National Park, 956, 960
Klamath Lake Wildlife Project, described, 401, 403
Knapp, —, 546
Kneipp, L. F., 989; opposes state park legislation, 362–363, 370
Knoxville (Tenn.), 926, 1151
Knudsen, William S., and Porcupine Mountains land, 1097, 1098
Kofa Mountain Bighorn Refuge, establishment and administration of, 822, 830–831, 839, 858
Kotok, E. I., 1106
Krum Elbow Creek, 694
Ku Klux Klan, 970
Kump, Herman G., 561

Labor, Department of, 46; and CCC, 132, 134, 136; and Columbia Basin project, 141, 1001

Labor, Secretary of, *Frances Perkins,* letters and memorandum of, 131, 237, 272, 854, 890; memorandum to, 129; on Committee on Water Flow, 254; on National Resources Board, 281; at CCC conference, 844 n.
Lacey Wildlife Act (1900), 688 n.; President's authority under, 214
Ladd, Carl E., 68 n.; drafts letters for FDR, 83 n., 87 n.
Ladies' Home Journal, 55
La Follette, Robert M., 129 n.; introduces forestry bill, 922 n.
La Follette-Costigan Public Works Bill (1933), 130, 131
La Guardia, Fiorello H., 974 n.
Lake Champlain, 749
Lake County (Ore.), 418
Lake Crescent, 700 n., 952
Lake Erie, pollution of, 86, 96; canal to, from Ohio River, proposed, 879 n.
Lake Mattamuskeet, 265
Lake Mead, 934, 947, 950
Lake Michigan, 198
Lake Okeechobee, 387
Lake Ozette, 750
Lake Placid (N. Y.) FDR's speech at (text), 419
Lake Quinault, 700, 750
Lake states, forest problem in, 485, 525, 746, 763, 890
Lake States Forest Experiment Station, 177 n.
Lake Wales Citrus Growers Association, 625
Lakin, B. W., 228
Lamoille Valley, 559 n.
Lamont, Robert P., 108
Land grant colleges, 437, 569; wildlife study by, proposed, 360 n.; and Cooperative Farm Forestry Act, 630 n.; work of, with TVA, 926
Landon, Alfred M., letters to, 279, 344; at drought conference, 541, 546, 557 n.
Land Planning Committee, recommendation of, on forest policy, 351; report, ignored by Great Plains Committee, 575
Land Policy Committee, *see* Agriculture, Department of
Land Program Administration, 321
Land use policies and programs, *in:* New York, 81, 94, 105–107, 920, Montana, 105, Europe, 109, Oregon, 429, southern pine area, 761, Northern Great Plains, 821, 825, Northwest, 827, Southwest, 994, West, 1014, Tennessee Valley, 1015; na-

tionally, 98, 107, 109, 113–114, 120, 149, 204, 226, 230, 236, 239, 281, 290, 297, 299, 456, 459, 476, 487, 527–528, 530, 540, 543, 569, 705, 712, 720–721, 757, 759–760, 762, 834, 835, 946, 1007, 1013
Lane, Franklin K., 286
Langer, William, 705
Langley, James C., letter to, 97
Langlie, Arthur B., letters to, 1095, 1101
Larooco, FDR's cruises on, 54 n., 59
Las Vegas Wash., 947
Latta, Maurice A., letter to, 1123
Lea, Robert W., letter of, 187
League of American Sportsmen, 4
League of Nations, 1154
League of Women Voters, 895 n.
Leavitt, Scott, 569
Lebanon, 1159
LeCron, James D., letter of, 713
Lee, Josh, 805
Lee Highway, 932
Leggett, Eugene, at drought conference, 544–548
Legislative Appropriation Act (1932), 332
LeHand, Marguerite A., 62, 142 n., 180 n., 713; letter of, 920; letter to, 753
Lehman, Herbert H., 419
Lemme, Edward H., 96
Lend-Lease Agreements, 1126, 1166
Lenox (Mass.), FDR's speech at (text), 47
Leonard, Roy S., 1106 n.
Leopold, Aldo, 557; on wildlife committee, 201 n., 234
Levy, A. J., 5, 6
Lilienthal, David E., 203, 926 n., 1156; memorandum of, 1157; drafts Roosevelt speech, 1015 n.; drafts California authority bill, 1031; supports extension of TVA concept, 1161
Linaka, Russell W., 995
Little Colorado River, 1050
Little Waters report, *sent to:* FDR, 444, Congress, 459, 627, engineering schools, 563
Livingston v. Moore, 953
Locke, S. B., 197 n.; telegram of, 669
Lodwick, —, 545
Loehr, Rodney C., 164 n.
Lonergan, Augustine, 215, 669; letter of, 197; letters to, 198–200; introduces water pollution bills, 568, 773, 915 n.
Long, James L., 5
Long Island Game Protective Association, 12 n., 29

Lorwin, Lewis L., 1166
Los Angeles (Calif.), water supply, 427; supplies Kings Canyon power data, 897, 905, 911
Los Angeles County (Calif.), 782
Louisiana, 1139; proposed national forest purchases in, 140, 161, 169; forestry in, 157; game refuges, 250, 285; flood control, 733
Louisville (Ky.) *American*, 83
Louisville (Ky.) *Times*, 893, 1058
Low, Augustus, Jr., letter to, 17
Lowdermilk, Walter C., at Soil Erosion Service conference, 338 n.; visits Near East, 989
Luckey, Henry C., letter to, 589
Ludlow, Louis, 514 n.
Luecke, John, letter to, 746; urges study of Michigan cut-over area, 890
Lumber Code, *see* National Recovery Administration Lumber Code
Lumbering, *in:* New York, 11, 14, 15, 16, 23, 91 n., national parks and forests, 74–75, 1054, 1059, 1106–1110, Okefenokee Swamp, 319, Olympic Peninsula, 467, 700, 836, 952, 956, 1059, 1096, 1102, 1110, Michigan, 1077, 1078, 1084, 1098, Quetico-Superior, 1087; destructive methods of, 78, 153, 310, 411 n., 512, 809, 928, 986, 989, 1056, 1090, 1092–1093; stabilization of industry, 120; rate of, and remaining timber, 130, 1018–1019, 1022; control of, through NRA, 150–155, 178, 184, 186, 228–229, 242, 260–261, 307; control of, by Federal Government, opposed, 339 n.; by selective cutting, 710, 989; vital to war effort, 1167
Lumber Survey Committee, report of, 1018–1019, 1022
Lyon, J. B. and Co., letter to, 1

McAdoo, William G., 772; introduces bill to enlarge Yosemite Park, 621; on Congressional forestry committee, 847
McAtee, W. L., 634
McCarl, John R., rules on Shelterbelt, 287 n., 295
McCarran, Patrick A., offers amendment to Taylor Grazing Bill, 263, 276; asks CCC aid on irrigation project, 717
McClellan, John L., letter of, 662; letters to, 674, 1114; introduces flood control legislation, 655 n., 667
McClure, James G. K., letter of, 870; letter to, 872

Mawhinney, R. J., opinion, on Federal pollution control, 197, 198
Maybank, Burnet R., 1016; letter to, 996
Mead, Elwood, *see* Reclamation Bureau, Commissioner of
Medicine Lake, 250
Meier, C. R. D., letter to, 496
Mellett, Lowell, 991 n.; to publicize Shelterbelt, 902; reports on conservation conference, 1007 n.
Meloy, Andrew D., letter of, 9
Merced Falls (Calif.), 621
Meriwether County (Ga.), 583
Merriam, Charles E., 620, 659, 1111 n.; letters of, 613, 854, 890; memorandum for, 884; planning board activities of, 281, 889, 946
Merriam, Frank C., letter to, 271
Merriam, John C., 201 n.
Merrimack River, 333, 485, 660
Mexico, 1126; Migratory Bird Treaty with, 220, 221, 557, 561, 1021; and wildlife conference, 446; and Big Bend National Park, 933, 1135
Miami Conservancy District, 614
Miami (Fla.), 356, 1026 n.
Michener, Earl C., 477 n.
Michigan, 678; proposed national forest purchases in, 124, 140, 485, 1082; forest land problem, 746, 763, 809, 890, 928; farm wood lot tax law, 787; proposed national park in, 1077–1078, 1097
Michigan, University of, 787
Michigan Forest Land Purchase Bill (1938), 794
Michigan State College, 787
Middle East, 1145
Midwest Conservation Alliance, 378
Midwest Game and Fish Commissioners, 378
Migratory Bird Conservation Act (1929), 603, 688; funds for, 190, 225 n.; supplementary act, 231
Migratory Bird Conservation Commission, proposes more wildlife refuges, 190; more authority proposed for, 221 n.
Migratory Bird Hunting Stamp Act (1934), 557 n.; revenue from, 225 n., 233 n., 378, 1021; amended, 367–368, 388, 391, 393, 409, 557
Migratory Bird Treaty, 151, 1021; enforcement, 231; amended, 533 n.; extended to Mexico, 557, 561
Miles City (Mont.), 569, 647
Milford (Utah), 569
Millar, A. C., letter to, 341

Miller, C. Blackburn, letter to, 595
Miller, John E., 1031
Miller, John F., 891 n.
Miller, Leslie A., letter to, 424; protests withdrawal of grazing lands, 223
Milwaukee (Wis.), 1167 n.
Mineral Leasing Act (1920), 480
Mineral resources, 1007, 1166; studies of, 437; *issue of development of, in:* national parks and monuments, 451, 455, 471, 480, 503, 700, 885, 952, 1064, national forests, 551, 555, game preserves, 582, 603, Upper Michigan, 746 n., recreational areas, 954, 1013; National Resources Planning Board and, 946
Mines, Bureau of, 1150; *studies and reports of, on:* mapping of Alaska for minerals, 451, Idaho mine-to-market roads, 551, 555, manganese in Olympic Peninsula, 952
Mining World, 1014, 1020; letter to, 1013
Minnesota, 631, 705; proposed national forest purchases in, 140, 485; CCC in, 146; stream pollution control in, 198; Quetico-Superior question in, 280, 538 n., 570, 572, 741, 751, 765, 811, 841, 886, 1078 n., 1087; drought, 527 n.; cut-over areas, 746, 890, 928
Mississippi, proposed national forest purchases in, 124, 140, 159, 161, 163, 169; forestry in, 157; game refuges, 273
Mississippi Forestry Association, 93
Mississippi River, 192, 205, 210, 226, 237 n., 250, 485, 520, 766, 805; control of, 34, 387, 581, 604, 610–612, 614, 618, 626, 647, 660, 775, 1015; studies and surveys of, 206–207, 216, 696; regional authority proposed for valley, 333, 636, 1139; pollution, 679 *See also* Ohio-Lower Mississippi Flood Control Plan
Mississippi River Commission, 501; authority of, 255, 636, 637
Mississippi Valley Committee, 255, 459, 563, 613, 614, 660; purpose, 210; studies and reports, 216, 279, 332, 387, 499; becomes part of National Resources Board, 310 n.; proposes conservation congress, 726 n.
Mississippi Wildlife Refuge, 250
Missouri, proposed national forest purchases in, 124, 159, 485, 833; CCC in, 146; drought conference for, 544; economic conditions, 828
Missouri River, 196, 202, 205, 210, 237 n., 292 n., 334, 529; flood control,

Muscle Shoals, 130; FDR's visit to, 126, 300; message to Congress on, 137; phosphate production at, 638

Muskingum Watershed Conservancy District, 614

Myers, William I., 379, 415, 713; letter to, 835; at drought conference, 544–548; on Land Committee, 834

Nance, James, 547

Nathan, Robert R., 1093

National Academy of Sciences, 437; proposes study of Forest Service-Park Service lands, 870

National Agricultural Conference, 299; letter of, 297

National Antiquities Act, *see* American Antiquities Act

National Association of Audubon Societies, *see* Audubon Societies, National Association of

National Capital Park and Planning Commission, 247, 248, 498

National Committee for the Preservation of Yosemite National Park, 31, 32

National Conference on State Parks, 457 n.

National Conservation Association, 11 n.

National Conservation Congress, FDR delegate to, 33

National Cooperative Council, 712

National Cooperative Reforestation Plan, described, 774; criticized by FDR, 777; revision of, proposed, 792

National Emergency Council, 332, 358 n., 464, 465, 523

National Farmers' Union, 1144; opposes proposed conservation department, 712

National Farm Land Program, 107

National Fertilizer Association, 300

National Forest Administration Act, *see* National Forest Reservation Act

National Forest Association, 725

National Forest Establishment Act (1891), 510

National Forest Reservation Act (1897), 510, 569, 987

National Forest Reservation Commission, purchase of forest lands by, 124, 140, 156, 159–160, 163, 240, 244, 351, 484, 794, 993, 1020; and Fulmer bill, 353 n., 382; furthers Quetico-Superior program, 765, 886

National Forest Survey Act Amendment (1944), 1167

National forests, 149, 303, 445, 631 n., 654, 657, 828, 891, 935, 950; timber production, 97 n., 750, 1059, 1082, 1089, 1107, 1108, 1123 n.; reforestation, 113; enlargement and preservation, 123, 125, 138–140, 148, 152, 153, 156–163, 165, 169, 217, 228, 236, 239–240, 244, 260, 286, 290, 312, 342–343, 485, 524–525, 538, 564, 615, 758, 795, 833, 837, 849, 886, 987, 1020, 1036, 1045, 1104, 1167; as employment source, 124, 130, 342, 350; CCC in, 131 n., 566, 1080; nurseries for, 173 n., 1082; and NRA Lumber Code, 186; grazing in, 245, 270, 276, 311, 442, 540, 543, 984, 987; recreation in, 296 n., 370, 702, 804, 807; extent of, 351; relation of, to national parks, 370, 495, 510, 856, 870–872, 1013, 1078; and Colorado-Big Thompson Project, 725; proposed transfer of, to Interior, 971, 1054; President's authority over, 1013; and McNary Forestry Bill, 1123

National Geographic Magazine, 194

National Grange, 220 n.; urges Taylor Grazing Bill veto, 263 n.; and Upstream Engineering Conference, 623; opposes proposed conservation department, 712; suggests changes in Fulmer bill, 921–922

National Industrial Recovery Act (1933), and lumber industry, 150–154, 160, 164, 178, 187; appropriations, available for Federal land purchases, 163, 265; Soil Erosion Service established under, 236 n., 332, 348; invalidation, 366 n., 466 n.; and National Resources Committee, 884; and Olympic National Park, 1096. *See also* National Recovery Administration Lumber Code

National Lumber Manufacturers Association, 178, 989; and NRA Lumber Code, 155, 160, 164, 186, 228 n., 366

National Monuments, *see* National Parks and Monuments

National Parks and Monuments, 657; *proposed:* Hetch Hetchy, 31, Everglades, 55, Olympic, 769, 960–961, 1101, 1110, Kings Canyon, 804, 807, 911, Admiralty Island, 869, 885, 894, Big Bend, 933, Boulder Dam, 934, Porcupine Mountains, 1077–1078, 1084; enlargement, 75 n., 495, 624; CCC in, 131 n., 286, 325, 526, 566, 654, 1037; expenditures for, 236;

policy and law governing establishment, 286, 872, 947, 950, 1013, 1020, 1061, 1124, 1148; recreation in, 296 n., 526, 872; reclamation and power projects and, 369, 647, 658, 725; primitive areas and wildlife, 445, 592; proposed transfer of, to Agriculture, 712; Ickes' views on, 725; bill for roads in, vetoed, 932; number of, ready for dedication, 1016; and proposed amendment to Antiquities Act, 1020; mining and prospecting in, 451, 455, 471, 480, 503, 1064; encroachment on, by Army, 1070

National Parks Association, invites FDR to be trustee, 58; proposes primeval parks, 592; protests Big Thompson bill, 648; criticized, 1000

National Park Service, 540, 702, 725, 1101 n.; *actions, authority and policies of, with respect to:* C. & O. Canal park, 241, protection of Alaskan bears, 266, CCC, 331, 756, 829, 844, state park bill, 363, Everglades wildlife area, 434, recreational areas, 523, 1009 n., national monument in Vermont, 558–559, reclamation use of Yellowstone Lake, 647 n., Katahdin national park, 649, Great Smoky Mountains National Park, 652, 1121–1122, water resources of arid regions, 677, Appalachian parkway, 704, commercial activities, 710, Quetico-Superior area, 741, Olympic National Park, 812, 818 n., 857, 956–957, wildlife, 831, power development in Kings Canyon National Park, 891, Grand Canyon National Monument, 931, Everglades, 943, Lake Mead recreation area, 947, National Parks Association, 1000, soil conservation, 1010, Washington State Planning Council, 1013, mining in national parks and monuments, 1064; FDR enlarges jurisdiction of, 286; needs public support, 457, dispute of, with Forest Service, 467, 807, 870, 872, 1078; original function of, 592; Presidential letter drafted by, 652; criticized, 950; revenue produced by, 1078

National Park Service, Director of, *Arno B. Cammerer*, 434, 468, 471; memoranda of, 649, 741, 769; letter to, 605; Olympic National Park policy of, 750

National Park Service, Director of, *Newton B. Drury*, memorandum of, 1098; visits Porcupine Mountains, 1084 n.; suggests General Motors do-

nate Porcupine Mountains lands, 1097, 1098; efforts of, in behalf of Calaveras Sequoia Grove, 1104

National Park Service Act (1916), 1102

National Plan for American Forestry, discussed, 138, 152, 153, 160 n., 178, 228, 244, 380, 569, 989

National Planning Agency, proposed, 587, 636

National Planning Board, 178, 237 n., 437, 636; commended by Cabinet committee, 272; work of, with state boards, 279; abolition, 281. *See also* National Resources Board; National Resources Committee; National Resources Planning Board

National Power Policy Committee, 587 n., 753; drafts power authority bill, 626; to plan use of Grand Coulee power surplus, 962

National Pulp and Paper Requirements in Relation to Forest Conservation, 404

National Reclamation Association, 912, 1130–1131

National Recovery Administration Lumber Code, 182, 197, 366 n.; 380, 713; *recommendations on, by:* Shepard, 150–153, 160, Wallace, 154, 164, 178; FDR's wishes concerning, 155, 166, 184, 191, 313; relation of, to Paper and Pulp Code, 184, 187–188, 191; analysis of, 185–186, 242–244, 339 n.; FDR confers with lumbermen on, 228–229; proposed amendments to, 232; proposed legislation in aid of, 253, 307–308, 374; enforcement, 260–261

National Recovery Administrator, *Hugh S. Johnson*, letter of, 232; and NRA Lumber Code, 155, 166, 188 n.

National recreational areas, 1013

National Research Council, 634

National Resources Board, 297 n., 302, 753; establishment, 272, 281, 466; to report on reclamation projects, 292, 293; Presidential letter drafted by, 299; *recommendations and reports of, on:* national planning and natural resources, 299, 309, 310, 343, forest lands, 351, 356, 380, water planning and flood control, 375, 387, 501, 612; to aid wildlife projects, 322, 323; to plan research program, 324; importance of, 372; abolition, 372 n.

National Resources Committee, 568 n., 569, 661, 730, 749; memorandum to, 611; organization, 372; relies on other agencies, 375; and national and state water policies, 394; *reports and studies on:* Upper Rio Grande Basin, 421, 425, Everglades, 434, 908, general program and progress, 436–437, 755, 867, 967, water pollution, 438, 601, 810, 832, 854, 868, 914, drainage basin development and flood control, 444, 459–461, 487–488, 492, 498–500, 502, 549, 563, 604, 607, 613, 619, 655, 659–660, 666, 671, 677, 696–697, 757, 766, 775–776, 781–782, 797–798, 808, recreational area programs, 523, national forest roads, 551, Great Plains, 560, 562, 574–575, 815–816, 821, 825, 906, public works program, 584, northern Lake States, 746, 890, 928, Northwest, 827, 906, land planning, 834–835, Ohio Valley planning, 848, Beaver-Mahoning and Clark Hill projects, 879, Whitney Dam, 917; FDR's opinion of, 466; Presidential letters drafted by, 466, 740, 746, 752, 825–827, 835, 867, 872; and Interior Department, 626; sponsors state planning conference, 730 n.; problem of continuance of, 843, 865–867, 883–884, 889; avoids Olympic National Park dispute, 857; to coordinate Great Plains water conservation, 913

National Resources Planning Board, 951 n., 1009, 1042; letter and memorandum to, 983, 992, establishment, 889, n.; *reports and studies on:* Kings River and Tulare Lake projects, 923, 1002, Great Plains water conservation, 936–938, 942, 992, 1003, Columbia Basin, 962, 977, Cumberland Basin, 965, general progress, 967, Coolidge Dam, 983, national forest policy (proposed), 993, Gila Basin Project, 994, Lower Colorado River Basin, 1001, regional authorities, 1031–1032, 1060, 1062, 1094, post-war public works, 1036; program, 946, 1111; savings effected by, 972; appropriations for, 981–982, 1099; Presidential letters drafted by, 1001, 1026; model for state planning boards, 1026; criticizes Gillette Water Pollution Bill, 1055; abolition, 1099 n., 1111

National Rivers and Harbors Congress, 884

National Tribute Grove, 1149 n.

National Wildlife Conference, *see* North American Wildlife Conference

National Wildlife Federation, 392 n.

National Wildlife Week, 745

National Youth Administration, to study recreational area programs, 523;

aids upstream engineering conference, 623; aids war work, 1079, 1081; bill to abolish, 1079 n., 1080

Navajo Indians, 830; letter of, 347; letter to, 1050

Navy, Department of the, 1040 n.; FDR's service with, 26, 29, 33, 34, 37; and wildlife conservation, 1034

Nebraska, 378, 1130; tree planting in, 78, 170, 172, 177; CCC in, 146; water conservation in, 207, 1105 n.; dust storms and drought in, 426, 452, 548, 560; Northern Great Plains Committee report on, 821, 826, 907; rehabilitation program for, 825

Nebraska, University of, 532

Nebraska National Forest, 177

Neely, Matthew M., 1136 n.; supports wildlife conservation, 561

Neligh (Nebr.), 1024

Nelson, Donald, 1092; and forest conservation, 1093

Neskahi, Allen, 347

Nevada, grazing in, 263, 298, 953; CCC in, 717; proposed Boulder Dam state park in, 934, 935, 947, 954

Newbold, Thomas J., 67

New Deal, 298; and national forest problem, 989

Newell, Frederick H., 569

New England, national forest purchases in, 485; flood control in, 587; proposed national parkway and park in, 704, 747; hurricane in, 862

New England Flood Control Compacts, proposed, 755, 786

New England Regional Planning Commission, 437

Newfound Gap, 1016

Newhalem (Wash.), 1107

Newhalem Creek, 1107

New Hampshire, 485, 618; proposed national forest purchases in, 124, 140, 944; game refuge needed in, 285; flood problem, 345, 531, 587

New Jersey, 704, 749; proposed national forest purchases in, 124; stream pollution in, 198; CCC in, 219 n.

New Jersey State Board of Conservation, 219 n.

New Mexico, 746, 884; reclamation, 421, 656, 994; dust storms, 452; manganese deposits, 952; grazing permit system, 953

New River, 786

New York (N. Y.), 704, 1166; proposal of, to use Dutchess County water, 63, 694; pollution of waters near, 197, 355, 678

New York Board of Trade, 25
New York Central Railroad, 175
New York Rod and Gun Editors Association, FDR's greetings to (text), 580
New York State, 306, 452, 704; conservation in, 2–3, 35–38, 52, 56–57, 65, 76–78, 80, 82, 84–85, 87, 91–92, 93 n., 95, 97, 101–104, 113, 115–117, 229, 268, 285, 354, 419, 579, 602, 628, 630, 1046; land problem, 46, 47, 72–73, 81–83, 94, 105–107, 109, 694; park development, 69–70, 85, 145, 175, 1085; water pollution in, 86, 96, 198, 355, 361; unemployment relief, 110 n., 119–120, 124, 180, 920, CCC in, 183
New York State Agricultural Society, FDR speaks to, 81 n.
New York State College of Forestry, 49, 62 n., 65 n., 381, 918, 1063; supervises FDR's tree plantings, 88, 128, 182, 256, 329, 632, 646, 711, 819, 873, 995; prepares Dutchess County forestry plan, 99; forestry-relief work plan of, 119 n.; studies chestnut blight, 824
New York State Conservation Commission, letter to, 56; creation and functions, 9 n., 22, 49, 57, 65 n.; helps draft FDR conservation bill, 23; legislation concerning, 36; FDR orders trees from, 52
New York State Conservation Department, 85 n., 123, 579, 596; development of Forest Preserve by, 102–103, 104 n.; reports on FDR's reforestation-employment plan, 124; functions, 419
New York State Council of Parks, 61, 69
New York State Fish, Game and Forest League, 9
New York State Forest, Fish and Game Commission, 9 n.
New York State Forest Preserve, protection of, 71, 82, 102–104, 106, 122
New York State Forestry Association, FDR a member, 35, 76; invites FDR to speak to, 37
New York State Museum, 69, 70
New York State Press Association, FDR speaks to, 73 n.
New York State Reforestation Amendment, 93; FDR urges passage of, 82, 85
New York State Senate, Forest, Fish and Game Committee, FDR's work on, 2, 4, 8, 21, 24, 35, 76, 78, 268,

419, 1136; holds hearings, 3, 6, 14, 20, 23
New York Times, 74, 75, 336, 459 n., 581 n.
New York Zoological Society, criticizes Agriculture Department, 859 n.; requests wartime wildlife protection, 1028
Niagara Falls, 1166
Niagara River, 96
Nicolet National Forest, 510
Nichols, Al., 547
Nicholson, John F., 544
Nielson, Harvey, 303
Niemeyer, F. W., 544
Nishi, Nal, 347
Nitrates, 783
Nixon, Robert G., 1159 n.
Norbeck, Peter, 337
Norbeck-Andresen Migratory Game Preservation Act (1929), 220
Norcross, Frank H., 953
Norrie State Park, establishment, 145, 175
Norris, George W., 1060; letters of, 206–207, 945, 974, 1049; letters and memorandum to, 209–210, 1029, 1048; responsible for TVA, 137, 1015; position of, on: regional authorities, 196, 202, 203, 587 n., 626, 636 n., 706, 753, Flood Control Bill of 1938, 798 n., proposed transfer of Forest Service, 978, Shelterbelt, 1067; offers flood control resolution, 226 n.; introduces farm forestry legislation, 516 n., 630 n.
Norris Dam, FDR's statement on (text), 478
Norris-Doxey Cooperative Farm Forestry Act (1937), 787; described, 516, 630, 919; and Shelterbelt, 600, 628, 998
Norris-Jones Farm Forestry Bill (1936), 537 n.; described, 515–516, 630
Norris-Rankin Regional Authorities Bill (1937), Wallace's view of, 626; FDR's view of, 633, 636 n., 637; described, 706
North American Wildlife Conference, 460, 462, 472; plans for, 445–446, 557; FDR's message to (text), 463
North Bend Timber Company, 1107
North Carolina, proposed national forest purchases in, 124, 140, 156 n., 161, 169; forestry in, 217 n.; parkway and park in, 526, 605, 652, 704, 813; paper industry in, 729
North Dakota, 378, 485, 705; CCC in, 146; drought and dust storms in,

O'Neal, Edward A., 297; letters to, 299, 975

Ontario (Canada), Quetico-Superior area in, 538 n., 570, 751, 765, 841, 886, 1087

Ontonago County (Mich.), 794

Order of Backwoodsmen, 30 n.

Oregon 276, 599, 1128; wildlife refuges in, 250, 265, 401, 442; Government land purchases in, 418, 429; forest conditions, 512, 522, 1089, 1123 n.; FDR's visits to, 701–702; apple growing in, 962

Oregon and California Revested Lands, 1089, 1123 n.

Organ Pipe Cactus National Monument, 1064

Osage County (Calif.), 93 n.

Osborn, Fairfield, letter to, 1028

Osborne, Lithgow, 419; letters to, 354, 881

Osborne, Thomas M., 8, 419

Oswego County (N. Y.), 89 n.

Ottawa (Canada), 841

Ottawa National Forest, 794

Ouachita River, 485

Outland, George E., 1146 n.

Overfield, William, letter to, 52

Overly, Fred J., memorandum of, 957

Overton Flood Control Act (1936), 614

Ozark Mountains, 485; population, 828; national forest program in, 833

Pacific Coast, in danger of forest fires, 1079–1080, 1086

Pacific Northwest, 884; forest exploitation in, 522, 758, 1074, 1089, 1102; migration to, 827, 906; public power movement in, 1048, 1060

Pacific Northwest Regional Planning Commission, 437; reports on migration from Great Plains, 827

Pacific-Yukon highway, 740

Pack, Charles L., letter and memorandum of, 112, 113; letters to, 114, 417; views of, on FDR reforestation-employment plan, 111, 118

Paducah (Ky.), 614, 618

Page, John C., see Reclamation Bureau, Commissioner of

Palestine, 1159

Palisades Interstate Park, 53, 62 n., 69, 70, 85, 183

Palm Beach (Fla.), 471

Palmer, C. M., 71 n.

Panama Canal Zone, 21, 286

Pan American Union, 1145

Park, Guy B., 541, 544

Parker, Joseph E., 641

Parker, Robert M., 13

Parran, Thomas, Jr., N. Y. State Health Commissioner, 96. See also Public Health Service, Surgeon General

Parrott, Forrest, 547, 548

Passamaquoddy Project, 637

Patrons of Husbandry, see National Grange

Patton, James G., 1151; letter of, 1144

Paul, Charles E., 696

Payne, George H., letter to, 36

Payne, John B., 39, 42

Pearson, L. B., 1170

Pearson, Thomas G., 59

Pearson Forest Taxation Act (Mich.), 787

Pecos River, 884

Peery, George C., 526

Pennsylvania, 426, 704, 749, 1085; proposed national forest purchases in, 113, 124, 140; water pollution in, 198, 1005; virgin forest in, 343; CCC in, 844

Pennsylvania Forestry Association, 343

Pennsylvania Sanitary Water Board, 198; and water pollution legislation, 780 n., 1005

Penobscot River, 485

Pensacola (Fla.), 985

Peoples, Christian J., 862

Perkins, Frances, see Labor, Secretary of

Perkins, Milo, 533 n.

Permanent Appropriation Repeal Act (1934), 406, 687

Perry, John, 347

Persia, see Iran

Person, Harlow S., 444 n., 554; FDR speech drafted by, 553 n.; on Great Plains Committee, 577

Persons, W. Frank, 136 n.

Pete, Billy, 347

Petersham (Mass.), 78

Peterson, J. Hardin, 1146

Petroleum, 1007; in Alaska, 39; and Anglo-American Agreement, 1138

Pettis, C. R., 56 n.; letters to, 57, 65

Philadelphia (Pa.), 704, 1073 n.

Phillips, John C., 634

Phosphate Resources of the United States, 784 n.

Phosphates, produced by TVA, 300, 1015; importance, 638, 640, 783–784

Pierce, C. C., letter of, 199

Pierce, Walter M., introduces forest conservation bill, 1036 n., 1045

665; Presidential letter drafted by, 449; transfer of, to Agriculture, proposed, 712, 975 n.; disputes of, with Army Engineers, 923; and Agriculture Department, 992 n.; and power development, 1048

Reclamation, Bureau of, Commissioner, *Elwood Mead,* 292; relations of, with Biological Survey, 322, 352 n., 401, 442; death, 509

Reclamation, Bureau of, Commissioner, *John C. Page,* 529, 554, 906 n., 976; memoranda of, 728, 977; appointment, 509; on Great Plains committees, 577, 821; and Big Thompson project, 643; a conservationist, 725

Reclamation, Bureau of, Commissioner, *Harry W. Bashore,* 1140 n.

Reclamation Act (1902), 267, 449, 643, 656, 797, 900; provisions, 728

Reclamation and irrigation, issues in 1920 campaign, 39, 40, 42, 45, 46; Government aid for, opposed, 107 n.; *projects (undertaken and proposed):* Columbia Basin, 141, 237 n., 286, 976–977, Casper-Alcova, 167, Arkansas Basin, 192, 965, Missouri Basin, 207, 1130–1131, 1140, 1143, Mississippi Valley, 210, Snake River, 278, Colorado River, 278, 1001, Central Valley, 432, Great Plains, 545, 547, 577, 825, 900, 906 n., 907, 912–913, 916, 937–938, 1003, 1017, Colorado-Big Thompson, 643, 648, 658, 724–725, Yellowstone National Park, 647, 795, Arch Hurley, 656, Kings River-Kern River, 891, 923, 1002, 1042–1043, 1116, 1119–1120, 1150, Cumberland Basin, 965, Gila Basin, 994, Arkansas-White River, 1114; CCC used in, 566, 717, 1037; and flood control, 222, 487, 797; Agriculture Department funds for, reduced, 224; planning and policy for, 226, 254, 259, 292, 460, 492, 587, 626, 705, 725, 1029, 1139; Tugwell proposal for, 236; and resettlement, 547; and work relief, 683, 703; and 1937 Water Conservation Act, 686; history of, 728

Reclamation Fund Act (1910), 724

Reconstruction Finance Corporation, *relation of, to:* Columbia River project, 141, forest credits, 160, 244, 253, 423, flood control loans, 766, national forest policy, 993, water pollution legislation, 1055, acquisition of national forest lands, 1074, 1077, 1078, 1082, 1091, 1098

Reconstruction Finance Corporation, Chairman of, *Jesse H. Jones,* 1077; views of, on forest credit, 379; drafts flood control loan bill, 766

Reconstruction Finance Corporation Act (1932), 356

Recreation, 153, 237 n., 660, 704, 1014; and state parks and forests, 82, 85, 102, 103, 122, 321, 363, 419 n.; and wildlife restoration, 214; and national parks and forests, 241, 248, 286, 296 n., 526, 621, 647, 702, 741, 758, 804, 807, 870, 872, 905, 944, 952, 960, 984, 1016; CCC and, 321, 566, 1037; legislation for, 370, 523, 1013, 1020; at Boulder Dam and Lake Mead, 427, 934; in Missouri Basin, 520; TVA and, 969, 1015; and proposed transfer of Forest Service, 970; in Colorado River canyon, 1009

Recreational Area Bill (1935), *see* State Park-Recreational Area Bill

Recreational Area Programs Act (1936), 523

Recreational Demonstration Projects Act (1942), 1085

Recreational Demonstration Projects Bill (1939), 940

Recreation Development of the Tennessee River System, 969

Redington, Paul G., letter of, 190

Red River, 485, 786, 805; regional authority for, proposed, 636, 965

Red River of the North, development of basin, 437, 549, 636, 746

Reed, Franklin, 160, 186 n., 228; approves Shepard forestry plan, 151 n.

Regional authorities, 607; planning and legislation for, 309, 333–334, 345, 587, 626, 706, 753, 1030–1032, 1048, 1060, 1062, 1150–1151, 1156–1157; FDR urges creation of, 636–637, 660, 666; Congressional criticism of, 655 n.; need for, in Michigan, 746; Norris' conception of, 1049; proposed for Missouri Valley, 1128, 1130–1131, 1134, 1143–1144

Regional Planning Association of America, 64 n.

Rehabilitation in the Northern Great Plains, 815 n., 816, 821, 825, 826, 906 n.

Reid, Kenneth A., letter of, 773; letters to, 780, 1073

Reindeer Act (1937), 924

Relief Appropriation Acts, *see* Emergency Relief Appropriation Acts

Renne, —, 569

Rensselaer County (N. Y.), 69

Social Security Act (1935), 846

Society of American Foresters, 120, 151 n., 160, 712; letter of, 312; letter to, 313; meeting of, 88; FDR a member, 90, 100; opposes change in Forest Preserve law, 104; honors FDR, 308; approves Fulmer State Forest Bill, 376; FDR's message to, 949; favors state regulation of private forests, 1082

Soil conservation, 146, 149, 210, 212, 237 n., 286, 445, 476, 496, 517, 581, 585, 627, 631 n., 983 n., 1046; *problems of, in:* China, 16, 78, 268, 419, Tennessee Valley, 137, 926, 945, 1015, Arkansas Valley, 192, Upper Mississippi Valley, 216, West, 278 n., 303, 565, 569, 701, Big Horn River Basin, 293 n., Great Plains, 344, 543–546, 571, 577, 683, 752, Navajo lands, 347, 1050, South, 552, East, 583, 694, Michigan, 787, Georgia, 838, Haiti, 882, Olympic Peninsula, 955, Gila Basin, 994, Iran, 1159; *relation of, to:* reforestation, 91, 110, 125, 530, 762, 989, flood control, 226, 254, 426, 444, 459, 485, 487, 612, 623, 660, 720, 782, 796, overgrazing, 259, 414, deforestation, 310, 1136, agricultural overproduction, 452, wind storms, 504, 506, Shelterbelt, 537, regional authority idea, 587, individual liberty, 602, absentee land ownership, 625, phosphate deposits, 638, 783, 784; *work in aid of, by:* CCC, 131 n., 135, 321, 566, 675, 748, 1037, TVA, 137, Mississippi Valley Committee, 255, National Resources Board, 281, 501 n., Science Advisory Board, 302, Resettlement Administration, 412 n., Agricultural Adjustment Administration, 431, 456, 458, National Resources Committee, 492; legislation for, 270, 277, 349, 358, 481, 626; national objective, 458; distribution of information on, 511; Agriculture-Interior rivalry over, 712, 1008, 1010; interest of United Nations in, 1172. *See also* Soil Conservation Service; Soil Erosion Service

Soil Conservation and Domestic Allotment Act (1936), provisions, 476, 481, 585; administration, 1069

Soil Conservation Service, 444 n., 518, 519, 569, 614, 618, 665, 675, 971, 983, 987, 989, 1050, 1052, 1115 n., 1164; establishment, 348, 349, 437; and Copeland Flood Control Bill, 499; FDR describes work of, 542; and

Standard State Soil Conservation Districts Law, 585, 590, 597, 608; and Shelterbelt, 600, 998, 999, 1067; publishes report on headwaters control, 623 n.; to study Everglades water supply, 943

Soil Erosion Act (1935), 456; legislative history, 336, 348–349; described, 590, 597, 1067

Soil Erosion Service, 370, 459; establishment, 236 n.; to study national land policy, 290; Forest Service duplicates work of, 331; transfer of, to Agriculture, 332, 336, 338, 340; methods, 341

Soil—The Nation's Basic Heritage, 511

South, FDR's forest program in, 114, 919; national forest system in, 159, 163, 165, 169, 217; yellow pine in, 229; exploitation of forests, 262, 552, 708, 723, 729, 739, 758; standard of living, 300 n.; soil conservation in, 545, 546, 552, 746; Federal reforestation of private lands of, proposed, 761; Shelterbelt in, 1024

South America, 579

South Carolina, 169, 321, 530, 895; proposed national forest purchases in, 124, 140, 156 n., 161; proposed game refuges in, 285, 996; forest problem, 767; phosphate deposits, 784

South Dakota, 378, 994; CCC in, 146; dust storms and drought, 452, 527 n., 560, 906; farm survey of, 544; need of tree planting in, 548; rehabilitation program for, 821, 825, 907; and Belle Fourche River Basin Compact, 1118 n.

South Platte River, 724

Spalding Ranch, 250

Sparhawk, William N., 186 n.

Special Advisory Committee on Water Pollution, report, 438, 832, 842, 854; authorization, 848

Spence, Brent, letter of, 840; letter to, 1129; introduces water pollution bill, 1005 n.

Sperryville (Va.), 168 n.

Spokane (Wash.), FDR's speech at (text), 44

Spotswood Trail, 932

Spring, Samuel N., 62 n.; letter to, 256

Staatsburg (N. Y.), 145 n., 175

Stalin, Joseph, 1153, 1172 n.

Standard State Soil Conservation Districts Law, 585, 608; proposed, 590, 597

Stanton, E. M., letter to, 95

Starch, Elmer A., 1169 n.

Code, 151, 153, 160, 186, 228, 242, 244, 307; of sporting arms, 225 n., 360, 406; of waterways, 226; loss of, from Federal land acquisitions, 495, 575, 577, 621; problems of, in Northern Great Plains, 821

Taylor, Edward T., letters to, 768, 924; introduces grazing bill, 144 n., 227 n., 270, 464 n., 465; opposes Big Thompson project, 643

Taylor Grazing Act (1934), 418, 575; situation before enactment of, 223 n.; FDR's views of, 227, 238, 277, 447, 528, 540, 953; legislative history, 227 n., 245, 263, 267, 274–276, 540; Attorney General's opinion on, 269; provisions and administration, 270, 291, 543, 984, 987, 997; game ranges and, 311 n., 315, 335, 442–443, 450, 822, 830, 839; amendments, 413, 414, 416, 420, 424, 464–465; Wallace's criticism of, 569

Taylor Grazing Bill (1933), 569

Teheran Conference, 1117, 1159

Teller's Hill, 67

Temple, Lucia, letter to, 101

Tenant farming, 777, 806; in Great Plains, 543, 577; soil waste caused by, 625; and Shelterbelt, 1024

Tennant, John D., 228

Tennessee, 517, 1015, 1139; forest service of, 111, 112, 228; national forest purchases proposed in, 124, 140; reforestation problem, 147; national parks in, 526, 605, 652; phosphate deposits, 783, 784; CCC in, 863

Tennessee River, 131 n., 237 n., 485, 636; FDR's plan for, 126; Norris Dam and, 478; navigation and flood problems of, 614, 691, 1015, 1161

Tennessee Valley Authority, 309, 437, 587, 618, 626, 636, 637, 660, 666, 923, 1062, 1094 n., 1141 n., 1166; message to Congress on (text), 137; forestry and soil conservation under, 151, 157, 158, 169, 178, 332, 511, 849; objectives, costs and accomplishments of, 203, 204, 236, 300, 614, 691, 945, 969, 1015, 1030, 1049, 1060, 1134; phosphate production by, 300, 638, 784; model for other authorities, 706, 1128, 1143–1144, 1156; CCC and, 748, 756; FDR to visit, 926; qualifications of board members, 945; to plan Cumberland Basin development, 965; advises National Resources Planning Board, 994; FDR's opinion of, 1048, 1161 n.; Norris defends

concept of, 1049; state's rights under, 1139, 1151

Tennessee Valley Authority Act (1933), 137, 945, 969, 1049, 1161

Tennyson, Alfred, 653

Ten Thousand Islands, 59

Teton County (Wyo.), tax problem in, 495, 1146, 1148

Teton National Forest, 1078

Texas, 517, 701, 746, 884, 1139; CCC in, 146; proposed purchase of national forest lands in, 159, 161, 163; shelterbelts proposed in, 170, 177; dust storms and drought in, 452–454, 529, 560, 806; Soil Conservation Service program in, 585; reforestation proposed for, 761; Big Bend National Park in, 864, 933, 1135; planning agency for, proposed, 1026

Theodore Roosevelt Memorial, FDR speaks at, 458 n.

Third World Power Conference, 742; background, 518 n.; FDR's speech before, 534, (text) 553

Thom, William R., 490

Thomas, Elbert D., letters of, 298, 582; letters to, 305, 483, 603, 1079; opposes Federal recreational area on Colorado River, 1009 n.

Thomas, Elmer, 202, 203; memorandum to, 209; at drought conference, 547; responsible for Grand River Dam, 805

Thomason, R. Ewing, letter to, 933

Thompson, Ben, 1020

Thompson, Mrs. Lewis S., letter to, 145; gives land for state park, 175

Thurston, Lloyd, 477 n.

Tiffany, Ross K., and Olympic National Park, 952, 956

Tigris River, 989

Timber Conservation Board, 108

Timberline Lodge (Mount Hood), FDR's speech at (text), 702

Time, 920

Tinker, Earl W., memorandum of, 573; on Quetico-Superior Committee, 280 n.

Tionesta Tract (Pa.), 343

Tobey, Charles W., letter to, 944

Toepfer, Elsa, letter to, 1167

Tolley, Howard R., 1171; on Land Committee, 834

Tombigbee River, 1139

Tomlinson, Owen A., 1013, 1101

Tompkins County (N. Y.), 81

Tongass National Forest, 869

Top Lopping Law (N. Y.), 229, 419

Torkelson, Martin W., 890

Townsend, Curtis, 34

Warm Springs Foundation, *see* Georgia Warm Springs Foundation.

Warm Springs (Ga.), 72 n., 107, 126 n., 926, 1015; FDR uses pool at, 59, 61; standard of living in area of, 300; FDR's farm at, 410, 838; soil erosion at, 456. *See also* Georgia Warm Springs Foundation

Warne, —, 977

Warner National Game Refuge, 442 n.

War Production Board, 1106 n.; and lumber production, 1089, 1092–1093, 1102, 1107, unsympathetic to Olympic National Park, 1110

Warren, G. F., 83

Warren, Lindsay C., urged to aid National Resources Committee legislation, 865 n., 866

Washburn Expedition (1870), 457

Washington, 599, 701, 1128; reclamation and irrigation, 39, 44, 141, 421, 825; submarginal lands, 412; Olympic National Park and, 710, 770, 778, 788, 801, 812, 857, 952, 956, 960, 1101, 1102; wood pulp and timber production, 952, 956, 1089, 1095, 1106–1108; apple growing, 962; national parks and forests, 1013

Washington (D. C.), 704, 813

Washington Hollow (N. Y.), 707 n.

Washington State Forest Advisory Committee, 1095

Washington State Planning Council, and Olympic National Park, 700, 952, 956; controversy of, with Ickes, 1012–1013; defense of, 1014; opposes proposed national recreational area, 1020

Waterbury Dam, FDR visits, 531 n.

Water conservation, in New York, 13–15, 63, 71, 82, 84–85; in China, 16; and national parks, 31–32, 643, 647–648, 658, 724–725, 768, 790, 795; issue in 1920 campaign, 39, 42, 44; in West, 47, 278, 293 n., 303–304, 347, 421, 425, 427, 432, 449, 509, 520, 781–782, 804, 962, 976, 977, 994, 1001, 1060, 1062, 1119–1120; and CCC, 146, 566, 728, 1037; national planning and policy, 167, 259, 278, 281, 310, 371–372, 375, 387, 394, 437, 444, 459–462, 492, 543, 584, 588, 601 n., 627, 641, 655, 660, 664–666, 696, 701, 715, 721, 757, 805, 934, 944, 1002, 1007, 1042–1043, 1116, 1130–1131, 1134, 1139–1140, 1150, 1155; in Great Plains, 267, 277, 279, 509, 520, 540, 543–550, 556,

560, 562, 571, 575, 577, 641, 676–677, 683–686, 752, 806, 821, 825–826, 900, 906–907, 913, 916, 936–939, 941–942, 992, 1003, 1017, 1105, 1118, 1128; conferences on, 445, 623; general legislation for, 487, 733, 757, 808, 1123; by Soil Conservation Service, 585, 590; in South, 1114; in Saudi Arabia, 1117. *See also* Water pollution

Water Facilities Act, *see* Water Storage Facilities Act

Water Planning Committee, 310, 372, 375, 611, 614

Water pollution, 237 n.; *problems of, in:* Lake Erie and Niagara River, 86, 96, Mississippi River, 255, Hudson River, 355, 361, York River, 386, Maryland streams, 438, Ohio River, 651, 682, 840, 848, 1129, Lake Mead, 934; Lonergan campaign against, 197, 199–200, 215; state legislation for control of, 198; and river improvement program, 254; National Resources Board and, 324 n., 437; Resettlement Administration and, 412 n.; on agenda of North American Wildlife Conference, 445; Federal policy on, 507, 601 n., 669, 673, 679, 689, 693, 695, 714, 716, 820, 832, 842, 868; FDR urged to act against, 568; National Resources Committee and, 601, 659–660, 810, 814, 842, 854; Federal legislation for control of, 773, 780, 799, 810, 832, 840, 845–846, 851, 868, 893, 899, 909, 914–915, 1004–1005, 1055; FDR's views of, 868, 888, 1073; effect of defense program on, 1129

Water Power and Control Commission (N. Y.), 85

Water Resources Committee, 437, 492, 619, 620 n., 696, 797, 845, 846, 848, 916; to coordinate wildlife agencies, 577; *recommendations and reports on:* Joint Resolution on Flood Control, 659–660, New England compacts, 755, water pollution, 842, water conservation, 923; funds for, 697; consulted on WPA sewer projects, 714

Water Storage Facilities Act (1937), enactment and administration, 676–677, 684–686, 903, 936–939; proposed amendment, 992, 1017; and Great Plains Water Conservation Act, 1003

Watkins, —, 946

Use and Abuse

of

America's Natural Resources

An Arno Press Collection

Ayres, Quincy Claude. **Soil Erosion and Its Control.** 1936

Barger, Harold and Sam H. Schurr. **The Mining Industries, 1899–1939.** 1944

Carman, Harry J., editor. **Jesse Buel:** Agricultural Reformer. 1947

Circular from the General Land Office Showing the Manner of Proceeding to Obtain Title to Public Lands. 1899

Fernow, Bernhard E. **Economics of Forestry.** 1902

Gannett, Henry, editor. **Report of the National Conservation Commission, February 1909.** Three volumes. 1909

Giddens, Paul H. **The Birth of the Oil Industry.** 1938

Greeley, William B. **Forests and Men.** 1951

Hornaday, William T. **Wild Life Conservation in Theory and Practice.** 1914

Ise, John. **The United States Forest Policy.** 1920

Ise, John. **The United States Oil Policy.** 1928

James, Harlean. **Romance of the National Parks.** 1939

Kemper, J. P. **Rebellious River.** 1949

Kinney, J. P **The Development of Forest Law in America.** *Including,* Forest Legislation in America Prior to March 4, 1789. 1917

Larson, Agnes M. **History of the White Pine Industry in Minnesota.** 1949

Liebig, Justus, von. **The Natural Lawss of Husbandry.** 1863

Lindley, Curtis H. **A Treatise on the American Law Relating to Mines and Mineral Lands.** Two volumes. 2nd edition. 1903

Lokken, Roscoe L. **Iowa**—Public Land Disposal. 1942

McGee, W. J., editor. **Proceedings of a Conference of Governors in the White House, May 13–15, 1908.** 1909

Mead, Elwood. **Irrigation Institutions.** 1903

Moreell, Ben. **Our Nation's Water Resources**—Policies and Politics. 1956

Murphy, Blakely M., editor. **Conservation of Oil & Gas: A Legal History, 1948.** 1949

Newell, Frederick Haynes. **Water Resources: Present and Future Uses.** 1920.

Nimmo, Joseph, Jr. **Report in Regard to the Range and Ranch Cattle Business of the United States.** 1885

Nixon, Edgar B., editor. **Franklin D. Roosevelt & Conservation, 1911–1945.** Two volumes. 1957

Peffer, E. Louise. **The Closing of the Public Domain.** 1951

Preliminary Report of the Inland Waterways Commission. 60th Congress, 1st Session, Senate Document No. 325. 1908

Puter, S. A. D. & Horace Stevens. **Looters of the Public Domain.** 1908

Record, Samuel J. & Robert W. Hess. **Timbers of the New World.** 1943

Report of the Public Lands Commission, with Appendix. 58th Congress, 3d Session, Senate Document No. 189. 1905

Report of the Public Lands Commission, Created by the Act of March 3, 1879. 46th Congress, 2d Session, House of Representatives Ex. Doc. No. 46. 1880

Resources for Freedom: A Report to the President by The President's Materials Policy Commission, Volumes I and IV. 1952. Two volumes in one.

Schoolcraft, Henry R. **A View of the Lead Mines of Missouri.** 1819

Supplementary Report of the Land Planning Committee to the National Resources Board, 1935–1942

Thompson, John Giffin. **The Rise and Decline of the Wheat Growing Industry in Wisconsin** (Reprinted from *Bulletin of the University of Wisconsin,* No. 292). 1909

Timmons, John F. & William G. Murray, editors. **Land Problems and Policies.** 1950

U.S. Department of Agriculture—Forest Service. **Timber Resources for America's Future:** Forest Resource Report No. 14. 1958

U.S. Department of Agriculture—Soil Conservation Service and Forest Service. **Headwaters Control and Use.** 1937

U.S. Department of Commerce and Labor—Bureau of Corporations. **The Lumber Industry,** Parts I, II, & III. 1913/1914

U.S. Department of the Interior. **Hearings before the Secretary of the Interior on Leasing of Oil Lands.** 1906

Whitaker, J. Russell & Edward A. Ackerman. **American Resources: Their Management and Conservation.** 1951